AMERICAN
VOLUME II
Reconstruction through the Present

Fourteenth Edition

Editor

Robert James Maddox
Pennsylvania State University
University Park

Robert James Maddox, distinguished historian and professor of American history at Pennsylvania State University, received a B.S. from Fairleigh Dickinson University in 1957, an M.S. from the University of Wisconsin in 1958, and a Ph.D. from Rutgers in 1964. He has written, reviewed, and lectured extensively, and is widely respected for his interpretations of presidential character and policy.

Annual Editions
A Library of Information from the Public Press
Dushkin/McGraw-Hill
Sluice Dock, Guilford, Connecticut 06437

The Annual Editions Series

ANNUAL EDITIONS is a series of over 65 volumes designed to provide the reader with convenient, low-cost access to a wide range of current, carefully selected articles from some of the most important magazines, newspapers, and journals published today. ANNUAL EDITIONS are updated on an annual basis through a continuous monitoring of over 300 periodical sources. All ANNUAL EDITIONS have a number of features that are designed to make them particularly useful, including topic guides, annotated tables of contents, unit overviews, and indexes. For the teacher using ANNUAL EDITIONS in the classroom, an Instructor's Resource Guide with test questions is available for each volume.

VOLUMES AVAILABLE

Abnormal Psychology
Adolescent Psychology
Africa
Aging
American Foreign Policy
American Government
American History, Pre-Civil War
American History, Post-Civil War
American Public Policy
Anthropology
Archaeology
Biopsychology
Business Ethics
Child Growth and Development
China
Comparative Politics
Computers in Education
Computers in Society
Criminal Justice
Criminology
Developing World
Deviant Behavior
Drugs, Society, and Behavior
Dying, Death, and Bereavement

Early Childhood Education
Economics
Educating Exceptional Children
Education
Educational Psychology
Environment
Geography
Global Issues
Health
Human Development
Human Resources
Human Sexuality
India and South Asia
International Business
Japan and the Pacific Rim
Latin America
Life Management
Macroeconomics
Management
Marketing
Marriage and Family
Mass Media
Microeconomics

Middle East and the
  Islamic World
Multicultural Education
Nutrition
Personal Growth and Behavior
Physical Anthropology
Psychology
Public Administration
Race and Ethnic Relations
Russia, the Eurasian Republics,
  and Central/Eastern Europe
Social Problems
Social Psychology
Sociology
State and Local Government
Urban Society
Western Civilization,
  Pre-Reformation
Western Civilization,
  Post-Reformation
Western Europe
World History, Pre-Modern
World History, Modern
World Politics

Cataloging in Publication Data
Main entry under title: Annual Editions: American history, vol. two: Reconstruction through the present. 14/E.
   1. United States—History—Periodicals. 2. United States—Historiography—Periodicals. 3. United States—Civilization—Periodicals. I. Title: American history, vol. two: Reconstruction through the present.
ISBN 0–697–36308–2   973'.05   75–20755

© 1997 by Dushkin/McGraw-Hill, Guilford, CT 06437, A Division of The McGraw-Hill Companies.

Copyright law prohibits the reproduction, storage, or transmission in any form by any means of any portion of this publication without the express written permission of Dushkin/McGraw-Hill, and of the copyright holder (if different) of the part of the publication to be reproduced. The Guidelines for Classroom Copying endorsed by Congress explicitly state that unauthorized copying may not be used to create, to replace, or to substitute for anthologies, compilations, or collective works.

Annual Editions® is a Registered Trademark of Dushkin/McGraw-Hill,
A Division of The McGraw-Hill Companies.

Fourteenth Edition

Printed in the United States of America

Printed on Recycled Paper

Editors/Advisory Board

Members of the Advisory Board are instrumental in the final selection of articles for each edition of ANNUAL EDITIONS. Their review of articles for content, level, currentness, and appropriateness provides critical direction to the editor and staff. We think that you will find their careful consideration well reflected in this volume.

EDITOR

Robert James Maddox
Pennsylvania State University
University Park

ADVISORY BOARD

Arthur H. Auten
University of Hartford

Edward H. Beardsley
University of South Carolina

Neal A. Brooks
Essex Community College

Bruce Dudley
Prince George's Community College

Nancy Gentile-Ford
Bloomsburg University

Melvin G. Holli
University of Illinois

Harry Russell Huebel
Texas A & M University

William Hughes
Essex Community College

Wilma King
Michigan State University

Larry Madaras
Howard Community College

Arthur F. McClure
Central Missouri State University

Ronald McCoy
Emporia State University

Rameth Owens
Clemson University

Robert Pierce
Foothill College

Irvin D. Solomon
University of South Florida - Ft. Myers

James R. Sweeney
Old Dominion University

Staff

Ian A. Nielsen, Publisher

EDITORIAL STAFF

Roberta Monaco, Developmental Editor
Addie Raucci, Administrative Editor
Cheryl Greenleaf, Permissions Editor
Deanna Herrschaft, Permissions Assistant
Diane Barker, Proofreader
Lisa Holmes-Doebrick, Program Coordinator

PRODUCTION STAFF

Brenda S. Filley, Production Manager
Charles Vitelli, Designer
Shawn Callahan, Graphics
Lara M. Johnson, Graphics
Laura Levine, Graphics
Mike Campbell, Graphics
Libra A. Cusack, Typesetting Supervisor
Juliana Arbo, Typesetter
Jane Jaegersen, Typesetter
Marie Lazauskas, Word Processor
Larry Killian, Copier Coordinator

To the Reader

In publishing ANNUAL EDITIONS we recognize the enormous role played by the magazines, newspapers, and journals of the *public press* in providing current, first-rate educational information in a broad spectrum of interest areas. Many of these articles are appropriate for students, researchers, and professionals seeking accurate, current material to help bridge the gap between principles and theories and the real world. These articles, however, become more useful for study when those of lasting value are carefully *collected, organized, indexed,* and *reproduced* in a *low-cost format*, which provides easy and permanent access when the material is needed. That is the role played by ANNUAL EDITIONS. Under the direction of each volume's *academic editor,* who is an expert in the subject area, and with the guidance of an *Advisory Board,* each year we seek to provide in each ANNUAL EDITION a current, well-balanced, carefully selected collection of the best of the public press for your study and enjoyment. We think that you will find this volume useful, and we hope that you will take a moment to let us know what you think.

Historical works used to concentrate heavily on dramatic crises in history, on individuals—usually white men—who wielded great power in government or in industry, and on military conflict. More recently scholars have been concentrating on other areas of interest: minority groups, women, and the environment, to name just a few. There also has been a tendency to examine the lives of ordinary people as opposed to those leaders who by definition are unique. New techniques of research have been developed to overcome the fact that ordinary people rarely leave manuscript collections or voluminous diaries.

Even the more traditional categories of history, such as political, economic, and diplomatic, are being approached in new ways. Military historians of World War II, for instance, previously focused mostly on strategies, generals, and great battles. Now much is being done on subjects such as the lives and backgrounds of ordinary soldiers, the contributions of women, and the deplorable treatment of African Americans who were asked to serve their country while being treated as second-class citizens.

These new approaches by no means invalidate continuing interest in those who made large differences as *individuals*. Presidents such as Woodrow Wilson and Franklin D. Roosevelt had to make decisions affecting thousands if not millions of lives. Martin Luther King Jr.'s eloquent oratory and inspiring presence permitted him to exert moral and spiritual leadership that an individual of lesser gifts could not have hoped to achieve.

This volume attempts to present a selection of articles balanced between the new accent on inclusion of hitherto neglected individuals and groups and the more traditional analyses of well-known leaders such as Franklin D. Roosevelt, Dwight D. Eisenhower, and Martin Luther King Jr. If the evaluations received of previous editions holds true, some readers will think too much emphasis has been placed on one aspect while other readers will complain there is too little. That is why we encourage teachers and students to let us know what they consider the strengths and weaknesses of this volume.

Annual Editions: American History, Volume II, contains a number of features designed to make it "user friendly." These include a *topic guide* to help locate articles on specific subjects; the *table of contents extracts* that summarize each essay with key concepts in boldface; and a comprehensive *index*. Articles are organized into six units. Each unit is preceded by an overview that provides background for informed reading of the articles, briefly introduces each one, and presents challenge questions. If you have any suggestions for improving the format, please tell us.

There will be a new edition of *Annual Editions: American History, Volume II,* in two years, and at least half the present articles will be replaced. By completing and mailing the postpaid article rating form included in the back of the book, you will help us judge which articles should be retained and which should be dropped. You can also help to improve the next edition by recommending (or better yet, sending along a copy of) articles that you think should be included. A number of essays in this edition have come to our attention in this way.

Robert James Maddox
Editor

Contents

To the Reader iv
Topic Guide 2

UNIT 1

Reconstruction and the Gilded Age

Four articles examine the development of the United States after the Civil War. Society was changed enormously by Western expansion and technology.

Overview 4

1. **The New View of Reconstruction,** Eric Foner, *American Heritage,* October/November 1983. 6
   Prior to the 1960s, according to Eric Foner, *Reconstruction* was portrayed in history books as "just about the darkest page in the American saga." This article presents a balanced view of the era and suggests that even though Reconstruction failed to achieve its objectives, its "animating vision" still has relevance.

2. **The First Chapter of Children's Rights,** Peter Stevens and Marian Eide, *American Heritage,* July/August 1990. 12
   In 1874 there were no legal means to save a child from abuse. Little Mary Ellen McCormack's testimony in court that year touched off a controversy over *the role of government in family matters* that exists to this day.

3. **A New View of Custer's Last Battle,** Richard Allan Fox Jr., *American History Illustrated,* September/October 1993. 17
   George Armstrong *Custer's "last stand"* against the Sioux and Northern Cheyenne warriors at Little Big Horn in 1876 has been described in numerous accounts. According to legend, the brave cavalry leader stood firing in the center of his steadily diminishing body of troopers until he too was cut down. However, new archaeological evidence shows that the battle actually was fought quite differently.

4. **Reinventing Government, 1882,** Bernard A. Weisberger, *American Heritage,* February/March 1994. 24
   "To the Victor Belong the Spoils" was a phrase used to justify the awarding of government jobs to loyal members of the winning party. Over time, the civil service was invented to replace the discredited patronage system. Periodically, *civil service reform* is proposed that attempts to replace this system with one based on nonpartisanship and merit.

UNIT 2

The Emergence of Modern America

Six articles review the beginnings of modern America. Key issues of this period are examined, including immigration, the dawn of manned flight, racial consciousness, and poverty in the early twentieth century.

Overview 26

5. ***Plessy v. Ferguson* Mandate,** Jean West Mueller and Wynell Burroughs Schamel, *Social Education,* February 1989. 28
   Homer Plessy was a mulatto who was arrested for sitting in the white section of a segregated train. Jean West Mueller tells of the 1896 Supreme Court decision that established the *"separate but equal"* doctrine. It remained the law of the land until 1954.

6. **Our First Southeast Asian War,** David R. Kohler and James Wensyel, *American History Illustrated,* January/February 1990. 30
   In 1898 the United States fought a short, victorious *war with Spain.* When President William McKinley decided to acquire the Philippine Islands from Spain, however, a bloody insurrection began that lasted for years. David Kohler and James Wensyel claim that this struggle should have afforded lessons about Vietnam for American policymakers 60 years later.

The concepts in bold italics are developed in the article. For further expansion please refer to the Topic Guide and the Index.

7. **Intervention,** Ivan Musicant, *American History,* February 1995.
   The United States has attempted to protect and enforce its strategic interests in the Caribbean for more than a century. Ivan Musicant examines the use of armed force during the early period of intervention, with emphasis on *the Spanish-American War* of 1898 and on securing the Panama Canal.
   37

8. **How We Lived,** *U.S. News & World Report,* August 28–September 4, 1995.
   Interviews with several centenarians provide personal testimony about *the way people lived at the turn of the century.* It was a time when housewives collected rainwater to do laundry, and many families faced daily harships that even included Indians and outlaws.
   44

9. **Wings for Man,** Doug McIntyre, *American History Illustrated,* January/February 1994.
   Wilbur and Orville Wright realized one of humanity's oldest dreams—prolonged, *controlled flight*—and changed the world. Doug McIntyre describes their long preparations for this feat and their subsequent struggles with competitors over patent rights.
   49

10. **Learning to Go to the Movies,** David Nasaw, *American Heritage,* November 1993.
    Despite the initial success in 1896 of what was billed as "Edison's Vitascope," *the earliest projected movies* failed to sustain popularity. Improved equipment and the introduction of plotted stories made "nickelodeons" a huge success. These in turn were replaced by ever more ornate theaters to attract the "better classes."
    56

UNIT 3

From Progressivism to the 1920s

Seven articles examine American culture in the early twentieth century. The economy began to reap the benefits of technology, women gained the right to vote, and Henry Ford ushered in mass production.

Overview
62

11. **Doctor Wiley and His Poison Squad,** Bernard A. Weisberger, *American Heritage,* February/March 1996.
    The "father" of the *Pure Food and Drug Act* of 1906 was a longtime enemy of "adulterated" foods that were increasingly being sold nationwide. Harvey Wiley's zealous efforts to enforce the act earned him a host of enemies and resulted in his resignation from government service in 1912.
    64

12. **Woodrow Wilson, Politician,** Robert Dallek, *The Wilson Quarterly,* Autumn 1991.
    Unfortunately best remembered for his failure to bring the United States into the *League of Nations, Woodrow Wilson* was a "brilliant democratic politician" who was elected on a wave of progressive reform sentiment. Robert Dallek argues that Wilson's first presidential term marks one of the "three notable periods of domestic reform in twentieth-century America."
    66

13. **Madam C. J. Walker,** A'Lelia Bundles, *American History,* July/August 1996.
    Despite repeated rebuffs, successful businesswoman C. J. Walker gained admittance to the previously all-male National Negro Business League. A'Lelia Bundles tells how this self-made millionaire fought for the *rights of women and blacks.*
    72

The concepts in bold italics are developed in the article. For further expansion please refer to the Topic Guide and the Index.

14. **Alcohol in American History,** David F. Musto, *Scientific American,* April 1996.   77
Over the course of American history, popular attitudes and legal responses to *the use of alcohol and other drugs* have gone from toleration to a peak of disapproval and back again in cycles of approximately 70 years. David Musto discusses current campaigns to stop alcohol abuse against the backdrop of past crusades, culminating in the Prohibition era of the 1920s.

15. **Why Suffrage for American Women Was Not Enough,** Elisabeth Perry, *History Today,* September 1993.   83
Despite *having won the vote,* most women accepted the notion that they should not compete with men in politics and that "their proper role was to serve others and to work for idealistic causes." Elisabeth Perry illustrates her thesis by tracing the careers of four energetic women: Belle Moskowitz, Eleanor Roosevelt, Frances Perkins, and Molly Dewson.

16. **Citizen Ford,** David Halberstam, *American Heritage,* October/November 1986.   87
Henry Ford once boasted, "I invented the modern age." His Model T Ford revolutionized the automobile industry, as did his introduction of the $5 workday. Ford's domination of the market reached a peak in the early 1920s, then began to slip because the willful genius "remained locked in the past."

17. **When White Hoods Were in Flower,** Bernard A. Weisberger, *American Heritage,* April 1992.   102
The original *Ku Klux Klan* emerged in the South under Reconstruction. Its purpose was to frighten free blacks and their white supporters and to keep them from voting. The organization reemerged in the 1920s. This time its enemies were Jews, Catholics, and foreigners as well.

UNIT 4

From the Great Depression to World War II

Six selections discuss the severe economic and social trials of the Great Depression of the thirties, the slow recovery process, and the enormous impact of World War II on America's domestic and foreign social consciousness.

Overview   104

18. **1933: The Rise of the Common Man,** Lewis Lord, *U.S. News & World Report,* October 25, 1993.   106
"We are at the end of our string," *lame-duck president Herbert Hoover* said on the day of Franklin Roosevelt's inauguration. "There is nothing more we can do." Lewis Lord describes how Roosevelt and his advisers proved Hoover wrong.

19. **The Draft,** Edward Oxford, *American History,* October 1994.   109
Stringent budgets during the 1930s kept the American army small and poorly equipped. With wars going on in both Europe and Asia, President Franklin Roosevelt obtained legislation instituting *the first peacetime draft.* Edward Oxford explains how the system worked and its profound effects on Americans.

20. **Home Front,** James W. Wensyel, *American History,* June 1995.   116
"World War II was fought and won on the assembly line as much as on the battle line." James Wensyel shows how practically *every aspect of civilians' lives was affected by the war:* their work, their leisure, and the foods they ate.

The concepts in bold italics are developed in the article. For further expansion please refer to the Topic Guide and the Index.

UNIT 5

From the Cold War to the 1990s

Eleven articles cover the post-World War II period in the United States. The Truman Doctrine influenced America's foreign policy, equality of education became the law of the land, the Vietnam War changed the way America looked at conflict, and the poor of America increasingly affected society's conscience.

21. **Operation Overlord from the Inside,** William L. O'Neill, *The New Leader,* June 6–20, 1994.   130
    Despite careful planning and a massive military buildup, *the Allied invasion of France* was by no means a sure thing. William O'Neill's review of Stephen Ambrose's book, *D-Day, June 6, 1944: The Climatic Battle of World War II,* analyzes the difficulties confronted and the decisions made that led to a successful operation.

22. **The Man of the Century,** Arthur Schlesinger Jr., *American Heritage,* May/June 1994.   132
    Historians have debated *Franklin Roosevelt's role in foreign affairs* for 50 years, and they have come to drastically different conclusions. Arthur Schlesinger argues that whatever his failings, Roosevelt, of all the statesmen active during that time, "saw most clearly into the grand movements of history."

23. **The Biggest Decision: Why We Had to Drop the Atomic Bomb,** Robert James Maddox, *American Heritage,* May/June 1995.   139
    Some critics have argued that Japan was so close to surrender during the summer of 1945 that the *use of atomic bombs* was unnecessary to end the war. Robert Maddox shows that this criticism is mistaken. The Japanese army, which controlled the situation, was prepared to fight to the finish, and it hoped to inflict such hideous casualties on invading forces that the United States would agree to a negotiated peace.

Overview   144

24. **Good-Bye to Isolationism,** Lee Edwards, *The World & I,* June 1995.   146
    The United States failed to join *the League of Nations* after World War I and concentrated on isolationist actions to avoid political commitments. Lee Edwards shows how differently the United States acted after World War II, when the frigid cold war atmosphere developed. As a result, emphasis was placed upon the Truman Doctrine, the Marshall Plan, and the formation of the North Atlantic Treaty Organization, all of which committed the United States to the role of free world leader.

25. **The G.I. Bill May Be the Best Deal Ever Made by Uncle Sam,** Edwin Kiester Jr., *Smithsonian,* November 1994.   150
    Experts predicted that only a relatively small percentage of veterans would take advantage of the *G.I. Bill's educational provisions.* Instead, about 2.2 million veterans rightly call this "one of the most important pieces of legislation in American history." It enabled these men and women to obtain educations that would otherwise have been impossible for many of them.

26. **Echoes of a Distant War,** Bernard A. Weisberger, *American Heritage,* July/August 1994.   154
    Just 5 years after the defeat of fascism and Japanese militarism, the United States sent its troops to fight a different enemy in *Korea.* Bernard Weisberger analyzes the frustrations involved during an age of apparently unlimited American power.

The concepts in bold italics are developed in the article. For further expansion please refer to the Topic Guide and the Index.

27. **TV's Wonder Years,** Edward Oxford, *American History,* February 1996. 156

Although invented decades earlier, television attained widespread popularity only in the years following World War II. Edward Oxford examines what some have called *the "Golden Age" of television.* There were original dramas of quality, live telecasts of established works, and some excellent reporting. There also was a great deal of fluff: sitcoms, game shows, and corny comedians. Then, as now, questions are asked about what television ought to be as opposed to what it was.

28. **Looking Back on Ike,** John P. Rossi, *The World & I,* December 1991. 161

In a 1962 poll of historians to rank and rate U.S. presidents, Dwight Eisenhower came in twenty-second, tied with Chester A. Arthur. Thirty years later, another pool ranked him ninth. John Rossi argues that such exercises tell us more about changing ideas and fads than about actual performance. He surveys *Eisenhower's accomplishments* and concludes that Ike's overall record "was a good, if not great one."

29. **The Boycott That Changed Dr. King's Life,** Clayborne Carson, *The New York Times Magazine,* January 7, 1996. 166

The Reverend Martin Luther King Jr. was a reluctant leader of the Montgomery, Alabama, bus boycott that began in December 1955. He emerged from this incident to become the most powerful figure in the 1960s *civil rights movement.*

30. **Trumpet of Conscience: A Portrait of Martin Luther King Jr,** Stephen B. Oates, *American History Illustrated,* April 1988. 169

Loved and admired by many, feared and detested by some, *Martin Luther King Jr.* was one of the great leaders in American history. A prize-winning biographer describes King's life, achievements, and tragic death.

31. **Reagan's Rise,** Gerard J. De Groot, *History Today,* September 1995. 175

Student unrest during the late 1960s and early 1970s aroused widespread fear and anger. Gerard De Groot shows how *Ronald Reagan* played masterfully upon these emotions in his campaign for the governorship of California. "By turning a relatively small problem of campus unrest into a massive conspiracy to overthrow democratic society," De Groot writes, "Reagan established himself as a leader worthy of national attention."

32. **Looking Back at Watergate,** Allen N. Sultan, *USA Today Magazine (Society for the Advancement of Education),* November 1994. 179

A number of administrations became enmeshed in scandals during U.S. history, and Allen Sultan argues that the illegal activities carried on within *the Richard Nixon presidency* were so vast that they dwarfed previous cases. The most well-known event, the 1972 Watergate break-in, should be remembered as a "most important event in the history of constitutional philosophy of the nation."

UNIT 6

New Directions for American History

Six articles discuss the current state of American society and the role the United States plays in the world.

33. **Final Days of South Vietnam,** Harry G. Summers Jr., *American History,* April 1995. — 183
    One of the last Americans to leave Saigon, Vietnam, recalls the *final defeats of the South Vietnamese forces.* Colonel Harry Summers regards the long U.S. involvement in Vietnam as a "well-intentioned but fatally flawed war."

34. **How the Seventies Changed America,** Nicholas Lemann, *American Heritage,* July/August 1991. — 188
    After the tumultuous era of the 1960s, the following decade seemed like nothing much more than a breathing space before what came next. Nicholas Lemann argues to the contrary: that *the great problems of the seventies*—economic stagnation, social fragmentation, and the need for a new world order—are yet to be solved.

Overview — 192

35. **The Suburban Century Begins,** William Schneider, *The Atlantic Monthly,* July 1992. — 194
    The 1990 Census revealed that *half the nation's population now lives in the suburbs.* William Schneider analyzes the political, social, and economic implications of this phenomenon for the future.

36. **The Disuniting of America** and **The Painful Demise of Eurocentrism,** Arthur M. Schlesinger Jr. and Molefi Kete Asante, *The World & I,* April 1992. — 203
    Multiculturalism and "political correctness" have been and will continue to be hotly debated within and outside our schools. Arthur Schlesinger argues that the way these matters have been implemented will exacerbate the very conditions they are intended to cure. Molefi Asante questions Schlesinger's "understanding of American history and his appreciation of diversity." He goes on to criticize what he regards as the narrowness and distortions produced by "Eurocentric scholars."

37. **Revolution in Indian Country,** Fergus M. Bordewich, *American Heritage,* July/August 1996. — 215
    Beginning in the 1970s, the U.S. government abandoned the long-standing policy of trying to integrate Native Americans into mainstream America in favor of *recognizing tribal sovereignty.* Fergus Bordewich assesses the implications of this new policy for the future.

38. **Muddled Masses: The Growing Backlash against Immigration Includes Many Myths,** Frederick Rose, *Wall Street Journal,* April 26, 1995. — 222
    It is generally believed that earlier immigrants to this country pulled themselves out of poverty by their own efforts, while more recent newcomers are costing American taxpayers billions of dollars in welfare and health care. "But there is a problem with the conventional wisdom about *yesterday's self-reliant immigrants,*" according to Frederick Rose. "It's wrong."

39. **The American Environment: The Big Picture Is More Heartening than All the Little Ones,** John Steele Gordon, *American Heritage,* October 1993. 225
In June 1969 the Cuyahoga River in Ohio was so polluted that it actually caught fire, with flames roaring five stories high. Today it "has changed greatly for the better and continues to improve." John Gordon believes that we must maintain the *commitment to environmental improvement* in all areas.

40. **America after the Long War,** Daniel Deudney and G. John Ikenberry, *Current History,* November 1995. 236
The collapse of the Soviet Union and the end of the cold war brought enormous *changes in international relations.* Daniel Deudney and G. John Ikenberry argue that these developments will cause equally enormous changes at home. They argue that "there is evidence that the domestic order forged by the cold war is coming apart ushering in a period of political disarray and posing daunting new challenges for parties and presidents."

Index 241
Article Review Form 244
Article Rating Form 245

The concepts in bold italics are developed in the article. For further expansion please refer to the Topic Guide and the Index.

Topic Guide

This topic guide suggests how the selections in this book relate to topics of traditional concern to American history students and professionals. It is useful for locating articles that relate to each other for reading and research. The guide is arranged alphabetically according to topic. Articles may, of course, treat topics that do not appear in the topic guide. In turn, entries in the topic guide do not necessarily constitute a comprehensive listing of all the contents of each selection.

TOPIC AREA	TREATED IN	TOPIC AREA	TREATED IN
African Americans	1. New View of Reconstruction 5. *Plessy v. Ferguson* Mandate 13. Madam C. J. Walker 17. When White Hoods Were in Flower 30. Trumpet of Conscience 36. Disuniting of America/Painful Demise of Eurocentrism	Government	4. Reinventing Government, 1882 5. *Plessy v. Ferguson* Mandate 11. Doctor Wiley and His Poison Squad 12. Woodrow Wilson, Politician 18. 1933: Rise of the Common Man 28. Looking Back on Ike 31. Reagan's Rise 40. America after the Long War
Asians	6. Our First Southeast Asian War 26. Echoes of a Distant War 33. Final Days of South Vietnam	Immigrants	38. Muddled Masses
		King, Martin L., Jr.	30. Trumpet of Conscience
Aviation	9. Wings for Man	Korean War	26. Echoes of a Distant War
Business	16. Citizen Ford	Movies	10. Learning to Go to the Movies
Children	2. First Chapter of Children's Rights	Multiculturalism	36. Disuniting of America/Painful Demise of Eurocentrism
Cold War	24. Good-Bye to Isolationism 26. Echoes of a Distant War 28. Looking Back on Ike 40. America after the Long War	Native Americans	3. New View of Custer's Last Battle 37. Revolution in Indian Country
Culture	10. Learning to Go to the Movies 27. TV's Wonder Years 35. Suburban Century Begins 36. Disuniting of America/Painful Demise of Eurocentrism	Nixon, Richard	32. Looking Back at Watergate
		Politics	4. Reinventing Government, 1882 11. Doctor Wiley and His Poison Squad 12. Woodrow Wilson, Politician 15. Why Suffrage for American Women Was Not Enough 28. Looking Back on Ike 31. Reagan's Rise 32. Looking Back at Watergate 40. America after the Long War
Custer, George A.	3. New View of Custer's Last Battle		
Depression, Great	18. 1933: The Rise of the Common Man		
Diplomacy	22. Man of the Century 24. Good-Bye to Isolationism	Progressivism	11. Doctor Wiley and His Poison Squad 12. Woodrow Wilson, Politician
Environment	39. American Environment		
Ford, Henry	16. Citizen Ford		

TOPIC AREA	TREATED IN	TOPIC AREA	TREATED IN
Racism	1. New View of Reconstruction 5. *Plessy v. Ferguson* Mandate 13. Madam C. J. Walker 17. When White Hoods Were in Flower 30. Trumpet of Conscience 36. Disuniting of America/Painful Demise of Eurocentrism 37. Revolution in Indian Country	Society (continued)	25. G.I. Bill 27. TV's Wonder Years 34. How the Seventies Changed America 35. Suburban Century Begins 36. Disuniting of America/Painful Demise of Eurocentrism
Reagan, Ronald	31. Reagan's Rise	Technology	9. Wings for Man 16. Citizen Ford 39. American Environment
Reconstruction	1. New View of Reconstruction	Urban Problems	34. How the Seventies Changed America
Reform	2. First Chapter of Children's Rights 4. Reinventing Government, 1882 11. Doctor Wiley and His Poison Squad 12. Woodrow Wilson, Politician 15. Why Suffrage for American Women Was Not Enough 18. 1933: Rise of the Common Man 30. Trumpet of Conscience 39. American Environment	Vietnam War	33. Final Days of South Vietnam
		West, The	3. New View of Custer's Last Battle
		Wilson, Woodrow	12. Woodrow Wilson, Politician
		Women	13. Madam C. J. Walker 15. Why Suffrage for American Women Was Not Enough
Roosevelt, Franklin D.	22. Man of the Century	World War II	19. The Draft 20. Home Front 21. Operation Overlord 22. Man of the Century 23. Biggest Decision
Society	2. First Chapter of Children's Rights 8. How We Lived 10. Learning to Go to the Movies 14. Alcohol in American History 18. 1933: Rise of the Common Man 19. The Draft 20. Home Front		

Reconstruction and the Gilded Age

The Civil War destroyed the institution of slavery, but it left undefined the status of freed peoples. Some Northerners wanted to give every black family "40 acres and a mule" to provide them with a stake in society. This proved to be too radical a notion for the time, with the result that most freedpeople were forced to work for whatever their former masters would pay them. Indeed, through much of the South what became known as "Black Codes" constituted efforts to force blacks into a condition of servitude. In "The New View of Reconstruction," Eric Foner describes Northern efforts to protect the rights and interests of blacks in the South. Reconstruction eventually collapsed in the face of Southern resistance, but it provided an "animating vision" for the future.

Westward expansion continued after the Civil War, and those Native Americans who stood in its path were shunted off onto "reservations" or hunted down if they resisted. At times they stood and fought, and occasionally they won. George Armstrong Custer's "last stand" at the battle of Little Big Horn has been retold in countless forms. "A New View of Custer's Last Battle," by Richard Fox, uses archaeological evidence to show that the usual descriptions of the way the battle was fought are incorrect.

Every year millions of children are referred to protective agencies as victims of abuse. An ongoing dilemma has been to define the point at which society can intervene to shield youngsters from mistreatment at the hands of their parents. The 1874 trial involving little Mary Ellen McCormack that broke new ground in trying to resolve this issue is described in "The First Chapter of Children's Rights."

The use of patronage has long been an integral part of the American political process. Successful candidates reward their supporters by appointing them to public offices. "To the Victor Belong the Spoils," as one politico put it. This practice invited corruption and often placed individuals in positions for which they were entirely unsuited. The essay "Reinventing Government, 1882," tells of an early effort to replace the spoils system with one based on merit regardless of political affiliation.

Looking Ahead: Challenge Questions

"Radical" Republicans sought to reconstruct Southern society in a way that would protect the rights of freedpeople. Discuss the ways Southerners resisted. Was radical Reconstruction doomed to fail?

At what point does acceptable punishment become child abuse? Who decides? What is the proper role of governmental agencies in seeking out and punishing child abusers?

How could white Americans defend the treatment meted out to Native Americans? Discuss how prejudices try to justify the mistreatment of people defined as "different."

UNIT 1

The New View of Reconstruction

Whatever you were taught or thought you knew about the post–Civil War era is probably wrong in the light of recent study

Eric Foner is Professor of History at Columbia University and author of Nothing but Freedom: Emancipation and Its Legacy.

IN THE PAST twenty years, no period of American history has been the subject of a more thoroughgoing reevaluation than Reconstruction—the violent, dramatic, and still controversial era following the Civil War. Race relations, politics, social life, and economic change during Reconstruction have all been reinterpreted in the light of changed attitudes toward the place of blacks within American society. If historians have not yet forged a fully satisfying portrait of Reconstruction as a whole, the traditional interpretation that dominated historical writing for much of this century has irrevocably been laid to rest.

Anyone who attended high school before 1960 learned that Reconstruction was an era of unrelieved sordidness in American political and social life. The martyred Lincoln, according to this view, had planned a quick and painless readmission of the Southern states as equal members of the national family. President Andrew Johnson, his successor, attempted to carry out Lincoln's policies but was foiled by the Radical Republicans (also known as Vindictives or Jacobins). Motivated by an irrational hatred of Rebels or by ties with Northern capitalists out to plunder the South, the Radicals swept aside Johnson's lenient program and fastened black supremacy upon the defeated Confederacy. An orgy of corruption followed, presided over by unscrupulous carpetbaggers (Northerners who ventured south to reap the spoils of office), traitorous scalawags (Southern whites who cooperated with the new governments for personal gain), and the ignorant and childlike freedmen, who were incapable of properly exercising the political power that had been thrust upon them. After much needless suffering, the white community of the South banded together to overthrow these "black" governments and restore home rule (their euphemism for white supremacy). All told, Reconstruction was just about the darkest page in the American saga.

Originating in anti-Reconstruction propaganda of Southern Democrats during the 1870s, this traditional interpretation achieved scholarly legitimacy around the turn of the century through the work of William Dunning and his students at Columbia University. It reached the larger public through films like *Birth of a Nation* and *Gone With the Wind* and that best-selling work of myth-making masquerading as history, *The Tragic Era* by Claude G. Bowers. In language as exaggerated as it was colorful, Bowers told how Andrew Johnson "fought the bravest battle for constitutional liberty and for the preservation of our institutions ever waged by an Executive" but was overwhelmed by the "poisonous propaganda" of the Radicals. Southern whites, as a result, "literally were put to the torture" by "emissaries of hate" who manipulated the "simple-minded" freedmen, "inflaming the negroes' egotism" and even inspiring "lustful assaults" by blacks upon white womanhood.

In a discipline that sometimes seems to pride itself on the rapid rise and fall of historical interpretations, this traditional portrait of Reconstruction enjoyed remarkable staying power. The long reign of the old interpretation is not difficult to explain. It presented a set of easily identifiable heroes and villains. It enjoyed the imprimatur of the nation's leading scholars. And it accorded with the political and social realities of the first half of this century. This image of Reconstruction helped freeze the mind of the white South in unalterable opposition to any movement for breaching the ascendancy of the Democratic party, eliminating segregation, or readmitting disfranchised blacks to the vote.

NEVERTHELESS, THE demise of the traditional interpretation was inevitable, for it ignored the testimony of the central participant in the drama of Reconstruction—the black freedman. Furthermore, it was grounded in the conviction that blacks were unfit to share in political power. As Dunning's Columbia colleague John W. Burgess put it, "A black skin means membership in a race of men which has never of itself succeeded in subjecting passion to reason, has never, therefore, created any civilization of any kind." Once objective scholarship and modern experience rendered that assumption untenable, the entire edifice was bound to fall.

The work of "revising" the history of

1. New View of Reconstruction

Reconstruction began with the writings of a handful of survivors of the era, such as John R. Lynch, who had served as a black congressman from Mississippi after the Civil War. In the 1930s white scholars like Francis Simkins and Robert Woody carried the task forward. Then, in 1935, the black historian and activist W.E.B. Du Bois produced *Black Reconstruction in America,* a monumental reevaluation that closed with an irrefutable indictment of a historical profession that had sacrificed scholarly objectivity on the altar of racial bias. "One fact and one alone," he wrote, "explains the attitude of most recent writers toward Reconstruction; they cannot conceive of Negroes as men." Du Bois's work, however, was ignored by most historians.

It was not until the 1960s that the full force of the revisionist wave broke over the field. Then, in rapid succession, virtually every assumption of the traditional viewpoint was systematically dismantled. A drastically different portrait emerged to take its place. President Lincoln did not have a coherent "plan" for Reconstruction, but at the time of his assassination he had been cautiously contemplating black suffrage. Andrew Johnson was a stubborn, racist politician who lacked the ability to compromise. By isolating himself from the broad currents of public opnion that had nourished Lincoln's career, Johnson created an impasse with Congress that Lincoln would certainly have avoided, thus throwing away his political power and destroying his own plans for reconstructing the South.

The Radicals in Congress were acquitted of both vindictive motives and the charge of serving as the stalking-horses of Northern capitalism. They emerged instead as idealists in the best nineteenth-century reform tradition. Radical leaders like Charles Sumner and Thaddeus Stevens had worked for the rights of blacks long before any conceivable political advantage flowed from such a commitment. Stevens refused to sign the Pennsylvania Constitution of 1838 because it disfranchised the state's black citizens; Sumner led a fight in the 1850s to integrate Boston's public schools. Their Reconstruction policies were based on principle, not petty political advantage, for the central issue dividing Johnson and these Radical Republicans was the civil rights of freedmen. Studies of congressional policy-making, such as Eric L. McKitrick's *Andrew Johnson and Reconstruction,* also revealed that Reconstruction legislation, ranging from the Civil Rights Act of 1866 to the Fourteenth and Fifteenth Amendments, enjoyed broad support from moderate and conservative Republicans. It was not simply the work of a narrow radical faction.

EVEN MORE STARTLING was the revised portrait of Reconstruction in the South itself. Imbued with the spirit of the civil rights movement and rejecting entirely the racial assumptions that had underpinned the traditional interpretation, these historians evaluated Reconstruction from the black point of view. Works like Joel Williamson's *After Slavery* portrayed the period as a time of extraordinary political, social, and economic progress for blacks. The establishment of public school systems, the granting of equal citizenship to blacks, the effort to restore the devastated Southern economy, the attempt to construct an interracial political democracy from the ashes of slavery, all these were commendable achievements, not the elements of Bowers's "tragic era."

Unlike earlier writers, the revisionists stressed the active role of the freedmen in shaping Reconstruction. Black initiative established as many schools as did Northern religious societies and the Freedmen's Bureau. The right to vote was not simply thrust upon them by meddling outsiders, since blacks began agitating for the suffrage as soon as they were freed. In 1865 black conventions throughout the South issued eloquent, though unheeded, appeals for equal civil and political rights.

With the advent of Radical Reconstruction in 1867, the freedmen did enjoy a real measure of political power. But black supremacy never existed. In most states blacks held only a small fraction of political offices, and even in South Carolina, where they comprised a majority of the state legislature's lower house, effective power remained in white hands. As for corruption, moral standards in both government and private enterprise were at low ebb throughout the nation in the postwar years—the era of Boss Tweed, the Credit Mobilier scandal, and the Whiskey Ring. Southern corruption could hardly be blamed on former slaves.

Other actors in the Reconstruction drama also came in for reevaluation.

Until recently, Thaddeus Stevens had been viewed as motivated by irrational hatred of the Rebels (left). Now he has emerged as an idealist in the best reform tradition.

1. RECONSTRUCTION AND THE GILDED AGE

Most carpetbaggers were former Union soldiers seeking economic opportunity in the postwar South, not unscrupulous adventurers. Their motives, a typically American amalgam of humanitarianism and the pursuit of profit, were no more insidious than those of Western pioneers. Scalawags, previously seen as traitors to the white race, now emerged as "Old Line" Whig Unionists who had opposed secession in the first place or as poor whites who had long resented planters' domination of Southern life and who saw in Reconstruction a chance to recast Southern society along more democratic lines. Strongholds of Southern white Republicanism like east Tennessee and western North Carolina had been the scene of resistance to Confederate rule throughout the Civil War; now, as one scalawag newspaper put it, the choice was "between salvation at the hand of the Negro or destruction at the hand of the rebels."

At the same time, the Ku Klux Klan and kindred groups, whose campaign of violence against black and white Republicans had been minimized or excused in older writings, were portrayed as they really were. Earlier scholars had conveyed the impression that the Klan intimidated blacks mainly by dressing as ghosts and playing on the freedmen's superstitions. In fact, black fears were all too real: the Klan was a terrorist organization that beat and killed its political opponents to deprive blacks of their newly won rights. The complicity of the Democratic party and the silence of prominent whites in the face of such outrages stood as an indictment of the moral code the South had inherited from the days of slavery.

By the end of the 1960s, then, the old interpretation had been completely reversed. Southern freedmen were the heroes, the "Redeemers" who overthrew Reconstruction were the villains, and if the era was "tragic," it was because change did not go far enough. Reconstruction had been a time of real progress and its failure a lost opportunity for the South and the nation. But the legacy of Reconstruction—the Fourteenth and Fifteenth Amendments—endured to inspire future efforts for civil rights. As Kenneth Stampp wrote in *The Era of Reconstruction*, a superb summary of revisionist findings published in 1965, "If it was worth four years of civil war to save the Union, it was worth a few years of radical reconstruction to give the American Negro the ultimate promise of equal civil and political rights."

As Stampp's statement suggests, the reevaluation of the first Reconstruction was inspired in large measure by the impact of the second—the modern civil rights movement. And with the waning of that movement in recent years, writing on Reconstruction has undergone still another transformation. Instead of seeing the Civil War and its aftermath as a second American Revolution (as Charles Beard had), a regression into barbarism (as Bowers argued), or a golden opportunity squandered (as the revisionists saw it), recent writers argue that Radical Reconstruction was not really very radical. Since land was not distributed to the former slaves, they remained economically dependent upon their former owners. The planter class survived both the war and Reconstruction with its property (apart from slaves) and prestige more or less intact.

Not only changing times but also the changing concerns of historians have contributed to this latest reassessment of Reconstruction. The hallmark of the past decade's historical writing has been an emphasis upon "social history"—the evocation of the past lives of ordinary Americans—and the downplaying of strictly political events. When applied to Reconstruction, this concern with the "social" suggested that black suffrage and officeholding, once seen as the most radical departures of the Reconstruction era, were relatively insignificant.

RECENT HISTORIANS have focused their investigations not upon the politics of Reconstruction but upon the social and economic aspects of the transition from slavery to freedom. Herbert Gutman's influential study of the black family during and after slavery found little change in family structure or relations between men and women resulting from emancipation. Under slavery most blacks had lived in nuclear family units, although they faced the constant threat of separation from loved ones by sale. Reconstruction provided the opportunity for blacks to solidify their preexisting family ties. Conflicts over whether black women should work in the cotton fields (planters said yes, many black families said no) and over white attempts to "apprentice" black children revealed that the autonomy of family life was a major preoccupation of the freedmen. Indeed, whether manifested in their withdrawal from churches controlled by whites, in the blossoming of black fraternal, benevolent, and self-improvement organizations, or in the demise of the slave quarters and their replacement by small tenant farms occupied by individual families, the quest for independence from white authority and control over their own day-to-day lives shaped the black response to emancipation.

In the post–Civil War South the surest guarantee of economic autonomy, blacks believed, was land. To the freedmen the justice of a claim to land based on their years of unrequited labor appeared self-evident. As an Alabama black convention put it, "The property which they [the planters] hold was nearly all earned by the sweat of *our* brows." As Leon Litwack showed in *Been in the Storm So Long*, a Pulitzer Prize–winning account of the black response to emancipation, many freedmen in 1865 and 1866 refused to sign labor contracts, expecting the federal government to give them land. In some localities, as one Alabama overseer reported, they "set up claims to the plantation and all on it."

In the end, of course, the vast majority of Southern blacks remained propertyless and poor. But exactly why the South, and especially its black population, suffered from dire poverty and economic retardation in the decades following the Civil War is a matter of much dispute. In *One Kind of Freedom*, economists Roger Ransom and Richard Sutch indicted country merchants for monopolizing credit and charging usurious interest rates, forcing black tenants into debt and locking the South into a dependence on cotton production that impoverished the entire region. But Jonathan Wiener, in his study of postwar Alabama, argued that planters used their political power to compel blacks to remain on the planta-

1. New View of Reconstruction

Reconstruction governments were portrayed as disastrous failures (left) because elected blacks were ignorant or corrupt. In fact, postwar corruption cannot be blamed on former slaves.

tions. Planters succeeded in stabilizing the plantation system, but only by blocking the growth of alternative enterprises, like factories, that might draw off black laborers, thus locking the region into a pattern of economic backwardness.

If THE THRUST OF recent writing has emphasized the social and economic aspects of Reconstruction, politics has not been entirely neglected. But political studies have also reflected the postrevisionist mood summarized by C. Vann Woodward when he observed "how essentially nonrevolutionary and conservative Reconstruction really was." Recent writers, unlike their revisionist predecessors, have found little to praise in federal policy toward the emancipated blacks.

A new sensitivity to the strength of prejudice and laissez-faire ideas in the nineteenth-century North has led many historians to doubt whether the Republican party ever made a genuine commitment to racial justice in the South. The granting of black suffrage was an alternative to a long-term federal responsibility for protecting the rights of the former slaves. Once enfranchised, blacks could be left to fend for themselves. With the exception of a few Radicals like Thaddeus Stevens, nearly all Northern policy-makers and educators are criticized today for assuming that, so long as the unfettered operations of the marketplace afforded blacks the opportunity to advance through diligent labor, federal efforts to assist them in acquiring land were unnecessary.

Probably the most innovative recent writing on Reconstruction politics has centered on a broad reassessment of black Republicanism, largely undertaken by a new generation of black historians. Scholars like Thomas Holt and Nell Painter insist that Reconstruction was not simply a matter of black and white. Conflicts within the black community, no less than divisions among whites, shaped Reconstruction politics. Where revisionist scholars, both black and white, had celebrated the accomplishments of black political leaders, Holt, Painter, and others charge that they failed to address the economic plight of the black masses. Painter criticized "representative colored men," as national black leaders were called, for failing to provide ordinary freedmen with effective political leadership. Holt found that black officeholders in South Carolina mostly emerged from the old free mulatto class of Charleston, which shared many assumptions with prominent whites. "Basically bourgeois in their origins and orientation," he wrote, they "failed to act in the interest of black peasants."

In emphasizing the persistence from slavery of divisions between free blacks and slaves, these writers reflect the increasing concern with continuity and conservatism in Reconstruction. Their work reflects a startling extension of revisionist premises. If, as has been argued for the past twenty years, blacks were active agents rather than mere victims of manipulation, then they could not be absolved of blame for the ultimate failure of Reconstruction.

Despite the excellence of recent writing and the continual expansion of our knowledge of the period, historians of Reconstruction today face a unique dilemma. An old interpretation has been overthrown, but a coherent new synthesis has yet to take its place. The revisionists of the 1960s effectively established a series of negative points: the Reconstruction governments were not as bad as had been portrayed, black supremacy was a myth, the Radicals were not cynical manipulators of the freedmen. Yet no convincing overall portrait of the quality of political and social life emerged from their writings. More recent historians have rightly pointed to elements of continuity that spanned the nineteenth-century Southern experience, especially the survival, in modified form, of the plantation system. Nevertheless, by denying the real changes that did occur, they have failed to provide a convincing portrait of an era characterized above all by drama, turmoil, and social change.

Building upon the findings of the past twenty years of scholarship, a new portrait of Reconstruction ought to begin by viewing it not as a specific time period, bounded by the years 1865 and 1877, but as an episode in a prolonged historical process—American society's adjustment to the consequences of the Civil War and emancipation. The Civil War, of course, raised the decisive questions of America's national existence: the relations between local and national authority, the definition of citizenship, the balance between force and consent in generating obedience to

1. RECONSTRUCTION AND THE GILDED AGE

authority. The war and Reconstruction, as Allan Nevins observed over fifty years ago, marked the "emergence of modern America." This was the era of the completion of the national railroad network, the creation of the modern steel industry, the conquest of the West and final subduing of the Indians, and the expansion of the mining frontier. Lincoln's America—the world of the small farm and artisan shop—gave way to a rapidly industrializing economy. The issues that galvanized postwar Northern politics—from the question of the greenback currency to the mode of paying holders of the national debt—arose from the economic changes unleashed by the Civil War.

Above all, the war irrevocably abolished slavery. Since 1619, when "twenty negars" disembarked from a Dutch ship in Virginia, racial injustice had haunted American life, mocking its professed ideals even as tobacco and cotton, the products of slave labor, helped finance the nation's economic development. Now the implications of the black presence could no longer be ignored. The Civil War resolved the problem of slavery but, as the Philadelphia diarist Sydney George Fisher observed in June 1865, it opened an even more intractable problem: "What shall we do with the Negro?" Indeed, he went on, this was a problem "*incapable* of any solution that will satisfy both North and South."

As Fisher realized, the focal point of Reconstruction was the social revolution known as emancipation. Plantation slavery was simultaneously a system of labor, a form of racial domination, and the foundation upon which arose a distinctive ruling class within the South. Its demise threw open the most fundamental questions of economy, society, and politics. A new system of labor, social, racial, and political relations had to be created to replace slavery.

The United States was not the only nation to experience emancipation in the nineteenth century. Neither plantation slavery nor abolition were unique to the United States. But Reconstruction was. In a comparative perspective Radical Reconstruction stands as a remarkable experiment, the only effort of a society experiencing abolition to bring the former slaves within the umbrella of equal citizenship. Because the Radicals did not achieve everything they wanted, historians have lately tended to play down the stunning departure represented by black suffrage and officeholding. Former slaves, most fewer than two years removed from bondage, debated the fundamental questions of the polity: What is a republican form of government? Should the state provide equal education for all? How could political equality be reconciled with a society in which property was so unequally distributed? There was something inspiring in the way such men met the challenge of Reconstruction. "I knew nothing more than to obey my master," James K. Greene, an Alabama black politician later recalled. "But the tocsin of freedom sounded and knocked at the door and we walked out like free men and we met the exigencies as they grew up, and shouldered the responsibilities."

You NEVER SAW a people more excited on the subject of politics than are the negroes of the south," one planter observed in 1867. And there were more than a few Southern whites as well who in these years shook off the prejudices of the past to embrace the vision of a new South dedicated to the principles of equal citizenship and social justice. One ordinary South Carolinian expressed the new sense of possibility in 1868 to the Republican governor of the state: "I am sorry that I cannot write an elegant stiled letter to your excellency. But I rejoice to think that God almighty has given to the poor of S. C. a Gov. to hear to feel to protect the humble poor without distinction to race or color.... I am a native borned S. C. a poor man never owned a Negro in my life nor my father before me.... Remember the true and loyal are the poor of the whites and blacks, outside of these you can find none loyal."

Few modern scholars believe the Reconstruction governments established in the South in 1867 and 1868 fulfilled the aspirations of their humble constituents. While their achievements in such realms as education, civil rights, and the economic rebuilding of the South are now widely appreciated, historians today believe they failed to affect either the economic plight of the emancipated slave or the ongoing transformation of independent white farmers into cotton tenants. Yet their opponents did perceive the Reconstruction governments in precisely this way—as representatives of a revolution that had put the bottom rail, both racial and economic, on top. This perception helps explain the ferocity of the attacks leveled against them and the pervasiveness of violence in the postemancipation South.

The spectacle of black men voting and holding office was anathema to large numbers of Southern whites. Even more disturbing, at least in the view of those who still controlled the plantation regions of the South, was the emergence of local officials, black and white, who sympathized with the plight of the black laborer. Alabama's vagrancy law was a "dead letter" in 1870, "because those who are charged with its enforcement are indebted to the vagrant vote for their offices and emoluments." Political debates over the level and incidence of taxation, the control of crops, and the resolution of contract disputes revealed that a primary issue of Reconstruction was the role of government in a plantation society. During presidential Reconstruction, and after "Redemption," with planters and their allies in control of politics, the law emerged as a means of stabilizing and promoting the plantation system. If Radical Reconstruction failed to redistribute the land of the South, the ouster of the planter class from control of politics at least ensured that the sanctions of the criminal law would not be employed to discipline the black labor force.

AN UNDERSTANDING OF this fundamental conflict over the relation between government and society helps explain the pervasive complaints concerning corruption and "extravagance" during Radical Reconstruction. Corruption there was aplenty; tax rates did rise sharply. More significant than the rate of taxation, however, was the change in its incidence. For the first time, planters and white farmers had to pay a signifi-

1. New View of Reconstruction

Some scholars exalted the motives of the Ku Klux Klan (left). Actually, its members were part of a terrorist organization that beat and killed its political opponents to deprive blacks of their rights.

cant portion of their income to the government, while propertyless blacks often escaped scot-free. Several states, moreover, enacted heavy taxes on uncultivated land to discourage land speculation and force land onto the market, benefiting, it was hoped, the freedmen.

As time passed, complaints about the "extravagance" and corruption of Southern governments found a sympathetic audience among influential Northerners. The Democratic charge that universal suffrage in the South was responsible for high taxes and governmental extravagance coincided with a rising conviction among the urban middle classes of the North that city government had to be taken out of the hands of the immigrant poor and returned to the "best men"—the educated, professional, financially independent citizens unable to exert much political influence at a time of mass parties and machine politics. Increasingly the "respectable" middle classes began to retreat from the very notion of universal suffrage. The poor were no longer perceived as honest producers, the backbone of the social order; now they became the "dangerous classes," the "mob." As the historian Francis Parkman put it, too much power rested with "masses of imported ignorance and hereditary ineptitude." To Parkman the Irish of the Northern cities and the blacks of the South were equally incapable of utilizing the ballot: "Witness the municipal corruptions of New York, and the monstrosities of negro rule in South Carolina." Such attitudes helped to justify Northern inaction as, one by one, the Reconstruction regimes of the South were overthrown by political violence.

IN THE END, THEN, neither the abolition of slavery nor Reconstruction succeeded in resolving the debate over the meaning of freedom in American life. Twenty years before the American Civil War, writing about the prospect of abolition in France's colonies, Alexis de Tocqueville had written, "If the Negroes have the right to become free, the [planters] have the incontestable right not to be ruined by the Negroes' freedom." And in the United States, as in nearly every plantation society that experienced the end of slavery, a rigid social and political dichotomy between former master and former slave, an ideology of racism, and a dependent labor force with limited economic opportunities all survived abolition. Unless one means by freedom the simple fact of not being a slave, emancipation thrust blacks into a kind of no-man's land, a partial freedom that made a mockery of the American ideal of equal citizenship.

Yet by the same token the ultimate outcome underscores the uniqueness of Reconstruction itself. Alone among the societies that abolished slavery in the nineteenth century, the United States, for a moment, offered the freedmen a measure of political control over their own destinies. However brief its sway, Reconstruction allowed scope for a remarkable political and social mobilization of the black community. It opened doors of opportunity that could never be completely closed. Reconstruction transformed the lives of Southern blacks in ways unmeasurable by statistics and unreachable by law. It raised their expectations and aspirations, redefined their status in relation to the larger society, and allowed space for the creation of institutions that enabled them to survive the repression that followed. And it established constitutional principles of civil and political equality that, while flagrantly violated after Redemption, planted the seeds of future struggle.

Certainly, in terms of the sense of possibility with which it opened, Reconstruction failed. But as Du Bois observed, it was a "splendid failure." For its animating vision—a society in which social advancement would be open to all on the basis of individual merit, not inherited caste distinctions—is as old as America itself and remains relevant to a nation still grappling with the unresolved legacy of emancipation.

The First Chapter of Children's Rights

More than a century ago an abused child began a battle that is still being fought today

Peter Stevens and Marian Eide

In the quiet New York courtroom, the little girl began to speak. "My name is Mary Ellen McCormack. I don't know how old am. . . . I have never had but one pair of shoes, but can't recollect when that was. I have had no shoes or stockings on this winter. . . . I have never had on a particle of flannel. My bed at night is only a piece of carpet, stretched on the floor underneath a window, and I sleep in my little undergarment, with a quilt over me. I am never allowed to play with any children or have any company whatever. Mamma has been in the habit of whipping and beating me almost every day. She used to whip me with a twisted whip, a raw hide. The whip always left black and blue marks on my body. I have now on my head two black and blue marks which were made by mamma with the whip, and a cut on the left side of my forehead which was made by a pair of scissors in mamma's hand. She struck me with the scissors and cut me. I have no recollection of ever having been kissed, and have never been kissed by mamma. I have never been taken on my mamma's lap, or caressed or petted. I never dared to speak to anybody, because if I did I would get whipped. . . . Whenever mamma went out I was locked up in the bedroom. . . . I have no recollection of ever being in the street in my life."

At the beginning of 1874 there were no legal means in the United States to save a child from abuse. Mary Ellen's eloquent testimony changed that, changed our legal system's view of the rights of the child.

Yet more than a century later the concerns that arose from Mary Ellen's case are still being battled over in the courts. The classic dilemmas of just how deeply into the domestic realm the governmental arm can reach and what the obligations of public government are to the private individual take on particular urgency in considering child abuse.

Early in 1989, in the case of *DeShaney v. Winnebago County,* the Supreme Court declared that the government is not obligated to protect its citizens against harm inflicted by private individuals. DeShaney brought the case before the court in a suit against county social service agencies that had failed to intervene when her estranged husband abused their son, Joshua, who, as a result of his father's brutality, suffered permanent brain damage. The father was convicted, but his former wife believes that fault also lies with the agencies, whose failure to intercede violated her son's Fourteenth Amendment right not to be deprived of life or liberty without due process of the law. Chief Justice William H. Rehnquist wrote that intervening officials are often charged with "improperly intruding into the parent-child relationship." Justice William J. Brennan, Jr., dissenting, wrote: "Inaction can be every bit as abusive of power as action, [and] oppression can result when a State undertakes a vital duty and then ignores it."

The difficulty in bringing Mary Ellen McCormack into the New York Supreme Court in 1874 grew from similar controversy over the role of government in family matters, and Mary Ellen's sad history is not so different from Joshua DeShaney's.

When Mary Ellen's mother, Frances Connor, immigrated to the United States from England in 1858, she took a job at the St. Nicholas Hotel in New York City as a laundress. There she met an Irishman named Thomas Wilson who worked in the hotel kitchen shucking oysters. They were married in April 1862, shortly after Wilson had been drafted into the 69th New York, a regiment in the famous Irish Brigade. Early in 1864 she gave birth to their daughter, whom she named Mary after her mother and Ellen after her sister.

The birth of her daughter seems to have heralded the beginning of Frances Wilson's own decline. Her husband was killed that same year in the brutal fighting at Cold Harbor, Virginia, and with a diminished income she found it necessary to look for a job. In May 1864, unable to pay someone to watch the baby while she was at work, she gave Mary Ellen over to the care of a woman named Mary Score for two dollars a week, the whole of her widow's pension. Child farming was a common practice at that time, and many women made a living taking in unwanted children just as others took in laundry. Score lived in a tenement in the infamous warrens of Mulberry Bend, where thousands of immigrants crowded into small, airless rooms, and it is likely that providing foster care was her only means of income.

FINALLY FRANCES WILSON BECAME unable to pay for the upkeep of her child; three weeks after the payments ceased, Score turned Mary Ellen over to the Department of Charities. The little girl—whose mother was never to see her

2. First Chapter of Children's Rights

again—was sent to Blackwells Island in July 1865. Her third home was certainly no more pleasant than Mulberry Bend. Mary Ellen was among a group of sick and hungry foundlings; fully two-thirds of them would die before reaching maturity.

The same slum-bred diseases that ravaged the children on Blackwells Island had also claimed all three children of a couple named Thomas and Mary McCormack. So when Thomas frequently bragged of the three children he had fathered by another woman, his wife was more receptive to the idea of adopting them than she might otherwise have been. Those children, he told her, were still alive, though their mother had turned them over to the care of the city.

The child belonged to the animal kingdom; perhaps the Society for Prevention of Cruelty to Animals could save her.

On January 2, 1866, the McCormacks went to the Department of Charities to reclaim one of the children Thomas's mistress had abandoned. The child they chose as their own was Mary Ellen Wilson. Because the McCormacks were not asked to provide any proof of relation to the child and gave only the reference of their family doctor, there is no evidence that Thomas was in any way related to the child he brought home that day. More than a month later an indenture was filed for Mary Ellen in which the McCormacks promised to report on her condition each year. There were no other requirements.

Shortly after bringing the child home, Thomas McCormack died, and his widow married a man named Francis Connolly. Little more than that is known of the early childhood of Mary Ellen. She came to her new home in a flannel petticoat, and when her clothing was removed from Connolly's home as evidence six years later, there was barely enough to fill a tiny suitcase. She was beaten, set to work, deprived of daylight, and locked in closets for days at a time; she was rarely bathed, never kissed, and never addressed with a gentle word. During the six years she lived with Connolly, only two reports on her progress were filed with the Commissioners of Charities and Correction.

Late in 1873 Etta Angell Wheeler, a Methodist caseworker serving in the tenements of New York City, received a disturbing report. It came from Margaret Bingham, a landlord in Hell's Kitchen, and told of a terrible case of child abuse. The child's parents had been tenants of Bingham for about four years, and almost immediately after they moved in, Bingham began to observe how cruelly they treated their child, Mary Ellen. They confined her in close quarters during hot weather, kept her severely underdressed in cold, beat her daily, and left her unattended for hours at a time. On several occasions Bingham tried to intervene; each time the child's mother said she would call upon the fullest resources of the law before she would allow any interference in her home. Finally Bingham resorted to threat: The beatings and ill treatment would have to stop, or the family would be evicted. When her plan backfired and the family left, Bingham, in a last-ditch effort, sent for Etta Wheeler. In order to observe Mary Ellen's predicament, Wheeler went to the Connollys' neighbor, an ailing tubercular woman named Mary Smitt. Enlisting Smitt's aid, she proposed that Mary Ellen be sent over each day to check on the patient. Smitt reluctantly agreed, and on the pretext of inquiring about this sick neighbor, Wheeler knocked on Mary Connolly's door.

Inside she saw a "pale, thin child, bare-foot, in a thin, scanty dress so tattered that I could see she wore but one garment besides.

"It was December and the weather bitterly cold. She was a tiny mite, the size of five years, though, as afterward appeared, she was then nine. From a pan set upon a low stool she stood washing dishes, struggling with a frying pan about as heavy as herself. Across the table lay a brutal whip of twisted leather strands and the child's meager arms and legs bore many marks of its use. But the saddest part of her story was written on her face in its look of suppression and misery, the face of a child unloved, of a child that had seen only the fearsome side of life. . . . I never saw her again until the day of her rescue, three months later. . . ."

Though social workers often witnessed scenes of cruelty, poverty, and grief, Wheeler found Mary Ellen's plight especially horrifying. She went first to the police; they told her she must be able to furnish proof of assault in order for them to act. Charitable institutions she approached offered to care for the child, but first she must be brought to them through legal means. There were none. Every effort Wheeler made proved fruitless. Though there were laws to protect children—laws, in fact, to prevent assault and battery to any person—there were no means available for intervention in a child's home.

Finally Wheeler's niece had an idea. The child, she said, was a member of the animal kingdom; surely Henry Bergh, the founder of the American Society for the Prevention of Cruelty to Animals, who was famous for his dramatic rescue of mistreated horses in the streets of New York, might be willing to intervene. Within the hour Wheeler had arranged a meeting with Bergh. Despite its apparent strangeness, this sort of appeal was not new to Bergh. Once before he had tried to intervene in a case of child abuse and had failed. This time he was more cautious.

"Very definite testimony is needed to warrant interference between a child and those claiming guardianship," Bergh told Wheeler. "Will you not send me a written statement that, at my leisure, I may judge the weight of the evidence and may also have time to consider if this society should interfere? I promise to consider the case carefully."

WHEELER PROVIDED A STATEMENT IMMEdiately, including in it the observations of neighbors to whom she had spoken. Bergh was convinced. "No time is to be lost," he wrote his lawyer, Elbridge T. Gerry. "Instruct me how to proceed."

The next day Wheeler again visited the sick woman in Hell's Kitchen and found in her room a young man who, on hearing Wheeler's name, said, "I was sent to take the census in this house. I have been in every room." Wheeler then knew him to be a detective for Bergh.

On the basis of the detective's observations and the testimony provided by Etta Wheeler, Bergh's lawyers, Gerry and Ambrose Monell, appeared before Judge Abraham R. Lawrence of the New York Supreme Court to present a petition on behalf of Mary Ellen. They showed that Mary Ellen was held illegally by the Connollys, who were neither her natural parents nor her lawful custodians, and went on to describe the physical abuse

1. RECONSTRUCTION AND THE GILDED AGE

Mary Ellen endured, the marks and bruises on her body, and the general state of deprivation that characterized her existence. They offered a list of witnesses willing to testify on behalf of the child and concluded by stating that there was ample evidence to indicate that she was in clear danger of being maimed or even killed. The lawyers requested that a warrant be issued, the child removed from her home and placed in protective custody, and her parents brought to trial.

Bergh testified that his efforts on behalf of the child were in no way connected to his work with abused animals and that they did not make use of the special legal provisions set up for that purpose. Because of Bergh's association with animal rescue, to this day the case is often described as having originated in his conviction that the child was a member of the animal kingdom. Bergh, however, insisted that his actions were merely those of any humane citizen and that he intended to prevent cruelties inflicted on children through any legal means available.

Judge Lawrence issued a warrant under Section 65 of the Habeas Corpus Act as requested. This provision read in part: "Whenever it shall appear by satisfactory proof that any one is held in illegal confinement or custody, and that there is good reason to believe that he will . . . suffer some irreparable injury, before he can be relieved by the issuing of a *habeas corpus* or *certiorari,* any court or officer authorized to issue such writs, may issue a warrant . . . [and] bring him before such court or officer, to be dealt with according to law."

THE PRESS OF THE DAY HAILED GERRY'S use of Section 65 of the Habeas Corpus Act as brilliant. The act was rarely invoked, and the legal means for removing a child from its home were nonexistent. In using the little-known law, Gerry created a new method for intervention.

That same day, April 9, 1874, Mary Ellen was taken from her home and brought into Judge Lawrence's court. Having no adequate clothing of her own, the child had been wrapped in a carriage blanket by the policemen who held her in custody. A reporter on the scene described her as "a bright little girl, with features indicating unusual mental capacity, but with a care-worn, stunted, and prematurely old look. . . . no change of custody or condition could be much for the worse."

The reporter Jacob Riis was present in the court. "I saw a child brought in . . . at the sight of which men wept aloud, and I heard the story of little Mary Ellen told . . . that stirred the soul of a city and roused the conscience of a world that had forgotten, and as I looked, I knew I was where the first chapter of children's rights was being written." Her body and face were terribly bruised; her hands and feet "showed the plain marks of great exposure." And in what almost instantly seemed to condemn Mrs. Connolly before the court, the child's face bore a fresh gash through her eyebrow and across her left cheek that barely missed the eye itself. Mary Ellen was to carry this scar throughout her life.

Jacob Riis "saw a child brought in at the sight of which men wept aloud, and heard the story that roused the conscience of a world."

Interestingly, there is no further mention in the ample reports surrounding Mary Ellen's case of her foster father, Francis Connolly. He was never brought into court, never spoke publicly concerning the child. All her life Mary Ellen exhibited a frightened timidity around men, yet it was against her foster mother that she testified.

On the evening of her detention, Mary Ellen was turned over to the temporary custody of the matron of police headquarters. The next day, April 10, the grand jury read five indictments against Mary Connolly for assault and battery, felonious assault, assault with intent to do bodily harm, assault with intent to kill, and assault with intent to maim. Once the stepmother had been brought into the legal system, there were ample means to punish her.

Mary Ellen herself was brought in to testify against the woman she had called her mother. On her second appearance in court she seemed almost wholly altered. She was clothed in a new suit, and her pale face reflected the kindness that surrounded her. She carried with her a new picture book, probably the first she had ever owned. She acted open and uninhibited with strangers, and interestingly, seemed to show no great fear of her mother or any apparent enmity toward her.

The lawyers Gerry and Monell gathered several witnesses against Mary Connolly, among them neighbors, Wheeler, and Mary Ellen herself. Margaret Bingham said she had seen the child locked up in a room and had told other neighbors, but they said there was no point in interfering since the police would do nothing. Bingham had tried to open the window of the child's room to let in some air, but it would not lift more than an inch. As a constant presence and reminder, a cowhide whip was locked in the room with the child. Wheeler recounted her first visit to Mary Ellen, during which the child washed dishes that seemed twice her size and was apparently oblivious of the visitor's presence. The whip lay on the table next to her. The next day, when Wheeler came by again, the child was sewing, and the whip lay on a chair near her.

Then it was the mother's turn to testify. On the witness stand Mary Connolly showed herself to be a woman of some spirit. Despite her treatment of the child, there is something compelling in Connolly's strength and humor. At one point the prosecutor asked if she had an occupation beyond housekeeping. "Well," she said, "I sleep with the boss." As the trial wore on, she became enraged at Gerry's prodding questions; finally she accused him of being "ignorant of the difficulties of bringing up and governing children." Yet she admitted that contrary to regulations, in the six years she had Mary Ellen in her custody, she had reported on her condition to the Commissioners of Charities and Correction only twice.

Two indictments were brought against Connolly, the first for her assault on the child with scissors on April 7, the second for the continual assaults inflicted on the child throughout the years 1873 and 1874. After twenty minutes of deliberation the jury returned a verdict of guilty of assault and battery. Connolly was sentenced to one year of hard labor in the city penitentiary, then known as the Tombs. In handing down this sentence, the judge defined it not only as a punishment to Connolly but also as a statement of precedence in child-abuse cases.

Mary Ellen never returned to the Connollys' home. In the ensuing months the publicity that her case received brought in many claims of relation. But on investigating, her guardian, Judge Lawrence, discovered the stories were fictions, and he finally placed the child in the Sheltering Arms, a home for grown girls; soon after, she was moved to the Woman's Aid Society and Home for Friendless Girls. This mirrors another critical problem in the system's treatment of minors. All juveniles were handled by the Department of Charities and Correction, and whether they were orphaned or delinquent, their treatment was the same. And so it was that the ten-year-old Mary Ellen was placed in a home with mostly delinquent adolescents.

Etta Wheeler knew this was wrong for Mary Ellen, and she expressed her hesitations to Judge Lawrence. He, in turn, consulted with Henry Bergh, and eventually they agreed to turn the girl over to Etta Wheeler herself. Unable to imagine giving up her work in the slums of New York City but believing that Mary Ellen deserved a better environment, Wheeler brought the child to her mother in North Chili, New York. Wheeler's mother became ill shortly afterward, and Mary Ellen was raised mostly by Wheeler's sister.

"HERE BEGAN A NEW LIFE," WHEELER wrote. "The child was an interesting study, so long shut within four walls and now in a new world. Woods, fields, 'green things growing,' were all strange to her, she had not known them. She had to learn, as a baby does, to walk upon the ground,—she had walked only upon floors, and her eye told her nothing of uneven surfaces. . . . But in this home there were other children and they taught her as children alone can teach each other. They taught her to play, to be unafraid, to know her rights and to claim them. She shared their happy, busy life from the making of mud pies up to charming birthday parties and was fast becoming a normal child."

The happiness of her years in the upstate New York countryside lies in stark contrast to her early childhood. And indeed, as Wheeler wrote, she learned by example the ways of normal childhood. She grew up strong and well, learning how to read and playing with friends and pet kittens. In 1875 Wheeler reported to Gerry that Mary Ellen was growing up as a normal child. "She has some faults that are of the graver sort. She tells fibs and sticks to them bravely, steals lumps of sugar & cookies and only confesses when the crumbs are found in her pocket—in short she is very much like other children, loving—responding to kindness & praise, hating a task unless there be a play, or a reward thereof, and inevitably 'forgetting' what she does not wish to remember—what children do not do some or all of these forbidden things! She is a favorite with nearly all the people who have come to know her."

When she was twenty-four, Mary Ellen married a widower named Louis Schutt and with him had two children, Etta—named after the woman who had rescued her—and Florence. She adopted a third, orphaned child, Eunice. She also raised Louis Schutt's three children from his first wife.

In 1911 Wheeler visited her protégé in her home, "finding her well and happy. . . . The family income is small, but Mary Ellen is a prudent housewife & they are comfortable. The two daughters are promising girls." The eldest daughter, Etta, worked industriously through that summer, finished high school, and became a teacher. Florence followed her sister's path, teaching first grade for thirty-eight years. When she retired, the elementary school in North Chili was renamed in her honor. Eunice earned a business degree, married, and raised two sons.

Florence remembers her mother as a solemn woman who came alive whenever she listened to Irish jigs and especially to "The Irish Washerwoman." She was unfailingly generous with her time and her affection. Her years in North Chili had saved her from the vicious cycle abused children often suffer of becoming abusers themselves. According to Florence her mother was capable of sternness and certainly willing to punish her daughters, but the terrible experiences of her early childhood never spilled into her own child rearing. As Etta Wheeler wrote, "To her children, two bright, dutiful daughters, it has been her joy to give a happy childhood in sharp contrast to her own."

ETTA AND FLORENCE OFTEN ASKED THEIR mother about the Connollys, but Mary Ellen was reluctant to speak of her early years. She did show her daughters the scars on her arms where she had been burned with a hot iron, and of course they could see the scissors scar across her face. Florence distinctly recalls that in the few times they spoke of her mother's years in New York City, she never mentioned a woman inflicting her injuries; it was always a man.

In October of 1913 Mary Ellen Schutt attended a meeting of the American Humane Society in Rochester. She was accompanied by Etta Wheeler, who was there to present a paper entitled "The Finding of Mary Ellen." The paper concluded: "If the memory of her earliest years is sad, there is this comfort that the cry of her wrongs awoke the world to the need of organized relief for neglected and abused children."

Mary Ellen was survived by three daughters—and by a movement that would help avert tragedies like hers.

Mary Ellen died on October 30, 1956, at the age of ninety-two. She was survived by her two daughters, her adopted daughter, three stepchildren, three grandchildren, and five great-grandchildren. More important, she was survived by the beginning of a movement to prevent the repetition of tragedies like her own. On December 15, 1874, Henry Bergh, Elbridge Gerry, and James Wright founded the New York Society for the Prevention of Cruelty to Children (SPCC) with the ample assistance of Cornelius Vanderbilt. It was the first organization of its kind in America. At the outset of their work the founders signed a statement of purpose: "The undersigned, desirous of rescuing the unprotected children of this city and State from the cruelty and demoralization which neglect and abandonment engender, hereby engage to aid, with their sympathy and support, the organization and working of a Children's Protective Society, having in view the realization of so important a purpose."

The SPCC saw its role essentially as a legal one. As an agent or a friend of the court, the society endeavored to intervene on the behalf of children, enforcing the laws that were in existence to prevent cruelty toward them and at the same time introducing new legislation on their behalf.

At the first meeting of the SPCC on December 16, 1874, Gerry stressed the fact that the most crucial role of the society lay in the rescue of children from abusive situations. From there, he

1. RECONSTRUCTION AND THE GILDED AGE

pointed out, there were many excellent groups available to care for and shelter children and many state laws to punish abusive parents. He went on to predict that as soon as abusers learned that the law could reach them, there would be few cases like that of Mary Ellen.

Bergh was less optimistic. At the same meeting, he pointed out that neglected and abused children were to become the mothers and fathers of the country and that unless their interests were defended, the interests of society in general would suffer.

In its first year the SPCC investigated more than three hundred cases of child abuse. Many people felt threatened by the intrusion of the government into their private lives; discipline, they believed, was a family issue, and outside influence was not only unwelcome but perhaps even unconstitutional. When, with the aid of a state senator, James W. Booth, Gerry introduced in the New York legislature a law entitled "An Act to Prevent and Punish Wrongs to Children," the proposal was immediately and vigorously attacked. The New York *World* wrote that Bergh was to be authorized to "break into the garrets of the poor and carry off their children upon the suspicion of spanking." According to the *World,* the law would give Bergh "power to discipline all the naughty children of New York. . . . We sincerely hope that it may not be finally kicked out of the legislature, as it richly deserves to be, until the public mind shall have had time to get itself thoroughly enlightened as to the state of things in which it has become possible for such a person as Mr. Bergh to bring the Legislature to the point of seriously entertaining such an impudently senseless measure. This bill is a bill to supersede the common law in favor of Mr. Bergh, and the established tribunals of justice in favor of an irresponsible private corporation." The bill was passed in 1876, however, and became the foundation upon which the SPCC performed its work.

From its initial concentration on preventing abuse in the home, the society broadened its franchise to battle neglect, abandonment, and the exploitation of children for economic gain. In 1885, after considerable effort by the SPCC and in the face of yet more opposition, Gerry secured passage of a bill that made labor by children under the age of fourteen illegal.

As THE EXPLOSIVE STORY OF THE DEATH of Lisa Steinberg in the home of her adoptive parents revealed to the nation in 1987, abuse still haunts American society. There are still legal difficulties in removing a child from an abusive situation. In 1987 the House Select Committee on Children, Youth, and Families reported that the incidence of child abuse, particularly sexual abuse and neglect, is rising; in 1985 alone almost two million children were referred to protective agencies. In part, the committee said, this increase was due to a greater awareness of the issue, and there has also been an increased effort to educate children themselves about situations that constitute abuse or molestation and about ways to get help.

Despite a plethora of programs designed to address abuse, the committee concluded that not enough is being done. The most effective programs were found to be those that worked to prevent the occurrence of abuse at the outset through education in parenting techniques, through intervention in high-risk situations, such as unwanted pregnancies, and through screening for mental and emotional difficulties. However, funding for public welfare programs has fallen far below the demands, and what funding there is must frequently be diverted to intervene in more and more sensational and hopeless cases.

If there is still much hard, sad work ahead, there is also much that has been accomplished. And all of it began when Mary Ellen McCormack spoke and, in speaking, freed herself and thousands of other children from torment.

Peter Stevens, who lives in Quincy, Massachusetts, writes frequently on historical themes. Marian Eide is a graduate student in the Comparative Literature and Critical Theory Program at the University of Pennsylvania. We would like to thank Dr. Stephen Lazoritz for his contributions to the research of this article. Lazoritz, a pediatrician specializing in child-abuse cases, first became interested in Mary Ellen's history when, preparing for a lecture on child abuse, he read "The Great Meddler," Gerald Carson's profile of Henry Bergh in the December 1967 issue of American Heritage. Lazoritz was fascinated by the child and traced her history through a trail of documents and newspaper articles. In the story of Mary Ellen's childhood he found the roots of a movement to prevent child abuse in which he is very much involved today. Lazoritz's youngest daughter was born during his pursuit of the case. Her name is Mary Ellen. Thanks, too, to the New York Society for the Prevention of Cruelty to Children, whose archives contain full documentation of the Mary Ellen case.

Article 3

BATTLES WON AND LOST

A New View of Custer's Last Battle

For more than a century, accounts of George Armstrong Custer's fatal 1876 encounter with Sioux and Northern Cheyenne warriors in Montana's Little Big Horn Valley almost uniformly painted a picture of a determined resistance by men of the U.S. Seventh Cavalry before they were finally overwhelmed by superior numbers. But after applying the principles of historic archaeology to evidence gathered from the battlefield and re-evaluating the surviving historical record, the author draws some surprisingly different—and perhaps controversial—conclusions.

Richard Allan Fox, Jr.

Richard A. Fox is an Assistant Professor in the Department of Anthropology at the University of South Dakota. In the mid-1980s, he codirected the Custer Battlefield Archaeological Project. He coauthored two books on the project, Archaeological Insights into the Custer Battle *(1987) and* Archaeological Perspectives on the Battle of the Little Big Horn *(1989).*

Elbert Hubbard's 1905 vision of George Armstrong Custer's final battle measures the romance of that famous frontier encounter. As Hubbard told it, the outcome came down to a matter of endurance. With his command surrounded by hostile warriors, Custer realized how tenuous the situation had become. In desperation, he dispatched a message to General Alfred Terry, pleading for help. Then came noon "and buzzards began to gather in the azure." The afternoon dragged on; the sun sank. "Custer warned his men that sleep was death." The dawn of a new day approached. Daylight found Terry still struggling to reach the beleaguered expedition with reinforcements. Finally, Custer and his men ran out of ammunition. Then the Indians closed in and it was over. Sadly, Terry had fallen an hour or two short.

Although fanciful in the extreme—actually, the final engagement between Custer's troops and their antagonists probably unfolded in no more than two hours, with the decisive fighting taking much less than an hour—Hubbard's image reflects the heroic aura that still continues to surround the events of June 25, 1876, when Lieutenant Colonel Custer and more than two hundred of his men from the U.S. Seventh Cavalry died in the fabled clash with Sioux and Northern Cheyenne warriors on a hillside overlooking Montana's Little Big Horn River.

Even today it is popular to imagine a gallant if futile defense by Custer's cavalry that, if not sustained to the last man and the last bullet, certainly involved a determined struggle. But a study of archaeological evidence gathered during recent years—especially when combined with long-ignored Indian testimony and tradition—points to the likelihood of a different kind of ending for the mythic Custer and his troopers.

BACKGROUND ON THE 1876 CAMPAIGN

During the 1850s, increasing contact with the western Indian tribes led to formulation of U.S. Government policies designed to confine the natives to reservations. One such tract was the Great Sioux Reservation that encompassed much of what is now western Da-

This article is based on the author's research for Archaeology, History, and Custer's Last Battle: The Little Big Horn Reexamined *(416 pages, illustrated, $29.95), published by the University of Oklahoma Press, Norman 73070, 800-627-7377.*

1. RECONSTRUCTION AND THE GILDED AGE

kota. The Black Hills, considered sacred by the Sioux, lay in the heart of the vast reserve.

Treaty obligations of 1851 and 1868 guaranteed to the Sioux that the reservation would not pass from their possession. In 1874, however, word of gold deposits in the Black Hills spread, precipitating an influx of white entrepreneurs. Within a year, the white populace in the region grew significantly, and political pressures to open the Black Hills to permanent white settlement magnified. Eventually the U.S. Government drastically reduced the size of the Great Sioux Reservation, and the Indians lost their sacred lands entirely. Many, disenchanted with the repeated treaty violations, left the reservation to return to their old way of life. They moved west, often to join non-treaty brethren roaming unceded lands in the Montana and Wyoming territories.

Government officials perceived the Sioux wanderings as threats, not only to existing Indian policies but also to the security of settlers pushing ever westward. Thus in late 1875 and early 1876, the U.S. Army devised plans to intercept the Indians and return them to the reservation. According to a loosely formulated strategy, three Army columns would converge on the Indians in pincer-like fashion. One column, under the command of General Terry, included the Seventh U.S. Cavalry Regiment led by Lieutenant Colonel Custer. Terry's column left Fort Abraham Lincoln (on the Missouri River near Bismarck, North Dakota) on May 17, 1876, and marched westward, expecting to find the Indians in what is now southern Montana.

Responding to intelligence reports, the Seventh Cavalry, some six hundred men strong, separated from General Terry's command on June 22 and headed toward the Little Big Horn River with orders to scout the country and locate the Indians. The rest of the column under General Terry, along with a second column under Colonel John Gibbon, were to join Custer in the vicinity of the Little Big Horn on June 26.

In the early morning hours of June 25, from a hilltop vantage point called the Crow's Nest, Custer's scouts spied signs of an Indian encampment on the west bank of the Little Big Horn River. Custer, fearing that his force had in turn been detected by Indian scouts, decided to attack.

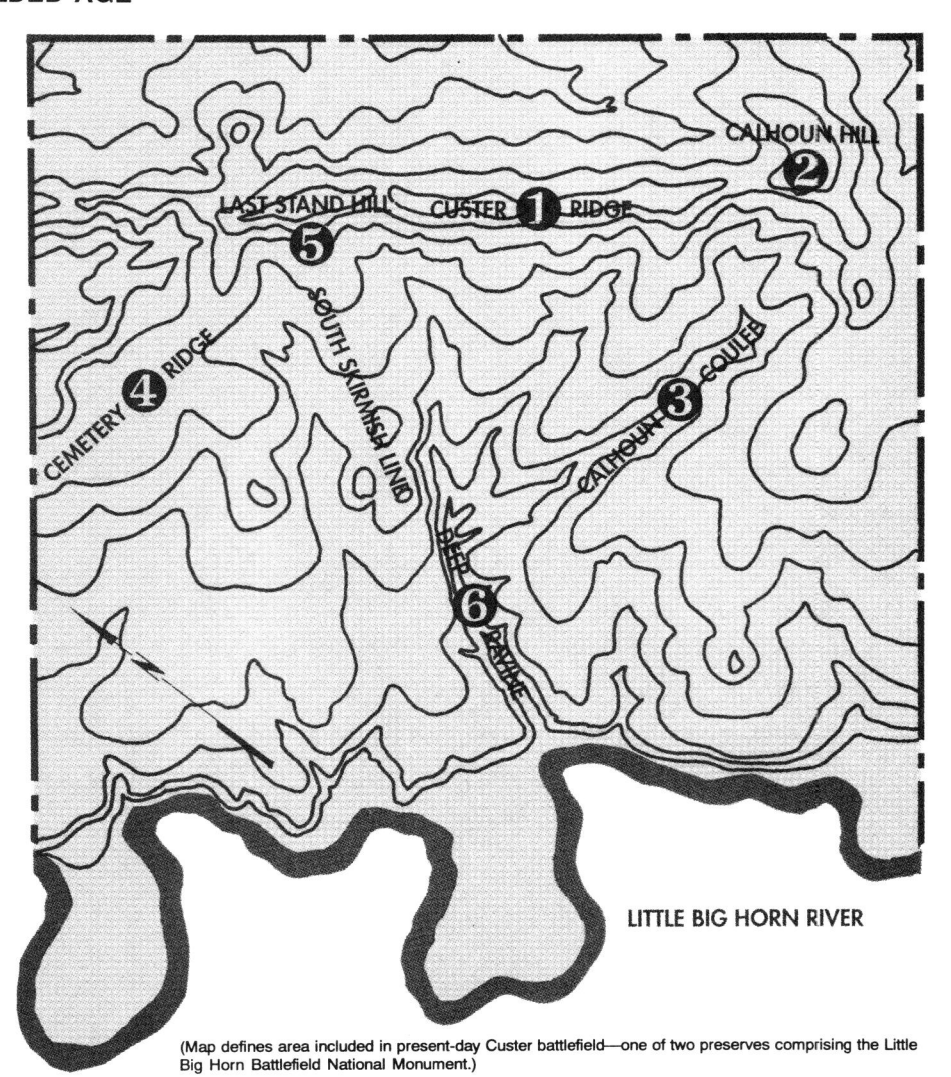

(Map defines area included in present-day Custer battlefield—one of two preserves comprising the Little Big Horn Battlefield National Monument.)

The author argues that after nearly reaching the Indian encampment at Medicine Tail Ford (out of view to right of this map of the Custer Battlefield), Custer and two of his companies regained the heights, crossed Custer Ridge (1), and then descended on a reconnaisance to another river crossing, "Ford D" (north of the encampment and out of view to the left of the map). His three remaining companies, under Captain Myles Keogh, remained on and near Calhoun Hill (2). During Custer's absence, Indians began to infiltrate and threaten Keogh's position. Subsequent engagements with warriors at Calhoun Coulee (3), on Calhoun Hill, and along the ridge to the north led to the sudden unanticipated collapse of Keogh's forces. Custer, who by this time had returned to Cemetery Ridge (4) to await expected reinforcement by three companies under Captain Frederick Benteen, was now forced to advance to Last Stand Hill (5) to provide assistance. There the cavalry commander and many of his remaining men were overwhelmed; others, however, reached Deep Ravine (6) before becoming the last to perish.

As the twelve companies of the Seventh Cavalry descended westward through broken country toward the river, Custer divided his regiment into three battalions and detached one company to escort the slower-moving pack train that carried ammunition and supplies. Captain Frederick W. Benteen, commanding three companies (approximately 125 men), received orders to ride toward the southwest, ostensibly to block a possible escape by the Indians. The remaining eight companies, led by Custer, then continued west down a small tributary of the Little Big Horn, today known as Reno Creek. At a point several miles above the river valley, the column surprised a party of Sioux; at nearly the same time the soldiers saw a cloud of dust rising in the direction of the en-

3. New View of Custer's Last Battle

campment. Custer detached Major Marcus Reno with three companies (roughly 130 men), ordering him to charge into the valley and attack the tepee village.

Custer, commanding the last battalion of five companies (about 210 men), promised to support Reno's assault. But instead of following in Reno's wake as the major had expected, he veered north, evidently intent on striking the village from farther downriver.

Reno's force, descending into the valley and crossing the Little Big Horn, encountered resistance at the edge of what proved to be a huge Indian encampment. After dismounting and forming a skirmish line, the cavalrymen withdrew into timber adjacent to the river, where they remained for about thirty minutes. Then, threatened by infiltrating Indians, Reno abandoned this position. Pursued by warriors, the retreating cavalrymen scrambled in confusion and disorder across the river and up the bluffs on the far side, losing about forty of their number in the process.

The arrival of Reno's shaken command on the bluffs coincided with the approach of Benteen's battalion, which had been recalled by Custer. Reno's predicament compelled Benteen to forgo joining his commander. Aided by Benteen and the eventual arrival of the pack train under Captain Thomas McDougall, Reno's battalion began to reorganize. The Indians, meanwhile, disengaged and moved several miles downriver to meet the new danger posed by Custer's battalion.

This threat had developed in Medicine Tall Coulee, where two companies of Custer's cavalry, descending the coulee and reaching the ford on the Little Big Horn River, exchanged gunfire with warriors. The cavalrymen then left the coulee and continued north along the heights to the area that now comprises the Custer Battlefield [see map].[1] Here, fighting ultimately intensified, and here Sioux and Cheyenne warriors wiped out Custer's battalion.

It is also here that the application of historical archaeology has provided clues that can help us to piece together a picture of what most likely happened during Custer's final battle.

BATTLEFIELD ARCHAEOLOGY

When a prairie fire swept across the Custer Battlefield in August 1983, clearing the terrain of obscuring vegetation, it became practicable for the first time in this century to conduct an archaeological investigation that could conceivably provide answers to many of the questions that had gone begging for more than a hundred years.

During the next two summers, National Park Service archaeologist Douglas D. Scott and the author led teams of metal detector operators and other volunteers on a systematic survey of nearly the entire Custer Battlefield (the river bottoms excepted) to locate and recover battle-related artifacts.

The archaeological record extracted from the field during 1984–85 provided significant evidence relating to Custer's final battle—including about two thousand recovered artifacts that ranged from bullets, cartridges coins, horse trappings, and buttons to human remains.[2] The perspective provided by the application of what is known as historical archaeology to this material residue has generated new insights into the probable movements and behavior of Custer and his troops during this decisive action.

These clues paint a picture that is inconsistent with the traditional image of a determined struggle between cavalrymen and Indians—the gallant "Last Stand" of lore. Instead, a study of the distribution of certain artifact types indicates that in most sectors of the field the soldiers resisted but little.

The archaeological record from the Custer Battlefield is inconsistent with a determined struggle. Indeed, the distribution of certain artifact types indicates that at most battle sectors, the soldiers resisted but little.

This picture is consistent with numerous narratives from the historical record, in which warriors who had participated in the fighting recounted fear, panic, and flight among the Army troops. Indeed, archaeology and history together paint a Custer battle quite unlike that presented by most white chroniclers.

Recovered cartridges from Army and Indian firearms, combined with data regarding the exact locations at which they were found, provided the archaeological team with its most useful source of information for analyzing Custer battle events.

Each soldier carried a single-shot Springfield carbine and a Colt revolver—each of which employed distinctive ammunition. Thus the recovery of expended cartridges (casings) from the government firearms provided a fairly reliable record of how often and in what locales the soldiers fired their weapons.

Relatively few Colt casings were found, indicating that sidearms played a minor role in the fray. The distribution of recovered Springfield casings, moreover, revealed that only at what is known as Calhoun Hill did the cavalrymen engage in organized firing with their rifles.[3] Sectors further to the north—at the Keogh area, on Last Stand Hill, and along what is termed the South

---

[1] In 1992 the National Park Service officially changed the name of the Montana site (encompassing both the 667-acre Custer Battlefield and the 160-acre Reno-Benteen Battlefield) from the Custer Battlefield National Monument to the Little Bighorn Battlefield National Monument.

[2] Already available was a less-than-perfect record of where the cavalrymen had died during the battle. When Terry's column arrived following the action, his men interred the fallen soldiers in hastily prepared graves marked by wooden stakes. Similar markers were substituted in 1877 when officers' remains were exhumed for reburial according to their families' wishes, and again in 1881 when troopers' bones were moved to a mass grave atop Last Stand Hill. In 1890, the 252 marble memorial stones visible today were placed on the battlefield. Since only 210 of Custer's command had died there, it is presumed that the additional markers were intended to memorialize those killed in the Reno-Benteen sector.

[3] Situated at the eastern corner of the Custer Battlefield, Calhoun Hill takes its name from Lieutenant James Calhoun, Custer's brother-in-law, whose Company L fought and died there.

1. RECONSTRUCTION AND THE GILDED AGE

Skirmish Line—exhibited little evidence of tactically organized resistance by the troopers, at least with firearms.[4]

Although collectors have undoubtedly removed artifacts from the battlefield over the years, historical evidence suggests that this practice has not significantly compromised the archaeological record. Lieutenant George Wallace (a Reno fight survivor), for example, went over Custer's field in the aftermath of the catastrophic battle. He observed piles of Springfield casings at Calhoun Hill, "but very few elsewhere." Similarly, Lieutenant Charles Roe, who arrived with Terry, noted generally that "very few cartridge shells were found." Equally telling is the testimony of Lieutenant Charles DeRudio (also with Reno) concerning Last Stand Hill. DeRudio remembered seeing only "a few shells" on this hillock—a recollection consistent with the archaeological findings.

The grim reality of Custer's "Last Stand" is not the determined, glorious defense of legend. Rather the picture is of an offensive-minded battalion unexpectedly overcome by disintegration.

When a cartridge is fired and then ejected, the gun's firing pin and ejector mechanism leave marks—called signatures—on the expended cartridge case. Signatures are often peculiar to a firearm type. Signature analysis of Custer battle specimens revealed that warriors possessed at least forty-one different types of firearms, including Henry, Winchester, and Spencer repeating rifles. Indian warriors not only had Custer's troops outnumbered, they were also much better armed than the soldiers.

Firing pins and extractor mechanisms also vary between individual firearms within a type. When examined microscopically, these unique signatures, complemented by the recorded location at which each casing was found, make it not only possible to discern where guns were fired but also to reconstruct the movement of individual firearms—and hence the men who used them—across a battlefield.

Such tracking was possible in numerous instances for both soldiers and warriors at the Little Big Horn battlefield. For the cavalry, unique signatures reveal that some troopers manned two skirmish lines on Calhoun Hill. At least at this one spot, tactical stability existed for a time.

Skirmish-line patterning is absent from all other sectors occupied by Custer's troops. This suggests that a breakdown in stability, or "tactical disintegration" (to use the term employed by those who study battlefield behavior), took place. Based on the archaeological evidence, it appears that disintegration of the Custer force began in the Calhoun Hill vicinity. The discovery of a tight cluster of Springfield casings on Calhoun Hill indicates that at some point soldiers ceased skirmishing and bunched together.

Two unique signatures among the Springfield casings found in a cluster on Calhoun Hill were duplicated in the area last occupied by Captain Myles Keogh's command, indicating that some cavalrymen fled north from Calhoun Hill. Bunching and flight can be expected of men under psychological stress. Typically, flight is toward safety, real or perceived. The direction of flight indicates, therefore, that other cavalry units still survived north of Calhoun Hill when Calhoun's force collapsed.

REEVALUATING THE HISTORICAL RECORD

"I tell no lies about dead men," Sitting Bull assured a white interviewer in 1877 when he stated that the "men who came with [Custer] were as good [as] men who ever fought." In 1881 Low Dog told the same story: "The white warriors stood their ground bravely, and none of them made any attempt to get away." And in 1905 Rain-in-the-Face said that "I had always thought that white men were cowards, but I had great respect for them after [the Custer battle]."

There are more Indian testimonies like these—mostly from the native leaders. But do they accurately reflect the cavalrymen's performance on that 25th day of June, 1876? Could such accounts instead reflect a human propensity well described by French artillery officer Ardant du Picq, a contemporary of Custer? To paraphrase du Picq, "the vanquished always console themselves, and the victors never contradict."

Did the warriors who recounted bravery among their adversaries simply relate what their white audiences wished to hear? Was the Custer battle in fact something less than a glorious, determined Last Stand?

Like material remains, the primary historical record of the Custer battle is rich and varied. Indian eyewitness accounts number in the hundreds—and many contradict those just noted. Indeed, conduct attendant to flight—panic and fear—is described, often as metaphor, in many of the Indian narratives of soldier behavior.

Runs the Enemy, for instance, recalled that the troopers' rush from Calhoun Hill resembled a "stampede of buffalo." Gall, Dewey Beard, Moving Robe, and others remembered that in the Keogh sector, warriors using clubs, knives, and hatchets jumped among the soldiers. Horned Horse recollected that fighting in that same area "was just like this [fingers intertwined], Indians and white men." Hollow Horn Bear remembered the fleeing soldiers acting as if drunk. Red Feather saw them shot from behind, and White Bull recounted that some were jerked from their horses. Indeed, there is not much evidence in the Keogh sector for firing by the warriors.

RECONSTRUCTING CUSTER'S LAST BATTLE

Here, based on an analysis of archaeological evidence from the battlefield and the historical record, is what probably took place during Custer's final, catastrophic battle:

What ended in a chaotic confrontation began without even a hint of alarm in Medicine Tail Coulee, about two-

---

[4] The Keough sector, which is dotted with fifty-eight marble markers to indicate where Captain Myles Keogh and members of his command fell, is situated on the eastern perimeter of the Battlefield between Calhoun Hill and Last Stand Hill—the spot where Custer himself is presumed to have died. The South Skirmish Line is a ridge running south from Last Stand Hill.

thirds of a mile south of the present Custer Battlefield boundary. Custer's five companies entered the drainage in battalion formation, then split into two wings. The right wing (companies C, I, and L, commanded by Keogh) ascended to high ground directly above the stream and waited there, just over a mile from the Little Big Horn River. Meanwhile the left wing (companies E and F, commanded by Captain George Yates and accompanied by Custer and his staff) rode down the coulee, eventually reaching its mouth at a river crossing known today as Medicine Tail Ford. Directly across the Little Big Horn River from the troopers lay the northern limit of the Indian encampment—the Cheyenne camp circle.

Scant numbers of warriors were present at the ford when the cavalrymen arrived—most already having rushed south to meet Reno's assault. By Bobtail Horse's account not more than ten Indians initially met the Army riders, and these increased to only thirty or so. Dull Knife, who was among them, exclaimed, "It's no use, we cannot stop them!" Mad Wolf also sensed a precarious situation, cautioning, "No one should charge yet, the soldiers are too many." Though few in number, the warriors did fire, and the troopers responded with a volley or two.

Certainly, the few warriors at Medicine Tail expected the cavalrymen to charge across the ford into the village. But the anticipated charge never took place—producing the most enigmatic of all Custer battle conundrums. The soldiers had closed to within easy striking distance of the village, but did not attack! Why?

Very simply, Custer did not cross Medicine Tail Ford because the village was virtually empty. His quarry—the noncombatants—had fled at the first hint of Reno's attack, first to the northern camps, then north and west out of the village. Lone Bear, Two Eagles, and Lights agreed that villagers "scattered down the stream [river], and up in the hills." Several sketches left by Indian informants—including Red Hawk, White Bull, Standing Bear, and Flying Hawk—depict hiding places in ravines approximately abreast of Last Stand Hill.

Whatever Custer's intent had been prior to reaching Medicine Tail Ford, he now intended to capture refugees. That was the mission of the expedition—to return the Indians to their reservation. Capturing the noncombatants would render the warriors, now busy with Reno, helpless; the village could be sacked later. Custer had learned this much eight years earlier on the Washita, in the Oklahoma Territory, where he surprised Black Kettle's Cheyenne band.

The exodus of noncombatants fueled the subsequent strategic movements undertaken by Custer and the two companies of the left-wing force. Drawn by the fleeing villagers, they rode back out of Medicine Tail Coulee and north along Custer Ridge, then back down into the valley to a river crossing known today as "Ford D," north of the present Custer Battlefield boundary.[5]

This reconnaissance to the river established for Custer the existence of a suitable ford; determined that it lay a reasonable distance from the village; and allowed a closeup assessment of the fleeing villagers. With this vital intelligence gathered, Custer and the riders of the left wing turned about and returned to Cemetery Ridge (so-named for the national cemetery later situated there) to await reinforcements.

Meanwhile Keogh's right wing, again functioning in a passive role, ascended to the heights of the Custer Battlefield, where it remained in reserve. Positioned to receive Benteen's three companies, which Custer had recalled even before entering Medicine Trail Coulee, this force was also well-situated to check the few warriors who had followed the two wings up the hillside. Dismounting his riders, Keogh deployed Company L in skirmish formation on Calhoun Hill; he placed the remaining two companies in reserve, probably in what is known as the Keogh sector between Calhoun Hill and Last Stand Hill.

During the left wing's absence, the number of warriors on the hillside gradually increased as the Indians cautiously infiltrated Keogh's positions. Fighting, according to many native accounts, was desultory. Nonetheless warriors eventually got very close to Keogh's troops, some threatening the riderless horses—a strategy reported by Gall, the Hunkpapa Sioux leader.

Threats to the cavalry mounts, and the nearness of warriors, finally demanded relief. Captain Keogh dispatched one of his reserve companies (Company C) into Calhoun Coulee, where many Indians had by now gathered. Wooden Leg recalled this "charge," as he termed it. The company, about forty strong, sent the antagonists scattering.

Then, according to Indian accounts, Cheyenne warrior Lame White Man rallied the warriors. This was the beginning of the end for the cavalrymen; Company C collapsed and fled toward Calhoun Hill.

In response, the men in L Company (who had originally faced south to counter the warriors emerging from Medicine Tail Coulee) shifted their skirmish line position, firing west to cover the men of Company C.

Confusion among Keogh's troops emboldened other warriors, including Crazy Horse and Gall, who joined in the attack. Soon panic engulfed L Company. Now, with both companies broken, the survi-

---

[5] All previous analyses of the Custer battle have ignored or discounted this reconnaissance by cavalrymen to Ford D—which nevertheless is noted in Indian narratives.

vors from C and L bunched together. Some soldiers fired, leaving the cluster of casings found during the 1984–85 survey. Then they fled into the Keogh sector toward Company I, now also under attack by Two Moons and others.

Warriors pursued C and L survivors, and their movements can be tracked by the signatures on spent cartridges they ejected along the way. By now the entire right wing of Custer's battalion had disintegrated. Routed survivors, with warriors among them, fled the Keogh sector, rushing toward Last Stand Hill. Disintegration of the right wing had forced Custer to abandon his position on Cemetery Ridge and advance to Last Stand Hill to provide assistance.

Of approximately 120 men in Keogh's companies, about twenty made it to Last Stand Hill. There they linked up with Custer and the eighty-five or so soldiers of the left wing. The command had been reduced to about 105 men.

Now only half the original battalion remained, and there—on Last Stand Hill—the survivors were surrounded. Though matters had evolved into a desperate situation, Custer and his officers evidently restored some measure of control. Warriors, moments earlier aggressive and bold, reverted again to stealth tactics.

According to Hollow Horn Bear, the siege that followed lasted "just a few minutes." Two Moons recalled that a trumpeter blew a call, whereupon about forty-five men—five mounted, the others on foot—dashed from Last Stand Hill toward the river. The mounted soldiers, as He Dog put it, tried to get away to the south. But they did not make it.

The mounted men probably intended to ride to Reno for help.[6] And the forty or so troopers who rushed from Last Stand Hill on foot probably did so to divert attention from the riders, allowing them the opportunity to escape.

The troopers—E Company as we now know—succumbed to panic induced by a heavy Indian attack. Iron Hawk recalled the Sioux charge that carried the Indians right into the terrified soldiers. The company disintegrated. Bear Lying Down thought the troopers acted as if drunk. According to Lights, soldiers fired wildly in the air, and warriors wrenched their guns away. The attack caused E Company to "swerve," as one Indian put it, toward a rugged coulee now called Deep Ravine. Many, such as Good Voiced Elk and Standing Bear, recalled that surviving soldiers jumped into the coulee. Once there, the fighting evolved into a hide-and-seek affair as soldiers struggled on their own.

Meanwhile, the siege at Custer Hill had taken its toll. It was a grim siege—not the swirling, glorious finale of history. About sixty men had remained behind when E Company rushed from the hill. Of these, some twenty more subsequently fled toward Deep Ravine—leaving about forty, including the general, to die on Last Stand Hill. Their deaths, and this hill, have more than anything else immortalized the Custer battle—the "Last Stand" of frontier lore.

The last fighting of the Custer battle, however, did not take place on Last Stand Hill. Instead, the struggle ended in and around the tangled brush of Deep Ravine. Flying Hawk, American Horse, and Young Two Moons said exactly that, echoing Respects Nothing, who reported, "[The soldiers] at Custer Hill were all killed before those were down along the ravine."

In all, the fighting had lasted about ninety minutes—around an hour of subdued exchanges as cautious warriors infiltrated, followed by the dissolution of tactical stability—when "the battle became furious" as Foolish Elk described it. Gall, Crow King, and other participants estimated the "furious" activity as lasting about thirty minutes.

Iron Hawk summarized the whole affair. Referring to the transition from stability to disintegration, he said: "Custer's men in the beginning shot straight, but later they shot like drunken men, firing into the ground, into the air, wildly in every way." Two Moons described the panic this way: "They acted and shot their guns like something was wrong with them, [like they] had too much of that whiskey." And, according to Waukutemonie, "most of the soldiers acted as though they were drunk. Many of them threw down their guns."

References to soldiers abandoning their guns are numerous. This behavior puzzled the Indians, Gall included. They seemed not to understand that close-in fighting—characteristic of much of the Custer battle—rendered the single-shot carbine sorely ineffective. Conversely, many warriors—more than two hundred based on firearm signature analysis projections—carried repeating rifles. The repeaters were very effective at close range, dealing destruction as much in the debilitating effects of shock as in the killing.

Captain Benteen went over the field on June 28, searching for clues. Writing to his wife a month after the fight, he noted that "[Custer's battalion] was probably thrown into a panic at the first check received—and gotten in just the condition that indian [sic] would get a herd of buffalo."

Lieutenant Luther Hare helped to bury the dead. Late in life he confided, "The men were struck with panic and did not fight well." Paints Himself Brown summed it up: "Pretty soon the soldiers started to run and we went after them, but it wasn't long before they were all killed or wounded."

CONCLUSIONS

And so Custer's last battle ended. Experienced observers will note that the picture painted here is wholly at odds with conventional explanations, which are invariably built around a fatalistic theme that superior numbers forced the battalion to defend itself on Custer Ridge. While some proponents of this scenario contend that the soldiers were driven there, others argue that they were caught on the ridge and forced into their gallant Last Stand. But would not a battalion on the defensive leave traces of resistance everywhere it went?

The archaeological evidence for such a determined defense does not exist. Only at Calhoun Hill do we find the material remains of organized firing. Elsewhere, archaeological finds in no way support an organized, even stubborn resistance. Instead, the residue of battle reveals hints of a battalion on the offensive. With this foundation, the confusing, often contradictory historical record can be sorted. In the process, the picture of an offensive-minded battalion unexpectedly overcome by disintegration springs from the documents.

Archaeology provided the foundation for this realization. But it might have been deduced on theoretical grounds. Modern studies of combat show that collapse usually comes suddenly and when least expected. Indeed, decisive battles are seldom the result of attrition

---

[6] As previously noted, attacking warriors had forced Reno and Benteen into a defensive position, where they remained until June 27. Losses for the two battalions totaled about fifty.

3. New View of Custer's Last Battle

through prolonged resistance. Rather, psychological collapse almost always precedes physical collapse. Military scholars are quick to caution, however, that psychological debilitation is not cowardice, the utter absence of a willingness to fight.

Archaeology, the historical record, and studies of behavior in battle are in agreement. When the general's battalion reached Custer Ridge, it was on the offensive. Hordes of Indians bent on destruction did not drive it there, nor was denouement immediately forthcoming. This view of Custer's last battle—provided by the findings of historical archaeology—forces a reconsideration of events that preceded the action on Custer Ridge. Such an understanding helps explain why the Custer battle happened as it did.

Stephen Jay Gould once noted that most impediments to scientific understanding are conceptual locks, not factual locks. Gould was not referring to the Custer battle—but he might as well have been doing so. In fatalistic versions, Custer is driven to or at least corralled on Custer Ridge, and he went no further. Throngs of Indians saw to that; they stopped him in his tracks. The doomed battalion had no choice but to hastily throw out its defense—soldiers on the southern end of the ridge (Calhoun Hill) and soldiers on the northern end—Last Stand Hill. Then came the onslaught with the defenders sandwiched from the north by Crazy Horse, among others, and from the south by Gall. Thus it is that accounts describing the left wing's operations on Cemetery Ridge and its trip to Ford D go unrecognized or are dismissed out-of-hand as untrustworthy. Often they are simply ignored. But now, focused by archaeology, these accounts must be included in the story of Custer's last battle.

Massive disturbances on the Cemetery Ridge, including construction of a national military cemetery there, unfortunately have compromised the archaeological record on this landform. Material evidence for troops on this ridge is therefore circumstantial. Historical accounts, however, mesh nicely with the circumstantial evidence. Indeed, Two Moons stated explicitly that troopers rode from behind Custer Ridge down into the valley. We cannot tell unit affiliation from his description, but it can be safely deduced from ancillary data. Two Moons spoke of the left wing. So did Sitting Bull when he reported that troopers rode up Cemetery Ridge to Custer Hill. Runs the Enemy also mentioned the action on Cemetery Ridge, and White Bull sketched a cavalry position there. White accounts mention that ridge as well. Lieutenant Philo Clark interviewed Custer battle warriors in 1877 at Camp Robinson, Nebraska. One informant provided the lieutenant with a map showing troop movements off Custer Ridge to Ford D.

Several strands of Cheyenne oral tradition preserve the movements of what we now know as the left wing in great detail. According to tradition, this force met little resistance during its descent to Ford D, and on its return delayed on Cemetery Ridge for about twenty minutes. A sketch made by Captain Henry Freeman, an officer with Terry, marks a spot on Cemetery Ridge where the delay may have occurred. Freeman noted in his map key that some soldiers had "made a stand" at this location. Freeman's spot corresponds to a notation—"Custer first met the Indians here" on a map drawn by Captain R. E. Freeman, who interviewed Custer battle warriors in 1876 at Standing Rock Agency in Dakota Territory.

Clearly the general's battalion remained on the offensive as it operated from Custer Ridge. Mobility is the key to cavalry, and Custer, riding with the left wing, exercised that advantage. Custer therefore chose to wait for the anticipated arrival of Reno and Benteen, preferring to close the distance between his two wings as he did. He took the left wing out of the valley, and moved onto Cemetery Ridge. Meanwhile, the right wing remained on and around Calhoun Hill. Now a mile (as the horse goes) separated the two wings—a patently offensive posture. But, the wait brought neither Benteen nor Reno. It did, however, bring many more warriors, then disaster for Custer and 210 men of his Seventh Cavalry.

Reinventing Government, 1882

They had the perfect remedy for the bloated bureaucracy: the civil service

Bernard A. Weisberger

The explicit premise behind this column, it should be clear to regular readers, is borrowed from Ecclesiastes (or Koheleth) and declares that "there is no new thing under the sun." It is sometimes hard to justify; I am not sure what Ecclesiastes would have made of DNA or computers. But at times the message virtually cries aloud to whoever will listen. In the autumn of last year, President Clinton and Vice President Gore unveiled a mighty plan to shrink the bloated and wasteful federal bureaucracy and thereby in effect "reinvent government."

At a well-staged press conference on the White House lawn Clinton and Gore promised to cut out at least a quarter of a million redundant jobs and infuse federal job-holders with a new, "consumer-oriented" spirit in which cost efficiency and customer satisfaction would become cherished values.

Well, I'm not one to quarrel with the intention, but shucks, folks, we've heard it all before, slightly more than a century ago, when the very civil (or uncivil) service now under siege was itself invented to take the place of a discredited patronage system that replaced all officeholders every time an administration changed. In its place, one of the reformers promised, there would arise a new administrative apparatus with members chosen by merit guaranteed through competitive examination of applicants drawn from the ranks of "educated, earnest, patriotic, and ingenuous youths."

The messages behind the reform efforts, then and now, are similar even in point of harboring internal contradictions. Both would democratically reward taxpayers by giving them more service for less money; the early civil service advocates did not make economy a major point, but they did hope to win savings through cutting graft and incompetence. Both, however, also exhale an aura of elitism. The old reformers wanted to get "good men"—that is, from the prosperous and better-educated classes—into office. The thrust of the Gore reforms will be to run the government in a businesslike way, which can easily mean cutting out services that don't have enough of a "market" to justify their costs—or whose recipients can't afford to hire lobbyists in their defense.

The similarities become clearer by a look at our early pre-reform bureaucratic history. How we vote to "manage" government services reflects our changing and often inconsistent views on precisely what government should or should not do. President Washington continued the inherited British system of naming political sympathizers to office; to do otherwise, he argued, would undercut his policies and "be a sort of political suicide." Jefferson's appointments were few, but they were distributed among friends to his administration.

Andrew Jackson thought the duties of officeholders were (or should be) simple enough for any voter to master. Because experience was not an important qualification, personnel could be changed frequently to keep government in contact with plain folks. He called the principle "rotation in office," and it is still very much alive in the term-limitation movement.

Throughout the 1840s and 1850s most of the patronage jobs were in the Post Office, Treasury, and (after 1849) Interior departments. By 1865 about fifty-three thousand such workers, accounting for a yearly payroll of some thirty million, were regularly replaced after elections. Their appointments technically came from the White House, but they were actually named by senators and representatives whose choices the Presidents simply ratified, often finding competing claims among applicants a nuisance. One of the best Lincoln jokes deals with his response to catching a mild case of smallpox. At last, he said, he had something he could give to everybody.

Naturally the practice of spoilsmanship, though democratic in theory, came to stink of corruption. Officeholders paid for their appointments or were "assessed" for regular party contributions or both. Conscientious bureau chiefs had to put up with hacks, no-shows, and dolts assigned to them because they happened to have the right congressional sponsors. "At present there is no . . . system save that of chaos; no test of integrity save that of partisanship; no test of qualification save that of intrigue," complained a magazine article in 1868. It could not have been all that bad. The government did, after all, function. Still, it was bad enough to launch a reform drive that kept accumulating momentum like an avalanche.

A first bill to fill some federal jobs by examination was tentatively introduced in the Senate and tabled without a fight in 1864. A second and more carefully debated (but never passed) measure was proposed in 1867 by Rhode Island's Rep. Thomas A. Jenckes. But it was not until fifteen years later that the Pendleton Act, generally considered the starting point of the modern civil service system, was sent to the desk of President Chester A. Arthur and signed. The story of those years gives interesting insight into both the mentality and mechanics of reform legislation.

For example, though Jenckes's motives may have been simon-pure, he picked up early support from fellow Republicans who were, in 1867, locked in battle with President Andrew Johnson over Reconstruction policy. Johnson was threatening to build up a cadre of supporters by awarding them the patronage that would normally have gone to his congressional opponents. That was reason enough for his foes to smile on a merit system. When Johnson was subdued, however, a number of Jenckes's backers simply lost interest.

With their own choice, Ulysses S. Grant, in power in 1871, Republicans passed a measure that authorized the President to propose new regulations for strengthening the efficiency of the government's various bureaus. He began bravely enough by naming a blue-ribbon advisory board—the first Civil Service Commission—to make recommendations for installing a merit system. But congressional defenders of the spoils tradition rendered the board cosmetic by refusing to appropriate any money for its operation. Grant wound up following the old pattern.

The outrage of reformers at his failures deepened their feeling that at root the problem was moral; the country was no longer in the hands of disinterested gentlemen who were above politics. Henry Adams, son and grandson of Massachusetts-born Presidents, complained that Grant did not appoint enough men like Attorney General Ebenezer Hoar, a representative of old New England, "holding his moral rules on the sole authority of his own conscience, indifferent to opposition whether in or out of his party."

It was the "impractical" antipolitical gentility of the reformers, in fact, that infuriated their enemies most. In 1877 Rutherford B. Hayes, Grant's successor, under reform pressure, replaced Alonzo Cornell, the collector of the Port of New York, for compelling his customhouse employees to do political legwork. Cornell's boss and protector, Sen. Roscoe Conkling, delivered a celebrated outburst that declared that the reformers were "the man-milliners, . . . the dilettanti and carpet knights of politics," who forgot that "parties are not built up by deportment, or by ladies magazines, or gush." All the actors in the drama were Republican, but it was a Democratic senator from Ohio, George Pendleton, who, in December of 1880, dropped into the hopper the measure for a Civil Service Examination Board that would eventually carry the day.

The reform efforts then and now are so similar they even have basically the same internal contradictions.

By that time the defenders of the merit approach were making ever more generous claims for what it might do. Typical of their arguments was the speech of an Indiana state legislator sometime after the Pendleton Act finally became an accomplished fact. Asking for a similar state enactment, he said that the removal of patronage would make both parties "purer and cleaner." The "demoralizing solicitations" that took up the time of politically appointed bureau chiefs would cease, and they would devote their "undivided energy" to their jobs. All in all, civil service was an idea whose time had arrived: "The thinking people of the nation demand it."

But thinking people, who rarely constitute a majority, needed an extra boost in 1880 to have their way. It came in July of 1881, when President James A. Garfield was mortally wounded by a shot from the hand of a disappointed and mentally unbalanced office seeker. The "crime," said one editorial, "acted on public opinion very like a spark on a powder-magazine." It fell on a "mass of popular indignation all ready to explode." Congress reconvened in December with an understood mandate for some kind of action on civil service. The machinery clanked and groaned for a year, but final passage in the Senate came in December, with no Republican and only five Democrats voting against it. It was gaveled quickly through the House, 155 to 47, and signed in January of 1883 by President Chester A. Arthur, ironically an ally of Cornell and Conkling.

That was, of course, only the beginning. Over many years and administrations the scope of civil service coverage was widened, and other issues and enactments also contributed to the ongoing growth of government in America. The only moral to be drawn, if any, is that the entire question is too complicated for simplistic argument or swift and neat resolution. Government seems indeed to be too damned big, but what neutral hand will pare it down with justice for all? What consensus will support a general reduction of government operations when so many of us are government's beneficiaries in one way or another? I predict that the question will be a live one for as long as the balancing of public and private concerns, the essential dance of democracy, goes on.

The Emergence of Modern America

UNIT 2

The face of America changed greatly during the decades following the Civil War. Huge economic combinations came to dominate the marketplace, and individuals often referred to as "robber barons" amassed fortunes previously unheard of. Laborers, on the other hand, found themselves completely unable to protect their interests—especially during recessions. Farmers often had to pay exorbitant shipping and storing charges to monopolistic railroads, only to find that the prices they received for their crops were too low to cover their costs. The essay "How We Lived" presents interviews with several centenarians about the way they lived at the turn of the century.

Despairing of having their troubles addressed by either of the two major political parties, in 1892 discontented farmers and their allies launched the People's Party, better known as the Populists. They favored government intervention to regulate business and to make cheaper credit available to them. The Populists gained strength the following year when the worst depression in the nation's history struck, resulting in large-scale unemployment, violent strikes, and farm foreclosures.

Populist influence peaked in 1896 when the party endorsed Democratic candidate William Jennings Bryan for the presidency. Bryan, a gifted orator, campaigned tirelessly while Republican candidate William McKinley stayed mostly at home. The Democrat-Populists failed to attract large numbers of urban voters, however, because of differences over issues such as inflation. The gradual return of prosperity and the onset of the Spanish-American War in 1898 undermined the movement.

Following the collapse of Radical Reconstruction, white Southerners pushed blacks out of the electoral process and instituted formal segregation with regard to public facilities. When the case of Homer Plessy, a mulatto who was arrested for sitting in the white section of a segregated train, reached the Supreme Court, the Court enunciated the "separate but equal doctrine" that sanctioned segregation until it was overturned in 1954.

The Spanish-American War was one of the most popular conflicts in our history. Apparently fought for a just cause—the liberation of Cuba from Spanish misrule—this short, victorious war resulted in the opportunity for overseas U.S. expansion. President McKinley's decision in 1898 to acquire the Philippine Islands resulted in an insurrection that lasted for years. David Kohler and James Wensyel describes this struggle in their report, "Our First Southeast Asian War." They believe that the Philippine-American War provided lessons for American policymakers that could be applied to Vietnam 60 years later.

Two articles in this unit deal with technology. "Wings for Man," by Doug McIntyre, describes how Wilbur and Orville Wright achieved one of humanity's oldest dreams. On December 17, 1903, Orville made the first sustained, controlled flight by a powered aircraft. It would change the world forever. McIntyre describes how these two hardworking, inventive men realized their goal and their subsequent destructive battles to protect their invention through lawsuits.

Motion pictures had been around for a long time, but until the first decade of the twentieth century they were little more than novelties. By the middle of the first decade of the 1990s, "nickelodeons" were springing up by the thousands. Most were drab, dirty little places that critics condemned as squalid dens of iniquity. Later, luxurious theaters were built in order to "secure the patronage of a better class of people," as one owner put it. "Learning to Go to the Movies" chronicles the growth of what the author refers to as this "great democratic art form."

Looking Ahead: Challenge Questions

Can the study of history provide lessons for the present and future? What are some of the similarities between the 1890s and the 1990s?

How might those in charge of American policies in Vietnam have profited from a study of the Philippine insurrection?

What impact did the *Plessy v. Ferguson* decision have on racial practices in the South? Facilities were separate, but were they ever equal?

Plessy v. Ferguson Mandate

Jean West Mueller and
Wynell Burroughs Schamel

During the era of Reconstruction, black Americans' political rights were affirmed by three constitutional amendments and numerous laws passed by Congress. Racial discrimination was attacked on a particularly broad front by the Civil Rights Act of 1875. This legislation made it a crime for an individual to deny "the full and equal enjoyment of any of the accommodations, advantages, facilities, and privileges of inns, public conveyances on land or water, theaters and other places of public amusement; subject only to the conditions and limitations established by law, and applicable alike to citizens of every race and color."

In 1883, the Supreme Court struck down the 1875 act, ruling that the Fourteenth Amendment did not give Congress authority to prevent discrimination by private individuals. Victims of racial discrimination were told to seek relief not from the federal government, but from the states. Unfortunately, state governments were passing legislation that codified inequality between the races. Laws requiring the establishment of separate schools for children of each race were most common; however, segregation was soon extended to encompass most public and semipublic facilities.

Beginning with passage of an 1887 Florida law, states began to require that railroads furnish separate accommodations for each race. These measures were unpopular with the railway companies that bore the expense of adding Jim Crow cars. Segregation of the railroads was even more objectionable to black citizens who saw it as a further step toward the total repudiation of three constitutional amendments. When such a bill was proposed before the Louisiana legislature in 1890, the articulate black community of New Orleans protested vigorously. Nonetheless, despite the presence of 16 black legislators in the state assembly, the law was passed. It required either separate passenger coaches or partitioned coaches to provide segregated accommodations for each race. Passengers were required to sit in the appropriate areas or face a $25 fine or a 20-day jail sentence. Black nurses attending white children were permitted to ride in white compartments, however.

In 1891, a group of concerned young black men of New Orleans formed the "Citizens' Committee to Test the Constitutionality of the Separate Car Law." They raised money and engaged Albion W. Tourgée, a prominent Radical Republican author and politician, as their lawyer. On May 15, 1892, the Louisiana State Supreme Court decided in favor of the Pullman Company's claim that the law was unconstitutional as it applied to interstate travel. Encouraged, the committee decided to press a test case on intrastate travel. With the cooperation of the East Louisiana Railroad, on June 7, 1892, Homer Plessy, a mulatto (7/8 white), seated himself in a white compartment, was challenged by the conductor, and was arrested and charged with violating the state law. In the Criminal District court for the Parish of Orleans, Tourgée argued that the law requiring "separate but equal accommodations" was unconstitutional. When Judge John H. Ferguson ruled against him, Plessy applied to the State Supreme Court for a writ of prohibition and certiorari. Although the court upheld the state law, it granted Plessy's petition for a writ of error that would enable him to appeal the case to the Supreme Court.

In 1896, the Supreme Court issued its decision in *Plessy v. Ferguson*. Justice Henry Brown of Michigan delivered the majority opinion, which sustained the constitutionality of Louisiana's Jim Crow law. In part, he said:

> We consider the underlying fallacy of the plaintiff's argument to consist in the assumption that the enforced separation of the two races stamps the colored race with a badge of inferiority. If this be so, it is not by reason of anything found in the act, but solely because the colored race chooses to put that construction upon it.... The argument also assumes that social prejudices may be overcome by legislation, and that equal rights cannot be secured except by an enforced commingling of the two races.... If the civil and political rights of both races be equal, one cannot be inferior to the other civilly or politically. If one race be inferior to the other socially, the Constitution of the

5. *Plessy v. Ferguson* Mandate

United States cannot put them upon the same plane.

In a powerful dissent, conservative Kentuckian John Marshall Harlan wrote:

I am of the opinion that the statute of Louisiana is inconsistent with the personal liberty of citizens, white and black, in the State, and hostile to both the spirit and the letter of the Constitution of the United States. If laws of like character should be enacted in the several States of the Union, the effect would be in the highest degree mischievous. Slavery as an institution tolerated by law would, it is true, have disappeared from our country, but there would remain a power in the States, by sinister legislation, to interfere with the blessings of freedom; to regulate civil rights common to all citizens, upon the basis of race; and to place in a condition of legal inferiority a large body of American citizens, now constituting a part of the political community, called the people of the United States, for whom and by whom, through representatives, our government is administered. Such a system is inconsistent with the guarantee given by the Constitution to each State of a republican form of government, and may be stricken down by congressional action, or by the courts in the discharge of their solemn duty to maintain the supreme law of the land, anything in the Constitution or laws of any State to the contrary notwithstanding.

Indeed, it was through the Supreme Court's decision in *Brown v. Board of Education of Topeka, Kansas* and congressional civil rights acts of the 1950s and 1960s that systemic segregation under state law was ended. In the wake of those federal actions, many states amended or rewrote their state constitutions to conform with the spirit of the Fourteenth Amendment. But for Homer Plessy the remedies came too late....

BATTLES WON AND LOST

Our First Southeast Asian War

America's turn-of-the-century military campaign against Philippine insurgents consumed three years, involved 126,000 troops, and cost 4,000 lives. The lessons we learned could have been used in Vietnam sixty years later.

David R. Kohler and James W. Wensyel

David R. Kohler, Commander, U.S. Navy, is a Naval Special Warfare officer who has served multiple tours in UDT (underwater demolition) and SEAL (sea, air, land) teams. He has a master's degree in national security affairs from the Naval Postgraduate School in Monterey, California.

James W. Wensyel, a retired Army officer, is the author of three published books and numerous articles. His article on the crash of the dirigible Shenandoah *appeared in the February 1989 issue of* American History Illustrated. *He resides with his wife Jean in Newville, Pennsylvania.*

Guerrilla warfare . . . jungle terrain . . . search and destroy missions . . . benevolent pacification . . . strategic hamlets . . . terrorism . . . ambushes . . . free-fire zones booby traps . . . waning support from civilians at home. These words call forth from the national consciousness uncomfortable images of a war Americans fought and died in not long ago in Southeast Asia. But while the phrases may first bring to mind America's painful experience in Vietnam during the 1960s and '70s, they also aptly describe a much earlier conflict—the Philippine Insurrection—that foreshadowed this and other insurgent wars in Asia.

The Philippine-American War of 1898–1902 is one of our nation's most obscure and least-understood campaigns. Sometimes called the "Bolo War" because of the Filipino insurgents' lethally effective use of razor-sharp bolo knives or machetes against the American expeditionary force occupying the islands, it is often viewed as a mere appendage of the one-hundred-day Spanish-American War. But suppressing the guerrilla warfare waged by Philippine nationalists seeking self-rule proved far more difficult, protracted, and costly for American forces than the conventional war with Spain that had preceded it.

America's campaign to smash the Philippine Insurrection was, ironically, a direct consequence of U.S. efforts to secure independence for other *insurrectos* halfway around the world in Cuba. On May 1, 1898, less than a week after Congress declared war against Spain, a naval squadron commanded by Commodore George Dewey steamed into Manila Bay to engage the Spanish warships defending that nation's Pacific possession. In a brief action Dewey achieved a stunning victory, sinking all of the enemy vessels with no significant American losses. Destroying the Spanish fleet, however, did not ensure U.S. possession of the Philippines. An estimated 15,000 Spanish soldiers still occupied Manila and the surrounding region. Those forces would have to be rooted out by infantry.

President William McKinley had already ordered a Philippine Expeditionary Force of volunteer and regular army infantry, artillery, and cavalry units (nearly seven thousand men), under the command of Major General Wesley Merritt, to "reduce Spanish power in that quarter [Philippine Islands] and give order and security to the islands while in the possession of the United States."

Sent to the Philippines in the summer of 1898, this limited force was committed without fully considering the operation's potential length and cost. American military and government leaders also failed to anticipate the consequences of ignoring the Filipino rebels who, under Generalissimo Don Emilio Aguinaldo y Famy, had been waging a war for independence against Spain for the past two years. And when American insensitivity toward Aguinaldo eventually led to open warfare with the rebels, the American leaders grossly underestimated the determination of the seemingly ill-trained and poorly armed insurgents. They additionally failed to perceive the difficulties involved in conducting military operations in a tropical environment and among a hostile native population, and they did not recognize the burden of fighting at the end of a seven-thousand-mile-long logistics trail.

Asian engagements, the Americans learned for the first time, are costly. The enterprise, so modestly begun, eventually saw more than 126,000 American

6. Our First Southeast Asian War

officers and men deployed to the Philippines. Four times as many soldiers served in this undeclared war in the Pacific as had been sent to the Caribbean during the Spanish-American War. During the three-year conflict, American troops and Filipino insurgents fought in more than 2,800 engagements. American casualties ultimately totaled 4,234 killed and 2,818 wounded, and the insurgents lost about 16,000 men. The civilian population suffered even more; as many as 200,000 Filipinos died from famine, pestilence, or the unfortunate happenstance of being too close to the fighting. The Philippine war cost the United States $600 million before the insurgents were subdued.

The costly experience offered valuable and timeless lessons about guerrilla warfare in Asia; unfortunately, those lessons had to be relearned sixty years later in another war that, despite the modern technology involved, bore surprising parallels to America's first Southeast Asian campaign.

ORIGINS

America's war with Spain, formally declared by the United States on April 25, 1898, had been several years in the making. During that time the American "yellow press," led by Joseph Pulitzer's *New York World* and William Randolph Hearst's *New York Journal,* trumpeted reports of heroic Cuban *insurrectos* revolting against their cruel Spanish rulers. Journalists vividly described harsh measures taken by Spanish officials to quell the Cuban revolution. The sensational accounts, often exaggerated, reminded Americans of their own uphill fight for independence and nourished the feeling that America was destined to intervene so that the Cuban people might also taste freedom.

Furthermore, expansionists suggested that the revolt against a European power, taking place less than one hundred miles from American shores, offered a splendid opportunity to turn the Caribbean into an American sea. Businessmen pointed out that $50 million in American capital was invested in the Cuban sugar and mining industries. Revolutions resulting in burned cane fields jeopardized that investment. As 1898 opened, American relations with Spain quickly declined.

In January 1898 the U.S. battleship *Maine* was sent to Cuba, ostensibly on a courtesy visit. On February 15 the warship was destroyed by a mysterious explosion while at anchor in Havana harbor, killing 262 of her 350-man crew. The navy's formal inquiry, completed on March 28, suggested that the explosion was due to an external force—a mine.

On March 29, the Spanish government received an ultimatum from Washington, D.C.: Spain's army in Cuba was to lay down its arms while the United States negotiated between the rebels and the Spaniards. The Spanish forces were also told to abolish all *reconcentrado* camps (tightly controlled areas, similar to the strategic hamlets later tried in Vietnam, where peasants were regrouped to deny food and intelligence to insurgents and to promote tighter security). Spain initially rejected the humiliation of surrendering its arms in the field but then capitulated on all points. The Americans were not satisfied.

On April 11, declaring that Spanish responses were inadequate, President McKinley told a joint session of Congress that "I have exhausted every effort to relieve the intolerable condition . . . at our doors. I now ask the Congress to empower the president to take measures to secure a full and final termination of hostilities in Cuba, to secure . . . the establishment of a stable government, and to use the military and naval forces

Manila-bound soldiers on a troopship pulling away from a San Francisco pier watch as the last man climbs aboard (right). At the height of the Spanish-American War, President William McKinley sent a seven-thousand-man expeditionary force to occupy the Philippines; during the next three years nearly twenty times that number of Americans would become involved in operations against Filipino insurgents.

2. THE EMERGENCE OF MODERN AMERICA

of the United States . . . for these purposes. . . ."

Congress adopted the proposed resolution on April 19. Learning this, Spain declared war on the 24th. The following day, the United States responded with its own declaration of war.

The bulk of the American navy quickly gathered on the Atlantic coast. McKinley called for 125,000 volunteers to bolster the less than eighty-thousand-man regular army. His call was quickly oversubscribed; volunteers fought to be the first to land on Cuba's beaches.

The first major battle of the war, however, was fought not in Cuba but seven thousand miles to the west—in Manila Bay. Dewey's victory over Spanish Admiral Patricio Montojo y Pasarón (a rather hollow victory as Montojo's fleet consisted of seven unarmored ships, three of which had wooden hulls and one that had to be towed to the battle area) was wildly acclaimed in America.

American leaders, believing that the Philippines would now fall into America's grasp like a ripe plum, had to decide what to do with their prize. They could not return the islands to Spain, nor could they allow them to pass to France or Germany, America's commercial rivals in the Orient. The American press rejected the idea of a British protectorate. And, after four hundred years of despotic Spanish rule in which Filipinos had little or no chance to practice self-government, native leaders seemed unlikely candidates for managing their own affairs. McKinley faced a grand opportunity for imperialistic expansion that could not be ignored.

The debate sharply divided his cabinet—and the country. American public opinion over acquisition of the Philippines divided into two basic factions: imperialists versus anti-imperialists.

The imperialists, mostly Republicans, included such figures as Theodore Roosevelt (then assistant secretary of the navy), Henry Cabot Lodge (Massachusetts senator), and Albert Beveridge (Indiana senator). These individuals were, for the most part, disciples of Alfred Thayer Mahan, a naval strategist who touted theories of national power and prestige through sea power and acquisition of overseas colonies for trade purposes and naval coaling stations.

The anti-imperialists, staunchly against American annexation of the Philippines, were mainly Democrats. Such men as former presidents Grover Cleveland and Rutherford B. Hayes, steel magnate Andrew Carnegie, William Jennings Bryan, union leader Samuel Gompers, and Mark Twain warned that by taking the Philippines the United States would march the road to ruin earlier traveled by the Roman Empire. Furthermore, they argued, America would be denying Filipinos the right of self-determination guaranteed by our own Constitution. The more practical-minded also pointed out that imperialistic policy would require maintaining an expensive army and navy there.

Racism, though demonstrated in different ways, pervaded the arguments of both sides. Imperialists spoke of the "white man's burden" and moral responsibility to "uplift the child races everywhere" and to provide "orderly development for the unfortunate and less able races." They spoke of America's "civilizing mission" of pacifying Filipinos by "benevolent assimilation" and saw the opening of the overseas frontier much as their forefathers had viewed the western frontier. The "subjugation of the Injun" (wherever he might be found) was a concept grasped by American youth—the war's most enthusiastic supporters (in contrast to young America's opposition to the war in Vietnam many years later).

The anti-imperialists extolled the sacredness of independence and self-determination for the Filipinos. Racism, however, also crept into their argument, for they believed that "protection against race mingling" was a historic American policy that would be reversed by imperialism. To them, annexation of the Philippines would admit "alien, inferior, and mongrel races to our nationality."

As the debate raged, Dewey continued to hold Manila Bay, and the Philippines seemed to await America's pleasure. President McKinley would ultimately cast the deciding vote in determining America's role in that country. McKinley, a genial, rather laid-back, former congressman from Ohio and one-time major in the Union army, remains a rather ambiguous figure during this period. In his Inaugural Address he had affirmed that "We want no wars of conquest; we must avoid the temptation of territorial aggression." Thereafter, however, he made few comments on pacifism, and, fourteen weeks after becoming president, signed the bill annexing Hawaii.

Speaking of Cuba in December 1897, McKinley said, "I speak not of forcible annexation, for that cannot be thought of. That, by our code of morality, would be criminal aggression." Nevertheless, he constantly pressured Madrid to end Spanish rule in Cuba, leading four months later to America's war with Spain.

McKinley described experiencing extreme turmoil, soul-searching, and prayer over the Philippine annexation issue until, he declared, one night in a dream the Lord revealed to him that "there was nothing left for us to do but to take them all [the Philippine Islands] and to educate the Filipinos, and uplift, and civilize, and Christianize them." He apparently didn't realize that the Philippines had been staunchly Roman Catholic for more than 350 years under Spanish colonialism. Nor could he anticipate the difficulties that, having cast its fortune with the expansionists, America would now face in the Philippines.

PROSECUTING THE WAR

Meanwhile, in the Philippine Islands, Major General Wesley Merritt's Philippine Expeditionary Force went about its job. In late June, General Thomas Anderson led an advance party ashore at Cavite. He then established Camp Merritt, visited General Aguinaldo's rebel forces entrenched around Manila, and made plans for seizing that city once Merritt arrived with the main body of armed forces.

Anderson quickly learned that military operations in the Philippines could be difficult. His soldiers, hastily assembled and dispatched with limited prior training, were poorly disciplined and inadequately equipped. Many still wore woolen uniforms despite the tropical climate. A staff officer described the army's baptism at Manila: " . . . the heat was oppressive and the rain kept falling. At times the trenches were filled with two feet of water, and soon the men's shoes were ruined. Their heavy khaki uniforms were a nuisance; they perspired constantly, the loss of body salts inducing chronic fatigue. Prickly heat broke out, inflamed by scratching and rubbing. Within a week the first cases of dysentery, malaria, cholera, and dengue fever showed up at sick call."

During his first meeting with Dewey, Anderson remarked that some American leaders were considering annexation of the Philippines. "If the United States intends to hold the Philippine Islands," Dewey responded, "it will make things

6. Our First Southeast Asian War

awkward, because just a week ago Aguinaldo proclaimed the independence of the Philippine Islands from Spain and seems intent on establishing his own government."

A Filipino independence movement led by Aguinaldo had been active in the islands since 1896 and, within weeks of Dewey's victory, Aguinaldo's revolutionaries controlled most of the archipelago.

Aguinaldo, twenty-nine years old in 1898, had taken over his father's position as mayor of his hometown of Kawit before becoming a revolutionary. In a minor skirmish with Spanish soldiers, he had rallied the Filipinos to victory. Thereafter, his popularity grew as did his ragtag but determined army. Aguinaldo was slight of build, shy, and soft-spoken, but a strict disciplinarian.

As his rebel force besieged Manila, Aguinaldo declared a formal government for the Philippines with himself as president and generalissimo. He proclaimed his "nation's" independence and called for Filipinos to rally to his army and to the Americans, declaring that "the Americans . . . extend their protecting mantle to our beloved country . . . When you see the American flag flying, assemble in numbers: they are our redeemers!" But his enthusiasm for the United States later waned.

Stymied by the Filipinos' use of guerrilla warfare, the Americans were forced to change their strategy.

Merritt put off Aguinaldo's increasingly strident demands that America recognize his government and guarantee the Filipinos' independence. Aguinaldo perceived the American general's attitude as condescending and demeaning.

On August 13, Merritt's forces occupied Manila almost without firing a shot; in a face-saving maneuver the Spanish defenders had agreed to surrender to the Americans to avoid being captured—and perhaps massacred—by the Filipino insurgents. Merritt's troops physically blocked Aguinaldo's rebels, who had spent weeks in the trenches around the city, from participating in the assault. The Filipino general and his followers felt betrayed at being denied a share in the victory.

Further disenchanted, Aguinaldo would later find his revolutionary government unrepresented at the Paris peace talks determining his country's fate. He would learn that Spain had ceded the Philippines to the United States for $20 million.

Officers at Merritt's headquarters had little faith in the Filipinos' ability to govern themselves. "Should our power . . . be withdrawn," an early report declared, "the Philippines would speedily lapse into anarchy, which would excuse . . . the intervention of other powers and the division of the islands among them."

Meanwhile, friction between American soldiers and the Filipinos increased. Much of the Americans' conduct betrayed their racial bias. Soldiers referred to the natives as "niggers" and "gugus," epithets whose meanings were clear to the Filipinos. In retaliation, the island inhabitants refused to give way on sidewalks and muscled American officers into the streets. Men of the expeditionary force in turn escalated tensions by stopping Filipinos at gun point, searching them without cause, "confiscating" shopkeepers' goods, and beating those who resisted.

On the night of February 4, 1899 the simmering pot finally boiled over. Private William "Willie" Walter Grayson and several other soldiers of Company D, 1st Nebraska Volunteer Infantry, apprehended a group of armed insurgents within their regimental picket line. Shots were exchanged, and three Filipino *insurrectos* fell dead. Heavy firing erupted between the two camps.

In the bloody battle that followed, the Filipinos suffered tremendous casualties (an estimated two thousand to five thousand dead, contrasted with fifty-nine Americans killed) and were forced to withdraw. The Philippine Insurrection had begun.

GUERRILLA WARFARE

The Americans, hampered by a shortage of troops and the oncoming rainy season, could initially do little more than extend their defensive perimeter beyond Manila and establish a toehold on several islands to the south. By the end of March, however, American forces seized Malolos, the seat of Aguinaldo's revolutionary government. But Aguinaldo escaped, simply melting into the jungle. In the fall, using conventional methods of warfare, the Americans first struck south, then north of Manila across the central Luzon plain. After hard marching and tough fighting, the expeditionary force occupied northern Luzon, dispersed the rebel army, and barely missed capturing Aguinaldo.

Believing that occupying the remainder of the Philippines would be easy, the Americans wrongly concluded that the war was virtually ended. But when the troops attempted to control the territory they had seized, they found that the Filipino revolutionaries were not defeated but had merely changed strategies. Abandoning western-style conventional warfare, Aguinaldo had decided to adopt guerrilla tactics.

Aguinaldo moved to a secret mountain headquarters at Palanan in northern Luzon, ordering his troops to disperse and avoid pitched battles in favor of hit-and-run operations by small bands. Ambushing parties of Americans and applying terror to coerce support from other Filipinos, the insurrectionists now blended into the countryside, where they enjoyed superior intelligence information, ample supplies, and tight security. The guerrillas moved freely between the scattered American units, cutting telegraph lines, attacking supply trains, and assaulting straggling infantrymen. When the Americans pursued their tormentors, they fell into well planned ambushes. The insurgents' barbarity and ruthlessness during these attacks were notorious.

The guerrilla tactics helped to offset the inequities that existed between the two armies. The American troops were far better armed, for example, carrying .45-caliber Springfield single-shot rifles, Mausers, and then-modern .30-caliber repeating Krag-Jorgensen rifles. They also had field artillery and machine guns. The revolutionaries, on the other hand, were limited to a miscellaneous assortment of handguns, a few Mauser repeating rifles taken from the Spanish, and antique muzzle-loaders. The sharp-edged bolo knife was the revolutionary's primary weapon, and he used it well. Probably more American soldiers were hacked to death by bolos than were killed by Mauser bullets.

As would later be the case in Vietnam, the guerrillas had some clear advantages. They knew the terrain, were inured to the climate, and could generally count on a friendly population. As in Vietnam, villages controlled by the insurgents provided havens from which the guerrillas could attack, then fade back into hiding.

Americans soon began to feel that they

2. THE EMERGENCE OF MODERN AMERICA

were under siege in a land of enemies, and their fears were heightened because they never could be sure who among the population was hostile. A seemingly friendly peasant might actually be a murderer. Lieutenant Colonel J. T. Wickham, commanding the 26th Infantry Regiment, recorded that "a large flag of truce enticed officers into ambushes . . . Privates Dugan, Hayes, and Tracy were murdered by town authorities . . . Private Nolan [was] tied up by ladies while in a stupor; the insurgents cut his throat . . . The body of Corporal Doneley was dug up, burned, and mutilated . . . Private O'Hearn, captured by apparently friendly people was tied to a tree, burned over a slow fire, and slashed up . . . Lieutenant Max Wagner was assassinated by insurgents disguised in American uniforms."

As in later guerrilla movements, such terrorism became a standard tactic for the insurgents. Both Filipinos and Americans were their victims. In preying on their countrymen, the guerrillas had a dual purpose: to discourage any Filipinos disposed to cooperate with the Americans, and to demonstrate to people in a particular region that they ruled that area and could destroy inhabitants and villages not supporting the revolution. The most favored terroristic weapon was assassination of local leaders, who were usually executed in a manner (such as beheading or burying alive) calculated to horrify everyone.

By the spring of 1900 the war was going badly for the Americans. Their task forces, sent out to search and destroy, found little and destroyed less.

The monsoon rains, jungle terrain, hostile native population, and a determined guerrilla force made the American soldiers' marches long and miserable. One described a five-week-long infantry operation: " . . . our troops had been on half rations for two weeks. Wallowing through hip-deep muck, lugging a ten-pound rifle and a belt . . . with 200 rounds of ammunition, drenched to the skin and with their feet becoming heavier with mud at every step, the infantry became discouraged. Some men simply cried, others slipped down in the mud and refused to rise. Threats and appeals by the officers were of no avail. Only a promise of food in the next town and the threat that if they remained behind they would be butchered by marauding bands of insurgents forced some to their feet to struggle on."

News reports of the army's difficulties began to erode the American public's support for the war. "To chase barefooted insurgents with water buffalo carts as a wagon train may be simply ridiculous," charged one correspondent, "but to load volunteers down with 200 rounds of ammunition and one day's rations, and to put on their heads felt hats used by no other army in the tropics . . . to trot these same soldiers in the boiling sun over a country without roads, is positively criminal. . . . There are over five thousand men in the general hospital."

Another reported that the American outlook "is blacker now than it has been since the beginning of the war . . . the whole population . . . sympathizes with the insurgents. The insurgents came to Pasig [a local area whose government cooperated with the Americans] and their first act was to hang the 'Presidente' for treason in surrendering to Americans. 'Presidentes' do not surrender to us anymore."

U.S. troops found the tropical climate and Southeast Asian terrain almost as deadly as combat. Thousands of soldiers were incapacitated by dysentery, malaria, and other tropical maladies. The first troops sent to the archipelago wore unsuitable woolen uniforms; these men, photographed in 1900, had at least been issued ponchos for use during the rainy season.

NEW STRATEGIES

Early in the war U.S. military commanders had realized that, unlike the American Indians who had been herded onto reservations, eight million Filipinos (many of them hostile) would have to be governed in place. The Americans chose to emphasize pacification through good

6. Our First Southeast Asian War

works rather than by harsh measures, hoping to convince Filipinos that the American colonial government had a sincere interest in their welfare and could be trusted.

As the army expanded its control across the islands, it reorganized local municipal governments and trained Filipinos to take over civil functions in the democratic political structure the Americans planned to establish. American soldiers performed police duties, distributed food, established and taught at schools, and built roads and telegraph lines.

As the war progressed, however, the U.S. commanders saw that the terrorism practiced by Aguinaldo's guerrillas was far more effective in controlling the populace than was their own benevolent approach. Although the Americans did not abandon pacification through good works, it was thereafter subordinated to the "civilize 'em with a Krag" (Krag-Jorgensen rifle) philosophy. From December 1900 onward, captured revolutionaries faced deportation, imprisonment, or execution.

The American army also changed its combat strategy to counter that of its enemy. As in the insurgents' army, the new tactics emphasized mobility and surprise. Breaking into small units—the battalion became the largest maneuver force—the Americans gradually spread over the islands until each of the larger towns was occupied by one or two rifle companies. From these bases American troops began platoon- and company-size operations to pressure local guerrilla bands.

Because of the difficult terrain, limited visibility, and requirement for mobility, artillery now saw limited use except as a defensive weapon. The infantry became the main offensive arm, with mounted riflemen used to pursue the fleeing enemy. Cavalry patrols were so valued for their mobility that American military leaders hired trusted Filipinos as mounted scouts and cavalrymen.

The Americans made other efforts to "Filipinize" the war—letting Asians fight Asians. (A similar tactic had been used in the American Indian campaigns twenty years before; it would resurface in Vietnam sixty years later as "Vietnamization.") In the Philippines the Americans recruited five thousand Macabebes, mercenaries from the central Luzon province of Pampanga, to form the American officered Philippine Scouts. The Macabebes had for centuries fought in native battalions under the Spanish flag—even against their own countrymen when the revolution began in 1896.

Just as a later generation of American soldiers would react to the guerrilla war in Vietnam, American soldiers in the Philippines responded to insurgent terrorism in kind, matching cruelty with cruelty. Such actions vented their frustration at being unable to find and destroy the enemy. An increasing number of Americans viewed all Filipinos as enemies.

"We make everyone get into his house by 7 P.M. and we only tell a man once," Corporal Sam Gillis of the 1st California Volunteer Regiment wrote to his family. "If he refuses, we shoot him. We killed over 300 natives the first night. . . . If they fire a shot from a house, we burn the house and every house near it."

Another infantryman frankly admitted that "with an enemy like this to fight, it is not surprising that the boys should soon adopt 'no quarter' as a motto and fill the blacks full of lead before finding out whether they are friends or enemies."

That attitude should not have been too surprising. The army's campaigns against the Plains Indians were reference points for the generation of Americans that took the Philippines. Many of the senior officers and noncommissioned officers—often veterans of the Indian wars—considered Filipinos to be "as full of treachery as our Arizona Apache." "The country won't be pacified," one soldier told a reporter, "until the niggers are killed off like the Indians." A popular soldiers' refrain, sung to the tune of "Tramp, tramp, tramp, the boys are marching," began, "Damn, damn, damn the Filipinos," and again spoke of "civilizing 'em with a Krag."

Reprisals against civilians by Americans as well as insurgents became common. General Lloyd Wheaton, leading a U.S. offensive southeast of Manila, found his men impaled on the bamboo prongs of booby traps and with throats slit while they slept. After two of his companies were ambushed, Wheaton ordered that every town and village within twelve miles be burned.

The Americans developed their own terrorist methods, many of which would be used in later Southeast Asian wars. One was torturing suspected guerrillas or insurgent sympathizers to force them to reveal locations of other guerrillas and their supplies. An often-utilized form of persuasion was the "water cure," placing a bamboo reed in the victim's mouth and pouring water (some used salt water or dirty water) down his throat, thus painfully distending the victim's stomach. The subject, allowed to void this, would, under threat of repetition, usually talk freely. Another method of torture, the "rope cure," consisted of wrapping a rope around the victim's neck and torso until it formed a sort of girdle. A stick (or Krag rifle), placed between the ropes and twisted, then effectively created a combination of smothering and garroting.

The anti-imperialist press reported such American brutality in lurid detail. As a result, a number of officers and soldiers were court-martialed for torturing and other cruelties. Their punishments, however, seemed remarkably lenient. Of ten officers tried for "looting, torture, and murder," three were acquitted; of the seven convicted, five were reprimanded, one was reprimanded and fined $300, and one lost thirty-five places in the army's seniority list and forfeited half his pay for nine months.

Officers and soldiers, fighting a cruel, determined, and dangerous enemy, could not understand public condemnation of the brutality they felt was necessary to win. They had not experienced such criticism during the Indian wars, where total extermination of the enemy was condoned by the press and the American public, and they failed to grasp the difference now. Press reports, loss of public support, and the soldiers' feeling of betrayal—features of an insurgent war—would resurface decades later during the Vietnam conflict.

SUCCESS

Although U.S. military leaders were frustrated by the guerrillas' determination on one hand and by eroding American support for the war on the other, most believed that the insurgents could be subdued. Especially optimistic was General Arthur MacArthur, who in 1900 assumed command of the seventy thousand American troops in the Philippines. MacArthur adopted a strategy like that successfully used by General Zachary Taylor in the Second Seminole War in 1835; he believed that success depended upon the Americans' ability to isolate the guerrillas from their support in the villages. Thus were born "strategic hamlets," "free-fire zones," and "search and destroy" missions, concepts the Ameri-

2. THE EMERGENCE OF MODERN AMERICA

can army would revive decades later in Vietnam.

MacArthur strengthened the more than five hundred small strong points held by Americans throughout the Philippine Islands. Each post was garrisoned by at least one company of American infantrymen. The natives around each base were driven from their homes, which were then destroyed. Soldiers herded the displaced natives into *reconcentrado* camps, where they could be "protected" by the nearby garrisons. Crops, food stores, and houses outside the camps were destroyed to deny them to the guerrillas. Surrounding each camp was a "dead line," within which anyone appearing would be shot on sight.

Operating from these small garrisons, the Americans pressured the guerrillas, allowing them no rest. Kept off balance, short of supplies, and constantly pursued by the American army, the Filipino guerrillas, suffering from sickness, hunger, and dwindling popular support, began to lose their will to fight. Many insurgent leaders surrendered, signaling that the tide at last had turned in the Americans' favor.

In March 1901, a group of Macabebe Scouts, commanded by American Colonel Frederick "Fighting Fred" Funston, captured Aguinaldo. Aguinaldo's subsequent proclamation that he would fight no more, and his pledge of loyalty to the United States, sped the collapse of the insurrection.

As in the past, and as would happen again during the Vietnam conflict of the 1960s and '70s, American optimism was premature. Although a civilian commission headed by William H. Taft took control of the colonial government from the American army in July 1901, the army faced more bitter fighting in its "pacification" of the islands.

As the war sputtered, the insurgents' massacre of fifty-nine American soldiers at Balangiga on the island of Samar caused Brigadier General Jacob W. "Hell-Roaring Jake" Smith, veteran of the Wounded Knee massacre of the Sioux in 1890, to order his officers to turn Samar into a "howling wilderness." His orders to a battalion of three hundred Marines headed for Samar were precise: "I want no prisoners. I wish you to kill and burn, the more you kill and burn the better it will please me. I want all persons killed who are capable of bearing arms against the United States." Fortunately, the Marines did not take Smith's orders literally and, later, Smith would be court-martialed.

On July 4, 1902 the Philippine Insurrection officially ended. Although it took the American army another eleven years to crush the fierce Moros of the southern Philippines, the civil government's security force (the Philippine Constabulary), aided by the army's Philippine Scouts, maintained a fitful peace throughout the islands. The army's campaign to secure the Philippines as an American colony had succeeded.

American commanders would have experienced vastly greater difficulties except for two distinct advantages: 1) the enemy had to operate in a restricted area, in isolated islands, and was prevented by the U.S. Navy from importing weapons and other needed supplies; and 2) though the insurgents attempted to enlist help from Japan, no outside power intervened. These conditions would not prevail in some subsequent guerrilla conflicts in Asia.

In addition to the many tactical lessons the army learned from fighting a guerrilla war in a tropical climate, other problems experienced during this campaign validated the need for several military reforms that were subsequently carried out, including improved logistics, tropical medicine, and communications.

The combination of harsh and unrelenting military force against the guerrillas, complemented by the exercise of fair and equitable civil government and civic action toward those who cooperated, proved to be the Americans' most effective tactic for dealing with the insurgency. This probably was the most significant lesson to be learned from the Philippine Insurrection.

LESSONS FOR THE FUTURE

Vietnam veterans reading this account might nod in recollection of a personal, perhaps painful experience from their own war.

Many similarities exist between America's three-year struggle with the Filipino *insurrectos* and the decade-long campaign against the Communists in Vietnam. Both wars, modestly begun, went far beyond what anyone had foreseen in time, money, equipment, manpower, casualties, and suffering.

Both wars featured small-unit infantry actions. Young infantrymen, if they had any initial enthusiasm, usually lost it once they saw the war's true nature; they nevertheless learned to endure their allotted time while adopting personal self-survival measures as months "in-country" lengthened and casualty lists grew.

Both wars were harsh, brutal, cruel. Both had their Samar Islands and their My Lais. Human nature being what it is, both conflicts also included acts of great heroism, kindness, compassion, and self-sacrifice.

Both wars saw an increasingly disenchanted American public withdrawing its support (and even disavowing its servicemen) as the campaigns dragged on, casualties mounted, and news accounts vividly described the horror of the battlefields.

Some useful lessons might be gleaned from a comparison of the two conflicts. Human nature really does not change—war will bring out the best and the worst in the tired, wet, hungry, and fearful men who are doing the fighting. Guerrilla campaigns—particularly where local military and civic reforms cannot be effected to separate the guerrilla from his base of popular support—will be long and difficult, and will demand tremendous commitments in resources and national will. Finally, before America commits its armed forces to similar ventures in the future, it would do well to recall the lessons learned from previous campaigns. For, as the Spanish-born American educator, poet, and philosopher George Santayana reminded us, those who do not learn from the past are doomed to repeat it.

Recommended additional reading: Benevolent Assimilation: The American Conquest of the Philippines, 1899–1902 *by Stuart C. Miller (Yale University Press, 1982);* In Our Image: America's Empire in the Philippines *by Stanley Karnow (Random House, 1989);* Little Brown Brother *by Leon Wolff (Doubleday & Co., Inc., 1961);* Muddy Glory *by Russell Roth (Christopher Publishing House, 1981); and* Soldiers in the Sun *by William T. Sexton (Books for Libraries Press, 1971).*

Intervention

For more than a century—from Panama in 1885 to Haiti in 1994—the U.S. employed its armed forces in the Caribbean to protect and enforce its strategic interests.

Ivan Musicant

Award-winning military historian Ivan Musicant's books include The Banana Wars: A History of United States Military Intervention in Latin America from the Spanish-American War to the Invasion of Panama *(Macmillan, 1990) and* United States Armored Cruisers: A Design and Operational History *(Naval Institute Press, 1985).*

For the thirtieth time, United States armed forces have landed on Caribbean shores, this time in Haiti, to sweep clean what old, deaf Assistant Secretary of State Alvee Adee in 1915 called "the public nuisance at our doors." Why Haiti? Why the Caribbean at all? Because eons ago the accidental formation of land and sea masses shaped the North American continent into a colossus that—like a giant meat axe poised overhead—dominates its Central-American and Caribbean neighbors. Strategic geography dictates political events; the United States can no more ignore the Caribbean than Great Britain can disregard the North Sea.

The Isthmus of Panama and its canal—shielded on the Atlantic side by an island chain of sentry boxes extending two thousand miles from Key West to Trinidad—constitutes the strategic chokepoint of the Western Hemisphere. For the United States, defending this hemispheric jugular vein by stabilizing regional politics and controlling the Atlantic sea approaches is the nut-kernel of interventionist policy in the Caribbean and Central America.

Motivations, however, shift with the changing currents of international and domestic events. U.S. actions in the Caribbean before the Civil War were an extension of Manifest Destiny as military forces pacified Central-American way stations for an America expanding across the continent. The defense of the Panama Canal was the overriding strategic consideration for interventions during the classic "Banana Wars" era of 1899–1934. And several rationales have provided justification for U.S. military involvements from the 1960s to the present: the Cold War for landings in the Dominican Republic in 1965 and Grenada in 1983; security issues for invading Panama in 1989; and humanitarian considerations and U.S. domestic politics for the occupation of Haiti in 1994.

If any Americans needed a lesson regarding the absolute necessity for a transisthmian canal, it came during the Spanish-American War, when the U.S. battleship *Oregon,* stationed on the mist-shrouded waters of Puget Sound, had to make a sixty-seven-day 15,770-mile voyage around South America to join other fleet units concentrated in the Caribbean. A canal through the isthmus, it was obvious to U.S. strategists, would have cut the voyage by two-thirds. Future conflicts with enemy maritime powers would doubtless require a more rapid concentration of the fleet.

Transit from ocean to ocean via Panama was hardly a new idea. In 1519, Spain completed the Western Hemisphere's first transcontinental highway, a two-donkey cobbled isthmian track, as the great post road of its empire. By 1534 the Spaniards had dredged the twisting Chagres River, allowing water traffic for a thirty-odd-mile segment of the Atlantic Pacific crossing. But for the remaining fifteen miles, the path across the isthmus ran unchanged for the next 321 years.

In 1831, after the Spanish American wars of independence, New Granada, later called Colombia, annexed the territory of Panama atop its coast.

The simultaneous discovery of gold in California and the United States victory over Mexico in 1848 stretched the national polity unbroken across North America. But without the transcontinental railroad that would be built twenty years hence, the arduous overland trek from St. Louis to the Pacific slope could take six months. By contrast, travel via steamer from New York to Panama, then by flatboat and mule across the isthmus, and finally aboard another ship to San Francisco took less than eight weeks. Panama became the linchpin of American hemispheric expansion.

In Colombia, the American minister negotiated a permanent American presence on the isthmus. The treaty which remained in effect until 1903, served upon the United States the right and duty under international law to maintain the security of the line of transit.

In 1855 the American-owned Panama Railroad Company opened for business: the single-track, forty-eight-mile railway ran from Aspinwall (renamed Colón in 1890) on the Atlantic side to Panama City on the Pacific shore. The monumental engineering feat brought thousands of Caribbean and Central American laborers to the isthmus. In 1856, joined by local "disorderly elements" in Panama City, they rioted, killing fifteen Americans and wounding fifty more. The subsequent arrival of the U.S. Navy sloop *St. Mary's* in Panama City's harbor, with her guns cleared for action, brought temporary calm. Some months

2. THE EMERGENCE OF MODERN AMERICA

later the first American landing on the isthmus took place when 160 sailors and Marines from the frigate *Independence,* armed with a pair of boat howitzers, cleared the railroad terminal of rioters and prepared to defend the line of transit against attack. Some practice volleys and a battery drill with the howitzers convinced the mob to disperse.

In 1885 the United States returned to Panama. Following the Colombian presidential election of 1884, an insurrection sparked by the Liberal "outs" had swept across that nation. Meanwhile Ferdinand de Lesseps, builder of the Suez Canal, had begun his ill-fated isthmian-ditch venture, bringing "thousands of desperate and vicious characters" to Panama City. On March 11, 1885, in anticipation of trouble, the United States screw sloop *Galena* anchored in the harbor of Aspinwall on Panama's Caribbean shore.

Within a week, a Colombian revolution swept across the isthmus. In Panama City Colombian General Rafael Aizpuru declared himself president of the "Sovereign State of Panama." His followers turned on the railroad, destroying rolling stock, switches, and the telegraph.

At Aspinwall, the *Galena* landed sixteen Marines and a dozen sailors to guard the railroad's Atlantic terminal. Further adding to the chaos was the "army" of Pedro Prestan, a xenophobic Haitian, with a particular hatred for white Americans. For two weeks, Prestan's gang extorted and terrorized Aspinwall, destroying a good part of the railroad in the process. When Prestan demanded some arms that had just arrived by steamer, took hostages, and threatened to kill every American in reach, the *Galena's* commanding officer landed every additional available man, 112 seamen. But to the consternation of all, they served only to reinforce the guard around the wharf and did not confront Prestan directly.

On April 1, Colombian reinforcements coming up the railroad from Panama City defeated Prestan near Aspinwall. The remnants of his band ran amok and torched the wooden town to ashes before being taken prisoner and hanged by the Colombians.

In Panama City General Aizpuru again declared himself President of Panama and swore vengeance on every American. From Aspinwall, the American consul cabled the State Department, "More force here or Americans must abandon Isthmus." On April 1, Navy Secretary William C. Whitney committed the United States to full-scale intervention: 460 Marines, 280 sailors, six

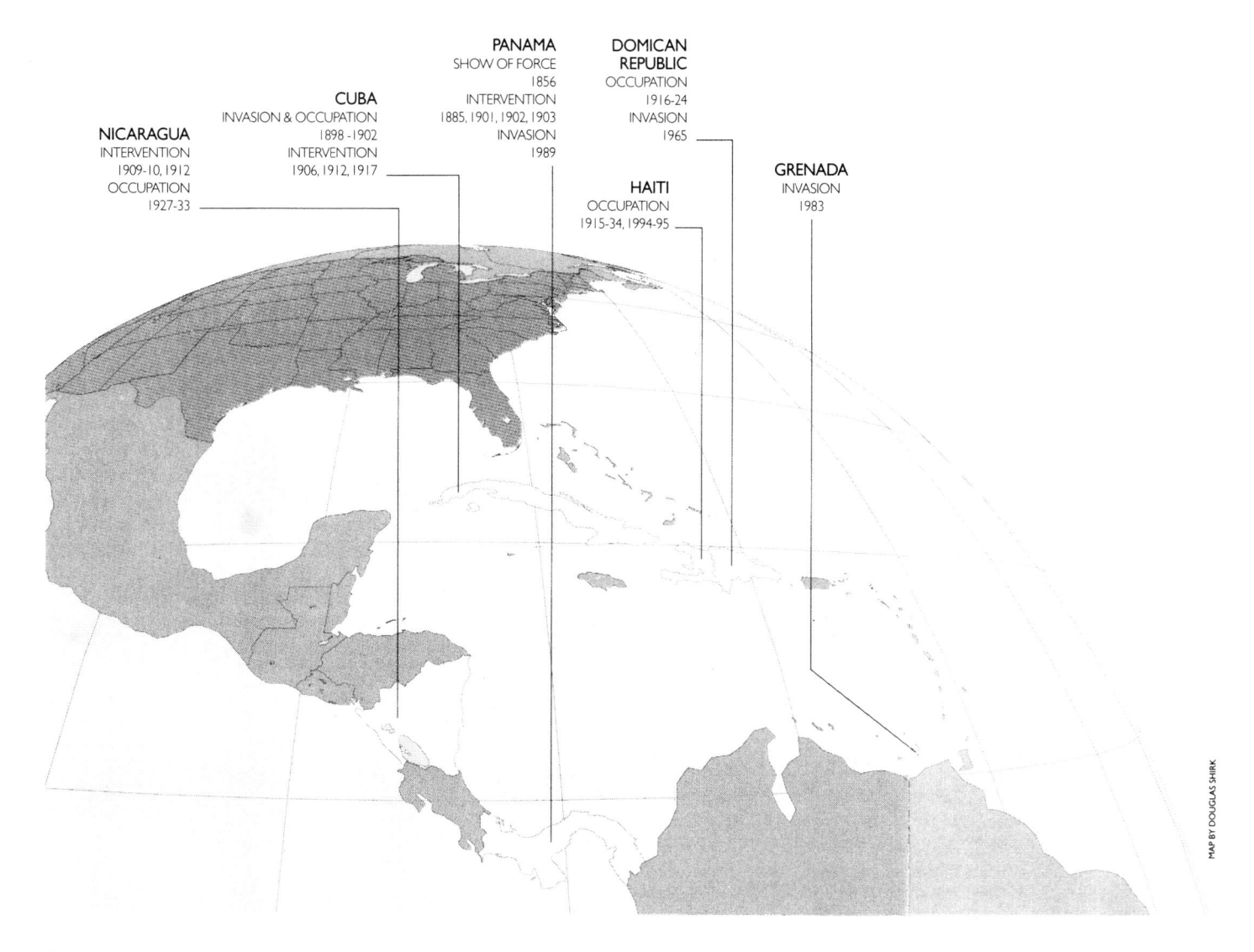

NICARAGUA
INTERVENTION
1909-10, 1912
OCCUPATION
1927-33

CUBA
INVASION & OCCUPATION
1898-1902
INTERVENTION
1906, 1912, 1917

PANAMA
SHOW OF FORCE
1856
INTERVENTION
1885, 1901, 1902, 1903
INVASION
1989

DOMICAN REPUBLIC
OCCUPATION
1916-24
INVASION
1965

HAITI
OCCUPATION
1915-34, 1994-95

GRENADA
INVASION
1983

MAP BY DOUGLAS SHIRK

7. Intervention

three-inch field guns, and three Gatlings—the largest American overseas expedition between the Mexican and Spanish-American wars. So poor were the Navy's resources at this point in history that the men sailed in civilian steamers and the Marines had to borrow entrenching tools and rubber ground sheets from the Army

On the Pacific side at Panama City the sloop *Shenandoah* landed 125 sailors and Marines to defend the railroad depot. On the 10th, the screw frigate *Tennessee* and sloop *Swatara* anchored at Aspinwall. The steamer *City of Para* brought the first contingent of Marines. They rigged a flatcar with boilerplate armor, mounted a one-pounder Hotchkiss revolving cannon, and chugged down the line to Panama City; the first train in six weeks. When the *Acapulco* arrived with the remainder of the troops, Commander Bowman H. McCalla took command of forces ashore.

On learning that Aizpuru had thrown up barricades in Panama City, McCalla resolved to occupy the town. Against 500 rebels of various stripes, American forces numbered 824 Marines and sailors. It all transpired like a textbook exercise in minor tactics. "The several columns advanced without music," McCalla reported, "the Marines in two lines deployed for street fighting, the Gatlings and field pieces between the lines."

There was no resistance. Four days later a battalion of Colombian troops arrived by sea to re-establish control. The Americans, however, would be back.

In February 1895, a small group of Cuban rebels launched the final War of Cuban Liberation against a delusional, rusty Spain. Almost immediately the war impacted on the United States. The American sensationalist press ("new journalism," William Randolph Hearst called it) recounted stories of Spanish atrocities, real and imagined, in high-stakes circulation wars. Press-driven public opinion in turn drove American politics, especially the Republican-controlled Congress, to demand Cuban recognition, even if it led to war with Spain. But contrary to belief, America's "yellow press" did not drive American policy as it did public opinion and politics.

Neither Democratic President Grover Cleveland nor his Republican successor William McKinley (who assumed office in 1897) desired an independent Cuba, and both forcefully pressed Spain to legislate overdue reforms and grant the island a true degree of political autonomy. Withstanding enormous domestic pressures, each offered in vain their good offices to mediate the peace and political future between Spain and Cuba.

The United States government could not permit this running sore to continue perpetually, however, and the descent to war began in February 1898. The publication of a stolen letter written by Spain's Washington envoy, humiliatingly critical of President McKinley and suggesting cynical methods to convince the United States of Spain's intentions in Cuba, brought a diplomatic storm. One week later, on February 15, an explosion aboard the U.S.S. *Maine* (today generally thought to have been accidental) sank the battleship in Havana harbor, killing 252 seamen and Marines. The Navy court of inquiry fixed no blame, but laid the cause to "probably a submarine mine."

On April 11, recognizing that nothing short of "subjugation or extermination" would end the three-year bloodletting, President McKinley presented his special Cuba message to Congress, asking the body to authorize "the military and naval forces of the United States" to intervene in the Cuban war. Congress voted out a Joint Resolution indistinguishable from a declaration of war. Before any formalities, the Navy's North Atlantic Squadron began the blockade of Cuba. Citing the Joint Resolution as an overtly hostile act, Spain declared war on April 24. The U.S. Congress followed suit the next day.

The U.S. Navy was ready, the U.S. Army was not. On May 1, Commodore George Dewey's Asiatic Squadron pounced on the decrepit Spanish naval force at Manila Bay in the Philippines, destroying it utterly. In the Caribbean, an elusive Spanish squadron of four armored cruisers and two destroyers slipped past the American scouts into Santiago de Cuba. Immediately the Navy concentrated its overwhelming forces in a close blockade.

Once the Spanish ships were blocked up in port, the U.S. Army's V Corps, nearly 17,000 troops, amidst chaotic logistic nightmares, boarded a convoy of civilian steamers at Tampa, Florida. On June 22 they landed unopposed in the surf at Daiquirí, eighteen miles east of Santiago. Against them stood a regional Spanish garrison of nearly 34,000 men, with 119,000 more scattered throughout the island. Rear Admiral William Sampson, commanding the North Atlantic Squadron, wanted the Army to capture the Spanish harbor forts, neutralizing the minefields. That done, he could steam into Santiago harbor and destroy the enemy fleet at its moorings. General William Shafter opted to fight for the city itself.

The dilemma resolved itself in the hard-fought battle for San Juan heights, key to the city. Shafter's dispositions were bad, the Spanish fought very well, and it was hardly the comic opera sometimes depicted. At great personal danger, Theodore Roosevelt *did* lead the advance of the dismounted cavalry up the hill and was a true hero in the fight.

The Spanish naval squadron was doomed. On July 3, obeying suicidal orders to break through the blockade, Admiral Pascual Cervera led his ships on the death ride of the Spanish Navy. In a running fight along the coast, the four armored cruisers and two destroyers were picked off one by one and run aground.

The overwhelming naval victory at Santiago gave the United States strategic control of the sea. Puerto Rico fell almost without a fight. "An hour or two at Manila," said the Navy's Captain Albert Barker, "an hour or two at Santiago, and the maps of the world were changed." In the Treaty of Paris, Spain ceded Puerto Rico, the Philippines, and Guam to the United States, which had now achieved an empire virtually by default.

Pending full independence, Cuba entered the jurisdiction of the U.S. War Department, which established a transitional military government over the island, lasting until May 1902.

When Cuba eventually did get her freedom, it came with heavy baggage. Written into her constitution was a guarantee, the Platt Amendment, giving prior consent to any future American military intervention and agreeing to the sale of land for a naval base. The United States settled on Guantanamo Bay which, combined with Puerto Rico, placed an American naval presence on the key waterways providing Atlantic access to the as yet unbuilt isthmian canal.

U.S. military forces intervened in Cuba again when the island nation lapsed into civil war in 1906; when a black-led "race" rebellion erupted in eastern Cuba in 1912; and in 1917 to

2. THE EMERGENCE OF MODERN AMERICA

arbitrate a stolen election on the eve of the United States entry into World War I.

The United States now possessed an empire stretching from Manila Bay to Guantanamo Bay. "When one half of the Anglo-Saxon race holds the waterway between the Mediterranean and Indian Ocean," observed the *London Spectator*, "what could be more appropriate than the other half should hold that between the Atlantic and the Pacific?"

In Colombia, a civil war between the Conservative government and Liberal rebels had raged since 1899, taking more than 100,000 lives. In November 1901, a Liberal army seized Colón (formerly Aspinwall), prompting a Colombian request for American intervention. Although the U.S. Navy had dispatched vessels to Colón, at first the United States declined to become directly involved. It made no difference which faction or party controlled the isthmus, as long as the trains moved. But when British and French warships arrived, the Navy Department ordered ashore a landing force of three hundred Marines and sailors from the battleship *Iowa* and gunboat *Marietta*. Officers of the three navies parleyed the surrender of the Liberals, and by mid-December conditions returned to normal.

The United States, meanwhile, had become actively involved in obtaining a "canal zone" for the inevitable project. The problem was that the builder's concession and most of the railroad shares were owned by the French New Panama Canal Company which had to be bought out. Further, the Colombian government had to be convinced to surrender a degree of zonal sovereignty. The U.S. Congress would not permit these matters to drag on interminably. If sale and agreement were not reached within reasonable times, the United States would transfer its canal project to Nicaragua, which offered several distinct geographical advantages.

In 1902—simultaneous with the delicate negotiation—the line of transit was threatened when two thousand ragged government soldiers surrendered to an equally tatterdemalion Liberal host. The trains ceased to run. President Theodore Roosevelt and the Navy Department ordered naval forces forward. In mid-September, the cruiser *Cincinnati's* landing force took over railroad security. On the Pacific side, the battleship *Wisconsin*, flagship of Rear Admiral Silas Casey's Pacific Squadron, joined the ancient gun-boat *Ranger*. And from Philadelphia and Norfolk steamed transports carrying nearly one thousand Marines "and the necessary color guard." They immediately mounted guard on the trains and took control of the line of transit, brushing away some angry Liberal gestures.

In Colombia, the Conservative government forces soon defeated the Liberals in the field, enabling eight thousand bedraggled scarecrows to be sent to Panama. When Admiral Casey considered their numbers sufficient to maintain security he began withdrawing U.S troops.

During the winter and spring of 1903 the continuing negotiations between the United States and Colombia over the canal treaty ruptured and collapsed over the issue of increased American payments, something the Roosevelt administration considered "contemptible" extortion. There was fear in Colombian circles that the United States might simply seize the isthmus and dictate its own terms. Graver still was the scenario predicted by the Colombian minister in Washington: "The 'Republic of Panama' may declare itself independent and the canal treaty may be made with it." That is exactly what happened.

In the summer of 1903, in New York and Panama City insurrectionary agents for the "Republic of Panama" fomented a not-very-secret rebellion. The Roosevelt administration knew about it (as did anyone who read a newspaper), welcomed it, and prepared for the event. But the U.S. government neither plotted nor funded the revolt. "Our policy before the world," advised Assistant Secretary of State Alvee A. Adee, "should stand, like Mrs. Caesar, without suspicion." On both the Atlantic and Pacific coasts, U.S. naval and Marine forces deployed to within a day's steaming of the isthmus. In Panama City coup leaders bought off key Colombian officers. Panama Railroad officials, mostly Americans, played critical roles in ensuring success.

On November 2, 1903, the gunboat *Nashville* arrived at Colón. The next day as the plotters were about to declare the Republic, the small Colombian cruiser *Cartagena* steamed in, carrying five hundred men of the *Tiradores* (Sharpshooters) Battalion. If these troops got to Panama City the rebellion would die aborning. The problem was neatly solved by the Panama Railroad. There were only enough cars for the Colombian commander and his staff, sighed the general superintendent—the bulk of the *Tiradores* would have to wait in Colón until other cars could be rounded up, and they would have to pay cash for the tickets.

That afternoon of November 3, the *Tiradores'* commander and staff, after arriving in Panama City, were arrested by turncoat Colombian officers. The Panama rebels immediately declared the Republic, and word was telegraphed to the U.S. State Department.

Back in Colón, the *Tiradores* threatened to put that town to the torch and kill every American unless they got a train. The skipper of the *Nashville* landed his force, forty-two sailors and Marines, and maneuvered to bring his ship's four-inch guns to bear on the enraged Colombian soldiery.

At any moment a full-scale firefight could have erupted. But it all turned out to be anticlimax: "Sighted USS *Dixie*," penned the *Nashville's* officer of the deck. Carrying a battalion of Marines, the American transport settled the question of the Panama revolt. The Marines marched through the shanty streets of Colón, and the sullen *Tiradores* sailed for home. On November 6, the United States granted formal recognition to the new Republic of Panama.

A treaty was drafted in near-record time. Panama granted to the United States "in perpetuity" all rights to a "zone of land" for the digging, operation, and protection "of the Canal to be constructed." Thus was obtained the anvil upon which was forged the key to America's hemispheric defense and global grand strategies for the next four decades.

Nicaragua, where the canal nearly happened, lies in the center of Central America. It has been a sharp thorn to its neighbors and, because of its rippling effect on Panama, to the United States. José Santós Zelaya, Liberal *caudillo* president, attempted to impose Nicaraguan hegemony in Central America and in 1907 invaded Honduras. The State Department considered Zelaya a medieval tyrant "guilty of murder and rape" and ordered naval vessels to Nicaragua's Atlantic and Pacific coasts.

In 1909 a Conservative revolution toppled Zelaya, though it left the Liberals in power. Frustrated, Secretary of

7. Intervention

State Philander Knox complained to President William Howard Taft that "there should be some conventional right to intervene in Central American affairs promptly without waiting for outbreaks and with a view to averting rather than quelling disturbances."

In December 1909, the transport *Buffalo* carried a 750-man Marine Nicaraguan Expeditionary Force to Corinto (described by Marine Major Smedley Butler as "the hottest place this side of hell"), on Nicaragua's Pacific shore. On the Atlantic side, the continuing civil war threatened the port of Bluefields. Gunboat landing parties established neutral zones within the town limits. By August the Conservatives had achieved victory

The Taft administration recognized the new government and initiated a program of "Dollar Diplomacy," described by Secretary Knox as "dollars instead of bullets." It did not work. By the spring of 1912 the Nicaraguan government was on very shaky legs. Events swept out of control with a revolt by the Conservative minister of war, General Mena, and the Liberals dynamiting Managua's Fort La Loma. The Conservative president, Adolfo Díaz appealed for American intervention.

On the Pacific and Atlantic coasts, U.S. gunboats landed parties to guard the legation at Managua and the port of Bluefields. Up from Panama came a Marine battalion to bolster the Managua force. Major units of the U.S. Pacific Fleet arrived off Corinto, and a provisional Marine regiment under Colonel Joseph Pendleton sailed from Philadelphia.

The big battle occurred on October 3, when the Marines, supported by sailors and artillery, stormed the Liberal positions at Cayotepe. At León, the traditional Liberal stronghold, 1,300 Marines and bluejackets attacked and occupied the city, defeating a drunken, rioting garrison and ending the revolt. Before year's end American forces, save for legation guards, were withdrawn. "I think nearly everybody," said "Uncle Joe" Pendleton, "was glad to see us, and I think they were impressed with the idea the United States means to see that revolutions in Nicaragua are done with."

On July 28, 1915, 340 Marines and sailors from the armored cruiser *Washington* landed at Bizoton, just outside Port-au-Prince, Haiti, marking the beginning of nineteen years of U.S. occupation there—the longest of the Banana Wars.

Haiti had no parties, only factions, and political succession happened through coup or revolution. Between 1838 and the arrival of the Americans, there were 102 of them. President Woodrow Wilson attempted to force certain reforms on several Haitian governments, only to be met with disdainful dismissal. World War I, and the fact that Germany had large investments in Haiti, only heightened United States apprehension. By 1915 Haiti was in a state of political, social, and economic collapse.

In July of that year a new civil war panicked Haitian President Vilbrun Guillaume Sam into butchering perhaps two hundred opposition family members in Port-au-Prince. Sam and his police chief were in turn slaughtered by the city mob, their heads were paraded about on poles, and parts of their bodies were publicly eaten. Offshore on the *Washington,* Rear Admiral William Caperton watched events horribly unfold. The diplomatic community pleaded with him to land forces to restore order in the capital. His quick response did exactly that.

A rapid buildup, with the 1st Marine Brigade presence eventually numbering about four thousand men, brought an initial peace of sorts. The Haitian army was disbanded immediately. Within two weeks of the intervention, an American guided legislative election brought a pliant puppet to the presidential palace. A treaty of cooperation transformed Haiti into an American protectorate under the auspices of the Navy Department. U.S. officers administered the customs service, police and prisons, public health and sanitation, supervised government finances and education, and commanded a new Haitian *gendarmerie.* The Franco-Haitian *élite,* traditional skimmers of the national purse, were for intents disenfranchised.

Peace and stability did not come without military operations. There were several campaigns against the *cacos,* extortionist mountain thieves who had hitherto served whichever faction paid the most to retain or topple a presidency.

Until the close of World War l, no one in the United States much cared about what was happening in Haiti, but war's end brought with it scandal and public view. In an effort to construct modern paved roads, the American administration employed the ancient French system of the *corvée,* road-gang work in lieu of taxes. The Marine brigade had been depleted by calls to greater duty in France, and much of the labor recruitment and overseeing was done by the Haitian *gendamierie.* The system was historically capable of tremendous abuse. Bribery, extortion, and ill-treatment were common. Large numbers of workers deserted into the ranks of the *cacos,* and the spark was struck for a major uprising against the American presence.

Charlemagne Masséna Péralte, a *"gros nègre,"* sworn enemy of the puppet government and its American masters, launched a *caco* insurrection in the fall of 1918. The Haitian *gendarmerie* proved woefully inept, and the job fell to the Marine brigade, bolstered with aircraft and combat veterans from the Great War.

On the night of October 6, 1919, Charlemagne led several hundred followers in a raid on Port-au-Prince and was nearly wiped out by a counterattack of Marines and *gendarmerie.* Later in the month, two Marine Corps enlisted men and sixteen handpicked *gendarmes* staged an elaborate ruse, entered Charlemagne's camp, and killed him with two .45-cal. bullets to the heart. To convince Haiti of the *gros nègre's* death, the corpse was tied to a door, photographed, and publicly displayed. It was an extraordinary act of political stupidity. Appearing Christ-like, upright in his bonds, Charlemagne became an instant martyr.

Taken together, the abuses of the *corvée* and the episode with Charlemagne brought loud calls in the U.S. Congress and press for an investigation of the Haiti mess. The Marine Corps, so recently hailed for its heroic conduct on the Western Front, was now vilified. "American Marines," went one hysterical account in the *New York Times,* "opened fire with machine guns from airplanes upon defenseless Haitian villages, killing men, women, and children in the open market place." The Haitian *elite* spread obscene tales of villagers "devoured by war dogs imported from the Philippines."

A U.S. Senate committee went to Haiti in 1921, resulting in appointment of a High Commissioner to govern in place of the Navy Department and a reduction of the Marines. In 1930, the United States being in the well of the Great Depression, the occupation's military and civilian functions were increas-

2. THE EMERGENCE OF MODERN AMERICA

ingly transferred to Haitians. On August 14, 1934, the 2nd Marine Regiment, sole remnant of nineteen years in Haiti, boarded their transport at Port-au-Prince. "Neither the Haitians, the American public, nor the Marines," noted the *Denver News,* "will feel very badly about it if they never go back."

The Dominican Republic, wrote an American observer, "is about the size of Ireland and has caused almost as much trouble." The nation that shares the island of Hispaniola with Haiti had known almost no peace. Its internal problems stemmed from *caudillismo,* the recurrent symptom of military strongmen. Externally troubles grew from massive, constant overextension of credit and terribly ruinous debts. International law permitted military force as a means of collection.

In July 1904, the Dominican Republic defaulted, again. To force payment, France, Italy, and Belgium threatened to seize the customs house in the capital port, Santo Domingo. The administration of President Theodore Roosevelt could not permit that. In an unofficial preamble to the "Roosevelt Corollary" of the Monroe Doctrine, the president said, "If we intend to say 'Hands off' to the powers of Europe, then sooner or later we must keep order ourselves." In January 1905, the United States took control over the Dominican customs houses, parceling debts to creditors and operating funds to the Dominican government.

In 1914, an American-supervised election brought *caudillo* Juan Isidro Jiménez to office. In return for continued support, President Woodrow Wilson demanded an American financial advisor at the treasury and an American officered constabulary. Jiménez agreed but the Dominican legislature did not, and that body threatened impeachment. On May 1, 1916, war minister General Desiderio Arias forced Jiménez out.

Within days, five companies of Marines were dispatched from neighboring Haiti and Guantanamo Bay and joined with ships' landing parties to form a provisional regiment. On May 15, they occupied Santo Domingo. General Arias escaped north. "Considerable anti-American sentiment," wired the U.S. minister. The bloodless *entre* disguised what would become eight fruitless years of occupation to no purpose.

The Marines, reinforced to more than eight hundred men by Joe Pendleton's 4th Regiment, with artillery four-wheel-drive prime movers, and Ford Model-T cars, skirted the island by water, and landed at Monte Cristi on the north coast. From there, Pendleton marched, skirmished, and fought seventy miles inland to Arias' stronghold at Santiago, where the ex-war minister surrendered.

The political mess began when the compromise president refused on constitutional grounds to accept an American commander for the Dominican national guard. In disastrous coercion, the U.S. minister halted all customs-house revenues into the country. The economy and attendant bureaucracy stopped dead. Threats of armed resistance brought martial law to the capital. By November President Wilson and the State Department, spooked by Arias' pro-German leanings and convinced that the country was incapable of self-reform, declared the Dominican Republic "in a state of military occupation ... subject to military government." Marine and naval officers assumed cabinet positions. Colonel Joe Pendleton, for instance, became Minister of War and Navy Interior and Police; not even Haiti had been so humiliated.

As in Haiti, the Dominican Republic's infrastructure, penal system, public education, public health, and sanitation were given thorough overhauls. But none of these reforms really mattered. The occupation had no unifying program beyond keeping order and training a nonpartisan constabulary. Widespread resistance in the countryside erupted, aided in part by traditional *gavillero* bandits. A movement of national liberation blossomed, becoming especially effective during the drawdown of American forces in the whole region during World War I. Again, as in Haiti, isolated atrocities achieved national attention in the United States.

By 1920 no one could think of any reason for staying on. The Marines were withdrawn from the rural areas and concentrated in the cities. A Dominican-officered national police took up its duties. A new constitution, elections, and transitional government were put in place. In the summer of 1924 the last of the Marines left without lament.

The final American military intervention during the classic period of the Banana Wars took place in Nicaragua from 1927 to 1934 and augured some very uncomfortable parallels with the future Vietnam War. The latest strife pitted the Liberal "outs" against the Conservative "ins," and for the first time Soviet-influenced Communism replaced Germany as the chief menace to United States' hemispheric security. The scare spread to where the Associated Press saw "the specter of a Mexican-fostered Bolshevistic hegemony intervening between the United States and the Panama Canal." Raising the Red scare, the Conservative Nicaraguan regime of Adolfo Díaz desperately sought overt American assistance. The State Department didn't bite, and instead slapped an arms embargo on the whole country. Having just untangled itself from the Dominican tar pit, the U.S. government had no wish to fall into another. Ships' landing forces went ashore in some ports to establish neutral safe zones, but nothing beyond that.

Meantime, the civil war raged on, with the Liberals gaining strength. In January 1927, President Calvin Coolidge announced the sale of ammunition to the Díaz government. The same month, the 2nd Battalion, 5th Marines arrived to protect communications between Managua and the sea. In February the Liberals under General José Moncada inflicted severe defeats on the government army. Deserting soldiers and endemic bandits ravaged the countryside. Díaz formally requested American military intervention. It was refused, but more American forces poured in to guard ports and railroads. When the British threatened to send warships to protect their nationals, the Roosevelt Corollary kicked in. More reinforcements were sent, forming the 2nd Marine Brigade that included an aviation squadron. The civil war deadlocked.

In May 1927 former U.S. Secretary of War Henry Stimson negotiated an eminently fair solution, providing for a Marine-officered, Nicaraguan *guardia* and American-supervised elections during the coming year. The Marines would then go home. In the United States, part of the aware public did not see it that way. Charges of "imperialism" were hurled at the Coolidge administration, and the normally sane Republican Senator George Norris considered the agreement "shocking to every peace-loving citizen in civilization."

Another who felt sold out, and who refused to be a party to the peace, was a difficult Liberal field commander with

7. Intervention

messianic ambitions, Augusto Cesar Sandino, whose men called themselves *Sandinistas*. For six frustrating years the Marines and *guardia* would fight them up and down the Nicaraguan mountains. The *Sandinistas* proved excellent at ambush, and mercilessly inhuman as captors.

The jungle battles took on the tint of modern warfare, providing a precursor to what future American generations would experience on Guadalcanal and in Vietnam. Air power was used extensively and Marine aviators perfected the technique of dive-bombing in support of ground troops and air evacuation of wounded from the battlefield. Automatic weapons were used by both sides to a degree not previously seen in the Banana Wars. Aircraft carriers were present twice. Wide-ranging riverine operations were conducted.

In the United States, and a good part of the world, the charismatic Sandino's stock (much as Ho Chi Minh's later) rose astonishingly high. Large demonstrations massed in front of the White House carrying placards reading "Wall Street not Sandino is the Real Bandit." Marines embarking for Nicaragua were urged to desert to Sandino and his "war for freedom."

The 1928 Nicaraguan presidential election, a model of American democratic efficiency, brought the Liberals to power. For Sandino, it mattered not. His war was not with the United States at all, but against any Nicaraguan government, whatever its leanings. On more than one occasion he offered large bribes to Marine officers to quit the country, leaving him a free hand.

By 1929, Sandino's bands were compressed north, against the Honduran border. In Washington, as pressure mounted in Congress and the press, President-elect Herbert Hoover made prompt withdrawal from Nicaragua a priority. Military responsibility for Sandino shifted to the *guardia*. Marine units were pulled out, from nearly 6,000 men on election day to 2,215 inside a year. Sandino cooperated by taking off to Mexico, leaving his forces confused, demoralized, and bandit-ridden. In Nicaraguan elections, Liberals gained more legislative seats. In the spring of 1930, Sandino returned, and the war burst anew

Henry Stimson, now secretary of state, initiated a complete policy review. Understanding that military victory over Sandino was impossible without a massive commitment of American troops, he determined to get the Marines out completely. American public opposition to the Nicaraguan campaign became deeper and more widespread. Hundreds of people were arrested in pro-*Sandinista* rallies. By spring 1931, Marine ground troops were down to 745 men. There would be no more for Nicaragua.

On March 31, an earthquake hit Managua, killing 2,000 people and injuring 3,500 more. Sandino considered the quake a "divine gesture" of his favor in heaven. He struck east to the fruit plantations. American companies begged for protection. Stimson refused, calling them "a pampered lot of people . . . who think they have a right to call for troops whenever any danger apprehends." Emboldened by the American reticence, the *Sandinistas* raided throughout the country. Stimson authorized Marines as train guards, but held firm in his refusal to commit reinforcements.

Through 1932 the guerilla war continued unabated. In the November Nicaraguan presidential elections, both Liberals and Conservatives offered Sandino the opportunity to participate and offered a seat in any subsequent "national unity" government. He refused. On January 1, 1933, the Marines departed Nicaragua.

Immediately after the American withdrawal, Sandino made peace with the government and disbanded his forces. Just over a year later, he and his brother were kidnapped and murdered on orders from the Liberal-appointed chief of the *guardia*, Antonio Somoza.

Thus ended the classic period of the Banana Wars; subsequent interventions are historical footnotes. In April 1965, President Lyndon Johnson's inflated fear of Castro-inspired Communism sent strong forces into the Dominican Republic. President Ronald Reagan's turn came in October 1983 at Grenada. In a comic quest to "stand tall," his administration fabricated a patently false excuse of endangered medical students to overthrow a thuggish Left regime, but at the cost of a minor American military debacle. President George Bush's 1989 intervention in Panama had legitimacy in terms of canal security. And President Bill Clinton's 1994 actions in Haiti were driven by domestic politics, the effect of Haitian immigration on American institutions, and finally the utter inability of Haiti to govern and administer itself humanely.

Based on history's lessons, at least one thing is certain: the current American military intervention on Caribbean shores will not be the last one.

How We Lived

They were so mundane, then, the habits that now seem worthy of Ripley's Believe It or Not: *Housewives collected rainwater in barrels to wash their clothes. In the days before toilet paper, people used pages from the Sears, Roebuck and Co. catalog. The job of running a home at the turn of the century, especially a prairie home like the one in west Texas run by* **Mary McQuerry,** *104, required enormous endurance. Some 1.6 million families received land under the program between 1863 and 1967 and like many of them, McQuerry's family arrived on its land by covered wagon:*

... My day began at 4 a.m. My husband, James, and I milked about 130 dairy cows by hand. He'd load the wagon to head for the creamery while I gathered wood for the stove and began the first of my many trips to the water well. It took maybe an hour for the oven to heat up right and then I made breakfast from scratch—eggs, biscuits, homemade jellies and jams, bacon from our hogs. The stove was great in the winter, but when it was canning season in the summer, it was brutal. Canning peaches took me two or three days of constant work at the stove in the Texas heat in July. But if I didn't make them, we didn't eat in the winter.

Mondays were wash days. You scrubbed on a board, then stirred them in boiling water and then through two rinse tubs and some bluing. It took till early afternoon. Tuesday was ironing day. The irons were 6 or 7 pounds. You heated them in the fireplace and the process took all day. I did gardening a lot during the rest of the week. And Sunday I rested. Before church, I'd catch a chicken and pin it to the ground under my foot. Then I'd pull its head off with my hands. I never got the hang of wringing their necks.

Beyond daily hardships, life on the frontier contained other perils, according to **Pauline McCleve,** *100, who recounts her memories of desolate Arizona:*

... There were Indians and outlaws all around. They would steal our cattle, and there would be killings. My father always rode with six-shooters at each side. It was just part of the attire. Sometimes he'd wear two gun belts—four guns, in all. Billy the Kid came by the house one day before I was born and wanted to kill my mother's dog for barking at him. But the Indian that was with him said, "No! No!" So they went away. When people in the town found out,

> ## PAULINE MCCLEVE, 100
>
> **Her parents were Mormon pioneers in Arizona. She now lives in Tempe and for 50 years ran a beauty salon.** *Family Profile:* **married for 65 years; husband is deceased; five children.** *Family lore:* **Before she married, her mother accidentally shot a hole in her father's hat at a picnic. "Mother never did shoot well," the father opined.** *Beauty secret:* **As a child, she made shampoo from yucca root.** *Midwife's bill for delivery of her first baby:* **$10.**

they formed a posse to try to catch Billy. They didn't. But two men who were separated from the posse were found shot and killed by the outlaws.

In cities, a small army of tradesmen and merchants moved through neighborhoods. **Sidney Amber,** *109, describes early San Francisco:*

... My mother left the milk jug in front of the door. In the morning the milkman came and filled it up. The tea man delivered tea for 25 cents per pound. And the vegetable man or fruit man came in a wagon on the street, hollering: "Fresh fruit! Fresh vegetables!" You went out to look it over. They'd usually come every other day. Wood and coal were delivered. And so was ice—they cut it to the size you wanted.

Buying meat meant a trip to the butcher, recalls **Annie Cecelia Maddigan Healey,** *101:*

... There was no refrigeration. They had a big room out in back, and they used to put great big blocks of ice, and they'd hang the critters up, like a lamb or a pig. And you'd say you want some pork chops, and he'd go in this room with a cleaver—crack, crack—and get the chops and throw the fat away in a barrel.

Indoor plumbing was an urban luxury 100 years ago. The first major sewer system was designed in 1885 in Chicago. Utility companies were providing about 3 billion gallons of water a day in 1900, compared with 41 billion gallons' in 1990. The first large-scale purification was launched by a Jersey City company in 1908, and chlorination quickly spread. Before all that, most kept chamberpots by their beds for middle-of-the-night emergencies or relied on outhouses. **Miriam Eliason,** *104, recalls living in her later home of Zion, Ill:*

... Everybody had a privy on the end of the lot at the alley, and away from the well so [sewage] wouldn't seep into the water supply. A man would come along once a week with a big covered wagon that had a galvanized can. He'd clean out the privy and dump [the waste] in his wagon. In the wintertime, he had a charcoal affair on the side of his wagon to set the can on to thaw the waste out. It would be frozen.

If you didn't have running water says **Bernice Isaacson,** *100, you just made do:*

... When we first moved to the Minnesota north woods, we had to borrow drinking water from neighbors who lived more than a mile away. There was a pond on our ground, and my uncle said that we would have to use that water. I said, "Oh, there's worms in there." He said, "If they can live in there, it's pure." We got a pailful and Grandma took a tea towel and strained it and put it on the stove and sterilized it. I remember all those black wiggler worms and polliwogs in that cloth.

Homes were mostly outfitted with handmade goods or things bought from catalogs. Though Benjamin Franklin introduced the first mail-order catalog to America in 1744, it didn't become a truly national market force until a decade after 1886 when Richard Sears and Alvah Roebuck published a 196-page catalog. Circulation of the catalog grew from 318 in 1897 to more than 1 million in 1904 as it became a staple in homes like **Bernice Isaacson**'s:

... We ordered most everything from Sears, Roebuck catalogs. When my aunt and uncle's house in Iowa burned down some time around 1910, they ordered everything from Montgomery Ward. We laughed about it because they ordered everything down to an eggbeater. But the first thing I bought after I began to work is a lady's desk from Sears. It's still in the other room.

CONVENIENCES

"Everything changed with electricity," says **Pauline McCleve**. *Just weeks after Thomas Edison lit a filament in October 1879, Charles Brush thrilled Cleveland residents by illuminating the town square. By 1888, 53 municipalities had light and power systems; that number rose to 800 municipal systems by 1900. Government regulation began in states in 1907 and the federal government broke up the monopoly power of big utility holding companies in 1935. Families greeted the arrival of electrical household devices like magical talismans. McCleve still speaks with rapture about "my beautiful Blue Bird washing machine" and other advances:*

... A man down the street had a vacuum cleaner and would rent it to people. My mother used to take the rugs up twice a year and take them out on the line and beat them to get the dirt out. But once she used that vacuum cleaner, she never had to take them up again.

Two years after Alexander Graham Bell patented the telephone in 1876, the first commercial phone exchange opened in New Haven. The phone's use exploded after that: There were 150,000 phones in the country in 1887 and 2,371,000 by 1902. That's 1 for every 33 Americans. They opened vast new worlds, though at first the newfangled contraption mystified some like **Pauline McCleve**'s *father:*

... I followed Papa down to the post office, where he was going to make his first phone call. A little local girl was missing, and he wanted to know if they had found her. He picked up the phone

SIDNEY AMBER, 109

He owned two restaurants in Los Angeles and still works as maître d' today; also ran two retail stores and did graphic arts. *Family profile:* **two marriages; both wives deceased; no children.** *Celebrities he has known:* **singer Al Jolson, magician Harry Houdini, heavyweight champion Jack Johnson.** *Price of his first Cadillac:* **$800.** *Vivid memories:* **his mother being thrown from bed in the 1906 San Francisco earthquake; Lindbergh baby kidnapping.**

and was screaming into it, thinking that the person he was talking to was so far away that he had to yell. The postmaster, John Dilavitz, finally said, "Dick, you don't have to yell. Just use your ordinary voice."

Everybody was on a party line, says **Jennie Brown**, *101, so "you didn't tell any secrets."* **Bernice Isaacson** *says making calls was a pretty elaborate event:*

... A neighbor helped me get a summer job with the phone company when I was a freshman in high school about 1910. I learned to "throw the plugs." Callers had to pick up the phone, put it to their ear and then ring by winding it. Then, I'd help with their connections. They put me on long distance when I was 15. People would tell me where they wanted to call, then hang up and wait a half-hour till I could call back.

HEALTH

Killer diseases and the complications of giving birth and getting sick were omnipresent in homes at the turn of the century. The scourges included polio, measles and mumps (for which vaccines were invented in 1954, 1963 and 1967, respectively) and influenza. **Leola Peoples**, *101, had medical training and volunteered in Washington, D.C., to fight the 1918 flu epidemic that killed 675,000 Americans overall between September 1918 and June 1919:*

... We worked in a makeshift hospital. People would bring bodies in and just drop them in a bed anywhere. I went to work one night, passed 25 beds, and all of them had dead bodies. They couldn't even get enough caskets to bury them. The government gave us whiskey and quinine to give to the sick. That's all they knew as treatments.

There were just two of us black volunteers. A lot of the others were Catholic sisters, and many died. For 700 patients, they had two doctors and 12 nurses. They couldn't get anybody to work, because they were scared. But even with that, the old head nurse didn't want us to eat with the other volunteers because we were black. Can you imagine? We were putting our lives in danger, but she didn't want us to be eating in there with the white people! I never went back in that cafeteria anymore.

When you got sick yourself, says **Miriam Eliason**, *even common complaints could be frightful:*

... I wasn't a very healthy child. My father tried to cure my problem with my tonsils by painting them with iodine. When that didn't work, he took me one day on a big old-fashioned bicycle to the doctor's office. They laid me on a table, my father held my head and another man held my feet on the table. The doctor stood over me with that long, shiny instrument, and my mouth was propped open. My screams and struggles were in vain, and the blood was wiped up with towels. And I rode home

2. THE EMERGENCE OF MODERN AMERICA

on the bicycle. They didn't have any such thing as painkillers in those days.

Quarantine signs were a commonplace sight. The family of **Joseph Hankinson,** *100, paid dearly when scarlet fever struck:*

...My sister died of it in three days. My mother was at her sister's funeral—my aunt—and Mother came home to find her daughter was dead. When my other sister got sick, we were quarantined—a sign with big red letters right on our front door: "NOTICE: KEEP OUT!" After she got better, they [health authorities] fumigated the house, stuck a pipe through the front door after corking up all the windows and pumped something in.

Childbirth was hardly routine. **Ora Glass,** *103:*

...I gave birth in a regular hospital in Omaha. I don't remember having any painkillers. After the birth, I stayed in the hospital to be a wet nurse, because I had so much milk and my boy only took one breast because one breast has an inverted nipple. He didn't like that one. Sometimes, they'd pump the milk out of my breast to feed other babies, and sometimes they'd bring the white babies in. About three or four needed nourishment every day—something was wrong with their mothers. I stayed in the hospital for a few months just to help these babies out.

The hospital was segregated. A lot of Negro mothers in there said, "I don't see how you can do that." I said, "They need nourishment. Why be so cruel when you can help somebody? If my baby needed it, I'd be happy for somebody to help him."

WOMEN AT WORK

Women entered the work force in increasing numbers after the turn of the century: Five million worked outside the home in 1900. That figure grew to 10.4 million in 1930 and, spurred by the women's movement, hit 30 million by 1970. Many of the things women did by hand are now done by technology or cheaper labor abroad. **Annie Healey** *worked in mills in Middleboro, Mass., as a teenager in the 1910s:*

...When I was 14 years old my father went to town hall and got permission for me to work at the Star Mill that made beautiful, woolen men's suits. I worked from 6:30 in the morning when the bell rang until 6 at night. At noon, I had three quarters of an hour off for lunch and I'd go home for it. When we moved farther away, I got a job when I was around 15 in a factory where they made candy boxes and shoe boxes. We worked six days a week from 7 until 5, for 50 cents a day. I used to give my mother all the money because my family was buying a house. At first, unions helped get rid of things like child labor, but then they caused some trouble. In Middleboro, we lost three factories after unions got higher wages for workers. The factories were moved to Mexico.

LEOLA PEOPLES, 101

She attended Meharry Medical School in Nashville and got a medical license in 1915. But her training was not equal to that of whites and her poor clientele often couldn't pay, so she moved to the North and became a porter, waitress and nurse's aide. *Family profile:* **married briefly; now lives in Manhattan.** *Favorite memory:* **In 1918, to keep her brother in school, she gambled $5 on a horse race and won $350. He ultimately graduated from Harvard Law School.**

The medical training **Leola Peoples** *got made her one of the first black women to get a physician's license in Georgia. But schools for blacks were so poor that she never learned the more advanced techniques of her white counterparts. She found she could earn more money in the North by being a waitress and working for the railroad:*

...I worked in a little hospital in Forsyth, Ga., after I got my doctor's license. I delivered a lot of babies, but all you did then was wash your hands and try to help them pull the baby out. They hadn't heard of C-sections, so women with breech babies often just died.

Few people could pay, so I didn't make money there or in the hospital where I worked in Baldwin, Ala., so I moved to Atlantic City and learned how to be a waitress. There was an old Irish fisherman who saw me on the boardwalk and said, "You got a sad face today." I told him I'd like to be a waitress. I helped him carry fish into the restaurant and was hired.

The most money I ever made in my life was during World War II, working for the Pennsylvania Railroad. The tips were great on the run from Boston to Washington. You'd give [the great actor] Paul Robeson orange juice and coffee and he'd leave a $2.50 tip. When the men came back from the war, they laid the women off.

I became a nurse's aide at Columbia Presbyterian Medical Center in New York and helped some beautiful people. Elizabeth Taylor always suffered from back pain—a slipped disk. She was a nice patient, a good tipper. She'd leave all her jewels right on the table. We'd say, "Miss Taylor, put your stuff away. Anybody can pick that up." She'd laugh. "I don't care, I can get some more."

One of the toughest businesses for women to break into was journalism. **Marjory Stoneman Douglas,** *105, didn't have that much trouble, though, because her father founded and edited the* Miami Herald:

...I'd been in Miami a short while when my father asked me to fill in for the society editor, who was off because her mother was sick. I worked from the house. I'd call up two or three women from the women's club to get the news, and the *Herald* would send a boy on a motorcycle to get my copy. After a short period of filling in, I took over the society editor's job full time.

Once in a while my column would make a difference to somebody. In the early 1920s, a story came out that a North Dakota boy named Martin Tabert was arrested here and put in a labor camp as a vagrant. He was beaten to death in the labor camp. The news of his death shocked me so much I wrote a simple ballad [about it]. It received enormous attention. It was read in Tallahassee in the Legislature and as a result they abolished beating in the labor camps forever.

8. How We Lived

PROHIBITION

Everyone has stories about how his family or friends got around the law banning alcohol that was enacted in 1919. **Dominic Cali,** *102, says everybody made his own beer without fear of reprisal from the 1,550 federal prohibition agents. Still, 500,000 were convicted of alcohol-related activities and paid $75 million in fines during Prohibition. Some companies found enterprising ways to skirt the law, says* **Tom Lane, 101:**

...You could get a cask of [prefermented juice] from California, and it came with a little leaflet that said something like, "Do not put a hose into the cask, and let it stand for one month or it will turn into wine and that is against the law." They told you just how to make it!

There were as many as 219,000 illegal saloons at the height of Prohibition. And violence became part of the liquor business. The national murder rate rose from 6 per 100,000 of population to 10 per 100,000 in 1933. **Sadie Nickelson,** *100, describes how violence seeped into her hometown, Thermopolis, Wyo.:*

...Prohibition was the worst thing the government ever did. It made more trouble—shootings and killings. Once, there was a man who had a load of whiskey who had to cross a bridge at Gooseberry Creek. The local game warden, the only one who had the authority to stop the car and search it, approached the car. But when he looked in, the driver shot him dead.

That wasn't the only fatality. A local farmer, just as a curiosity, decided to watch from behind some trees as a shipment of whiskey came through. The fellow [who] was driving the car just shot him, even though he was innocent—wasn't a threat at all.

CLOTHING

Function prevailed over fashion in clothes for most at the dawn of the century. Onetime seamstress **Lucille Mosditchian,** *100, knew how important it was to make clothes well:*

...Clothing had to be perfect or you couldn't sell it. In those days, I mostly made dresses for women. Like most women, I wore dresses all the time around the house. I never thought that women would wear pants like they do now. The first pair of pants I wore, my husband nearly killed me. They didn't believe in that those days. But I felt good in them.

But when folks got interested in fashion, **Sidney Amber** *remembers, they went all out:*

...Women always wore gloves, a hat, a bustle, long skirts. They always looked very beautiful in their garments. A hat would cost around $2.50, $2.75, and that's for a very gorgeous hat with a

---

SADIE NICKELSON, 100

She was a homesteader in Thermopolis, Wyo.; worked as a cowgirl doing ranch work. Still lives there. *Family profile:* **married twice (she and her first husband walked to a preacher's house and got him to perform the service on the spot); two children; one grandchild; three great-grandchildren.** *Childhood lore:* **She discovered an Indian grave site at the top of a tree. Later, she lived in a boxcar turned into a home for railroad workers like her father.**

---

beautiful plume on it. But now, hats are of the past.

In upscale families, clothes were changed at different parts of the day. **Miriam Eliason:**

...My mother always dressed up in the afternoon. After she'd get the dinner dishes washed, she'd wear a skirt and a dressing sack. Women also wore cotton pants with legs that would overlap in the back. There wasn't any underwear. They wore two or three long petticoats, too. My mother would sweat; her dress would be wet.

MANNERS

Many centenarians are unhappy about the coarsening of everyday life. The views of 102-year-old **Mary Corinne Rosebrook,** *a onetime Latin teacher are typical:*

...I think that generally speaking there's more informality and relaxation these days. But I think manners mattered more some years ago. There have to be some standards. There's nothing unjust about that. In my schools we always had high standards, and the children had reason to respect the authorities. Schools used to be a safe place, but it doesn't seem that way today.

Ora Glass *recalls that formal schooling in manners was common:*

...When I was young we took a course at the YMCA on table manners and how to act at different receptions and the like, on how you're supposed to address people. Today, some places you go to even the clerks in the stores aren't very mannerly. Some are so rude.

A becoming modesty is what **Pauline McCleve** *remembers about the way her parents related to each other.*

...We bathed in a tin tub when we were growing up. Once, I went in the bathroom and found that even though Mother was all alone, she had put chairs up and quilts around to protect the view of her bathing. I said, "Mother, you put those barriers up and you're all alone here except for Father." She said she was afraid he might come in while she was bathing, and she didn't want him to see her bathing.

DEALING WITH OTHERS

Many of these centenarians say they experienced profound love, enjoyed their families and communities and regret that today's families and relationships don't seem as satisfying as theirs. But that was not a universal circumstance. Relations between men and women were often shrouded in mystery, according to **Marjory Stoneman Douglas:**

2. THE EMERGENCE OF MODERN AMERICA

... In the early 1900s, girls weren't brought up to be competitive, unless you consider their attractiveness to males. We were more or less sheltered from everything and especially from sex. In junior and senior year [at Wellesley College], we had lectures behind locked doors. One girl fainted when the lecturer showed a picture of a pregnant woman. In zoology class, we saw pictures of copulating earthworms, and a good deal was said about frogs. But outside of the general idea that something had to happen between the male and female, we were completely vague. I had some dim idea it had something to do with the navel.

Racial segregation was a deeply wounding and debilitating reality, recalls **Leola Peoples:**

If you were black, you had to go to the black section of everything. If you rode a train, you had to ride right up in front by the engine where you'd get all that smoke. When I got to Atlantic City from the South, black people could not bathe in the ocean with the whites. I guess white people didn't want to go in the water with the black folks.

After I moved to New York, I went to Brooklyn a lot to see Jackie Robinson play. They used to throw bottles at him from the seats. But he stuck with it. He sure helped his people.

Black people fought like heck for civil rights. But then we had our own troubles. Mayor John Lindsay [of New York] was a good leader. They had a riot up here in the late 1960s that started at a five-and-dime store. He came up here on a big truck with a big bullhorn. He rode through 125th Street and said, "This isn't getting you anywhere. Put down those bottles and rocks you're throwing. I know what you're going through. I just want you to remember that the man underneath today could be on top tomorrow."

Mary Okinaga, *100, was one of the 110,000 Japanese-Americans sent to internment camps in 1942 during World War II—even though she had been in the United States for 25 years, considered herself "a full American" and blamed Japan for starting the war:*

... I was in San Francisco when Pearl Harbor happened. When the executive order [establishing the internment camps] came out, I personally didn't fight against it. The government took us by train. We could bring only what we could carry in our hands.

I went to Heart Mountain, Wyo. It was snowing when I got there, and I didn't like the cold. But I got used to it. I was a janitor in the hospital inside the camp. I got $6 a month for the work, and there was no other place to spend that money, so I saved some up.

At the end of the war, we went back to San Francisco. Everything in our home had been looted. All gone. I had stored some of my personal belongings at the Buddhist temple's storage place. And when I came back, it was gone, too.

BERNICE ISAACSON, 100

Her mother died when she was 6; her father was an alcoholic. She was raised by relatives. Now lives in Omaha. *Family profile:* **married at 20; husband deceased; two sons; four grandchildren; seven great-grandchildren.** *First job:* **telephone operator as a young teenager, earning $5 a week; specialized in long-distance calls at age 15.** *Earliest memory:* **at age 2½, singing "McKinley's elected, Bryan's a fool, sitting on a haystack, looking like a mule!"**

Wings For Man

The right men at the right time and place in history, Wilbur and Orville Wright applied their natural inventiveness, mechanical skills, extraordinary foresight, and great tenacity to achieve one of mankind's oldest and most nearly impossible dreams—prolonged, controlled human flight. In doing so, they radically changed their world, and ours.

Doug McIntyre

Los Angeles writer Doug McIntyre is author of Ride the Wind, *a screen biography of the Wrights, as well as numerous television comedies, including* Married . . . With Children, WKRP in Cincinnati, *and* Full House.

On the bitter-cold morning of December 17, 1903, Wilbur Wright watched as his nervous brother Orville lay prone on the bottom wing of their first powered airplane. The two men squinted their eyes from the sting of blowing sand and the sharp winter winds that gusted at more than twenty miles an hour across the isolated section of North Carolina's Outer Banks known as the Kill Devil Hills.

The product of three and a half years of research and experimentation, the Wrights' 1903 "Flyer" weighed more than six hundred pounds and measured forty feet from wingtip to wingtip. Above Orv's head was a tank of explosive gasoline; a few inches to his right were the roaring steel engine and whirling chain-drive transmission. Behind him spun the airplane's two eight-foot blades. He was well aware that the steel bracing wires that surrounded him were sharp enough to draw blood on contact. No wonder he was nervous.

John Daniels was also nervous. As a member of the United States Life Saving Corps he was no stranger to physical danger, having often risked death to pluck shipwreck victims from the treacherous waters off the North Carolina coast. Today, however, standing behind Orville's Korona camera, he faced a different challenge. Daniels had been asked by the Wrights to photograph the first moment of human flight. He had never touched a camera in his life.

In a sense, while inventing the airplane, Wilbur and Orville Wright also invented themselves. "The Wright Brothers" became a corporate entity that all but obscured the individuals.

At 10:35 A.M. Orville threw the trip switch that released the Flyer from its tether. The machine gathered speed as it rolled down the "Grand Junction Railroad," the Wright's four-dollar launching system of two-by-fours and bicycle hubs. Wilbur ran beside the machine, holding its right wingtip steady. When Orv judged the speed to be sufficient, he pulled back on the elevator control, and the world's first airplane left the ground.

The five lucky witnesses—Daniels, two other members of the nearby lifesaving station, and two local residents—cheered. They had just seen a miracle!

In his excitement, Daniels was not sure if he had remembered to squeeze the bulb and trip the camera's shutter. It was not until weeks later, back in their darkroom in Dayton, Ohio, that Wilbur and Orville saw the proof they would need to back their claim of "first to fly." The Wright Flyer was captured two feet off the ground, with Orv prone on the lower wing and Wilbur frozen in wonder for all eternity. Daniels' first photograph remains the most famous in the annals of invention and perhaps the most famous in American history.

From the time we were little children, my brother Orville and myself lived together, played together, worked together, in fact, thought together." So wrote Wilbur in 1912. It was an exaggeration.

As a young boy Wilbur was much closer to his older brothers, Reuchlin and Lorin. Orville had many boyhood friends, including the African-American poet Paul Laurence Dunbar. However, Orv's favorite companion—as a child and into adulthood—was his sister Katharine.

Wilbur and Orville *did* grow to be as close as twins, but this happened over many years. In a sense, while inventing the airplane, they also invented themselves. "The Wright brothers" became a corporate entity that has obscured the individuals.

Wilbur was born in Millville, Indiana in 1867, to Milton and Susan Wright. His father, a bishop in the Church of the United Brethren in Christ, named his third son after Wilbur Fisk, a preacher he admired.

In 1871 the Bishop moved his family to Dayton, Ohio, where Orville soon was born in the upstairs bedroom at 7 Hawthorn Street. This simple two-story house would remain the family's primary residence until 1914 when Orville, the Bishop, and Katharine—born three years

From American History Illustrated, *January/February 1994, 30-42, 66, 69. © 1994 by Cowles Magazines, Inc. Reprinted through the courtesy of Cowles Magazines, Inc., publisher of* American History Illustrated.

2. THE EMERGENCE OF MODERN AMERICA

to the day after Orv—moved to a mansion in suburban Oakwood.

As youngsters both Wright boys earned above-average grades, but neither officially graduated from high school. Orv was the born inventor, having inherited mechanical dexterity from his mother. As a child he was fascinated by printing; over time this hobby evolved into the brothers' first career. For many years, "Wright & Wright Job Printers" operated on Dayton's racially integrated west side. The young men edited and published local newspapers on an ingenious printing press they had built from scrap lumber and an old buggy top, with a tombstone serving as the press bed.

The Wrights claimed that their interest in flight began in early childhood when their father, who traveled extensively on church business, returned home with a toy "bat." This rubber-band-powered helicopter-like toy made a tremendous impact upon the boys. They played with it until it fell to pieces; rebuilt it many times; and eventually made larger versions that failed to fly as well as the smaller original. Disenchanted they drifted off to other interests but never forgot their first taste of "flight."

As the Wrights matured, America seemed to go crazy; bicycle madness swept the nation. In the 1880s it was called "wheeling," and Americans couldn't buy bicycles fast enough. The sudden proliferation of "wheels" created a demand for good mechanics. As Wilbur and Orv's reputation for mechanical creativity spread, a second career—bicycle repairing—was virtually thrust upon them.

Orville, the more reckless and impetuous of the two, purchased a brand-new bicycle for the astounding sum of $160. Wilbur bought a used "wheel" for $80. The brothers' personalities were reflected in how they rode. Will preferred long quiet rides in the country, while Orv fancied himself a "scorcher" and won several medals in YMCA races.

Eventually the Wrights built and sold their own line of bicycles. This not only provided a steady, if modest, income; it also gave the Wrights basic engineering skills they would later put to use in building flying machines. That time was rapidly approaching—but first Wilbur and Orville would each have a brush with death.

In 1885, while playing shinny (an early form of ice hockey), Wilbur was struck in the mouth by an opposing player's stick. His teeth were knocked out, and he suffered severe trauma. The family became deeply concerned as Wilbur's recovery dragged on for months, then years. Wilbur withdrew into himself. He no longer went to work and rarely left the house. He complained of heart palpitations and began to speculate that he would not live long. Prior to his accident, Will had expressed an interest in attending Yale University and becoming a teacher. He now dropped his college plans, telling his father that "my health has been such that it might be time and money wasted."

During Will's convalescence, Susan Wright, Wilbur and Orville's mother, was seriously ill with tuberculosis. Wilbur spent what little energy he had caring for his dying mother. When not by her side he was invariably buried in a book, absorbing vast stores of knowledge. He read on a variety of subjects, including the works of Robert Ingersoll, the famous agnostic. Learning was encouraged in the Wright home. The Bishop's religious principles never prohibited the brothers from examining any area of interest. "We were lucky enough," wrote Orville in 1940, "to grow up in an environment where there was always much encouragement to children to pursue intellectual interests; to investigate whatever aroused curiosity. In a different kind of environment, our curiosity might have been nipped long before it could have borne fruit."

The Wilbur Wright who emerged after his hockey accident and the death of his mother was a very different person from the rudderless Wilbur who had followed his younger brother's lead. With his health restored, Wilbur was now confident and self-assured. He had not only studied books during his convalescence; he had evaluated his own strengths and weaknesses. Will concluded that he wasn't cut out for a life in business. Science was his passion—if only he could find the proper venue in which to make his mark.

In Europe, a German engineer named Otto Lilienthal had gained international fame by experimenting with flying machines. Unlike many of the crackpots who earned ridicule and scorn, Lilienthal was a respected man whose public flights drew large crowds and numerous photographers. During his five years of gliding experiments, Lilienthal had accumulated a total of five minutes of actual flight time. As paltry as this might seem, it made him the world's most experienced aviator.

On August 9, 1896, while gliding from his man-made hill near Berlin, Lilienthal's machine was overturned by a sudden gust. His method for controlling the glider required him to shift his body to the left or right to rebalance the craft. "Weight shifting," as it was known, was both slow and dangerous. Lillenthal's glider plunged to the ground, and the crash snapped his neck. Allegedly, his final words were: "Sacrifices must be made."

Back in Dayton, meanwhile, another life-or-death struggle was in progress. Orville had contracted typhoid fever from contaminated well water. For weeks he hovered near death, slipping in and out of a coma. It was during Orv's illness that Wilbur read a newspaper obituary detailing Lilienthal's death. When Orville's fever finally broke, Wilbur, his childhood interest in flight re-awakened, filled his ears with talk of flying machines. Wilbur had found his venue, but the dynamics of the brothers' relationship had changed. From now on Wilbur would lead, not follow.

What happened over the next five years is one of the great American tales, a story so archetypal as to almost define Yankee ingenuity and rugged individualism. It began with a letter.

On May 30, 1899, Wilbur picked up a pen and a sheet of Wright Cycle Company stationary and wrote to Samuel Langley, a well-known flying-machine inventor and secretary of the Smithsonian Institution. He requested copies of the museum's publications on aeronautics as well as a list of other writings on the subject.

Wilbur's letter remains the most important letter the Smithsonian has ever received: "I have been interested in the problem of mechanical and human flight ever since as a boy I constructed a number of bats [helicopters] of various sizes after the style of Cayley's and Pénaud's machines," he wrote. "My observations since have only convinced me more firmly that human flight is possible and practicable. It is only a question of knowledge and skill just as in all acrobatic feats. Birds are the most perfectly trained gymnasts in the world . . . and it may be that man will never equal them . . . [but] I believe that simple flight at least is possible to man. . . . I wish to avail myself of all that is already known and then, if

9. Wings for Man

possible, add my mite to help the future worker who will attain final success."

This remarkable letter is significant on three counts. First, it reflects how much research Wilbur had already done. In addition to studying birds, he was familiar with the work of early European experimenters. Secondly, it is clear he did not think that he would invent the airplane; rather some "future worker" would "attain final success." Finally, and most significantly, he made no mention of Orville. This letter, and most of the hundreds of others that Wilbur penned between 1899 and 1902, are written in the first-person singular. Wilbur's famous quotation about how he and Orv "thought together" was apparently not a sentiment he held from the start.

"It is possible to fly without motors, but not without knowledge and skill."

Wilbur Wright

In response to Wilbur's request, the Smithsonian sent him pamphlets on human flight, including some by the late Lilienthal. Also recommended was Octave Chanute's book, *Progress in Flying Machines*. On May 13, 1900, Wilbur wrote to Chanute: "For some years now I have been afflicted with the belief that flight is possible to man. My disease has increased in severity and I feel that it will soon cost me an increased amount of money if not my life. . . . It is possible to fly without motors, but not without knowledge and skill. This I conceive to be fortunate, for man, by reason of his greater intellect, can more reasonably hope to equal birds in knowledge, than to equal nature in the perfection of her machinery."

The language of Wilbur's preamble to Chanute is not only beautiful, it is revealing. It indicates that he had dismissed motors as a detail, not the key to flight. This was a point missed by many of his contemporaries, most notably Dr. Langley, who spent years and thousands of tax dollars developing state-of-the-art engines.

What the letter tells us about Wilbur's state of mind is even more significant. Wilbur Wright was a young man who foresaw early death. When viewed through this prism, perhaps his subsequent condescending treatment of Orville was actually brotherly love, not selfishness. Wilbur would not allow Orv to fly until 1902. Since Wilbur did not believe he had long to live anyway, it made sense for him to risk his neck on their imperfect flying machines, sparing his brother. At the very least, his premonitions of death may have given urgency to his work.

Wilbur concluded that the first major necessity in achieving human flight was the development of a control system. His years in the bicycle business had taught him that it was possible to ride a machine that is inherently unstable. The rider achieves balance by making tiny adjustments as he moves over an ever-changing terrain. So too, thought Wilbur, must an airplane pilot adjust his machine to maintain balance and control in the rapidly changing environment of the sky. What good are powerful engines and wings that lift if you have no control in flight? As obvious as this point seems today, virtually all of the Wright's rivals—including Alexander Graham Bell, Sir Hiram Maxim, John Montgomery, and Albert Santos-Dumont—put their chief efforts into designing wings and/or engines. Most viewed control as a detail rather than as essential for flight.

In 1899 Wilbur built a small kite to test a method of control that he called "wing warping." Modern airplanes still incorporate this breakthrough discovery in the form of ailerons. When the tip of one wing is turned up, the tip of the opposite wing turns down. The resulting change in air pressure over the wing surfaces causes the machine to roll in the opposite direction from the down-turned wingtip.

Wilbur discovered wing warping while fiddling with a bicycle tire innertube box. In a spectacular example of creative visualization, he saw the top and bottom surfaces of the box as the upper and lower wings of a biplane. When twisting the box, the corners flared; one up, one down. This is what birds' wings do in flight. He knew that he had discovered something important.

With his kite tests a success and with encouragement from Chanute, Wilbur was now ready to leave the safety of the bike shop: "If you are looking for perfect safety," he later wrote, "you will do well to sit on a fence and watch the birds; but if you really wish to learn, you must mount a machine and become acquainted with its tricks by actual trial."

Why Kitty Hawk? Chanute told Wilbur that the United States Weather Bureau could provide a list of locations offering strong winds and soft sand upon which to land. As chance would have it, a U.S. Life Saving Station located near the lyrically named village of Kitty Hawk doubled as a weather bureau outpost. Wilbur's letter of inquiry was passed along to Kitty Hawk postmaster Bill Tate, who sent Will a friendly reply. According to Tate, the *only* thing Kitty Hawk had was strong winds and soft sand.

On September 6, 1900 Wilbur left Dayton to make the five-hundred-mile journey to the Outer Banks islands of North Carolina. Orville elected to stay behind and run the bike shop—further evidence that flying machines were still primarily Wilbur's passion.

It took Wilbur six days, traveling by train, horse, boat, and on foot to reach Kitty Hawk. Orville, unable to resist sharing in his brother's adventure, arrived two weeks later. His companionship, mechanical skills, and the supplies he brought with him made Orv more than welcome.

The Wrights' arrival made quite an impression on the villagers. Extremely poor, the local inhabitants eked out a living fishing and farming the poor, sandy soil. The Wrights' modest incomes made them wealthy men amongst the Kitty Hawkers. Their ability to pay cash for fresh eggs disrupted the local barter economy.

Will and Orv were the big attractions in town for reasons other than economics; they were spectacular oddballs! In their bowler hats, jackets and ties, they could be seen running up and down the beach, flying their big glider as a kite. The locals were divided: some were fascinated by the brothers; others were convinced the visitors were dabbling with the Devil. The "Bankers'" mindset is best summed up in a popular expression of the day: "If God had meant for man to fly, he would have given us wings."

Wilbur and Orville's first flying season ran from September 13 through October 23, 1900. It could be more accurately described as a "kiting season," since they attempted only one manned flight.

Wilbur, who had used Lilienthal's tables of air pressure when designing his machine, had expected it to be capable of flights of up to 300 meters. However, the glider generated only about half the projected lift—reducing the earthbound

2. THE EMERGENCE OF MODERN AMERICA

Wrights to flying their glider as a tethered kite, loaded with seventy-five pounds of chain.

In 1901 the Wrights returned to Kitty Hawk, arriving on July 10. They hoped to get in hours of practice, thanks to the additional lift generated by their new and vastly larger machine. The 1901 glider had lifting surfaces totaling 315 square feet—the largest machine anyone had ever attempted to fly. However, it too failed to produce enough lift.

Frustration in the air was only one of the problems the brothers faced that summer. Their tent and shed provided little shelter from the horrendous storms and gale-force winds that rolled in from the ocean. But even the hardships of inclement weather paled alongside the suffering inflicted by swarms of bloodthirsty mosquitoes. Orville, describing their ordeal in a letter to his sister Katharine, complained that "it was the most miserable existence I have ever passed through. The agonies of typhoid fever with its attending starvation are as nothing in comparison.... The sand and grass and trees and hills and everything were crawling with [mosquitoes]. They chewed us clean through our underwear and socks.... Misery! Misery!"

On August 22 the Wrights packed up their equipment and left for home. On the train to Dayton, a disillusioned Wilbur told Orv that "not within a thousand years would man ever fly."

Back in Dayton, the Wrights threw themselves into their neglected bike business, pushing talk of flying machines to the back burner. Then, Wilbur received a timely invitation. Octave Chanute wanted him to speak to the Western Society of Engineers in Chicago. "Nagged" into accepting by Katharine, Will was forced to re-examine the work that he and Orville had done up to that point. While drafting the speech, Will and Orv became convinced that their lift problem was the result of errors in Lilienthal's air pressure tables and not in their construction techniques. They determined to prove Lilienthal wrong, and resolved to never again rely on data they did not develop themselves. This marked a milestone in the brothers' career: no longer simply engineers, they were becoming theoretical scientists.

Orville described the months of November and December 1901 as the happiest of the brothers' lives. "Wilbur and I" he said, "could hardly wait for the morning to come. To get at something that interested us. *That's happiness!*"

In their bicycle-shop-turned-laboratory, the brothers constructed a small wind tunnel powered by the same gas engine that ran the shop's machinery. Inside the tunnel they placed two ingenious devices called "balances"—one to measure lift; the other, drag.

As crude as they appeared, these balances—cobbled by Orville from bicycle spokes and hacksaw blades—were remarkable instruments; exact mechanical analogues to the mathematical formulas for calculating lift and drag. They worked brilliantly, producing new tables of air pressure whose precision has been confirmed by modern computers. The 1902 Wright glider would be the first flying machine based on accurate data and designed by modern scientific methods.

The Wrights' lab work was important in one more significant respect: it marked Wilbur's acceptance of Orville as a full and equal partner. "My machine" no longer appeared in Wilbur's letters. From this point on it would be "our machine."

The third flying season ran from August 28 through October 28, 1902. With the lift problem behind them, both brothers rolled up flight time. Quickly, Wilbur and Orville became the world's most experienced aeronauts. The new machine functioned perfectly—except for one perplexing and potentially fatal flaw. For no apparent reason, the glider would, sporadically, fall from the sky in a "tail spin."

One night Orville drank a pot of coffee and then found himself unable to sleep. As he tossed in his bunk, it struck him that the tailspin problem could be eliminated by making the tail a movable rudder, rather than a fixed surface. This was the final piece of the puzzle. The Wrights now had a glider with a system that effectively controlled all three axes: the elevator for "pitch," wing warping for "roll," and a movable rudder for "yaw." Three-axis control is the key to flight. The discovery of this principle and the development of a system for achieving it are the Wrights' greatest contributions to aircraft technology. Everything that flies, from a hang glider to the Space Shuttle, still incorporates these epoch-making innovations.

Wilbur and Orville now had a practical glider. During the fall of 1902 they made more than seven hundred flights (375 in one week alone), with their longest glide covering 622.5 feet in twenty-six seconds. It was time to add an engine and propellers.

Back in Dayton, Wilbur and Orville soon discovered that obtaining an engine powerful enough to lift their machine, yet light enough to be carried aloft, wasn't going to be easy. Most of the big-name engine makers couldn't produce a motor light enough, and those who could refused to sell one to the Wrights for fear of being associated with flying machines.

With significant help from Charlie Taylor, a Dayton machinist the brothers had hired to run the bike shop in their absence, they built their own lightweight internal combustion engine producing twelve horsepower. The crankshaft was turned by hand on their lathe from a nineteen-pound bar of steel; only the aluminum crankcase was made outside the bike shop, cast by a local foundry from a mold provided by the Wrights.

"After running the engine and propellers a few minutes to get them in working order, I got on the machine at 10:35 for the first trial. . . . On slipping the rope the machine lifted from the track just as it was entering on the fourth rail."

Orville Wright's diary entry for December 17, 1903

Having solved one problem the Wrights now ran into a stone wall—propellers. They had envisioned that this would be the easiest part of their work, anticipating a trip to the library to obtain ship propeller data, and then applying that knowledge to design "airscrews." The brothers were astonished to discover that no such data existed on ship propellers; all had been made on a trial-and-error basis. While it is desirable for a

9. Wings for Man

ship's propeller to be efficient, it is not essential. An airplane, however, will not leave the ground with an inefficient prop.

The "Great Propeller Debate" has passed down into Wright family lore. During an interview, ninety-seven-year-old Ivonette Wright-Miller, Wilbur and Orville's niece (and the last person alive who flew with them as a passenger), recalled that her uncles argued "so long and loud they would end up converted to the other's side, only to have the argument start up again, with each brother arguing the other's original position, 'Tis so! 'Tis not!'"

Orville described the complexity of their dilemma: "With the machine moving forward, the air flying backward, the propellers turning sidewise, and nothing standing still, it seemed impossible to trace the various simultaneous reactions."

The Wrights' solution was brilliant. They made a theoretical assumption: a propeller is merely a wing that rotates. If they could predict a wing's performance in a straight path, why couldn't they predict its performance in a spiral? This assumption revolutionized the concept of aircraft propulsion. Wright propellers generated thrust and lift.

There was no argument over the transmission system. Drawing on their bike-building experience, Wilbur and Orville used chains and sprockets to spin their props. They now had everything they needed. It was time to fly.

The Wrights' fourth and most momentous flying season saw them back at Kitty Hawk from September 25 through December 19, 1903. Plagued by a myriad of mechanical and weather delays, the brothers finally had their first powered airplane ready for takeoff on the morning of December 14.

Wilbur won the coin toss for the first shot at human flight. However, a "pilot error" on his part resulted in a crash seconds after liftoff. Although the plane had left the ground, the brothers considered this a "hop," not a "flight."

It took several days to make repairs. During this delay, the weather turned bitter cold, and winter set in. The Wrights feared that they might not get to fly at all in 1903.

On the morning of December 17, the winds were gusting above thirty miles an hour. Despite the grave risks involved in flying an untested machine in air this turbulent, the brothers, for once in their lives, literally threw caution to the wind.

This time, Orville would go first. His first effort produced a twelve-second flight of approximately 120 feet. This is the historic flight immortalized in Daniel's photograph. Wilbur went next, flying 175 feet. Then Orville made his second attempt, this time reaching the 200-foot mark. The shortness of these flights had nothing to do with machine failure. Wilbur and Orville simply lacked experience controlling the heavy 1903 Flyer. If anything, it responded too well, with the slightest movement of the elevator control causing the machine to dart toward earth.

Wilbur later would write to Chanute, declaring that "those who understand the real significance of the conditions under which we worked will be surprised rather at the length than the shortness of the flights made with an unfamiliar machine after less than one minute's practice."

After their initial flight of December 17, 1903, the Wright brothers found that the newspapers did not believe their story. This turned out to be both good and bad for the brothers: good because it protected their technology while their patents were processed, and bad because it made it hard for the Wrights to market their machine.

Orville added in 1913: "With all the knowledge and skill acquired in thousands of flights in the last ten years, I would hardly think today of making my first flight in a strange machine in a twenty-seven mile wind. . . . I look on with amazement upon our audacity in attempting flights with a new and untried machine under such circumstances."

On the fourth flight of the day, Wilbur flew for fifty-nine seconds, spanning a distance of 852 feet. Elated, the brothers made plans to fly the four miles from their camp at Kill Devil Hills to Kitty Hawk village. In an instant their plans were dashed. A huge gust flipped the machine over and cartwheeled it down the beach. The 1903 Flyer was reduced to a jumble of broken spars and ribs. It never flew again. It didn't have to.

The Wrights' famous flight of December 17, 1903 is usually where history drops their story, but it is actually just the second-act curtain in an exciting three-act drama.

Upon arriving home, the Wrights discovered that the newspapers did not believe their story, or misunderstood what they had accomplished. This consequence proved to be both a blessing and a curse for the brothers. The blessing was that it protected their technology while their patents worked their way through the bureaucracy. The curse was that it made it hard for the Wrights to market the machine and for many years deprived them of the glory that should have been theirs.

In 1904 and 1905 the Wrights flew from a cow pasture eight miles north of Dayton. It was at Huffman Prairie, now part of Wright-Patterson Air Force Base, that the brothers perfected their machine and taught themselves how to fly. The first circles and figure eights made by an airplane were flown above Torrance Huffman's field. Word eventually leaked out of the experiments after the Wrights were seen by passengers on a trolley car. With a record flight of twenty-four miles in thirty-eight minutes under their belts, the Wrights stopped flying for more than two years while they tried to find a buyer for their machine.

The U.S. government had been burned by flying machines in the past (investing $50,000 in Dr. Langley's failure, for example), and the Wrights' offer to provide a practical airplane was rejected out of hand. Insulted by their own country's "snub," Wilbur and Orville then traveled to England, France, and Germany in hopes of making a deal.

Their mission was complicated by unforeseeable obstacles. A sale in France was blocked by a lapse in judgement by their old friend Octave Chanute.

The brothers' relationship with Chanute had soured over time, with Chanute accusing the Wrights of being too secretive. In March 1903, Chanute had traveled to Paris to speak at an Aéro-Club banquet. During his lecture he not only implied that the Wrights were his stu-

2. THE EMERGENCE OF MODERN AMERICA

dents; he also let stand the impression that their work had been financed by him. To make matters worse, he showed slides of the Wrights' gliders and told the French about wing warping. The rebirth of European interest in heavier-than-air flight can be traced directly to Chanute.

Fortunately for Wilbur and Orville, Chanute's understanding of wing warping was limited, so his talk didn't give away the store. However, he created the impression that it was just a matter of time before French aviators would have airplanes of their own, so why should France spend money on an American machine?

The brothers knew that nobody else understood the true nature of the flying problem. Still, by 1906 a few brave souls had coaxed machines into the air. These "flights" prompted the Wrights' rivals, and the press, to dismiss Orv and Will as frauds. One Paris newspaper ran this banner headline over a story on the brothers: "Flyers or Liars?"

Why Wilbur and Orville didn't simply make a demonstration flight has never been easy to explain. They had become paranoid that a rival would see their machine and steal its secrets, making it impossible for them to recoup their investment. (Their patent attorney had preached secrecy.) However, the primary reason may have been emotional. The Wrights simply couldn't let go of their "baby." Bishop Wright publicly boasted that his three youngest children never left the "paternal roof."

Wilbur and Orville appear to have inherited their father's possessiveness.
Finally, in 1908 everything changed. A consortium of French businessmen agreed to purchase a Wright machine. At almost the same time, the U.S. government accepted a new bid from the brothers to supply the Signal Corps with an airplane. After a quick trip to Kitty Hawk to brush up on their rusty flying skills, the brothers split up to meet the deadlines on their contracts.

In France, in Wilbur's words, "princes and millionaires are as thick as thieves." Huge crowds came out to watch him fly. He astonished the Europeans with the grace of his machine and his skill as its pilot, making flights of more than two hours in length. There was no longer any doubt that the Wrights' claim of "first to fly" was true. The same newspapers that had called them "liars" now hailed them as *"Les Premiers Hommes-oiseaux!"*—first among the "bird men!"

Orville went to Fort Myer, Virginia, where he flew before large crowds, including President Taft, senators, and congressmen. It was while he was there that Orville suffered the only serious accident of his career. During a flight with Lieutenant Thomas Selfridge as his passenger, a propeller cracked, cutting a bracing

Unlike many of the inventors of the latter part of the nineteenth century and the first part of the twentieth century, the Wright brothers can claim total credit for their invention; they provided a large paper trail that documents each step of their systematic program of aeronautical research.

wire. The machine crashed, breaking Orv's leg and killing Selfridge. Still, the American public had seen enough to know that the "air age" had arrived.

Back home, the brothers were honored with parades, medals, and trips to the White House. Everywhere they went, huge throngs gathered to see them, speak with them, touch them. Wilbur and Orville were repelled by the hysteria, just as another famous American aviator would be a generation later. The fuss and hoopla was anathema to the pathologically shy Wrights. Orville categorically refused to speak in public, and Wilbur once declined a request for a speech by quipping, "I know of only one bird that talks, the parrot, and they don't fly very high."

Soon after their world triumph, the Wrights found themselves embroiled in messy patent infringement suits—usually initiated by them. The ugliest and most celebrated involved rival aviator Glenn Curtiss. The Wrights won every case but in the process lost the war. To protect their claims of priority in court, the brothers could not make significant changes in their aircraft designs; a big change could be interpreted by the airplane-ignorant courts as an admission by the inventors that their original designs were flawed. So, while they were frozen in 1908 technology, Curtiss and others were free to innovate. Quickly, Wright airplanes became obsolete.

The psychological and physical demands of testifying in court and giving endless depositions destroyed Wilbur's health. In 1912 he contracted typhoid fever, the same illness that Orville had battled in 1896. On May 30, Wilbur died at the family home in Dayton. His premonition of early death had come true. He was only forty-five years old.

When Wilbur died, his place in history was anything but assured. To this day, rumors persist about "flights" made by other aviators prior to December 17, 1903. In Brazil, Santos-Dumont is still hailed as the "father of flight." Books have appeared over the years claiming credit for Connecticut's Gustav Whitehead. Frenchman Gabriel Voisin went to his grave debunking the Wrights. Tourists in California can visit a monument to John Montgomery, a glider pilot of dubious achievement, who died in 1911 in a craft that Wilbur had warned him was a death trap.

Ironically, the greatest threat to the Wrights' place in history turned out to be the Smithsonian Institution. In conjunction with Curtiss, the Smithsonian credited its beloved secretary, the late Dr. Langley, with inventing the airplane.... Correcting this gross distortion became Orville's obsession, and ultimately resulted in his sending the 1903 Flyer into exile in England, where it remained until 1948.

Finally, however, Orville's protracted battle with Curtiss and the Smithsonian culminated in a final triumph: the establishment of the Wrights' priority as conquerors of the sky. Whatever doubts serious scholars may have harbored were finally put to rest with publication of *The Papers of Wilbur and Orville Wright* in 1953.

Orv spent the years after Wilbur's death in a laboratory originally intended for both brothers. He tinkered with whatever caught his fancy (spending months on an automatic record changer, for example). He produced no major inventions of his own.

Until his death of a heart attack in 1948, Orville was, literally, a living legend. So quietly had he lived that when his obituary appeared in newspapers most people outside of Dayton were sur-

9. Wings for Man

prised to learn that he had still been alive.

What the Wrights might have accomplished had Wilbur not died so young is one of the great "what ifs?" Wilbur himself shed some light on the vicissitudes of invention in a 1906 letter to Chanute: "If the wheels of time could be turned back . . . it is not at all probable that we would do again what we have done. . . . It was due to a peculiar combination of circumstances which might never occur again."

More so than Thomas Edison, Robert Fulton, or Samuel Morse, the Wrights can claim total credit for the invention that brought them lasting fame. Lifelong diarists, prolific letter writers, and amateur photographers of considerable skill, Wilbur and Orville left a paper trail that documents each step in their systematic program of aeronautical research. They invented more than wings of strength, a lightweight engine, and efficient propellers. They also perfected three-axis control-pitch, yaw, and roll, the three dimensions of flight. They tested their theories in the air, teaching not only themselves how to fly, but the rest of us as well. From humble beginnings, these two bachelor bicycle makers built everything themselves. They paid for their work from their own earnings, risked their lives repeatedly on imperfect gliders, and triumphed with no desire for glory, only a just demand for what was rightfully theirs. It is as much the quality of their character as the brilliance of their work that earns Wilbur and Orville Wright lasting fame in the pantheon of American heroes.

Perhaps the most eloquent testament to their achievement is one simple line from Orville's diary, dated June 7, 1903: "Isn't it astonishing that all these secrets have been preserved for so many years just so that we could discover them!"

Suggested additional reading: The authoritative biography of the Wright brothers is *The Bishop's Boys* by Tom Crouch (W. W. Norton, 1989). An illustrated work fascinating to both young people and adults is *The Wright Brothers: How They Invented the Airplane* by Russell Freedman (Holiday House, 1991). Other pictorial volumes of interest include *Kitty Hawk and Beyond* by Ronald R. Geibert and Patrick B. Nolan (Wright State University Press, 1990), and *How We Invented the Airplane* by Orville Wright (Dover, 1988).

Learning to Go to the Movies

The great democratic art form got off to a very rocky start. People simply didn't want to crowd into a dark room to look at a flickering light, and it took nearly twenty years for Americans and motion pictures to embrace each other.

David Nasaw

On July 5, 1896, the Los Angeles *Times* greeted the imminent arrival of Thomas Alva Edison's moving-picture projector with enormous enthusiasm: "The vitascope is coming to town. It is safe to predict that when it is set up at the Orpheum and set a-going, it will cause a sensation as the city has not known for many a long day."

Thousands of city residents had already viewed moving pictures by peering into the eyeholes of peep-show machines on display in saloons, railroad terminals, and amusement parlors, but these images were no bigger than a postcard. Never before had anyone seen moving pictures projected big as life on a screen.

The commercial possibilities of such an exhibition seemed boundless, and inventors, electricians, and showmen on two continents had been hard at work on a "screen machine" for several years. That the one about to make its debut at the Orpheum vaudeville theater had not actually been invented by Edison was kept secret by its promoters. The Edison name was much too valuable to compromise by suggesting that there might be others who were the Wizard's equal in imagination and technical skill.

The projector that bore Edison's name had, in fact, been invented by Thomas Armat, a Washington, D.C., bookkeeper, and his partner, C. Francis Jenkins, a government stenographer. After months of tinkering, separately and together, the two men had in the summer of 1895 put together a workable projector, named it the Phantoscope, and arranged to exhibit it at the Cotton States and International Exposition in Atlanta, Georgia, in September of the same year.

John Ripley Collection, Kansas State Historical Society, Topeka

The partners borrowed money from relatives to erect an outdoor tent theater on the fairgrounds, arranged for a series of newspaper articles on their wondrous invention, and printed complimentary tickets. When the expected crowds failed to materialize, in

---

Tally's back room with its three chairs and seven peepholes was arguably the nation's first motion-picture theater.

---

large part because fairgoers were not willing to pay a quarter for an amusement they knew nothing about, Armat and Jenkins hired a barker who invited visitors to enter free and pay at the exit only if they were satisfied. The offer worked, but the customers it attracted entered the theater with only the vaguest idea of what they were going to see. Never having viewed projected moving pictures before, they did not know that the theater had to be darkened. "The moment the lights turned off for the beginning of the show a panic ensued," wrote the film historian Terry Ramsaye some thirty years later. "The visitors had a notion that expositions were dangerous places where pickpockets might be expected on every side. This was, the movie audience thought, just a new dodge for trapping the unwary in the dark."

Jenkins and Armat never did figure out how to introduce their moving pictures to prospective audiences. They ended up losing the fifteen hundred dollars they had borrowed, and the rights to their projector were eventually sold to the company that licensed and distributed Edison's peep-show machines.

The Los Angeles debut of the Phantoscope, renamed Edison's Vitascope, went off without a hitch. The Orpheum Theater was filled with vaudeville patrons who, though not accustomed to sitting in the dark, had no reason to fear that they would be assaulted by those seated next to them. The Los Angeles *Times* carried a complete description of the exhibition for those who had been unfortunate or unadventurous enough not to buy tickets in advance or to secure standing room at the last minute:

"The theatre was darkened until it was as black as midnight. Suddenly a strange whirling sound was heard. Upon a huge white sheet flashed forth the figure of Anna Belle Sun, [a dancer whose real name was Annabelle Whitford] whirling

---

From *American Heritage*, November 1993, pp. 78-80, 82, 84-88, 90, 92. Adapted from *Going Out: The Rise and Fall of Public Amusements* by David Nasaw. © 1993 by David Nasaw. Reprinted by permission of BasicBooks, a division of HarperCollins Publishers, Inc.

through the mazes of the serpentine dance. She swayed and nodded and tripped it lightly, the filmy draperies rising and falling and floating this way and that, all reproduced with startling reality, and the whole without a break except that now and then one could see swift electric sparks. . . . Then, without warning, darkness and the roar of applause that shook the theater; and knew no pause till the next picture was flashed on the screen. This was long, lanky Uncle Sam who was defending Venezuela from fat little John Bull, and forcing the bully to his knees. Next came a representation of Herald Square in New York with streetcars and vans moving up and down, then Cissy Fitzgerald's dance and last of all a representation of the way May Irwin and John C. Rice kiss. [*The May Irwin Kiss,* perhaps the most popular of the early films, was a fifteen-second close-up of the embrace in the closing scene of the musical comedy *The Widow Jones.*] Their smiles and glances and expressive gestures and the final joyous, overpowering, luscious osculation was repeated again and again, while the audience fairly shrieked and howled approval. The vitascope is a wonder, a marvel, an outstanding example of human ingenuity and it had an instantaneous success on this, its first exhibition in Los Angeles."

It was through lengthy newspaper descriptions like this one that prospective customers first learned about the magic of moving pictures. Note how the article begins with mention of the darkened theater and refers to the darkness again in mid-paragraph. Note too the reference to "swift electric sparks." Neither audiences nor critics understood how the projectors worked, nor were they convinced that the electricity used to project the pictures was harmless.

After two weeks of sold-out performances, the projector and its operators left the Orpheum for a tour of nearby vaudeville houses. But it turned out that theaters outside Los Angeles could not provide the electrical power needed to run the projector, so the machine was hauled back to Los Angeles and installed in the back of Thomas Tally's amusement parlor.

In the front of his store, Tally had set up automatic phonograph and peep-show machines that provided customers, for a nickel a play, with a few minutes of scratchy recorded sound or a few seconds of flickering moving images. Tally now partitioned off the back of his parlor for a "vitascope" room. To acquaint the public with what he billed as the "Wizard's latest wonder," he took out ads in the Los Angeles newspapers: "Tonight at Tally's Phonograph Parlor, 311 South Spring St, for the first time in Los Angeles, the great Corbett and Courtney prize fight will be reproduced upon a great screen through the medium of this great and marvelous invention. The men will be seen on the stage, life size, and every movement made by them in this great fight will be reproduced as seen in actual life."

Tally's back room was arguably the nation's first moving-picture theater. But although the technology for projecting moving images was in place, people turned out to be reluctant to enter a dark room to see pictures projected on a sheet. Unable to lure customers into his "theater," Tally did the next best thing. He punched holes in the partition separating the larger storefront from the vitascope room and, according to Terry Ramsaye, invited customers to "peer in at the screen while standing in the comfortable security of the well lighted phonograph parlor. . . . Three peep holes were at chair level for seated spectators, and four somewhat higher for standees—standing room only after three admissions, total capacity seven. The price per peep hole was fifteen cents."

As Tally and other storefront proprietors quickly discovered, it was not going to be easy to assemble an audience for moving pictures. Projectors were difficult to run and impossible to repair; the electrical current or batteries they ran on seldom worked properly; and the films were expensive, of poor quality, and few.

Harry Davis, a Pittsburgh showman, attached the tony Greek word for theater to the lowly five-cent coin.

But most important, customers balked at entering darkened rooms to see a few minutes of moving pictures. In April 1902 Tally tried again to open an "Electric Theater" but was forced to convert it to vaudeville after six months.

It was the same story everywhere. As a disgusted Oswego, New York, operator reported, at first the vitascope drew

Library of Congress

2. THE EMERGENCE OF MODERN AMERICA

"crowded houses on account of its novelty. Now everybody has seen it, and, to use the vernacular of the 'foyer,' it does not 'draw flies.'"

Although projected films failed to attract customers to storefront theaters during their first decade of life, they were nonetheless being introduced to millions of vaudeville fans. "Dumb" acts—animals, puppets, pantomimists, magic-lantern slides, and *tableaux vivants*—had traditionally opened and closed the show because, being silent, they would not be disturbed by late arrivals or early departures. The movies were, the managers now discovered, the perfect dumb acts: they were popular, cheaper than most live performers, didn't talk back or complain about the accommodations, and could be replaced weekly.

Most of the early projectors held only fifty feet, or sixteen seconds, of film, which if looped and repeated five or six times could be stretched out to almost two minutes. Seven or eight films, displayed one after another in this fashion, lasted fifteen to twenty minutes, the perfect length for a vaudeville "turn."

The first moving pictures, shot in Edison's Black Maria studio in New Jersey, had been of vaudeville, musical theater, and circus acts. But audiences turned out to prefer pictures that moved across the frame: waves crashing onto a beach, trains barreling down their tracks, soldiers parading, horses racing. At the vitascope's debut performance at Koster & Bial's vaudeville theater in New York City, the crowd cheered loudest on seeing *Rough Sea at Dover,* the one picture shot outside the studio. Still, in the vaudeville halls the "living pictures" constituted one act among many.

Only in the middle of the first decade of the 1900s, after enormous improvements in the quality of the projectors and the production and distribution of films, was a new generation in show business ready to try again to lure customers into a moving-picture theater. What made the moment right was the fact that after 1903 the manufacturers—as the film producers referred to themselves—grew concerned that their customers were weary of the same old "actualities" and began to make pictures that told stories.

Although it was not possible to tell much of a story in a few silent minutes, audiences were captivated by the new films. As demand increased, the manufacturers developed assembly-line production methods, distributors streamlined the process of getting the films to exhibitors, and businessmen opened storefront theaters to exhibit the increasingly sophisticated product.

The first freestanding moving-picture theater was probably the work of Harry Davis, Pittsburgh's most prosperous showman. In April of 1904 Davis opened an amusement arcade near his Grand Opera House. When a fire burned it down, he rented a larger storefront, but instead of outfitting it as an arcade he filled the room with chairs, gaily decorated the exterior, and, attaching the high-toned Greek word for theater to the lowly five-cent coin, advertised the opening of a "nickelodeon." It was an instant success.

Although Davis was certainly the first exhibitor to use the name *nickelodeon,* similar experiments were taking place in other parts of the country. Marcus Loew on a visit to his Cincinnati arcade in 1905 learned from his manager that a rival across the river in Covington, Kentucky, had come up with a marvelous new "idea in entertainment. . . . I went over with my general manager—it was on Sunday . . . and I never got such a thrill in my life. The show was given in an old-fashioned brownstone house, and the proprietor had the hallways partitioned off with dry goods cases. He used to go to the window and sell the tickets to the children, then he went to the door and took the tickets, and after he did that he locked the door and went up and operated the machine. . . . I said to my companion, 'This is the most remarkable thing I have ever seen.' The place was packed to suffocation." Loew returned

---

Nickelodeon owners realized they had to meld the openness of the saloon with the selectivity of the hotel.

---

to Cincinnati and opened his own screen show the following Sunday. "The first day we played I believe there were seven or eight people short of five thousand and we did not advertise at all. The people simply poured into the arcade. That showed me the great possibilities of this new form of entertainment." Back in New York City, Loew rented space for similar picture-show theaters alongside each of his arcades.

Across the country arcade owners shut off the backs of their storefronts or rented additional space for picture shows, while vaudeville managers, traveling exhibitors, and show businessmen left their jobs to set up their own nickel picture shows.

There was a great deal of money to be made in the fledgling business, but nickelodeon owners had to work hard to introduce their product. They could not afford to advertise heavily in the papers, but they could and did design their storefront facades to call attention to their shows—with oversized entrances, attraction boards, posters, and as many light bulbs as they had room for. To draw the attention of passersby, they set up phonographs on the street outside and hired live barkers: "It is only five cents! See the moving-picture show, see the wonders of Port Said tonight, and a shrieking comedy from real life, all for five cents. Step in this way and learn to laugh!"

The din became such that local shopkeepers complained it was interfering with business. In Paterson, New Jersey, the Board of Aldermen outlawed "phonographic barkers" after complaints from storekeepers, among them M. L. Rogowski, who claimed that the "rasping music, ground out for hours at a time, annoyed his milliners until they became nervous."

With the aural accompaniment of the barkers the visual displays of glittering light bulbs, and word of mouth, city residents began to throng the new theaters. Contemporary commentators used terms like *madness, frenzy, fever,* and *craze* to describe the rapidity with which nickel theaters went up after about 1905. By November of 1907, a little more than two years after the opening of the first one, there were already, according to Joseph Medill Patterson of *The Saturday Evening Post,* "between four and five thousand [nickel shows] running and solvent, and the number is still increasing rapidly. This is the boom time in the moving-picture business. Everybody is making money . . . as one press-agent said enthusiastically, 'this line is a Klondike.'"

10. Learning to Go to the Movies

It is, from our vantage point in the 1990s—suffused as we are by television, radio, CD players, and VCRs—difficult to recapture the excitement caused by the appearance of these first nickel theaters. For the bulk of the city's population, until now shut out of its theaters and commercial amusements, the sudden emergence of not one but five or ten nickel shows within walking distance must have been nothing short of extraordinary.

Imagine for a moment what it must have meant to be able to attend a show for a nickel in your neighborhood. City folk who had never been to the theater or, indeed, to any commercial amusement (even the upper balcony at a vaudeville hall cost a quarter) could now, on their way home from work or shopping or on a Saturday evening or Sunday afternoon, enter the darkened auditorium, take a seat, and witness the latest technological wonders, all for five cents.

One understands the passion of the early commentators as they described in the purplest of prose what the moving-picture theater meant to the city's working people. Mary Heaton Vorse concluded a 1911 article in *The Outlook* by referring to the picture-show audiences she had observed on Bleecker Street and the Bowery in New York City, "You see what it means to them; it means Opportunity—a chance to glimpse the beautiful and strange things in the world that you haven't in your life; the gratification of the higher side of your nature; opportunity which, except for the big moving picture book, would be forever closed to you."

The nickelodeon's unprecedented expansion did not go unnoticed by the critics of commercialized popular culture who had for a century complained about and organized against the evils of saloons, bawdy houses, honky-tonks, prizefights, and variety theaters. For the anti-vice crusaders and child savers, the nickel shows presented an unparalleled threat to civic morality, precisely because they were so popular with the city's young and poor.

Although they grossly exaggerated the "immorality" of the pictures and the danger to those who saw them, the anti-vice crusaders and reformers were correct in claiming that never before had so many women, men, and children, most of them strangers to one another, been brought together to sit in the closest physical proximity in the dark for twenty to thirty minutes. The Vice Commission of Chicago believed that "many liberties are taken with young girls within the theater during the performance when the place is in total or semi-darkness. Boys and men slyly embrace the girls near them and offer certain indignities." The New York Society for the Prevention of Cruelty to Children presented case after case of such depravities. "This new form of entertainment," it claimed in its 1909 annual report, "has gone far to blast maidenhood. . . . Depraved adults with candies and pennies beguile children with the inevitable result. The Society has prosecuted many for leading girls astray through these picture shows, but GOD alone knows how many are leading dissolute lives begun at the 'moving pictures.'"

John Ripley Collection, Kansas State Historical Society, Topeka

While the anti-vice crusaders complained about the moral dangers, other reformers and a number of industry spokesmen worried about the physical conditions inside the "nickel dumps." Not only were the storefront theaters dark, dirty, and congested, but the stench inside was often overpowering. Investigators hired by the Cleveland commission investigating local movie theaters claimed that the "foul air" in the theaters was so bad that even a short stay was bound to result in "sneezing, coughing and the contraction of serious colds."

The Independent reported in early 1910 that the city's "moving picture places" had "become foci for the dissemination of tubercle bacilli," and *Moving Picture World* warned exhibitors to clean up their theaters before it was too late. "Should a malignant epidemic strike New York City, and these conditions prevail, the result might be a wholesale closing down of these germ factories."

Tuberculosis and head colds were not the only, or even the most serious, threats to the safety of movie patrons. In the early years of the storefront theaters, the danger of fire breaking out in the projection booth and sweeping through houses that lacked adequate exits was ever-present, especially since the film stock was highly flammable. There were close to one thousand theater fires in 1907 alone.

While nickelodeon owners and operators were reaping a bonanza, it had become apparent to manufacturers, distributors, and trade-journal editors that the industry had to do something about conditions inside the theaters to forestall government action and broaden the audience base. Homer W. Sibley of *Moving Picture World* warned his colleagues in August of 1911, "the 'dump' is doomed, and the sooner the cheap, ill-smelling, poorly ventilated, badly managed rendezvous for the masher and tough makes way for the better class of popular family theater the better it will be for the business and all concerned."

The enormous success of the nickelodeon was, paradoxically, blocking future growth of the moving-picture business. Potential customers who preferred not to mingle with the lower orders stayed away. In the vaudeville theaters the "refined" could, if they chose, sit safe from the rabble in the more expensive box and orchestra seats. There were no such sanctuaries in the nickel and dime theaters, where customers could sit wherever they pleased.

Nickelodeon owners began to realize that to attract an audience large enough to fill and refill their theaters twenty to thirty times a day, they would have to meld into one institutional space the openness of the saloon and the selectivity of the hotel. They had to welcome all who sought entrance to their amusements, while simultaneously "appearing" to screen their customers and admit only those who were, as Henry James had described the clientele of the American hotel, "presumably 'respectable,' . . . that is, not discoverably anything else."

The trick of remaining open to the street and its passersby while keeping out the riffraff was accomplished by designing an imposing exterior and entrance. The penny arcades had opened their fronts to encourage passersby to "drop in." The nickel theaters re-enclosed them, pulling back their doors about six feet from the sidewalk, in effect extending the distance between the theater and

2. THE EMERGENCE OF MODERN AMERICA

the street. This recessed, sheltered entrance functioned as a buffer or filter between the inside of the theater and the tumult outside. Framing this recessed entrance, massive arches or oversized columns jutted out onto the sidewalk. Thus the nickelodeon owners colonized the sidewalks in front of their establishments, shortening—while emphasizing—the distance between the amusements within and the workaday world outside.

Theater owners did all they could to convince customers that they would be

By the mid-1910s a huge, heterogeneous urban public had been taught to feel comfortable in movie houses.

safe inside, no matter whom they sat next to in the dark. To guarantee their customers' good behavior, the exhibitors began to hire and parade uniformed ushers through the largest theaters and flashed signs on the screen warning patrons that those who misbehaved would quickly be banished from the house and prosecuted by the law.

The industry also accepted new fire-safety legislation, but perhaps the most important step the exhibitors took to allay the public's anxieties about health hazards was to install new and expensive ventilation systems that, they claimed, removed not only bad odors but germs as well. A. L. Shakman, owner of a Broadway theater, proudly proclaimed that there were "no clothing or body odors noticeable even during the capacity hours of the 81st Street Theater, for the simple reason that the air is changed by dome ventilators every twenty minutes. The air is just as sweet and pure in the balcony as it is downstairs." The Butterfly Theater in Milwaukee advertised that its 'Perfect Ventilation" system provided customers with a "Complete Change of Air Every Three Minutes."

To convince the city's respectable folk that the movie theaters, though cheap, were safe and comfortable, the exhibitors assiduously courted the local gentry, businessmen, and politicians and invited them to their

John Ripley Collection, Kansas State Historical Society, Topeka

opening celebrations. The Saxe brothers of Milwaukee launched their Princess Theatre in 1909 with a gala invitation-only theater party, organized, as the owners told the Milwaukee *Sentinel*, "in the effort to secure the patronage of a better class of people." Mayor David S. Rose not only attended but gave the dedicatory address.

Gala openings like this had become routine occurrences by the late 1910s. Just as Barnum propelled Tom Thumb into the rank of first-class attractions by arranging and publicizing the midget's audience with the Queen of England, so did the exhibitors signify that their theaters were first-class entertainment sites by celebrating the patronage of the crowned heads of their communities.

Even though the moving pictures would not reach the pinnacle of their respectability until the early twenties, with the building of the movie palaces, the industry had by the middle 1910s educated a huge and heterogeneous urban public that they could visit movie theaters without danger to their pocketbooks, their reputations, or their health.

When the social researcher George Bevans was writing *How Workingmen Spend Their Spare Time* in late 1912 and early 1913, he discovered that no matter what the men's particular jobs, how many hours a week they worked, whether they were single or married, native-born or immigrant, earned less than ten dollars or more than thirty-five, they unfailingly spent more of their spare time at the picture show than anywhere else. William Fox claimed that the saloons in the vicinity of his theaters "found the business so unprofitable that they closed their doors. . . . If we had never had prohibition," he later told Upton Sinclair, "the

motion pictures would have wiped out the saloon."

More and more what drew these audiences was the emergence of the movie star from the ranks of the wholly anonymous players of a decade earlier. Actors in the early story films had borrowed their gestures, poses, grins, and grimaces from melodrama and pantomime. Villains all dressed, acted, and moved the same way, as did the other stock characters: the heroes, heroines, and aged mothers. Any child in the audience could tell who the villain was (the man in the long black coat), why he acted as he did (he was evil), and what he was going to do next. By 1909 or so critics and audiences alike appeared to be growing weary of these histrionics, and players adopted instead a "more natural" or "slower" acting style. As cameras moved in closer to capture increasingly subtle and personalized expressions, audiences began to distinguish the players from one another. Since the manufacturers never divulged their actors' given names, the fans had to refer to them by their brand names—the Vitagraph Girl, or the Biograph Girl.

It didn't take long for manufacturers to recognize the benefits of exploiting their audience's curiosity. Kalem was the first to identify its actors and actresses by name, in a group photograph published as an advertisement in the January 15, 1910, *Moving Picture World* and made available to exhibitors for posting in their lobbies. In that same year, Carl Laemmle, a distributor who was preparing to manufacture his own films, hired Florence Lawrence to star in them for the then exorbitant salary of fifteen thousand

*The reception accorded **The Birth of a Nation** marked the distance movies had traveled since their disastrous debut.*

dollars a year. To make sure the public knew that the Biograph Girl would now be appearing exclusively in IMP pictures, Laemmle engineered the first publicity coup. In March of 1910 he leaked the rumor that Miss Lawrence had been killed in a St. Louis streetcar accident and then took out a huge ad in *Moving*

10. Learning to Go to the Movies

Picture World to announce that the story of her demise was the "blackest and at the same time the silliest lie yet circulated by enemies of the 'Imp.'"

It took only a few years for the picture players to ascend from anonymity to omnipresence. The best evidence we have of the stars' newfound importance is the salaries the producers were willing to pay them. On Broadway Mary Pickford had earned $25 a week. In 1910 Carl Laemmle lured her away from Biograph, her first movie home, with an offer of $175 a week. Her starting salary with Adolph Zukor at Famous Players in 1914 was $20,000 a year, soon raised to $1,000 a week and then, in January of 1915, to $2,000 a week and half the profits from her pictures. In June of 1916 another contract raised her compensation to 50 percent of the profits of her films against a guaranteed minimum of $1,040,000 a year, including at least $10,000 every week, a bonus of $300,000 for signing the contract, and an additional $40,000 for the time she had spent reading scripts during contract negotiations. And this was only the beginning.

The stars were worth the money because their appearance in films not only boosted receipts but added a degree of predictability to the business, a predictability that was welcomed by the banks and financiers that in the 1920s would assume a larger role in the picture business. The most reliable, perhaps the only, predictor of success for any given film was the presence of an established star.

The stars were not only bringing new customers into the theaters but incorporating a movie audience scattered over thousands of different sites into a vast unified public. "Stars" were by definition actors or actresses whose appeal transcended every social category, with the possible exception of gender. As the theater and now film critic Walter Prichard Eaton explained in 1915, "The smallest town . . . sees the same motion-picture players as the largest. . . . John Bunny and Mary Pickford 'star' in a hundred towns at once."

John Ripley Collection, Kansas State Historical Society, Topeka

The reception accorded *The Birth of a Nation* that same year marked the distance the movies had traveled since their disastrous debut in Armat and Jenkins's tent just twenty years earlier. While African-Americans and their supporters strenuously protested the film's appalling portrayal of blacks and succeeded in forcing state and municipal censors to cut many scenes, white Americans of every age group, economic status, neighborhood, and ethnicity lined up at the box offices to see D. W. Griffith's Civil War epic.

The Birth of a Nation would eventually make more money than any film of its time and be seen by an audience that extended from prosperous theatergoers who paid two dollars in the first-class legitimate theaters to the women, children, and men who viewed it at regular prices in their neighborhood moving-picture houses. Even the President of the United States, as the promotions for the film asserted, had seen *The Birth of a Nation* and was now a moving-picture fan.

The ultimate confirmation of a picture show's respectability came only a few years later, during World War I, when the federal government, concerned that its propaganda messages might not reach the largest possible audience through the available print media, decided to send its "Four-Minute Men" into the nation's movie theaters. (The speakers were so named to reassure audiences and theater owners that their talks would be brisk.)

As President Wilson proclaimed in an open letter to the nation's moviegoers in April 1918, the picture house had become a "great democratic meeting place of the people, where within twenty-four hours it is possible to reach eight million citizens of all classes." There was nothing wrong with going to the movies while a war was being fought across the Atlantic, the President declared in his letter: "The Government recognizes that a reasonable amount of amusement, *especially* in war time, is not a luxury but a necessity."

61

From Progressivism to the 1920s

Most reform movements in our history have developed during periods of economic distress. Progressivism arose during a period of relative prosperity. Its leadership consisted largely of middle- and upper-middle-class white men and women. They were well educated and were drawn from both political parties. The movement developed at all levels: local, state, and federal. Progressives stood for clean government, regulation of the large economic interests and, above all, greater democratic participation in the political process through reforms such as referenda and the use of long ballots. To charges that they were radicals, Progressives replied that they merely

UNIT 3

wanted to use the power of government to create a more equitable society.

One reform that drew a popular response was the campaign against impure and falsely labeled foods, medicines, and drugs. The publication in 1906 of Upton Sinclair's novel, *The Jungle,* helped ensure success of the Pure Food and Drug Act that year. Sinclair's popular book described in detail the foul and unsanitary conditions found in the meatpacking industry. Bernard Weisberger, in "Doctor Wiley and His Poison Squad," tells how one zealous bureaucrat helped get legislation on federal food and drug regulation through Congress and his attempts to see that it was strictly enforced.

Woodrow Wilson is remembered primarily as the president who failed to get the United States into the League of Nations because of his unwillingness to compromise with his political enemies. He was elected president in 1912 on a wave of progressive sentiment, not because he was supposed to be an expert on foreign policy. During his first term in office he was able to get through Congress an impressive number of reform bills. The essay "Woodrow Wilson, Politician" assesses his performance and concludes that his administration constituted one of the three most notable periods of reform in this century. America's entry into World War I, for all practical purposes, ended the Progressive era.

The 1920s witnessed a curious blend of political conformity and social and intellectual ferment. Neither Warren Harding nor Calvin Coolidge were activist presidents, and it is doubtful that they could have accomplished much even if they had been, given the tenor of the times. There was a flourishing in all the arts, however, and many intellectuals began challenging conventional wisdom on all levels. It was also the age of the "flapper," the hip flask, and the Stutz Bearcat automobile. The "Roaring Twenties" had its downside as well: organized crime flourished and there was increased repression of racial and ethnic groups.

In "Alcohol in American History," David Musto traces the course of temperance and prohibition movements through our past, culminating in the "Great Experiment" of the 1920s. Although Prohibition did achieve some success against alcohol-related illnesses such as cirrhosis, it failed miserably to convince the majority of Americans to forgo the consumption of beer, wine, and liquor. It also contributed directly to the growth of organized crime as bootlegging became a most rewarding enterprise. This essay compares earlier movements with more recent campaigns against alcohol abuse.

Two articles in this unit address women's issues. In "Madam C. J. Walker," the remarkable story of a black woman born to former slaves and who became a millionaire through merchandising beauty products is presented by her great-great-granddaughter, A'Lelia Bundles. But wealth was not enough for Walker. She used her money and her influence to fight for the rights of women and blacks. Then, Elisabeth Perry, in "Why Suffrage for American Women Was Not Enough," argues that despite having won the right to vote, women continued to accept the notion that they should not compete with men in the political arena. Perry traces the careers of four energetic suffragists.

By 1925 Henry Ford's motor company was turning out a Model T every 10 seconds. How this erratic genius revolutionized the automobile industry is described by David Halberstam in "Citizen Ford." As time wore on, however, his unwillingness to adapt to new ideas caused his company to lose its competitive edge. By the 1930s, a business magazine referred to him as "the World's Worst Salesman."

The 1920s were characterized by a great deal of ethnic and racial discrimination. The first Ku Klux Klan had been organized during the Reconstruction period to cow freedpeople and their allies into submission. The second Klan emerged during the 1920s, and it came to wield enormous power in several sections of the country. In "When White Hoods Were in Flower," Bernard Weisberger describes how this group targeted Jews, Catholics, and foreigners, as well as blacks.

Looking Ahead: Challenge Questions

Describe the political and economic goals most Progressives sought. What did the legislation passed during Woodrow Wilson's first administration accomplish?

What social conditions and attitudes lead to the formation of hate groups such as the Ku Klux Klan? How do you think people justify belonging to such groups?

After reading the article "Why Suffrage for American Women Was Not Enough," discuss why you believe that while women attained the right to vote, they still believed it to be unseemly to compete with men in politics.

Doctor Wiley and His Poison Squad

The father of the Pure Food and Drug Act was as hard on his allies as he was on his foes

Bernard A. Weisberger

As Congress reassembled last autumn, the press reported an upsurge in campaign contributions by tobacco companies to fight new efforts to combat smoking—especially by declaring nicotine an addictive substance that can be regulated by the U.S. Food and Drug Administration. The industry regards the FDA as fondly as a whale would look on Captain Ahab. So, it seems, do a number of food-processing and pharmaceutical companies. Conservative complaints about the "regulatory burden" supposedly handcuffing American manufacturers often target the FDA for being too slow or too persnickety in deciding what products are allowable on the market without undue risk. But the agency catches it from both sides; consumer organizations occasionally worry that it's too complaisant in bending the rules when Congress leans on it to spare corporations fiscal pain. A federal regulator's lot is not an 'appy one.

Well, it never was. And the FDA's specific history has been stormy from the opening paragraph. For those who think that regulation is a net dropped on the American economy by left-wing plotters during the New Deal, it may be enlightening to learn that while the Food, Drug, and Cosmetic Act currently in force does indeed date from 1938, the antecedent of the present-day FDA was set up in 1927 under Calvin Coolidge. What is more, the original Pure Food and Drug Act, the primal fount of consumer protection by Washington, dates from 1906. It placed enforcement powers in the Bureau of Chemistry of the Department of Agriculture, to the vast satisfaction of that bureau's chief, who had waged a long, passionate campaign against what he saw as the outrageous and sometimes lethal frauds of the meatpacking, canning, and other food-processing corporations of the day as well as their partners in crime who peddled patent medicines.

The crusader's name was Harvey Wiley. Like many members of the Progressive flock, he came from a Midwestern evangelical background, and he translated the quest for salvation into worldly battles against political and economic unrighteousness. Born in Indiana in 1844 to a farmer who was also a Campbellite preacher, the young Wiley as a freshman at Hanover College in Indiana found the "consolations of religion sweeter than all." But when his studies led him to graduate work in chemistry at Harvard and Berlin, he put science at least on a par with faith as a great avenue to moral and spiritual improvement, and he forsook sectarianism. All religions could join "to lead forward the human race into the freer light of truth and the fresher air of brotherly love." Brotherly love was slightly compromised in his case by a feeling enunciated later in life that "I had the good fortune to be ranged on the side of right in every important contest I can remember."

He got a professorship of chemistry at Purdue, and while there he helped write a report for the Indiana State Board of Health condemning adulterated food as an underrated danger. Those who thought of him as something of a crank were not entirely wrong; he was obsessed with nutrition and framed its problems in moral rather than medical terms. At his life's end he insisted "that it is *sin to be sick*."

In 1883, after a quarrel with Purdue's president, Wiley moved to Washington to become chief chemist for the Department of Agriculture and to follow his cause with the total dedication of a bachelor who believed that only by "an intensively active life can I find relief from . . . awful ennui of Soul." A period of cutbacks during the second Cleveland administration (1893–97) sharpened his bureaucratic turf-defense skills and confirmed his boyhood Republicanism. So he was a seasoned advocate and adversary by the time he took the fight for federal food and drug regulation to Congress. Unresting and uncompromising—but with considerable wit and charm—he published articles, gave speeches, and testified before committees considering legislation on the subject.

It was needed. Adulteration of food—sanded sugar, watered milk, sawdust-enhanced flour—was a scam of biblical antiquity, and states already had laws against it. But the growth of a nationwide food industry put most products into interstate commerce and therefore beyond the reach of state regulation. In addition, late-nineteenth-century technology produced additives—coloring agents and preservatives (like benzoate of soda and copper sulfate and various bleaches for flour)—that were potentially dangerous to the unwarned. Wiley and other reformers cried out for honest labeling and for legal and enforceable standards of what was and was not "adulterated," which would be set by the department's experts, administered nonpolitically, and enforced in the courts.

From *American Heritage*, February/March 1996, pp. 14, 16. © 1996 by Forbes, Inc. Reprinted by permission of *American Heritage* magazine, a division of Forbes, Inc.

11. Doctor Wiley and His Poison Squad

Bills to that effect were introduced as early as 1897 but failed in several successive Congresses. Experienced reformers expected as much and continued their efforts. So did Wiley. He ran an experiment within the department on the dangers of preservatives, enlisting a "Poison Squad" of a dozen heroic young male employees who submitted to rigidly controlled diets, frequent examinations, and the collection of their urine and feces for analysis. He worked the banquet circuit, producing charming little poems to woo listeners, like one whose title was "I Wonder What's in It?"

The pepper perhaps contains co-
  coanut shells
And the mustard is cottonseed meal;
The coffee, in sooth, of baked chicory
  smells
And the terrapin tastes like roast
  veal.

Patent medicines—especially so-called proprietary over-the-counter remedies, whose ingredients were a trade secret—were of less interest to Wiley, but the war on them brought valuable allies and publicity to the pure-food cause. *The Ladies' Home Journal* ran editorials denouncing many popular nostrums like Peruna, Hostetter's Stomach Bitters, and Lydia Pinkham's Vegetable Compound as fakes, often full of alcohol and narcotics, brazenly claiming to cure everything from asthma to ulcers.

A major breakthrough came in 1906 with the publication of Upton Sinclair's novel of conditions in the packinghouses of Chicago, *The Jungle.* When Sinclair's book, based on his own researches, showed that filth, floor sweepings, rats, and parts of an occasional unlucky workman sometimes went into the grinders and pickling vats to emerge as canned meat, the public was disgusted. Theodore Roosevelt seated himself more firmly on the pure-food bandwagon. "Mr. Dooley" summed up his reaction: "Tiddy was toying with a light breakfast an' idly turnin' over th' pages iv th' new book.... Suddenly he rose fr'm th' table, an' cryin': 'I'm pizened,' begun throwin' sausages out iv th' window." The ninth one, Mr. Dooley explained, struck Sen. Albert J. Beveridge (Indiana) on the head "an' made him a blond." The senator rushed into the White House to discover "Tiddy engaged in a hand-to-hand conflict with a potted ham."

Opponents raised every conceivable objection: the slippery-slope argument, the freedom-of-property argument, the pretended horror at the lack of faith in consumer intelligence. The Proprietary [Medicine] Association of America warned, "If the Federal government should regulate Interstate traffic in drugs on the basis of their therapeutic value, why not regulate traffic in theology, by excluding... all theological books which Dr. Wiley... should find to be 'misleading in any particular.'" Nevertheless, the Pure Food and Drug Act was passed and signed into law on June 30, 1906. (TR later claimed all the credit, ignoring Wiley.)

The strength of the opposition was really felt when it came time to enforce the act. The final bill contained many compromises, and the food and pharmaceutical industries now did their best to weaken the standards proposed by the Department of Agriculture. Their lobbyists had access not only to Congress but to the White House, which turned out to be Wiley's undoing. He was sincere and intemperate; but so was Roosevelt, whose reformism usually stopped well short of any risk of serious political costs. Wiley provoked TR's wrath in ways that led the President to call him "nagging, vexatious [and] foolish." Wiley simply thought that he was trying to tell buyers exactly what they were paying for—dangerous or not—which he called the "application of ethics to digestion."

In a battle with a President and the President's Secretary of Agriculture, the contentious bureaucrat was bound to lose in the long run. He won some battles, and his personnel and budget continued to prosper and flourish; but he could not get the cooperation of the solicitor general in prosecuting fraud cases, and he was outflanked and reversed on many labeling and standards decisions. The situation got no better under Taft than Roosevelt, and in 1912 Wiley resigned.

He was by no means a dispirited loser. The previous year, at age sixty-six, he had married a suffragette half his age with whom he had long been in love. Two months after resigning he became the father of a baby boy; a second would follow later. Wiley's high spirits infused his new "job" of lecturing and writing for the cause. He had a special position at *Good Housekeeping* magazine, not only as a columnist but as a czar of advertisements, awarding or withholding the famous seal of approval.

He lived for another eighteen years after his resignation, never fully realizing his hopes to see "the food law of the country... administered for the public good as intended." Absolutist that he was, he could hardly have hoped for total success. At best, pure food and drug laws are complicated and hard to administer. Scientific data are not always clear and conclusive about what impairs health, and the law is full of defensive ambiguities in the definition of fraud. All the same, it does no harm to remember that this scrappy warrior helped remind his generation that there is a "public" in the republic that can be injured by private greed, and that it is a worthwhile objective of politics to enlist in that public's defense.

Woodrow Wilson, Politician

The idealistic architect of a postwar world order that never came into being: such is the popular image of President Woodrow Wilson. What it omits is the savvy, sometimes ruthless politician whose achievements in the domestic sphere were equalled by only two other 20th-century presidents, Franklin Delano Roosevelt and Lyndon Baines Johnson. Robert Dallek here restores the whole man.

Robert Dallek

Robert Dallek is professor of history at the University of California, Los Angeles. He is the author of several books on political and diplomatic history, including Franklin D. Roosevelt and American Foreign Policy, 1932–1945 *(1979), which won a Bancroft Prize, and, most recently,* Lone Star Rising: Lyndon Johnson and His Times, 1908–1960 *(1991).*

Few presidents in American history elicit more mixed feelings than Woodrow Wilson. And why not? His life and career were full of contradictions that have puzzled historians for 70 years. A victim of childhood dyslexia, he became an avid reader, a skilled academic, and a popular writer and lecturer. A deeply religious man, who some described as "a Presbyterian priest" with a dour view of man's imperfectability, he devoted himself to secular designs promising the triumph of reason and harmony in domestic and world affairs. A rigid, self-exacting personality, whose uncompromising adherence to principles barred agreement on some of his most important political goals, he was a brilliant opportunist who won stunning electoral victories and led controversial laws through the New Jersey state legislature and the U.S. Congress. A southern conservative and elitist with a profound distrust of radical ideas and such populists as William Jennings Bryan, he became the Democratic Party's most effective advocate of advanced progressivism. A leading proponent of congressional influence, or what he called "Congressional Government," he ranks with Theodore Roosevelt, Franklin D. Roosevelt, Harry S. Truman, and Lyndon B. Johnson as the century's most aggressive chief executives. An avowed pacifist who declared himself "too proud to fight" and gained reelection in 1916 partly by reminding voters that he had "kept us out of war," he made military interventions in Latin America and Europe hallmarks of his two presidential terms.

There is no greater paradox in Wilson's life and career, however, than the fact that his worst failure has become the principal source of his historical reputation as a great American president. Administrative and legislative triumphs marked Wilson's service as president of Princeton, governor of New Jersey, and president of the United States. But most Americans who would concede Wilson a place in the front ranks of U.S. chief executives would be hard pressed to name many, if any, of these achievements. To them, he is best remembered as the president who preached self-determination and a new world order. (And not only to Americans: An upcoming Wilson biography by Dutch historian J. W. Schulte Nordholt is subtitled *A Life for World Peace.*) In the 1920s and '30s, when America rejected participation in the League of Nations and a political or military role in a world hellbent on another total war, Wilson's reputation reached a low point. He was a good man whom bankers and munitions makers had duped into entering World War I. He had also led America into the fighting out of the hopelessly naive belief that he could make the world safe for democracy and end all wars.

American involvement in World War II reversed Wilson's historical standing. Now feeling guilty about their isolationism and their rejection of his vision of a world at peace, Americans celebrated him as a spurned prophet whose wisdom and idealism deserved renewed acceptance in the 1940s. A new world league of self-governing nations practicing collective security for the sake of global stability and peace became the great American hope during World War II. When the fighting's outcome proved to be the Soviet–American Cold War, Americans saw it as another setback for Wilson's grand design. Nevertheless, they did not lose faith in his ultimate wisdom, believing that democracy and the international rule of law would eventually have to replace tyranny and lawless aggression if the world were ever to achieve lasting peace.

Now, with America's triumph in the Cold War and the Soviet–American confrontation all but over, the country has renewed faith in a world order akin to what Woodrow Wilson proposed in 1918. The idea took on fresh meaning when President Bush led a coalition of U.N.-backed forces against Iraq's attack upon and absorption of Kuwait. The triumph of coalition arms seemed to vindicate Wilson's belief that collective action through a world body could reduce the likelihood and effectiveness of attacks by strong states against weaker ones and thus make international acts of aggression obsolete.

Yet present hopes for a new world order can plummet overnight—and with them Wilson's standing. If Wilson's rep-

12. Woodrow Wilson

utation as a great president rests upon his vision of a new era in world affairs and the fulfillment of some part of that design in our lifetimes, his place in the forefront of U.S. presidents seems less than secure.

Will the ghost of Wilson be plagued forever by the vagaries of world politics? Only if we fail to give scrutiny to his full record. A careful reassessment of Wilson's political career, especially in domestic affairs, would go far to secure his place as a great American president who has much to tell us about the effective workings of democratic political systems everywhere.

FOR ALL HIS IDEALISM AND ELITISM, Wilson's greatest triumphs throughout his career rested on his brilliance as a democratic politician. He was the "great communicator" of his day—a professor who abandoned academic language and spoke in catch phrases that inspired mass support. He was also a master practitioner of the art of the possible, a leader with an impressive talent for reading the public mood and adjusting to it in order to advance his personal ambition and larger public goals. This is not to suggest that his career was an uninterrupted success. He had his share of spectacular failures. But some of these he converted into opportunities for further advance. And even his unmitigated failures had more to do with circumstances beyond his control than with flaws in his political judgment.

Wilson's early life gave little indication of a master politician in the making. Born in 1856 in Staunton, Virginia, the third of four children, he was the offspring of devout Scotch Presbyterian divines. Thomas Woodrow, his maternal grandfather, came from Scotland to the United States, where he ministered to congregations in small Ohio towns. Jesse Woodrow Wilson, Wilson's mother, was an intensely religious, austere Victorian lady with no sense of humor and a long history of psychosomatic ailments. Joseph Ruggles Wilson, Woodrow's father, was a brilliant theologian and leading light in the southern Presbyterian church, holding pulpits in Staunton, Virginia; Augusta, Georgia; Columbia, South Carolina; and Wilmington, North Carolina. Joseph Wilson enjoyed a reputation as an eloquent and powerful speaker whose "arresting rhetoric and cogent thought" made him one of the leading southern preachers and religious teachers of his time. Woodrow Wilson described his father as the "greatest teacher" he ever knew. Yet theological disputes and clashes with other strong-willed church leaders drove Joseph, who advocated various reforms, from one pulpit to another and left him with a sense of failure that clouded his life. One Wilson biographer notes that "by mid-career, Joseph Wilson was in some ways a broken man, struggling to overcome feelings of inferiority, trying to reconcile a God of love with the frustration of his ambition for success and prominence within the church." To compensate for his sense of defeat, Joseph invested his vaunting ambition in his son Woodrow, whom he hoped would become the "very great man" Joseph himself had wished to be.

Although Joseph imparted a love of literature and politics to his son, Bible readings, daily prayers, and Sunday worship services were centerpieces of Woodrow's early years. His father also taught him the transient character of human affairs and the superiority of religious to secular concerns. Joseph left little doubt in the boy's mind that he foresaw for him a career in the ministry as "one of the Church's rarest scholars . . . one of her most illustrious reformers . . . or one of her grandest orators." But Joseph's defeats in church politics in Woodrow's formative adolescent years soured father and son on Woodrow's entrance into the ministry.

Instead, Woodrow, with his father's blessing, invested his ambitions in a political career. As Richard Hofstadter wrote, "When young Tommy Wilson sat in the pew and heard his father bring the Word to the people, he was watching the model upon which his career was to be fashioned." Before college, he hung a portrait of British Prime Minister William Gladstone above his desk and declared: "That is Gladstone, the greatest statesman that ever lived. I intend to be a statesman, too." During his years as a Princeton undergraduate (1875–79), he rationalized his determination to enter politics by describing it as a divine vocation. A career as a statesman was an expression of Christian service, he believed, a use of power for the sake of principles or moral goals. Wilson saw the "key to success in politics" as "the pursuit of perfection through hard work and the fulfillment of ideals." Politics would allow him to spread spiritual enlightenment to the yearning masses.

Yet Wilson, as one of his later political associates said, was a man of high ideals and no principles, which was another way of saying that Wilson's ambition for self-serving political ends outran his commitment to any particular philosophy or set of goals. Like every great American politician since the rise of mass democracy in the 19th century, Wilson allowed the ends to justify the means. But Wilson never thought of himself as an opportunist. Rather, he considered himself a democrat responsive to the national mood and the country's most compelling needs. It is possible to scoff at Wilson's rationalization of his willingness to bend to current demands, but we do well to remember that the country's greatest presidents have all been men of high ideals and no principles, self-serving altruists or selfish pragmatists with a talent for evoking the vision of America as the world's last best hope.

Wilson's path to high political office, like so much else in his life, ran an erratic course. Legal studies at the University of Virginia, self-instruction, and a brief law practice in Atlanta were meant to be a prelude to a political career. But being an attorney had little appeal to Wilson, and he decided to become a professor of politics instead. Consequently, in 1883, at the age of 27, he entered the Johns Hopkins University Graduate School, where he earned a Ph.D. for *Congressional Government* (1885). His book was an argument for a Congress more like the British Parliament, a deliberative body in which debate rather than contending interests shaped legislation. For 17 years, from 1885 to 1902, he taught at Bryn Mawr, Wesleyan, and Princeton, beginning at the last in 1890. By 1898 he had grown weary of what he derisively called his "talking profession," and during the next four years he shrewdly positioned himself to become the unanimous, first-ballot choice of Princeton's trustees as the university's president.

WILSON'S EIGHT YEARS AS PRESIDENT OF Princeton (1902–1910) were a prelude to his later political triumphs and defeats. During the first three years of his Princeton term, Wilson carried off a series of dazzling reforms. Offended by the shallowness of much instruction at Princeton and animated by a desire to make it a special university like Oxford and Cambridge, where undergraduate education emphasized critical thinking rather than "the ideal of making a living," Wilson

3. FROM PROGRESSIVISM TO THE 1920s

introduced a preceptorial system. It aimed at transforming Princeton "from a place where there are youngsters doing tasks to a place where there are men doing thinking, men who are conversing about the things of thought. . . ." As a prerequisite to the preceptorial system, Wilson persuaded the faculty to reorganize the University's curriculum and its structure, creating 11 departments corresponding to subjects and requiring upperclassmen to concentrate their studies in one of them. Wilson's reforms, biographer Arthur S. Unk asserts, "mark him as an educational statesman of originality and breadth and strength." His achievement was also a demonstration of Wilson's political mastery—a case study in how to lead strong-minded, independent academics to accept a sea change in the life of a conservative university.

The fierce struggles and bitter defeats of Wilson's next five years are a measure of how difficult fundamental changes in higher education can be without the sort of astute political management Wilson initially used. Between 1906 and 1910 Wilson fought unsuccessfully to reorganize the social life of undergraduates and to determine the location and nature of a graduate college. In the first instance, Wilson tried to deemphasize the importance of campus eating clubs, which had become the focus of undergraduate life, and replace them with residential colleges, or quadrangles, where students would live under the supervision of unmarried faculty members residing in the colleges. Wilson viewed the clubs as undemocratic, anti-intellectual, and divisive, and the quadrangle plan as a sensible alternative that would advance the university's educational goals and national standing. Wilson assumed that he could put across his plan without the sort of consultation and preparation he had relied on to win approval for the preceptorial system. But his failure to consult alumni, faculty, and trustees was a major political error that led to his defeat. Likewise, he did not effectively marshal the support he needed to win backing for his graduate-school plan, and again it made his proposal vulnerable to criticism from opponents.

Physical and emotional problems caused by strokes in 1906 and 1907 may partly account for Wilson's defeats in the quadrangle and graduate-school fights. But whatever the explanation for his poor performance in these academic struggles, they were by no means without political benefit to Wilson. In fact, what seems most striking about these conflicts is the way Wilson converted them to his larger purposes of running first for governor of New Jersey and then for president of the United States.

Colonel George Harvey, a conservative Democrat who owned a publishing empire that included the *New York World* and *Harper's Weekly,* proposed Wilson for the presidency as early as 1906. Although Wilson made appropriate disclaimers of any interest in seeking the White House, the suggestion aroused in him the longing for high political station that he had held for some 30 years. In response to Harvey's efforts, Wilson, who was already known nationally as a speaker on issues of higher education, began speaking out on economic and political questions before non-university audiences. His initial pronouncements were essentially conservative verities calculated to identify him with the anti-Bryan, anti-Populist wing of the Democratic Party. "The nomination of Mr. Wilson," one conservative editor wrote in 1906, "would be a good thing for the country as betokening a return of his party to historic party ideals and first principles, and a sobering up after the radical 'crazes.' " In 1907 Wilson prepared a "Credo" of his views, which, Arthur Unk says, could hardly have failed to please reactionaries, "for it was conservative to the core." It justified the necessity of great trusts and combinations as efficient instruments of modern business and celebrated individualism. In 1908 Wilson refused to support Bryan for president and rejected suggestions that he become his vice-presidential running mate.

During the next two years, however, Wilson shifted decidedly to the left. Mindful of the mounting progressive temper in the country—of the growing affinity of middle-class Americans for reforms that would limit the power of corporations and political machines—Wilson identified himself with what he called the "new morality," the need to eliminate fraud and corruption from, and to restore democracy and equality of opportunity to, the nation's economic and political life. His academic fights over the quadrangles and graduate school became struggles between special privilege and democracy. In a speech to Princeton's Pittsburgh alumni in the spring of 1910, Wilson attacked the nation's universities, churches, and political parties as serving the "classes" and neglecting the "masses." He declared his determination to democratize the colleges of the country and called for moral and spiritual regeneration. Incensed at his conservative Princeton opponents, who seemed the embodiment of the privileged interests, and eager to make himself a gubernatorial and then national candidate, Wilson invested idealism in the progressive crusade, leaving no doubt that he was ready to lead a movement that might redeem America.

New Jersey Democratic boss James Smith, Jr., seeing Wilson as a conservative opportunist whose rhetoric would appease progressives and whose actions would favor the corporations and the bosses, arranged Wilson's nomination for governor. Wilson seemed to play his part perfectly during the campaign, quietly accepting Smith's help even as he declared his independence from the party machine and espoused the progressive agenda—the direct primary, a corrupt-practices law, workmen's compensation, and a regulatory commission policing the railroads and public utilities. On election day Wilson swept to victory by a 50,000-vote margin, 233,933 to 184,573, and the Democrats gained control of the normally Republican Assembly. Once in the governor's chair, Wilson made clear that he would be his own man. He defeated Smith's bid for election to the U.S. Senate by the state legislature and skillfully assured the enactment of the four principal progressive measures. As he told a friend, "I kept the pressure of opinion constantly on the legislature, and the programme was carried out to its last detail. This with the senatorial business seems, in the minds of the people looking on, little less than a miracle in the light of what has been the history of reform hitherto in the State." As Wilson himself recognized, it was less a miracle than the product of constant pressure on the legislature at a time when "opinion was ripe on all these matters." Wilson's break with the machine and drive for reform reflected a genuine commitment to improving the lot of New Jersey's citizens. Most of all, they were a demonstration of how an ambitious politician in a democracy bends to the popular will for the sake of personal gain and simultaneously serves legitimate public needs.

WILSON'S NOMINATION FOR PRESIDENT BY a deeply divided Democratic convention

12. Woodrow Wilson

in the summer of 1912 was an extraordinary event in the history of the party and the nation. Wilson himself called it "a sort of political miracle." Although Wilson was the frontrunner in 1911 after speaking trips to every part of the nation, by May 1912 aggressive campaigns by Missouri's Champ Clark, speaker of the House of Representatives, and Alabama Representative Oscar W. Underwood made Wilson a decided underdog. When Clark won a majority of the delegates on the 10th ballot, it seemed certain that he would eventually get the two-thirds vote needed for the nomination. In every Democratic convention since 1844, a majority vote for a candidate had translated into the required two-thirds. But 1912 was different. Wilson won the nomination on the 46th ballot after his managers struck a bargain, which kept Underwood's 100-plus delegates from going to Clark. William Jennings Bryan gave Wilson essential progressive support, and the party's most powerful political bosses—the men who, in the words of one historian, had been Wilson's "bitterest antagonists and who represented the forces against which he had been struggling"—decided to back him.

Wilson's campaign for the presidency was another milestone in his evolution as a brilliant democratic politician. He entered the election without a clear-cut campaign theme. The tariff, which he initially focused on, inspired little popular response. In late August, however, after conferring with Louis D. Brandeis, Wilson found a constructive and highly popular campaign theme. Persuading Wilson that political democracy could only follow from economic democracy or diminished control by the country's giant business trusts, Brandeis sold him on the New Freedom—the idea that regulated competition would lead to the liberation of economic enterprise in the United States. This in turn would restore grassroots political power and control. Wilson accurately sensed that the country's mood was overwhelmingly favorable to progressive reform, especially the reduction of the economic power of the trusts. He also saw correctly that Theodore Roosevelt's plea for a New Nationalism—regulated monopoly and an expanded role for federal authority in the economic and social life of the nation—impressed most voters as too paternalistic and more a threat to than an expansion of freedom. As a result, Wilson won a plurality of the popular vote in the four-way contest of 1912, 42 percent to a combined 58 percent for William Howard Taft, TR, and socialist Eugene V. Debs. Wilson's victory in the electoral column was far more one-sided, 435 to 99 for TR and Taft. His victory was also a demonstration of his talents as a speaker who could satisfy the mass yearning for a new era in national affairs.

Wilson's election represented a triumph of democratic hopes. After nearly five decades of conservative rule by the country's business interests, the nation gave its backing to a reform leader promising an end to special privilege and the economic and political democratization of American life. "Nobody owns me," Wilson declared at the end of his campaign, signaling his readiness to act in behalf of the country's working and middle classes. Despite his own largely conservative background, his political agility and sensitivity to popular demands made it likely that he would not disappoint progressive goals.

His first presidential term represents one of the three notable periods of domestic reform in 20th-century America. What makes it particularly remarkable, notes historian John Milton Cooper, is that Wilson won his reforms without the national emergencies over the economy and civil rights that respectively confronted the country during the 1930s and the 1960s. Wilson, in other words, lacked "the peculiarly favorable political conditions" aiding Franklin Roosevelt and Lyndon Johnson.

Wilson's successful leadership rested on his effective management of his party and Congress. Following the advice of Texas Representative Albert S. Burleson, a superb politician who became postmaster general, Wilson filled his cabinet with "deserving" Democrats and allowed Burleson to use patronage "ruthlessly to compel adoption of administration measures." Despite Bryan's ignorance of foreign affairs, for example, his prominence persuaded Wilson to make him secretary of state. Wilson's readiness to set a bold legislative agenda found support from both a 73-member Democratic majority in the House and a decisive majority of Democratic and Republican progressives in the Senate. The 28th president quickly proved himself to be an able manipulator of Congress. Eager to create a sense of urgency about his legislative program and to establish a mood of cooperation

Among Wilson's progressive measures was the Underwood Tariff of 1914, the first downward revision of the tariff since the Civil War.

between the two branches of government, Wilson called a special congressional session at the start of his term and then spoke to a joint meeting of both houses. Indeed, he was the first president to appear in person before Congress since John Adams. Presenting himself as a colleague rather than "a mere department of the Government hailing Congress from some isolated island of jealous power," Wilson returned repeatedly to Capitol Hill for conferences to advance his reform program.

In the 18 months between the spring of 1913 and the fall of 1914, Wilson pushed four key laws through the Congress. The Underwood Tariff of October 1914 was the first downward revision of the tariff since the Civil War; it was inspired more by a desire to reduce the cost of living for lower- and middle-class Americans than by any obligation to serve the interests of industrial giants. Wilson drove the bill through the upper house by exposing the lobbyists representing businesses that sought "to overcome the interests of the public for their private profit." Making the tariff law all the more remarkable was the inclusion of the first graduated income tax in U.S. history. Shortly thereafter, Wilson won passage of the most enduring domestic measure of his presidency, the reform of the country's banking and money system. Insisting on public, centralized control of banks and the money supply rather than a private, decentralized system, Wilson once again came before Congress to influence the outcome of this debate. The Federal Reserve Act of December 1913 combined

3. FROM PROGRESSIVISM TO THE 1920s

elements of both plans, providing for a mix of private and public control. Although further reforms would occur later to make the Federal Reserve system a more effective instrument for dealing with national economic problems, the Wilson law of 1913 created the basic elements of the banking system that has existed for almost 80 years. During the next nine months, by keeping Congress in continuous session for an unprecedented year and a half, Wilson won passage of the Clayton Antitrust and Federal Trade Commission acts, contributing to the more effective regulation of big business and greater power for organized labor.

In November 1914, Wilson announced that his New Freedom program had been achieved and that the progressive movement was at an end. A man of fundamentally conservative impulses (which he believed reflected those of the nation at large), Wilson did not wish to overreach himself. His announcement bewildered advanced progressives, who had been unsuccessfully advocating a variety of social-justice measures Wilson considered too radical to support. Herbert Croly, the editor of the *New Republic*, charged that "any man of President Wilson's intellectual equipment who seriously asserts that the fundamental wrongs of a modern society can be easily and quickly righted as a consequence of a few laws . . . casts suspicion either upon his own sincerity or upon his grasp of the realities of modern social and industrial life." Similarly, Wilson's refusal to establish a National Race Commission and his active commitment to racial segregation in the federal government incensed African-American leaders who had viewed him as a likely supporter of progressive measures for blacks.

Though he did little to reverse course on helping blacks, Wilson stood ready to return to the progressive position for the sake of reelection in 1916. "I am sorry for any President of the United States who does not recognize every great movement in the Nation," Wilson declared in July 1916. "The minute he stops recognizing it, he has become a back number." The results of the congressional elections in 1914 convinced Wilson that the key to success in two years was a campaign attracting TR's Progressive backers to his standard. Consequently, in 1916, he elevated Louis D. Brandeis to the Supreme Court and signed seven additional reform bills into law. Among other things, these laws brought relief to farmers and workers and raised income and inheritance taxes on wealthy Americans. The election results in November vindicated his strategy. Wilson gained almost three million popular votes over his 1912 total and bested Charles Evans Hughes, who headed a reunited Republican party, by 23 electoral votes. On this count alone, Wilson's two consecutive victories as the head of a minority party mark him as one of the century's exceptional American politicians.

WHY DID WILSON'S POLITICAL ASTUTEness desert him during his second term in his handling of the Versailles Treaty and the League of Nations? The answer is not naiveté about world politics, though Wilson himself believed "it would be the irony of fate if my administration had to deal chiefly with foreign affairs." In fact, the same mastery of Congress he displayed in converting so many significant reform bills into law between 1913 and 1916 was reflected in his creation of a national consensus in 1917 for American participation in the Great War.

At the start of the fighting in 1914, Wilson declared America neutral in thought and deed. And though Wilson himself had a decidedly pro-British bias, he understood that the country then was only mildly pro-Allied and wanted no part in the war. His policies initially reflected these feelings. Only as national sentiment changed in response to events in Europe and on the high seas, where German submarine violations of U.S. neutral rights drove Americans more decisively into the Allied camp, did Wilson see fit to prepare the country for and then lead it into the war. His prewar leadership became something of a model for Franklin Roosevelt in 1939–41 as he maneuvered to maintain a national majority behind his responses to World War II.

Wilson's failure in 1919–20, or, more precisely, the collapse of his political influence in dealing with the peacemaking at the end of the war, consisted of a number of things—most of them beyond his control. His Fourteen Points, his formula for making the world safe for democracy and ending all wars, was beyond the capacity of any political leader to achieve, then and now. Yet there is every reason to believe that Wilson enunciated his peace aims assuming that he would have to accept compromise agreements on many of his goals, as indeed he did in the Versailles negotiations. A number of these compromises on the Fourteen Points went beyond what he hoped to concede, but he recognized that the conclusion of the fighting had stripped him of much of his hold over America's allies and limited his capacity to bend the strong-minded French, British, and Italian leaders to his will or to influence the radical revolutionary regime in Russia. Events were moving too fast in Europe and all over the globe for him to make the world approximate the postwar peace arrangements he had enunciated in 1918.

Faced by such circumstances, Wilson accepted the proposition that a League of Nations, including the United States, would be the world's best hope for a stable peace. Wilson's prime objective after the Versailles conference was to assure American participation in the new world body. But the political cards were stacked against him. After six years of Democratic rule and a growing conviction in Republican Party circles that the Democrats would be vulnerable in 1920, Senate Republicans made approval of the Versailles Treaty and American participation in the League partisan issues which could redound to their benefit. Moreover, between 1918 and 1920, Wilson's deteriorating health, particularly a major stroke in the fall of 1919, intensified a propensity for self-righteousness and made him uncharacteristically rigid in dealing with a political issue that cried out for flexibility and accommodation. As Edwin A. Weinstein has persuasively argued in his medical and psychological biography of Wilson, "the cerebral dysfunction which resulted from Wilson's devastating strokes prevented the ratification of the Treaty. It is almost certain that had Wilson not been so afflicted, his political skills and facility with language would have bridged the gap between [opposing Senate] resolutions, much as he had reconciled opposing views of the Federal Reserve bill . . . or had accepted the modifications of the Treaty suggested in February, 1919."

WILSON'S POLITICAL FAILURE IN 1919–20 was a striking exception in a career marked by a substantial number of political victories. His defeat and its consequences were so stunning that they have eclipsed the record of prior achievements and partly obscured Wilson's contributions to American history.

But it is not only the disaster of 1919–20 that is responsible. Mainstream academia today dismisses political history and particularly the study of powerful leaders as distinctly secondary in importance to impersonal social forces in explaining historical change. What seems lost from view nowadays is just how essential strong and skillful political leadership remains in bringing a democracy to accept major reforms. Wilson is an excellent case in point. For all the public's receptivity to progressivism in the first two decades of the century, it took a leader of exceptional political skill to bring warring reform factions together in a coalition that could enact a liberal agenda. By contrast, Wilson's physical incapacity in 1919 assured the defeat of American participation in a world league for 25 years. This is not to say that an American presence in an international body would have dramatically altered the course of world affairs after 1920, but it might have made a difference, and the collapse of Wilson's leadership was the single most important factor in keeping the United States on the sidelines.

Did social and economic and a host of other factors influence the course of U.S. history during Wilson's time? Without a doubt. But a leader of vision and varied abilities—not all of them purely admirable—was needed to seize the opportunities provided by history and make them realities. To forget the boldness of Wilson's leadership, and the importance of political leaders generally, is to embrace a narrow vision of this nation's past—and of its future.

Madam C. J. Walker

Born in Delta, Louisiana, to former slaves, Sarah Breedlove Walker founded a business that made her the first female African-American millionaire.

A'Lelia Bundles

A'Lelia Perry Bundles is Madam Walker's great-great-granddaughter and biographer. She is presently writing a biography of four generations of Walker women for Scribner.

Buoyed by a wave of recent good fortune, Madam C. J. Walker arrived in Chicago for her first National Negro Business League (NNBL) convention in 1912 eager to tell the other delegates about her bustling new Indianapolis factory and her surging monthly sales receipts. This 44-year-old former washerwoman was confident the mostly male membership would welcome her as a worthy colleague once they heard how she had turned a $1.50 investment into a thriving hair-care products company in just seven years. But first she had to convince Booker T. Washington, the group's founder and America's most influential black leader, to carve out a slot for her on his already overbooked program.

Walker was among those who admired Washington's exemplary personal journey from slave to educator to presidential advisor. Although by 1912 his gradualistic, accommodationist approach to civil rights was being challenged within the black community by a new generation of more progressive activists like W. E. B. DuBois of the National Association for the Advancement of Colored People (NAACP), Washington still retained his preeminent position.

Walker, who had met Washington at least twice before, suspected he might be reluctant to grant her a forum. Two years earlier, when she had written to him seeking advice and investment capital, he had brushed her off with replies that were noncommittal at best, condescending at worst. When she wrote again in late 1911 seeking an invitation to his annual Negro Conference at Tuskegee Institute—the Alabama school he had founded in 1881—he openly discouraged her from attending, because of his skepticism of female entrepreneurs.

Undaunted, and presumably uninvited, Walker arrived on Tuskegee's campus in January 1912. Determined to grab Washington's attention, she personally delivered to his home a letter of reference from the newly installed secretary of Indianapolis's "colored" Young Men's Christian Association (YMCA) and made another plea to address the group. Her persistence was rewarded, not with an audience during the regular sessions of the conference, but with ten minutes at the well-attended evening chapel.

Anticipating another challenge from Washington, Walker began a quiet, behind-the-scenes campaign for a place on the speakers' rostrum as soon as she registered in Chicago. With the help of Indianapolis *Freeman* publisher George Knox, a long-time NNBL member and Washington associate, she hoped to melt Washington's coolness toward her.

On Wednesday evening, Walker and the two thousand delegates and guests greeted Washington's annual speech with a foot-stomping standing ovation that reverberated from the altar of the Institutional Church to its rafters. "The men and women of our race of this generation hold in their hands the future of the generations that are to follow," she heard him say. "This is in an especial sense true of the Negro business man and woman. If we do not do our duty now in laying the proper foundation for economic and commercial growth, our children, and our children's children will suffer because of our inactivity or shortness of vision."

Awaiting a reply to her request to speak, Walker must have savored Washington's words. Who better to illustrate his description of a successful businesswoman than she? Washington had probably seen her well-equipped factory during a visit to Indianapolis the previous summer. He knew she provided jobs for hundreds of Walker agents and "hair culturists" who were selling her products across the country. Inveterate reader that he was, he could not have missed her advertisements in the NAACP's *Crisis* magazine. And he must have read the news of her $1,000 contribution to the Indianapolis YMCA in late 1911. If anyone was doing her part to "lay the proper foundation" of which he had spoken, it was she.

13. Madam C. J. Walker

Madam Walker, shown here with Booker T. Washington (to her left) and other black leaders at the dedication of the Indianapolis YMCA in 1913, had to fight for the right to be heard at that gathering. Speaking from the audience, she told the attendees that she had risen from the cotton fields of the South to the washtub and the cook kitchen. From there, she said, "... I promoted myself into the business of manufacturing hair goods and preparations."

Earlier in the evening Walker had probably listened carefully as Julia H. P. Coleman, a pharmacist and hair-care-products manufacturer, described the growing demand among black women for pomades, shampoos, and hair oils. No doubt Walker leaned forward intently the next morning as Anthony Overton, founder of the Overton Hygienic Company claimed that his sales of baking powder, hair pomades, face powder, and toilet articles had made his business the "largest Negro manufacturing enterprise in the United States."

As Overton completed his remarks, Walker's fellow Hoosier, George Knox, stood and addressed Booker T. Washington from the audience. "I arise to ask this convention for a few minutes of its time to hear a remarkable woman ... Madam Walker. The lady I refer to is the manufacturer of hair goods and preparations." Although he respected Knox—like himself a former slave who had prospered—Washington curtly dismissed his suggestion. "But Mr. Knox, we are taking up the question of life membership," he replied, then recognized another speaker.

That evening, as Sears, Roebuck & Company president Julius Rosenwald dispensed business advice to an attentive packed house, Walker must have wondered how Washington could continue to deny her. Surely the presence of Rosenwald, a major contributor to Tuskegee Institute as well as to the fund to build YMCAs in black communities across the country, must have reminded Washington that Walker's $1,000 contribution in Indianapolis was the largest any black woman had yet made to the effort.

By Friday—the third and final day—a frustrated Walker resolved to confront Washington. During the morning session, as members of the National Bankers' Association recounted the development of black-owned banks, Walker mustered her nerve while battling her anger and impatience. Timing, she knew was crucial. At just the right moment, as Washington prepared to call upon yet another banker, Walker seized her chance.

"Surely you are not going to shut the door in my face," she forcefully announced from the audience. "I feel that I am in a business that is a credit to the womanhood of our race." After tabulating her impressive, mounting annual income, she aimed a not so subtle jab at Washington. "I have been trying to get before you business people and tell you what I am doing."

"I am a woman who came from the cotton fields of the South," the now stately and well-dressed Walker continued with increasing assurance. "I was promoted from there to the washtub. Then I was promoted to the cook kitchen. And from there I promoted myself into the business of manufacturing

3. FROM PROGRESSIVISM TO THE 1920s

hair goods and preparations. Everybody told me I was making a mistake by going into this business, but I know how to grow hair as well as I know how to grow cotton . . . I have built my own factory on my own ground!"

In a setting so controlled by Washington's directives, Walker's remarks must have startled the audience. How could she have been so bold as to challenge this influential dispenser of favors, this advisor to presidents, this dinner guest of the wealthy? But her brazenness paid off, gaining, if not Washington's wholehearted acceptance, at least enough grudging respect that she was invited back the following two years as a scheduled speaker.

"I am a woman who came from the cotton fields of the South. I was promoted from there to the washtub. Then I was promoted to the cook kitchen. And from there I promoted myself into the business of manufacturing hair goods and preparations."

At the dedication of the Indianapolis YMCA in July 1913, Walker finally received Washington's recognition when he publicly praised her philanthropic generosity, then later wrote to her, in a tone very different from his earlier letters: "I want to thank you for the courtesies you showed me while in your magnificent home. You have indeed a model home and a business we should all be proud of."

A few weeks later, as Walker waited her turn as an *invited* speaker at the fourteenth annual NNBL conference in Philadelphia, Washington graciously welcomed the woman he had initially snubbed: "I now take pleasure in introducing to the convention, one of the most progressive and successful businesswomen of our race—Madam C. J. Walker."

After her remarks, Washington told the delegates, "We thank her for her excellent address and for all she has done for our race. You talk about what the men are doing in a business way. Why if we don't watch out, the women will excel us." For Walker, there were few more deeply satisfying moments.

Perhaps she might have preferred a less contentious start to her relationship with Washington, but a lifetime of adversity had taught Walker to cherish the rewards of triumphing over obstacles. Born Sarah Breedlove in 1867 on a Delta, Louisiana, plantation, this daughter of former slaves transformed herself from an uneducated farm laborer and laundress into a celebrated entrepreneur, philanthropist, and social activist.

Orphaned at age seven—when her parents died, possibly during an outbreak of yellow fever—she often said, "I got my start by giving myself a start." Motherless and fatherless, hungry and sometimes homeless, the young Sarah and her older sister, Louvenia, survived by working in the cotton fields around Delta, and Vicksburg, Mississippi.

Marriage at age 14 to Moses McWilliams was her escape from life with her sister's husband, whom she later described as "cruel." On her husband's death just six years later, in 1887, Sarah became a twenty-year-old widow with a two-year-old daughter. She was compelled to move again, this time up river to St. Louis where gas lamps brightened city nights and where she had heard that washtubs and "white folks' dirty clothes" replaced cotton bolls and the threat of nightriders.

In this energetic river city Sarah Breedlove McWilliams earned a reputation as a first-class laundress, but she wanted more than a washerwoman's wage for herself and her daughter, Lelia (later known as A'Lelia Walker). "As I bent over the washboard and looked at my arms buried in the soapsuds," she later remembered, "I said to myself, 'What are you going to do when you grow old and your back gets stiff?' This set me to thinking, but with all my thinking, I couldn't see how I, a poor washerwoman, was going to better my condition."

What she did see all around her were the trappings of a more comfortable life—in the homes of her clients as she dropped off their wash; in the mannerisms and fashions of the educated, urbanized black women in her church, on the faces of the women who rode downtown in horse-drawn carriages.

Worn as her own clothes must have been, she still prided herself on her appearance, on the starch in her dresses and the perfectly ironed collars and cuffs. But her hair was another matter. It was thin, unhealthy, patchy, and frayed. Like many women of the time,

Walker trained a force of African-American women as "hair culturists" to sell and demonstrate her products. The Walker agents (below), assembled in Philadelphia in 1917 for the first convention of the Madam C. J. Walker Hair Culturists Union of America, were told to use their own success to advance other women.

13. Madam C. J. Walker

she suffered from alopecia, a stress-, diet-, and hygiene-related scalp ailment characterized by excessive, infectious dandruff that made her nearly bald. She tried homemade remedies and store-bought products, including the hair pomades of another black, St. Louis businesswoman, Annie Malone, who had founded her own company in 1900.

Apparently finding some benefit from Malone's products, McWilliams moved to Denver in 1905 to sell Malone's "Wonderful Hair Grower." But by the spring of 1906, she had trained her eyes on more lucrative horizons. In January 1906, after she married Charles Joseph Walker—an ambitious, if sometime luckless, promoter—the couple explored ways to combine their complementary talents of her marketing ability and his knack for creating newspaper advertising. In the fashion of many women proprietors of her era, she adopted the title, "Madam," and attached to it her husband's name. She stopped selling Malone's "Wonderful Hair Grower" and started mixing her own formula, which she claimed had been revealed to her in a dream after she had prayed for a remedy to restore her hair.

"God answered my prayer, for one night I had a dream and in that dream a big black man appeared to me and told me what to mix up for my hair," she told a reporter. "I put it on my scalp, and in a few weeks my hair was coming in faster than it had ever fallen out. I tried it on my friends; it helped them. I made up my mind I would begin to sell it."

To promote her own products, the new "Madam C. J. Walker" traveled for a year and a half on a dizzying crusade through the heavily black South and Southwest, demonstrating her scalp treatments, selling her tins of Glossine and Wonderful Hair Grower, and devising sales and marketing strategies. In 1908, she temporarily moved her base to Pittsburgh and opened Lelia College—which she named for her daughter—to train Walker "hair culturists." By early 1910, she had settled in Indianapolis, then the nation's largest inland manufacturing center, and there built a factory, a hair and manicure salon, and another training school. When she attended the NNBL convention in 1912, she claimed a thousand Walker agents. Around the same time, she also divorced Charles Joseph Walker, business differences having spilled over into the couple's personal life.

Much of Walker's ascendancy as a businesswoman came from her instincts and her ability to discern what other women like herself wanted and needed. In an era when even the most respectable black woman's morality was questioned and sullied by detractors of African Americans, middle-class black women in particular placed tremendous pressure on themselves to conform to the Victorian behavior and dress that prevailed in America at the turn of the century. Entwined with the fashions and the idealized dictates of upper-class society were also Euro-American standards of beauty that prized white skin and long, straight hair. Even within the African-American community, mulatto women, whose appearance was often more European than African, were often favored.

Because Walker's unabashedly Negroid facial features and hair were like those of most African-American women, she understood the wishes of her sisters to be attractive to themselves and to men in a society that assigned both caste and class on the basis of skin color and hair texture. Acutely aware of the debate about whether black women should alter the appearance of their natural hair, Walker insisted years later that her hair-care system was not intended as a "hair straightener," but rather as a grooming method to heal and condition the scalp to promote hair growth.

An intense advocate of racial pride, she did not fully reconcile the insidious pressure both from within the black community and from society as a whole to conform to European tastes even when she and her agents were among the hair culturists who popularized the use of the metal straightening comb. "Right here let me correct the erroneous impression held by some that I claim to straighten hair," she once told a reporter. "I want the great masses of my people to take greater pride in their personal appearance and to give their hair proper attention."

At a time when ninety percent of African Americans lived in the South and most working black women were field laborers and household domestics, few people were contemplating, let alone exalting, their natural beauty. In fact, mainstream newspapers, magazines, and books were more likely to portray black women in unflattering, stereotypical images.

Walker, convinced that she had identified an unfulfilled need with her products and her grooming system, offered both personal attention and pampering, as well as economic self-sufficiency. To foster cooperation among her agents and to protect them from competitors, Walker organized them into local and state clubs of the Madam C. J. Walker Hair Culturists Union of America. Then, beginning in 1917, she held what must have been among the first annual convention for American businesswomen.

As her business grew, Walker became increasingly conscious of her power and her obligation to, as she often said, "help my race." Of her contributions to black preparatory schools and colleges, orphanages, and retirement homes, as well as to social and cultural organizations and institutions, she said: "My object in life is not simply to make money for myself or to spend it on myself in dressing or running around in an automobile, but I love to use a part of what I make in trying to help others."

After moving to New York City's Harlem in 1916, she became increasingly involved in the NAACP's anti-lynching movement, eventually contributing $5,000 to the organization's political and educational fund to end mob violence. In July 1917, when white thugs in East St. Louis murdered more than three dozen blacks, Walker joined other Harlem leaders in the Negro Silent Protest Parade. The massive, anti-lynching demonstration drew some ten thousand black New Yorkers who marched somberly and speechlessly down Fifth Avenue to the cadence of muffled drums, with banners and posters held high, to protest Jim Crow laws, mob violence, and disenfranchisement.

A few days later, Walker—along with James Weldon Johnson; Abyssinian Baptist Church minister Adam Clayton Powell, Sr.; Harlem realtor John E. Nail; and *New York Age* publisher Fred Moore—boarded a train to Washington to meet with President Woodrow Wilson. Their mission was to present a petition favoring legislation to make lynching a federal crime.

Although they knew that Wilson, the first southern-born president since the Civil War, had instituted racial segregation in federal buildings shortly after being elected, the group hoped he would listen to what they had to say. But because he had also hesitated to condemn lynching publicly—apparently for fear of alienating his southern constituency—it

3. FROM PROGRESSIVISM TO THE 1920s

probably did not surprise Walker and the others when he declined to meet with them, dispatching instead his secretary Joseph Patrick Tumulty. The group had every reason to be insulted, but they were not deterred, using their energy later that day on Capitol Hill to lobby senators and congressmen for an anti-lynching bill and a congressional investigation into the riots.

A few weeks later, at their first annual Walker agents' convention in Philadelphia, Walker advised the delegates and guests "to remain loyal to our homes, our country and our flag" despite the recent violence. Aware of the sensitive, wartime atmosphere—and stalwart in her support of the black American troops in Europe—Walker reminded her audience, "This is the greatest country under the sun. But we must not let our love of country, our patriotic loyalty cause us to abate one whit in our protest against wrong and injustice. We should protest until the American sense of justice is so aroused that such affairs as the East St. Louis riot be forever impossible."

For the rest of her life, Walker used her wealth and visibility to promote social and political causes in which she believed and to encourage women to pursue business opportunities and economic independence. By the time she died in 1919 at her estate in Irvington-on-Hudson, New York, she had helped to create the role of the twentieth-century self-made American businesswoman; established herself as a pioneer of the modern black hair-care and cosmetics industry; and had set standards in the African-American community for corporate and community giving.

Tenacity and perseverance, faith in herself and in God, quality products and "honest business dealings" were the elements and strategies she prescribed for aspiring entrepreneurs who requested the secret to her rags-to-riches ascent. "There is no royal flower-strewn path to success," she once commented. "And if there is, I have not found it for if I have accomplished anything in life it is because I have been willing to work hard."

Madam Walker marketed her products aggressively, including in her advertisements (above, top) the assurance that "All Mme. Walker's Inventions are reliable...." In 1910, Walker established the permanent national headquarters of her business in Indianapolis, Indiana, a city located at the heart of America's transportation network. She built a factory (above, bottom) that became a city landmark. Today, both the factory and Madam Walker's Irvington, New York, home are national historic landmarks.

Alcohol in American History

National binges have alternated with enforced abstinence for 200 years, but there may be hope for moderation

David F. Musto

David F. Musto, a professor of child psychiatry and history of medicine at Yale University, has studied attitudes toward alcohol and other drugs since the 1960s. He received a B.A. in classical languages from the University of Washington in 1956, an M.A. in the history of science and medicine from Yale in 1961, and an M.D. from Washington in 1963. He has been a member of the alcohol policy panel of the National Academy of Sciences and the Connecticut Drug and Alcohol Commission. Musto spent his medical internship at the Pennsylvania Hospital in Philadelphia, where the pioneering temperance author Benjamin Rush was an attending physician in the late 18th century.

The young American ship of state floated on a sea of distilled spirits. In the period immediately after the American Revolution, a generally favorable view of alcoholic beverages coincided with rising levels of consumption that far exceeded any in modern times. By the early decades of the 19th century, Americans drank roughly three times as much alcohol as they do in the 1990s.

The country also had its abstemious side. Even as consumption of alcohol was reaching unprecedented levels, an awareness of the dangers of drink began to emerge, and the first American temperance movement took hold. At its peak in 1855, 13 of 40 states and territories had adopted legal prohibition. By the 1870s, public opinion had turned back, and liquor was flowing freely again; then, around the turn of the century, a movement for abstinence gained steam, culminating in the 13-year experiment of Prohibition that began in 1920.

Over the history of the U.S., popular attitudes and legal responses to the consumption of alcohol and other mood-altering substances have oscillated from toleration to a peak of disapproval and back again in cycles roughly 70 years long. Although other nations appear to have embraced the virtues of moderation, the U.S. continues to swing slowly back and forth between extremes.

The length of these trends may explain why most people are unaware of our repetitive history. Few contemporary Americans concerned about the abuse of illegal drugs, for example, know that opiate use was also a burning issue in the first decades of the 20th century, just as few of today's nutrition and exercise enthusiasts know about their health-minded predecessors from the same period. Furthermore, a phenomenon analogous to political correctness seems to control discourse on alcohol and other "vices"; when drinking is on the rise and most believe that liquor poses little risk to life and health, temperance advocates are derided as ignorant and puritanical; in the end stage of a temperance movement, brewers, distillers, sellers and drinkers all come under harsh attack. Citizens may come of age with little knowledge of the contrary experiences of their forebears. Even rigorous studies that contradict current wisdom may be ignored—data showing both the damaging and beneficial effects of alcohol appear equally susceptible to suppression, depending on the era.

It now appears that a third era of temperance is under way in the U.S. Alcohol consumption peaked around 1980 and has since fallen by about 15 percent. The biggest drop has been in distilled spirits, but wine use has also waned. Beer sales have fallen less, but nonalcoholic brews—replicas of Prohibition's "near beer"—have been rising in popularity.

The shift in attitude is apparent in the cyclic movement of the legal drinking age. In 1971 the 26th Amendment to the Constitution—the most rapidly ratified in the nation's history—lowered the voting age to 18. Soon after, many state legislatures lowered the drinking age to conform to the voting age. Around 1980, however, states started rolling back the drinking age to 21. Surprisingly, the action was praised even among the 18- to 20-year-olds it affected. In 1984 the U.S. government, which cannot itself mandate a national drinking age, threatened to withhold federal highway funds from any state or territory that did not raise its drinking age to 21. Within a short time every state and the District of Columbia were in compliance. Puerto Rico has been the only holdout.

ALCOHOL, DRIVING AND YOUTH

Drunk driving is the most recent catalyst for public activism against alcohol abuse. At the end of the 1970s, two groups appeared with the goal of combating alcohol-related accidents: Remove Intoxicated Drivers (RID) on the

3. FROM PROGRESSIVISM TO THE 1920s

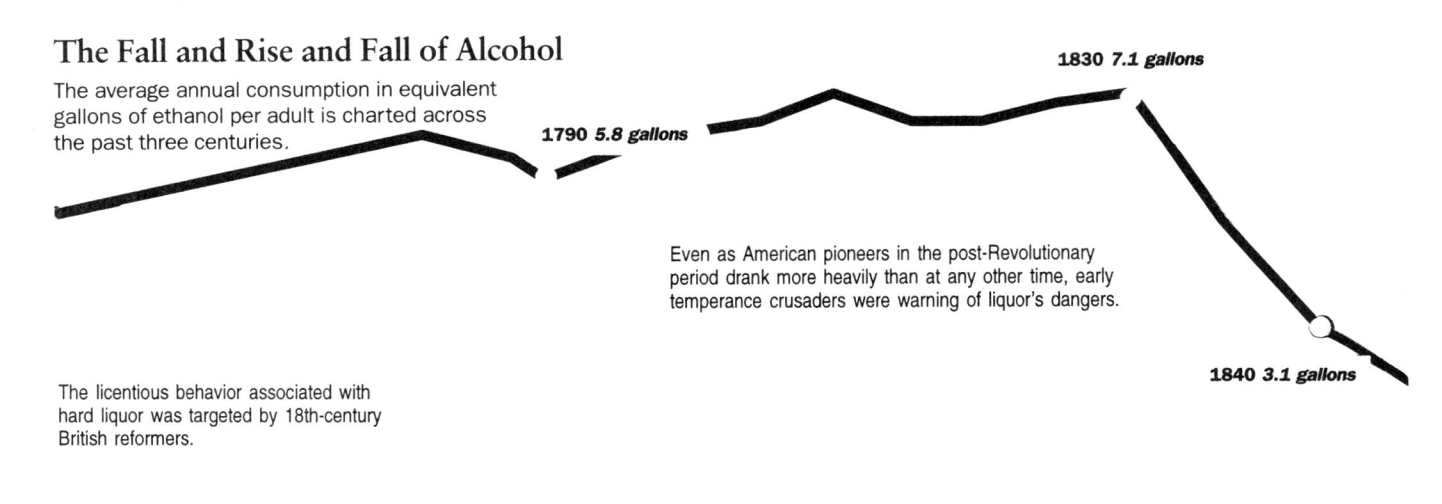

The Fall and Rise and Fall of Alcohol

The average annual consumption in equivalent gallons of ethanol per adult is charted across the past three centuries.

1790 *5.8 gallons*

1830 *7.1 gallons*

Even as American pioneers in the post-Revolutionary period drank more heavily than at any other time, early temperance crusaders were warning of liquor's dangers.

1840 *3.1 gallons*

The licentious behavior associated with hard liquor was targeted by 18th-century British reformers.

1700		1800		
London Gin Epidemic, 1710–1750	Revolutionary War, 1775–1783		War of 1812	Opening of Erie Canal, 1825

East Coast and Mothers Against Drunk Driving (MADD) in California. Both groups attacked weak drunk-driving laws and judicial laxness, especially in cases where drivers may have been repeatedly arrested for drunk driving—including some who had killed others in crashes—but never imprisoned.

Across the nation RID and MADD have strengthened the drunk-driving laws. Although sometimes at odds with each other, both have successfully lobbied for laws reducing the legal threshold of intoxication, increasing the likelihood of incarceration and suspending drivers' licenses without a hearing if their blood alcohol levels exceed a state's legal limit, typically about 0.1 percent.

In 1981 Students Against Driving Drunk (SADD) was established to improve the safety of high school students. The group promotes a contract between parents and their children in which the children agree to call for transportation if they have been drinking, and the parents agree to provide it. As a result, however, RID and MADD have accused SADD of sanctioning youthful drinking rather than trying to eliminate it.

Political action has reinforced the prevailing public beliefs. In 1988 Congress set up the Office of Substance Abuse Prevention (OSAP) under the auspices of the Department of Health and Human Services. The OSAP provided what it called "editorial guidelines" to encourage media to adopt new ways of describing drug and alcohol use. Instead of referring to "responsible use" of alcohol, for example, the office suggested

that newspapers and magazines should speak simply of "use, since there is a risk associated with all use." This language suggests that there is no safe threshold of consumption—a view also espoused by the American Temperance Society in the 1840s and the Anti-Saloon League early in this century. The OSAP also evaluated information on alcohol and drugs intended for distribution to schools and communities. It asserted that "materials recommending a designated driver should be rated unacceptable. They encourage heavy alcohol use by implying it is okay to drink to intoxication as long as you don't drive."

Another example of changing attitudes is the history of beliefs about alcohol's effects on fetal development. In the early 1930s, after Prohibition had ended, Charles R. Stockard of Cornell University, a leading authority on embryology, published animal studies that suggested minimal effects on fetal development. At about the same time, Harold T. Hyman of the Columbia University College of Physicians and Surgeons reviewed human experiments and found that "the habitual use of alcohol in moderate amounts by the normal human adult appears to be without any permanent organic effect deleterious in character."

FETAL ALCOHOL SYNDROME

Then, in the 1970s, researchers at the University of Washington described what they called fetal alcohol syndrome, a set of physical and mental abnormalities in children born to women who imbibed during pregnancy. At first, the syndrome appeared to require very heavy consumption, but after further investigation these researchers have come to assert that even a tiny amount of alcohol can cause the disorder. Drinks consumed at the earliest stage of embryonic development, when a woman may have no idea that she is pregnant, can be a particularly potent teratogen. Since 1989, all alcoholic beverages must bear a warning label for pregnant women from the U.S. Surgeon General's office.

Societal reaction to these findings has resulted in strong condemnation of women who drink any alcohol at all while pregnant. In a celebrated Seattle case in 1991, a woman nine months and a couple of weeks pregnant (who had abstained from alcohol during that time) decided to have a drink with her meal in a restaurant. Most embryologists agree that a single drink at such a late stage of pregnancy produces minimal risk. The waiters, however, repeatedly cautioned her against it; she became angry; the waiters lost their jobs. When the story became known, letters appeared in a local newspaper questioning her fitness as a mother. One University of Washington embryology expert even suggested that pregnant women should no longer be served alcohol in public.

The current worry over the effect of small amounts of alcohol during pregnancy is particularly interesting because belief in alcohol's ability to damage the

14. Alcohol in American History

Women were at the forefront of the second wave of antialcohol movements. The issue helped to legitimize their participation in political life, because alcohol abuse impinged on the family sphere to which women had been relegated.

Beverage manufacturers, especially brewers, tried to fight back against temperance movements by portraying their product as a healthy part of the national culture.

1860 *2.1 gallons*

1890 *2.1 gallons*

1850 — 1880

Maine temperance law, 1851   Civil War, 1861–1865   WCTU founded, 1874

fetus is a hallmark of American temperance movements in this and the past century. Indeed, as far back as 1726, during the English "gin epidemic," the College of Physicians of London issued a formal warning that parents drinking spirits were committing "a great and growing evil which was, too often, a cause of weak, feeble, and distempered children." There is little question that fetal alcohol syndrome is a real phenomenon, but the explosion in diagnosed cases in conjunction with changing social attitudes merits closer scrutiny.

THE FIRST TEMPERANCE MOVEMENT

Like today's antialcohol movement, earlier campaigns started with temperance and only later began pushing abstinence. In 1785 Benjamin Rush of Philadelphia, celebrated physician and inveterate reformer, became America's most prominent advocate of limited alcohol use. Tens of thousands of copies of his booklet, *An Inquiry into the Effects of Ardent Spirits upon the Human Mind and Body*, were distributed throughout the young nation. Like many of his compatriots, Rush censured spirits while accepting the beneficent effects of milder beverages. His "moral thermometer" introduced a striking visual tool to illustrate the graduated effects of beer and wine (health and wealth) and spirits (intemperance, vice and disease). When reformers "took the pledge" in the early years of the 19th century, it was a pledge to abstain from distilled spirits, not all alcoholic beverages.

The same kind of distinction had been made almost a century earlier in England, during an antispirits crusade in response to the gin epidemic. Rapidly increasing consumption of cheap distilled spirits swamped London during the first half of the 18th century. Gin was blamed for a dramatic rise in deaths and a falling birth rate. William Hogarth's powerful prints *Gin Lane* and *Beer Street* were designed to contrast the desolation caused by gin with the healthy prosperity enjoyed by beer drinkers. Despite the exhortations of Rush and others, until the 1830s most Americans believed that strong alcoholic drinks imparted vitality and health, easing hard work, warding off fevers and other illnesses, and relieving colds and snakebite. Soldiers and sailors took a daily ration of rum, and whiskey had a ceremonial role for marking any social event from a family gathering to an ordination. Even as concern grew, so did the distilling business. Annual consumption peaked around 1830 at an estimated 7.1 gallons of alcohol per adult.

TOTAL ABSTENTION

The creation of the Massachusetts Society for the Suppression of Intemperance in 1812 heralded the first organized antidrinking crusade on a state level. Through the inspiration and determination of one of the most dynamic writers and speakers of the century, the Reverend Lyman Beecher, the tide began to turn in earnest. That same year the annual meeting of the Connecticut Congregational Church received a report on the enormous rise in drinking and concluded, regretfully, that nothing could be done about it. An outraged Beecher demanded that a new report be written, then produced one himself overnight. He called for a crusade against alcohol. In 1826 Beecher limned the specifics of his argument in his epochal *Six Sermons on Intemperance*.

Beecher's words swept hundreds of thousands into America's first temperance movement. One of his signal contributions was to throw out compromise—how can you compromise with a poison? He extended the condemnation of spirits to all alcohol-containing beverages and denounced "prudent use."

"It is not enough," Beecher declaimed, "to erect the flag ahead, to mark the spot where the drunkard dies. It must be planted at the entrance of his course, proclaiming in waving capitals—THIS IS THE WAY TO DEATH!!" Beecher's argument that abstinence is the inevitable final stage of temperance gradually won dominance. In 1836 the American Temperance Society (founded in 1826) officially changed its definition of temperance to abstinence.

Not until 1851 did Maine pass its groundbreaking prohibition law but after that, things moved quickly. By 1855 about a third of Americans lived under democratically achieved laws that pro-

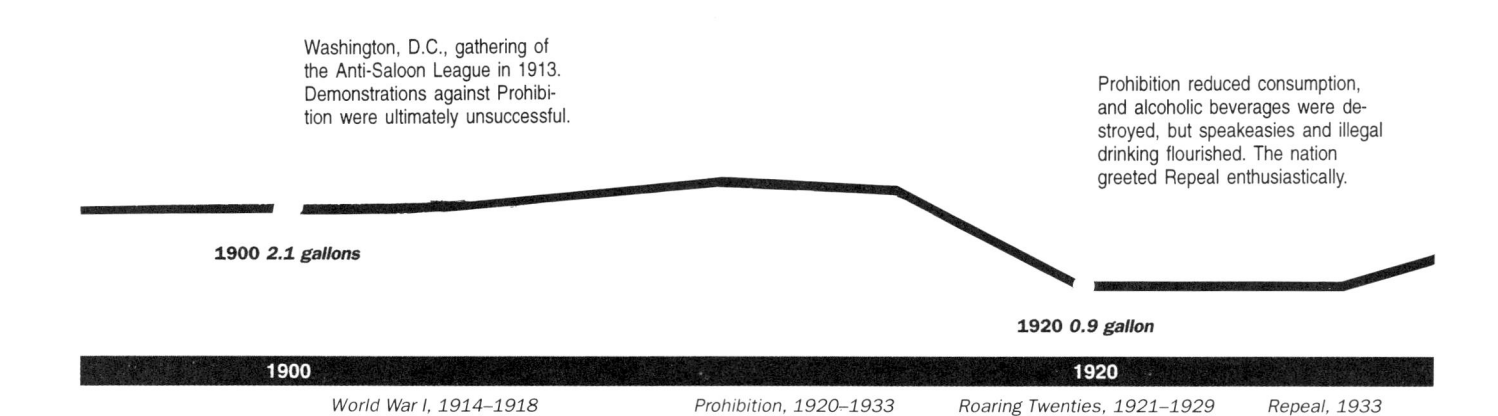

3. FROM PROGRESSIVISM TO THE 1920s

Washington, D.C., gathering of the Anti-Saloon League in 1913. Demonstrations against Prohibition were ultimately unsuccessful.

Prohibition reduced consumption, and alcoholic beverages were destroyed, but speakeasies and illegal drinking flourished. The nation greeted Repeal enthusiastically.

1900 *2.1 gallons*

1920 *0.9 gallon*

1900 | 1920

World War I, 1914–1918 — Prohibition, 1920–1933 — Roaring Twenties, 1921–1929 — Repeal, 1933

hibited the sale of alcohol. Alcohol consumption fell to less than a third of its pretemperance level and has never again reached the heights of the early republic.

THE WOMAN'S CRUSADE

As the first temperance movement was reaching its peak, another moral debate claimed national attention: slavery. Proabstinence forces began to lose their political strength, especially during the Civil War, when the federal government raised money by means of an excise tax on liquor. Starting in the 1860s, some states repealed their prohibitions, courts in others found the statutes unconstitutional, and prohibition laws in yet other states and territories fell into disuse.

Nevertheless, important antialcohol events continued. The most dramatic, the Woman's Crusade, began in Ohio in 1873. Large groups gathered and employed hymn singing and prayers to sway onlookers against saloons. Out of this movement evolved the Women's Christian Temperance Union (WCTU). Although it is now associated only with prohibition in the popular mind, during the union's prime it pushed for far broader reforms: its platform included equal legal rights for women, the right of

---

Down the Memory Hole

Deeply held attitudes can rewrite popular history. An 1848 lithograph of George Washington saying farewell to his officers shows the father of his country drinking a toast with his compatriots. In the 1876 edition the wineglasses and bottle are gone. If teetotalism was the only moral lifestyle, Washington could not possibly be a drinker.

Indeed, late in the first temperance movement, the American Tract Society "reprinted" Philadelphia physician Benjamin Rush's essay against distilled spirits but abruptly truncated the text before his praise of wine and beer. On the other side, many people today may find it more comfortable to remember First Lady Eleanor Roosevelt, for example, as a compassionate social reformer than as an ardent supporter of Prohibition.

N. CURRIER (LEFT) and CURRIER & IVES (RIGHT), MUSEUM OF THE CITY OF NEW YORK

14. Alcohol in American History

First Lady Betty Ford was later a founder of alcohol and drug clinics.

Soldiers, dry during the first world war, drank during the second.

Victims Wall put up by Mothers Against Drunk Driving in Washington, D.C., in 1990 displayed photographs of people who died in alcohol-related crashes.

1940 *1.56 gallons*

1980 *2.76 gallons*

1940			1990
World War II, 1939–1945	MADD founded, 1980	Federal support for age 21 drinking law, 1984	Warning labels on alcoholic beverages, 1989

women to vote, the institution of kindergartens and an attack on tobacco smoking.

Opposition to alcohol legitimized women's participation in national political life. Because women had been relegated to defense of the home, they could reasonably argue that they had a duty to oppose alcohol and saloons—which were efficiently separating men from their paychecks and turning them into drunken menaces to their families.

In each era of reform, people have tried to influence the education of children and to portray alcohol in a new, presumably more correct light. Today the federal Center for Substance Abuse Prevention (CSAP, the successor to the OSAP) works through prevention materials distributed to schools, but the champion of early efforts was the WCTU's Department of Scientific Temperance Instruction. It successfully fought for mandatory temperance lessons in the public schools and oversaw the writing of approved texts. Pupils would learn, among other things, that "the majority of beer drinkers die of dropsy"; "when alcohol passes down the throat it burns off the skin, leaving it bare and burning"; and "alcohol clogs the brain and turns the liver quickly from yellow to green to black."

The WCTU's multifarious agenda hampered its effectiveness, though, and in 1895 national leadership of the antialcohol movement was seized by the Anti-Saloon League, which went on to become the most successful single-issue group in American history. At first, the new organization had as its ostensible goal only abolition of the saloon, a social cesspool that had already elicited wide public outcry. As sentiment against alcohol escalated, however, so did the league's intentions, and finally it aimed at national prohibition.

In 1917, aided by a more general national push for health and fitness, what would become the 18th Amendment passed in both houses of Congress by a two-thirds majority. Two years later it became part of the Constitution, coming into effect in January 1920. In the span of one generation, antialcohol campaigns had reached a point where prohibition seemed reasonable to a political majority of Americans. Although brewers and vintners had attempted to portray their products as wholesome, they could not escape the rising tide against intoxicating beverages of any kind.

The first temperance movement had rallied a broad segment of society alarmed at excessive drinking of spirits; only later did the concern move to alcohol in general. Similarly, this second temperance movement initially focused on that widely criticized feature of urban life, the saloon, and then gradually took aim at all drinking.

THE GREAT EXPERIMENT

Prohibition lasted almost 14 years. On the positive side, the incidence of liver cirrhosis reached an all-time low: the death rate from the condition fell to half its 1907 peak and did not start to increase again until the amendment was repealed. On the negative side, Prohibition was a blatant failure at permanently convincing a large majority of Americans that alcohol was intrinsically destructive, and it made a significant contribution to the growth of already entrenched criminal organizations. These factors—combined after 1929 with the specious hope that revival of the alcoholic beverage industry would help lift the nation out of the Great Depression—all brought about the overwhelming national rejection of Prohibition in 1933.

As we look at the ways in which the U.S. has addressed issues related to alcohol, we might ask whether prohibition is the inevitable—if brief—culmination of temperance movements. Is our Puritan tradition of uncompromising moral stances still supplying righteous energy to the battle against alcohol? During the 1920s, when many nations of the Western world turned against alcohol, a sustained campaign in the Netherlands led by the workers' movement and religious groups reduced alcohol consumption by 1930 to a very low level, but without legal prohibition. Likewise in Britain: the antialcohol movement reduced consumption even though it did not result in legal bans. Apparently, each nation has its own style of control.

Underlying the U.S. travail with alcohol is the persistence of a sharp dichotomy in the way we perceive it: alcohol is either very good or very bad. Those who oppose alcohol doubt that it might have any value in the diet; those who support it deny any positive effect of prohibition. Compromise seems unthinkable for either side.

Dealing with alcohol on a practical level while maintaining either a totally favorable or totally condemnatory attitude is fraught with trouble. The backlash to Prohibition made discussion of the ill effects associated with alcohol extremely difficult, because those worried about drinking problems would often be labeled as straitlaced prudes. Not until another 50 years had passed and new generations had emerged did grass-roots movements such as RID and MADD arise and, without apology, promote new laws against drinking. Yet public acceptance of such restrictions on alcohol consumption has a natural limit that can be exceeded only with great danger to the temperance movement itself: that is the lesson of Prohibition.

During the past 15 years, groups such as RID, MADD and the CSAP, aided by advances in medical understanding, have been transforming the image of alcohol into a somber picture heretofore unknown to the current cohort of Americans. This reframing may bring about a healthy rebalancing of our perception of alcohol. But how far will this trend go?

Can we find a stance toward drink that will be workable in the long term? Or will we again achieve an extreme but unsustainable position that will create a lengthy, destructive backlash? There are some signs of moderation—in particular, recent pronouncements by the U.S. Department of Agriculture that it should be considered permissible for men and women to consume a glass of wine a day to reduce their risk of heart disease—but it is still unclear whether the U.S. will be able to apply history's lessons.

FURTHER READING

DELIVER US FROM EVIL: AN INTERPRETATION OF AMERICAN PROHIBITION. Norman H. Clark. W. W. Norton and Company, 1976.

THE ALCOHOLIC REPUBLIC: AN AMERICAN TRADITION. W. J. Rorabaugh. Oxford University Press, 1979.

TEMPERANCE AND PROHIBITION IN AMERICA: A HISTORICAL OVERVIEW. Paul Aaron and David Musto in *Alcohol and Public Policy: Beyond the Shadow of Prohibition*. Edited by M. Moore and D. Gerstein. National Academy Press, 1981.

DRINKING IN AMERICA: A HISTORY. Mark E. Lender and James K. Martin. Free Press, 1987.

THE TURNING POINT: REPEALING PROHIBITION, Chapter 2. DRINKING, Chapter 3. In *Bad Habits*, by John Burnham. New York University Press, 1993.

Why Suffrage for American Women Was Not Enough

With Hillary Clinton in the White House as the most political First Lady since Eleanor Roosevelt, the role of women in American politics is in sharp focus. Elisabeth Perry explains here, via four case-histories, why American women did not break through in politics between the wars, despite having won the vote.

Elisabeth Perry

Elisabeth Perry directs the graduate programme in Women's History at Sarah Lawrence College, in Bronxville, N.Y. Her most recent publication, The Challenge of Feminist Biography: Writing the Lives of Modern American Women *(Champaign: University of Illinois, 1992) was co-edited with Sara Alpern, Joyce Antler, and Ingrid Winther Scobie.*

As a result of the autumn elections in 1992, a year the American media billed as 'The Year of the Woman', the numbers of women holding elective office in the United States rose to unprecedented heights. The percentage of women office holders at state level climbed to 22.2 per cent for state-wide elected executives and 20.4 per cent for legislators. At the national level, the number of female US Senators tripled (from two to six), while the number in the House of Representatives rose from twenty-eight to forty-seven (there is a forty-eighth, who represents the District of Columbia, but she has no vote). Even with this impressive progress, however, women's share of elective office in the United States remains relatively small.

It is not hard to explain why. Deeply ingrained global traditions have long kept women out of public, authoritative roles. But why have these traditions remained so entrenched in the United States, ostensibly one of the most advanced, modernised countries of the world? A close look at American women's political history in the immediate post-suffrage era might provide a few clues.

American women won the vote in 1920 with the ratification of the Nineteenth Amendment to the federal Constitution. Women had worked for this goal since 1848, when Elizabeth Cady Stanton, a reformer active in the campaigns to abolish slavery and also a temperance advocate, organised a public meeting in Seneca Falls, New York, to discuss women's rights. Many observers ridiculed her demand for the vote. By the turn of the century, this demand had become the focal point of the entire women's movement. Suffrage for women was eventually won in a number of the states, and then nationwide in August, 1920.

By the time this event occurred, women were no longer political novices. For decades they had been organising conventions, giving public speeches, writing editorials, campaigning door-to-door, petitioning and marching. These activities gave them vast political expertise, as well as access to wide networks of other women activists and of male political leaders. This combination of expertise and contacts ought to have placed them at the centre of American political life. It did not.

The winning of female suffrage did not mark the end of prejudice and discrimination against women in public life. Women still lacked equal access with men to those professions, especially the law, which provide the chief routes to political power. Further, when women ran for office—and many did in the immediate post-suffrage era—they often lacked major party backing, hard to come by for any newcomer but for women almost impossible unless she belonged to a prominent political family. Even if successful in winning backing, when women ran for office they usually had to oppose incumbents. When, as was often the case, they lost their first attempts, their reputation as 'losers' made re-endorsement impossible.

American political parties did try to integrate women into their power structures after suffrage. They courted women's votes, especially in the early 1920s, when a 'woman's voting bloc' seemed real. In addition, the parties formed 'women's divisions' or created a committee system of equal numbers of committee women and committee men (with the latter usually choosing the former). But when party leaders sought a candidate for preferment, they tended to look for 'a good man', seldom imagining that a woman might qualify. In short, in the years immediately after suffrage most party leaders confined women to auxiliary, service roles. They expected women to help elect men but not seek office themselves. That party men in the early 1920s held to such an expectation is hardly surprising. That many of the most politically 'savvy' American women went along with them is more difficult to understand.

In the post-suffrage United States, although there were many strong, executive-type women with considerable political expertise, none of them became the vanguard of a new, office-seeking female

---

This article first appeared in *History Today*, September 1993, pp. 36-41. © 1993 by History Today, Ltd. Reprinted by permission.

3. FROM PROGRESSIVISM TO THE 1920s

Courtesy of Elisabeth Perry

Belle Moskowitz with Eleanor Roosevelt at a 1924 political meeting, and (right) a 1931 portrait of Belle Moskowitz by the celebrated photographer, Lewis Hine.

political leadership. Because of women's long exclusion from the vote and political parties, these women had worked for change only in a nonpartisan fashion from within their own gender sphere. After suffrage, in part because men kept them there, they accepted the notion that separate roles for women in politics ought to continue.

The reasons for this acceptance are complex, and probably differ from woman to woman. Some women felt most comfortable operating from within their own sphere. In single-sex groups, they made lifelong friendships with women who shared their interests and problems. In addition, in women's groups they did not have to compete with men for positions of authority. A deep suspicion of electoral politics was yet another important factor. Political women distrusted the world of electoral politics. It was a man's world, a world filled with 'dirty games' that men had been trained to play, and indeed were forced to play, if they wanted to 'get ahead'. For these women, it held few allures. Educated and middle-class, they had not been brought up to be career-orientated or personally ambitious. Rather, they had been taught that their proper role was to serve others and to work for idealistic causes. The winning of the vote did little to change this socialisation.

These were some of the views of women's role in politics held by both men and women in the 1920s. The careers of four suffragists, all politically active in the post-suffrage era and all of whom could have held elective office had circumstances differed, serve to illustrate how these views affected individual lives. The four do not comprise a balanced 'sample', for they were all based in New York City and were all active in the Democratic Party. They are exemplars, however, because they thrived in a hotbed of women's activism in the post-suffrage era. If any woman could have risen into electoral political prominence during that era, she would have been a New York City Democrat.

My first example is Belle Lindner Moskowitz (1877–1933). A shopkeeper's daughter born in Harlem, New York, she spent her early career as a social worker on the city's Lower East Side. After her marriage in 1903, while her children were growing up, she did volunteer work until, by the 1910s, she had developed a city-wide reputation as an effective social and industrial reformer. Although considering herself an independent Republican, in 1918, the first year New York State women voted, because of Democrat Alfred E. Smith's reputation as an advocate for labour, she supported him for governor.

After organising the women's vote for him, Moskowitz proposed that Governor-elect Smith establish a 'Reconstruction Commission' to identify and propose solutions for the state's administrative, social, and economic problems. Smith not only formed the Commission but appointed her its executive director. During the one year of its existence (1919–20), it outlined Smith's legislative programme and launched Moskowitz's career as his closest political advisor. From 1923 on, she ran his state re-election campaigns and guided the legislative enactment of his policies, all the while preparing the ground for his nomination by the Democratic Party as presidential candidate in 1928. In that year, she directed national publicity for the campaign and served as the only woman on the national Democratic Party executive committee.

Al Smith lost that election to Herbert Hoover. But because Belle Moskowitz had played such a central role in his career throughout the 1920s, by the time of his presidential race she was a nationally known political figure. Still, her fame depended on his. Smith had offered her a number of government posts but she had refused them. She believed, and rightly so, that her work from behind the scenes would in the end give her more power than the holding of any bureaucratic, appointive office. Thanks to her, Smith, a man whose formal education had ended at the age of thirteen, was able

Courtesy of Elisabeth Perry

to pursue his legislative programme with enough success to become a viable presidential candidate. But because of her self-effacement, when Smith failed to win the presidency and then lost his party leadership role to Franklin Delano Roosevelt, her career was eclipsed along with his. Future generations of political women would not see her example as an inspiration or model for their own careers.

More famous than Moskowitz, Anna Eleanor Roosevelt (1884–1962) became known worldwide for the role she played as the wife of Franklin Roosevelt, four-

84

15. Suffrage for American Women

term president during the Great Depression and Second World War. Most portraits of Eleanor focus on her activities after 1933, when Franklin became president, until his death in 1945, when she became a United Nations delegate and moral force in world politics. What is less well known is that, before FDR became president, even before he became governor of New York, she had accumulated a vast amount of political experience and influence in her own right.

Unlike Moskowitz, Eleanor Roosevelt was born into wealth and privilege, but endured an unhappy childhood. A measure of fulfillment came to her through her education and volunteer social work. She married Franklin in 1905, bore him several children, and fostered her husband's promising political career. In 1920, this career reached its first culmination when he ran, unsuccessfully, for vice-president. By then their marriage was on shaky ground. Although in 1918 Eleanor had discovered Franklin's affair with Lucy Mercer, the couple had resolved to keep the marriage together. In 1921, Franklin was stricken with polio and withdrew from politics. Franklin's political manager and publicist, Louis Howe, convinced Eleanor to keep her husband's name alive by becoming active herself in women's organisations. Once involved in this work, Eleanor confirmed what she had discovered during her husband's earlier campaigns. She liked politics.

But primarily from within her own sphere. She took up volunteer work for four New York City women's groups: the League of Women Voters and Women's City Club, the Women's Trade Union League, and the Women's Division of the State Democratic Party. For this latter group, from 1925 to 1928 she developed and edited a newspaper that, in bridging the gap between upstate and downstate Democrats, formed a critical base for Al Smith and her husband's future support. Through her other groups she worked for legislation on a variety of important issues: public housing for low-income workers; the dissemination of birth control information, the reorganisation of the state government, and shorter hours and minimum wages for women workers.

To accomplish her goals, she gave talks on the radio and published articles. Journalists interviewed her. She travelled all around the state during and in between campaigns to keep local party leaders connected with one another. She ran the women's campaigns for the Democrats at the state level in 1924 and national level in 1928. As a result, she became a well known figure, almost as well known as her husband, at both state and national level. But when her husband won the governorship in 1928, she gave up all activity. She knew where her duty lay—to become Albany's First Lady, not to hold office herself.

By 1928, in the crucible of New York women's politics, Eleanor Roosevelt had forged for herself acute political skills. These would serve her well as she continued until her husband's death to support his political agendas and afterwards to pursue more directly her own. By 1928, however, she herself had become so prominent that had she wanted she could have run for office and probably won. It did not even occur to her to do so. That was not what women did, especially not women married to ambitious men.

The first woman in the United States to hold cabinet rank was Frances Perkins (1880–1965). Even though she held public office my argument holds true for her as well: her post was appointive, not elective, and she asserted to the end of her life that she had never been interested in a political career. Better educated than either Moskowitz or Roosevelt (she graduated from Mt. Holyoke College), Perkins had a background similar to theirs. After working as a teacher and in a social settlement, she became secretary of the New York Consumers' League, a group seeking labour legislation to improve factory safety and health conditions for all workers. Although always known as 'Miss' Perkins, she was married and bore one child, but her husband suffered from mental illness and was later unable to earn a living. This circumstance gave her a keen interest in finding well paid jobs. Like Moskowitz, she came to admire Al Smith and in 1918 worked for his election as governor. Unlike Moskowitz, when Smith offered her a job as a State Industrial Commissioner, she accepted. This post became the launching pad from which she entered Roosevelt's cabinet in 1933.

Still, when she reflected on her career years later, she denied being a 'career woman' with political ambitions. Doors had opened for her and she had gone through them. She had never dreamed of being Secretary of Labor or Industrial Commissioner, she said. A 'series of circumstances' and her 'own energies' had thrown her into 'situations' where she had assumed responsibility and then was asked to assume more. Before she knew it she 'had a career'.

Here again is an accomplished, talented woman who had matured through social reform and suffrage politics in the 1910s and then moved into appointive office. As she plied her way, although she wanted and needed to work, ideas of personal advancement or career ambition were seldom at the forefront of her thinking. Convinced even at the moment of Roosevelt's elevation of her that she was probably unworthy, she accepted the offer as a 'call to service'. Once she attained office, fearful that men would resist answering to her, she took on the look, dress, and behaviour of a schoolmarm so as to appear less threatening to them. Despite all of her accomplishments, the gender stereotypes and constraints of her time prevailed.

My last example from the period is Mary W. (Molly) Dewson (1874–1962). Like Perkins, Dewson was well educated. After graduating from Wellesley College and holding some research jobs, she became Superintendent of Probation at the nation's first reform school for girls and then executive secretary of the Massachusetts Commission on the Minimum Wage. Never married, she maintained a lifelong partnership with a friend, Polly Porter, with whom she farmed in Massachusetts and did suffrage and war work. Eventually, under the mentorship of Eleanor Roosevelt, Dewson moved into Democratic state and then national politics. Her personal ambitions remained severely limited, however.

When Dewson assessed women's political progress since suffrage, she confessed that their opportunities had barely expanded. usually on the basis of their 'looks, money', or a 'late husband's service to the party', they had received only ceremonial party positions. In these circumstances, Dewson decided that the only way to build women's political strength was through separate women's divisions. As head of the Women's Division of the Democratic National Committee, she organised women workers for FDR's campaigns and co-ordinated support for his programmes between elections. In so doing, she played roles essential to the success of the Democratic Party during the New Deal initiative. Like Perkins, Dewson followed a cautious philosophy in working with men: she took on a maternal or 'aunty'

3. FROM PROGRESSIVISM TO THE 1920s

A 1917 photograph of Molly Dewson who co-ordinated a separate women's effort in the Democratic Party between the wars, but from a traditionalist standpoint.

pose and disclaimed any relationship to feminism. She also turned down posts when they threatened her partnership with Polly Porter. Only in her old age did she finally enter a political race in her own right. But the race she chose was in a solidly-Republican district where she had no chance of winning.

Among the most politically adept of their generation, all four of these women pursued political goals in the 1920s but none as a man would have done. Moskowitz achieved an important advisory role but lost all her power at the fall of her mentor. Roosevelt sacrificed her own needs to those of her husband. Perkins reached high office but masked her strength and denied personal ambition. Dewson often put domestic happiness before career fulfilment and, like Perkins, downplayed her feminism. Others of their generation who had been leaders in the suffrage struggle acted similarly.

When younger women growing up in the 1920s and 30s looked at their political forbears, Belle Moskowitz, Eleanor Roosevelt, Frances Perkins, and Molly Dewson were among the few successful ones they saw. But younger women wanted real careers, not roles as an amanuensis to a man or as a behind-the-scenes campaigner. But 'real careers' were denied them. Either men discriminated against them and kept them out of the central circles of power, or when they married they discovered that domestic life and a political career just did not mix.

The door was open to women in politics in the 1920s. But, as Molly Dewson once said, the battle was uphill and most women got quickly discouraged. By accommodating themselves to a reality they could not control, they participated in the perpetuation of a 'separate spheres ideology' long after it had outlived its relevance. Looking back at them from the standpoint of 1993 we might judge these women as 'old fashioned'. But we ought not reject them as important role models. As smart, wily, and skilled political strategists, they have much to teach us. We must reject not them but the constraints that held them back.

Some of those constraints are still with us. Throughout the 1992 campaign, questions about women's appropriate roles in politics continued to surface. They dominated the controversies that swirled around Hillary Clinton, wife of Democratic presidential candidate, Bill Clinton. What role had she played in his years as governor of Arkansas? Why did she keep her maiden name when they were married? What was the quality of their married life together? Had she been a good mother or was she one of those career-orientated, ambitious feminists?

At its national convention in August, the Republican Party exploited popular doubts about Hillary Clinton's ability to operate in the traditional mode of the political wife. In an unprecedented move, convention organisers asked the wives of its candidates, Barbara Bush and Marilyn Quayle, to speak. The shared theme of the women's speeches, 'traditional' family values, sent out a clear message: political wives must adhere strictly to giving priority to their husbands' careers.

The Democratic Party response disturbed many feminists, but it was probably essential to victory. Hillary Clinton got a makeover. She baked cookies and, in response to rumours that she was childless, trotted out her daughter Chelsea at every possible occasion. Still, when Bill Clinton and his running mate, Albert Gore, Jr., made their victory speeches on election night, women heard some new words on national television. In describing their future government, for the first time in history both president and vice-president-elect included the category of 'gender' as an important test of the diversity they envisioned.

Despite their personal openness to women in government, Hillary Clinton remained vulnerable to further attacks. As a lawyer with a distinguished record of accomplishment concerning the rights of children, she took active part in her husband's transition team discussions. Later, she received an appointment as unpaid head of a task force addressing one of the nation's most pressing problems, the lack of a national health insurance system. In response to a query by the press as to how reporters should refer to her, she asked them to use all three of her names, Hillary Rodham Clinton. The charges flew. Ambitious feminist. Power mad. Who is in charge here? In March 1993, on a flight over Washington DC, an airline pilot joked over the loudspeaker, 'Down below you can see the White House, where the president and her husband live'.

If, on the brink of the twenty-first century, the wife of the President of the United States still cannot perform in an authoritative role without questions being raised about the appropriateness of her behaviour how could the women of the 1920s have stood a chance? Today's 'Hillary factor' shows just how far we have come and how far we have to go before women can at last take up citizenship roles equal to those of men.

FOR FURTHER READING:

Blanche W. Cook, *Eleanor Roosevelt*, volume I (Viking, 1992); J. Stanley Lemons, *The Woman Citizen. Social Feminism in the 1920's* (University of Illinois, 1973); George W. Martin, *Madam Secretary Frances Perkins* (Houghton Mifflin, 1976); Elisabeth Israels Perry, *Belle Moskowitz: Feminine Politics and the Exercise of Power in the Age of Alfred E. Smith* (Routlege, 1992); Susan Ware, *Partner and I: Molly Dewson, Feminism, and New Deal Politics* (Yale University Press, 1987).

Citizen Ford

He invented modern mass production. He gave the world the first people's car, and his countrymen loved him for it. But at the moment of his greatest triumph, he turned on the empire he had built—and on the son who would inherit it.

David Halberstam

Part One
THE CREATOR

Late in the life of the first Henry Ford, a boy named John Dahlinger, who more than likely was Ford's illegitimate son,* had a discussion with the old man about education and found himself frustrated by Ford's very narrow view of what schooling should be. "But, sir," Dahlinger told Ford, "these are different times, this is the modern age and—" Ford cut him off. "Young man," he said, "I invented the modern age."

The American century had indeed begun in Detroit, created by a man of simple agrarian principles. He had started with scarcely a dollar in his pocket. When he died, in 1947, his worth was placed at $600 million. Of his most famous car, the Model T, he sold 15,456,868. Mass production, he once said, was the "new messiah," and indeed it was almost God to him. When he began producing the Model T, it took twelve and a half hours to make one car. His dream was to make one car every minute. It took him only twelve years to achieve that goal, and five years after that, in 1925, he was making one every ten seconds. His name was attached not just to cars but to a way of life, and it became a verb—to *fordize* meant to standardize a product and manufacture it by mass means at a price so low that the common man could afford to buy it.

When Ford entered the scene, automobiles were for the rich. But he wanted none of that; he was interested in transportation for men like himself, especially for farmers. The secret lay in mass production. "Every time I reduce the charge for our car by one dollar," he said early in the production of the T, "I get a thousand new buyers," and he ruthlessly brought the price down, seeking—as the Japanese would some sixty years later—size of market rather than maximum profit per piece. He also knew in a shrewd, intuitive way what few others did in that era, that as a manufacturer and employer he was part of a critical cycle that expanded the buying power of the common man. One year his advertising people brought him a new slogan that said, "Buy a Ford—save the difference," and he quickly changed it to "Buy a Ford—SPEND the difference," for though he was innately thrifty himself, he believed that the key to prosperity lay not in saving but in spending and turning money over. When one of the children of his friend Harvey Firestone boasted that he had some savings, Ford lectured the child. Money in banks was idle money. What he should do, Ford said, was spend it on tools. "Make something," he admonished, "create something."

For better or worse Ford's values were absolutely the values of the common man of his day. Yet, though he shared the principles, yearnings, and prejudices of his countrymen, he vastly altered their world. What he wrought reconstituted the nature of work and began a profound change in the relationship of man to his job. Near the end of this century it was clear that he had played a major part in creating a new kind of society in which man thought as much about leisure time as about his work. Ironically, the idea of leisure itself, or even worse, a leisure culture, was anathema to him. He was never entirely comfortable with the fruits of his success, even though he lived in a magnificent fifty-six-room house. "I still like boiled potatoes with the skins on," he said, "and I do not want a man standing back of my chair at table laughing up his sleeve at me while I am taking the potatoes' jackets off." Of pleasure and material things he was wary: "I have never known what to do with money after my expenses were paid," he said, "I can't squander it on myself without hurting myself, and nobody wants to do that."

Only work gave purpose: "Thinking men know that work is the salvation of the race, morally, physically, socially. Work does more than get us our living; it gets us our life."

---

*Dahlinger, who died in 1984, was baptized in the Ford christening gown and slept as an infant in the crib Henry had used as a baby. His mother was a secretary at the Ford company. —Ed.

3. FROM PROGRESSIVISM TO THE 1920s

As a good farm boy should, he hated alcohol and tobacco, and he once said that alcohol was the real cause of World War I—the beer-drinking German taking after the wine-drinking Frenchman. His strength, in his early years—which were also his good years—was in the purity of his technical instincts. "We go forward without facts, and we learn the facts as we go along," he once said. Having helped create an urbanized world where millions of God-fearing young men left the farm and went to the cities, he was profoundly uneasy with his own handiwork, preferring the simpler, slower America he had aided in diminishing. For all his romanticizing of farm life, however, the truth was that he had always been bored by farm work and could not wait to leave the farm and play with machines. They were his real love.

When Ford was born, in 1863, on a farm in Dearborn, Michigan, the Civil War was still on. His mother died at the age of thirty-seven delivering her eighth child. Henry was almost thirteen at the time. He had idolized her, and her death was a bitter blow. "I thought a great wrong had been done to me," he said. Later in his life he not only moved the house in which he grew up to Greenfield Village, and tracked down the Ford family's very own stove, whose serial number he had memorized, he also had a cousin who resembled his mother dress up in an exact imitation of the way she had and wear her hair in just the same style.

His father's people were new Americans. When the great potato blight had struck Ireland in 1846, ruining the nation's most important crop, that country had been devastated. Of a population of eight million, one million had died, and one million had emigrated to America. Among the migrants was William Ford, who had set off to the magic land with two borrowed pounds and his set of tools. He was a skilled carpenter, and when he arrived, he moved quickly to Michigan, where some of his uncles had already settled, and found work laying railroad track. With his savings he bought some land and built a house, in awe of an America that had so readily allowed him to do so. To William Ford, Ireland was a place where a man was a tenant on the land, and America was a place where he owned it.

Henry Ford started school when he was seven. The basic books were the McGuffey Reader; they stressed moral values but included sections from Dickens, Washington Irving, and other major writers, which enticed many children into a genuine appreciation of literature. Although Ford loved McGuffey, he did not like books or the alien ideas they sometimes transmitted. "We read to escape thinking. Reading can become a dope habit. . . . Book-sickness is a modern ailment." By that he meant reading that was neither technical nor functional, reading as an end in itself, as a pleasure without a practical purpose. But he was wary even of practical volumes. "If it is in a book, it is at least four years old, and I don't have any use for it," he told one of his designers.

What he truly loved was machinery. From the start, he had a gift for looking at a machine and quickly understanding it, not only to repair it but to make it work better. "My toys were all tools," he wrote years later. "They still are!" In his early teens he designed a machine that allowed his father to close the farm gate without leaving his wagon. Watches fascinated him. When he was given a watch at thirteen, he immediately took it apart and put it back together. He soon started repairing watches for his friends. His father complained that he should get paid for this, but he never listened, for it was a labor of love.

His father wanted him to become a farmer, but it was a vain hope. Henry Ford hated the drudgery of the farm. In 1879 he entered his seventeenth year, which in those days was considered maturity. On the first day of December of that year, he left for Detroit, a most consequential departure. He walked to the city, half a day's journey.

DETROIT WAS A TOWN OF 116,000, A PLACE of foundries and machine shops and carriage makers. There were some nine hundred manufacturing and mechanical businesses, many of them one-room operations but some of them large. It was an industrial city in the making. Ten railroads ran through it. As New York City, in the next century, would be a mecca for young Americans interested in the arts, Detroit was just becoming a city with a pull for young men who wanted to work with machines. The surge in small industries was beginning, and a young man who was good with his hands could always find a job.

Ford went to work at James Flower & Brothers, a machine shop with an exceptional reputation for quality and diversity of product. As an apprentice there, Ford was immersed in the world of machinery, working among men who, like himself, thought only of the future applications of machines. He made $2.50 a week, boarded at a house that charged him $3.50 a week, and walked to work. His salary left him a dollar a week short, and as a good, enterprising young man, he set out to make up the difference. Hearing that the McGill Jewelry Store had just gotten a large supply of clocks from another store, Ford offered to clean and check them. That job added another two dollars to his weekly salary, so he was now a dollar a week ahead.

His fascination with watches led him to what he was sure was a brilliant idea. He would invent a watch so elementary in design that it could be mass-produced. Two thousand of them a day would cost only thirty cents apiece to make. He was absolutely certain he could design and produce the watch; the only problem, he decided, was in marketing 600,000 watches a year. It was not a challenge that appealed to him, so he dropped the

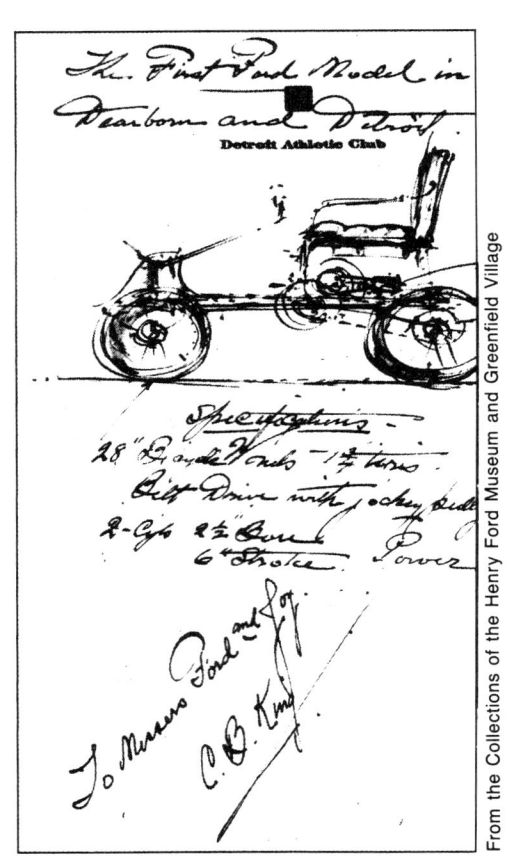

On the fiftieth anniversary of Ford's first car, in 1946, his adviser Charles Brady King made this sketch of it.

16. Citizen Ford

Ford at Detroit Edison in 1893.

By 1896, at the age of thirty-three, Ford finally had his first car on the street. He couldn't sleep for forty-eight hours before driving it.

project. The basic idea, however, of simplifying the product in order to mass-produce it, stayed with him.

He went from Flower & Brothers to a company called Detroit Dry Dock, which specialized in building steamboats, barges, tugs, and ferries. His job was to work on the engines, and he gloried in it, staying there two years. There was, he later said, nothing to do every day but learn. In 1882, however, at the age of nineteen, he returned to the farm, and his father offered him eighty acres of land to stay there. William Ford did that to rescue his wayward son from the city and his damnable machines; Henry Ford took it because he momentarily needed security—he was about to marry Clara Bryant. Nothing convinced him more of his love of machines than the drudgery of the farm. Again he spent every spare minute tinkering and trying to invent and reading every technical magazine he could. He experimented with the sawmill on the farm; he tried to invent a steam engine for a plow. Crude stationary gasoline engines had been developed, and Ford was sure a new world of efficient gasoline-powered machines was about to arrive. He wanted to be part of it. In 1891, with all the timber on the farm cut, he asked Clara to go back to Detroit with him. "He just doesn't seem to settle down," his father said to friends. "I don't know what will become of him."

The last thing Henry Ford was interested in was settling down. He intended, he told his wife, to invent a horseless carriage. But first he needed to know a good deal more about electricity. So he took a job with Detroit Edison at forty-five dollars a month. The city had grown dramatically in the few years since he had first arrived; its population was now more than 205,000. The railroads had begun to open up the country, and, except for Chicago, no town in America had grown as quickly. Detroit now had streetlights. There were more machine shops than ever before. In this city the age of coal and steam was about to end.

By 1896, at the age of thirty-two, Ford finally had his first car on the street. He was so excited by the prospect of his inaugural ride that he barely slept for the forty-eight hours before it. He had been so obsessed and preoccupied during the creation of the car that not until it was time for the test drive did he find that the door of the garage was too small for it to exit. So he simply took an ax and knocked down some of the brick wall to let the automobile out. A friend rode ahead on a bike to warn off traffic. A spring in the car broke during the ride, but they fixed it quickly. Then Henry Ford went home so he could sleep for a few hours before going to work. Later he drove the car out to his father's farm, but William Ford refused to ride in it. Why, he asked, should he risk his life for a brief thrill?

Henry Ford sold that first car for $200 and used the money to start work immediately on his next. It was considerably heavier than the first, and he persuaded a lumber merchant named William Murphy to invest in the project by giving him a ride. "Well," said Murphy when he reached home safely, "now we will organize a company." In August 1899 Murphy brought together a consortium of men who put up $15,000 to finance Ford's Detroit Automobile Company. Ford thereupon left Detroit Edison to work full time on his car.

In February 1900, at the threshold of the twentieth century, Ford was ready to take a reporter from the Detroit *News Tribune* for a ride. The car, he said, would go twenty-five miles an hour. The reporter sensed that he was witness to the dawn of a new era. Steam, he later wrote, had been the "compelling power of civilization," but now the shriek of the steam whistle was about to yield to a new noise, the noise of the auto. "What kind of a noise is it?" the reporter asked. "That is difficult to set down on paper. It is not like any other sound ever heard in this world. It was not like the puff! puff! of the exhaust of gasoline in a river launch; neither is it like the cry! cry! of a working steam engine; but a long, quick, mellow gurgling sound, not harsh, not unmusical, not distressing; a note that falls with pleasure on the ear. It must be heard to be appreciated. And the sooner you hear its newest chuck! chuck! the sooner you will be in touch with civilization's latest lisp, its newest voice." On the trip, Ford and the reporter passed a harness shop. "His trade is doomed," Ford said.

Ford, however, was not satisfied. The cars he was making at the Detroit Automobile Company were not far behind the quality of the cars being made by Duryea or Olds, but they remained too expensive for his vision. Ford desperately wanted to make a cheaper car. His stockholders were unenthusiastic. By November 1900 the company had died. But Ford was as determined as ever to make his basic car, and he decided that the way to call attention to himself and pull ahead of the more than fifty competing auto makers was to go into racing. In 1901 he entered a race to be held in Grosse Pointe. He won and became, in that small, new mechanical world, something of a celebrity. That propelled him ahead of his competitors.

Two years later, in 1903, he set out to start the Ford Motor Company. He was forty years old and had, he felt, been apprenticing long enough. There were 800 cars in the city at that time, and some owners even had what were called motor houses to keep them in. Ford soon worked up his plan for his ideal, inexpensive new car, but he needed money—$3,000, he thought, for the supplies for the prototype (the actual cost was $4,000).

3. FROM PROGRESSIVISM TO THE 1920s

He got the financing from a coal dealer named Alexander Malcomson. Ford and Malcomson capitalized their original company for $150,000, with 15,000 shares. Some of the early investors were not very confident. John Gray, Malcomson's uncle, made a 500 percent return on his early investment but went around saying that he could not really ask his friends to buy into the company. "This business cannot last," he said. James Couzens, Malcomson's assistant, debated at great length with his sister, a schoolteacher, on how much of her savings of $250 she should risk in this fledging operation. They decided on $100. From that she made roughly $355,000. Couzens himself managed to put together $2,400 to invest, and from that, when he finally sold out to Ford in 1919, he made $29 million.

This time Ford was ready. He was experienced, he hired good men, and he knew the car he would build. "The way to make automobiles," he told one of his backers in 1903, "is to make one automobile like another automobile . . . just as one pin is like another pin when it comes from a pin factory, or one match is like another match when it comes from a match factory." He wanted to make many cars at a low price. "Better and cheaper," he would say. "We'll build more of them, and cheaper." That was his complete vision of manufacturing. "Shoemakers," he once said, "ought to settle on one shoe, stove makers on one stove. Me, I like specialists."

But he and Malcomson soon split over the direction of the company: Malcomson, like Ford's prior backers, argued that fancy cars costing $2,275 to $4,775 were what would sell. At the time, nearly half the cars being sold in America fell into this category; a decade later, largely because of Ford, those cars would represent only 2 percent of the market. Malcomson wanted a car for the rich; Ford, one for the multitude. Though the early models were successful—the company sold an amazing total of 1,700 cars in its first 15 months—it was the coming of the Model T in 1908 that sent Ford's career rocketing.

It was the car that Henry Ford had always wanted to build because it was the car that he had always wanted to drive—simple, durable, absolutely without frills, one that the farmer could use and, more important, afford. He was an agrarian populist, and his own people were farmers, simple people; if he could make their lives easier, it would give him pleasure. He planned to have a car whose engine was detachable so the farmer could also use it to saw wood, pump water, and run farm machinery.

THE MODEL T WAS TOUGH, COMPACT, AND light, and in its creation Ford was helped by breakthroughs in steel technology. The first vanadium steel, a lighter, stronger form developed in Britain, had been poured in the United States a year before the planning of the Model T. It had a tensile strength nearly three times that of the steel then available in America, yet it weighed less and could be machined more readily. Ford instantly understood what the new steel signified. He told one of his top men, Charles Sorensen, that it permitted them to have a lighter, cheaper car.

The T was a brilliantly simple machine: when something went wrong, the average owner could get out and fix it. Unimproved dirt tracks built for horses, which made up most of the nation's roads and which defeated fancier cars, posed no problem for it. Its chassis was high, and it could ride right over serious bumps. It was, wrote Keith Sward, a biographer of Ford, all bone and muscle with no fat. Soon the Ford company's biggest difficulty was in keeping up with orders.

Because the Model T was so successful, Ford's attention now turned to manufacturing. The factory and, even more, the process of manufacturing, became his real passions. Even before the T, he had been concerned about the production process. In 1906 he had hired an industrial efficiency expert named Walter Flanders and offered him a whopping bonus of $20,000 if he could make the plant produce 10,000 cars in 12 months. Flanders completely reorganized the factory and beat the deadline by two days. He also helped convince Ford that they needed a larger space. Flanders understood that the increasing mechanization meant that the days of the garage-shop car maker were over. There was a process now, a *line,* and the process was going to demand more and more money and employees. Flanders understood that every small success on the line, each increment that permitted greater speed of production (and cut the cost of the car), mandated as well an inevitable increase in the size of the company. "Henceforth the history of the industry will be the history of the conflict of giants," he told a Detroit reporter.

Ford at the turn of the century.

The way to make cars, Ford said in 1903, is to make one like another, "just as one pin is like another pin, or one match like another match."

FORD THEREUPON BOUGHT HIS HIGHLAND Park grounds. Here he intended to employ the most modern ideas about production, particularly those of Frederick Winslow Taylor, the first authority on scientific industrial management. Taylor had promised to bring an absolute rationality to the industrial process. The idea was to break each function down into much smaller units so that each could be mechanized and speeded up and eventually flow into a straight-line production of little pieces becoming steadily larger. Continuity above all. What Ford wanted, and what he soon got, was a mechanized process that, in the words of Keith Sward, was "like a river and its tributaries," with the subassembly tributaries

16. Citizen Ford

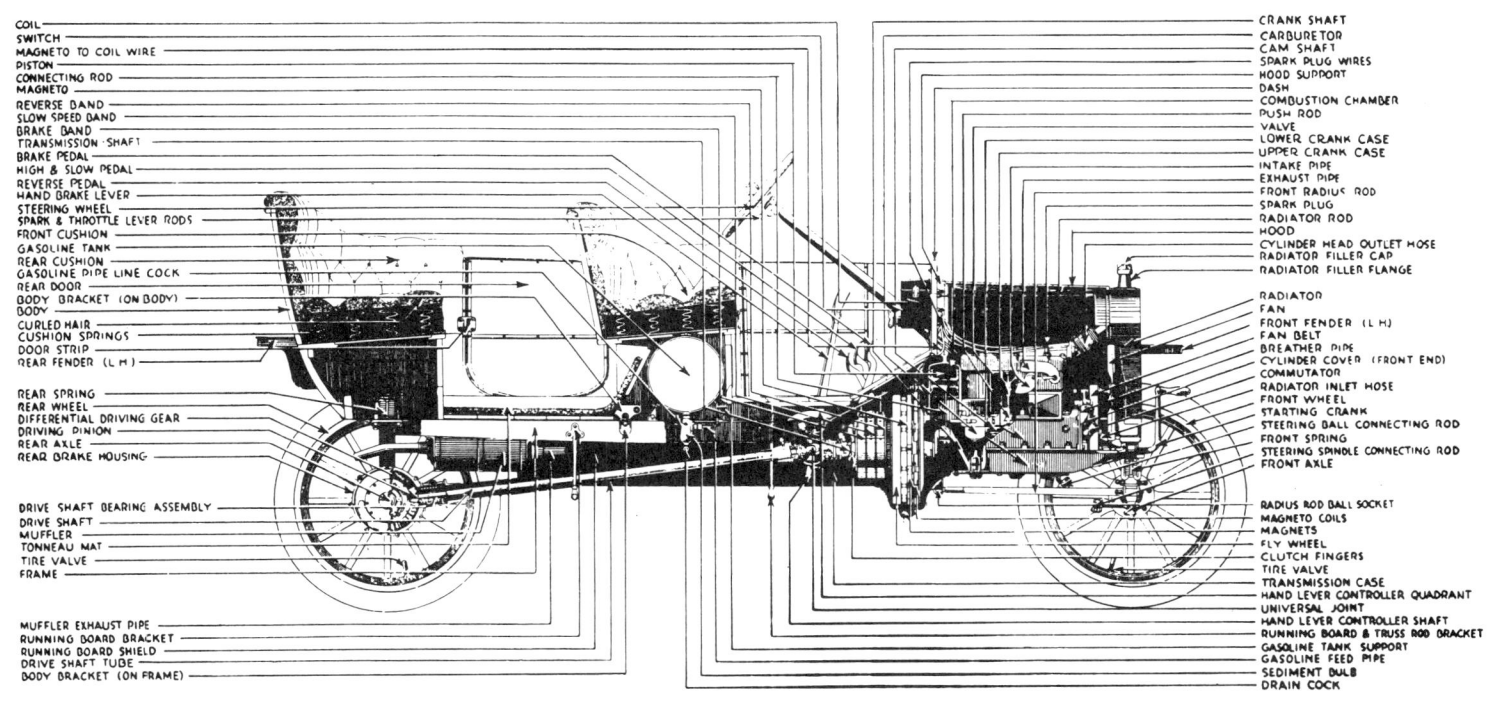

The Ford company issued this diagram showing every component of the Model T in 1913, five years after the car's birth. It was accompanied by the explanation, "The better you know your car the better will you enjoy it."

---

merging to produce an ever-more-assembled car.

The process began to change in the spring of 1913. The first piece created on the modern assembly line was the magneto coil. In the past a worker—and he had to be skilled—had made a fly-wheel magneto from start to finish. An employee could make 35 or 40 a day. Now, however, there was an assembly line for magnetos. It was divided into 29 different operations performed by 29 different men. In the old system it took twenty minutes to make a magneto; now it took thirteen.

Ford and his men quickly imposed a comparable system on the assembly of engines and transmissions. Then, in the summer of 1913, they took on the final assembly, which, as the rest of the process had speeded up, had become the great bottleneck. Until then the workers had moved quickly around a stationary metal object, the car they were putting together. Now the men were to remain stationary as the semifinished car moved up the line through them.

One day in the summer of 1913, Charles Sorensen, who had become one of Ford's top production people, had a Model T chassis pulled slowly by a windlass across 250 feet of factory floor, timing the process all the while. Behind him walked six workers, picking up parts from carefully spaced piles on the floor and fitting them to the chassis. It was an experiment, but the possibilities for the future were self-evident. This was the birth of the assembly line, the very essence of what would become America's industrial revolution. Before, it had taken some thirteen hours to make a car chassis; now they had cut the time of

From the Collections of the Henry Ford Museum and Greenfield Village

An oddly wistful 1912 portrait.

assembly in half, to five hours and fifty minutes. Not satisfied, they pushed even harder, lengthening the line and bringing in more specialized workers for the final assembly. Within weeks they could complete a chassis in only two hours and thirty-eight minutes.

Now the breakthroughs came even more rapidly. In January of 1914 Ford installed his first automatic conveyor belt. It was, he said, the first moving line ever used in an industrial plant, and it was inspired by the overhead trolley that the Chicago meat-packers employed to move beef. Within two months of that innovation, Ford could assemble a chassis in an hour and a half. It was a stunning accomplishment, but it merely whetted his zeal. Everything now had to be timed, rationalized, broken down into smaller pieces, and speeded up. Just a few years before, in the days of stationary chassis assembly, the best record for putting a car together had been 728 minutes of one man's work; with the new moving line it required only 93 minutes. Ford's top executives celebrated their victory with a dinner at Detroit's Pontchartrain Hotel. Fittingly, they rigged a simple conveyor belt to a five-horsepower engine with a bicycle chain and used the conveyor to serve the food

3. FROM PROGRESSIVISM TO THE 1920s

When Ford began making the Model T, the company's cash balance was $2 million; when production ceased, it was $673 million.

around the table. It typified the spirit, camaraderie, and confidence of the early days.

Henry Ford could now mass-produce his cars, and as he did so, he cut prices dramatically. In 1909 the average profit on a car had been $220.11; by 1913, with the coming of the new, speeded-up line, it was only $99.34. But the total profits to the company were ascending rapidly because he was selling so many more cars. When the company began making the Model T, its cash balance was slightly greater than $2 million. Nineteen years and more than 15 million cars later, when Ford reluctantly came to the conclusion that he had to stop making the T, the company balance was $673 million. But this was not the kind of success that merely made a company richer; it was the beginning of a social revolution.

Ford himself knew exactly what he had achieved—a breakthrough for the common man. "Mass production," he wrote later, "precedes mass consumption, and makes it possible by reducing costs and thus permitting both greater use-convenience and price-convenience." The price of the Model T touring car continued to come down, from $780 in the fiscal year 1910-11 to $690 the following year, to $600, to $550, to, on the eve of World War l, $360. At that price he sold 730,041 cars. He was outproducing everyone in the world.

IN 1913 THE FORD MOTOR COMPANY, with 13,000 employees, produced 260,720 cars; the other 299 American auto companies, with 66,350 employees, produced only 286,770. Cutting his price as his production soared, he saw his share of the market surge—9.4 percent in 1908, 20.3 in 1911, 39.6 in 1913, and with the full benefits of his mechanization, 48 percent in 1914. By 1915 the

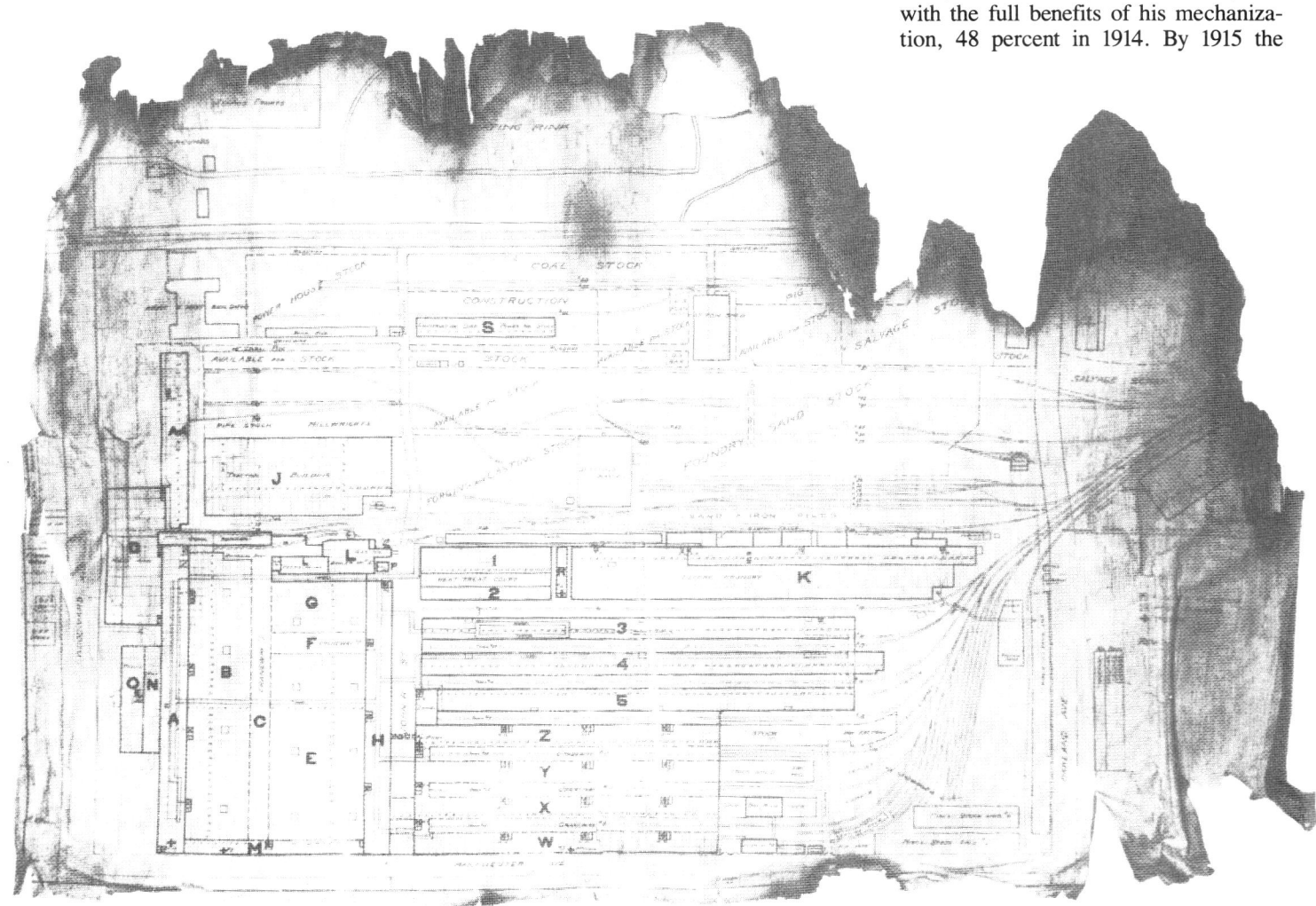

From the Collections of the Henry Ford Museum and Greenfield Village

The only surviving plan of the production line that changed the world and made Ford a billionaire is this badly charred 1918 blueprint of the Highland Park plant.

company was making $100 million in annual sales; by 1920 the average monthly earning after taxes was $6 million. The world had never seen anything remotely like it. The cars simply poured off the line. An early illuminated sign in Cadillac Square said, "Watch the Fords Go By." Ford's dreams, in a startlingly brief time, had all come true. He had lived his own prophecy.

There was a moment, however, in 1909 when Ford almost sold the entire company. William C. Durant, the entrepreneur who put General Motors together from several fledgling companies, felt him out about selling the company. An earlier offer of $3 million had fallen through because Ford wanted cash. This time, his company more successful, Ford demanded $8 million. But again he wanted what he called "gold on the table."

Durant couldn't get the financing.

Ford's timing in holding on to his company, it turned out, had been exquisite. There was no point in designing an Everyman's Car unless the average man could buy fuel cheaply as well. The coming of Ford was almost perfectly synchronized with the discovery in the American Southwest of vast new reserves of oil.

If, as has been said, the American century and the oil century were one and the same thing, then that century began on January 10, 1901, in a field just outside of Beaumont, Texas. The name of the field was Spindletop, so called because of the spindly pines that grew there. For years local children had tossed lighted matches into the field; as the flames hit the strong petroleum vapors seeping up through the soil, there would be a satisfying bang. But anyone who believed that there was real oil beneath the ground was thought an eccentric. Oil was not found in Texas; it was found in places like Pennsylvania, West Virginia, and Ohio. Those states were all Standard Oil territory, and the Rockefeller people had no interest in the Southwest. "I will drink any drop of oil west of the Mississippi," boasted John D. Archbold of Standard.

It was Patillo Higgins, a Beaumont man, who had insisted that there was oil underneath Spindletop, and he had been trying to tap it for several years. It had cost him $30,000 of his own money, and he owed friends an additional $17,000. As each attempt had failed and he had been forced to go to others for financial help in order to continue drilling, his own share of the operation shrank. Higgins's faith had never flagged, but he had become more and more a figure of ridicule in his hometown. "Millionaire," his neighbors nicknamed him. The drilling had gotten harder and harder; just before New Year's Day they had gone through 140 feet of solid rock. That had taken them to a level of 1,020 feet. On January 10 it happened. A geyser of oil roared out of the ground and shot a hundred feet above the derrick. No one had ever seen anything like it before; with it, the word *gusher* came into use.

At first no one could figure out how much oil the field was producing. Some said 30,000 barrels a day, some said

The Model T and its creator, 1921.

As he became one of the most popular men in America, the forces he had set in motion began to summon the darkness in his character.

40,000. Capt. Anthony Lucas, who had become a partner of Higgins, said 6,000, because he had never heard of a larger hole in America. In fact, that one gusher was producing 100,000 barrels a day, roughly 60 percent of the total American production. One new well at Spindletop produced as much as the total from all the 37,000 wells back East in the Rockefeller territory. Within a short time there were five more hits. Eventually analysts found that the oil from the first six holes, some 136 million barrels annually, more than twice surpassed what Russia, then the world's leading petroleum producer, could generate.

Spindletop changed the nature of the American economy and, indeed, the American future. Before the strike, oil was used for illumination, not for energy. (Until 1911 the sales of kerosene were greater than the sales of gasoline.) Spindletop inaugurated the liquid-fuel age in America. The energy of the new age was to be oil, and America suddenly was rich in it.

Texas was providing the gas; Henry Ford was providing the cars. The only limits on him were those imposed by production, and he continued to be obsessed by it. He wanted to put as much of his money as he could back into the factory. He hated bankers and financial people anyway, and he did not want to waste the company's money on stockholders. They were, to his mind, parasites, men who lived off other men's labor. In 1917 the Dodge brothers, who had manufactured many of the early components for Ford and who had been rewarded with sizable amounts of stock, sued him for withholding stock dividends. Some $75 million was at stake. During the trial, Ford testified that putting money back into the plant was the real fun he got from being in business. Fun, the opposing attorney retorted, "at Ford Motor Company expense." Retorted Ford, "There wouldn't be any fun if we didn't try things people said we can't do."

That was the trial in which he referred to the profits he was making as "awful," and when questioned about that by attorneys for the other side, he replied, with absolute sincerity, "We don't seem to be able to keep the profits down." Ford lost the suit, and the court ordered him to pay $19 million in dividends, $11 million of which went to him. The decision probably persuaded him to take as complete control of the company's stock as he

3. FROM PROGRESSIVISM TO THE 1920s

The major production problems had been solved, but labor problems lay ahead when this picture of workers in the Highland Park plant was taken in the 1920s.

could, so that as little money would be wasted as possible. Money to stockholders was a waste, money gone idle; money for the factory was not.

Out of that suit came both the means and the determination to build the River Rouge plant, his great industrial masterpiece, a totally independent industrial city-state. Nothing in the period that followed was too good for the Rouge: it had the best blast furnaces, the best machine tools, the best metal labs, the best electrical systems, the most efficient efficiency experts. Dissatisfied with the supply and quality of the steel he was getting, Ford decided to find out how much it would cost to build a steel plant within the Rouge. About $35 million, Sorensen told him. "What are you waiting for?" asked Ford. Equally dissatisfied with both the availability and the quality of glass, he built a glass factory at the Rouge as well. The price of glass had been roughly thirty cents a square foot early in the life of the T; soon it had soared to $1.50 a foot. With the glass plant at the Rouge, the price came down to twenty cents a foot.

At the Rouge, barges carrying iron ore would steam into the inland docks, and even as they were tying up, huge cranes would be swinging out to start the unloading. Some sixty years later Toyota would be credited for its just-in-time theory of manufacturing, in which parts arrived from suppliers just in time to be part of the final assembly. But in any real sense that process had begun at the Rouge. As Eiji Toyoda, of the Toyota family said in toasting Philip Caldwell, the head of Ford, who in 1982 was visiting Japan: "There is no secret to how we learned to do what we do, Mr. Caldwell. We learned it at the Rouge."

All of this, the creation of the Rouge as the ultimate modern plant, speeded up production even more. Before the opening of the Rouge as an auto plant in 1920 (it had produced submarine chasers for World War I in 1918), it had taken 21 days from the receipt of raw material to the production of the finished car. The Rouge cut that time to 14 days. With the opening of the Rouge steel plant in 1925, it took only 4 days.

The Rouge was Henry Ford's greatest triumph, and with its completion he stood alone as the dominant figure in America and the entire developed world. He had brought the process of manufacture to its ultimate moment; he had given the world the first people's car and by dint of his inventive genius had become

America's first billionaire. He was an immensely popular man as well, the man who had lived the American dream. But even then, forces he had helped set in motion would begin to summon forth the darkness in his character.

Part Two
THE DESTROYER

Henry Ford's strengths eventually became his weaknesses. One notorious example was staying with his basic car far too long, ignoring technological change in the cars themselves while obsessively pursuing technological change in their manufacture. From the very start he fought off every attempt to perfect the Model T. In 1912, while he was off on a trip to Europe, his top engineers made some changes intended to improve the car. Their version of the T was lower and some twelve inches longer. It was a better, smoother-riding vehicle, and his associates hoped to surprise and please him. When he returned, they showed it to him. He walked around it several times, finally approaching the left-hand door and ripping it off. Then he ripped off the other door. Then he smashed the windshield and bashed in the roof of the car with his shoe. During all this he said nothing. There was no doubt whose car the T was and no doubt who was the only man permitted to change it. For years anyone wanting to improve a Ford car ran into a stone wall.

What had been another Ford strength, his use of manpower, also turned sour. The early workers at Ford had been skilled artisans, tinkering with designs as they worked. A job at Ford's, as it was known, had been desirable because Henry Ford was at the cutting edge of technology, always trying to do things better, and men who cared about quality wanted to be a part of his operation. In the early days he had his pick of the best men in Detroit. But the mechanized line changed the workplace. These new jobs demanded much less skill and offered much less satisfaction. The pressure to maximize production was relentless. Men who had prided themselves on their skills and had loved working with machines found themselves slaves to those machines, their skills unsummoned. The machines, they discovered to their rage, were more important than they were. The more the plant was mechanized, the more the work force began to unravel.

At the peak of his power, about 1914.

Every year on his birthday, Ford said, he put on one old shoe to remind himself that he had once been poor and might be poor again.

Men began walking out of the Ford plant.

The turnover in the labor force in 1913, the year of the great mechanization, was 380 percent. It soon became even worse. In order to keep one hundred men working, Ford had to hire nearly a thousand. Ford and his principal business partner, James Couzens, realized they had to stabilize the work force. So they came up with the idea of the five-dollar day—that is, of doubling the existing pay. There were some who thought it was Couzens's idea, though Ford later took credit for it. Perceived by many observers as an act of generosity, it was also an act of desperation. Ford calculated that a five-dollar day would attract the best workers, diminish labor unrest, and thus bring him even greater profits. Besides, he believed, it was a mistake to spend money on the finest machinery and then put those precious machines into the hands of disgruntled, unreliable, perhaps incompetent men.

Ford's instincts were right. Not only did the decision solidify the work force; it was so successful a public relations gesture that it allowed Ford to cut back sharply on his advertising. He liked to refer to it as one of the finest cost-cutting moves he had ever made and insisted that he had no philanthropic intent. This denial of altruism, a young Detroit theologian named Reinhold Niebuhr said later, was "like the assurance of an old spinster that her reputation as a flirt has been grossly exaggerated." Indeed in 1914, 1915, and 1916, the first three years of the five-dollar wage, the Ford Motor Company's profits after taxes were $30 million, $20 million, and $60 million.

To workingmen, the five-dollar day was electrifying. Ford had also instituted an eight-hour workday and with it a third shift, and the day after his announcement of the new wage, 10,000 men turned up at the gates of the plant looking for work. Ford had wanted the pick of workers; the pick he now had. For days the crowds grew, and policemen were needed to keep them under control. It was probably the first time that the fruits of the oil-fueled industrial age had reached down to the average worker. A worker had a grim and thankless job that rarely let him get ahead. He would end his life as he began it, and his children were doomed to the same existence. Now, however, with cheap oil and mass production, the industrial cycle was different. It was more dynamic; it generated much more profit and many more goods, which required customers with money to buy them. The worker became the consumer in an ever-widening circle of affluence.

Ford became perhaps the greatest celebrity of his time. Reporters hung out at his office, and his every word was quoted. That both helped and hurt him, because although he was a certifiable genius in manufacturing and perhaps a semi-genius for a long time in business, much of what he said was nonsense, albeit highly quotable nonsense. On cigarettes: "Study the history of almost any criminal, and you will find an inveterate cigarette smoker." On Jews: "When there is something wrong in this country, you'll find Jews." The Jews, he thought, were particularly unproductive people, and he once vowed to pay a thousand dollars to anyone who would bring him a Jewish farmer, dead or alive. He hated the diet of Americans of his generation—"Most people dig their graves with their teeth," he once said. He was prophetic about the nutritional uses of the soybean and intuitive about the value of whole wheat bread, and he wanted his friends to eat no bread but whole wheat. He felt that people who wore glasses were making a serious mistake; they should throw away their glasses and exercise their eyes. For almost all his adult life, he used unadulterated kerosene as a hair cream. He did this because he had observed, he said, that men who worked in the oil fields always had good heads of hair. "They get their hands filled with the oil, and they are always rubbing their hands through their hair," he said, "and that is the reason they have good hair." One of the jobs of E. G. Liebold, his private secretary, was to keep a gallon of No. 10 light kerosene on hand for Ford's hair and constantly to watch that it did not turn rancid.

On one occasion someone noticed that his shoes did not match; he replied that every year on his birthday he put on one old shoe to remind himself that he had once been poor and might be poor again.

He was in some ways a shy man. In the old Ford factory his office had a window through which he used to crawl in order to escape visitors. Nonetheless he was acutely aware that his name was the company name and that his personal publicity generally helped the company. All news from the Ford Motor Company was about him. He was also a hard man, and he became harder as he became older. He distrusted friendship and thought it made him vulnerable: friends might want something from him. He used a company group called the Sociological Department—allegedly started to help workers with personal problems in finances or health—to check up on employees and find out whether they drank at home or had union sympathies. If they were guilty of either, they were fired. For all his populism, he always took a dim view of the average employee. Men worked for two reasons, he said. "One is for wages, and one is for fear of losing their jobs." He thought of labor in the simplest terms—discipline. He once told a journalist named William Richards, "I

From the Collections of the Henry Ford Museum and Greenfield Village

Edsel and Henry Ford stand with the ten millionth Model T—and the original quadricycle, Ford's first car—shortly after the T made a transcontinental trip in 1924.

have a thousand men who, if I say, 'Be at the northeast corner of the building at 4:00 A.M.,' will be there at 4:00 A.M. That's what we want—obedience."

Even in the days before he became isolated and eccentric, he liked playing cruel tricks on his top people. He loved pitting them against one another. A favorite ploy was to give the identical title to two men without telling either about the other. He enjoyed watching the ensuing struggle. The weaker man, he said, would always back down. He liked the idea of keeping even his highest aides anxious about their jobs. It was good for them, he said. His idea of harmony, his colleague Charles Sorensen wrote, "was constant turmoil." The same sort of thing was going on in the factories. The foremen, the men who ruled the factory floor, were once chosen for their ability; now, increasingly, they were chosen for physical strength. If a worker seemed to be loitering, a foreman simply knocked him down. The rules against workers talking to each other on the job were strict. Making a worker insecure was of the essence. "A great business is really too big to be human," Ford himself once told the historian Allan Nevins.

Slowly, steadily, in the twenties, Henry Ford began to lose touch. He had played a critical role in breeding new attitudes in both workers and customers. But as they changed, he did not, and he became more and more a caricature of himself. "The isolation of Henry Ford's mind is about as near perfect as it is possible to make it," said Samuel Marquis, a Detroit minister who had headed the Sociological Department when its purpose had been to help the employees and who later became its harshest critic.

The Ford Motor Company was no longer a creative operation focused on an exciting new idea and headed by an ingenious leader. For its engineers and designers, the company, only a decade earlier the most exciting place to work in America, was professionally a backwater. Sycophants rose, and men of integrity were harassed. Rival companies were pushing ahead with technological developments, and Ford was standing pat with the Tin Lizzie. His own best people became restless under his narrow, frequently arbitrary, even ignorant, policies. He cut off anyone who disagreed with him. Anyone who might be a threat within the company because of superior leadership ability was scorned as often and as publicly as possible.

EVENTUALLY HE DROVE OUT BIG BILL Knudsen, the Danish immigrant who was largely responsible for gearing up the Ford plants during World War I and was widely considered the ablest man in the company. Knudsen was a formidable production man who had been in charge of organizing and outfitting the Model T assembly plants; he had set up fourteen of them in two years. But his prodigious work during World War I made him a target of perverse attacks by Henry Ford. Knudsen was a big, burly man, six foot three and 230 pounds, and he drank, smoked, and cursed, all of which annoyed the puritanical Ford. Worse, Knudsen was clearly becoming something of an independent figure within the company. He was also drawing closer to Ford's son, Edsel, believing him a young man of talent, vision, and, most remarkable of all, sanity. Together they talked of trying to improve the Model T. All of this merely infuriated the senior Ford and convinced him that Knudsen was an intriguer and becoming too big for his place. Ford took his revenge by making a great show of constantly countermanding Knudsen's production decisions. Knudsen became frustrated with these public humiliations and with the company's failure to move ahead technologically. He finally told his wife that he did not think he could work there any longer. He was sure he was going to have a major confrontation with Henry Ford.

"I can't avoid it if I stay," he said, "and I can't stay and keep my self-respect. I just can't stand the jealousy of the place any more."

"Then get out," she said.

"But I'm making $50,000 a year. That's more money than we can make anywhere else."

"We'll get along," she said. "We did before you went to work there."

In 1921 he quit, virtually forced out. "I let him go not because he wasn't good, but because he was too good—for me," Ford later said.

Knudsen went to General Motors for a starting salary of $30,000, but GM soon put him in charge of its sluggish Chevrolet division. It was the perfect time to join GM. Alfred P. Sloan, Jr., was putting together a modern automotive giant, building on Ford's advances in simplifying the means of production and bringing to that manufacturing success the best of modern business practices. Within three years of Knudsen's arrival, GM became a serious challenger to Ford.

By the early twenties the rumblings from Ford's dealers were mounting. They begged him to make changes in the Model T, but he had become so egocentric that criticism of his car struck him as criticism of himself. Ford defiantly stayed with the Model T. Perhaps 1922 can be considered the high-water mark of Ford's domination of the market. The company's sales were never higher, and with an average profit of $50 a car, it netted more than $100 million. From then on it was downhill. As Chevy made

In 1927, last year of the Model T.

After he built his fifteen millionth Model T, Ford's domination over a market that he himself had created came to an end.

its challenge, the traditional Ford response—simply cutting back on the price—no longer worked. The success of that maneuver had been based on volume sales, and the volume was peaking. From 1920 to 1924 Ford cut its price eight times, but the thinner margins were beginning to undermine Ford's success. The signs got worse and worse. For the calendar year ending February 1924, the Ford company's net profit was $82 million; of that only $41 million came from new cars, and $29 million came from the sales of spare parts. If anything reflected the stagnation of the company, it was that figure.

In 1926 Ford's sales dropped from 1.87 million to 1.67. At the same time, Chevy nearly doubled its sales, from 280,000 to 400,000. America's roads were getting better, and people wanted speed and comfort. In the face of GM's continuing challenge, Henry Ford's only response was once again to cut prices—twice in that year. The Model T was beginning to die. Finally, in May of 1927, on the eve of the manufacture of the fifteenth million Model T, Henry Ford announced that his company would build a new car. The T was dead. His domination over a market that he himself had created was over. With that he closed his factories for retooling, laying off his workers (many of them permanently).

The new car was the Model A. It had shock absorbers, a standard gearshift, a gas gauge, and a speedometer, all things that Chevy had been moving ahead on and that Ford himself had resisted installing. In all ways it seemed better than its predecessor, more comfortable, twice as powerful, and faster. When it was finally ready to be revealed, huge crowds thronged every showplace. In Detroit one hundred thousand people turned up at the dealerships to see the unveiling. In order to accommodate the mob in New York City, the manager moved the car to Madison Square Garden. Editorials ranked the arrival of the Model A along with Lindbergh's solo transatlantic flight as the top news story of the decade. The car was an immense success. Even before it was available, there were 727,000 orders on hand. Yet its success was relatively short-lived, for once again Henry Ford froze his technology. Even the brief triumph of the Model A did not halt the downward spiral of the company. Henry Ford remained locked into the past. The twenties and thirties and early forties at Ford were years of ignorance and ruffianism. Henry Ford grew more erratic and finally senile. At the end of his life he believed that World War II did not exist, that it was simply a ploy made up by the newspapers to help the munitions industry. No one could reach the old man any more. His became a performance of spectacular self-destructiveness, one that would never again be matched in a giant American corporation. It was as if the old man, having made the company, felt he had a right to destroy it.

With Knudsen's departure, the burden of trying to deal with Ford fell on his son, Edsel. Gentle and intelligent, Edsel Ford reflected the contradictions in his

3. FROM PROGRESSIVISM TO THE 1920s

The trim little Model A appeared in 1927: "Excitement could hardly have been greater," said the New York *World* of the crowd shown here, "had Pah-Wah, the sacred white elephant of Burma, elected to sit for seven days on the flagpole of the Woolworth Building."

father's life. He had been born while the Fords were still poor. (As a little boy, Edsel had written Santa Claus a letter complaining: "I haven't had a Christmas tree in four years and I have broken all my trimmings and I want some more.") By the time he entered manhood, his father was the richest man in the country, unsettled by the material part of his success and ambivalent about the more privileged life to which his son was being introduced. Henry Ford wanted to bestow on his son all possible advantages and to spare him all hardship, but, having done that, he became convinced that Edsel was too soft to deal with the harsh, brutal world of industry, symbolized by nothing better than the Ford Motor Company.

Edsel was not a mechanical tinkerer himself, but he had spent his life in the auto business, and he knew who in the company was good and who was not; he was comfortable with the engineers and the designers. Edsel knew times were changing and that the Ford Motor Company was dying. During his father's worst years, Edsel became a magnet for the most talented men in the company, who came to regard his defeats as their defeats. He was a capable executive, and an exceptionally well-trained one: his apprenticeship was full and thorough—and it lasted thirty years. Absolutely confident in his own judgment about both people and cars, Edsel Ford was beloved by his friends and yet respected in the automobile business for his obvious good judgment. "Henry," John Dodge, Henry Ford's early partner and later his rival, once said, "I don't envy you a damn thing except that boy of yours."

Edsel was the first scion of the automotive world. He married Eleanor Clay, a member of the Hudson family that ran Detroit's most famous department store. They were society, and the marriage was a great event, the two worlds of Detroit merging, the old and the new, a Ford and a Clay. Henry Ford hated the fact that Edsel had married into the Detroit elite and had moved to Grosse Pointe. He knew that Edsel went to parties and on occasion took a drink with his friends, not all of whom were manufacturing people and some of whom were upper class—worse, upper-class citified people—and was sure all this had corrupted him. It was as if Edsel, by marrying Eleanor, had confuted one of Henry Ford's favorite sayings: "A Ford will take you anywhere except into society."

ON TOP OF ALL HIS OTHER BURDENS, it was Edsel's unfortunate duty to represent the future to a father now absolutely locked in a dying past. Genuinely loyal to his father, Edsel patiently and lovingly tried to talk Henry Ford into modernizing the company, but the old man re-

16. Citizen Ford

Reluctant author of the Model A, 1928.

By the 1930s the business community had begun to turn against Ford: Fortune called him "the world's worst salesman."

garded his son's loyalty as weakness and spurned him and his advice.

When everyone else in the company agreed that a particular issue had to be brought before the old man, Edsel became the designated spokesman. With Knudsen now gone, he usually stood alone. He was probably the only person who told the truth to his father. Others, such as Sorensen, were supposed to come to Edsel's defense during meetings with Henry, but they never did. Sorensen, brutal with everyone else in the company but the complete toady with the founder, always turned tail in the face of Henry Ford's opposition.

All the while the competition was getting better faster. Chevy had hydraulic brakes in 1924; Ford added them fourteen years later. Because Chevy had already gone to a six-cylinder car, Edsel pleaded even more passionately with his father to modernize the Ford engine. A six, his father retorted, could never be a balanced car. "I've no use for an engine," he said, "that has more spark plugs than a cow has teats." After all, he had built one back in 1909, and he had not liked it.

The six-cylinder engine, more than any other issue, stood between the two Fords. The quintessential story about Henry Ford and the six-cylinder engine—for it reflects not just his hatred of the new but his contempt for his son as well—concerns a project that Edsel and Laurence Sheldrick, the company's chief engineer, had been working on. It was a new engine, a six, and Edsel believed he had gotten paternal permission to start experimenting with it. He and Sheldrick labored for about six months and they were delighted with the prototype. One day when they were just about ready to test it, Sheldrick got a call from Henry Ford.

"Sheldrick," he said, "I've got a new scrap conveyor that I'm very proud of. It goes right to the cupola at the top of the plant. I'd like you to come and take a look at it. I'm really proud of it."

Sheldrick joined Ford for the demonstration at the top of the cupola, where they could watch the conveyor work. To Sheldrick's surprise, Edsel was there too. Soon the conveyor started. The first thing riding up in it, on its way to becoming junk, was Edsel Ford's and Larry Sheldrick's engine.

"Now," said the old man, "don't you try anything like that again. Don't you ever, do you hear?"

In 1936, his company under mounting pressure, Henry Ford reluctantly built a six-cylinder engine. It went into production a year later. But moves like this were too late. By 1933, *Fortune,* reflecting the growing scorn and indeed the contempt of the business community that Henry Ford had once dazzled, called him "the world's worst salesman."

He became more and more distant from the reality of his own company. As he became more senile and more threatened by growing pressure from a restive labor force, he began to cut back on the power of Charlie Sorensen and grant it instead to Harry Bennett, who was head of the company's security forces. Sorensen had been a savage man, hated by many, capable of great cruelty, eager to settle most disputes with his fists, but at least he knew something about production. Bennett was worse. An ex-seaman who had boxed professionally under the name of Sailor Reese, he had come to power in the post-World War I days, when his assignment was to hire bullies and ex-cons and wrestlers and boxers to help control the plant and keep the union out. Bennett was well suited for that role. His was an empire within an empire, and that inner empire was built on fear. He padded his pockets with Ford money—the finances of the company were in chaos. He built at least four houses with his appropriated wealth. His rise exactly paralleled the decline of the old man, and he played on all the fears the old man had, especially fear of labor and fear of kidnapping. Ford was convinced that Bennett, with his connections in the underworld, could stop any attempt to kidnap his son or grandchildren. Ford loved the fact that Bennett used force to intimidate people. "Harry gets things done in a hurry," he liked to say.

To the distress of Ford's family, Bennett's power over Henry grew almost without check in the 1930s, when the founder was in his seventies. Board meetings were a travesty. Often Ford did not show up. Or he would walk in at the last minute with Bennett and after a few minutes say, "Come on, Harry, let's get the hell out of here. We'll probably change everything they do anyway." Once a magazine writer was in a car with Ford and Bennett, and he asked Ford who was the greatest man he had ever known—after all, in so rich and varied a career he had known quite a few exceptional people. Ford simply pointed at Bennett.

At the very end he used Bennett as his principal weapon against his son. The last years were truly ugly. Sure that he was protected by Ford, Bennett harassed Edsel mercilessly. The old man took obvious pleasure in Edsel's humiliations. Already emotionally beaten down by his father, Edsel had become a sick man. He had remained loyal to his father and endured his humiliations while healthy. Now, battling stomach cancer, he had less and less to fight back with. Edsel's last years were very difficult, as he struggled to expedite the war-production work his father hated while at the same time resisting his illnesses. In 1942 Edsel got undulant fever from drinking milk from his father's dairy; Ford disapproved of

3. FROM PROGRESSIVISM TO THE 1920s

pasteurization. The old man blamed it on Edsel's bad habits. In 1943 Edsel died. He was only forty-nine. Almost everyone who knew both Henry and Edsel Ford thought the son had really died of a broken heart.

This was the final, malevolent chapter in Henry Ford's own life. Not only had he destroyed his son, he had all but ruined a once-great industrial empire. By the middle of the war, the Ford Motor Company was in such poor shape that high government officials pondered whether to take it over, for the government had to keep the giant going. Without the stimulus of the war and the work it eventually brought the company, it is possible that Ford might have failed completely. As the government debated, two women stepped forward. Clara Bryant Ford and Eleanor Clay Ford, one Henry Ford's wife and the other Edsel's widow, had watched it all with dismay— the old man's senility, the crushing of Edsel, the rise of Bennett—but with a certain helplessness. "Who is this man Bennett who has such power over my husband and my son?" Clara Ford once asked. She had hated the fact that Bennett and Sorensen had both taken it upon themselves to speak for Henry against Edsel and had participated in and encouraged his destruction. Now both women feared that the same forces might prevent young Henry, Edsel's son, from ascending and assuming power.

Henry Ford II had been serving in the Navy during the war, enjoying a taste of personal freedom. But in August 1943, thanks to intervention by his mother and grandmother, he got orders sending him back to Detroit; the nation's highest officials feared that, after Edsel's death, Harry Bennett might actually take over the company. Young Henry returned reluctantly, but he was the firstborn of Edsel Ford, and familial obligation demanded it. He had no illusions about the challenge ahead. He was well aware that, except for a very few men, the Ford Motor Company was a corrupt and corrupting place.

BENNETT AND SORENSEN IMMEDIATELY began belittling him, Bennett by undoing what Henry was attempting to do each day and Sorensen by demeaning him in front of other people and by always calling him "young man." "He might just as well have called me Sonny," Henry later told friends. Henry Ford II might have titular power—he was named vice president in December 1943—and the power of blood, but unless his grandfather moved aside and Bennett left the company, he would never be able to take control. Even Sorensen was in the process of being destroyed by Bennett, and young Henry seemed very vulnerable. Again Eleanor Clay Ford put her foot down and forced an issue. Widowhood had stirred in her the kind of indignation her husband had always lacked. He had been too loyal to challenge his father, but now Edsel's company stock was hers to vote. She threatened to sell it unless old Henry moved aside in favor of his grandson. Her son would not be destroyed as her husband had been. Clara Bryant Ford backed her completely. They fought off the old man's excuses and his delaying ploys. With that threat, and a sense that these women were intensely serious, Henry Ford finally, furiously, gave up, and Henry Ford II took control.

The young man—he was just twenty-eight—had not served the long apprenticeship his father had, and he had only the scantest knowledge of the vast and complicated world he inherited. But it soon became clear that he was shrewd and tough. Through the most unsparing work he mastered the business; and he got rid of Harry Bennett. "You're taking over a billion-dollar organization here that you haven't contributed a thing to!" Bennett yelled. But, having no other recourse, he left.

In the end Henry Ford II broke all of Bennett's cronies and put an end to the bad old era. But there was no way to escape the complex legacy of the founder.

Once a popular figure with the average man, Henry Ford had become known as one of the nation's leading labor baiters. He had helped usher in a new age of economic dignity for the common man, but he could not deal with the consequences. His public statements during the Depression were perhaps the most pitiless ever uttered by any capitalist. He repeatedly said that the Depression was good for the country and the only problem was that it might not last long enough, in which case people might not learn enough from it. "If there is unemployment in America," he said, "it is because the unemployed do not want to work." His workers, embittered by his labor policies, marched against him and were put down by Bennett's truncheons and guns. His security people were so vicious that when Ford's workers marched against the company, the workers wore masks over their faces to hide their identities—something rare in America. Nothing could have spoken more eloquently of tyrannical employment practices.

IN BUSINESS HENRY FORD WAS OVERTAKEN by General Motors, which relentlessly modernized its design, its production, and its marketing. GM fed the appetites Ford had helped create. In addition, GM inaugurated a dynamic that haunted the Ford company for the next fifty years; buyers started out driving Fords when they were young and had little money, but slowly, as their earnings rose, they graduated to more expensive GM cars. As a workingman's hero, Ford was replaced by FDR. What had once been charming about his eccentricity now became contemptible.

Nothing reflected his failures more tellingly than the fate of the River Rouge manufacturing complex. It was an industrial masterpiece, and it should have stood long after his death as a beacon to the genius of its founder. But the treatment of human beings there had been so mean and violent, the reputation of the Rouge so scurrilous, that in the postwar era it stood as an embarrassment to the new men running Ford, a reputation that had to be undone.

The bequeathment had other unfortunate aspects. By fighting the unions so unalterably for so long, Ford and the other Detroit industrialists had ensured that, when the unions finally won power, they would be as strong as the companies themselves, and that there would be a carry-over of distrust and hatred. There were other, more concrete, burdens as well. Because he had been locked in the past and had frozen his technology, the company was on the verge of bankruptcy.

Probably no major industrial company in America's history was ever run so poorly for so long. By the beginning of 1946, it was estimated, Ford was losing $10 million a month. The chaos was remarkable, but some of it, at least, was deliberate. The old Henry Ford hated the government and in particular the federal income tax, and by creating utter clerical confusion he hoped to baffle the IRS. He also hated bookkeepers and accountants; as far as he was concerned, they were parasitical. When Arjay Miller, who later became president of the company, joined Ford in 1946, he was told to get the profit forecast for the next month.

16. Citizen Ford

Miller went down to the Rotunda, where the financial operations were centralized, or at least supposed to be. There he found a long table with a lot of older men, who looked to him like stereotypes of the old-fashioned bookkeeper. These men were confronted by bills, thousands of bills, and they were dividing them into categories—A, B, C, D. The piles were immense, some several feet high. To Miller's amazement the bookkeepers were actually estimating how many million dollars there were per foot of paper. That was the system.

Miller asked what the estimates for the following month's profits were. One of the men working there looked at him and asked, "What do you want them to be?"

"What?" asked Miller.

"I can make them anything you want."

He meant it, Miller decided. It was truly a never-never land.

It was not surprising, then, that the young Henry Ford, seeking to bring sense to the madness he found all around him, turned to an entirely new breed of executive—the professional managers, the bright, young financial experts who knew, if not automobiles and manufacturing plants, then systems and bottom lines. To them Henry Ford II gave nearly unlimited power. And they, in turn, would in the years to come visit their own kind of devastation on the company. The legacy of what the old man had done in his last thirty years left a strain of tragic unreason in the inner workings of the company. So, once again did the past influence the future. For the past was always present.

TO FIND OUT MORE There has been a great deal written about Henry Ford—in fact two large new biographies have come out this year—but one older book that David Halberstam found particularly readable was Keith Sward's "irreverent" *The Legend of Henry Ford,* originally published in 1948 and reissued as a paperback by Atheneum in 1968. There is also, he said, a "very good small book" by Anne Jardim, *The First Henry Ford,* published by the MIT Press in 1970. Allan Nevins's trilogy, *Ford,* much praised by scholars, is no longer in print but is still available in libraries. For a vivid sense of the man's life, readers can visit Henry Ford's Greenfield Village in Dearborn, Michigan, which is open year-round. Writing about this "stupendous" museum in the December 1980 issue of American Heritage, Walter Karp said that the collection reflects Ford's mind so intimately that it becomes almost a three-dimensional autobiography.

When White Hoods Were in Flower

Bernard A. Weisberger

This month's historical reflections are inspired by the presidential candidacy of David Duke, a former Imperial Wizard of the Ku Klux Klan, whose elevation to at least marginal respectability reminds me uncomfortably of a time when the Klan was functioning openly and aboveground and was a very palpable force in American politics.

The "original" Knights of the Ku Klux Klan, the "invisible empire" of hooded nightriders immortalized in *The Birth of a Nation* and *Gone with the Wind,* got its start in 1866 in the defeated former Confederacy. Whatever its exact origins, its purpose soon became to drive freed blacks and their Northern allies away from the polling places and back into a state of economic and political subservience. It "persuaded" by fires, floggings, and lynchings. Forget the romantic mush; it was an outlawed terrorist organization, designed to undo Reconstruction. And with its help, Reconstruction was undone. But so, by 1872, was the Klan. However, in 1915 it underwent a second ten- to fifteen-year incarnation, of which more in a moment. That is the main story here.

During the 1950s a third, "new" Klan—or perhaps several successive new Klans—emerged, in reaction to the legal dismantling of Jim Crow, sometimes called the Second Reconstruction. Like the original KKK, the groups functioned in the South, and they were responsible for bombings and the gunshot murders of at least five civil rights workers. Post-1970 Klans have had a large, changing, Cold War-influenced list of enemies, allies, and strategies. All have led a furtive existence under legal surveillance and almost universal repudiation.

But it wasn't so with that "middle" Klan that lived in the atmosphere of World War I and the 1920s. That one targeted Catholics, Jews, and foreigners as well as blacks. In so doing, it expanded its base beyond Dixie and had more national influence than is pleasant to think about.

The evidence? How about a parade of forty thousand robed and proud-of-it Klansmen down Pennsylvania Avenue in Washington, D.C.? Or a state—Indiana—whose KKK "Grand Dragon" held a political IOU—one of many—from the mayor of Indianapolis promising to appoint no person to the Board of Public Works without his endorsement? Or a Democratic National Convention of 1924 that split down the middle of a vote to condemn the Klan by name, with just over half the delegates refusing?

This new Klan was the creation of Alabama-born "Colonel" William J. Simmons, who resuscitated fading memories of the original Knights in a Thanksgiving Day cross-burning ceremony atop Stone Mountain, Georgia, in 1915. Its credo not only pledged members to be "true to the faithful maintenance of White Supremacy" but restricted the membership to "native born American citizens who believe in the tenets of the Christian religion and owe no allegiance . . . to any foreign Government, nation, political institution, sect, people or person." The "person" was the Pope, and the new KKK tapped into a long-standing tradition of nativism that went back at least as far as the American or Know-Nothing party of the 1850s, which flared transiently in the cloudy political skies just before the Civil War.

Simmons kept and improved on the primal Klan's ritual mumbo jumbo, including secret initiations and an array of officeholders with titles like Imperial Wizard, Exalted Cyclopes, and Grand Goblin. He struck an alliance with a publicist named Edward Clarke who helped devise a deft recruiting scheme. Recruiters called Kleagles signed up members for local chapters (Klaverns) at ten dollars a head. The Kleagle kept four dollars; one dollar went to the state's King Kleagle, fifty cents to the Grand Goblin, and so on up the chain of command, with two dollars to Simmons himself.

For many native-born, white, Gentile Americans, joiners by nature, the new Klan became a special lodge, like the Elks, the Rotarians, or Woodmen of the World, for which Simmons had been a field organizer. There were four million Klansmen by 1924, according to some estimates, in a population that turned out only about thirty million voters in that year's presidential election. So it became prudent for some politicians, President Harding included, to join the KKK or at least seek its support. According to Wyn C. Wade, author of *The Fiery Cross,* one of the latest books on the Klan, the number of municipal officials elected nationwide by Klan votes has yet to be counted. The organization likewise had input in the choice of more than a dozen senators and eleven governors.

The Klan's greatest victories were in Indiana, whose Grand Dragon, purple-robed David C. Stephenson, was a gifted publicist who organized a women's auxiliary and staged barbecues and picnics, which he visited by dropping from the sky in an airplane with gilded wings. He made enough on the regalia and literature concessions to live in princely style, with lots of clandestine booze and women available. And he endorsed a slate of state candidates that swept Indiana's Republican Convention in 1924 and followed Calvin Coolidge to victory in the fall. Stephenson's dreams of the future for himself included a Senate seat and perhaps even the White House.

What made these astonishing successes possible? Was the whole country gripped by a fever of hatred? Yes and no. Racism and xenophobia actually were enjoying a favorable climate. The KKK's rebirth in 1915 coincided with the success of *The Birth of a Nation,* which depicted the original Klan as a necessity to save Southern civilization from barbaric blacks egged on by Radical Republican plunderers. This was not much of an exaggeration of the "official" version of Reconstruction then embalmed in scholarly histories, but D. W. Griffith's cinematic skills burned it into the popular mind.

At the same time, a wave of immigration from Southern and Eastern Europe troubled "old stock" Americans. In 1924 the immigration laws were rewritten specifically to keep out such indigestible Catholic and Jewish hordes, as they were considered.

THEN THERE WAS THE EXPERIENCE OF World War I, in which "100 percent Americanism" was enforced by vigilante groups and by the government, armed with Espionage and Sedition acts. Following that, the Bolshevik Revolution inaugurated a Red scare that brought a frantic search for "agitators" to arrest or deport.

All these forces predisposed potential Klan members to accept its exclusionary message without much analysis—and to overlook incidents of violence. But there was more. Thousands of fundamentalist Christians, beleaguered and bewildered by the Progressive Era victories of evolution and the social gospel—not to mention jazz, gin, and short skirts—saw the Klan as the savior of oldtime religion.

The KKK played to their anxiety by supporting Prohibition and the teaching of religion in the schools. Had the Moral Majority then been in existence, it might have absorbed some who instead became Klan followers.

It was the onrush of change, the shakeups brought by radio and film and the auto, that spooked so many Americans. My friend David Chalmers, author of *Hooded Americanism,* put it neatly to me by phone. "They couldn't blame Henry Ford or Charles Steinmetz [the socialist engineering genius of the General Electric Company], but happily they found 'the dago on the Tiber' " instead.

In the 1920s the KKK expanded its base beyond Dixie and had far more national influence than is pleasant to think about.

But change could not be held back for long. In the mid-twenties the Klan's strength dropped off dramatically, to forty-five thousand by 1930. There were many reasons. One was internal feuding among Klan leaders over control of the organization's assets. Another was the exposure of Klan-led bombings, beatings, threats, and atrocities by courageous newspapers like the Indianapolis *Times,* the Memphis *Commercial Appeal,* and the Columbus (Georgia) *Enquirer-Sun.* They resisted boycotts and other forms of pressure in the heart of the enemy's country and told the truth. So did many courageous politicians who repudiated the votes of bigotry. Revelations that some Klan officials were given to liquor, loot, and lechery also defaced the "knightly" image. The biggest scandal of all sent Grand Dragon Stephenson to jail for the brutal rape of Madge Oberholtzer, a young state employee, who afterward committed suicide. Stephenson, outraged that the Indiana authorities did not set him above the law, avenged himself by squealing on his political puppets and ruining their subsequent careers.

AND OVER TIME THE SECOND KLAN WAS repudiated because it collided with the fundamental American values of inclusiveness and pluralism. The trouble is that it also expressed equally durable American attitudes: the ongoing quest for an unalloyed "Americanism," the perverse pressure to conform to a single majority standard, and the tendency to substitute mob "justice" for the unsatisfying ambiguities of legal verdicts.

It seems that current historians, unencumbered by having lived through the period's hostilities, are more inclined to explain than to condemn the Klan of the twenties. Most of its members, they suggest, were tradition-bound outsiders to the emerging new urban money culture, more frightened than vicious. I am unpersuaded, even while acknowledging that "good" people can join "bad" associations out of understandable frustrations. But the Klan could not be separated from its hateful implications then, and the Klan spirit cannot be so separated now, however prettified, sanitized, and shorn of wacky costumes and titles. Scapegoating of "the other," assurances that "we" must safeguard our system, our heritage, and our values from "them"—these notions inevitably carry implications of violence and repression.

Yet under certain conditions they can become widespread, unless watched and guarded against. As the evidence presented shows, it has happened. Here. And not so long ago.

From the Great Depression to World War II

Many Americans enjoyed an unprecedented prosperity during the Republican era of the 1920s. Ownership of automobiles, telephones, and radios skyrocketed. However, some groups, such as farmers, did not do as well as others. The middle- and upper-middle-classes, however, received ever larger shares of the wealth. An estimated nine million individuals began playing the stock market in hopes of making fortunes. Various devices were utilized to enable them to purchase stock with what amounted to borrowed money. Warnings from some economists that the stock market was shaky went unheeded. Then, on "Black Thursday," October 24, 1929, the market crashed. Efforts to shore it up helped a bit, but prices continued to plummet during the months that followed.

President Herbert Hoover tried repeatedly to assure the public that business conditions were fundamentally sound. His words grew more hollow as time went on. Confidence was badly shaken, and many firms began retrenching in hopes that they could ride the situation out. Laying off workers and scaling back on inventories only made the situation worse. The nation headed into the worst depression in its history.

Hoover used more federal programs to stimulate recovery than had any of his predecessors, yet he was widely perceived as a do-nothing president who cared little about the common people. Hoover was not unfeeling, but he feared that instituting the large-scale economic programs many critics were clamoring for might

UNIT 4

ultimately destroy the entire system. He and his party went down to a humiliating defeat in the election of 1932.

Franklin Delano Roosevelt had compiled an admirable record as governor of New York, but the truth is that almost anyone would have defeated the reviled Hoover. Roosevelt had no grand theory about dealing with the Depression. What he did do, especially during the "first 100 days" of his administration, was to introduce a mass of remedial legislation. Some were designed to provide immediate relief to the unemployed, others to reform the system. Lewis Lord, in "1933: The Rise of the Common Man," contrasts Roosevelt's approach to the problem with that of Hoover.

President Woodrow Wilson had hoped to create a lasting peace after World War I through the League of Nations. Whether American participation in the League would have changed anything cannot be known, but the organization proved to be helpless in resolving various crises during the 1930s. Aggressor nations such as Nazi Germany, Japan, and Italy found that they could achieve their goals without fear of punishment. For its part, the United States tried to insulate itself from foreign conflicts through a series of neutrality acts designed to treat both parties with rigid impartiality.

Roosevelt acted hesitantly through the mid-1930s, but he developed a growing conviction that this nation had to take a more active role in deterring aggression. Against mounting criticism that he was leading the country into war, he took a number of steps such as trading American destroyers for British bases and instituting the Lend-Lease program to help those nations fighting aggressors. He adopted an increasingly harsh position toward the Japanese in an effort to pry them out of China. Economic pressures had the opposite effect from what was intended: instead of strengthening the hands of Japanese moderates, they instead convinced militants that Japan had to acquire the materials it needed by force. This led to the Japanese attack on Pearl Harbor in 1941. Arthur Schlesinger, in "The Man of the Century," analyzes Roosevelt's foreign policies through this period until his death and awards him high marks overall.

Two articles in this unit address the profound effects the war had on American society. Budgetary constraints had kept American armed forces pitifully weak during the 1930s. In 1940 Roosevelt obtained legislation that instituted the first peacetime conscription in our history. "The Draft," by Edward Oxford, shows how the system worked and evaluates its effects on society. Then, a broad range of ways in which society was reorganized and how it functioned to further the war effort is examined by James Wensyel in "Home Front."

The Soviet Union had been fighting Germany on the eastern front since June 1941. As early as the spring of 1942, Roosevelt had promised the Russians that the United States and Great Britain would launch a cross-channel invasion of France to relieve pressure on the Soviets. The invasion did not come to pass until June 1944, and even then it was an iffy proposition. In "Operation Overlord from the Inside," William O'Neill examines the decisions that were made that led to the success of this enormous undertaking.

Germany surrendered on May 7, 1945, but Japan still fought on. Although it had suffered defeat after defeat as Allied forces drew closer to the Japanese home islands, military hard-liners demanded that the war continue. The American invasion of Okinawa in April led to a bloody struggle that lasted until late June. The first large-scale use of kamikaze planes at Okinawa provided a frightening preview of things to come if the United States had to invade Japan proper. "The Biggest Decision: Why We Had to Drop the Atomic Bomb" shows that President Harry S. Truman, assuming that an invasion would be necessary, used atomic bombs to shorten the war and to save lives. He had no reason to believe, as some critics have charged, that the Japanese were near surrender and would have done so if only they could retain their sacred emperor.

Looking Ahead: Challenge Questions

Discuss some of Roosevelt's New Deal programs that were designed to promote relief and recovery. What were the underlying assumptions about what had to be done?

How equitably did the draft work? Once the United States entered the war, how was society mobilized to provide the vast array of food and materials necessary to win the war?

Discuss alternatives to using atomic bombs. What do you think would have happened had Truman refrained from using them and an invasion of the Japanese home islands took place?

1933
The Rise of the Common Man

Lewis Lord

It had happened in Russia only 15 years before, and mere days had passed since it occurred in Germany. Now, on March 4, 1933, fears abounded that chaos and totalitarianism soon would strike the United States of America. Herbert Hoover awoke that cold, dreary Saturday, his final morning in the White House, to word that Illinois and New York had joined a long list of states where all the banks had ceased to function. "We are at the end of our string," the president-reject conceded. "There is nothing more we can do."

What, indeed, could anyone do to curb the Great Depression, then in its fourth grim year? Working women could help, several women's magazines suggested, by giving men their jobs. Deport all aliens so more paychecks can go to real Americans, counseled Texas's Rep. Martin Dies. Ship America's 12 million blacks to Africa, proposed Theodore Bilbo, Mississippi's soon-to-be senator. A retired major recommended killing old people "of no use to themselves or anyone else." John Dewey, the educator, favored the death of something less personal. "Capitalism," he said, "must be destroyed."

The hapless Hoover had waited in vain for capitalism to cure itself, with no help from Washington. "Economic wounds," he said, "must be healed by the action of the cells of the economic body—the producers and consumers themselves." But producers quit producing and consumers stopped consuming. Industries operated at less than half their 1929 capacity, and probably a third of the work force was out of work. Despair ruled the land. People slept in sewer pipes in Oakland and hunted food in garbage dumps in Chicago. When a puny child in Appalachia complained of being hungry, her teacher told her to go home and eat. "I can't," the girl replied. "It's my sister's turn to eat."

Hoover's secretary of war, bracing for an Inauguration Day revolt by "reds and possible Communists," massed troops near big cities. East Coast businessmen plotted ways to get out of town in case the jobless cut telephone lines and barricaded highways. The chief of the American Farm Bureau Federation warned of a coming "revolution in the countryside," while Alf Landon, the Republican governor of Kansas, declared "the iron hand of a national dictator" preferable to a paralyzed economy. Franklin D. Roosevelt, the president-elect, sensed what was at stake. A friend told him that if he succeeded, he would go down in history as the greatest president ever and that if he failed, he would be known as the worst. "If I fail," Roosevelt replied, "I shall be the last one."

That Saturday, millions turned on their Philcos and Zeniths to hear Roosevelt's answer to calamity. For months, the 51-year-old New York governor had promised little except a vague "new deal for the American people," especially "the forgotten man at the bottom of the economic pyramid." Now, in his inaugural address, the new president's voice rang out: "This great nation will endure as it has endured, will revive and will prosper. So, first of all, let me assert my firm belief that the only thing we have to fear is fear itself." The crowd stood almost silent in the cold wind. "This nation asks for action, and action now." For the first time since 1929, the capital heard genuine cheers. "We must act, and act quickly." The paraplegic president left the applauding throng like a cocky prizefighter, shaking his hands over his head. Wrote Will Rogers: "If he burned down the Capitol, we would cheer and say, 'Well, we at least got a fire started.'"

Roosevelt did not torch the Capitol, as Adolf Hitler's Nazis had done with Berlin's Reichstag only days earlier. Nor did he seek dictatorial power or set people against people as Hitler was doing. Instead, as 1933 unfolded, this one man who seemed to understand what Americans had in common much better than they themselves had ever known would pull together the nation's degraded down and outs and scared-as-hell upper crust. He would lift up a generation of his countrymen and set back on course a national dream that, though battered and transformed, has endured ever since. "We have had our revolution," *Collier's* magazine would observe that year, "and we like it."

The foundation for saving the middle class was set immediately. FDR chose as his first New Deal patient the banks, most of them reeling from hemorrhages of deposits. Rather than nationalize the system, as Germany did, he closed every bank in the land until examiners ruled them sound. On his eighth day in office, he told a national radio audience why the shutdown was necessary, explaining the crisis so well, Will Rogers said, that even bankers could understand it. Such "fireside chats" would come to represent something new, a bond across the airwaves between the leader and the people, one that in some countries would be a force for evil. In America, for the most part, the tie would reinforce democracy. That week, 3 of every 4 banks reopened. Banks were safe, people concluded, because FDR said so. Cash stashed under mattresses suddenly became bank deposits, and the stock market jumped 15 percent. Raymond Moley, then a top Roosevelt aide, would later become one of his harshest critics, but his assessment

18. 1933: The Rise of the Common Man

The Way We Were

Alphabet Soup
The New Deal created 59 new agencies. Growth in federal employees from 1932 to 1936: 46 percent. The agencies included the Federal Theatre Project to produce plays with the help of 3,350 out-of-work actors, and the Federal Writers' Project to compile oral histories and travel guides. Number of commercially published FWP works: 378.

Domestic Demagogues
Populists like Father Charles Coughlin and Louisiana's Huey Long held great sway. In 1933, Coughlin's weekly radio show won a preference poll against the New York Philharmonic broadcast, 187,000 to 12,000. By 1935, Long's Share-Our-Wealth organization, which backed a $2,000-a-year guaranteed income, had 7 million members. Long was assassinated that year.

Opening the Floodgates
The 18th Amendment to the Constitution—enacted in 1920 to outlaw the sale of beverages with more than 0.5 percent alcohol—was repealed in 1933. During the era, a new subculture arose, with women and men drinking together in "speakeasies." In 1930, members of the Women's Organization for National Prohibition Reform: 60,000

Radio Days
The '30s were the "Golden Age of Radio." U.S. homes with radios in 1920: 500,000; in 1930: 14 million. Commercial stations that began in the '30s: 212. Radio advertising revenues in 1930: $40 million; in 1935: $112 million. In October 1938, 6 million heard Orson Welles's broadcast of "War of the Worlds." Many thought the Martian invasion was real, setting off panic in the New York City area.

Big Screens and Small
The Depression arrived almost simultaneously with the "talkies." Weekly U.S. moviegoers, 1930: 115 million; U.S. population: 122 million. U.S. feature films in the '30s: 5,009; in the '80s: 3,774. The most eagerly awaited film of the decade was 1939's *Gone With the Wind*. Meanwhile, by 1938, there were still only 20,000 television sets in service in New York City.

The Long March
In October 1934, Mao Zedong's Red Army began a yearlong, 6,000-mile trek to escape government forces and establish itself throughout China, crossing 24 rivers and 18 mountain ranges, and occupying 62 cities. Troops who began the march: 100,000; who survived: 33,000. After the march, Mao's forces devised communist strategies and, in 1949, took over China.

Re-election Roundup
In the 1936 presidential election, FDR defeated Republican Alf Landon by a landslide, with 61 percent of the popular vote. Still, that same year, Adolf Hitler did somewhat better in a vote of confidence from the German people. Share of votes for Hitler as *führer* in 1936: 99 percent. Other political parties allowed to compete in Germany that year: zero.

Peace in Our Time
On Sept. 30, 1938, British Prime Minister Neville Chamberlain met Hitler in Munich in hopes of averting war and agreed that Germany could annex Czechoslovakia's Sudetenland. Number of days before Hitler broke the Anglo-German nonaggression agreement by invading Poland: 336; number of days after invasion Chamberlain served as prime minister: 219.

---

of what happened that March never changed: "Capitalism was saved in eight days."

It was saved by a distinctively American form of pragmatic planning. All that spring, lights burned late in the White House as Moley and other "Brain Trusters" looked for ways to rescue farmers, revive industries and feed the hungry. "Take a method and try it," Roosevelt urged. "If it fails, try another. But above all, try something." He was asked what he would say when people questioned the ideology behind the Tennessee Valley Authority, a massive public-power scheme some saw as creeping socialism. "I'll tell them it's neither fish nor fowl," he laughed, "but whatever it is, it will taste awfully good to the people of the Tennessee Valley." Some plans fell short, including one aimed at easing hunger in the long run. "People don't eat in the long run," snapped Harry Hopkins, in charge of relief. "They eat every day."

An entirely different way of thinking about American government emerged, with a blizzard of programs known by initials: AAA, CCC, NLRB, HOLC, FERA, FDIC. Everyone seemed to pitch in. For the NRA, or National Recovery Act, the presidents of General Motors and General Electric huddled with labor bosses to create "codes" telling businesses how much to charge customers and pay workers. Sears, Roebuck rescinded a 10 percent pay cut, and dozens of firms raised wages. Pratfalls abounded. "What Is America Up to?" asked a London newspaper after a Jersey City tailor drew 30 days in jail for charging 35 cents to press a suit instead of the 40 cents the NRA's Tailoring Industry Code required. (Two years later, the Supreme Court would kill the NRA, and FDR would try something else.)

The WPA, or Works Progress Administration, put 3½ million of the jobless to work on roads, parks and buildings. Former businessmen who couldn't afford overalls wore business suits to lay sewer pipes. "I hate to think what would have happened if this work hadn't come," a Montana ditch digger said. "I'd sold or hocked everything. And my kids were hungry. I stood in front of the window of the bake shop and wondered just how long it would be before I got desperate enough to pick up a rock and heave it through that window and grab some bread to take home."

During the decade, Roosevelt would become 20th-century America's most loved and most hated public figure. The well-to-do despised him as "that man," the aristocrat who betrayed his class, while Georgia sharecroppers and California pea pickers adorned their shacks with FDR portraits made from news photos glued to cardboard. A reporter quizzed a North Carolina millworker about his enthusiasm for the president: Didn't he realize that FDR's crackpot notions would wreck America? The worker didn't know that, but he did know this: "Roosevelt is the only man we ever

4. FROM THE GREAT DEPRESSION TO WORLD WAR II

Eyewitness
Down and Out in the Dust Bowl

Cleo Frost, now 77, was 18 years old in 1934 when she and her family left their Sallisaw, Okla., home, bound for California, part of the migration westward by thousands of unrooted people from the dust bowl.

"All you could see was the top of the corn out of the dust. It would drift, so you'd only see the tops of the fence posts. People would cut open old potato sacks, put them over the windows and turn the water on them to try to stop the dust.

"When we decided to come out to California, my dad went to the store that had lent him $35 for that year's crop. 'We're not leaving to beat the bills but to pay them,' he said. And when we came out here, in six weeks we had all of that $35 paid off.

"There were 16 of us, including four young children. My brother bought a Chevrolet truck in Tulsa. We put blankets in the center for the kids to sleep on. Just before Oklahoma City, we stopped in a motel. Before we went to bed, we shook the dust out of the sheets. Mama was scared to death of the dust. So she got some of my dad's handkerchiefs, wet them in water and put them over our faces for us to breathe through. When we got up the next morning, those handkerchiefs looked brown.

"When we stopped in McFarland, Calif., Mr. Lessley was in the store getting groceries when he saw our Oklahoma license plates. He was from Sallisaw, too. And he told us where to go to get work, at the Twin Pines Ranch about a mile out of town.

"I tell you, the Lord did watch over us."

---

had in the White House who would understand that my boss is a son of a bitch."

The New Deal's reforms would endure, from Social Security and accessible home mortgages to cheap electricity and a supervised stock market. And early on there would come a sure sign that business was picking up: Executives who had begged the government to do something began complaining that it did too much. But the New Deal would not cure America's economic woes—to end the Depression, FDR would swap his "Dr. New Deal" hat for a "Dr. Win the War" cap. Only then, during the massive spending for World War II, would unemployment slip below 15 percent.

The New Deal's start would prove more vital than its finish. Long before political scientists concluded he had created the modern presidency, long before economists decided he had saved capitalism, long before historians ranked him beside Washington and Lincoln as "great," a man who couldn't walk put America on its feet. Nothing summed up 1933's new mood better than a Walt Disney cartoon that hit the movie screens in uplifting color. When the Three Little Pigs sang "Who's Afraid of the Big Bad Wolf?" few missed the symbolism.

The Draft

Draftees formed the heart and sinew of America's fighting forces during World War II. When their "number came up," ten million men answered the call to arms.

Edward Oxford

New York writer Edward Oxford has contributed more than two dozen major articles to American History. *His last contribution—the special D-Day Plus 50 Years issue—appeared in June 1994.*

With the arrival of 1940, Depression-weary Americans dared hope that the new decade would bring better days. But the first months of the year had a bitter taste. As a storm of war swept across Europe and Asia, people on Main Street began to wonder whether even the vast expanses of the Atlantic and Pacific oceans could for long keep the ominous clouds at a safe distance. War and rumors of war filled newspaper headlines and conversations.

There yet lived hundreds of thousands of American men, no longer young, who had done battle in "the war to end all wars." They had been part of the American Expeditionary Forces whose resolute doughboys, back in 1917-18, had trained, fought, and in considerable numbers, died for freedom's cause.

Now the sons of the fathers had come of age. And now again, week after week, American families glimpsed the horror-faces of war in newspaper photographs, magazine layouts, and newsreels. Young American men, seeing those stricken faces, tried not to behold in them their own.

As the threat loomed larger, anxious Americans sought to hold on to some measure of happiness in their lives. *Fantasia, The Philadelphia Story,* and *My Little Chickadee* brightened motion-picture screens. Sports fans cheered Joe DiMaggio, Don Budge, Joe Louis, Sammy Baugh, and Whirlaway. Big-band fans bought the latest recordings by Benny Goodman, Artie Shaw, and Glenn Miller. Couples learned the "Lindy Hop," and a young singer named Frank Sinatra sang "I'll Never Smile Again."

By mid-1940, however, it was no longer possible to pretend that events in Europe and Asia were not America's concern. The time had clearly come for its citizens and their representatives in Washington to ponder the nation's course.

Pulled in one direction by isolationists and in the other by interventionists, Americans were caught in a quandary. Many, especially in small towns and rural areas, had traditionally advocated no U.S. involvement in Europe's affairs. Although news of Axis aggression now brought the wisdom of this stance into question, a considerable isolationist sentiment persisted and was brought to bear on the debates surrounding proposals to aid the struggling British and to strengthen America's defenses.

The "America First" Committee—which attracted such known figures as Eddie Rickenbacker, Alice Roosevelt Longworth, and Lillian Gish—argued forcefully that the United States had more to lose by becoming embroiled in the conflict, especially if Britain were to fall, than it did from coming to a peaceful understanding with a victorious Germany. At the opposite end of the spectrum, playwright Robert Sherwood, whose *There Shall Be No Night* showed audiences how to stand up to totalitarianism, expressed the save-Europe sentiment by running a newspaper advertisement headed "Stop Hitler Now!"

The debate came to focus on the matter of military preparedness. Many Americans held on to the wistful hope that a volunteer army would still be adequate for the troubled times. But Army Chief of Staff George Marshall disagreed, stating forcefully that "paper plans no longer will suffice. The security of our country depends on more trained men. There is no other way to do it."

In Washington, D.C.'s summer heat, the struggle to reach a national consensus began. Senator Edward R. Burke of Nebraska and New York Congressman James W. Wadsworth co-sponsored a bill calling for peacetime military conscription—an action unprecedented in the nation's history. During the third week of June 1940, the bill began its legislative journey through Congress.

A Gallup poll taken at the end of May had indicated that U.S. citizens were divided half-for, half-against conscription. Weeks later, however, France fell before Hitler's onslaught, leaving Britain to stand alone. News accounts told of the Royal Air Force's stirring fight against waves of German bombers. The unforgettable voice of Prime Minister Winston Churchill sounded on radios across America in tribute to the R.A.F. defenders: "Never in the field of human conflict was so much owed by so many to so few."

Listening Americans considered whether they, too, owed something to such brave men; whether, somehow, the Battle of Britain was but prologue to the Battle of America; and whether, will it or not, they soon must take arms against forces that would not otherwise be brought to a halt. By early August, when a new poll was taken, two-thirds of the American people favored some form of draft.

The various individuals and groups who lobbied against conscription "made a weird hash," according to *Time* magazine. Some, like clergyman Harry Emerson Fosdick, could not reconcile war with their religious principles. Labor leader John L. Lewis declared that only a fool would expect that Americans "are gong to send their sons to be butchered in another foreign war." Socialist Norman

4. FROM THE GREAT DEPRESSION TO WORLD WAR II

Thomas and members of the Communist Party also took an isolationist stance that included opposition to conscription.

The draft bill came before the Senate in late August, and the House debate began early in September. The intemperate words and attention-getting antics of pro- and anti-draft factions frequently sank to distasteful levels that obscured the genuine concerns felt by both sides. A mock petition circulating on the streets of New York lampooned the likes of Nebraska's Senator George Norris, who, while conceding that "dictators would like to conquer the U.S.," would not support peacetime conscription because it was "contrary to the spirit of human freedom." Addressed to Adolf Hitler, Benito Mussolini, and Emperor Hirohito, the petition "most respectfully" requested "that any aggressive intention you might have toward the United States be graciously deferred until the United States has been given ample time to strengthen its Army, Navy, and Air Force by the volunteer system."

Florida's Claude Pepper, speaking in favor of the draft bill on the Senate floor, was hanged in effigy near the Capitol building by a women's group calling itself the Congress of American Mothers. Montana's isolationist Senator Burton Wheeler, clad in a white suit, climaxed his three-hour anti-draft address by admonishing his fellow senators that with the passage of this bill "you slit the throat of the last democracy still living—you accord to Hitler his greatest and cheapest victory to date. On the headstone of American democracy he will inscribe: 'Here lies the foremost victim of the war of nerves.'"

On the steps of the Capitol, "Pauline Revere," a young woman in colonial costume, rode a white horse bearing a sign that read: "Mobilize for Peace and Defeat Conscription." Dressed in widows' garb, six women kept a silent vigil in the Senate and House galleries.

In the House, Congresswomen Clara McMillan of South Carolina and Frances Bolton of Ohio, both of whom had sons of draft age, took the floor to debate the issue. McMillan supported the draft; if men had to go into battle, she maintained, they should be trained. Bolton, however, argued that there was "more danger than defense" in conscription.

Debate on the House floor finally became so intense that a pro-draft Kentucky congressman delivered a hard right-cross to the head of his anti-draft Ohio counterpart, whom he called "a traitor." The House Doorkeeper rated the fist-fight the liveliest he had witnessed during fifty years of service.

Meanwhile, President Franklin D. Roosevelt, facing a strong challenge from Wendell Willkie as he sought re-election to his third term in office, tried to stay clear of the politically explosive issue.

While the lawmakers went about their deliberations, German bombers stepped up their assault on England. "Every time they bombed London," one pro-draft legislator later observed, "we gained a vote or two in the House or Senate."

In its final form, shaped by thirty-three amendments, the Selective Training and Service Act passed its final hurdle on September 14 by an almost

19. The Draft

two-to-one margin in both houses of Congress. Two days later President Roosevelt, sitting at his desk in the White House, picked up a pen and signed: "Approved Sept. 16, 1940. Franklin D. Roosevelt. 3:08 P.M. E.S.T."

Roosevelt's pen-strokes marked a dramatic change in the nation's view of itself. The United States would require its citizens to learn the art of self-defense in peacetime. The Selective Service Act expressed America's answer to aggression.

The new conscription law sought men—citizens and resident aliens alike—between the ages of twenty-one and thirty-six. No more than 900,000 could be called up in peacetime. They would be required to serve for only one year, but that would be followed by ten years of reserve duty. Those drafted would not go overseas (except to serve in American possessions), and "sympathetic regard" would be provided for those who claimed dependents. Fines and/or imprisonment awaited anyone failing to comply with the law. Such, at least, was the way the draft started out.

The giant first step—national Registration Day—was set for October 16.* Public officials—from the president to governors to mayors—heralded the day. Radio stations and newspapers announced and re-announced the date. Bars and nightclubs posted "R-Day" reminder-signs. The Selective Service System, from its national headquarters in Washington, urged men in the affected age group: "If in doubt, register. If you are required to register—and fail to do so—you will face the probability of punishment."

The great sign-in began at 7 A.M. on that crisp, cool Wednesday. To 125,000 registration centers across the land—the same locations that served as election polling places—came the young men of America from all walks of life and all ethnic backgrounds.

During the next fourteen hours, Uncle Sam recorded the basic facts concerning some 16,500,000 men—the huge first contingent from which he would call the new defenders of the nation. More than a million volunteer register-clerks signed the men in at the rate of a million an hour and assigned each a number between 1 and 8,500.

There was, that memorable day, a singular sense of patriotic spirit in the air. Circus midgets and blind men guided by friends appeared for registration. Here and there, a handful of individuals—such as eight Union Theological Seminary students in Manhattan—publicly stated their refusal to register. But, in a remarkable display of like-mindedness, those whose civic duty was to register did so. The massive registration went almost perfectly—a testament to the temper of the times.

On October 29, Americans witnessed the next step in building the nation's military preparedness: the drawing of draft numbers. The U.S. draft lottery began at noon in the federal government's large Departmental Auditorium, near the Mall in Washington, D.C. Klieg lights shown down on a ten-gallon fishbowl—the same glass container used in the 1917 drawing of World War I draft numbers—that held 9,000 robin's-egg-blue capsules, each containing a registration serial number.*

Looking tired and drawn from campaigning, President Roosevelt made his way to a lectern on the auditorium stage. In his address, broadcast by radio to an anxiously waiting nation, he called the process about to begin a "muster," rather than a draft or a conscription, thus evoking images of America's minutemen at Concord and Lexington. "Ever since the first muster," he stated, "our democratic army has existed for one purpose only: the defense of our freedom. It is for that one purpose and that one purpose only, that you will be asked to answer the call for training."

The auditorium, packed with 1,500 men and women—some of them the parents of draft-registrants—was silent as a blindfolded Secretary of War Henry Stimson reached into the big jar, picked up a capsule, and handed it to the president. With newsreel cameras rolling, Roosevelt opened the capsule and intoned: "The first number is one-five-eight."

Man the GUNS—Join the NAVY

LIBRARY OF CONGRESS.

A woman in the auditorium cried out. Mrs. Mildred Bell's twenty-one-year-old son Harry had the registration serial number 158. At that moment he was shopping for furniture in a Washington, D.C. suburb with his bride-to-be and would not learn of his luck for several hours. Harry Bell and other "158s" across the country would be the first in their draft board regions to be considered for induction.*

More than a hundred journalists reported news of the numbers as they continued to be drawn that day. For a while, random volunteers—veterans, onlookers, government clerks—had the chance to draw a capsule from the bowl. Then, after 150 or so capsules had been opened, crews trained by Selective Service headquarters took over. Anyone interested could get an empty blue capsule for a souvenir.

As each number was plucked out of its capsule, an official camera photographed it next to a clock that showed the exact time of its selection. The individual numbers were then attached to large, gummed sheets of cardboard, which would become the master record of the drawing.

By mid-afternoon Selective Service teams were chalking the numbers on a

---

*Five more registrations were held before the process became a continuous one in 1942. From then on American males would register automatically when they turned eighteen.

*Each local draft board was limited to 8,500 registrants. However, just to be safe, the Selective Service System opted for placing 9,000 numbers in the lottery bowl.

*In due time, Bell was inducted into the U.S. Army. He served with distinction in the European Theater, where he was wounded in action. He survived the war and passed away in 1990.

4. FROM THE GREAT DEPRESSION TO WORLD WAR II

big blackboard at the rate of eight or so a minute. The procedure went on through the night, ending at 5:48 A.M. on October 30. Now 16,500,000 American men knew the order in which they would be considered for the call to colors.

A mood of mingled excitement, pride, and solemnity had taken hold. A *Washington Post* editorial observed that "the men and women and families called upon to sacrifice personal wishes to the national welfare have cause for both the regret and the happiness that comes from unselfish service."

Across America, young men in the "158" number-group learned—to their befuddlement or delight—that Uncle Sam, in his random selecting, was pointing his finger directly at them.

Some holders of "158" were proud, some resentful. Reactions ranged from celebration to consternation. At Victor's Tavern, in Queens, a shout went up as Roosevelt announced that first number, for among the crowd listening was twenty-one-year-old Jim Cody, who held 158. Single, healthy, and jobless, Jim lived with his grandparents. "I'm proud to be called," he later told a reporter. "I'm willing to go. Military training will be good for me."

George Tsatsaronis, a thirty-one-year-old alien who had emigrated from Greece five years earlier, got the news in the coffee shop of which he was part-owner. Through an interpreter, he said: "Good. It's good. I would like to serve America. I could be a cook in the Army. I am a good cook."

Interior decorator Irving Heyman, a married man with two children, was cutting slip covers when he heard his number-group announced over the radio. "I had to drop my shears," he recounted. "I would go in a second if I were single. But they need me—the wife and the kids—at home."

Somehow, in a way few citizens could then comprehend, America had suddenly changed. The people had known a time for peace. Soon enough they would know a time for war.

As the land made its spin beneath the next day's sun, crowds of young American men gathered outside draft boards to peer at the first lists of numbers posted on the wall in sets of hundreds. As the men stared at the columns of figures, each tried to understand, in the larger scheme of things, just where he stood. "If it's gotta be, it's gotta be," Samuel Hookoff told a reporter. A half-smiling Joe Sloss observed: "At last I'll get away from that hardware store." Theodore Browning related that "I got no job. I got no way to get one. The Army, I don't care for it, I guess. But maybe they'll make a man out of me." Speaking for perhaps tens of thousands of other men, one spotted his number, grimaced, and muttered: "My (blankety-blank-blank) lucky day."

The first of the newly chosen reported early on November 18, 1940 to armories, induction stations, and school buildings. Among those to present themselves for service that wintry morning was John Lawton, of Everett, Massachusetts. A single twenty-one-year-old, Lawton had been out of work for much of the year. Now the government had given him an occupation: he was a soldier. A local newspaper said Lawton had "the distinction of being the very first of the inductees." Though there was no way of accurately saying who was the first man "to go." His picture appeared on the front page as such.

Lawton was one of eleven men lined up shoulder to shoulder in a Boston armory in front of an American flag. "You are the first men in the United States to be inducted under the law," Captain Harold Linderson informed them. "You've got a lot to live up to. We're expecting a lot from you." The men somberly recited the oath of service, then took the required one step forward. The captain told them: "You're in the Army now." Lawton, along with 236 other inductees from New England, would reach Fort Devens that night.

By train, bus, and truck, rookies rolled into training sites from Camp Upton, New York to Fort Ord, California. The newcomers didn't much like the look of their new homes, and the waiting sergeants didn't much like the looks of the new arrivals. Hometown newspapers duly printed names of the newest "boys in uniform."

By the beginning of December 1941, the Selective Service had gathered in the 900,000 men the system had sought. Then came the first Sunday of the month—December 7—and with the Japanese attack on Pearl Harbor, the war's scope became world-wide.

On the morning after the "date which will live in infamy," thousands of young American men, eager to do their patriotic duty, lined up outside recruiting stations. The United States and Great Britain declared war on Japan. By Thursday of that week Germany and Italy had in turn declared war on the United States.

The surprise assault swept away America's last thoughts of isolationism, stirred to action a nation whose will had been held hostage by doubt, and gave grim fulfillment to Roosevelt's prophecy that "this generation has a rendezvous with destiny."

As "Remember Pearl Harbor" became America's battle cry, citizens everywhere volunteered to do whatever they could do to win the war—*their* war, now—against the Axis. Within a week after the Pearl Harbor attack, Congress removed the draft law's restriction against men serving overseas and lowered the minimum age to twenty. Draftees would serve as long as the war lasted—and for six months after it ended. Now a man was in for "duration plus six."

Almost overnight, the Selective Service System took on a powerful, almost intimidating, presence in the minds of millions of American men. General Lewis B. Hershey, its director—previously an abstract figure at a paper-laden desk in Washington—increasingly became the personification of a system whose workings would have a decisive impact upon the nation's fate. A steady, even-handed administrator, Hershey was handed the delicate and enormous task of seeing to it that the armed forces received the full complement of men they needed to wage and to win the war.

A descendant of anti-militarist Mennonites, Hershey nevertheless had specialized in drawing up Army conscription plans since 1926 and brought a unique combination of insights to bear on the problem of drafting men by the tens of thousands. Having learned from history, he saw to it that prospective draftees had no contact with the Army, which had made a muddle of the Union draft in the Civil War. Civilian coordination during World War I had proved a far better model. Throughout World War II, the work of finding and selecting draftees would rest with members of local draft boards across the nation.

As the United States took up arms, Hershey made it clear that the task awaiting those summoned to serve was nothing less than to "save America." And he gave voice to the thoughts crossing the minds of many of his fellow citizens

19. The Draft

when he stated that everyone "called from a family goes to serve that family and to protect it. All hoped for peace. War has come, actual war, with death and blood its companions." For whatever it might be worth to the men who would be drafted, the General at that desk in Selective Service headquarters in Washington, D.C., sensed and respected their feelings; harbored—much as a father—concern for their well-being; and saluted, soldier to soldier, the service and sacrifice they were being called upon to render.

There were jokes about the draft, at least in the beginning. A comic strip titled "Draftie" appeared; Bob Hope and Dorothy Lamour got laughs in the movie *Caught in the Draft;* and standup comedians rattled off one-liners about reveille, close-order drill, and twenty-mile hikes. But down deep—as they heard about service-life, saw the horror-scenes of battle in each day's newspaper, and pondered the odds of ever coming home safe and sound—draftees-to-be weren't smiling. If the joke was on anyone, it was on them.

Some 6,500 local draft boards from Maine to Oregon carried out the thankless work of actually selecting the men who would go into uniform. These groups of civilians—three to five local citizens on a board who served without pay—were federal officials with letters of appointment from President Roosevelt. Board members were usually white men in their forties or fifties. Some were veterans of World War I; the illustrious Sergeant Alvin York, for example, headed the draft board in Franklin County, Tennessee.

The eight-page questionnaire filled out by draft registrants became the prime document in a draft-board's assessment of each man. Thirteen classifications ranged from "1A" (fit for general military service), and "1B" (fit for limited service), to "4E" (conscientious objector), and "4F" (physically, mentally, or morally unfit for service).

To a telling degree, draft boards determined the makeup of America's World War II Army. Draft board No. 49, in the northwest section of Detroit, for instance, had jurisdiction over about 12,500 registrants, aged eighteen to sixty-five. As of mid-1943, the three-man board, working about twenty hours per week, had placed 2,300 of their registrants into the Army. Draft boards, as General Hershey put it, had to "do the unpleasant thing." The message from the front line to the rear was: "More bodies."

However great the need for fighting men, the Army chose not put aside its longstanding segregationist policies in order to fill the ranks. Additional black units were planned—the existing six totalled fewer than 4,500 men—but the service needed time to build the segregated facilities that would be required. Since the Army could not accommodate all the black registrants, call-ups were race-specific. Problems arising from this policy, which endangered mobilization, caused Hershey to insist that "the Army must revise its procedure to receive men in such order, without regard to color." The Army accordingly made changes in policy—but slowly and in modest increments.

Soon after being classified 1-A, a potential draftee received his induction notice in the mail. The order read: "Greeting: Having submitted yourself to a local board comprised of your neighbors for the purpose of determining your availability for training and service in the armed forces of the United States in the present emergency, you are hereby notified that you have now been selected for immediate military service." For some ten million American men, this "Greeting" was the most significant single piece of correspondence they would ever receive.

Once notified, the draftee had to report for the "physical." Doctors moved the men through on an almost assembly-line basis, evaluating perhaps twenty-five an hour at a typical induction center. For most self-conscious young men, it was the most comprehensive physical examination they had ever undergone. Selectees who passed were adjudged physically fit for "general service." Those who had minor defects were slotted for "limited service." Roughly one-third failed either of these categories.

The men also underwent a screening session with a psychiatrist who looked for signs of "NP"—neuropsychosis—an inexact term that covered everything from phobias to heavy sweating, which resulted in the rejection of one in every eight men. A psychiatrist who once screened 512 men in a single day remembered the "hectic days when my profiling consisted of four or five rapid-fire questions: 'How do you feel? Have you ever been sick? Are you nervous? How do you think you will get along in the Army?'" Almost always he would finally ask: "Do you like girls?"

Those who passed both examinations were then fingerprinted and signed their induction papers. Each man received a military serial number and was told to memorize it. "That Army serial number is yours for keeps," an Army sergeant would tell the rookies. "No one else will ever have it." Finally, inductees were assembled before an Army officer who administered the oath. Then the men were instructed to take one step forward.* As of that moment, though they did not yet wear uniforms, they were soldiers in the United States Army.

With this new status, the men found themselves under the provisions of "military law" and had to obey the rules as outlined in the "Articles of War." To underscore the inductees' new legal standing, a sergeant read Articles 58 and 61, dealing with desertion and "being absent without leave" (AWOL). It was the Army's way of saying "You had better show up."

As America's new conscripts began to flood into Army basic training camps at ever-increasing rates, growing numbers of other young men—reluctant to wait and "take their chances" with the draft—found their way to Army Air Corps, Navy, Marine Corps, and Coast Guard recruiting offices to voluntarily enlist.

The Navy's slogan—"Choose While You Can"—worked well. In the first months after Pearl Harbor, thousands of men scheduled to be drafted into the Army signed up with the sea arm. The guiding rule seemed to be: "Whatever you do, stay out of the Infantry."

America's manpower pool was something of a pudding, with everyone fighting for the spoon. Induction and recruiting stations, war plants, and the agricultural industry pushed and pulled against one another—trying to put men into combat boots, behind factory-floor lathes, or atop tractors.

Finally, on January 1, 1943, military policy-makers put an end to the time-honored volunteering. As of that date, a man had to be drafted into the armed forces. Men between the ages of eighteen

---

*In the draft's early stages, men sometimes took the oath on the day they reported to the center for departure to camp.

113

4. FROM THE GREAT DEPRESSION TO WORLD WAR II

and thirty-seven all became subject to the Selective Service System.

Even so, the Navy managed to "cream-skim" from the pool by refusing to accept men not meeting certain physical standards or who had been guilty of certain offenses. (To help meet its vast replacement needs, the Army took such men.)

In a radio address on October 12, 1942, less than a year into the war, President Roosevelt sounded the call for eighteen- and nineteen-year-olds. A couple of days later, Secretary Stimson declared that the "Army is getting too old." In draftee-heavy divisions, he pointed out, "the average age was up to twenty-eight years two months. That's too old!" Draft director Hershey stressed that the Army needed *young* men, men who could "jump from planes without breaking ankles, drive tanks in 130-degree temperature, or swim ashore."

They were being realistic. There had been much talk of "modern war"—battles fought with tanks, planes, artillery. But in point of fact, the premium was still on the foot soldiers who led ground actions and served as riflemen, machine-gunners, mortar men. The infantry—in keeping with the Latin root of the word—needed the young. On November 13, 1942, barely a month after FDR had asked that the draft age be lowered to eighteen, the law was amended in accordance with his bidding.

Fatherhood presented the draft-system with a poignant problem. The boards, who well respected marriage and family, were inclined to send bachelors to war first. "Pre-Pearl Harbor" fathers stood the best chance of obtaining deferments. Those whose children had been conceived after December 7, 1941 still figured into the deferment balance, but to a lesser degree.

The American Legion urged that "every eligible single man that can be registered" be removed from government and industry before fathers were taken. But Army and Navy leaders alike argued for the drafting of fathers—contending that their continued exemption would prolong the war. Steadily, draft boards stripped their rolls of single men until, by the last quarter of 1943, the boards started falling short of their quotas.

Finally, across the country, the draft boards had to face up to it; they began drawing upon fathers. In October 1943 fathers accounted for six per cent of that month's draft quota; by April 1944 they made up more than forty per cent.

Colleges—in the persons of their presidents, faculty members, and students—had viewed the draft with particular trepidation. In "Conscription Hits the Campus" in the May 1941 issue of *Harper's* magazine, Professor Gaynor Maddox wrote that certain college students "live in a dream world of escape formulations, self-centered in little greedy and shallow cynicisms. They putter half-heartedly over excuses while all history is in turmoil."

An athlete at a California university asserted that he would help defend America against Hitler—but only in the Army Air Corps. "I Don't intend to go into the infantry," he said. "A foot soldier's just one of a mob, and the whole gang may be slaughtered together." A senior, twenty-two years of age, believed in the draft, but "not for university men studying for careers. Fill up the ranks with Civilian Conservation Corps boys and the unemployed first."

With America in the war, however, the self-serving protestations of some college students faded. The draft proved a remarkably effective equalizer. Board members, themselves volunteers, were unimpressed by power and prestige. "We looked at each man as a man," one draft board member recalled, "no better, no worse, no more important, no less important than the next man."

Surprising numbers of men fit enough to live in peace were initially found unfit to fight in war. A husky young man not capable of detecting "low voice sounds at twenty feet in a quiet room" might be able to play football, yet be rejected by the Army because of poor hearing. A fellow who had half his teeth decayed could be a structural steel worker, but the Army would turn him down.

As manpower needs went up, however, acceptance standards went down. Under later rules, false teeth were no ban to induction as long as they were "well mounted, of good occlusion, and sufficient to sustain a man on the Army ration." Toward war's end, one soldier out of five wore glasses. The services even took some men who had only one eye.

The American public became increasingly upset as, with more and more men being required to go into uniform, others "less desirable"—individuals with venereal disease or convictions as felons, for example—were barred from service. A Pennsylvania congressman declared that there were "hobos, bums, wife-beaters, drunks, and dissipators of all kinds who should be put into uniform."

The military, in time, concurred. The Army eventually drafted 200,000 men who had venereal disease, treating them with sulfa drugs to make them fit for soldierly duties. And by war's end, more than 100,000 former felons wore the Army uniform—the vast majority of them serving honorably. Some 100,000 men unable to read or write also were accepted, taught the rudiments of English, and assigned to full-duty units.

A file of letters seven feet thick, preserved in the National Archive, attests to the volumes of "fan mail" addressed to Selective Service headquarters. Signed with such names as "Anonymous Citizen" and "True American," they "tattled" on relatives, neighbors, or acquaintances. One woman wrote to tell of her "shiftless" son-in-law, who "could do with" some Army discipline. A wife wrote: "Please locate my husband and put him in the service. He diserted [sic] his family and took another woman with him."

In the course of the war, the Federal Bureau of Investigation picked up thousands of men who had not registered, had not reported for induction, had failed to report for physical examination, or who simply were not carrying their draft cards. Upon confrontation, a culprit usually admitted to the error of his ways and then complied with the law. Some draft boards publicly posted the names of delinquents, shaming them into service. The F.B.I., wielding the threat of legal prosecution, nudged great numbers of reluctant young men into uniform.

Some, however, couldn't be nudged. One Kentuckian devised a most elaborate will-of-the-wisp scheme. By means of telephone calls and letters to his draft board, he impersonated every member of his family in an attempt to prove that he was dead, buried, and bereaved. Later, rather than sooner, the artful dodger was found—alive, well, and rue-

19. The Draft

ful. A federal judge sent him to a penitentiary for three years.

One New York City sharpie conducted a "school" where he taught selectees—for sizeable fees—how to fake deafness, mental disorders, or heart ailments in order to avoid being drafted. In Jersey City three men were fined $1,000 apiece for "selling" shipyard jobs (for sums ranging from $300 to $500 apiece) that qualified the holders for deferment from service.

At Orangeville, Pennsylvania, a young registrant and his girlfriend claimed they were married and had a baby. When the draft board asked to see the baby, the couple borrowed one from a relative. It was months before their deception came to light—whereupon the man was given a three-year prison term.

Men had fabricated all sorts of reasons in their attempts to evade the draft, but at least one told the cold truth. His reason for not wanting to be a soldier was one anyone could understand; he was afraid of being killed.

World War II so unified the American people against the Axis onslaught that organized pacifism as such almost vanished from the scene. Of the millions of men called forth to serve, only a minute fraction—fewer than 40,000 men—were classified as "Conscientious Objector." The "C.O." was required to show "sincerity of belief in religious teachings combined with a profound moral aversion to war." Peace sects, such as the Quakers, accounted for most of the conscientious objectors. Yet, when called by their draft boards, seventy-five per cent of the Quakers entered the armed forces unreservedly.

The law required that conscientious objectors assume some noncombat role within the military or perform a civilian service. About 25,000 C.O.s carried out non-fighting military duties. Many served on the battlefront—as ambulance drivers, medical aides, and stretcher-bearers. Said one: "The soldiers were fighting for the same things I believed in—peace in the world and democracy."

Some twelve thousand conscientious objectors served at former Civilian Public Service Corps camps scattered throughout the United States. They cleared underbrush, felled trees, and cut firebreaks in woodlands. Provided with food and clothing by various support groups, the C.O.s lead unexacting, almost indulgent, lives—in sharp contrast to the hard, discipline-ridden regimen that draftees and volunteers were called upon to endure. This state of affairs angered many Americans and disappointed those objectors who had hoped for more meaningful service.

Declared, unyielding resistance to the draft-call was rare. Some thirteen thousand men—among them four thousand Jehovah's Witnesses—went to prison for refusing to serve the nation in any way during the war.* This worked out to a remarkably small four-tenths of one per cent of all registrants, a figure much lower than the World War I rate.

The draft, in World War II, became a rite of passage. "I was just out of high school," recalls Herman Harrington, of Rensselaer, New York. "When my draft notice came, I figured I had to do my duty. Looking back, I was proud to do it."

John Mahoney, who lives in Chicago, remembers: "I registered on my eighteenth birthday. When I got called to the draft board, they had to look high and low for my papers. Did they find them? You betcha they did."

George Thomas, of Phoenix, Arizona, relates: "I was a kid then. I didn't know what to expect when I got drafted. But neither did the others. They were kids, too. We were in it together."

The G.I. Army, by far the largest of the services, had the greatest percentage of draftees in its ranks. It was a cross-section of America's young men, a collection of "the long and the short and the tall." They were the sons, brothers, husbands, and fathers of America. Not per-

*Jehovah's Witnesses had a hard time convincing local draft boards that each of their number was a "minister" and therefore eligible for deferment.

fect men, by any means. Common men, in the main. But men quite good enough, they would prove, to train, to stand fast, to fight, to be wounded and—if need be—to die for their nation's cause. Men able, strong, and brave enough to win World War II.

They would be a long time gone—a lot longer than they wanted to be. But most of them would come back. Older. Wearier. Bearing memories that would be hard to put behind them. Some, when they stepped foot from their troopship, got down and kissed the pier. Newspapers called them "heroes." They counted themselves lucky just to be alive.

Other men would not be back. They would live on in the recollections of those who had come home, but as haunting presences. For men of arms knew what became of the fallen.

More than 403,000 American servicemen were killed on the battlefront or in the line of duty during World War II. Some 670,000 others were wounded. They had gone to their rendezvous with destiny in places many of them had barely heard of, places they had never expected to see—Bizerta, Attu, Anzio, Kwajalein, Normandy, Remagen, the Ardennes, Mindanao, Iwo Jima, and Okinawa.

Dorothy South Alvey, who works in Washington, D.C. as a planner with today's Selective Service System, well remembers her days as an employee in a Leitchfield, Kentucky draft board in 1943. "The people had a patriotic feeling," she recalls. "I remember some young men who *wanted* to be called."

To this day Ms. Alvey keeps a copy of a memorial book titled "Gold Star Boys," containing photographs and brief biographical sketches of men from her home county "who didn't come back from the war." The pictures, some of them simple snapshots, show boyish faces of soldiers, sailors, Marines, and airmen, taken a half-century ago. "For those of us who knew them back home," she says of those who never returned, "all those young men are still with us, in our memories. We think of them as they were."

Article 20

Home Front

World War II was fought and won on the assembly line as much as on the battle line. The nation's massive war effort involved and affected the lives of all Americans.

James W. Wensyel

James W. "Skip" Wensyel, a previous contributor to American History *magazine, is a retired Army colonel and a licensed battlefield guide at Gettysburg National Military Park.*

As Americans turned the pages of their calendars at the beginning of December 1941, the United States was slowly emerging from the Great Depression that had crippled the nation for nearly a decade. The economy to be sure, was still soft, with more than 5 million Americans unemployed and 7.5 million workers earning less than 40 cents per hour. But when you could remember (as the author did) a Christmas when your parents, having only $3.50 to spend on food and presents for their four boys, compromised by wrapping oranges as gifts, it was a lot better than people had known for a long time.

For the first time in years most Americans had enough food on their tables and some change to jingle in their pockets. Retail sales were rising to $54 million in 1941 from $10 million the previous year. The national median income was $2,000, which bought a lot when a new car cost about $1,000 and a pound of good steak could be had for 23 cents.

But despite the signs of economic recovery Americans had good reason to be concerned about the future. For three years the United States had been able to remain aloof from the war that was sweeping across Europe. Now, however, in its ninth year under the leadership of President Franklin D. Roosevelt, the U.S. found itself drawn ever closer to the European conflict and into a confrontation with Japan in the Pacific as well. In 1940 Congress enacted the Selective Service

President Franklin D. Roosevelt's call for a declaration of war in response to Japan's December 7, 1941 attack on Hawaii was a summons to action for every citizen. Drawn together in unanimity of purpose, Americans on the home front mobilized themselves and their resources for a full commitment to the men on the fighting lines.

From *American History*, June 1995, pp. 44-63, 77, 78, 81. © 1995 by Cowles Magazine, Inc. Reprinted through the courtesy of Cowles Magazines, publishers of *American History*.

20. Home Front

> **WE ARE NOW IN THIS WAR**
> **We are all in it all the way**
>
> Every single man, woman and child is a partner in the most tremendous undertaking of our American history. We must share together the bad news and the good news, the defeats and the victories—the changing fortunes of war.
>
> (President Roosevelt, Address to the Nation, December 9, 1941)

and Training Act that saw more than sixteen million American men between the ages of twenty-one and thirty-six registered for military service. Under the provisions of the Lend-Lease Act passed by Congress in March 1941, the U.S. was providing war matériel, as well as food and medicine, to Great Britain. And to protect the convoys carrying those desperately needed supplies to Europe, we had armed our merchant ships, and the Navy was attacking German U-boats.

The world situation notwithstanding, most Americans greeted December 7, 1941 as a typical peaceful Sunday. Throughout the country families relaxed over their newspapers, attended church, washed their cars, or planned their Christmas shopping (department stores were closed for the Sabbath). With a little money that year, it promised to be a wonderful Christmas.

By evening, however, everything had changed. The suddenness, ferocity and surprise of the Japanese attack against the big U.S. Navy base and military airfields on the island of Oahu, Hawaii, left Americans confused, shocked, and stunned. For those old enough to understand, the name, the date, the act itself would be indelibly seared in their memories as if cameras had clicked in their minds and frozen "Pearl Harbor" there for all time.

Following news of the attack, Americans from Maine to Oregon waited for President Roosevelt to speak. Party affiliation and political philosophy no longer mattered. He was the president, and all Americans looked to their chief executive (and trusted him) to lead the nation in this time of crisis. In Washington, D.C., hundreds instinctively walked to the White House, where FDR was meeting with his Cabinet. Standing quietly before the darkened Executive Mansion, they began to sing, softly at first but then more strongly, *God Bless America* and other patriotic songs.

Shortly after noon on December 8, in an address to a joint session of Congress and the nation, President Roosevelt condemned the Japanese attack and requested an immediate declaration of war. The Senate complied, voting 82 to 0 for war against Japan. The House of Representatives, with one exception (Congresswoman Jeanette Rankin of Montana) concurred.

Three days later, Germany and Italy, supporting their Japanese ally, declared war against the United States. The waiting was over; in joining the fight against the Axis powers, America was now committed to a global conflict the likes of which had never before been seen.

With America at war, life on the home front began to change almost immediately. Robert Albert, then living near Fort MacArthur in San Pedro, California, remembers that even as the president addressed Congress, "things started moving fast for the military. We looked out to see Army vehicles blocking the streets to the beach below. "Barricades of coiled barbed wire had been erected to prevent passage. Soldiers were everywhere."

Christmas 1941 was a somber holiday. Families were being separated, and a great many Americans already were fighting in the Pacific. On December 24, Britain's Prime Minister Winston Churchill paid a surprise visit to America and the White House. While watching the annual lighting of the great Christmas tree, he remarked, "I spend this anniversary and festival far from my family. And yet I cannot truthfully say that I feel far from home."

FDR proclaimed New Year's Day 1942 a National Day of Prayer, and Americans greeted the new year with absolute confidence in victory. Signs of that certainty were everywhere. A street banner in Yuma, Arizona, proclaimed "TO HELL WITH JAPAN AND ALL HER FRIENDS." In an Alabama town a notice appeared in the window of Joe's Country Lunch: "Maybe you don't know there's a war on. Have gone to see what it's all about. Meanwhile good luck and best wishes until we all come home—Joe."

Even our ice cream treats—with such names as "Blackout Sundae," "Commando Sundae," and "Paratroop Sundae—it goes down easy"—reflected Americans' newfound patriotism. Some popular tunes, like *Jingle, Jangle, Jingle* or *Deep in the Heart of Texas,* reflected that same cheerfulness, but others—*White Christmas, Don't Get Around Much Anymore, I Left My Heart At The Stage Door Canteen,* and *You'd Be So Nice To Come Home To*—revealed the nationwide undercurrent of pensiveness and loneliness that would deepen as the war dragged on.

Anger at everything Japanese was not limited to adults. At fourteen years and a robust 115 pounds, this author tried to persuade Army recruiters to give me a uniform. Their friendly "Thanks, but no thanks," was repeated every month until I reached seventeen. And in Newburgh, New York, a nine-year-old girl (now my wife) was scolded for smashing her Japanese toy piano to pieces.

With the exception of Lieutenant Colonel Jimmy Doolittle's daring April 18 bombing raid on Japanese cities from the aircraft carrier *Hornet,* war news was not encouraging in 1942. At home, oil slicks from torpedoed merchant ships appeared on beaches from Cape Cod to the Gulf of Mexico. German submarine "wolf packs" lay a few miles offshore, preying on merchant ships silhouetted against the coastal lights. When bodies and debris began to float ashore, the Navy sealed off beaches to restrict news of the grim battle they were waging (and at that point losing) on our doorstep.

Americans had some of their first war heroes in Captain Colin P. Kelly, Jr., a B17 pilot who died while bombing a Japanese warship off the Philippines, and Second Lieutenant Alexander R. Nininger, Jr., posthumously awarded the Medal of Honor for his courage during fighting on the Bataan Peninsula. Church attendance grew as it would throughout the war, and more and more homes displayed blue-star emblems. As the war went on, gold stars would replace many of the blue ones, signifying the loss of another loved one.

For some, especially children, this change from blue to gold did more than anything else to bring home the horrible reality of war. Dianne Price's grandfather "had placed a small rectangular silk flag, emblazoned by three blue stars on

4. FROM THE GREAT DEPRESSION TO WORLD WAR II

a white background in our front window in honor of his three sons in the Army. After Uncle Eddy was killed, I remember a blue star was changed to gold. Grandma was never the same after that. My uncle's young wife was a basket case for a long time and my mother, who was trying to buoy everyone else up, almost had a nervous breakdown. For myself, I hated the war now I had seen, firsthand, how bad it could hurt."

As America prepared to send its armed forces abroad, so too did it begin to take precautions for the security of the home front. The Office of Civilian Defense (OCD) enlisted more than 12 million volunteers and organized most communities down to the block level, adding such expressions as "block warden," "blackout," and "dim-out" to our wartime vocabulary. Volunteers studied aircraft identification silhouettes and stored sandbags, helmets, flashlights, buckets, and hoses for use in the event of an air raid. In mock attacks Civil Air Patrol planes dropped flour-filled dummy bombs or wardens threw firecrackers to simulate exploding shells. Medical volunteers treated masses of ketchup-stained Boy Scout "casualties."

Residents hung opaque blackout curtains in their windows and when an alert sounded, carefully drew them and waited by candlelight or flashlight for the "all clear." Air raid wardens, official-looking in their white helmets and arm bands, meant business. If a light showed, the person responsible was sure to hear about it.

Air-raid drills "were a source of entertainment" for nine-year-old Cornelius Lynch and his three siblings. "It was always exciting to have the house pitch black, particularly if it coincided with the broadcast of *Inner Sanctum* or *Lights Out* on the radio. I found those programs scary-fun enough when the lights were on." Not all children shared

To unite Americans and build their determination to win the war, the Office of War Information distributed millions of posters. Wherever they went, people on the home front were exhorted to support the armed forces, join the defense industry, avoid waste, buy war bonds, and keep quiet.

118

that sense of excitement, however. For Louise Butler, near Washington, D.C., the wartime measures instilled fear. "The Germans were bombing other countries and sinking ships. It was logical to us that they would attempt to bomb our nation's capital. We knew that we weren't just exercising childish imagination because the government made us all wear dog tags stamped with name, address, and a long number so that in case of injury our parents would be notified we were in the hospital. In case of death they would know they were burying the right child."

Civil defense volunteer Eva Schillingburg recalls an air-raid drill in Baltimore: "It was very dark. I could not see where I was walking. My memory of the sidewalk guided me. How weird to be on a street in the city with no lights, no sound."

Initially some cities and towns had to improvise air-raid signals. Sepulveda, California, used a century-old cast-iron bell. Reading, Pennsylvania, used car horns beeping out the Morse Code "V", for Victory. Bell Telephone Laboratories developed a device to be used countrywide. This "Victory Siren" proved so ear-shattering, however, that some communities refused to install it.

All across America, civilian defense seemed to be an area where Americans, anxious to help, could contribute to the war effort. A meeting to recruit OCD volunteers in Hannibal, Missouri, packed the armory with four thousand applicants, while another fifteen thousand waited outside. When the mayor of Northport, Alabama, galloped through the streets on horseback calling for volunteers, eighty percent of the town's 2,500 residents responded.

The Ground Observer Corps (GOC), another branch of the OCD, attracted 600,000 plane spotters who manned posts up to three hundred miles inland, reporting every aircraft observed. Spotters at the twenty-four-hours-a-day posts included men, women, and children. In Nebraska three ladies, each over seventy, took turns serving as their town's "plane spotter" every day of the war.

The Civil Air Patrol (CAP) of the OCD recruited 100,000 private pilots who used their own aircraft to fly anti-

SAVE WASTE PAPER — IT IS A "WEAPON OF WAR!"

HE'S WATCHING YOU

He's *Sure* to get V---MAIL — Safest Overseas Mail

What did *you* do today ...for Freedom?

Today, at the front, he died...Today, what did *you* do?
Next time you see a list of dead and wounded, ask yourself:
"What have *I* done today for freedom?
What can I do tomorrow that will *save* the lives of
men like this and help them win the war?"

4. FROM THE GREAT DEPRESSION TO WORLD WAR II

submarine patrols, search for downed aircraft, tow targets, watch for fires, and carry critical food and medicine. By July 1942, CAP planes on antisubmarine patrols were armed with bombs, and by 1945 they had attacked fifty-seven U-boats, actually sinking a few.

OCD volunteers also organized block projects, explained government programs, sold war savings stamps, surveyed housing needs, recruited for the armed forces and for industry, distributed anti-black-market pledges, encouraged Victory Gardens and salvage campaigns, and performed many other useful services. When the Civil Defense was organized in his Pennsylvania hometown, fourteen-year-old Uzal Ent volunteered as a messenger. "I was proud of my white helmet and arm band, which proclaimed me a member of Civil Defense. In the darkness and solitude of my lonely post [during alerts], I fantasized German bombers attacking, and how I would act—very bravely of course."

The greatest potential danger to American security was thought to be German or Japanese saboteurs or intelligence agents within the United States. In June 1942 a German submarine landed four agents near Amagansett, Long Island. Several days later four more made it ashore near Ponte Vedra Beach, Florida. All spoke excellent English. When caught, the saboteurs were carrying U.S. currency bombs, timing devices, incendiary pistols, magnesium flares, and a long list of targets—factories, bridges, railroads, terminals, power plants, and dams. Apprehended before they could carry out any of the planned attacks, the infiltrators were tried in secrecy and found guilty of espionage. Six were executed; the remaining two received thirty-year sentences.

Concern about foreign agents led the FBI to round up thousands of Japanese, German, and Italian aliens and American citizens of the same ethnic backgrounds. Most German and Italian Americans were able to resume normal lives within a year, but 127,000 Japanese men, women, and children (many of whom were second- or third-generation American citizens) were—in accordance

When consumer goods began to become scarce, rationing was established under the Office of Price Administration to insure distribution of items on an equitable basis and to prevent runaway inflation. And, to supplement the nation's food supply, Americans planted "Victory Gardens" in almost any available plot of earth.

with Executive Order 9066 signed by President Roosevelt—given forty-eight hours to settle their affairs and report to designated collecting stations. "A Jap's a Jap," declared Army General John L. DeWitt, "it makes no difference whether he's an American or not."

Each internee was allowed to carry two suitcases and a duffel bag to one of the ten hastily built camps. By late 1942 most were permitted to leave the camps if they could find destinations inland, away from the Pacific coast, that would receive them. Two Japanese families moved to Leon Wahlbrink's town of St. Charles, Missouri. Their children, Itsu and Sammy "were surprisingly well accepted by their classmates and suddenly Japanese became different than 'Japs.'"

Life in the guarded internment camps was bleak, crowded, and disheartening, and most internees never regained the homes, businesses, and property they had been forced to abandon. Despite all this no Japanese American was charged with espionage or sabotage during the war, and some eight thousand *Nisei* served with great valor in American infantry units.

120

20. Home Front

To conserve irreplaceable cars and rubber, the government regulated tire ownership, reduced the speed limit, and restricted driving by rationing gasoline. With the needs of the military given priority on public transportation, civilian travelers endured long waits, crowded conditions, and altered schedules.

Perhaps the most important way that Americans on the home front contributed to the war effort was by producing the arms and equipment Allied forces needed to win the war. FDR set ambitious production goals for 1942: 60,000 airplanes, 48,000 tanks, 20,000 anti-aircraft guns. Although these totals were not reached, American industry learned from its mistakes and for the most part met or exceeded the even higher quotas set for 1943. By war's end Americans had produced a staggering total of almost 300,000 planes, 87,000 ships and landing craft, more than 100,000 tanks and self-propelled guns, 47 million tons of artillery shells, and 44 billion rounds of small-arms ammunition.

To achieve such goals, it became necessary to centralize coordination of personnel, equipment, facilities, raw materials, and industrial information. From January 1942 to September 1944, responsibility for this enormous undertaking fell to Donald M. Nelson, a Sears, Roebuck executive picked to head the War Production Board (WPB). With thousands of employees and volunteers, Nelson oversaw the war efforts of 13 million workers at 185,999 factories nationwide.

By May 1942 Nelson had 16,000 new plants operating around-the-clock shifts, and thousands of older factories had been converted to war industries. Former canneries now made parts for merchant ships; cotton-processing plants produced guns; bedspread manufacturers turned out mosquito netting; a soft drink company loaded shells with explosives; a shoe manufacturer forged cannon; and a former burial-vault builder now specialized in one-hundred-pound bombs.

Some of these almost miraculous changes were wrought by industrialists like Henry J. Kaiser and Henry Ford. With no previous experience in shipbuilding (he called ships' bows "front ends"), Kaiser introduced mass production and prefabrication techniques. In 1941 it took eight months to produce a Liberty ship, a version of a British tramp steamer that became our premier cargo carrier. Within two years, Kaiser cut that time to fourteen days. A record time was set when workers at his Richmond, California, plant assembled the *Robert E. Peary* in less than five days.

One of the largest defense plants in the U.S. was built by Henry Ford at Willow Run outside Detroit for the manufacture of B-24 Liberator bombers. Completed in six months, the $65-million plant consisted of a single building a half-mile long and nearly a quarter-mile wide. Raw materials were fed from railroad sidings and loading ramps at one end of the building and joined with assembled components en route to the far side of the plant, where completed B-24s rolled out onto a runway to be flight-tested.

The Willow Run facility encountered difficulties caused by repeated design changes in the complex aircraft; absenteeism among the employees forced to commute more than twenty miles from Detroit in an era of gas and tire rationing; and a general shortage of workers that was exacerbated by Ford's strict regulations and his refusal to hire women for factory positions. During its first year, Willow Run produced only one bomber a day, leading critics to dub the facility "Willit Run?" By 1944, however, streamlining increased production to one bomber every sixty-three minutes. By war's end, 8,685 planes had rolled off the Willow Run assembly line.

The shortage of workers [a]ffected all businesses. A sign on a diner read "Be polite to our waitresses. They are harder to get than customers." A newspaper advertised: "Wanted: Registered druggist; young or old, deaf or dumb. Must have license and walk without crutches. Apply Clover Leaf Drug Store."

One solution to the problem was the opening of previously male-only positions to women. Initially there was resistance; during the first six months after the bombing of Pearl Harbor, of the 750,000 women who applied for jobs in the defense industry only about 80,000 were hired. Necessity however, soon forced manufacturers to put aside their prejudices, and advertisements courting prospective women employees appeared, proclaiming "If you can drive a car, you can run a machine" or "If you've followed recipes exactly in making cakes, you can learn to load shells."

Single women, widows, wives, and those whose husbands were away at war responded in great numbers. In Marietta, Georgia, the eighty-year-old widow of Confederate General James Longstreet joined the 8:00 A.M. shift at the Bell Aircraft Company. By 1945 about 16.5 million women comprised 36 percent of the labor force.

"By late 1943 acute labor shortages meant that even a short, skinny sixteen-year-old girl with an eighth-grade education was employable," recalls Pennsylvanian Sonya Jason, who coated glider wings at a Heinz factory in Pittsburgh. Later Sonya moved to the state capital at Harrisburg, where she and coworkers "fought home-front battles—rent-gouging landladies, amorous girl-starved servicemen, shortages of everything, fatigue and boredom—all for $25 for a six-day week."

Some companies hired leading fashion designers such as Lily Dache to create uniforms for their women workers. These creations were not well received; American women did not like being told what to wear. When Vought-Sikorsky tried to ban sweaters at its aircraft plant, "Rosie the Riveters" ignored such restrictions. Other companies tried to do away with the popular "Veronica Lake" hairdo (long tresses covering one eye), but some female workers persisted until the movie star, as a patriotic gesture, altered her own hairstyle. Most companies

4. FROM THE GREAT DEPRESSION TO WORLD WAR II

simply asked that women workers wear "practical" clothing: slacks, sturdy shoes, hair in bandannas or net snoods.

Women proved their worth, and their presence usually improved working conditions for everyone through cleaner, better cafeterias and rest rooms; labor-saving lifts; and increased safety precautions. They also seemed to loaf less on the job and were less concerned with jockeying for the boss's favor. Despite their performance, however, women were not paid as much for their labor as their male counterparts, earning about forty percent of the salaries paid to men for the same work.

Like women, blacks seeking employment in the defense industry faced prejudice based on stereotypes. When the U.S. entered the war, most defense jobs were virtually closed to African Americans; one aircraft company for example, had ten black workers among 33,000 employees. When blacks threatened to stage a massive protest march on Washington in 1941, President Roosevelt issued Executive Order 8802 banning discrimination on the basis of race in the defense industry. To enforce the ban, the Fair Employment Practices Commission was established. Although successful in resolving some complaints, the commission lacked the enforcement authority necessary to bring about desegregation in defense plants. More blacks were hired and more acquired desirable job skills, but the overall economic situation of African Americans continued to lag far behind that of whites. The situation exploded into riots in several American cities in 1943 and led to a renewed activism that presaged the civil rights movement of the 1950s and '60s.

The national shortage of workers also resulted in the hiring of children under the age of sixteen in contravention of child labor laws, with an attendant rise in rates of truancy and school dropouts. In 1943, Lockheed Aircraft hired 1,500 boys as riveters, draftsmen, and electricians. For most youngsters, however, employment took the form of lesser jobs in drugstores, restaurants, or dime stores that had been vacated by adults now working in the defense industry.

Dorothy Martell, a young teacher at the time, saw her classes grow in size as male teachers entered the services. Then some of her older students "quit school and went to work in factories in Pittsburgh. One student came to visit

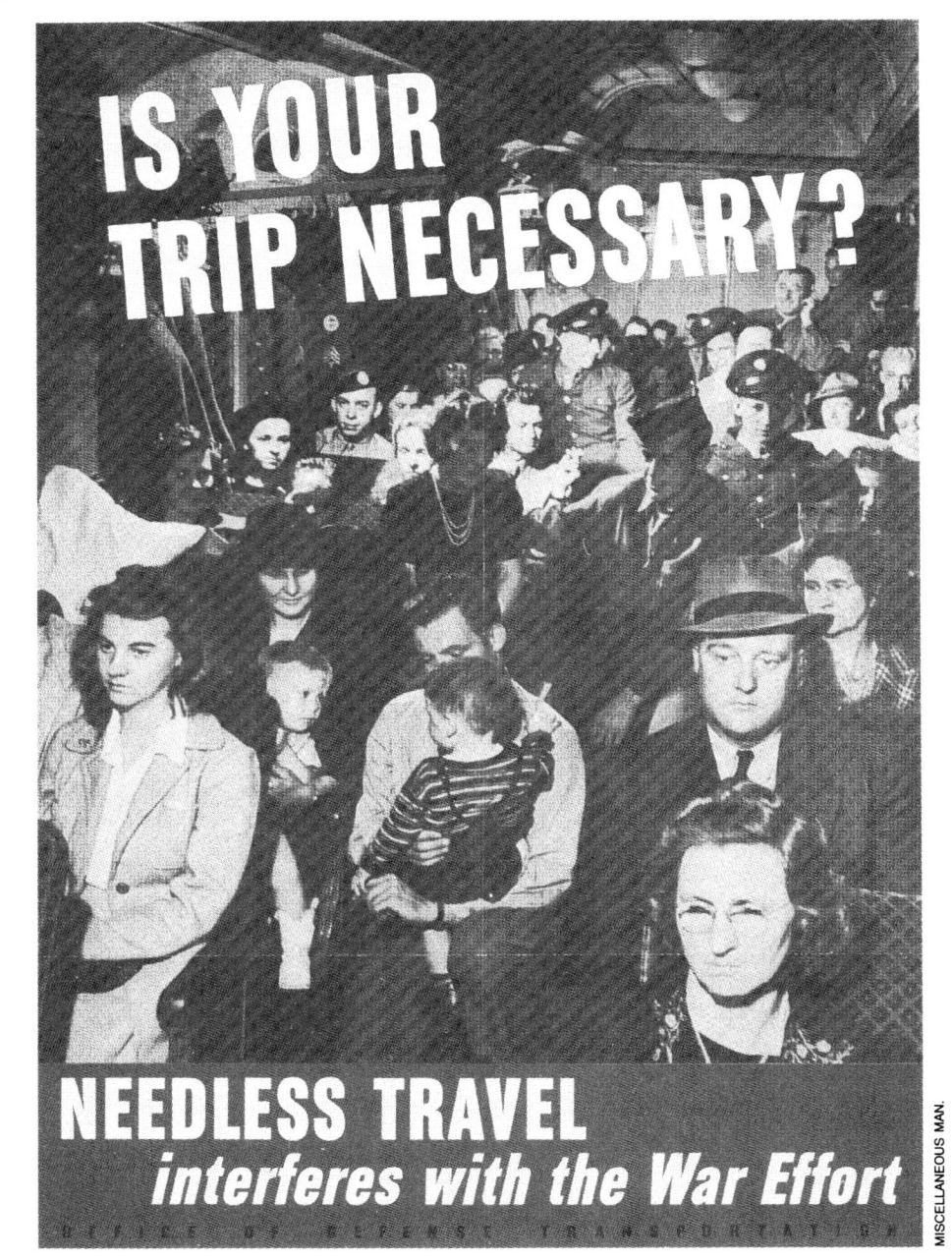

Metal items were salvaged enthusiastically by Americans of all ages for recycling into tanks, guns, and ammunition. The successful scrap drives resulted in huge heaps of "junk"; hard-pressed to keep up with the collection, the government nevertheless put it all to good use.

me, showed me his paycheck and noted that he was making more than I was. Furthermore, he told me that he had some influence and could get me a job if I wanted it."

As Americans followed jobs to their sources or loved ones to military bases, we became a transient society and certain areas of the country experienced sudden and enormous growth. Particularly congested were the shipyard centers of Mobile, Alabama; Hampton Roads, Virginia; San Diego, California; and Charleston, South Carolina, whose populations rose anywhere from thirty-eight to more than sixty-four percent.

The most obvious problem associated with this influx of new residents was finding adequate housing. Many of San Francisco's two million newcomers slept in garages on mattresses spread out on cement floors. Near San Pablo, a California Navy base, a family of four adults and seven children made do with two cots and a full-sized bed in an eight-by-ten-foot wooden shack. "Bomber City" near Ford's Willow Run plant housed 14,000 workers in trailers, dormitories, and prefabricated family units. At some sites, workers paid 25 cents to sleep in a "hot bed" during an eight-hour shift, then stood in long lines at restaurants and used shower or restroom facilities wherever they could find them.

The situation in the nation's capital typified the housing problem. In less than a year, twenty-seven prefabricated office buildings sprang up in the city. The Pentagon, the huge nerve center of the armed forces, followed. Almost 300,000 new government workers staffed these facilities. Housing for the newcomers was nearly non-existent. Since hotels limited stays to three days, many people made the rounds from one to another, never sure where they would rest that night. Hospitals induced childbirth when a room was vacant lest one not be available when the mother's time came.

Many wives followed their husbands to military training camps and then to ports of embarkation. Care-worn and

4. FROM THE GREAT DEPRESSION TO WORLD WAR II

often disheveled, with crying babies and heavy suitcases, they appeared at bus and train stations, endured outrageous rents, and cooked on portable stoves, all for the few hours they might have with their loved ones. When Sue Williams and her mother joined her stepfather, then a serviceman stationed in Charlotte, North Carolina, they lived in quarters that "consisted of one room and a closet-kitchen containing a table and a hot plate. My mother thought she should buy some food and cook a meal. Checking her purse, she found $1.50 and no ration stamps. This was Friday. Payday was Monday. She decided to go to the grocery store and beg, borrow or steal. Our family lived for three days on dehydrated potato soup and a loaf of bread."

During 1940–45, the number of families headed at least temporarily by women jumped from 770,000 to more than 2.7 million. Anthropologist Margaret Mead observed that when American men returned from the war they would find women "more interchangeable with men than they used to be, better able to fix a tire, or mend a faucet or fix an electrical connection, or preside at a meeting, or keep a treasurer's account, or organize a political campaign than when they went away."

With fathers and older brothers in uniform and mothers working, children were cared for by friends, grandparents, or often simply fended for themselves. With no daycare facilities, mothers left children wherever they could, providing as stable an environment as possible under the circumstances.

School children were very patriotic. They kept war maps; proudly displayed bits of uniforms; wore unit patches on their sleeves; read comic books such as "Spy Smasher," "GI Joe," or "Don Winslow of the Navy;" and used allowances to buy 10- and 25-cent defense stamps. "We fought the war daily in school," remembers Joseph Gregory, then a boy in Laurel Run, Pennsylvania. "Our tablets would be filled with aerial 'dog fights' which, to be sure, the sons of the emperor would always lose. My classmates and I must have downed three hundred Japanese Zeros each and at least that many German Messerschmidts without any of us even getting scratched."

Students took part in school air-raid drills, crouching beneath desks in the approved fashion until the "all clear" buzzer sounded. Young patriots picked streets, back yards, and attics clean of paper, tinfoil, rubber, iron, and tin cans (with the ends removed and the cans flattened) for scrap drives. In Robert Jollay's school in Dayton, Ohio, all the children "learned to KNIT! From the first to sixth grade, we knitted small, varied colored squares. These squares, which measured six by six inches, we were told, were sent to a central location and made into blankets for the troops. I've often wondered what became of my squares."

Even before Pearl Harbor, as the United States provided matériel for its allies and Americans raised funds for Bundles for Britain, the nation felt the war's effects on the availability of various commodities that originated in countries no longer open for trade. The U.S. entrance into the war and the consequent needs of the military and defense industry caused additional shortages of hundreds of ordinary items ranging from batteries, lawn mowers, and cigarettes to bobby pins, diapers, and soap. Paper match books vanished; so did zippers, only recently introduced in clothing.

The federal government established the Office of Price Administration (OPA) in April 1941 to oversee the marketplace so that goods in short supply could, through rationing, be made available to consumers on an equitable basis and to regulate prices in order to prevent runaway inflation. The OPA began by controlling raw materials used in manufacturing, then expanded to rationing many consumer goods.

On the local level, the OPA was represented by 5,500 ration boards staffed by volunteers, whose number eventually grew to 30,000. These boards issued "War Ration Book One" to consumers in May 1942. The ration stamps in each book represented "points" that were needed to buy the restricted items. Each individual received sixty-four red stamps (for meat, fish, and dairy products) and forty-eight blue Stamps (for processed foods) each month.

The number of points needed for a particular product varied with the scarcity of goods. Applesauce, for example, required ten blue points or stamps in March 1943 and twenty-five twelve months later; grapefruit juice, during the same period, went from twenty-three blue points to just four.

Housewives had the bewildering task of putting their family's ration stamps to best use, finding grocery stores stocking the items they needed, and arriving there with purses stuffed with the right number and kind of stamps. According to George Kaulbach, who lived in Atlanta with his family during the war years, "If someone needed an extra pair of shoes, meat and sugar coupons were offered in exchange. Everyone swapped for gas stamps. Some who did not use them sold them for a sporty price. All this was illegal, but it happened."

Sugar, the first item rationed, remained scarce until 1946 (newsman Walter Winchell whimsically wrote "Roses are Red/Violets are Blue/Sugar is Sweet, Remember?"). Each person was permitted to buy eight ounces of the sweetener a week, but grocers often did not have sugar in stock, causing housewives to find substitutes in saccharin, corn syrup, honey or molasses.

Meat rationing began on March 29, 1943 with each person allowed twenty-eight ounces per week. The number of points required varied with the type of meat and cut, as well as with its availability.

Butter was especially precious. A half-pound, when one could get it, might cost a week's supply of red stamps. It was something Louise Butler really missed. Then one day her mother returned from the store with a whole pound of the spread. "I slipped away with it to a hiding place behind the sofa. I ate just a little, and then a little more until it was half gone, three-quarters gone, and finally all gone. Mother never could figure out whom to blame. Every morning I was tortured by remorse as the family went without."

An artificially colored margarine developed as a substitute took the form of white lard-like cakes that came with an envelope of vegetable food coloring. When kneaded into the spread, the margarine might pass for anemic butter: unfortunately it still tasted like lard. "If you were blind, you didn't need the coloring because it didn't [a]ffect the taste," recalls George Kaulbach. "For the rest of us it was a necessity. Who wants to coat their toast with white grease?"

Coffee rationing, begun in November 1942, eased the following summer when South American supplies became available. The one pound authorized to each person was supposed to last for five

20. Home Front

weeks. Hotels stopped giving refills, and railroad diners did not serve coffee at all, except for breakfast. One woman, caught with a large supply she had gathered before rationing began, explained to authorities that "I'm just stocking up before the hoarders get it all."

Probably the biggest inconvenience caused by rationing on the home front came with the restrictions placed on the use of Americans' beloved automobiles. On February 2, 1942 the last wartime civilian automobile (a Ford) authorized by the OPA came off a Detroit assembly line. Americans had to be made to drive less, and cars had to last longer. Rubber, a product of territories occupied by Japan, and vitally important for the tires of both military and civilian vehicles, was especially scarce. A speed limit of thirty-five miles per hour was enacted to save wear and tear on the tires, and a massive scrap drive to recycle used rubber began.

The OPA cut tire production for civilian use from 4 million to 35,000 a month. No one was supposed to own more than four tires; anyone with extras was expected to turn them in. To prolong tire use drivers tried recapping and sometimes wrapped plastic, paper, or cornsilk between a worn inner tube and the tire itself. Eventually a synthetic rubber was developed, easing the shortage.

The unpopular notion of gasoline rationing to cut down on car use was introduced in certain areas as early as the spring of 1942, but took effect nationally in December of that year. Each car and truck was assigned a colored sticker emblazoned with a large letter to be affixed to its windshield. The letter indicated the quantity of gasoline the vehicle's driver could buy each week.

An "A" sticker, the one most Americans received, authorized the purchase of from three to five gallons per week. "B" stickers went to war workers, entitling them to exactly as much as they needed to get back and forth to work; those who required automobiles for their jobs but could not estimate precisely how much driving they would have to do (doctors, clergymen, and telegram deliverers) were issued a "C" sticker. Almost unlimited fuel went to emergency vehicles with "E" stickers, trucks marked with a "T", and a few civilians who qualified for an "X" sticker. No sticker, however, could guarantee that there would be any gasoline to buy. Long lines of thirsty automobiles could often be seen trailing gas delivery trucks to their destinations.

The need to conserve rubber, fuel, and metal also [a]ffected commercial transportation. Travel by airline, for those not in uniform, became a non-option. And with increased pressure on buses and trains, comfort while traveling became a distant memory. It was nothing to have to sit on a suitcase or stand for an eight-hour trip. Sue Williams was a child when she and her mother headed out by train from Bloomington, Illinois, to join her stepfather in Charlotte, North Carolina. "Train schedules and seating were dictated by military needs, and there was no guarantee that a train would go when or where it was scheduled, or that it would ever go," she remembers. "Our route should have been Bloomington-Cincinnati-Charlotte, switching trains at Cincinnati. It turned out to be Bloomington-Cincinnati-Washington-Richmond-Charlotte, with three switches and double the time."

To save electricity all Americans turned their clocks ahead one hour on February 2, 1942, putting the country on War Time. Fuel oil and coal rationing cut consumption for heating by one-third as folks at home donned sweaters in the evening, went to bed early and set thermostats at sixty-five degrees.

By February 1943 clothing, too, was becoming scarce. Each person was allowed two pairs of shoes a year, but most families pooled stamps to buy shoes for growing children. To conserve cloth, tailors fashioned "Victory Suits" with short jackets, narrow lapels, no vests, and one pair of trousers (no cuffs).

As a further means of combating shortages of rubber, paper, and critical metals, Americans held scrap drives. Everywhere there were reminders: a poster proclaiming "Slap the Japs with Scrap;" Bing Crosby singing "Junk Will Win the War" (not his best effort); or an old jalopy on its way to be recycled bearing the sign, "Praise the Lord, I'll Soon Be Ammunition."

Children turned in masses of tinfoil, tin cans, and old overshoes (scrap rubber was worth a penny a pound at most gas stations). A youngster in Maywood, Illinois—told that a P-51 fighter plane required 1,069 square feet of paper packaging for overseas shipment—collected one hundred tons of scrap paper.

Leon Wahlbrink, while in the first grade, got enthused about scrap drives. "All of us who collected scrap got to wear an arm band," he recalls. "I could not have been prouder to wear a Marine dress-uniform. On more than one Saturday I pulled my red wagon around town and proudly picked up scrap metal on the curb in front of people's homes."

Billy Kerr's high school in Baytown (then Goose Creek), Texas, had a nice Civil War bronze cannon mounted on a pedestal. "Unfortunately this historical memento went into, and served as the centerpiece of, a special brass, copper, and bronze scrap drive which also featured old razor blade injectors, wire, water faucets, and all sorts of weird cop-

Americans helped to finance the war by buying $135 billion in war savings bonds. School children bought savings stamps that, when they filled an album, were redeemable for a $25 bond.

4. FROM THE GREAT DEPRESSION TO WORLD WAR II

Hasten the Homecoming

BUY VICTORY BONDS

LIBRARY OF CONGRESS.

Back to Elm Street, U. S. A.

MISCELLANEOUS MAN.

per-containing items that only high school students could possibly locate."

Housewives—made aware that one pound of kitchen fat provided enough glycerine for a pound of black powder, which then equated to six artillery shells or fifty .30-caliber bullets—took what they had saved to the local butcher, who sometimes sweetened their reward with red ration stamps.

To increase the nation's food supply, Americans cultivated "Victory Gardens" wherever the ground would hold them—the Portland, Oregon zoo; Boston common; a downtown parking lot in New Orleans; Chicago's Arlington Race Track—in tracts ranging from eight-by-ten-feet backyard plots to hundreds of acres behind defense plants. The 20.5 million Victory Gardens cultivated in 1943 provided more than thirty percent of all the vegetables grown in America that year. Growing food was something the ordinary citizen felt good about—a tangible and tasty way to help the war effort.

There was some black marketing in rationed goods, but most home-front Americans played pretty straight. Sometimes they became angrier at "stoopers"—store owners who always seemed able to stoop behind their counters and come up with a scarce item for favored customers—than at black marketeers.

Americans—once again reaping the benefits of a healthy economy—also helped to finance the war. A five-percent surcharge, dubbed a "Victory Tax," was added to each wage-earner's federal income tax. To put more funds immediately at the government's disposal, employers were required to withhold taxes from workers' pay instead of allowing them to make a single payment each March. In addition to helping the national treasury these measures cut down on individual spending and thus prevented inflation from

More than three years after Pearl Harbor, the cherished dream of all Americans—the safe return home of loved ones—finally became a reality for most following V-E Day on May 8, 1945 and then V-J Day on August 15. Victory and peace had now been won—at the cost of 320,000 war dead and through the commitment of tens of millions of other men and women both in and out of uniform.

20. Home Front

getting out of control, a real danger during such an economic boom.

To further reduce the enormous debt incurred by the nation during the war, the government began the sale of war bonds. Sold in denominations ranging from $25 (ten-year maturity on the $18.75 purchase price) to $10,000, the bonds brought $135 billion into the national treasury.

War heroes, entertainers, and other popular figures on the home front helped to sell the bonds. Actress Betty Grable donated her nylons to the top bidder at a bond rally; Man O' War's horseshoes rewarded another; comedian Jack Benny's $75 violin brought a $1-million bid; and starlet Hedy Lamarr promised to reward any buyer of $25,000 worth of bonds with a kiss. Singer Kate Smith outdid all rivals when she sold $40 million in bonds during a sixteen-hour radio marathon.

The media and the entertainment industry played an important role in keeping the American public informed and in a positive frame of mind during the war years. In June 1942 President Roosevelt created the Office of War Information (OWI), charging it to "tell the people as much about the war as possible, as fast as possible, and with as few contradictions as possible." There was a lot of home-grown propaganda in the media's offerings but, all in all, reports from the battle lines were accurate and reached the public quickly. By 1944 CBS was devoting thirty percent of its air time to war news, and NBC's news coverage had grown from 1939's 3.6 percent to better than 20 percent. FDR himelf used radio, in a series of "fireside chats," to keep Americans informed of the war's progress.

American newspapers and radio had more than seven hundred reporters and correspondents stationed overseas at a given time; more than four hundred covered the D-Day Normandy landings. "Geography may not have been in the curriculum for those of us in the primary grades," recalls Leon Wahlbrink, "but I can guarantee that we learned it. Each day the newspapers printed maps of the war zones, and the front pages were covered with stories of the war's progress. Hans V. Kaltenborn, Gabriel Heater, and Edward R. Murrow were heard broadcasting war news every day. The programs originating from the battle areas made an indelible mark on my young mind."

The most popular American correspondent was Ernie Pyle, a slight (110 pounds), balding man in his forties who found his stories, not in generals' headquarters or Pentagon offices, but among the ranks of the beleaguered foot soldiers he accompanied into battle. Pyle's newspaper column appeared six times a week in 310 newspapers for an audience of more than 12 million readers. His writings brought the war home, perhaps even more clearly than today's television journalism, because he not only pictured war but made the reader *feel* it and *think* about it. He marched with the troops from Africa to Sicily to Italy to France; then he went to the Pacific theater—and was killed on the tiny atoll of Ie Shima near Okinawa. Over his grave his fellow soldiers placed a headstone: "On this spot the 77th Infantry Division lost a buddy, Ernie Pyle, 18 April 1945."

On newspaper "funny pages," comic-strip heroes went to war too. The Army had Privates Joe Palooka and Snuffy Smith. The Air Corps had Terry of "Terry and the Pirates" and Smilin' Jack. The Navy had Don Winslow and Dick Tracy (special duty with Naval Intelligence when he was not battling such criminals as Pruneface, 88 Keys, Brow or Flattop on the home front). Tillie the Toiler joined the WAACS, and Fritzie Ritz (of "Nancy") and Winnie Winkle took their places on assembly lines.

During the last months of the war, an irresistible cartoon—a bulb-nosed, scant-haired, wide-eyed man peering over some kind of wall, always with the simple message "Kilroy was Here"—appeared on the combat front and on virtually every public surface at home. The ubiquitous character epitomized the spirit of the American GI at war—omnipotent, irreverent, and *there*.

The OWI tried to guide Hollywood's movie-making efforts by suggesting that they not condemn *all* Germans and Japanese; show farm boys remaining on the farm instead of enlisting (food production was critical to the war effort); and not portray Chinese in menial positions, Englishmen living lavishly or GIs as cocky, bumptious, and undisciplined. Producers bought some of OWI's guidance, but ignored most of it.

The movie industry provided films with both recreational and propaganda value, as well as military and industrial training films. John O'Neill recalls that "on Saturday afternoons we would go to the movies and watch John Wayne and the Fighting Seabees capture an island to build an airstrip for our pilots. Then we watched a short, patriotic film urging us to buy War Bonds. 'Buy a Bond to Buy a Bomber and Send Your Name to War' was the slogan they used."

In retrospect, wartime films seem to have inspired us to fight the Nazis because they were the aggressor and had to be fought, but to seek the utter destruction of the Japanese because we hated what they had done to us at Pearl Harbor, Wake Island, and Bataan. Early movies did not dwell on the extent of America's losses at Pearl Harbor and seldom showed U.S. war dead. Some—*The Story of G.I. Joe* and *Guadalcanal Diary* among them—were good motion pictures, but mainly war movies such as *Mrs. Miniver, Thirty Seconds Over Tokyo, The Purple Heart, Objective Burma,* and *Wake island* were intended to arouse the nation's patriotism and will to win.

Movie stars and other celebrities also helped the war effort by entertaining servicemen at United Service Organization (USO) canteens across the country. The USO's three thousand canteens provided a club-like atmosphere for those away from home. When Vice President Harry S. Truman showed up to play for the troops at the canteen in the National Press Club building in Washington; D.C., his performance was enhanced by the presence of Hollywood star Lauren Bacall perched atop the piano. At the "Stage Door Canteen," in the basement of New York's Forty-Fourth Street Thea-

4. FROM THE GREAT DEPRESSION TO WORLD WAR II

ter, Broadway stars entertained, danced with servicemen, or helped by washing dishes, pouring coffee, or just chatting with those who stopped by. Hollywood's canteen attracted stars and starlets under the watchful eye of its first director, actress Bette Davis.

Music was a major source of enjoyment or comfort to war-weary Americans. There were patriotic songs—"Praise the Lord and Pass the Ammunition" "Remember Pearl Harbor," and Irving Berlin's "This is the Army, Mr. Jones"; sentimental favorites such as "Don't Sit Under the Apple Tree," and "Don't Get Around Much Anymore," which reflected the loneliness of loved ones separated by the war; and specially crafted numbers, most very short-lived, supporting such home front phenomena as bond drives ("Cash for Your Trash"), Victory Gardens ("Get Out and Dig, Dig, Dig"), and women defense workers ("Rosie the Riveter").

Despite the war, sports remained popular on the home front. When baseball commissioner Judge Kennesaw Mountain Landis addressed the question of cancelling professional baseball for the duration of the war, President Roosevelt replied that the sport was a "definite recreational asset to at least 20 million [Americans] and that in my judgment is thoroughly worthwhile."

Most professional athletes traded their team uniforms for new ones in the military but ball clubs fielded less skilled, draft-deferred players in their place. The St. Louis Browns signed Pete Gray, a one-armed outfielder who batted .218 during a seventy-seven-game season. One sports writer lamented that rosters of players were as full of unknown names as YMCA hotel registers. There were other problems to be overcome—night baseball was banned in many cities; rail travel from city to city was difficult; and baseballs were in short supply (eventually we accepted a different composition ball, but then argued whether hitters got an unfair advantage from the new ball).

Nonetheless, more than 4 million fans attended major-league baseball games in 1942, and Americans continued to support the game throughout the war years. In New York City the Yankees, Giants, and Dodgers played a three-team exhibition game to sell war bonds. Each team batted six times against rotating opponents. The score: Dodgers 5, Yankees 1, Giants 0; Uncle Sam $56.5 million.

More than six hundred players from the ten-team National Football League went into military service. The league continued during the war, but, due to the shortage of players, teams—the Philadelphia Eagles and the Pittsburgh Steelers in 1943, the Brooklyn Tigers and the new Boston Yanks in 1945—were forced to merge squads. College football, dominated by West Point's Army team, included service teams from such facilities as the Great Lakes Naval Training Center near Chicago and California's March Field among their ranks.

When Franklin D. Roosevelt won an unprecedented fourth term as president in November 1944, comedian Bob Hope teased, "I've always voted for Roosevelt as president; my *father* always voted for Roosevelt as president."

As that year drew to a close, more and more living room windows displayed service flags. Now however, because there had been many Western Union messengers bearing telegrams beginning "The War Department regrets to inform you . . . ," many of the blue stars had been replaced by gold. At Christmas Mrs. Belle Ellzey of Texas, who lost her son, Lieutenant John G. Ellzey, in France expressed the feelings of many an American mother: "I am so very homesick for him. It is Christmas—and . . . I cannot write to him, putting my tears into words, for my eyes stay strangely dry."

Finally by the spring of 1945 it was clear that the war would soon be over. But it was too soon to celebrate. On April 12 Americans were stunned to learn that President Roosevelt, having suffered a massive cerebral hemorrhage while at his "Little White House" near Warm Springs, Georgia, was dead.

The news flashed across the country with great force. Businesses closed. Theaters emptied. Traffic slowed to a halt. Newspaper "extras" hit the streets. All military units in the country were put on alert. A New York City cab driver stopped, parked, and cried, "It just doesn't seem possible." A hastily-closed shop in Pittsburgh bore the simple sign "He died." In Washington, a soldier probably spoke for most Americans when he confided, "I felt as if I knew him—and I felt as if he liked me."

For three days and nights radio programming was suspended, except for news broadcasts and religious music. After appropriate national ceremonies in Washington, Roosevelt's body was returned to his home in Hyde Park, New York, for burial. On a Sunday morning the funeral train chugged its way up the shore of the Hudson River past West Point and through Beacon, where the young girl who, four years before, had been scolded for breaking her Japanese toy piano, held her mother's hand and promised to always remember that day.

Less than a month later, on May 8, 1945, Germany officially surrendered, ending the war in Europe. The news touched off a frenzied celebration in the United States. Schools, offices, and defense plants emptied, and streets were filled with jubilant revelers who sounded whatever noisemakers they had. In St. Charles, Missouri, Leon Wahlbrink rushed off to join in the town's impromptu parade as "horns honked, church bells pealed, factory whistles went full blast for hours. It was a grand and glorious day."

Three months later, on the other side of the world, Japan surrendered. Three years, eight months, and seven days after the attack on Pearl Harbor, the war was over at a cost of more than a million American casualties.

The surviving soldiers, sailors, and airmen came home. They seemed older, a bit tense, impatient to do at once everything they had dreamed about during the past four years. And their language was pretty salty at times. Soon however, they picked up most of their prewar ways. Home-front emergency defense organizations were disbanded. Defense workers gave up (or were laid off from) wartime jobs, moving over to give the veterans their places.

"Perhaps my most significant memory from the early forties," sums up Cornelius Lynch, "is that overnight the world around me had changed dramatically and significantly.... For me, it was part of growing up but I realize now that it was more than simply a childhood I had left behind; it was another age."

The war, which had eradicated the last vestiges of the Great Depression and marked the U.S. as an economic and military superpower, also significantly altered Americans' perceptions of how things should be. Previously held assumptions about a "woman's place" or an African American's ability to get a job done would never again go unchallenged. "Female clothing became feminine [in the postwar years,] and veterans wanted their women to return home and stay there," says Sonya Jason, "but the genie could not be squeezed back into the bottle. Few of us who experienced the satisfaction of doing a demanding job and earning our own money could ever again be content to be dependent on anyone else, even the man we loved."

The American people had demonstrated a remarkable unanimity of purpose during almost four years of war. Although they never wavered in the belief that the Allies would prevail, Americans realized early on that winning would not be easy. But almost everyone, it seemed, felt a personal sense of responsibility to get the job done. On the home front, citizens pretty much did what their leaders asked—and a bit more. "To a boy growing from age six to ten, World War II, with all its horrors, was a romantic period," recalls Leon Wahlbrink. "I was fortunate that it did not tragically touch my most immediate family. Maybe it was just me at my young age, but the war seemed to be a time of unparalleled heroes and patriotism. We were proud to be Americans."

Fifty years later, the ranks of World War II veterans (both those in uniform and those who maintained the home front) have thinned. We wear bifocals now and aren't quite so concerned about the extra pounds and the receding hair (too late to worry about that) as we were when we were younger. Some of those who once wore uniforms still squeeze into them to fire rifle volleys at funerals or Veterans' Day rallies, while home-front veterans preserve their memories in other ways. But all of us remain very concerned about our country. May *that* characteristic of Americans never change.

The editors wish to express their appreciation to the numerous individuals who shared their home-front memories as part of this article.

Operation Overlord from the Inside

D-Day, June 6, 1944:
The Climactic Battle of World War II
By Stephen E. Ambrose
Simon & Schuster.
655 pp. $30.00.

Reviewed by
William L. O'Neill
Professor of history, Rutgers; author, "A Democracy at War: America's Fight at Home and Abroad in World War II"

Cornelius Ryan's classic *The Longest Day*, though still a wonderful read, came out in 1959 when much vital information about Operation Overlord remained classified or was otherwise unavailable. Thus a need existed that many historians were eager to fill, and early this spring books began pouring off the presses to coincide with the 50th anniversary of the momentous event.

There are at least two reasons why *D-Day, June 6, 1944* stands out in what is now a crowded field. Its first advantage is the author himself, Stephen Ambrose, one of the best and most widely read of contemporary military historians and biographers. He brings to his new work the narrative drive, thorough research and muscular prose he is justly famous for. Second, as the director of the Eisenhower Center at the University of New Orleans, Ambrose has been able to draw on some 1,400 oral histories and written memoirs contributed by D-Day veterans. This important collection, the largest number of firsthand accounts of a single battle in existence, has made it possible for him to fill his story with details and observations that could only come from men who had been there.

Ambrose begins by setting the stage in 10 chapters that describe the rival armies and commanders and the problems facing each side. The sequence ends with Eisenhower's decision, one of the most critical of the War, to move out on June 6 despite a heavy rain. Ike staked Overlord on his belief that the 36 hours of decent weather his chief meteorologist was predicting would arrive on schedule. Had he taken the safer course the attack would not have been mounted until two weeks later, when, as it happened, one of the worst storms in many years struck the English Channel. Either it would have wrecked the invasion or forced another delay, jeopardizing the element of surprise on which everything depended. And an Allied failure would have dragged out the War in Europe for another year at the minimum.

The next 21 chapters establish that, if posterity owes much to Eisenhower, it owes even more to those who were called upon to carry out the operation. There is a good deal of exciting battle narrative here, but Ambrose never loses control of the argument he is making virtually from the first page to the last: American productivity alone is not what won the War; American democracy was no less a factor, for it had produced men whose spirit and initiative could not be matched by opponents serving a dictatorship.

At the top, Eisenhower had complete charge of every aspect of the offensive, while the defense of Normandy was conducted by two field marshals, Erwin Rommel and Gerd von Runsted. They had contradictory defense plans, uncertain writs of authority, and were subject to constant interference from Hitler—who personally retained control of the all-important Panzer (armored) divisions. Indeed, a coherent response was impossible under these circumstances.

In contrast, the best American commanders knew that in battle flexibility is everything, and they had the freedom to act accordingly. Nobody demonstrated this better than Colonel Paul Good, who led the 175th Infantry Regiment. At the conclusion of a briefing he picked up the operation plan for D-Day, which was thicker than a big phone book, tossed it over his shoulder and told his officers: "Forget this goddamned thing. You get your ass on the beach. I'll be there waiting for you and I'll tell you what to do. There ain't anything in this plan that is going to go right." He was correct, especially about Omaha Beach, the most difficult of the five invasion sites, where almost everything did go wrong. Nevertheless, determined men in small uncoordinated groups, relying largely on their own ingenuity, managed to prevail. Only Americans, Ambrose believes, could have done this.

Yet if plans meant little after the attack started, they were critical before. Brilliantly executed deception moves—including a superb air campaign that virtually isolated Normandy from the rest of France while doing damage elsewhere—kept the Germans from knowing where the assault would take place and prevented Hitler from marshaling his numerically superior forces to repel it. The Allies did make a few mistakes. In particular, dropping two airborne divisions at night behind the Atlantic Wall—the chain of fortifications defending France's coast—caused immense confusion and needless casualties that a dawn drop would have avoided.

But the Germans, Ambrose notes, committed far more numerous and costly errors than the Allies. Moreover, Hitler's insistence on directing the battle

21. Operation Overlord

himself paralyzed his officers at every level. To cite one instance, the vitally important Panzer divisions deployed close to the beaches achieved full readiness by 2:00 A.M. on D-Day, but they were not authorized to counterattack until early afternoon when it was easy for naval gunners to turn them back. The German Navy and Air Force failed utterly to interfere with Allied movements.

Ambrose is scornful of the Atlantic Wall. Rommel reasoned that once ashore the Allies could not be driven off because supporting naval gunfire would break up his counterattacks, and therefore the invaders had to be stopped on the beaches. Runsted, Rommel's nominal superior as Commander in Chief West, disagreed. He wanted to concede the beaches and mass his forces inland beyond the range of the naval guns. Hitler split the difference, giving Rommel three panzer divisions and Runsted four—although none of them could move without the Führer's authorization.

As Ambrose sees it, Runsted was right. He dismisses Rommel's argument that counterattacks well inland would still fail because of Allied air power. Had Runsted's strategy been followed, Ambrose speculates, the Allied advance would have stalled at the Somme-Seine barrier. Yet when the Germans launched a Panzer counterattack on August 6 against the Americans who had broken out of Normandy, it was destroyed by rampaging tank-killers of the American tactical air arm. The subsequent rout was so complete that one terrified German unit actually surrendered to the U.S. 405th Fighter-Bomber Group.

This suggests that Rommel was right. If the Allies could be stopped at all, it had to be on the beaches. But Rommel lacked the means to do so, and probably still would not have succeeded with all seven Panzer divisions at his disposal. There seem to have been only two things that could have caused D-Day to go wrong: bad weather or German foreknowledge of the Allied landing sites. Absent either of those conditions, the Allies' overwhelming air and naval superiority, together with the vast stretch of coast to be defended, assured Germany's ruin. On D-Day the Atlantic Wall was pierced at all five points of attack, mostly within the first hour. The best the Germans could do was buy time; the outcome of the invasion was never in doubt.

Historians will of course always disagree on one or another point. It is unlikely, though, that any will produce a book like *D-Day, June 6, 1994,* with its wealth of detail, absorbing vignettes and rich anecdotal material. Take the following observation by a former ranger who survived the landing and 11 more months of combat. The Allied High Command, he remarked in his oral history, was right to ensure that "there be no experienced troops in the initial waves that hit the beach, because an experienced infantryman is a terrified infantryman, and they wanted guys like me who were more amazed than they were frozen with fear, because the longer you fight a war the more you figure your number's coming up tomorrow, and it really gets to be God-awful."

By the time darkness fell on June 6 some 175,000 men had gone ashore, of whom about 5,000 became casualties. This was a smaller number than many had expected, but D-Day was only the beginning of America's crusade in Europe. By the time it ended, General Omar N. Bradley recorded in his memoirs, "586,628 American soldiers had fallen—135,576 to rise no more. The grim figures haunted me. I could hear the cries of the wounded, smell the stench of death. I could not sleep: I closed my eyes and thanked God for victory."

The 50th anniversaries of many famous World War II events—the Battle of Midway, Guadalcanal, victory in North Africa, even Pearl Harbor—have passed practically unnoticed in the last two and a half years. The anniversaries yet to come, it appears, will be similarly neglected. D-Day alone holds a place in our collective memory of America's role in World War II. And Stephen Ambrose's compelling book reminds us very graphically of the great things this country once accomplished.

But in remembering D-Day we should not forget the cost of victory. During the War American families who lost loved ones overseas displayed gold stars in their windows. After D-Day, and because the fighting in the Pacific had gotten fiercer too, entire constellations of such stars came out all across America.

The Man of the Century

Of all the Allied leaders, argues FDR's biographer, only Roosevelt saw clearly the shape of the new world they were fighting to create

Arthur Schlesinger, Jr.

Arthur Schlesinger, Jr., is currently at work on a memoir.

After half a century it is hard to approach Franklin D. Roosevelt except through a minefield of clichés. Theories of FDR, running the gamut from artlessness to mystification, have long paraded before our eyes. There is his famous response to the newspaperman who asked him for his philosophy: "Philosophy? I am a Christian and a Democrat—that's all"; there is Robert E. Sherwood's equally famous warning about "Roosevelt's heavily forested interior"; and we weakly conclude that both things were probably true.

FDR's Presidency has commanded the attention of eminent historians at home and abroad for fifty years or more. Yet no consensus emerges, especially in the field of foreign affairs. Scholars at one time or another have portrayed him at every point across a broad spectrum: as an isolationist, as an internationalist, as an appeaser, as a warmonger, as an impulsive decision maker, as an incorrigible vacillator, as the savior of capitalism, as a closet socialist, as a Machiavellian intriguer plotting to embroil his country in foreign wars, as a Machiavellian intriguer avoiding war in order to let other nations bear the brunt of the fighting, as a gullible dreamer who thought he could charm Stalin into postwar collaboration and ended by selling Eastern Europe down the river into slavery, as a tightfisted creditor sending Britain down the road toward bankruptcy, as a crafty imperialist serving the interests of American capitalist hegemony, as a highminded prophet whose vision shaped the world's future. Will the real FDR please stand up?

Two relatively recent books illustrate the chronically unsettled state of FDR historiography—and the continuing vitality of the FDR debate. In *Wind Over Sand* (1988) Frederick W. Marks III finds a presidential record marked by ignorance, superficiality, inconsistency, random prejudice, erratic impulse, a man out of his depth, not waving but drowning, practicing a diplomacy as insubstantial and fleeting as wind blowing over sand. In *The Juggler* (1991), Warren F. Kimball finds a record marked by intelligent understanding of world forces, astute maneuver, and a remarkable consistency of purpose, a farsighted statesman facing dilemmas that defied quick or easy solutions. One-third of each book is given over to endnotes and bibliography, which suggests that each portrait is based on meticulous research. Yet the two historians arrive at diametrically opposite conclusions.

---

*If we can't as historians puzzle out what he **was**, we surely must as historians try to make sense of what he **did**.*

So the debate goes on. Someone should write a book entitled *FDR: For and Against,* modeled on Pieter Geyl's *Napoleon: For and Against.* "It is impossible," the great Dutch historian observed, "that two historians, especially two historians living in different periods, should see any historical personality in the same light. The greater the political importance of a historical character, the more impossible this is." History, Geyl (rightly) concluded, is an "argument without end."

I suppose we must accept that human beings are in the last analysis beyond analysis. In the case of FDR, no one can be really sure what was going on in that affable, welcoming, reserved, elusive, teasing, spontaneous, calculating, cold, warm, humorous, devious, mendacious, manipulative, petty, magnanimous, superficially casual, ultimately decent, highly camouflaged, finally impenetrable mind. Still, if we can't as historians puzzle out what he *was,* we surely must as historians try to make sense out of what he *did.* If his personality escapes us, his policies must have some sort of pattern.

What Roosevelt wrote (or Sam Rosenman wrote for him) in the introduction to the first volume of his *Public Papers* about his record as governor of New York goes, I believe, for his foreign policy too: "Those who seek inconsistencies will find them. There were inconsistencies of methods, inconsistencies caused by ceaseless efforts to find ways to solve problems for the future as well as for the present. There were inconsistencies born of insufficient knowledge. There were inconsistencies springing from the need of experimentation. But through them all, I trust that there also will be found a consistency and continuity of broad purpose."

Now purpose can be very broad indeed. To say that a statesman is in favor of peace, freedom, and security does not narrow things down very much. Meaning resides in the details, and in FDR's case the details often contradict each other. If I may invoke still another cliché, FDR's foreign policy seems to fit Churchill's description of the Soviet Union: "a riddle wrapped in a mystery inside an enigma." However, we too often forget

From American Heritage, *May/June 1994, pp. 82-88, 90-93. © 1994 by Forbes, Inc. Reprinted by permission of* American Heritage *magazine, a division of Forbes, Inc.*

22. Man of the Century

The young Assistant Secretary of the Navy stands with Admirals McKean, left, and Sims in 1919.

what Churchill said next: "But perhaps there is a key. That key is Russian national interest." German domination of Eastern Europe, Churchill continued, "would be contrary to the historic life-interests of Russia." Here, I suggest, may be the key to FDR, the figure in his carpet: his sense of the historic life-interests of the United States.

Of course, "national interest" narrows things down only a little. No one, except a utopian or a millennialist, is against the national interest. In a world of nation-states the assumption that governments will pursue their own interests gives order and predictability to international affairs. As George Washington said, "no nation is to be trusted farther than it is bound by [its] interest." The problem is the substance one pours into national interest. In our own time, for example, Lyndon Johnson and Dean Rusk thought our national interest required us to fight in Vietnam; William Fulbright, Walter Lippmann, Hans Morgenthau thought our national interest required us to pull out of Vietnam. The phrase by itself settles no arguments.

How did FDR conceive the historic life-interests of the United States? His conception emerged from his own long, if scattered, education in world affairs. It should not be forgotten that he arrived in the White House with an unusual amount of international experience. He was born into a cosmopolitan family. His father knew Europe well and as a young man had marched with Garibaldi. His elder half-brother had served in American legations in London and Vienna. His mother's family had been in the China trade; his mother herself had lived in Hong Kong as a little girl. As FDR reminded Henry Morgenthau in 1934, "I have a background of a little over a century in Chinese affairs."

FDR himself made his first trip to Europe at the age of three and went there every summer from his ninth to his fourteenth year. As a child he learned French and German. As a lifelong stamp collector he knew the world's geography and politics. By the time he was elected President, he had made thirteen trips across the Atlantic and had spent almost three years of his life in Europe. "I started . . . with a good deal of interest in foreign affairs," he told a press conference in 1939, "because both branches of my family have been mixed up in foreign affairs for a good many generations, the affairs of Europe and the affairs of the Far East."

Now much of his knowledge was social and superficial. Nor is international experience in any case a guarantee of international wisdom or even of continuing international concern. The other American politician of the time who rivaled FDR in exposure to the great world

133

4. FROM THE GREAT DEPRESSION TO WORLD WAR II

was, oddly, Herbert Hoover. Hoover was a mining engineer in Australia at twenty-three, a capitalist in the Chinese Empire at twenty-five, a promoter in the City of London at twenty-seven. In the years from his Stanford graduation to the Great War, he spent more time in the British Empire than he did in the United States. During and after the war he supervised relief activities in Belgium and in Eastern Europe. Keynes called him the only man to emerge from the Paris Peace Conference with an enhanced reputation.

Both Hoover and Roosevelt came of age when the United States was becoming a world power. Both saw more of that world than most of their American contemporaries. But international experience led them to opposite conclusions. What Hoover saw abroad soured him on foreigners. He took away from Paris an indignant conviction of an impassable gap between his virtuous homeland and the European snake pit. Nearly twenty years passed before he could bring himself to set foot again on the despised continent. He loathed Europe and its nationalist passions and hatreds. "With a vicious rhythm," he said in 1940, "these malign forces seem to drive [European] nations like the Gadarene swine over the precipice of war." The less America had to do with so degenerate a place, the Quaker Hoover felt, the better.

The patrician Roosevelt was far more at home in the great world. Moreover, his political genealogy instilled in him the conviction that the United States must at last take its rightful place among the powers. In horse breeder's parlance, FDR was by Woodrow Wilson out of Theodore Roosevelt. These two remarkable Presidents taught FDR that the United States was irrevocably a world power and poured substance into his conception of America's historic life-interests.

FDR greatly admired TR, deserted the Democratic party to cast his first presidential vote for him, married his niece, and proudly succeeded in 1913 to the office TR had occupied fifteen years earlier, Assistant Secretary of the Navy. From TR and from that eminent friend of both Roosevelts, Admiral Mahan, young Roosevelt learned the strategic necessities of international relations. He learned how to distinguish between vital and peripheral interests. He learned why the national interest required the maintenance of balances of power in areas that, if controlled by a single power, could threaten the United States. He learned what the defense of vital interests might require in terms of ships and arms and men and production and resources. His experience in Wilson's Navy Department during the First World War consolidated these lessons.

But he also learned new things from Wilson, among them that it was not enough to send young men to die and kill because of the thrill of battle or because of war's morally redemptive qualities or even because of the need to restore the balance of power. The awful sacrifices of modern war demanded nobler objectives. The carnage on the Western Front converted FDR to Wilson's vision of a world beyond war, beyond national interest, beyond balances of power, a world not of secret diplomacy and antagonistic military alliances but of an organized common peace, founded on democracy, self-determination, and the collective restraint of aggression.

Theodore Roosevelt had taught FDR geopolitics. Woodrow Wilson now gave him a larger international purpose in which the principles of power had a strong but secondary role. FDR's two mentors detested each other. But they joined to construct the framework within which FDR, who cherished them both, approached foreign affairs for the rest of his life.

As the Democratic vice presidential candidate in 1920, he roamed the country pleading for the League of Nations. Throughout the twenties he warned against political isolationism and economic protectionism. America would commit a grievous wrong, he said, if it were "to go backwards towards an old Chinese Wall policy of isolationism." Trade wars, he said, were "symptoms of economic insanity." But such sentiments could not overcome the disillusion and disgust with which Americans in the 1920s contemplated world troubles. As President Hoover told the Italian foreign minister in 1931, the deterioration of Europe had led to such "despair . . . on the part of the ordinary American citizen [that] now he just wanted to keep out of the whole business."

Depression intensified the isolationist withdrawal. Against the national mood, the new President brought to the White House in 1933 an international outlook based, I would judge, on four principles.

One was TR's commitment to the preservation of the balance of world power. Another was Wilson's vision of concerted international action to prevent or punish aggression. The third principle argued that lasting peace required the free flow of trade among nations. The fourth was that in a democracy foreign policy must rest on popular consent. In the isolationist climate of the 1930s, this fourth principle compromised and sometimes undermined the first three.

Diplomatic historians are occasionally tempted to overrate the amount of time Presidents spend in thinking about foreign policy. In fact, from Jackson to FDR, domestic affairs have always been, with a few fleeting exceptions—perhaps Polk, McKinley, Wilson—the presidential priority. This was powerfully the case at the start for FDR. Given the collapse of the economy and the anguish of unemployment, given the absence of obvious remedy and the consequent need for social experiment, the surprise is how much time and energy FDR did devote to foreign affairs in these early years.

He gave time to foreign policy because of his acute conviction that Germany and Japan were, or were about to be, on the rampage and that unchecked aggression would ultimately threaten vital interests of the United States. He packed the State Department and embassies abroad with unregenerate Wilsonians. When he appointed Cordell Hull Secretary, he knew what he was getting; his brain trusters, absorbed in problems at hand, had warned him against international folly. But there they were, Wilsonians all: Hull, Norman Davis, Sumner Welles, William Phillips, Francis B. Sayre, Walton Moore, Breckinridge Long, Josephus Daniels, W. E. Dodd, Robert W. Bingham, Claude Bowers, Joseph E. Davies. Isolationists like Raymond Moley did not last long at State.

Roosevelt's early excursions into foreign policy were necessarily intermittent, however, and in his own rather distracting personal style. Economic diplomacy he confided to Hull, except when Hull's free-trade obsessions threatened New Deal recovery programs, as at the London Economic Conference of 1933. He liked, when he found the time, to handle the political side of things himself. He relished meetings with foreign leaders and found himself in advance of most of them in his forebodings about Germany and Japan. He invited his ambassadors, especially his political appointees, to write directly to him, and nearly all took advantage of the invitation.

His diplomatic style had its capricious aspects. FDR understood what admirals and generals were up to, and he understood the voice of prophetic statesmanship. But he never fully appreciated the professional diplomat and looked with some disdain on the career Foreign Service as made up of tea drinkers remote from the realities of American life. His approach to foreign policy, while firmly grounded in geopolitics and soaring easily into the higher idealism, always lacked something at the middle level.

At the heart of Roosevelt's style in foreign affairs was a certain incorrigible amateurism.

At the heart of Roosevelt's style in foreign affairs was a certain incorrigible amateurism. His off-the-cuff improvisations, his airy tendency to throw out half-baked ideas, caused others to underrate his continuity of purpose and used to drive the British especially wild, as minutes scribbled on Foreign Office dispatches make abundantly clear. This amateurism had its good points. It could be a source of boldness and creativity in a field populated by cautious and conventional people. But it also encouraged superficiality and dilettantism.

The national mood, however, remained FDR's greatest problem. Any U.S. contribution to the deterrence of aggression depended on giving the government power to distinguish between aggressors and their victims. He asked Congress for this authority, first in cooperating with League of Nations sanctions in 1933, later in connection with American neutrality statutes. Fearing that aid to one side would eventually involve the nation in war, Congress regularly turned him down. By rejecting policies that would support victims against aggressors, Congress effectively nullified the ability of the United States to throw its weight in the scales against aggressors.

Roosevelt, regarding the New Deal as more vital for the moment than foreign policy and needing the support of isolationists for his domestic program, accepted what he could not change in congressional roll calls. But he did hope to change public opinion and began a long labor of popular education with his annual message in January 1936 and its condemnation of "autocratic institutions that beget slavery at home and aggression abroad."

It is evident that I am not persuaded by the school of historians that sees Roosevelt as embarked until 1940 on a mission of appeasement, designed to redress German grievances and lure the Nazi regime into a constructive role in a reordered Europe. The evidence provided by private conversations as well as by public pronouncements is far too consistent and too weighty to permit the theory that Roosevelt had illusions about coexistence with Hitler. Timing and maneuver were essential, and on occasion he tacked back and forth like the small-boat sailor that Gaddis Smith reminds us he was. Thus, before positioning the United States for entry into war, he wanted to make absolutely sure there was no prospect of negotiated peace: hence his interest in 1939–40 in people like James D. Mooney and William Rhodes Davis and hence the Sumner Welles mission. But his basic course seems pretty clear: one way or another to rid the world of Hitler.

Oddly, the revisionists accept geopolitics as an O.K. motive for the Soviet Union but deny it to the United States.

I am even less persuaded by the school that sees Roosevelt as a President who rushed the nation to war because he feared German and Japanese economic competition. America "began to go to war against the Axis in the Western Hemisphere," the revisionist William Appleman Williams tells us, because Germany was invading U.S. markets in Latin America. The Open Door cult recognizes no geopolitical concerns in Washington about German bases in the Western Hemisphere. Oddly, the revisionists accept geopolitics as an O.K. motive for the Soviet Union but deny it to the United States. In their view American foreign policy can never be aimed at strategic security but must forever be driven by the lust of American business for foreign markets.

In the United States, of course, as any student of American history knows, economic growth has been based primarily on the home market, not on foreign markets, and the preferred policy of American capitalists, even after 1920, when the United States became a creditor nation, was protection of the home market, not freedom of trade. Recall Fordney-McCumber and Smoot-Hawley. The preference of American business for high tariffs was equally true in depression. When FDR proposed his reciprocal trade agreements program in 1934, the American business community, instead of welcoming reciprocal trade as a way of penetrating foreign markets, denounced the whole idea. Senator Vandenberg even called the bill "Fascist in its philosophy, Fascist in its objectives." A grand total of two Republicans voted for reciprocal trade in the House, three in the Senate.

The "corporatism" thesis provides a more sophisticated version of the economic interpretation. No doubt we have become a society of large organizations, and no doubt an associational society generates a certain momentum toward coordination. But the idea that exporters, importers, Wall Street, Main Street, trade unionists, and farmers form a consensus on foreign policy and impose that consensus on the national government is hard to sustain.

It is particularly irrelevant to the Roosevelt period. If Roosevelt was the compliant instrument of capitalist expansion, as the Open Door ideologies claim, or of corporate hegemony, as the corporatism thesis implies, why did the leaders of American corporate capitalism oppose him so viciously? Business leaders vied with one another in their hatred of "that man in the White House." The family of J. P. Morgan used to warn visitors against mentioning Roosevelt's name lest fury raise Morgan's blood pressure to the danger point. When Averell Harriman, one of that rare breed, a pro–New Deal businessman, appeared on Wall Street, old friends cut him dead. The theory that Roosevelt pursued a foreign policy dictated by the same corporate crowd that fought him domestically and smeared him personally belongs, it seems to me, in the same library with the historiography of Oliver Stone.

4. FROM THE GREAT DEPRESSION TO WORLD WAR II

What was at stake, as FDR saw it, was not corporate profits or Latin American markets but the security of the United States and the future of democracy. Basking as we do today in the glow of democratic triumph, we forget how desperate the democratic cause appeared half a century ago. The Great War had apparently proved that democracy could not produce peace; the Great Depression that it could not produce prosperity. By the 1930s contempt for democracy was widespread among elites and masses alike: contempt for parliamentary methods, for government by discussion, for freedoms of expression and opposition, for bourgeois individualism, for pragmatic muddling through. Discipline, order, efficiency, and all-encompassing ideology were the talismans of the day. Communism and fascism had their acute doctrinal differences, but their structural similarities—a single leader, a single party, a single body of infallible dogma, a single mass of obedient followers—meant that each in the end had more in common with the other than with democracy, as Hitler and Stalin acknowledged in August 1939.

The choice in the 1930s seemed bleak: either political democracy with economic chaos or economic planning with political tyranny. Roosevelt's distinctive contribution was to reject this either/or choice. The point of the New Deal was to chart and vindicate a middle way between laissez-faire and totalitarianism. When the biographer Emil Ludwig asked FDR to define his "political motive," Roosevelt replied, "My desire to obviate revolution. . . . I work in a contrary sense to Rome and Moscow."

Accepting renomination in 1936, FDR spoke of people under economic stress in other lands who had sold their heritage of freedom for the illusion of a living. "Only our success," he continued, "can stir their ancient hope. They begin to know that here in America we are waging a great and successful war. It is not alone a war against want and destitution and economic demoralization. It is more than that: it is a war for the survival of democracy. We are fighting to save a great and precious form of government for ourselves and for the world."

Many people around the world thought it a futile fight. Let us not underestimate the readiness by 1940 of Europeans, including leading politicians and intellectuals, to come to terms with a Hitler-dominated Europe. Even some Americans thought the downfall of democracy inevitable. As Nazi divisions stormed that spring across Scandinavia, the Low Countries, and France, the fainthearted saw totalitarianism, in the title of a poisonous little book published in the summer by Anne Morrow Lindbergh, a book that by December 1940 had rushed through seven American printings, as "the wave of the future." While her husband, the famous aviator, predicted Nazi victory and opposed American aid to Britain, the gentle Mrs. Lindbergh lamented "the beautiful things . . . lost in the dying of an age," saw totalitarianism as democracy's predestined successor, a "new, and perhaps even ultimately good, conception of humanity trying to come to birth," discounted the evils of Hitlerism and Stalinism as merely "scum on the wave of the future," and concluded that "the wave of the future is coming and there is no fighting it." For a while Mrs. Lindbergh seemed to be right. Fifty years ago there were only twelve democracies left on the planet.

Roosevelt, however, believed in fighting the wave of the future. He still labored under domestic constraints. The American people were predominantly against Hitler. But they were also, and for a while more strongly, against war. I believe that FDR himself, unlike the hawks of 1941—Stimson, Morgenthau, Hopkins, Ickes, Knox—was in no hurry to enter the European conflict. He remembered what Wilson had told him when he himself had been a young hawk a quarter-century before: that a President could commit no greater mistake than to take a divided country into war. He also no doubt wanted to minimize American casualties and to avoid braking political promises. But probably by the autumn of 1941 FDR had finally come to believe that American participation was necessary if Hitler was to be beaten. An increasing number of Americans were reaching the same conclusion. Pearl Harbor in any case united the country, and Hitler then solved another of FDR's problems by declaring war on the United States.

We accepted war in 1941, as we had done in 1917, in part because, as Theodore Roosevelt had written in 1910, if Britain ever failed to preserve the European balance of power, "the United States would be obliged to get in . . . in order to restore the balance." But restoration of the balance of power did not seem in 1941, any more than it had in 1917, sufficient reason to send young men to kill and die. In 1941 FDR provided higher and nobler aims by resurrecting the Wilsonian vision in the Four Freedoms and the Atlantic Charter and by proceeding, while the war was on, to lay the foundations for the postwar reconstruction of the world along Wilsonian lines.

I assume that it will not be necessary to linger with a theory that had brief currency in the immediate postwar years, the theory that Roosevelt's great failing was his subordination of political to military objectives, shoving long-term considerations aside in the narrow interest of victory. FDR was in fact the most political of politicians, political in every reflex and to his fingertips—and just as political in war as he had been in peace. As a virtuoso politician he perfectly understood that there could be no better cloak for the pursuit of political objectives in wartime than the claim of total absorption in winning the war. He had plenty of political objectives all the same.

The war, he believed, would lead to historic transformations around the world. "Roosevelt," Harriman recalled, "enjoyed thinking aloud on the tremendous changes he saw ahead—the end of colonial empires and the rise of newly independent nations across the sweep of Africa and Asia." FDR told Churchill, "A new period has opened in the world's history, and you will have to adjust yourself to it." He tried to persuade the British to leave India and to stop the French from returning to Indochina, and he pressed the idea of UN trusteeships as the means of dismantling empires and preparing colonies for independence.

Soviet Russia, he saw, would emerge as a major power. FDR has suffered much criticism in supposedly thinking he could charm Stalin into postwar collaboration. Perhaps FDR was not so naive after all in concentrating on Stalin. The Soviet dictator was hardly the helpless prisoner of Marxist-Leninist ideology. He saw himself not as a disciple of Marx and Lenin but as their fellow prophet. Only Stalin had the power to rewrite the Soviet approach to world affairs; after all, he had already rewritten Soviet ideology and Soviet history. FDR was surely right in seeing Stalin as the only lever capable of overturning the Leninist doctrine of irrevocable hostility between capitalism and communism. As Walter Lippmann once observed, Roos-

22. Man of the Century

The biggest of the three smiles confidently between his allies at the Teheran Conference, 1943.

evelt was too cynical to think he could charm Stalin. "He distrusted everybody. What he thought he could do was to outwit Stalin, which is quite a different thing."

Roosevelt failed to save Eastern Europe from communism, but that could not have been achieved by diplomatic methods alone. With the Red Army in control of Eastern Europe and a war still to be won against Japan, there was not much the West could do to prevent Stalin's working his will in countries adjacent to the Soviet Union. But Roosevelt at Yalta persuaded Stalin to sign American-drafted Declarations on Liberated Europe and on Poland—declarations that laid down standards by which the world subsequently measured Stalin's behavior in Eastern Europe and found it wanting. And FDR had prepared a fallback position in case things went wrong: not only tests that, if Stalin failed to meet them, would justify a change in policy but also a great army, a network of overseas bases, plans for peacetime universal military training, and the Anglo-American monopoly of the atomic bomb.

In the longer run Roosevelt anticipated that time would bring a narrowing of differences between democratic and Communist societies. He once told Sumner Welles that marking American democracy as one hundred and Soviet communism as zero, the American system, as it moved away from laissez-faire, might eventually reach sixty, and the Soviet system, as it moved toward democracy, might eventually reach forty. The theory of convergence provoked much derision in the Cold War years. Perhaps it looks better now.

So perhaps does his idea of making China one of the Four Policemen of the peace. Churchill, with his scorn for "the pigtails," dismissed Roosevelt's insistence on China as the "Great American Illusion." But Roosevelt was not really deluded. As he said at Teheran, he wanted China there "not because he did not realize the weakness of China at present, but he was thinking father into the future." At Malta he told Churchill that it would take "three generations of education and training . . . before China could become a serious factor." Today, two generations later, much rests on involving China in the global web of international institutions.

As for the United States, a great concern in the war years was that the country might revert to isolationism after the war just as it had done a quarter-century before—a vivid memory for FDR's generation. Contemplating Republican gains in the 1942 midterm election, Cordell Hull told Henry Wallace that the country was "going in exactly the same steps it followed in 1918." FDR himself said

4. FROM THE GREAT DEPRESSION TO WORLD WAR II

privately, "Anybody who thinks that isolationism is dead in this country is crazy."

He regarded American membership in a permanent international organization, in Charles Bohlen's words, as "the only device that could keep the United States from slipping back into isolationism." And true to the Wilsonian vision, he saw such an organization even more significantly as the only device that could keep the world from slipping back into war. He proposed the Declaration of the United Nations three weeks after Pearl Harbor, and by 1944 he was grappling with the problem that had defeated Wilson: how to reconcile peace enforcement by an international organization with the American Constitution. For international peace enforcement requires armed force ready to act swiftly on the command of the organization, while the Constitution requires (or, in better days, required) the consent of Congress before American troops can be sent into combat against a sovereign state. Roosevelt probably had confidence that the special agreements provided for in Article 43 of the UN Charter would strike a balance between the UN's need for prompt action and Congress's need to retain its war-making power and that the great-power veto would further protect American interests.

He moved in other ways to accustom the American people to a larger international role—and at the same time to assure American predominance in the postwar world. By the end of 1944 he had sponsored a series of international conferences designed to plan vital aspects of the future. These conferences, held mostly at American initiative and dominated mostly by American agendas, offered the postwar blueprints for international organization (Dumbarton Oaks), for world finance, trade, and development (Bretton Woods), for food and agriculture (Hot Springs), for relief and rehabilitation (Washington), for civil aviation (Chicago). In his sweeping and sometimes grandiose asides, FDR envisaged plans for regional development with environmental protection in the Middle East and elsewhere, and his Office of the Coordinator for Inter-American Affairs pioneered economic and technical assistance to developing countries. Upon his death in 1945 FDR left an imaginative and comprehensive framework for American leadership in making a better world—an interesting achievement for a President who was supposed to subordinate political to military goals.

New times bring new perspectives. In the harsh light of the Cold War some of FDR's policies and expectations were condemned as naive or absurd or otherwise misguided. The end of the Cold War may cast those policies and expectations in a somewhat different light.

FDR's purpose was to safeguard the life-interests of the Republic in a world undergoing vast and fundamental transformations.

FDR's purpose, I take it, was to find ways to safeguard the historic life-interests of the Republic—national security at home and a democratic environment abroad—in a world undergoing vast and fundamental transformations. This required policies based on a grasp of the currents of history and directed to the protection of U.S. interests and to the promotion of democracy elsewhere. From the vantage point of 1994, FDR met this challenge fairly well.

Take a look at the Atlantic Charter fifty years after. Is not the world therein outlined by Roosevelt and Churchill at last coming to pass? Consider the goals of August 1941—"the right of all peoples to choose the form of government under which they will live," equal access "to the trade and to the raw materials of the world," "improved labor standards, economic advancement and social security," assurance that all "may live their lives in freedom from fear and want," relief from "the crushing burden of armaments," establishment of a community of nations. Is this not the agenda on which most nations today are at last agreed?

Does not most of the world now aspire to FDR's Four Freedoms? Has not what used to be the Soviet Union carried its movement toward the West even more rapidly than FDR dared contemplate? Has not China emerged as the "serious factor" FDR predicted? Did not the Yalta accords call for precisely the democratic freedoms to which Eastern Europe aspires today? Has not the UN, at last liberated by the end of the Cold War to pursue the goals of the founders, achieved new salience as the world's best hope for peace and cooperation?

Consider the world of 1994. It is manifestly not Adolf Hitler's world. The thousand-year Reich turned out to have a brief and bloody run of a dozen years. It is manifestly not Joseph Stalin's world. That world disintegrated before our eyes, rather like the Deacon's one-hoss shay. Nor is it Winston Churchill's world. Empire and its glories have long since vanished into the past.

The world we live in today is Franklin Roosevelt's world. Of the figures who, for good or for evil, bestrode the narrow world half a century ago, he would be the least surprised by the shape of things at the end of the century. Far more than the rest, he possessed what William James called a "sense of futurity." For all his manifold foibles, flaws, follies, and there was a sufficiency of all of those, FDR deserves supreme credit as the twentieth-century statesman who saw most deeply into the grand movements of history.

The Biggest Decision: Why We Had to Drop the Atomic Bomb

Robert James Maddox

Robert James Maddox teaches American history at Pennsylvania State University. His Weapons for Victory: Hiroshima Fifty Years Later *is published by the University of Missouri Press (1995).*

On the morning of August 6, 1945, the American B-29 *Enola Gay* dropped an atomic bomb on the Japanese city of Hiroshima. Three days later another B-29, *Bock's Car,* released one over Nagasaki. Both caused enormous casualties and physical destruction. These two cataclysmic events have preyed upon the American conscience ever since. The furor over the Smithsonian Institution's *Enola Gay* exhibit and over the mushroom-cloud postage stamp last autumn are merely the most obvious examples. Harry S. Truman and other officials claimed that the bombs caused Japan to surrender, thereby avoiding a bloody invasion. Critics have accused them of at best failing to explore alternatives, at worst of using the bombs primarily to make the Soviet Union "more manageable" rather than to defeat a Japan they knew already was on the verge of capitulation.

By any rational calculation Japan was a beaten nation by the summer of 1945. Conventional bombing had reduced many of its cities to rubble, blockade had strangled its importation of vitally needed materials, and its navy had sustained such heavy losses as to be powerless to interfere with the invasion everyone knew was coming. By late June advancing American forces had completed the conquest of Okinawa, which lay only 350 miles from the southernmost Japanese home island of Kyushu. They now stood poised for the final onslaught.

Rational calculations did not determine Japan's position. Although a peace faction within the government wished to end the war—provided certain conditions were met—militants were prepared to fight on regardless of consequences. They claimed to welcome an invasion of the home islands, promising to inflict such hideous casualties that the United States would retreat from its announced policy of unconditional surrender. The militarists held effective power over the government and were capable of defying the emperor, as they had in the past, on the ground that his civilian advisers were misleading him.

> Okinawa provided a preview of what an invasion of the home islands would entail. Rational calculations did not determine Japan's position.

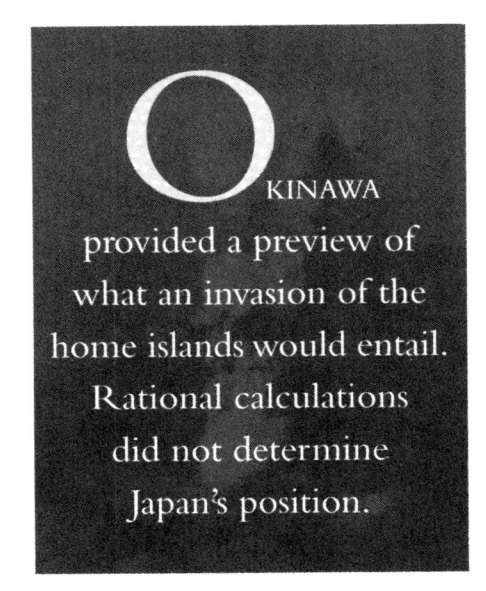

Okinawa provided a preview of what invasion of the home islands would entail. Since April 1 the Japanese had fought with a ferocity that mocked any notion that their will to resist was eroding. They had inflicted nearly 50,000 casualties on the invaders, many resulting from the first large-scale use of kamikazes. They also had dispatched the superbattleship *Yamato* on a suicide mission to Okinawa, where, after attacking American ships offshore, it was to plunge ashore to become a huge, doomed steel fortress. *Yamato* was sunk shortly after leaving port, but its mission symbolized Japan's willingness to sacrifice everything in an apparently hopeless cause.

The Japanese could be expected to defend their sacred homeland with even greater fervor, and kamikazes flying at short range promised to be even more devastating than at Okinawa. The Japanese had more than 2,000,000 troops in the home islands, were training millions of irregulars, and for some time had been conserving aircraft that might have been used to protect Japanese cities against American bombers.

Reports from Tokyo indicated that Japan meant to fight the war to a finish. On June 8 an imperial conference adopted "The Fundamental Policy to Be Followed Henceforth in the Conduct of the War," which pledged to "prosecute the war to the bitter end in order to uphold the national polity, protect the imperial land, and accomplish the objectives for which we went to war." Truman had no reason to believe that the proclamation meant anything other than what it said.

Against this background, while fighting on Okinawa still continued, the President had his naval chief of staff, Adm. William D. Leahy, notify the Joint Chiefs of Staff (JCS) and the Secretaries of War and Navy that a meeting would be held at the White House on June 18. The night before the conference Truman wrote in his diary that "I have to decide

4. FROM THE GREAT DEPRESSION TO WORLD WAR II

Japanese strategy—shall we invade Japan proper or shall we bomb and blockade? That is my hardest decision to date. But I'll make it when I have all the facts."

Truman met with the chiefs at three-thirty in the afternoon. Present were Army Chief of Staff Gen. George C. Marshall, Army Air Force's Gen. Ira C. Eaker (sitting in for the Army Air Force's chief of staff, Henry H. Arnold, who was on an inspection tour of installations in the Pacific), Navy Chief of Staff Adm. Ernest J. King, Leahy (also a member of the JCS), Secretary of the Navy James Forrestal, Secretary of War Henry L. Stimson, and Assistant Secretary of War John J. McCloy. Truman opened the meeting, then asked Marshall for his views. Marshall was the dominant figure on the JCS. He was Truman's most trusted military adviser, as he had been President Franklin D. Roosevelt's.

Marshall reported that the chiefs, supported by the Pacific commanders Gen. Douglas MacArthur and Adm. Chester W. Nimitz, agreed that an invasion of Kyushu "appears to be the least costly worthwhile operation following Okinawa." Lodgment in Kyushu, he said, was necessary to make blockade and bombardment more effective and to serve as a staging area for the invasion of Japan's main island of Honshu. The chiefs recommended a target date of November 1 for the first phase, code-named Olympic, because delay would give the Japanese more time to prepare and because bad weather might postpone the invasion "and hence the end of the war" for up to six months. Marshall said that in his opinion, Olympic was "the only course to pursue." The chiefs also proposed that Operation Cornet be launched against Honshu on March 1, 1946.

Leahy's memorandum calling the meeting had asked for casualty projections which that invasion might be expected to produce. Marshall stated that campaigns in the Pacific had been so diverse "it is considered wrong" to make total estimates. All he would say was that casualties during the first thirty days on Kyushu should not exceed those sustained in taking Luzon in the Philippines—31,000 men killed, wounded, or missing in action. "It is a grim fact," Marshall said, "that there is not an easy, bloodless way to victory in war." Leahy estimated a higher casualty rate similar to Okinawa, and King guessed somewhere in between.

King and Eaker, speaking for the Navy and the Army Air Forces respectively, endorsed Marshall's proposals. King said that he had become convinced that Kyushu was "the key to the success of any siege operations." He recommended that "we should do Kyushu now" and begin preparations for invading Honshu. Eaker "agreed completely" with Marshall. He said he had just received a message from Arnold also expressing "complete agreement." Air Force plans called for the use of forty groups of heavy bombers, which "could not be deployed without the use of airfields on Kyushu." Stimson and Forrestal concurred.

Truman summed up. He considered "the Kyushu plan all right from the military standpoint" and directed the chiefs to "go ahead with it." He said he "had hoped that there was a possibility of preventing an Okinawa from one end of Japan to the other," but "he was clear on the situation now" and was "quite sure" the chiefs should proceed with the plan. Just before the meeting adjourned, McCloy raised the possibility of avoiding an invasion by warning the Japanese that the United States would employ atomic weapons if there were no surrender. The ensuing discussion was inconclusive because the first test was a month away and no one could be sure the weapons would work.

In his memoirs Truman claimed that using atomic bombs prevented an invasion that would have cost 500,000 American lives. Other officials mentioned the same or even higher figures. Critics have assailed such statements as gross exaggerations designed to forestall scrutiny of Truman's real motives. They have given wide publicity to a report prepared by the Joint War Plans Committee (JWPC) for the chiefs' meeting with Truman. The committee estimated that the invasion of Kyushu, followed by that of Honshu, as the chiefs proposed, would cost approximately 40,000 dead, 150,000 wounded, and 3,500 missing in action for a total of 193,500 casualties.

That those responsible for a decision should exaggerate the consequences of alternatives is commonplace. Some who cite the JWPC report profess to see more sinister motives, insisting that such "low" casualty projections call into question the very idea that atomic bombs were used to avoid heavy losses. By discrediting that justification as a cover-up, they seek to bolster their contention that the bombs really were used to permit the employment of "atomic diplomacy" against the Soviet Union.

The notion that 193,500 anticipated casualties were too insignificant to have caused Truman to resort to atomic bombs might seem bizarre to anyone other than an academic, but let it pass. Those who have cited the JWPC report in countless op-ed pieces in newspapers and in magazine articles have created a myth by omitting key considerations: First, the report itself is studded with qualifications that casualties "are not subject to accurate estimate" and that the projection "is admittedly only an educated guess." Second, the figures never were conveyed to Truman. They were excised at high military echelons, which is why Marshall cited only estimates for the first thirty days on Kyushu. And indeed, subsequent Japanese troop buildups on Kyushu rendered the JWPC estimates totally irrelevant by the time the first atomic bomb was dropped.

Another myth that has attained wide attention is that at least several of Truman's top military advisers later informed him that using atomic bombs against Japan would be militarily unnecessary or immoral, or both. There is no persuasive evidence that any of them did so. None of the Joint Chiefs ever made such a claim, although one inventive author has tried to make it appear that Leahy did by braiding together several unrelated passages from the admiral's memoirs. Actually, two days after Hiroshima, Truman told aides that Leahy had "said up to the last that it wouldn't go off."

Neither MacArthur nor Nimitz ever communicated to Truman any change of mind about the need for invasion or expressed reservations about using the bombs. When first informed about their imminent use only days before Hiroshima, MacArthur responded with a lecture on the future of atomic warfare and even after Hiroshima strongly recommended that the invasion go forward. Nimitz, from whose jurisdiction the atomic strikes would be launched, was notified in early 1945. "This sounds fine," he told the courier, "but this is

23. Biggest Decision

only February. Can't we get one sooner?" Nimitz later would join Air Force generals Carl D. Spaatz, Nathan Twining, and Curtis LeMay in recommending that a third bomb be dropped on Tokyo.

Only Dwight D. Eisenhower later claimed to have remonstrated against the use of the bomb. In his *Crusade in Europe,* published in 1948, he wrote that when Secretary Stimson informed him during the Potsdam Conference of plans to use the bomb, he replied that he hoped "we would never have to use such a thing against any enemy," because he did not want the United States to be the first to use such a weapon. He added, "My views were merely personal and immediate reactions; they were not based on any analysis of the subject."

Eisenhower's recollections grew more colorful as the years went on. A later account of his meeting with Stimson had it taking place at Ike's headquarters in Frankfurt on the very day news arrived of the successful atomic test in New Mexico. "We'd had a nice evening at headquarters in Germany," he remembered. Then, after dinner, "Stimson got this cable saying that the bomb had been perfected and was ready to be dropped. The cable was in code . . . 'the lamb is born' or some damn thing like that." In this version Eisenhower claimed to have protested vehemently that "the Japanese were ready to surrender and it wasn't necessary to hit them with that awful thing." "Well," Eisenhower concluded, "the old gentleman got furious."

The best that can be said about Eisenhower's memory is that it had become flawed by the passage of time. Stimson was in Potsdam and Eisenhower in Frankfurt on July 16, when word came of the successful test. Aside from a brief conversation at a flag-raising ceremony in Berlin on July 20, the only other time they met was at Ike's headquarters on July 27. By then orders already had been sent to the Pacific to use the bombs if Japan had not yet surrendered. Notes made by one of Stimson's aides indicate that there was a discussion of atomic bombs, but there is no mention of any protest on Eisenhower's part. Even if there had been, two factors must be kept in mind. Eisenhower had commanded Allied forces in Europe, and his opinion on how close Japan was to surrender would have carried no special weight. More important, Stimson left for home immediately after the meeting and could not have personally conveyed Ike's sentiments to the President, who did not return to Washington until after Hiroshima.

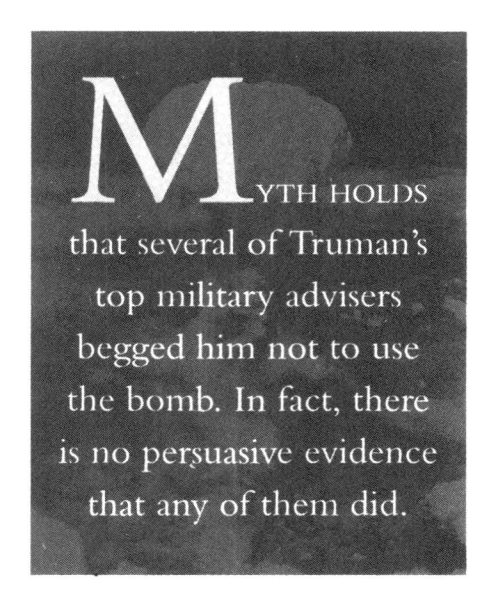

> MYTH HOLDS that several of Truman's top military advisers begged him not to use the bomb. In fact, there is no persuasive evidence that any of them did.

On July 8 the Combined Intelligence Committee submitted to the American and British Combined Chiefs of Staff a report entitled "Estimate of the Enemy Situation." The committee predicted that as Japan's position continued to deteriorate, it might "make a serious effort to use the USSR [then a neutral] as a mediator in ending the war." Tokyo also would put out "intermittent peace feelers" to "weaken the determination of the United Nations to fight to the bitter end, or to create inter-allied dissension." While the Japanese people would be willing to make large concessions to end the war, "For a surrender to be acceptable to the Japanese army, it would be necessary for the military leaders to believe that it would not entail discrediting warrior tradition and that it would permit the ultimate resurgence of a military Japan."

Small wonder that American officials remained unimpressed when Japan proceeded to do exactly what the committee predicted. On July 12 Japanese Foreign Minister Shigenori Togo instructed Ambassador Naotaki Sato in Moscow to inform the Soviets that the emperor wished to send a personal envoy, Prince Fuminaro Konoye, in an attempt "to restore peace with all possible speed." Although he realized Konoye could not reach Moscow before the Soviet leader Joseph Stalin and Foreign Minister V. M. Molotov left to attend a Big Three meeting scheduled to begin in Potsdam on the fifteenth, Togo sought to have negotiations begin as soon as they returned.

American officials had long since been able to read Japanese diplomatic traffic through a process known as the MAGIC intercepts. Army intelligence (G-2) prepared for General Marshall its interpretation of Togo's message the next day. The report listed several possible constructions, the most probable being that the Japanese "governing clique" was making a coordinated effort to "stave off defeat" through Soviet intervention and an "appeal to war weariness in the United States." The report added that Undersecretary of State Joseph C. Grew, who had spent ten years in Japan as ambassador, "agrees with these conclusions."

Some have claimed that Togo's overture to the Soviet Union, together with attempts by some minor Japanese officials in Switzerland and other neutral countries to get peace talks started through the Office of Strategic Services (OSS), constituted clear evidence that the Japanese were near surrender. Their sole prerequisite was retention of their sacred emperor, whose unique cultural/religious status within the Japanese polity they would not compromise. If only the United States had extended assurances about the emperor, according to this view, much bloodshed and the atomic bombs would have been unnecessary.

A careful reading of the MAGIC intercepts of subsequent exchanges between Togo and Sato provides no evidence that retention of the emperor was the sole obstacle to peace. What they show instead is that the Japanese Foreign Office was trying to cut a deal through the Soviet Union that would have permitted Japan to retain its political system and its prewar empire intact. Even the most lenient American official could not have countenanced such a settlement.

Togo on July 17 informed Sato that "we are not asking the Russians' mediation in *anything like unconditional surrender* [emphasis added]." During the following weeks Sato pleaded with his superiors to abandon hope of Soviet intercession and to approach the United States directly to find out what peace terms would be offered. "There is . . . no alternative but immediate unconditional surrender," he cabled on July 31, and he bluntly informed Togo that "your way of looking at things and the actual situation in the Eastern Area may be seen to be absolutely contradictory." The Foreign Ministry ignored his pleas and continued to seek Soviet help even after Hiroshima.

"Peace feelers" by Japanese officials abroad seemed no more promising from the American point of view. Although several of the consular personnel and military attachés engaged in these activities claimed important connections at home, none produced verification. Had the Japanese government sought only an assurance about the emperor, all it had to do was grant one of these men authority to begin talks through the OSS. Its failure to do so led American officials to assume that those involved were either well-meaning individuals acting alone or that they were being orchestrated by Tokyo. Grew characterized such "peace feelers" as "familiar weapons of psychological warfare" designed to "divide the Allies."

Some American officials, such as Stimson and Grew, nonetheless wanted to signal the Japanese that they might retain the emperorship in the form of a constitutional monarchy. Such an assurance might remove the last stumbling block to surrender, if not when it was issued, then later. Only an imperial rescript would bring about an orderly surrender, they argued, without which Japanese forces would fight to the last man regardless of what the government in Tokyo did. Besides, the emperor could serve as a stabilizing factor during the transition to peacetime.

There were many arguments against an American initiative. Some opposed retaining such an undemocratic institution on principle and because they feared it might later serve as a rallying point for future militarism. Should that happen, as one assistant Secretary of State put it, "those lives already spent will have been sacrificed in vain, and lives will be lost again in the future." Japanese hard-liners were certain to exploit an overture as evidence that losses sustained at Okinawa had weakened American resolve and to argue that continued resistance would bring further concessions. Stalin, who earlier had told an American envoy that he favored abolishing the emperorship because the ineffectual Hirohito might be succeeded by "an energetic and vigorous figure who could cause trouble," was just as certain to interpret it as a treacherous effort to end the war before the Soviets could share in the spoils.

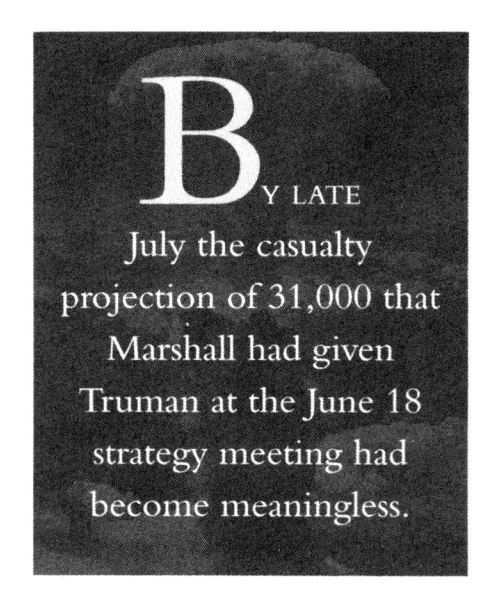

> BY LATE July the casualty projection of 31,000 that Marshall had given Truman at the June 18 strategy meeting had become meaningless.

There were domestic considerations as well. Roosevelt had announced the unconditional surrender policy in early 1943, and it since had become a slogan of the war. He also had advocated that peoples everywhere should have the right to choose their own form of government, and Truman had publicly pledged to carry out his predecessor's legacies. For him to have formally *guaranteed* continuance of the emperorship, as opposed to merely accepting it on American terms pending free elections, as he later did, would have constituted a blatant repudiation of his own promises.

Nor was that all. Regardless of the emperor's actual role in Japanese aggression, which is still debated, much wartime propaganda had encouraged Americans to regard Hirohito as no less a war criminal than Adolf Hitler or Benito Mussolini. Although Truman said on several occasions that he had no objection to retaining the emperor, he understandably refused to make the first move. The ultimatum he issued from Potsdam on July 26 did not refer specifically to the emperorship. All it said was that occupation forces would be removed after "a peaceful and responsible" government had been established according to the "freely expressed will of the Japanese people." When the Japanese rejected the ultimatum rather than at last inquire whether they might retain the emperor, Truman permitted the plans for using the bombs to go forward.

Reliance on MAGIC intercepts and the "peace feelers" to gauge how near Japan was to surrender is misleading in any case. The army, not the Foreign Office, controlled the situation. Intercepts of Japanese military communications, designated ULTRA, provided no reason to believe the army was even considering surrender. Japanese Imperial Headquarters had correctly guessed that the next operation after Okinawa would be Kyushu and was making every effort to bolster its defenses there.

General Marshall reported on July 24 that there were "approximately 500,000 troops in Kyushu" and that more were on the way. ULTRA identified new units arriving almost daily. MacArthur's G-2 reported on July 29 that "this threatening development, if not checked, may grow to a point where we attack on a ratio of one (1) to one (1) which is not the recipe for victory." By the time the first atomic bomb fell, ULTRA indicated that there were 560,000 troops in southern Kyushu (the actual figure was closer to 900,000), and projections for November 1 placed the number at 680,000. A report, for medical purposes, of July 31 estimated that total battle and non-battle casualties might run as high as 394,859 *for the Kyushu operation alone.* This figure did not include those men expected to be killed outright, for obviously they would require no medical attention. Marshall regarded Japanese defenses as so formidable that even after Hiroshima he asked MacArthur to consider alternate landing sites and began contemplating the use of atomic bombs as tactical weapons to support the invasion.

The thirty-day casualty projection of 31,000 Marshall had given Truman at the June 18 strategy meeting had become meaningless. It had been based on the assumption that the Japanese had about 350,000 defenders in Kyushu and that naval and air interdiction would preclude significant reinforcement. But the Japanese buildup since that time meant that the defenders would have nearly twice the number of troops available by "X-day" than earlier assumed. The assertion that apprehensions about casualties are insufficient to explain Truman's use of the bombs, therefore, cannot be taken seriously. On the contrary, as Winston Churchill wrote after a conversation with him at Potsdam, Truman was tormented by "the terrible responsibilities that rested upon him in regard to the unlimited effusions of American blood."

Some historians have argued that while the first bomb *might* have been required to achieve Japanese surrender, dropping the second constituted a needless barbarism. The record shows otherwise. American officials believed more than one bomb would be necessary because they assumed Japanese hard-liners would minimize the first explosion or attempt to explain it away as some sort of natural catastrophe, precisely what they did. The Japanese minister of war, for instance, at first refused even to admit that the Hiroshima bomb was atomic. A few hours after Nagasaki he told the cabinet that "the Americans appeared to have one hundred atomic bombs . . . they could drop three per day. The next target might well be Tokyo."

Even after both bombs had fallen and Russia entered the war, Japanese militants insisted on such lenient peace terms that moderates knew there was no sense even transmitting them to the United States. Hirohito had to intervene personally on two occasions during the next few days to induce hard-liners to abandon their conditions and to accept the American stipulation that the emperor's authority "shall be subject to the Supreme Commander of the Allied Powers." That the militarists would have accepted such a settlement before the bombs is farfetched, to say the least.

Some writers have argued that the cumulative effects of battlefield defeats, conventional bombing, and naval blockade already had defeated Japan. Even without extending assurances about the emperor, all the United States had to do was wait. The most frequently cited basis for this contention is the *United States Strategic Bombing Survey,* published in 1946, which stated that Japan would have surrendered by November 1 "even if the atomic bombs had not been dropped, even if Russia had not entered the war, and even if no invasion had been planned or contemplated." Recent scholarship by the historian Robert P. Newman and others has demonstrated that the survey was "cooked" by those who prepared it to arrive at such a conclusion. No matter. This or any other document based on information available only after the war ended is irrelevant with regard to what Truman could have known at the time.

What often goes unremarked is that when the bombs were dropped, fighting was still going on in the Philippines, China, and elsewhere. Every day that the war continued thousands of prisoners of war had to live and die in abysmal conditions, and there were rumors that the Japanese intended to slaughter them if the homeland was invaded. Truman was Commander in Chief of the American armed forces, and he had a duty to the men under his command not shared by those sitting in moral judgment decades later. Available evidence points to the conclusion that he acted for the reason he said he did: to end a bloody war that would have become far bloodier had invasion proved necessary. One can only imagine what would have happened if tens of thousands of American boys had died or been wounded on Japanese soil and then it had become known that Truman had chosen not to use weapons that might have ended the war months sooner.

From the Cold War to the 1990s

President Roosevelt's largest goal was to create a lasting peace after the defeat of the Axis powers. In order to do so, he believed, collaboration with the Soviet Union must continue in the postwar world. Roosevelt tried to persuade Soviet dictator Joseph Stalin that the United States and Great Britain could be trusted. Despite his efforts, cracks began appearing in the Grand Alliance even before World War II ended. Soviet actions in Eastern Europe, particularly with regard to Poland, caused Roosevelt to move toward a tougher position during the days before his death on April 12, 1945. His successor, Harry S. Truman, was thrust unexpectedly into a situation that would continue to deteriorate into what became known as the cold war.

The United States had failed to join the League of Nations after World War I, and it had spurned all other international commitments. Roosevelt feared a similar retreat after World War II. Lee Edwards, in "Good-Bye to Isolationism," shows how differently the nation acted this time. In the face of what many regarded as the global menace of communism, the United States assumed awesome obligations such as the Truman Doctrine, the Marshall Plan, and membership in the North Atlantic Treaty Organization. And, as discussed by Edwin Wiester in "Echoes of a Distant War," this nation found itself fighting in Asia only five years after V-J Day. Our enemies, first the North Koreans, then the Chinese, were widely believed to be acting as proxies for the Soviet Union.

At home, after some dislocation caused by demobilization and reconversion to a peacetime economy, Americans headed into a period of unprecedented prosperity. Many veterans, male and female, took advantage of what became known as "The G.I. Bill of Rights." Among other provisions, it provided tuition and living expenses for those who wanted to go to college. Millions of individuals took advantage of this act, many of whom would otherwise never have received college degrees. "The G.I. Bill May Be the Best Deal Ever Made by Uncle Sam" discusses the ramifications of this revolutionary legislation.

Production of consumer goods such as automobiles and home appliances had been suspended for the duration of the war. People with more money in their pockets than they had ever had before clamored to purchase cars, refrigerators, and their own homes. There was a new product on the market as well—television. Although invented during the 1920s, television started to become popular after World War II. By the end of the 1940s, four networks were producing a wide variety of shows that were watched by millions of viewers. The high and low points of television programming during this era are presented by Edward Oxford in "TV's Wonder Years."

After winning an upset victory over Republican candidate Thomas Dewey in 1948, Harry Truman's second administration encountered rough going. Developments such as the "fall" of China to the Communists, Soviet detonation of its first nuclear bomb years before most Americans thought possible, and the inconclusive Korean War caused a sense of frustration and bewilderment within the public. Many people were prepared to believe the charges being hurled by individuals such as Senator Joseph McCarthy that these setbacks had occurred because Truman, and Roosevelt before him, had been "soft"

UNIT 5

on communism and that their administrations were honeycombed with spies and Soviet sympathizers.

As the presidential election of 1952 approached, both political parties sought the popular Dwight D. Eisenhower to be their standard-bearer. Eisenhower opted for the Republican Party. A war hero without the stuffiness of Douglas MacArthur, "Ike" appealed to a great many voters as a regular fellow without pretense who would clean up the mess in Washington and end the war in Korea. Democrat candidate Adlai Stevenson never had a chance.

Eisenhower was an enormously popular president throughout his two administrations, though not with most intellectuals. Often he was depicted as a passive figurehead who allowed subordinates to run the show while he played golf or bridge. In "Looking Back on Ike," John Rossi shows that Eisenhower's stock has risen over the years in polls conducted among historians. His record, the article concludes, was "a good, if not great one."

There was a great deal of racial unrest during the Eisenhower years over the injustices that still permeated our society. Blacks and their allies, helped along by a Supreme Court decision that overturned the "separate but equal" doctrine, conducted sit-ins, marches, and other demonstrations to destroy segregation. The essay "Trumpet of Conscience: A Portrait of Martin Luther King Jr." tells the story of Reverend Martin Luther King Jr., who first achieved prominence during a 1955 boycott of segregated buses in Montgomery, Alabama. He went on to become the most eloquent spokesman and the most revered leader of the civil rights movement.

The 1960s began inauspiciously. President John Kennedy, who had won a paper-thin victory over Richard Nixon, promised to get the nation "moving again," but he was a fairly conventional politician. Things began to change radically by the middle of the decade. Events such as Kennedy's assassination in 1963, discontentment over continued racial oppression, perceived excessive materialism, and, above all, discontent over the escalating Vietnam War, spilled beyond the boundaries of conventional politics into protest marches and violent confrontations.

By the late 1960s the nation was in great turmoil, and some feared it might be torn apart. Many radical groups advocated violence to destroy what they called the "establishment," and law enforcement officials often responded with violence of their own. Riots took place in a number of cities and on college campuses. In "Reagan's Rise," Gerard De Groot tells how one politician manipulated widespread fear of student unrest to his own advantage.

The various activist movements of the late 1960s and early 1970s soon petered out. Observers disagreed as to the causes: simple weariness, the worsening of economic conditions, and the aging of a "special" generation of young people were a few of the answers offered. The presidential election of 1972 marked a watershed. Richard Nixon, who advocated all the traditional values, was reelected in a landslide against Democratic candidate George McGovern, who was perceived as a radical candidate.

Despite the dimensions of his victory Nixon perceived himself as an outsider, besieged and harassed by countless enemies who were "out to get him." McGovern had tried without success to focus attention on the forced entry by Republican operatives into Democratic National Headquarters at the Watergate complex in 1972. It soon developed, however, that the Watergate incident was but the tip of an iceberg. Despite efforts to contain the damage—"stonewalling," as it came to be known—revelation after revelation showed that the Nixon White House had engaged in a wide range of illegal and unconstitutional activities. Allen Sultan, in "Looking Back at Watergate," argues that the most harmful legacy of all those activities lumped under the name "Watergate" was the erosion of faith in the rule of law.

In "How the Seventies Changed America," Nicholas Lemann provides an overview of the decade with emphasis on problems such as economic stagnation and social fragmentation. The essay "Final Days of South Vietnam" chronicles the dismal collapse of an ally the United States had kept propped up for years at the cost of more than 50,000 American lives. The Vietnam conflict, according to Harry Summers, "was a well-intentioned but fatally flawed war."

Looking Ahead: Challenge Questions

Contrast American foreign policies after World War II with those of the post–World War I era. What lessons can be learned from the Korean War? From the Vietnam War?

Evaluate Martin Luther King Jr.'s impact on the civil rights movement. Explain his strategy of nonviolence.

What was the significance of all those transgressions of the Nixon administration that we refer to collectively as "Watergate"?

Describe your impression of the 1970s on U.S. history both economically and socially.

Good-Bye to Isolationism

Western weakness and Soviet expansionism forced the United States to become the leader of the free world.

Lee Edwards

Lee Edwards is senior editor for Current Issues of The World & I. *His latest book is a political biography of Barry Goldwater.*

With the successful conclusion of World War II, America sought a return to normalcy, believing that it would be possible, as in the past, to concentrate on domestic rather than foreign affairs. However, in sharp contrast to its isolationist actions in the post–World War I period, the nation took several prudent steps to ensure international peace.

First and foremost, the U.S. government hosted the founding of the United Nations in San Francisco in June 1945 and agreed to become a permanent member of the Security Council. It instructed Gen. Douglas MacArthur to remain in the Far East and oversee the political transition of imperial Japan to a modern democracy. And it concluded that the future of Europe, particularly that of Germany, could be safely placed in the hands of its wartime allies, Great Britain and the Soviet Union.

Accordingly, a massive demobilization was rapidly carried out. In May 1945, at the end of war with Germany the United States had an army of 3.5 million in Europe. By June 1946, there were only 400,000 U.S. troops left, mainly new recruits. Some 1.5 million men returned from the Pacific during the same period. The Air Force and Navy (including the Marines) carried out similar in-depth reductions.

However, while the nation was demobilizing and Congress was debating the extension of wage and price controls, some foreign-policy experts were expressing alarm over Soviet intentions. Their concern was intensified by Premier Joseph Stalin's February 1946 address, in which the communist dictator blamed World War II on "monopoly capitalism," stated that future conflicts were inevitable because of the "present capitalist development of the world economy," and called for Soviet expansion of heavy industry "and all kinds of scientific research" (including, presumably, strategic weapons) for the next 15 years if necessary.

His words disturbed many in Washington, including Supreme Court Justice William O. Douglas, who believed that Stalin's speech meant "the declaration of World War III." *Newsweek* referred to the address as the "most war-like pronouncement uttered by any statesman since V-J Day."

THE 'LONG TELEGRAM'

At this critical moment, George Kennan, deputy chief of mission in Moscow, sent his famous "long telegram" to the State Department in Washington. Frustrated by the inability of some officials to understand or accept the reality of Soviet aims and actions, he gave his superiors what he saw as "the whole truth" about the Soviet Union's objectives as well as a suggested U.S. response.

Prescient to a remarkable degree, the 8,000-word analysis made the following major points: (1) The USSR believed that it lived in antagonistic "capitalist encirclement," with which there could be no permanent peaceful coexistence; (2) Moscow would do everything possible to advance the relative strength of the Soviet Union; (3) Soviet suspicion of the world was based on the traditional Russian sense of insecurity; (4) the Soviets would seek to undermine the general political and strategic potential of major Western powers; and (5) all Soviet efforts on the international plane would be negative and destructive.

Yet, said Kennan, armed conflict between the Soviet Union and the United States was not inevitable, because Soviet power was "highly sensitive to the logic of force. For this reason, it can easily withdraw—and usually does—when strong resistance is encountered at any point."

Secretary of the Navy James Forrestal, a hard-line anti-Soviet, had the telegram reproduced by the hundreds and personally carried it to many high-ranking administration officials. There were, however, significant flaws in Kennan's analysis.

As international-affairs analyst Elizabeth Spalding points out, Kennan depicted Soviet doctrine, intentions, and policy as springing from a background of traditional Russian insecurity rather than communist ideology. He insisted that Moscow acted *only* under the "guise" of Marxism. In so arguing, he laid the groundwork for the revisionist argument that all Kremlin actions were based on geopolitical considerations and therefore could be politically assuaged.

Kennan was very selective in his recommendations, arguing that intervention in what he designated as Moscow's sphere of influence was futile and should be avoided. As Spalding puts it, Kennan "did not see that the Soviet Union was imperial and communist at the same time."

Others in Washington did not fail to make this crucial connection. In late February, Sen. Arthur Vandenberg of Michigan, the leading Republican spokesman on foreign affairs in the U.S. Senate and arguably the nation, delivered a major address on U.S.-Soviet re-

24. Good-Bye to Isolationism

> # COPING WITH COMMUNISM
>
> *In the frigid Cold War atmosphere, proposals like the Truman Doctrine were not only possible but expected by the American public.*
>
> *The Truman Doctrine was a rite of passage by which the once-isolationist United States became the leader of the noncommunist world.*
>
> *The Marshal Plan committed the United States to a policy of economic and political solidarity with other nations.*
>
> *NATO established the principle, for the first time in U.S. history, of tranoceanic military alliances in peacetime.*

lations. "What is Russia up to," he asked, from Manchuria to Eastern Europe "to our own United States?"

Vandenberg asserted that the Soviet Union was deliberately testing the resolve of the United States, which, in the interests of peace, should meet firmness with firmness. "We can live together in reasonable harmony," he said, "if the United States just as vigorously sustains its own purposes and its ideals upon all occasions as Russia does." Vandenberg's remarks were the first public criticism of the Soviet Union by a major American political figure since the end of World War II.

His analysis marked the beginning of a historic, bipartisan effort over the next three years that would produce the Truman Doctrine, the Marshall Plan, and NATO (the North Atlantic Treaty Organization), committing the United States to the role of leader of the free world in the Cold War.

THE 'IRON CURTAIN'

The following month, there occurred one of the most famous events of the post–World War II period: Winston Churchill's "Iron Curtain" speech in Fulton, Missouri. Introduced by President Harry Truman himself, Churchill intoned that "from Stettin in the Baltic to Trieste in the Adriatic," an "Iron Curtain" had descended across the European continent, behind which lay all the capitals of central and Eastern Europe, within "the Soviet sphere."

He cited a number of specific Soviet actions that warranted a firm response by the West, including pressure on nations on the Soviet Union's periphery like Greece, Turkey, and Persia (Iran), and subversion and espionage in noncommunist nations around the world. He warned that the bitter lesson of Munich would be repeated unless appropriate counteraction was taken.

Stalin immediately attacked Churchill, charging that the British statesman had sounded "a call to war with the Soviet Union." To the charge that the Soviet Union dominated its neighbors, Stalin explained that Soviet security required that neighboring governments be "loyal." He provided a fascinating insight into his understanding of political science by declaring that such nations as Yugoslavia, Bulgaria, and Poland were *more* democratic than Great Britain because each of them was ruled by a bloc of several parties while the British government was run by only one party the Labour Party with the opposition, including Churchill, barred from participation.

Truman entered the quickening debate by declaring, in an Army Day speech, that the United States had to remain militarily strong to "ensure peace in the world." He also stated that "economic reconstruction" was the first task for the people and governments of Europe. He promised that the United States would help in the reconstruction because:

- "We know that we ourselves cannot enjoy prosperity in a world of economic stagnation";
- "Economic distress, anywhere in the world, is a fertile breeding ground for violent political upheaval";
- "We feel it is right to lend a hand to our friends and allies who are recovering from wounds inflicted by our common enemy."

These three arguments—economic aid makes good economic sense, economic chaos produces political chaos, and it is morally right to help friends in need—were used frequently in 1947 and '48 to win congressional (and public) approval of the Truman Doctrine and the Marshall Plan. What was missing in Truman's address was the theme of anticommunism, which would be a major element in the forthcoming debate about U.S. foreign policy.

THE CLIFFORD-ELSEY MEMO

Although the White House was reluctant to declare officially that it was engaged in a cold war with the Soviet Union, a decisive step was taken in July when Truman asked Clark Clifford, his special counsel, to prepare a memorandum about the number of agreements that the Soviets had kept and broken. With his aide, George Elsey (who wrote much of the text), Clifford presented Truman with a remarkable 100,000-word top-secret document in late September 1946. The memorandum represented a consensus of opinion about the Soviet Union among the leading foreign-policy and defense experts in the Truman administration, including the secretary of state; the secretary of war, Admiral Leahy, who had been President Franklin D. Roosevelt's chief military adviser; the Joint Chiefs of Staff; and the director of central intelligence.

The document was unequivocal in its language, stating that "our ability to resolve the present conflict between Soviet and American foreign policies may determine whether there is to be a permanent peace or a third World War."

The Clifford-Elsey memorandum argued bluntly that the "language of military power" was the "only language" that disciples of power politics like the Soviet Union understood and the United States had to be prepared even "to wage atomic and biological warfare if necessary." In anticipation of the Truman Doctrine (and the Reagan Doctrine nearly 40 years later), it counseled that the United States should "support and assist all democratic countries that are in any way menaced or endangered by the U.S.S.R."

The Clifford-Elsey memorandum differed significantly from the Kennan telegram in several important aspects. The memorandum examined Soviet actions in terms of their ideological intentions.

5. FROM THE COLD WAR TO THE 1990s

It recognized that the Kremlin was engaged in a battle for world domination. It argued that because Soviet ideology and policies were global, America's purpose and response also had to be global.

THE BRITISH WITHDRAWAL

Now came one of those catalytic events on which history turns. The combination of one of the worst winters in history and the economic consequences of World War II reduced Great Britain in early 1947 to a state of near bankruptcy. The British Embassy in Washington informed the State Department that Britain could no longer meet its traditional responsibilities in Greece and Turkey and would have to pull out by no later than April 1.

What was needed was a coordinated plan to revive the agriculture, industry, and trade of the stricken countries.

As both Greece and Turkey were on the brink of economic and political collapse, only an American commitment could prevent a Soviet takeover of these strategically located countries. For the first time since the founding of the American Republic, there was no one to protect the United States and its international interests but the United States itself. Quite suddenly, a dangerous bipolar world confronted the United States.

Greece needed substantial amounts of aid, and quickly. The alternative, as Truman recalled in his memoirs, would be the loss of Greece and the extension of the "Iron Curtain" across the eastern Mediterranean. If Greece were lost, he wrote, Turkey would "become an untenable outpost in a sea of communism." America, he felt, had no choice but to help both Greece and Turkey and prevent Soviet expansionism.

Led by internationalists like Vandenberg in the Senate and Charles Eaton of New Jersey and Walter Judd of Minnesota in the House of Representatives, the Republican Congress passed Greek-Turkish aid (the Truman Doctrine) in May. As he signed the bill, Truman remarked that the legislation was "an important step in the building of the peace," adding that "the conditions of peace include, among other things, the ability of nations to maintain order and independence, and to support themselves economically."

Truman's explanation helped prepare the way for the much-larger task of economically assisting a profoundly distressed Europe.

EUROPE'S PLIGHT

The desperate straits in which the nations of Western Europe found themselves were spelled out by columnist Walter Lippmann, who warned that "the danger of a European economic collapse is the threat that hangs over all of us and all the world." None of the leading nations—Great Britain, France, Italy, or Germany—were recovering economically from World War II. If Britain were forced to withdraw from Germany, Lippmann wrote, the United States would find itself "isolated in Europe, face to face with the Russians."

To prevent such an ominous prospect, concluded Lippmann, "political and economic measures on a scale which no responsible statesman has yet ventured to hint at will be needed in the next year or two."

The Lippmann analysis was shared by high-ranking U.S. officials like Under Secretary of State Will Clayton, who advised the president, after spending six weeks on the Continent, that without substantial American aid, "economic, social and political disintegration will overwhelm Europe." A consensus formed in the Truman administration that what was needed was not simply more U.S. "relief" but a coordinated plan to revive the agriculture, industry, and trade of the stricken countries so that Europe might again become self-supporting.

Speaking at Harvard's commencement exercises in June 1947, Secretary of State George Marshall outlined a program to get "Europe on its feet economically" with the "full cooperation" of the United States. Vandenberg described Marshall's Harvard speech as a "shot heard 'round the world" but knew that it fell on many deaf ears in a Congress focused on reducing taxes and cutting government spending.

Aware that bipartisanship could be stretched only so far, Truman insisted that the proposed aid program be called the *Marshall* Plan, not the Truman Plan, and that key congressional supporters be either Republicans or noncontroversial Democrats. As part of its campaign, the White House encouraged members of Congress to personally inspect the European situation.

In fact, more than 200 representatives, nearly one-half of the House, visited Europe during 1947. Most became firm supporters of the Marshall Plan because of the reality of Europe's deepening plight. A typical comment was that of Rep. Everett Dirksen of Illinois, a onetime isolationist, who asserted that Congress had three options: withdraw from Europe, give "niggardly aid," or implement the Marshall Plan—"the choice we must make."

THE SOVIET RESPONSE

Validating the Clifford-Elsey thesis that the Soviet Union was ideologically driven, the Kremlin formed the Communist Information Bureau (Cominform), which immediately characterized the Marshall Plan as an act of Western "imperialism" and ordered the communist parties of France, Italy, Great Britain, and other countries to defend the "national independence and sovereignty of their countries."

French and Italian communists initiated widespread strikes in an attempt to bring down their governments. The Soviet pattern of subversion in Western Europe and expansion in Eastern Europe strengthened the conviction of Truman and his advisers that the Soviet Union had to be resisted, at the very least through economic-political measures like the Marshall Plan.

THE 'X' FACTOR

The rationale for a geopolitical response by America appeared in *Foreign Affairs* under the mysterious byline "X" (actually George Kennan). Kennan wrote that the main element of any U.S. policy toward the Soviet Union must be "a long-standing vigilant *containment* [emphasis added] of Russian expansive tendencies." He called for the "adroit and vigilant application of counter-force at a series of constantly shifting geographical and political points, corresponding to the shifts and maneuvers of Soviet policy."

However, as Spalding points out, Kennan again stressed the psychological origins of Soviet imperialism (as he had in his long telegram), asserting that the Soviets did not believe in communism but simply used it to justify their behavior. In sharp contrast, when Paul Nitze and his colleagues at the State Department wrote the seminal Cold War document, NSC 68, two years later, they stated that the "Soviet Union, unlike previous aspirants to hegemony, is animated by a new fanatic faith, antithetical to our own, and seeks to impose its absolute authority over the rest of the world."

As the Soviet Union tightened its grip on Eastern Europe in 1948 and tried to cut off Berlin (forcing Truman to initiate the famed Berlin airlift), the U.S. public's attitude toward the USSR hardened and the expectation of war increased. In March, after a communist coup in Czechoslovakia that stunned officials in every Western capital, pollster George Gallup asked the American public an open-ended question, "What policy do you think we should follow toward Russia?"

A plurality answered, "prepare to fight, build up armed forces." The other most frequent replies were "be firm, no appeasement" and "go to war." Seventy-three percent told Gallup that the United States was "too soft" in its policy toward the Soviet Union.

In such a frigid Cold War atmosphere, proposals like the Truman Doctrine, the Marshall Plan, and NATO were not only possible but expected by large segments of the American public. In fact, the United States decided that it had little choice but to act as it did, given these factors:

- Great Britain's strategic withdrawal from Greece and Turkey created a vacuum in the continental balance of power that the United States decided it had to fill or see filled by the Soviet Union.
- The impending economic collapse of Britain, France, and the rest of Western Europe in the winter of 1947 forced the United States to take large-scale action in the economic sphere.
- Soviet expansionism—including the establishment of puppet governments in Poland, Bulgaria, Romania, and Czechoslovakia; the demand to share in the policing of the Dardanelles; the support of communist strikes and political agitation in France and Italy; and the Berlin blockade—laid the foundation for a military response by the West.

The Truman Doctrine was a rite of passage by which the once-isolationist United States became the leader of the noncommunist world. The Marshall Plan committed the United States to a policy of economic and political solidarity with other nations. NATO established the principle, for the first time in American history, of transoceanic military alliances in peacetime.

THE ALTERNATIVES

In the immediate post–World War II period, the United States faced the following foreign policy alternatives:

Isolationism. But turning inward was no longer possible, given the realities of modern transportation and communication and the birth of a global economy.

A Fortress America. Not even the mighty United States could afford to build and maintain the gigantic air force, navy, and army that would be required.

Quite suddenly, a dangerous bipolar world confronted the United States.

Global welfarism. History, from the time of the Roman Empire to the present, demonstrated that it was impossible to permanently buy the good-will of others.

A genuine and effective collective security. It was the last alternative, based on reasoned internationalism and prudent national interests, that was selected by a farsighted, bipartisan coalition. It prevailed for the next four decades until, capped by the peace-through-strength policies of Presidents Ronald Reagan and George Bush, the Cold War was finally won without firing a single nuclear shot.

ADDITIONAL READING

Dean Acheson, *Present at the Creation: My Years in the State Department,* W. W. Norton & Co., New York, 1969.

George F. Kennan, *American Diplomacy 1900–1950,* University of Chicago Press, Chicago, 1951.

Harry S. Truman, *Memoirs, Volume One: Year of Decisions; Volume Two: Years of Trial and Hope,* Doubleday & Co., Garden City, N.Y., 1955 and 1956.

Arthur H. Vandenberg, Jr., ed., with the collaboration of Joe Alex Morris, *The Private Papers of Senator Vandenberg,* Houghton Mifflin Co., Boston, 1952.

The G.I. Bill May Be the Best Deal Ever Made by Uncle Sam

Also known as Public Law 346, it did a lot, including help millions of veterans to an education they would otherwise have missed.

Edwin Kiester Jr.

The author, who wrote on apprenticeships in March 1993, went to the University of Pittsburgh on the G.I. Bill, earning a degree in political science, 1950.

On that humid evening in May 1944, a reminiscent Les Faulk was saying nearly five decades later, he could see his future unrolling ahead of him, like frames of a wartime Movietone News. As he crossed the high school stage, clutching his brand-new diploma and switching the tassel on his mortarboard from right to left to signify his new graduate status, he figured that within weeks he would board a train for an Army camp and eventually wind up in the climactic battles of World War II.

If he were lucky—and Les had always been lucky—he would get to come home safely to the smoky western Pennsylvania industrial town where the grim days of the Great Depression were still vivid. Then he would look for work. If he were very lucky, he would move up from his high school occupations of caddying at the local golf course and racking balls in Kindler's poolroom. Maybe he'd even find what the town considered a "good job." That meant he might be stoking a steel-mill openhearth furnace or winding copper armatures in the Westinghouse generator plant.

College? Not for a young man from an Italian-speaking immigrant household—the name on Les' diploma read "Falcocchio." Not in a factory town where half the males saw so little future in the classroom that they dropped out of school at 16. Not in Turtle Creek, Pennsylvania, where before the war fewer than 5 percent of graduates went on to post-high school education, even a secretarial course or barber training. "College," Les remembered decades later, "that was for the teachers' kids or preachers' kids. For the rest of us, with names like Tarantini and Trkula, it was a distant dream."

So how had this white-haired 68-year-old, who still moved with the easy grace of a basketball point guard, managed to collect bachelor's and master's degrees and several credits toward his doctorate? How had he avoided the blue-collar life that seemed so certain in 1944, and spent 38 years as a teacher and elementary-school principal instead? Les raised his beer glass in toast to the 11 other 1944 Turtle Creek High School graduates who had gathered to shake hands, slap backs, display grandchildren's pictures and exchange embroidered memories about Mrs. Whittum's American history class.

"To the G.I. Bill!" Les said. "The G.I. Bill!" the others echoed.

The G.I. Bill of Rights, that is, a.k.a. Public Law 346, a.k.a. the Servicemen's Readjustment Act of 1944, clearly one of the most important pieces of legislation in American history. On June 22, 1944, as Pvt. Leslie Faulk was getting accustomed to the fit of G.I. fatigues, President Franklin D. Roosevelt signed the measure with so little fanfare that most major newspapers, overwhelmed with news of the Allied invasion of Europe, buried the story. Two years later people certainly took notice, though. American college campuses were flooded with young veterans (including 60,000 women and an estimated 70,000 African-Americans) who had never in their lives expected to be there.

Its impact can still be felt today. The G.I. Bill pulled a whole generation of Les Faulks up by their combat bootstraps and put them among the most educated and financially well-off generations in U.S. history. By granting a paid education to every qualified veteran, the bill transformed America's colleges and universities, cranked out a huge pool of trained professionals, changed the educational goals of the nation and fueled a giddy postwar boom. Suddenly a college degree was within the reach of millions—and remained that way.

A PRICE TAG OF $5.5 BILLION

There were two periods in American history when rapidly expanding education eventually translated into economic gain. One was after the land grant colleges were established in the 1860s. The other was the era of the G.I. Bill, clearly the most farsighted veterans program in history. G.I. Bill statistics are awesome. Out of 14 million eligibles, 2.2 million veterans jumped at the chance to attend college. At a cost of $5.5 billion, the first G.I. Bill turned out 450,000 engineers, 240,000 accountants, 238,000 teachers, 91,000 scientists, 67,000 doctors, 22,000 dentists, 17,000 writers and editors, and thousands of other professionals. Colleges that had languished during the Depression swiftly doubled and tripled in enrollment. More students signed up for engineering at the University of Pittsburgh in 1948 (70 percent of them veterans) than had in five years combined during the 1930s. By 1960 there were a thousand G.I. Bill-educated vets listed in *Who's Who*.

The astonishing thing about this human cascade is that practically nobody saw it coming. The measure squeaked through a Congressional committee only after some hardball lobbying by the American Legion and a midnight legislative rescue that its backers liked to compare to Paul Revere's ride. Moreover, the college-for-everyone clauses were really a kind of throw-in; the bill's real purpose was to keep the boys off the streets. Haunted by memories of the violent veterans' bonus march of the 1930s and gloomy warnings of a postwar depression with up to nine million unemployed, Congress made the main feature of the bill a program that guaranteed to veterans $20 a week in unemployment benefits for a year, which rapidly became known as the "52-20 Club."

FARM AND FACTORY, OR COLLEGE?

In 1944 everyone knew, absolutely *knew*, that only a handful of veterans would take advantage of Uncle Sam's offer to go to college. Experts predicted 8 to 12 percent. Veterans were expected to return posthaste to farms and factories. The *Saturday Evening Post* was so confident on this topic that it commissioned an article declaring that veterans had turned their backs on college. "G.I.'s Reject Education," a *Post* headline in the August 18, 1945, issue read. The G.I. Bill, an accompanying article stated, is "a splendid bill, a wonderful bill, with one conspicuous drawback. The guys aren't buying it." Two months after the article appeared, 88,000 veterans were "buying it." A year later there were a million.

Roosevelt's signature was hardly dry on the bill when the first applicant signed up. On June 23, 1944, the day after the White House ceremony, former corporal Don A. Balfour of Washington, D.C. called on John M. MacCammon, a Veterans Administration vocational officer. Balfour, who now owns an insurance agency near the White House, had been honorably discharged with poor eyesight. He was paying his way at George Washington University, editing the school paper, *The Hatchet,* and interviewed MacCammon for an article. "I asked Mr. MacCammon to explain the benefits to me," Balfour recalled. "Suddenly I said, 'Could I sign up for benefits?' He said, 'Certainly.' The forms hadn't even been printed, but by August I was officially on the G.I. Bill."

Although critics at first denounced the bill's educational benefits as a "handout" and predicted that "lazy" veterans would capitalize on them to shirk jobs, the 1944 bill guaranteed military personnel a year of education for 90 days' service, plus one month for each month of active duty, for a maximum of 48 months. Tuition, fees, books and supplies up to $500 a year would be paid directly to the college or university (at a time when private universities charged about $300 a year tuition and state universities considerably less). Single veterans were to receive a subsistence allowance of $50 a month, married veterans $75 a month.

That may not have been a bonanza, but it was plenty for a generation hardened by the Depression. In his book *The American Veteran Back Home,* sociologist Robert J. Havighurst followed 416 veterans who had returned to a prototypical town he called "Midwest." Twenty-eight percent—some of whom had not planned to go—used the G.I. Bill for college, he reported. He could have been talking about Les Faulk and the other young men of Turtle Creek '44. Of 103 male graduates in their high school class of 270, thirty earned college degrees, nearly ten times as many as had in the past; 28 of the 30 attended college under the G.I. Bill of Rights. The class produced ten engineers, a psychologist, a microbiologist, an entomologist, two physicists, a teacher-principal, three professors, a social worker, a pharmacist, several entrepreneurs, a stockbroker and a journalist (me). The next year's class matched the 30-percent college attendance almost exactly. The 110 male graduates of 1945 included a federal appellate judge and three lawyers, another stockbroker, a personnel counselor, and another wave of teachers and engineers.

For almost all of them, their college diploma was a family first. Some of their parents had not completed elementary school—a few could not read or write English.

For their children, however, the G.I. Bill became a ticket of admission to a better life. On our spring-night reunion, the gray-haired, mainly retired "boys of '44" told one another tales of how a handful of legislative paragraphs had changed their lives. As they nibbled pizza and sipped beer, they spoke of houses, jobs, travel, knowledge and career accomplishments far beyond their wildest dreams of many years before.

Joe Valentich, for instance, had grown up on Prospect Street in Turtle Creek, among a cluster of Slavic immigrants who provided the strong backs and muscles for western Pennsylvania industries. "I don't think I heard a word of English until I entered first grade," confided Valentich, a Croatian-American whose father worked in an alloy plant. But the Army veteran proudly displayed two books with the brain-twisting titles *Short Range Radio Telemetry for Rotating Instrumentation* and *Tube Type Dilatometers: Applications from Cryogenic to Elevated Temperatures*—and the byline "Joseph Valentich." After a high school machine-shop diploma, he had earned a degree in mathematics and 45 graduate credits in math and physics at Duquesne and Pitt, shouldering superhuman loads of up to 23 hours per semester to graduate early.

Les Faulk, who fought in Germany as a Seventh Army infantryman, "matured awfully fast in a foxhole." When he returned home, his father arranged a job for him as an apprentice bricklayer at a steel mill. The job lasted one day. "I went to the poolroom and said to my old boss, 'I'm going to college.' He said, 'I read that only one vet in 20 who enters college will finish.' I said, 'I'm going to be that one.' " Alvan Hoffman had held an after-school job as mechanic's helper before entering the Army Air Corps. "My dad said, 'I can give you meals and a roof over your head, but I can't afford college.' " After discharge, he earned bachelor's and master's degrees in engineering and traveled the world, briefing military personnel on survival techniques.

With few models to follow but in a hurry to catch up, many of the Turtle Creek graduates made capricious, hasty academic decisions—which nonetheless

5. FROM THE COLD WAR TO THE 1990s

paid off. Wyatt Young, center fielder on the baseball team, who had served in Europe with the Air Corps, chose a small West Virginia college he had never heard of, Bethany, because he was told a friend was going there. Bethany launched the farm boy on a successful career in advertising; he now owns a bookstore. Jim Graham, who became a university professor and then an aerospace engineer, applied to the engineering schools at Penn State and Cornell; he went to Cornell because it accepted him first. Navy veteran Alexander Yerman, the class valedictorian, applied for electrical engineering at Carnegie Tech (now Carnegie-Mellon). Told that the program was full, he simply switched to chemical engineering and built a career developing microchips.

Why go to Podunk U. when Uncle Sam will send you to Yale? *Time* magazine speculated in 1946. Bill Norris, Turtle Creek '45, now a U.S. Circuit Court judge in Los Angeles, and Layman Allen, professor of law and a research scientist at the University of Michigan, asked themselves that very question. When the two close friends learned about the G.I. Bill, Allen, who was stationed at Treasure Island, California, and Norris, at San Diego, met in Santa Barbara to discuss their educational future. Allen recalls: I told Bill that a Navy friend had suggested we try for Princeton. We were small-town boys, what did we know? Bill said, 'Where's Princeton?' " Both got in and graduated. Afterward Norris went on to Stanford Law School, clerked for Supreme Court Justice William O. Douglas, practiced law in Los Angeles, ran for attorney general of California and was appointed to the bench in 1980. Allen went to graduate school at Harvard and then on to Yale Law. He became a nationally known authority on the application of mathematical logic to the analysis of legal problems. "Princeton opened all those doors for us," Judge Norris says. "But the G.I. Bill opened the doors to Princeton."

The two were typical of the new crop of students. Norris was the fifth of six children. None of his brothers and sisters had gone to college, nor had his parents. When he and Allen entered high school, they signed up for the commercial track—typing and secretarial skills. "We didn't expect college," Norris says, "but we didn't want to get our hands dirty in the mill. The plant had this big building full of offices, and we thought it would be nice to wear clean shirts and flirt with all the secretaries."

One day their biology teacher, Miss Chilcote, stormed in and made them go with her to the principal's office. " 'What kind of school are you running?' she said. 'These boys shouldn't be in a commercial course. They could get scholarships to college.' She insisted that we be transferred to the academic track. We had a lot of credits to make up, but we did it," Norris recalls. In the class of 1945, the two took first and second honors.

FLOATING DORMITORIES AND QUONSET HUTS

Meanwhile, campuses all across America were being flooded by ambitious veterans. Some 11,000 ex-G.I.'s attended the University of Wisconsin in 1946, swelling the total enrollment from 9,000 the previous year to 18,000. Rutgers University's enrollment jumped from a prewar 7,000 to 16,000 by 1948. Stanford went from 3,000 to 7,000 students within a year; four-fifths of the men were vets. There simply were not enough beds, teachers, classrooms and laboratories.

Some ingenious makeshift living and teaching arrangements resulted. Quonset huts and surplus barracks mushroomed on once pristine campus lawns. Marietta College in Ohio obtained a surplus Coast Guard vessel and anchored it in the Muskingum River as a floating dormitory. Stanford converted a former military hospital into one- and two-room apartments.

Prewar student bodies had consisted of single men and single women. No one was prepared for the postwar deluge of married couples and families; on some campuses, half the veterans were married. The University of Iowa hastily assembled a trailer camp in what newspapers described as "a sea of mud." Veterans had to carry water in buckets to their apartments. They and their families tiptoed across boardwalks to a common lavatory-bathhouse to take showers while, according to one report, "little boys played peekaboo." The University of Wisconsin threw up a similar "vetsville" with a central water outlet, but eventually the school opened Badger Village, a 699-unit complex that had its own post office, fire department, chapel, grocery store, barbershop and elementary school.

Concurrently, the easygoing Joe College life depicted in "varsity show" movies disappeared. One of the first casualties was the freshman beanie, the distinguishing skullcap traditionally worn by newcomers on many campuses. No 25-year-old freshman who had gone through the Battle of the Bulge and had a wife and two kids was going to put up with such a thing. Out went other hallowed traditions, too. At the University of Iowa, a certain romantically shaded bench had always been reserved for courting couples—by prewar tradition, every woman student would be kissed there before she graduated. Veterans saw the bench as just another convenient spot for study and shooed the amorous away.

Vets often had little time for extracurricular activities, campus politics or social life, but they made their presence felt in athletics. While recent high school stars sat on the sidelines, teams were dominated by 24- and 25-year-olds, some fresh from service squads. Bob Chappuis, the star halfback of Michigan's 1947 championship team, was an ex-aerial gunner who had bailed out over Italy on his 21st mission. When Chappuis lost the Heisman Trophy, it was to Johnny Lujack of Notre Dame, who was back from three years as a Navy ensign.

Worse yet, women students preferred the dashing ex-servicemen, with their scars and battle jackets, to fuzzy-faced 18-year-olds. As for the vetsvilles, they had a life and an atmosphere unlike anything the campuses had seen before. Prior to World War II, a student could be expelled from many colleges if he or she got married. But veterans were creating families as fast as they could get to the altar; so many babies were born in one section of the University of Minnesota veterans' housing that it was nicknamed "Fertile Acres." Baby carriages were parked under the campus elms; drying diapers fluttered in place of college pennants. For the young wives, it was a hectic life under primitive conditions, with responsibility for governing the communities while their husbands studied and often worked part-time as well.

Between books and babies, there wasn't much social life, recalls one vet's wife who lived in Stanford Village. What there was revolved around meetings in the common laundry room and wives' gabfests in the children's play yards, which the "daddies" had constructed with scrounged scrap lumber.

"If there is a baby," a Columbia sociologist had solemnly intoned as late as 1945, "college is almost out of the question for any reasonable man." In fact, fathers turned out to be the most diligent students. Grade-point averages hit a record high at Stanford the first year the veterans were back. Flunk-outs and absenteeism hit an all-time low. Other Stanford students called the veterans "DARs"—"Damn Average Raisers."

The veterans' hurry-up pace revolutionized the colleges' old, easygoing schedule. Summer vacation almost disappeared. At Stanford before World War II, only 7 percent of the classrooms were occupied at 2 P.M. By 1946–47, classes were beginning at 7 A.M. and running until past the dinner hour. "Lights still blazed in the Quad at 11:30," the *Stanford Alumni Review* marveled.

Faculties, their ranks already depleted by the war, were stretched thin. Wallace Stegner, who taught literature and creative writing at Stanford, once recalled that his pre-G.I. Bill classes could be comfortably seated around a dining-room table. By 1947 he was teaching 160 students—and grading as many papers, since he had no graduate assistants to help him.

Professors at some universities were accustomed to prep school types who dutifully took notes but weren't all that interested in real lessons. Those teachers had a tough time dealing with grown men. One veteran recalled a student who interrupted a Contemporary Affairs lecture with "Don't tell me about China. I've been there." A Spanish professor directed a veteran to write a mistranslated sentence 100 times, as if he were in eighth grade. The vet simply laughed at him.

A minority of faculty deplored the driven young men who were "ruining" the college in their haste to gain a diploma and get to earning a living. They were missing the essence of college life, these professors complained. Said one Stanford professor of the faculty critics, "They couldn't cope with students who didn't swallow goldfish or hold all-night parties." But most found the atmosphere stimulating. Having taught at Pitt for more than 50 years, economics professor Reuben Slesinger recalled, "The vets were very good, very motivated."

The idea that Uncle Sam should help veterans with their education was not exactly new. After World War I, the states of New York and Wisconsin set up programs under which certain veterans could receive academic or vocational training at government expense. In 1941 Canada began considering such a plan. President Roosevelt, an Assistant Secretary of the Navy during World War I, had long been concerned about the government's role in planning for the veterans' return to civilian life. By 1942 the educational community, headed by the august American Council on Education, was quietly sketching out suggestions for veterans educational benefits. But the issue really began to move when it caught the attention of the American Legion, which had enormous political clout. To this day, several local Legion posts still claim they "originated" the G.I. Bill.

VETERANS' GROUPS WRANGLE OVER THE BILL

Eventually, after lining up political support and testing the waters, a Legion committee in fact prepared a draft bill. One winter evening in 1943, Legionnaire Harry Colmery sat down in a suite at the Mayflower Hotel in Washington, D.C. and wrote out the proposal in longhand. Hearst newspapers began a drumbeating campaign for the bill. Yet it was almost strangled at birth in a bizarre political turf battle and a fuss over tactics. It was saved, finally, only through a last-minute, cliff-hanger rescue worthy of Hollywood.

The Legion had thrown all its weight behind its "omnibus" bill (opponents called it an "ominous" bill), which lumped veterans' educational and medical benefits, on-the-job training, home and farm loans, and unemployment payments into one measure. Other veterans groups initially disagreed, urging Congress not to be "stampeded into hasty and possible unwise legislation." Some organizations worried that the omnibus tactic would allow opponents of individual features to gang up and defeat the whole package. The Disabled Veterans of America feared that wounded and disabled G.I.'s might be shortchanged if benefits were given to all.

Partly as a result, one version of Public Law 346 passed the Senate, while another passed the House. The bitter struggle to reconcile the two threatened the bill's survival. At stake were sharp differences about such issues as states' rights (would a new, perhaps state-controlled, office administer the funds or would the Federal Employment Service?), veteran eligibility (should it include all veterans or just those whose schooling had been interrupted?), and varying degrees of hostility to unemployment benefits (which some legislators thought likely to promote indolence).

The conference committee trying to sort things out contained seven Senators and seven Representatives. The Senators offered a compromise bill that three Representatives agreed to. But three others, led by the powerful states' rights proponent John Rankin of Mississippi, rejected it. The seventh and deciding voter, John Gibson, was back home in Georgia. He had submitted a proxy vote to Rankin, but when it turned out to be for the compromise, Rankin refused to honor it. On June 9, the conferees remained deadlocked, and Gibson was still away. Under the conference rules, the two committees had to agree by 10 o'clock the next morning or the G.I. Bill would die.

Opponents were confident the bill had been at least temporarily defeated. When the Legion decided that Gibson must somehow be hauled back bodily to cast the deciding vote it was already past 6 P.M. and nobody could find him. He was believed to be heading home to Douglas, Georgia, after a speech at Valdosta, 70 miles away. Later that evening the pro-bill *Atlanta Constitution* got into the act; a telephone operator started calling Gibson's home every five minutes. Radio stations broadcast an appeal for anyone knowing Gibson's whereabouts to "call operator 2 in Washington immediately."

Just after 11 P.M. Gibson answered his phone in Douglas. With a Georgia state motorcycle-police escort, he was driven to an Air Force base in Waycross and transferred to a military car, which raced through a slashing thunderstorm at 90 miles an hour toward Jacksonville, Florida, where the Legion had a plane waiting. At 6:37 A.M. on June 10, less than four hours before the deadline, Gibson's plane touched down in Washington. Promptly at 10 A.M. he appeared at the committee room and cast the deciding vote.

Echoes of a Distant War

The half-remembered Korean conflict was full of surprises, and nearly all of them were unpleasant

Bernard A. Weisberger

Korea is in the news again, and it's ugly news. North Korea may or may not have the capability to make nuclear weapons, and North Korea's aging dictator, Kim Il Sung, is unwilling to let international inspectors find out. The United Nations is talking of sanctions. The United States is pointedly scheduling military maneuvers with the army of the Republic of South Korea. Some of the media's self-chosen secretaries of state summon us, from their word processors, to sturdy firmness. Others warn that the unpredictable Kim should not be cornered, lest he provoke a second Korean War.

I don't know if that last is an impossible scenario. But the mere idea gives me the feeling of being trapped in a rerun. Nearly five years after the Cold War ended, we are talking about possible renewed hostilities with a chief character from its early phases. Kim is the oldest surviving Communist boss. He goes back beyond an era already ancient—the days of Khrushchev; Eisenhower, Adenauer, de Gaulle, Ho Chi Minh—to an almost paleolithic time when World War II strongmen like Truman, Stalin, and Chiang Kai-shek still walked the stage.

A great many people know nothing whatever about the original Korean War. It is a barely commemorated conflict, buried between the heroics of World War II, the "good war," and the torments of Vietnam, the bad one, which we lost. And it partakes of both traditions. It started as a neat epilogue to the great war against fascist aggression and ended as a curtain raiser to the frustrations of an age of limited power. It was full of surprises, almost all of them unpleasant.

To begin at the beginning, North and South Korea, like East and West Germany, were political fictions created by the post-1945 failure of the wartime Soviet-U.S. alliance. Korea was a single nation, divided into temporary Soviet and American occupation zones pending a final peace treaty with Japan, which had seized and annexed Korea.

The little peninsula was a rich prize, half of which fell into Stalin's lap cheaply in August of 1945, when the U.S.S.R. entered the war against Japan in its final days. Moscow's forces got to occupy Manchuria and northern Korea and help themselves to "reparations" from both places. In Korea the Soviets also dominated the political reorganization that was supposedly the prelude to all-Korean elections that would at last set up a free, single, democratic Korea. Kim Il Sung, a veteran of Korea's Communist underground, emerged at this time. He was thought by Americans to be a totally obedient Stalin puppet, but so was every Communist leader in those days—a somewhat simplistic assessment, as events showed.

In South Korea the reawakening of independent political life brought back a long-exiled figure, Dr. Syngman Rhee, who was seventy years old at the war's end. Rhee was a veteran nationalist, jailed and tortured by the Japanese in his youth. He was a popular autocrat whose limited brand of "democracy" had America's blessing, and when he won elections held in the South, Washington helped him build an army for his Republic of Korea and then withdrew its forces. The U.S.S.R. did likewise with Kim, whom it endowed with the leadership of the People's Democratic Republic of Korea. By 1950 Kim and Rhee—their man and ours—were glaring at each other from their respective capitals, Pyongyang and Seoul. Each wished passionately to depose the other "puppet" and unify Korea under his own rule. There were border clashes and provocations, threats (unpleasantly like those we are hearing today) and clear indications that either would use force if he could get his patron's backing.

But it was Kim who struck first. On June 25, 1950, his tanks rolled across the thirty-eighth parallel, which marked the border between South and North, and gave the world the first of a series of shocks. Number one was the attack itself, seemingly a crude act of aggression in imitation of Japan's grab of Manchuria, Mussolini's attack on Ethiopia, or Hitler's march into Austria. This searing parallel to the 1930s led American public opinion almost universally and instantly to agree that action was needed. *This* time international outlawry would be stopped in its tracks. And right at hand was the United Nations, the precise agency for calling in the international cops. The United States got a resolution authorizing "police action" rushed through the Security Council. The war thereby became technically a UN operation, though 90 percent of the forces, and the overall commander, Gen. Douglas MacArthur, were furnished by the Republic of Korea and the United States.

Now came the second great shock. The air and naval forces that President Truman immediately ordered to support the South Koreans were not enough to stop the invasion. Ground troops were needed, and MacArthur could deploy only his occupation forces, softened by years of garrison duty. Fed piecemeal into action, they were quickly overrun by North Korean divisions. By the end of August the soldiery of a "tiny" Asian nation had penned the UN forces in a perimeter around the port of Pusan and seemed on the verge of driving them completely off the peninsula.

26. Echoes of a Distant War

Then a thunderclap for our side. MacArthur had assembled an amphibious force from the reinforcements pouring into Japan, and on September 15 it landed at Inchon, on Korea's western coast, in a dramatic high-risk attack against strong positions in tricky tides—a gamble that, to MacArthur's delight, was brilliantly successful. Now it was the enemy that faced cutoff and entrapment. The North Koreans retreated pellmell; inside two weeks Seoul was back in UN hands, and American troops were surging northward above the thirty-eighth parallel, for the United Nations had authorized the then-untouchable MacArthur (though not without debate) not only to restore the status quo but to overrun North Korea and punish the aggressor.

That set up shock number three. The Chinese Communists, who had been in power since 1949, when Chiang Kai-shek and his Nationalist army were driven off the mainland and onto Taiwan, let it be known through neutrals that they would not tolerate a UN armed presence on their common border with North Korea, the Yalu River. MacArthur, who fancied himself a master of "Oriental" psychology, persuaded Washington to ignore these warnings and pushed on. At the end of October 1950 Chinese infantry entered the fighting against the Americans in force, although technically there was no state of war between Peking and Washington or Peking and Seoul. Within days the divided and outnumbered American and ROK forces were enveloped and driven into a bitter winter retreat. As the new year opened, Seoul fell to the Communists again. MacArthur then set the stage for the next scene.

For the general, who had spent the preceding fifteen years in Asia, the war with China, declared or not, was real and had to be pursued to victory. He wanted American bombers to hit Chinese and North Korean bases and "sanctuaries" in Manchuria and also wished to have Chiang's army sea-lifted from Taiwan to Korea. In the Cold War atmosphere these ideas were attractive to many Americans, but not to Truman and the Joint Chiefs of Staff. Preoccupied with confronting Stalin in Europe, they wanted no part of consuming land battles in Asia. MacArthur pushed his public quarrel with Washington up to, if not over, the edge of insubordination.

The American public dealt with the frustration of a victoryless war by forgetting the whole episode.

But he was up against another rocklike, if less flamboyant, individual in Truman. Politician though he was, the President was immovable when he thought he had the Constitution on his side. And so the fourth great shock: On April 11, 1951, Truman fired MacArthur amid a firestorm of public fury. MacArthur's dismissal was a turning point. After ten months of violent pendulum swings, the war settled into a new kind of conflict. None of the major powers wanted a full-scale engagement in Korea. What was needed was a peace of some kind with neither victory nor defeat. In July of 1951 truce talks began. They lasted for two years.

And in that time the real and most terrible Korean War was fought. The battle line stabilized more or less near the thirty-eighth parallel, and the fighting became a nasty and brutish affair, reminiscent of World War I, of small advances against strongly fortified positions with names like Pork Chop Hill and the Iron Triangle. Each gain cost hundreds, sometimes thousands, of lives. When final truce terms were approved on July 27, 1953 (over the strong objections of Rhee, and possibly Kim too), there was no exultation but mainly a kind of grim relief. Little was changed, except that a U.S. security treaty with Seoul pledged us to the future defense of the ROK against any attack, so as to leave no tempting doubt.

The American public, grudgingly forced to accept a victoryless war, seems to have dealt with frustration by forgetting the whole episode. There is just now under way a memorial in Washington to the thirty-three thousand Americans who died in Korea. Its returning veterans got no parades; they got a platter of benefits sharply reduced from that provided for the warriors of 1941–45. The United Nations, rather than being perceived as the force that had stopped aggression, fell into disrepute with some Americans for its failure to destroy North Korea. The United States settled into an era of diminished expectations of world perfection. Perhaps not diminished enough: The Korean War seems not to have prepared the public mind fully for the limits to power encountered later in Vietnam.

I don't wish to sound dismissive or to trivialize the vast suffering of soldiers and civilians on all sides. One could argue that the war was "won" to the extent that it may have discouraged further adventurism. Still, I wish it were possible to worry less about the surprises that a still divided Korea may bring us in the years to come.

Article 27

TV's Wonder Years

The classic television programs aired in the early 1950s captured the imagination of the American public and guaranteed a central place for the medium in our lives.

Edward Oxford

New York writer Edward Oxford has contributed more than two dozen articles to American History.

Something quite like magic took hold of the nation back in the mid-twentieth century. Across the country come evening, hundreds of thousands—and before long, millions—of families sat entranced before flickering television sets, as though huddled about some cosmic campfire. Americans watched in wonder as the first, magical images shone forth from their brand-new television sets. A many-splendored marvel had come into their living rooms.

Now projected into their own homes, were glimpses of high culture, serious drama, and blatant celebrity. Here were comedy headliners such as Milton Berle, Lucille Ball, Jack Benny, Jackie Gleason, Ernie Kovacs, Sid Caesar, and Jimmy Durante—with his eloquent fade-out of "Good night, Mrs. Calabash wherever you are..."; Captain Video with his zap-gun leading us into the space age; the musical virtuosity of Liberace at his schmaltzy piano, Perry Como crooning "Dream Along With Me (I'm on My Way to the Stars)," and Gene Autry serenading with "I'm Back in the Saddle Again"; news delivered with authority by Edward R. Murrow and John Cameron Swayze; live dramatic presentations featuring many future stars of Broadway and Hollywood; and sporting events ranging from the roller derby to baseball's World Series.

Television programming's remarkable montage of art, entertainment, culture, and hokum offered viewers a window into the human condition. One scholar observed that just as the "printing press five centuries before had begun to democratize learning, now television would democratize experience." Comedian Bob Hope called the new wonder "that piece of furniture that stares back at you."

However one described it, television was startling, intriguing, and more than somewhat baffling as to what, in its deepest

One of the most innovative early TV shows was *Captain Video and His Video Rangers,* which aired from 1949–1955. The tales of this futuristic "Guardian of the Safety of the World," starring first Richard Coogan and then Al Hodge (the radio voice of the Green Hornet, who is shown atop *TV Guide* page, above), beat out rival *Space Patrol* and *Tom Corbett—Space Cadet,* despite a prop budget of only $25.00 per week.

27. TV's Wonder Years

World War II brought television's forward march to a virtual halt, although the National Broadcasting Corporation (NBC) did produce *The War As It Happens,* a weekly program that began in February 1944. Transmission lines were taken over for war needs, and critical materials were diverted from the burgeoning television industry to production of radar components and bomb-sights. Americans simply added television to their list of dreams put on hold for the postwar world.

It did not take long, however, for television to find its place after the war ended. Thousands of men who had braved combat now strove to meet mortgage payments. For the first time in several generations, the number of Americans owning their own homes surpassed the number who rented. And, as the little house on the quiet street in the suburbs became reality for growing numbers of Americans, television sets began to assume their place as the home's centerpiece.

In the entertainment industry, television also took center-stage, leaving radio, motion pictures, sports, and even publishing scrambling in the wings. As of 1946, scattered stations around the country were telecasting programs. Within two years, four networks—the Columbia Broadcasting System (CBS), the American Broadcasting Company (ABC), and Dumont, in addition to NBC—were on the air for much of each day and evening. By 1950, the new medium had become the unmatched leader of show business. As such, it was to have a profound effect on the American scene.

Antennas by the tens of thousands sprouted from rooftops. The first family on the block to own a television set soon found itself beset by uninvited guests who stopped by to glimpse the wonder-box "just for a minute." One woman recalled: "We didn't like our cousins, but they had a television set. A few times a week we'd go to their house and watch television. It didn't matter what. Everything was a treat. Even so, there'd be bickering. Our family got our own set— and that worked out for the better, all the way around."

During the first decade or so of network television—from 1946 through 1955—the new medium underwent vast expansion and wild experimentation. Centered in New York— and initially resented and reviled by

sense, it signified—and just where, with its power to mesmerize, it would finally lead those who peered into its screen.

It had taken television a while to reach Americans. As of the late 1920s, the first, faltering images—jittering silhouettes, call letters, and blurred faces— had flickered onto one-by-two-inch screens in research laboratories. It was in 1930 that the first public television broadcast was made in America.

During the thirties, the few hundred proud owners of television receivers had, for the most part, nothing to look at but a blank screen and the hardwood cabinet that housed it. But, bit by bit, makeshift studios in New York, Chicago, and Los Angeles sporadically transmitted cartoons, comic monologues, and pantomimes. By the decade's end, the new medium was attracting attention with a variety of offerings that included scenes from the Broadway play *Susan and God;* a test-pattern image of Felix the Cat; composer George Gershwin rendering "Lola"; a Princeton-Columbia University baseball game; on-the-spot coverage of a man poised on a Manhattan hotel ledge, preparing to leap to his death; and President Franklin D. Roosevelt's opening of the 1939 World's Fair in New York.

5. FROM THE COLD WAR TO THE 1990s

LIFE IN FRONT OF "THE TUBE"

For years before TV took hold in America, families gathered in the evening to listen to their favorite radio programs, so the switch to television would seem to be a natural evolution. But "the tube" was more seductive; it made you afraid that you would miss something if you didn't pay attention. It was no longer as easy to sew, play a game, or do homework while listening; you had to be able to watch too.

Most early televisions were substantial pieces of furniture connected to a roof-top antenna cable, and couldn't be taken from room to room. So that dinner could be prepared quickly and people could eat without missing their favorite show, Swanson's introduced its line of "TV Dinners" in 1954, starting with a turkey entrée in a tray that could be taken right in front of the television set.

By 1953, viewers could buy *TV Guide* to help them keep track of the increasing number of new programs. The premier issue hit the newsstands the week of April 3-9 that year with *I Love Lucy*'s "Little Ricky" on the cover.

More and more companies aimed their advertisements at what would come to be called the "television generation." Ads for the latest models of television sets proliferated. Some sets, like the one mentioned in the 1949 ad shown here, could cost more than $2,000; for many at the time, a year's salary.

Most sets, however, were more reasonably priced, and Americans were buying them—between 1949 and '55 the number of families with televisions in the U.S. increased more than 1,500 percent. In only a few years, television had become a source of information, a primary form of entertainment, a babysitter or companion, and an important sector of the national economy. ★

Hollywood—television looked to radio, theater, and vaudeville for writers, directors, and performers. Television studios, bulging with microphone-booms, scenery, and cameras, overflowed into theaters, dance studios, and old movie houses.

Live drama became the distinguishing signature of television's golden years. Producers, for a time denied Hollywood stars and properties, brought both original dramas and adaptations of classics to America's television screens. A listing of some of the era's "anthology series" forms an honor roll of an under-appreciated portion of American letters and dramatic history: *Philco Playhouse, Armstrong Theater, Lux Video Theatre, Robert Montgomery Presents, Schlitz Playhouse of Stars,* and *Goodyear TV Playhouse.*

Millions of viewers who had never been to a stage performance suddenly had topflight, theatrical-quality presentations right in their living rooms. *Studio One* presented "The Twelve Angry Men"; *The U.S. Steel Hour* offered "No Time for Sergeants"; *Philco Television Playhouse* brought forth "A Trip to Bountiful." Rising stars from New York's theater world, such as Paul Newman, Kim Stanley, James Dean, Eva Marie Saint, Jack Lemmon, and Grace Kelly, found important roles.

In 1953, Paddy Chayefsky's poignant *Marty* crowned the era's original drama achievements. His tale of the not-so-handsome Bronx butcher and his pals, with its true-to-life settings and realistic street-talk, made a telling impact on the audience. Rod Steiger, who starred in this production, commented afterwards: "People from all over the country and all different walks of life, people of different races and creeds, sent me letters. The immense power of that medium!"

Live telecasts of established works—*The Petrified Forest, The Man Who Came to Dinner, Arsenic and Old Lace*—introduced those classics to whole new audiences. When, for example, television presented *Hamlet* in 1953, more people watched it at home in a single evening than had seen it on the stage in the 350 years since William Shakespeare put pen to paper.

For viewers seeking lighter fare, variety shows proliferated. Red Skelton introduced Clem Kaddidlehopper. Bud Abbot and Lou Costello asked "Who's on First?" Arthur Godfrey strummed his ukulele and gave a start to up-and-coming performers on his *Talent Scouts*. Kate Smith sang "When the Moon Comes

Over the Mountain." Jerry Lewis played "Lady of Spain" on a set of bedsprings under the watchful gaze of his partner, Dean Martin.

Ed Sullivan couldn't sing, dance, or tell jokes. And sometimes he forgot the names of the acts he was set to introduce. But as host of *The Toast of the Town,* the newspaper-columnist-turned-television-host proved the perfect foil for performers who *did* have talent. The "Great Stone Face" presided over a dazzling array of acts that ranged from classical pianists to ice-cube jugglers, from Shakespearean actors to barking seals, and from the Bolshoi Ballet to dancing dogs.

Sullivan's program went on the air in June 1948, just two weeks after Milton Berle made his raucous television debut. Before his show ended in 1971, impresario Sullivan presented some twenty thousand acts on his "really big shew."

For the manic-at-heart, Saturday evenings presented *Your Show of Shows,* ninety minutes of inspired lunacy built around the dynamic comedy of Sid Caesar and cohort Imogene Coca. As caveman, dandy, or mad professor, Caesar would twitch, snarl, yell, and explode his way through sketches, often taking scripts by such stellar talent as Mel Brooks, Neil Simon, and Woody Allen beyond their written limits into hysterical new dimensions.

Situation comedies fast became prime television fare. At first, plain-and-simple homeyness set the tone—as in *The Goldbergs* and *Mama*—with quiet insights into everyday family matters. And there would be more than a touch of the wholesome to be savored in *The Adventures of Ozzie and Harriet, Father Knows Best,* and *Make Room for Daddy.*

But "sitcoms," as they came to be termed, afforded ample room for caricature. In *The George Burns and Gracie Allen Show,* Gracie was the delightfully daffy one, George the resigned onlooker Typically, George, with his ever-present cigar, would deadpan something like: "Gracie believes everything she reads. She fried fish the other day, and I had to buy her a new dress. The recipe said, 'Roll in cracker crumbs.' "

Zaniest of the zany *I Love Lucy* was to prove a resounding favorite. Viewers, it seemed, could not get enough of this spoof of married life—particularly of Lucille Ball's indefatigable mugging. Week after week, her Lucy sought to reach out from the realm of domesticity toward a fuller measure of independence, with hilarious—sometimes disastrous—results.

During the episode aired January 19, 1953, Lucy gave birth to "Little Ricky Ricardo"; on that same day, real-life Lucille gave birth to Desi Arnaz, Junior. More television viewers watched the arrival of the fictitious Ricky than would tune in for President Dwight D. Eisenhower's inauguration the next day. The nation did indeed love Lucy, through 179 episodes that ran from 1951 to 1957.

Crime-solving also became a television staple. *Man Against Crime,* featuring Ralph Bellamy as a special investigator, and *Martin Kane, Private Eye* emerged as early successes in 1949. Writers were instructed that "somebody must be murdered, preferably early, with the threat of more violence to come."

Dragnet, the prototypical crime drama, began in early 1952. The widely popular show featured Jack Webb as Sergeant Joe Friday, badge No. 714 for the Los Angeles Police Department, ever in quest of "the facts, ma'am (or sir), just the facts." There were few fist fights, few bullets, few moments of violence of any kind.

Westerns, a genre that almost saturated television schedules by the late 1950s, enjoyed their first success when William Boyd brought his *Hopalong Cassidy* from the movie screen to the nation's TV sets in 1947. A year later, *The Lone Ranger,* the daring masked rider of the plains, made the switch from radio with his fiery horse, Silver, and his faithful Indian companion, Tonto. Gene Autry was one of the first western motion-picture stars to film a series especially for television. Roy Rogers, the "King of the Cowboys," co-starred with his wife, Dale Evans, and his horse, Trigger, in 101 episodes, each of which closed with the Sons of the Pioneers harmonizing "Happy Trails to You."

As the television medium gained acceptance, viewers came to expect coverage of important or interesting news stories. Live coverage of events as they transpired and broadcasts illustrated with still photography or film footage whet the nation's appetite for news. Catching the nightly news at suppertime or just before bedtime—with commentators such as Walter Cronkite, Chet Huntley David Brinkley and Douglas Edwards—quickly became part of most families' routines.

Meet the Press, which debuted in 1947, provided weekly press conferences with newsmakers from around the world. (Network television's longest-running program, it is still aired weekly) Vice-presidential candidate Richard Nixon turned to television for his famous "Checkers" speech during the 1952 campaign. Senator Estes Kefauver's investigation of organized crime fascinated audiences; at one point, a camera focused on the hands of reputed mobster Frank Costello while he time and again invoked his right to remain silent. *Broadcasting* magazine said of the spectacle: "Television's camera eye had opened the public's."

The era's most riveting televised moments may well have come during the so-called Army-McCarthy hearings of 1954. Wisconsin's Senator Joseph R. McCarthy's witch-hunt for communists within the U.S. government came undone, in part, because of his own ill-at-ease manner in front of the probing television cameras that carried the disturbing capitol hill drama into the nation's living rooms. Urbane telejournalist Edward R. Murrow helped to hasten McCarthy's fall from grace by presenting a highly critical view of him on *See It Now.* Commenting on the role played by television in bringing McCarthy down, the *New York Times* declared that "Television has come of age."

Of the medium's truth-sensing quality, producer Fred Friendly commented: "Television can show you the Atlantic and the Pacific, and television can show you the face of the moon. But it can also show you the face and heart of man. And perhaps what it does best is the latter."

Right from the start, television sought to satisfy the viewers' every mood and whim. The early-riser watched *Today* over breakfast. Telecast from a street-level studio, with New Yorkers on their way to work as the live audience, the show was affably hosted by Dave Garroway with the able assistance of one J. Fred Muggs, a chimpanzee. For insomniacs, *The Tonight Show* with Steve Allen—a mix of skits and chat meant to banish the cares of the day—debuted in 1954.

Game-shows such as *What's My Line?, Break the Bank, Beat the Clock,* and *Truth or Consequences* allowed those at home to watch studio contestants compete for prizes or stump celebrity panelists. Quick-witted Groucho Marx slyly needled contestants on *You Bet Your Life,* offering an added prize

5. FROM THE COLD WAR TO THE 1990s

to anyone who said the day's "secret word."

To youngsters, television brought perhaps the most wondrous moments of all. Freckle-faced marionette Howdy Doody, along with Buffalo Bob and Clarabell the Clown, delighted children in the Peanut Gallery and at home for 13 years, starting in 1947. Young and old alike took delight in *Kukla, Fran, and Ollie,* which featured puppeteer Burr Tillstrum, Fran Allison, and assorted creatures of the Kuklapolitan troupe. For the fanciful, *Mr. I. Magination* created a magical town where a child's wishes could come true. And, a quietly paced early-morning show, *Captain Kangaroo,* combined pure entertainment with stories and basic education.

Slightly older children marveled as Superman leaped tall buildings in a single bound; cheered as Lassie, the intrepid collie, made yet another rescue; and—mouse-cap ears properly affixed—joined in 1955 in singing the timeless words of *The Mickey Mouse Club* theme song.

For the first television generation, held spellbound by shows that were charming, wholesome, and benevolent, memories of the new medium would have a lasting impact. Radio had already opened new vistas to home audiences; now, no home was so small that it could not host a symphony orchestra or a football game. But there was something about actually being able to see the concert or the game that provided an extra sense of immediacy and intimacy.

Questions about what television *ought to be* were asked early and often. Essayist E. B. White opined that television "should be our Lyceum, our Chautauqua, our Misnky's, and our Camelot." But much as the medium raised expectations, it also raised concerns. "Television is the first truly democratic medium," critic Clive Barnes stated, "the first culture available to everybody and entirely governed by what the people want. The most terrifying thing is what the people want."

Comedian Fred Allen wisecracked: "Television permits people who haven't anything to do to watch people who can't do anything." And Edward R. Murrow noted the role of individual responsibility when he observed that "[Television] can teach, it can illuminate; yes, it can even inspire. But it can do so only to the extent that humans are determined to use it to those ends. Otherwise, it is merely lights and wires in a box."

The questions asked during television's formative years still crop up in discussions of the medium's potential. No one, pondering television's prospects a half-century ago, could foretell with much certainty what would come of this strange, compelling phenomenon. Many still wonder.

Looking Back on Ike

John P. Rossi

John P. Rossi is professor of history at La Salle University in Philadelphia.

In his wonderful essay on Gandhi, George Orwell observed that "regarded simply as a politician, and compared with the other leading political figures of our time, how clean a smell he has managed to leave behind." The same observation could be made of Dwight Eisenhower and his presidency. How good he looks now, in contrast to when he left the White House in 1961.

In 1962 Arthur Schlesinger, Jr., polled some seventy-five leading historians to rank and rate the American presidents. Ike came in twenty-second, tied with Chester A. Arthur! What a commentary on the judgment of the historical profession. But now in less than thirty years Ike has risen to ninth place, just behind his predecessor, Harry Truman, according to a survey of forty scholars by the Chicago Tribune.[1] What caused this startling reevaluation? Why have scholars and critics of the presidency shown a new appreciation for Ike's positive qualities? The explanation, I believe, tells us much about the way ideas move in our society and much about the fickleness of the concept of "reputation." It also should lead us to be careful of evaluation by academic scholars, who, despite their reputation for insight, are often just as influenced by fads as the public.

EISENHOWER'S SUCCESSORS

Part of Eisenhower's present appeal flows from the contrast with his successors. Seven men have held the presidency after Ike and, while it is too soon to make any firm evaluation of Reagan and Bush, I believe it is safe to say that none of Ike's successors will oust him from his ranking as a successful president. John Kennedy's reign was too short for much to be accomplished, and the initial enthusiasm for him in the aftermath of his tragic assassination has not held up to close scrutiny, despite the mythologizing of Schlesinger, Ted Sorensen, and others of the "Camelot" clique.

Lyndon Johnson's presidency remains mired in the swamps of the Big Muddy of Vietnam. While Johnson still seems bigger than life, what we know about him repels rather than attracts, as evidenced by Robert Caro's recent biography. Even Johnson's ambitious social and civil rights legislation, his War on Poverty, lost whatever glamour it once had in the late 1970s and the Reagan-oriented 1980s. I see no evidence of a positive reevaluation of Johnson taking place in the foreseeable future.

Richard Nixon has tried with limited success to revive his reputation by writing extensively on his role in American foreign policy. The American public is showing signs of forgiveness, but somehow I believe Watergate and Nixon's own smarmy self-justifications will keep

---

1. Steve Neal, "Why We Were Right to Like Ike," *American Heritage* (Dec. 1985): 49–65.

5. FROM THE COLD WAR TO THE 1990s

him from achieving presidential greatness. Impeachment will haunt his reputation for generations to come.

Gerry Ford is little more than a historical footnote. Jimmy Carter left office under a bigger cloud than any president since Herbert Hoover. Carter's reputation will rise because he wasn't that bad, and he has kept a low but appealing profile as reflected in his involvement in good works like the "Habitat for Humanity" program. But I see no signs either from popular writers or from scholars that his presidency can be rescued from the ash heap of history. For one thing, like Johnson and Nixon, Carter is totally lacking in a sense of humor, a quality that served both Kennedy and Reagan well. He also possesses a mean streak reminiscent of H. L. Mencken's description of Woodrow Wilson: the perfect example of the Christian cad.

Reagan could prove interesting. He bears some resemblance to Eisenhower in that he was an elderly, grandfatherly figure who was laughed at by his own contemporaries while remaining vastly popular in the polls. But it is still too early to tell whether he and his administration will be treated kindly by future generations. The memoirs have just started to appear, and the scholars are only beginning to go beyond journalistic investigations of his years in office.

Compared to these six presidents, Eisenhower seems a giant. An analysis of his presidency shows that the portrait of Ike as an amiable, good-natured, golf-playing, do-nothing, intellectually lazy president just doesn't hold up. We know that Ike rose early, read the press daily, had a full calendar five days a week, and often worked Saturdays and Sundays. He also held frequent meetings with the Democratic and Republican leadership in the evening over drinks, where business was effectively conducted.

Starting with talented journalists such as Murray Kempton and Garry Wills, the portrait of Ike began to be revised in the mid-1960s. Kempton showed that, contrary to popular opinion, Ike was an effective politician, successful in getting his way and even outmaneuvering old pros in Congress. Wills contrasted Eisenhower to Nixon and Johnson and showed not only a more appealing persona but an abler political leader and a more reflective statesman.

It is also important to remember that this initial reevaluation came against the backdrop of the turbulent sixties, with

---

PRÉCIS

Contrary to the usual depictions by critics, Dwight Eisenhower was no simple golf-playing, lazy, or intellectually limited president. This myth began to be shattered during the 1960s when journalists such as Garry Wills and Murray Kempton indicated that Ike was, in reality, both a capable political leader and a reflective statesman.

Historians too have gradually changed their assessments of his presidency. Arthur Schlesinger, Jr., asked seventy-five of them to rank Eisenhower in relation to other presidents. In 1962 he rated twenty-second. Less than thirty years later, in a poll of forty scholars conducted by the *Chicago Tribune*, he came in ninth.

Part of the reason for Eisenhower's present standing is the contrast of his accomplishments with the decade that followed: the violent, chaotic 1960s. Compared to this troubled time, the idyllic 1950s do not seem too bad. As a result, a more generous portrait of the Eisenhower era has emerged in popular culture, in particular in the television program *Happy Days*.

On a more serious level, the release of his private papers during the 1970s initiated a reassessment of Eisenhower by younger scholars untainted by liberal snobbery. They even disclosed, surprisingly, that Ike was a gifted prose stylist, in addition to being a superb judge both of men and political subtleties.

---

its public and private excesses. Ike, who seemed like the dopey fuddy-duddy of Herblock's cartoons in 1960, now looked awfully good in contrast to Johnson and Nixon's record of duplicity, or the rumors of Kennedy's philandering.

The 1950s suddenly didn't seem to be such a bad decade after all, especially when compared with the violence-ridden sixties with its sad record of urban riots, growth of a drug culture, political assassinations, and fifty-thousand deaths in Vietnam. Within a short time an idealized fifties portrait began to appear on TV in the incredibly popular series with the perfect Ike: *Happy Days*.

THE EISENHOWER DIARY

The release of Eisenhower's private papers in the 1970s began a positive scholarly reinterpretation of him. If anything, a new generation of scholars—younger and free from the liberal snobbery of people like Schlesinger and John Kenneth Galbraith—finds Ike increasingly appealing. Scholars as different and influential as his biographer, Stephen Ambrose, and historians like Robert Divine, Robert Ferrell, Charles Alexander, and Fred Greenstein have revealed an Eisenhower who was an effective executive, a superb judge of men and political re-

alities, and, most surprising of all, given his reputation for grammatical clumsiness, a fine writer of prose. The publication of Eisenhower's diary for the years 1935–1969 was a revelation. More profound than Truman's diary, it is filled with sharp portraits of contemporaries such as General MacArthur, General Marshall, and Senator Taft, and demonstrates a grasp of political subtleties worthy of FDR. It is difficult to imagine any of Ike's successors as president maintaining such a diary. The thought of a Reagan diary, for example, is almost too funny to contemplate. Two passages from Eisenhower's diary, written almost a decade apart, indicate its scope and reveal much about him.

In June 1942, Manuel Quezon, the president of the Philippines, offered Eisenhower an honorarium of $75,000 or $100,000 to thank him for his services in Manila in the 1930s. Ike refused, even though MacArthur had accepted $500,000. Ike's reasoning is both typical and revealing: While thanking Quezon, Eisenhower told him that accepting the money would create a false impression and "destroy whatever usefulness I may have to the allied cause in the present war."

Seven years later Gov. Tom Dewey of New York was trying to convince Ike to run for the presidency on the grounds that he was a public property who should not

28. Looking Back on Ike

Dwight Eisenhower campaigning for the presidency.

deny his talents to the nation. Of Dewey's praise Ike wrote, "Although I'm merely repeating someone else's expositions, the mere writing of such things almost makes me dive under the table." Can one imagine any of Ike's successors making such a self-effacing evaluation?

The Eisenhower reevaluation is rooted in a new look at what his administration accomplished and what kind of leader he was personally. Eisenhower ran for the presidency, despite a certain degree of reluctance, because he feared that continued Democratic, New Deal-type rule would mean one-party government for the United States. Eisenhower believed the Democrats' monopoly of the presidency was dangerous. They were winning, he wrote, by the

> doctrine of "spend and spend, elect and elect." It seemed to me that this had to be stopped or our country would deviate badly from the precepts on which we have placed so much faith—the courage and self-dependence of each citizen, the importance of opportunity as opposed to mere material security and our belief that American progress depended upon the work and sweat of all our citizens.

EISENHOWER'S LEADERSHIP

Eisenhower's views on domestic issues were strikingly conservative despite his reputation as the people's general. But on most international issues Eisenhower was close to the Democratic policies initiated by Truman after World War II. He believed in containment and was as rigidly anticommunist as Truman. Interestingly, Eisenhower's reflexive anticommunism was offset by a residual faith in the people. He once wrote that if the United States held the line politically then the gradual growth of education in Russia and Eastern Europe would undermine the Soviet system.

During the presidential primary campaign of 1952, Eisenhower seemed a moderate or even liberal Republican because his chief foe was the staunchly isolationist Sen. Robert Taft. In reality Eisenhower's main disagreement with Taft was on foreign policy, not domestic matters. In fact, Eisenhower was shocked to find that on certain measures—housing for instance—Taft went far beyond anything that he himself would support.

If there was a single compelling reason why Eisenhower sought the presidency, it was to complete the internationalizing of the Republican Party, which he feared was drifting back to prewar isolationism. In his diary during the 1952 election, he observed critically of Herbert Hoover, whom he admired: "I am forced to believe he is getting senile. God knows I'd personally like to get out of Europe and I'd like to see the United States able to sit at home and ignore the rest of the world. What a pleasing prospect until you look at the ultimate consequences, destruction."

Eisenhower's accomplishments over eight years hold up surprisingly well, especially when measured against the record of his successors. He was not an innovative president in the sense that FDR or Wilson was. Rather his success was as conservator or unifier—exactly what the nation yearned for after twenty years of an activist presidency. Where men like FDR, Johnson, and Nixon sought and coveted power, Eisenhower, according to his speechwriter, Emmet Hughes, "distrusted and discounted it." That seemed like a weakness in the 1950s. Today, having watched the way presidents abused their awesome power, such a limited view seems more appealing. Ike's greatest strength was the same quality that he demonstrated so well as supreme allied commander in Europe—he had a gift for reconciling different groups. In some ways, he was a political healer.

CRITICISMS OF EISENHOWER

One of the sharpest criticisms leveled at Eisenhower as president was his apparent lack of control over his administration. He was regarded as an aloof, ineffectual executive as compared to FDR or even Truman. Ike's press conferences, especially his tortured syntax, created the impression of a military leader who was out of place in the political arena—another Grant.

The publication of various scholarly monographs and especially the opening of the Eisenhower archives belie this estimate. Men who served in his administration, especially at the cabinet level, testified to Eisenhower's mastery. He viewed the cabinet as a collegial institution and allowed free discussion of all agenda topics. But as attested by Eisenhower's secretary of health, education, and welfare, Arthur Flemming, there was no doubt who was in charge: "Nothing was ever put to a vote, and it was clear we were talking about these matters as general advisers to him. He is the only person who voted." While it is true that Ike relied on some advisers more than others—John Foster Dulles on foreign policy, George Humphrey for economic matters, Jim Hagerty and Sherman Adams for press and congressional relations—there was no doubt who was boss. He overruled all of these advisers

5. FROM THE COLD WAR TO THE 1990s

when he felt it was necessary. But he did it cleverly.

His brother, Milton, who knew his way around bureaucratic realities, was impressed by the way Ike exercised executive authority:

> He was always building up the other fellow. He did this during the war, and it was perfectly natural for him to do it in the presidency. He wanted people to be responsible and to grow and develop. He never said: "I have told the secretary of agriculture to do so and so." Never. He might say, "I have approved the secretary's recommendation."[2]

This is close to Fred Greenstein's interpretation of Eisenhower's type of executive leadership as "hidden-hand." Eisenhower preferred to work from behind the scenes instead of constantly placing himself before the public. He saw how much of a problem that had been for the combative Truman during his presidency. Truman was in one scrape after another with Congress or the press, and it weakened his position. This difference in style of executive leadership is highlighted most dramatically in the way the two men dealt with Sen. Joseph McCarthy.

There is no issue on which Eisenhower was so criticized during his presidency as in his handling of McCarthy. Contemporaries in the press and in Congress called on Eisenhower to denounce McCarthy and his tactics. Ike refused on the often-quoted grounds that he wouldn't get down in the gutter with McCarthy. This was often portrayed as some form of political cowardice, as if Ike was afraid to confront McCarthy.

Eisenhower naively believed at first that McCarthy could be silenced on grounds of party loyalty. But after that failed, he was involved in the campaign to undermine and destroy the Wisconsin senator. The section of Greenstein's book dealing with the Eisenhower administration's isolation of McCarthy at the time of the Army-McCarthy crisis in late 1953—early 1954 is the clearest demonstration of the effective use of "hidden-hand" leadership. Through memos and interviews, Greenstein traces how active Eisenhower was in drawing the noose tighter around McCarthy despite appeals from the press for public denunciations. Ike believed that was exactly what McCarthy wanted. Truman's public attacks on McCarthy's red-baiting gave him an opportunity to reply and a way of sharing the headlines with the president. In effect, Truman raised McCarthy to his level. Ike never did.

Bryce Harlow, one of Eisenhower's advisers, argued that his handling of McCarthy was ultimately correct. "Truman attacked him personally, by name. Thereby he created a monster. Eisenhower killed him, and he did it by ignoring him.... The result proved him right." While this analysis is correct, the McCarthy question was one of the issues on which the image of a weak, befuddled president grew. Ike would have been better served if he had taken his case against the senator to the public. This image of weakness bothered his advisers more than it did Eisenhower. He believed he was right in his choice of tactics in the McCarthy case, and in the long run he was correct. Within a few months of his censure by the Senate at the end of 1954, McCarthy had been forgotten.

There is no issue on which Eisenhower was so criticized during his presidency as in his handling of McCarthy.

In the areas of foreign policy and military affairs, Eisenhower's administration came in for serious criticism from both journalists and scholars. He was portrayed as an indecisive, vacillating president who left America weaker at the end of his term than it was when he became president. One of the issues that John Kennedy exploited in his presidential campaign in 1960 was precisely this perception, of which the so-called missile gap was part. Eisenhower completely rejected this scenario. At the end of his administration, he said his proudest accomplishment was simple: "The United States never lost a soldier or foot of ground in my administration. We kept the peace."

KINDER EVALUATIONS OF EISENHOWER

In recent years, scholars examining Eisenhower's handling of foreign and military policy have been kinder to him. Again, he looks impressive in contrast to his successors. When he took office, Eisenhower confronted a thirty-month-long war in Korea that was sapping the nation's strength and poisoning its political life. He also recognized that the Korean conflict was causing serious differences with our allies in Europe. He was determined to end the war on acceptable grounds, and he succeeded in doing so by July 1953. His conduct of the negotiations with China was successful, in part because both sides wanted to end the war and also because Eisenhower convinced the Chinese that he might resort to nuclear weapons if they prolonged the war.

Despite his success in the Korean negotiations Eisenhower did not recklessly threaten nuclear war. He had no illusions about the ultimate cost of such a future conflict. In 1954 he told a group of military officers what a nuclear war would entail:

> No matter how well prepared for war we may be, no matter how certain we are that within twenty-four hours we could destroy Kuibyshev and Moscow and Leningrad and Baku and all the other places that would allow the Soviets to carry on war, I want you to carry this question home with you: Gain such a victory, and what do you do with it? Here would be a great area from the Elbe to Vladivostok and down through southeast Asia torn up and destroyed, without government, without its communications, just an area of starvation and disaster. I ask you what would the civilized world do about it? I repeat, there is no victory in any war except through our imaginations, through our dedication, and through our work to avoid it.

Never again during his presidency was Eisenhower drawn into a military conflict. Unlike Kennedy and Johnson, who escalated American involvement in Southeast Asia, Eisenhower scaled back

---

2. Richard A. Melanson, *Reevaluating Eisenhower: American Foreign Policy in the 1950s* (Urbana: University of Illinois Press, 1987), 17.

America's role. In the spring of 1954, when the French were on the eve of a collapse in Vietnam, immense pressure was brought to bear on Eisenhower to intervene. He rejected all such arguments on the unanswerable grounds that the country would not support such a conflict. Moreover, military arguments could not be used to sway him, as was the case with later presidents. Eisenhower was comfortable with his own military judgments. As Paul Carter has pointed out in his study of Eisenhower's decade, *Another Part of the Fifties,* Ike's refusal to intervene in Vietnam was the "only time in the course of six consecutive American presidencies that the United States stepped backward from, rather than more deeply into, Southeast Asia." Even left-wing historians like William Appleton Williams had to admit that Eisenhower knew how to say "enough" and no.

EISENHOWER: A SELF-CONFIDENT MAN

Eisenhower's refusal to countenance foreign policy adventures flowed from his sense of self-confidence. He had nothing to prove. Unlike his successors, he could not be overwhelmed with military arguments. He was concerned that the United States would have to avoid unnecessary conflicts because they would rob the nation of its most precious resource: its young people. Eisenhower also was anxious about the long-term consequences of expensive military commitments. In 1949 he noted in his diary that the key to America's national security was "to hold our position of strength without bankrupting ourselves." The seeds of Eisenhower's concern about the impact of the military-indusrial complex on American society can be found here a decade before his famous farewell speech. He stuck to these views throughout his presidency.

Eisenhower's eight years in office were prosperous ones for the United States.

In his handling of both domestic and international policy, Eisenhower revealed his real inclinations—he was a conservator. He disliked wasteful, unproductive spending and thus brought the military budget under control without weakening the nation. New spending begun during his administration was often not very imaginative, although the completion of the national highway system and the St. Lawrence Seaway were accomplishments that he could be proud of.

Eisenhower was no Republican in the style of the later conservative-movement Goldwater or Reagan. He had no time for those who thought you could dismantle the New Deal welfare state in one fell swoop. He once told his fervently right-wing brother, Edgar, that any party that tried to abolish social security, labor laws, or farm programs would soon disappear. In speaking of people who believed that was possible, including H. L. Hunt and other Texas millionaires, he told Edgar that their number is negligible and "they are stupid."

When Eisenhower left office, journalist and lifelong liberal Democrat William Shannon argued that he was a political failure. "'No national problem," he wrote, "whether it be education, housing, urban revitalization, agriculture or inflation, will have been advanced toward solution, nor its dimension significantly altered." This sentence purports to describe an eight-year period of unmatched prosperity in the United States, with the inflation rate averaging 1.47 percent per year, personal income rising by 28 percent, and real disposable income by 20 percent. Housing boomed as suburbs sprung up all over the country. America outproduced the world in farm goods, and education prospered as colleges continued to build in the aftermath of the GI Bill. In foreign policy, peace reigned. Eisenhower ended one war and, more significantly, avoided another. Not a bad record.

Eisenhower's eight years in office were prosperous ones for the United States. His administration gave the nation the peace and security it required to grow and expand after the twin traumas of the Depression and World War II. He took office when the nation was bitterly divided by political issues of war and anti-communism. Eisenhower's presidency was not without flaws: He was slow to respond to McCarthyism, he was woefully unprepared for the emergence of the civil rights movement, and he didn't grasp the depth of racism in America. But his overall record was a good, if not a great one.

The Boycott That Changed Dr. King's Life

Forty years later, new revelations.

"KING AND ATTORNEY IN COURTROOM, MONTGOMERY"

Text by Clayborne Carson
Drawings by Harvey Dinnerstein and Burt Silverman

Clayborne Carson is the director of the Martin Luther King Jr. Papers Project. This essay has been adapted from the introduction to the third volume of King's papers (which will also include some of these drawings), to be published in the fall.

By the time the Montgomery Improvement Association chose the 26-year-old Martin Luther King Jr. as its leader, the hours-old bus boycott by the black citizens of Montgomery, Ala., was already an overwhelming success. King would later write that his unanticipated call to leadership "happened so quickly that I did not have time to think it through. It is probable that if I had, I would have declined the nomination."

Although press reports at the time focused on his inspiring oratory, King was actually a reluctant leader of a movement initiated by others. (The boycott began on Dec. 5, 1955.) His subsequent writings and private correspondence reveal a man whose inner doubts sharply contrast with his public persona. In the early days of his involvement, King was troubled by telephone threats, discord within the black community and Montgomery's "get tough" policy, to which King attributed his jailing on a minor traffic violation. One night, as he considered ways to "move out of the picture without appearing a coward," he began to pray aloud and, at that moment, "experienced the presence of the Divine as I had never experienced Him before."

He would later admit that when the boycott began, he was not yet firmly committed to Gandhian principles. Although he had been exposed to those teachings in college, he had remained skeptical. "I thought the only way we could solve our problem of segregation was an armed revolt," he recalled. "I felt that the Christian ethic of love was confined to individual relationships."

Only after his home was bombed in late January did King reconsider his views on violence. (At the time, he was seeking a gun permit and was protected by armed bodyguards.) Competing with each other to influence King were two ardent pacifists: Bayard Rustin, a black activist with the War Resisters League, and the Rev. Glenn E. Smiley, a white staff member of the Fellowship of Reconciliation. Rustin was shocked to discover a gun in King's house, while Smiley informed fellow pacifists that King's home was "an arsenal."

By the time the Supreme Court struck down Montgomery's bus segregation policies, in November 1956, King had been permanently changed. "Living through the actual experience of the protest, nonviolence became more than a method to which I gave intellectual assent," he would later explain. "It became a commitment to a way of life."

After the boycott, King allowed himself to reflect on his growing fame and his own self-doubts. "Frankly, I'm worried to death," he said. "A man who hits the peak at 27 has a tough job ahead. People will be expecting me to pull rabbits out of the hat for the rest of my life."

29. Boycott That Changed Dr. King's Life

"MONTGOMERY BUS BOYCOTT"

Art for Equality's Sake

Harvey Dinnerstein and Burt Silverman, friends and fellow artists since high school in Manhattan, were both struck from afar by the Montgomery bus boycott. Inspired, they set out for Alabama. (The three drawings on the next page are by Dinnerstein, the others by Silverman.) As they later wrote, "We clung to the notion that Realism—an artist's way of looking at the world with critical appraisal—could be an invaluable tool in recording momentous events of our time."

"THE VICTORY SIGN"

5. FROM THE COLD WAR TO THE 1990s

"THE CENTER OF TOWN"

"OLD WOMAN WALKING, MONTGOMERY"

"WALKING TOGETHER, MONTGOMERY"

Trumpet of Conscience
A Portrait of Martin Luther King, Jr.

A noted biographer examines the life and legacy of the civil rights leader who may have been the most-loved and most-hated man in America during the turbulent 1960s.

Stephen B. Oates

Biographer and historian Stephen B. Oates is Paul Murray Kendall Professor of Biography and Professor of History at the University of Massachusetts, Amherst. He is the author of twelve books, including award-winning biographies of John Brown, Nat Turner, Abraham Lincoln, and Martin Luther King, Jr. His newest biography, William Faulkner: The Man and the Artist, *was published by Harper & Row in 1987. "This article on Martin Luther King," writes Oates, "is dedicated to the memory of James Baldwin, who had a powerful influence on me in the 1960s, when I was a young writer trying to understand the complexities of American race relations."*

He was M.L. to his parents, Martin to his wife and friends, Doc to his aides, Reverend to his male parishioners, Little Lord Jesus to adoring churchwomen, De Lawd to his young critics in the Student Nonviolent Coordinating Committee, and Martin Luther King, Jr., to the world. At his pulpit or a public rostrum, he seemed too small for his incomparable oratory and international fame as a civil rights leader and spokesman for world peace. He stood only five feet seven, and had round cheeks, a trim mustache, and sad, glistening eyes—eyes that revealed both his inner strength and his vulnerability.

He was born in Atlanta on January 15, 1929, and grew up in the relative comfort of the black middle class. Thus he never suffered the want and privation that plagued the majority of American blacks of his time. His father, a gruff, self-made man, was pastor of Ebenezer Baptist Church and an outspoken member of Atlanta's black leadership. M.L. joined his father's church when he was five and came to regard it as his second home. The church defined his world, gave it order and balance, taught him how to "get along with people." Here M.L. knew who he was—"Reverend King's boy," somebody special.

At home, his parents and maternal grandmother reinforced his self-esteem, praising him for his precocious ways, telling him repeatedly that he was *somebody*. By age five, he spoke like an adult and had such a prodigious memory that he could recite whole Biblical passages and entire hymns without a mistake. He was acutely sensitive, too, so much so that he worried about all the blacks he saw in Atlanta's breadlines during the Depression, fearful that their children did not have enough to eat. When his maternal grandmother died, twelve-year-old M.L. thought it was his fault. Without telling anyone, he had slipped away from home to watch a parade, only to find out when he returned that she had died. He was terrified that God had taken her away as punishment for his "sin." Guilt-stricken, he tried to kill himself by leaping out of his second-story window.

He had a great deal of anger in him. Growing up a black in segregated Atlanta, he felt the full range of southern racial discrimination. He discovered that he had to attend separate, inferior schools, which he sailed through with a modicum of effort, skipping grades as he went. He found out that he—a preacher's boy— could not sit at lunch counters in Atlanta's downtown stores. He had to drink from a "colored" water fountain, relieve himself in a rancid "colored" restroom, and ride a rickety "colored" elevator. If he rode a city bus, he had to sit in the back as though he were contaminated. If he wanted to see a movie in a downtown theater, he had to enter through a side door and sit in the "colored" section in the balcony. He discovered that whites referred to blacks as "boys" and "girls" regardless of age. He saw "WHITES ONLY" signs staring back at him in the windows of barber shops and all the good restaurants and hotels, at the YMCA, the city parks, golf courses, swimming pools, and in the waiting rooms of the train and bus stations. He learned that there were even white and black sections of the city and that he resided in "nigger town."

Segregation caused a tension in the boy, a tension between his parents' injunction ("Remember, you are *somebody*") and a system that constantly demeaned and insulted him. He struggled with the pain and rage he felt when a white woman in a downtown store slapped him and called him "a little nigger" . . . when a bus driver called him "a black son-of-a-bitch" and made him surrender his seat to a white . . . when he stood on the very spot in Atlanta where whites had lynched a black man . . . when he witnessed nightriding Klansmen beating blacks in the streets. How, he asked defiantly, could he heed the Christian injunction and love a race of people who hated him? In retaliation, he determined "to hate every white person."

Yes, he was angry. In sandlot games, he competed so fiercely that friends could not tell whether he was playing or fighting. He had his share of playground combat, too, and could outwrestle any of his peers. He even rebelled against his father, vowing never to become a preacher like him. Yet he liked the way Daddy King stood up to whites: he told them never to call him a boy and vowed to fight this system until he died.

5. FROM THE COLD WAR TO THE 1990s

Still, there was another side to M.L., a calmer, sensuous side. He played the violin, enjoyed opera, and relished soul food—fried chicken, cornbread, and collard greens with ham hocks and bacon drippings. By his mid-teens, his voice was the most memorable thing about him. It had changed into a rich and resonant baritone that commanded attention whenever he held forth. A natty dresser, nicknamed "Tweed" because of his fondness for tweed suits, he became a connoisseur of lovely young women. His little brother A.D. remembered how Martin "kept flitting from chick to chick" and was "just about the best jitterbug in town."

AT AGE FIFTEEN, HE ENTERED MOREHOUSE College in Atlanta, wanting somehow to help his people. He thought about becoming a lawyer and even practiced giving trial speeches before a mirror in his room. But thanks largely to Morehouse President Benjamin Mays, who showed him that the ministry could be a respectable forum for ideas, even for social protest, King decided to become a Baptist preacher after all. By the time he was ordained in 1947, his resentment toward whites had softened some, thanks to positive contact with white students on an intercollegiate council. But he hated his segregated world more than ever.

Once he had his bachelor's degree, he went north to study at Crozer Seminary near Philadelphia. In this mostly white school, with its polished corridors and quiet solemnity, King continued to ponder the plight of blacks in America. How, by what method and means, were blacks to improve their lot in a white-dominated country? His study of history, especially of Nat Turner's slave insurrection, convinced him that it was suicidal for a minority to strike back against a heavily armed majority. For him, voluntary segregation was equally unacceptable, as was accommodation to the status quo. King shuddered at such negative approaches to the race problem. How indeed were blacks to combat discrimination in a country ruled by the white majority?

As some other blacks had done, he found his answer in the teachings of Mohandas Gandhi—for young King, the discovery had the force of a conversion experience. Nonviolent resistance, Gandhi taught, meant noncooperation with evil, an idea he got from Henry David Thoreau's essay "On Civil Disobedience." In India, Gandhi gave Thoreau's theory practical application in the form of strikes, boycotts, and protest marches, all conducted nonviolently and all predicated on love for the oppressor and a belief in divine justice. In gaining Indian independence, Gandhi sought not to defeat the British, but to redeem them through love, so as to avoid a legacy of bitterness. Gandhi's term for this—Satyagraha—reconciled love and force in a single, powerful concept.

As King discovered from his studies, Gandhi had embraced nonviolence in part to subdue his own violent nature. This was a profound revelation for King, who had felt much hatred in his life, especially toward whites. Now Gandhi showed him a means of harnessing his anger and channeling it into a positive and creative force for social change.

AT THIS JUNCTURE, KING FOUND MOSTLY theoretical satisfaction in Gandhian nonviolence; he had no plans to become a radical activist in the segregated South. Indeed, he seemed destined to a life of the mind, not of social protest. In 1951, he graduated from Crozer and went on to earn a Ph.D. in theology from Boston University, where his adviser pronounced him "a scholar's scholar" of great intellectual potential. By 1955, a year after the school desegregation decision, King had married comely Coretta Scott and assumed the pastorship of Dexter Avenue Baptist Church in Montgomery, Alabama. Immensely happy in the world of ideas, he hoped eventually to teach theology at a major university or seminary.

But, as King liked to say, the Zeitgist, or spirit of the age, had other plans for him. In December 1955, Montgomery blacks launched a boycott of the city's segregated buses and chose the articulate twenty-six-year-old minister as their spokesman.* As it turned out, he was unusually well prepared to assume the kind of leadership thrust on him. Drawing on Gandhi's teachings and example, plus the tenets of his own Christian faith, King directed a nonviolent boycott designed both to end an injustice and redeem his white adversaries through love. When he exhorted blacks to love their enemies, King did not mean to love them

---

*See "The Father His Children Forgot" in the December 1985 issue of American History Illustrated.

as friends or intimates. No, he said, he meant a disinterested love in all humankind, a love that saw the neighbor in everyone it met, a love that sought to restore the beloved community. Such love not only avoided the internal violence of the spirit, but severed the external chain of hatred that only produced more hatred in an endless spiral. If American blacks could break the chain of hatred, King said, true brotherhood could begin. Then posterity would have to say that there had lived a race of people, of black people, who "injected a new meaning into the veins of history and civilization."

During the boycott King imparted his philosophy at twice-weekly mass meetings in the black churches, where overflow crowds clapped and cried as his mellifluous voice swept over them. In these mass meetings King discovered his extraordinary power as an orator. His rich religious imagery reached deep into the black psyche, for religion had been the black people's main source of strength and survival since slavery days. His delivery was "like a narrative poem," said a woman journalist who heard him. His voice had such depths of sincerity and empathy that it could "charm your heart right out of your body." Because he appealed to the best in his people, articulating their deepest hurts and aspirations, black folk began to idolize him; he was their Gandhi.

Under his leadership, they stood up to white Montgomery in a remarkable display of solidarity. Pitted against an obdurate city government that blamed the boycott on Communist agitation and resorted to psychological and legal warfare to break it, the blacks stayed off the buses month after month, and walked or rode in a black-operated carpool. When an elderly woman refused the offer of a ride, King asked her, "But don't your feet hurt?" "Yes," she replied, "my feet is tired but my soul is rested." For King, her irrepressible spirit was proof that "a new Negro" was emerging in the South, a Negro with "a new sense of dignity and destiny."

That "new Negro" menaced white supremacists, especially the Ku Klux Klan, and they persecuted King with a vengeance. They made obscene phone calls to his home, sent him abusive, sickening letters, and once even dynamited the front of his house. Nobody was hurt, but King, fearing a race war, had to dissuade angry blacks from violent retaliation. Finally, on November 13, 1956, the U.S. Supreme Court nullified the Alabama laws that enforced segregated buses, and handed King and his boycotters a resounding moral victory. Their protest had captured the imagination of progressive people all over the world and marked the beginning of a southern black movement that would shake the segregated South to its foundations. At the forefront of that movement was a new organization, the Southern Christian Leadership Conference (SCLC), which King and other black ministers formed in 1957, with King serving as its president and guiding spirit. Operating through the southern black church, SCLC sought to enlist the black masses in the freedom struggle by expanding "the Montgomery way" across the South.

The "Miracle of Montgomery" changed King's life, catapulting him into international prominence as an inspiring new moral voice for civil rights. Across the country, blacks and whites alike wrote him letters of encouragement; *Time* magazine pictured him on its cover; the National Association for the Advancement of Colored People (NAACP) and scores of church and civic organizations vied for his services as a speaker. "I am really disturbed how fast all this has happened to me," King told his wife. "People will expect me to perform miracles for the rest of my life."

But fame had its evil side, too. When King visited New York in 1958, a deranged black woman stabbed him in the chest with a letter opener. The weapon was lodged so close to King's aorta, the main artery from the heart, that he would have died had he sneezed. To extract the blade, an interracial surgical team had to remove a rib and part of his breastbone; in a burst of inspiration, the lead surgeon made the incision over King's heart in the shape of a cross.

THAT HE HAD NOT DIED CONVINCED KING that God was preparing him for some larger work in the segregated South. To gain perspective on what was happening there, he made a pilgrimage to India to visit Gandhi's shrine and the sites of his "War for Independence." He returned home with an even deeper commitment to nonviolence and a vow to be more humble and ascetic like Gandhi. Yet he was a man of manifold contradictions, this American Gandhi. While renouncing material things and giving nearly all of his extensive honorariums to SCLC, he liked posh hotels and zesty meals with wine, and he was always immaculately dressed in a gray or black suit, white shirt, and tie. While caring passionately for the poor, the downtrodden, and the disinherited, he had a fascination with men of affluence and enjoyed the company of wealthy SCLC benefactors. While trumpeting the glories of nonviolence and redemptive love, he could feel the most terrible anger when whites murdered a black or bombed a black church; he could contemplate giving up, turning America over to the haters of both races, only to dedicate himself anew to his nonviolent faith and his determination to redeem his country.

In 1960, he moved his family to Atlanta so that he could devote himself fulltime to SCLC, which was trying to register black voters for the upcoming federal elections. That same year, southern black students launched the sit-in movement against segregated lunch counters, and King not only helped them form the Student Nonviolent Coordinating Committee (SNCC) but raised money on their behalf. In October he even joined a sit-in protest at an Atlanta department store and went to jail with several students on a trespassing charge. Like Thoreau, King considered jail "a badge of honor." To redeem the nation and arouse the conscience of the opponent, King explained, you go to jail and stay there. "You have broken a law which is out of line with the moral law and you are willing to suffer the consequences by serving the time."

He did not reckon, however, on the tyranny of racist officials, who clamped him in a malevolent state penitentiary, in a cell for hardened criminals. But state authorities released him when Democratic presidential nominee John F. Kennedy and his brother Robert interceded on King's behalf. According to many analysts, the episode won critical black votes for Kennedy and gave him the election in November. For King, the election demonstrated what he had long said: that one of the most significant steps a black could take was the short walk to the voting booth.

The trouble was that most blacks in Dixie, especially in the Deep South, could not vote even if they so desired. For decades, state and local authorities had kept the mass of black folk off the voting rolls by a welter of devious obstacles and outright intimidation. Through 1961 and 1962, King exhorted President Kennedy to sponsor tough new civil rights legislation that would enfranchise southern blacks and end segregated public accommodations as well. When Kennedy shied away from a strong civil rights commitment, King and his lieutenants took matters into their own hands, orchestrating a series of southern demonstrations to show the world the brutality of segregation. At the same time, King stumped the country, drawing on all his powers of oratory to enlist the black masses and win white opinion to his cause.

Everywhere he went his message was the same. The *civil rights issue,* he said, *is an eternal moral issue that will determine the destiny of our nation and our world. As we seek our full rights, we hope to redeem the soul of our country. For it is our country, too, and we will win our freedom because the sacred heritage of America and the eternal will of God are embodied in our echoing demands. We do not intend to humiliate the white man, but to win him over through the strength of our love. Ultimately, we are trying to free all of us in America— Negroes from the bonds of segregation and shame, whites from the bonds of bigotry and fear.*

We stand today between two worlds— the dying old order and the emerging new. With men of ill-will greeting this change with cries of violence, of interposition and nullification, some of us may get beaten. Some of us may even get killed. But if you are cut down in a movement designed to save the soul of a nation, no other death could be more redemptive. We must realize that change does not roll in "on the wheels of inevitability," but comes through struggle. So "let us be those creative dissenters who will call our beloved nation to a higher destiny, to a new plateau of compassion, to a more noble expression of humaneness."

That message worked like magic among America's long-suffering blacks. Across the South, across America, they rose in unprecedented numbers to march and demonstrate with Martin Luther King. His singular achievement was that he brought the black masses into the freedom struggle for the first time. He rallied the strength of broken men and women, helping them overcome a lifetime of fear and feelings of inferiority. After segregation had taught them all their lives that they were *nobody,* King taught them that they were *somebody.* Because he made them believe in themselves and in the beauty of chosen suffering, he taught them how to straighten their backs (''a man can't ride you unless your back is bent'') and confront those who oppressed them. Through the technique of nonviolent resistance, he furnished them something no previous black leader had been able to provide. He showed them a way of controlling their pent-up anger, as he had controlled his own, and using it to bring about constructive change.

THE MASS DEMONSTRATIONS KING AND SCLC choreographed in the South produced the strongest civil rights legislation in American history. This was the goal of King's major southern campaigns from 1963 to 1965. He would single out some notoriously segregated city with white officials prone to violence, mobilize the local blacks with songs, scripture readings, and rousing oratory in black churches, and then lead them on protest marches conspicuous for their grace and moral purpose. Then he and his aides would escalate the marches, increase their demands, even fill up the jails, until they brought about a moment of ''creative tension,'' when whites would either agree to negotiate or resort to violence. If they did the latter, King would thus expose the brutality inherent in segregation and so stab the national conscience so that the federal government would be forced to intervene with corrective measures.

The technique succeeded brilliantly in Birmingham, Alabama, in 1963. Here Police Commissioner Eugene ''Bull'' Connor, in full view of reporters and television cameras, turned firehoses and police dogs on the marching protestors. Revolted by such ghastly scenes, stricken by King's own searching eloquence and the bravery of his unarmed followers, Washington eventually produced the 1964 Civil Rights Act, which desegregated public facilities—the thing King had demanded all along from Birmingham. Across the South, the ''WHITES ONLY'' signs that had hurt and enraged him since boyhood now came down.

Although SNCC and others complained that King had a Messiah complex and was trying to monopolize the civil rights movement, his technique worked with equal success in Selma, Alabama, in 1965. Building on a local movement there, King and his staff launched a drive to gain southern blacks the unobstructed right to vote. The violence he exposed in Selma—the beating of black marchers by state troopers and deputized possemen, the killing of a young black deacon and a white Unitarian minister—horrified the country. When King called for support, thousands of ministers, rabbis, priests, nuns, students, lay leaders, and ordinary people—black and white alike—rushed to Selma from all over the country and stood with King in the name of human liberty. Never in the history of the movement had so many people of all faiths and classes come to the southern battleground. The Selma campaign culminated in a dramatic march over the Jefferson Davis Highway to the state capital of Montgomery. Along the way, impoverished local blacks stared incredulously at the marching, singing, flag-waving spectacle moving by. When the column reached one dusty crossroads, an elderly black woman ran out from a group of old folk, kissed King breathlessly, and ran back crying, ''I done kissed him! The Martin Luther King! I done kissed the Martin Luther King!''

In Montgomery, first capital and much-heralded ''cradle'' of the Confederacy, King led an interracial throng of 25,000—the largest civil rights demonstration the South had ever witnessed—up Dexter Avenue with banners waving overhead. The pageant was as ironic as it was extraordinary, for it was up Dexter Avenue that Jefferson Davis's first inaugural parade had marched, and in the portico of the capitol Davis had taken his oath of office as president of the slave-based Confederacy. Now, in the spring of 1965, Alabama blacks—most of them descendants of slaves—stood massed at the same statehouse, singing a new rendition of ''We Shall Overcome,'' the anthem of the civil rights movement. They sang, ''Deep in my heart, I do believe, We have overcome—*today.*''

Then, within view of the statue of Jefferson Davis, and watched by cordons of state troopers and television cameras, King mounted a trailer. His vast audience listened, transfixed, as his words rolled and thundered over the loudspeaker: ''My people, my people listen. The battle is in our hands. . . . We must come to see that the end we seek is a society at peace with itself, a society that can live with its conscience. That day will be a day not of the white man, not of the black man. That will be the day of man as man.'' And that day was not long in coming, King said, whereupon he launched into the immortal refrains of ''The Battle Hymn of the Republic,'' crying out, ''Our God is marching on! Glory, glory hallelujah!''

Aroused by the events in Alabama, Washington produced the 1965 Voting Rights Act, which outlawed impediments to black voting and empowered the attorney general to supervise federal elections in seven southern states where blacks were kept off the rolls. At the time, political analysts almost unanimously attributed the act to King's Selma campaign. Once federal examiners were supervising voter registration in all troublesome southern areas, blacks were able to get on the rolls and vote by the hundreds of thousands, permanently altering the pattern of southern and national politics.

In the end, the powerful civil rights legislation generated by King and his tramping legions wiped out statutory racism in America and realized at least the social and political promise of emancipation a century before. But King was under no illusion that legislation alone could bring on the brave new America he so ardently championed. Yes, he said, laws and their vigorous enforcement were necessary to regulate destructive habits and actions, and to protect blacks and their rights. But laws could not eliminate the ''fears, prejudice, pride, and irrationality'' that were barriers to a truly integrated society, to peaceful intergroup and interpersonal living. Such a society could be achieved only when people accepted that inner, invisible law that etched on their hearts the conviction ''that all men are brothers and that love is mankind's most potent weapon for personal and social transformation. True integration will be achieved by true neighbors who are willingly obedient to unenforceable obligations.''

Even so, the Selma campaign was the movement's finest hour, and the Voting Rights Act the high point of a broad civil rights coalition that included the federal government, various white groups, and all the other civil rights organizations in addition to SCLC. King himself had best expressed the spirit and aspirations of that coalition when, on August 28, 1963, standing before the Lincoln Memorial, he electrified an interracial crowd of 250,000 with perhaps his greatest speech, ''I Have A Dream,'' in which he described in rhythmic, hypnotic cadences his vision of an integrated America. Because of his achievements and moral vision, he won the 1964 Nobel Peace Prize, at thirty-four the youngest recipient in Nobel history.

STILL, KING PAID A HIGH PRICE FOR HIS fame and his cause. He suffered from stomachaches and insomnia, and even felt guilty about all the tributes he received, all the popularity he enjoyed. Born in relative material comfort and given a superior education, he did not think he had earned the right to lead the impoverished black masses. He complained, too, that he no longer had a personal self and that sometimes he did not recognize the Martin Luther King people talked about. Lonely, away from home for protracted periods, beset with temptation, he slept with other women, for some of whom he had real feeling. His sexual transgressions only added to his guilt, for he knew he was imperiling his cause and hurting himself and those he loved.

Alas for King, FBI Director J. Edgar Hoover found out about the black leader's infidelities. The director already abhorred King, certain that Communist spies influenced him and masterminded his demonstrations. Hoover did not think blacks capable of organizing such things, so Communists had to be behind them and King as well. As it turned out, a lawyer in King's inner circle and a man in SCLC's New York office did have Communist backgrounds, a fact that only reinforced Hoover's suspicions about King. Under Hoover's orders, FBI agents conducted a ruthless crusade to destroy King's reputation and drive him broken and humiliated from public life. Hoover's men tapped King's phones and bugged his hotel rooms; they compiled a prurient monograph about his private life and showed it to various editors, public officials, and religious and civic leaders; they spread the word, Hoover's word, that King was not only a reprobate but a dangerous subversive with Communist associations.

King was scandalized and frightened by the FBI's revelations of his extramarital affairs. Luckily for him, no editor, not even a racist one in the South, would touch the FBI's salacious materials. Public officials such as Robert Kennedy were shocked, but argued that King's personal life did not affect his probity as a civil rights leader. Many blacks, too, declared that what he did in private was his own business. Even so, King vowed to refrain from further affairs—only to succumb again to his own human frailties.

As for the Communist charge, King retorted that he did not need any Russians to tell him when someone was standing on his neck; he could figure that out by himself. To mollify his political friends, however, King did banish from SCLC the two men with Communist backgrounds (later he resumed his ties with the lawyer, a loyal friend, and let Hoover be damned). He also denounced Communism in no uncertain terms. It was, he believed, profoundly and fundamentally evil, an atheistic doctrine no true Christian could ever embrace. He hated the dictatorial Soviet state, too, whose "crippling totalitarianism" subordinated everything—religion, art, music, science, and the individual—to its terrible yoke. True, Communism started with men like Karl Marx who were "aflame with a passion for social justice." Yet King faulted Marx for rejecting God and the spiritual in human life. "The great weakness in Karl Marx is right here," King once told his staff, and he went on to describe his ideal Christian commonwealth in Hegelian terms: "Capitalism fails to realize that life is social. Marxism fails to realize that life is individual. Truth is found neither in the rugged individualism of capitalism nor in the impersonal collectivism of Communism. The kingdom of God is found in a synthesis that combines the truths of these two opposites. Now there is where I leave brother Marx and move on toward the kingdom."

BUT HOW TO MOVE ON AFTER SELMA WAS a perplexing question King never successfully answered. After the devastating Watts riot in August 1965, he took his movement into the racially troubled urban North, seeking to help the suffering black poor in the ghettos. In 1966, over the fierce opposition of some of his own staff, he launched a campaign to end the black slums in Chicago and forestall rioting there. But the campaign foundered because King seemed unable to devise a coherent anti-slum strategy, because Mayor Richard Daley and his black acolytes opposed him bitterly, and because white America did not seem to care. King did lead open-housing marches into segregated neighborhoods in Chicago, only to encounter furious mobs who waved Nazi banners, threw bottles and bricks, and screamed, "We hate niggers!" "Kill the niggers!" "We want Martin Luther Coon!" King was shocked. "I've been in many demonstrations all across the South," he told reporters, "but I can say that I have never seen—even in Mississippi and Alabama—mobs as hostile and as hate-filled as I've seen in Chicago." Although King prevented a major riot there and wrung important concessions from City Hall, the slums remained, as wretched and seemingly unsolvable as ever.

That same year, angry young militants in SNCC and the Congress of Racial Equality (CORE) renounced King's teachings—they were sick and tired of "De Lawd" telling them to love white people and work for integration. Now they advocated "Black Power," black separatism, even violent resistance to liberate blacks in America. SNCC even banished whites from its ranks and went on to drop "nonviolent" from its name and to lobby against civil rights legislation.

Black Power repelled the older, more conservative black organizations such as the NAACP and the Urban League, and fragmented the civil rights movement beyond repair. King, too, argued that black separatism was chimerical, even suicidal, and that nonviolence remained the only workable way for black people. "Darkness cannot drive out darkness," he reasoned: "only light can do that. Hate cannot drive out hate: only love can do that." If every other black in America turned to violence, King warned, then he would still remain the lone voice preaching that it was wrong. Nor was SCLC going to reject whites as SNCC had done. "There have been too many hymns of hope," King said, "too many anthems of expectation, too many deaths, too many dark days of standing over graves of those who fought for integration for us to turn back now. We must still sing 'Black and White Together, We Shall Overcome.'"

In 1967, King himself broke with the older black organizations over the ever-widening war in Vietnam. He had first objected to American escalation in the summer of 1965, arguing that the Nobel Peace Prize and his role as a Christian minister compelled him to speak out for peace. Two years later, with almost a half-million Americans—a disproportionate number of them poor blacks—fighting in Vietnam, King devoted whole speeches to America's "immoral" war against a tiny country on the other side of

5. FROM THE COLD WAR TO THE 1990s

the globe. His stance provoked a fusillade of criticism from all directions—from the NAACP, the Urban League, white and black political leaders, *Newsweek, Life, Time,* and the *New York Times,* all telling him to stick to civil rights. Such criticism hurt him deeply. When he read the *Times*'s editorial against him, he broke down and cried. But he did not back down. "I've fought too long and too hard now against segregated accommodations to end up segregating my moral concerns," he told his critics. "Injustice anywhere is a threat to justice everywhere."

That summer, with the ghettos ablaze with riots, King warned that American cities would explode if funds used for war purposes were not diverted to emergency antipoverty programs. By then, the Johnson administration, determined to gain a military victory in Vietnam, had written King off as an antiwar agitator, and was now cooperating with the FBI in its efforts to defame him.

The fall of 1967 was a terrible time for King, the lowest ebb in his civil rights career. Everybody seemed to be attacking him—young black militants for his stubborn adherence to nonviolence, moderate and conservative blacks, labor leaders, liberal white politicians, the White House, and the FBI for his stand on Vietnam. Two years had passed since King had produced a nonviolent victory, and contributions to SCLC had fallen off sharply. Black spokesman Adam Clayton Powell, who had once called King the greatest Negro in America, now derided him as Martin Loser King. The incessant attacks began to irritate him, creating such anxiety and depression that his friends worried about his emotional health.

Worse still, the country seemed dangerously polarized. On one side, backlashing whites argued that the ghetto explosions had "cremated" nonviolence and that white people had better arm themselves against black rioters. On the other side, angry blacks urged their people to "kill the Honkies" and burn the cities down. All around King, the country was coming apart in a cacophony of hate and reaction. Had America lost the will and moral power to save itself? he wondered. There was such rage in the ghetto and such bigotry among whites that he feared a race war was about to break out. He felt he had to do something to pull America back from the brink. He and his staff had to mount a new campaign that would halt the drift to violence in the black world and combat stiffening white resistance, a nonviolent action that would "transmute the deep rage of the ghetto into a constructive and creative force."

OUT OF HIS DELIBERATIONS SPRANG A BOLD and daring project called the poor people's campaign. The master plan, worked out by February 1968, called for SCLC to bring an interracial army of poor people to Washington, D.C., to dramatize poverty before the federal government. For King, just turned thirty-nine, the time had come to employ civil disobedience against the national government itself. Ultimately, he was projecting a genuine class movement that he hoped would bring about meaningful changes in American society—changes that would redistribute economic and political power and end poverty, racism, "the madness of militarism," and war.

In the midst of his preparations, King went to Memphis, Tennessee, to help black sanitation workers there who were striking for the right to unionize. On the night of April 3, with a storm thundering outside, he told a black audience that he had been to the mountaintop and had seen what lay ahead. "I may not get there with you. But I want you to know tonight that we as a people *will* get to the promised land."

The next afternoon, when King stepped out on the balcony of the Lorraine Motel, an escaped white convict named James Earl Ray, stationed in a nearby building, took aim with a high-powered rifle and blasted King into eternity. Subsequent evidence linked Ray to white men in the St. Louis area who had offered "hit" money for King's life.

For weeks after the shooting, King's stricken country convulsed in grief, contrition, and rage. While there were those who cheered his death, the *New York Times* called it a disaster to the nation, the *London Times* an enormous loss to the world. In Tanzania, Reverend Trevor Huddleston, expelled from South Africa for standing against apartheid, declared King's death the greatest single tragedy since the assassination of Gandhi in 1948, and said it challenged the complacency of the Christian Church all over the globe.

On April 9, with 120 million Americans watching on television, thousands of mourners—black and white alike—gathered in Atlanta for the funeral of a man who had never given up his dream of creating a symphony of brotherhood on these shores. As a black man born and raised in segregation, he had had every reason to hate America and to grow up preaching cynicism and retaliation. Instead, he had loved the country passionately and had sung of her promise and glory more eloquently than anyone of his generation.

They buried him in Atlanta's South View Cemetery, then blooming with dogwood and fresh green boughs of spring. On his crypt, hewn into the marble, were the words of an old Negro spiritual he had often quoted: "Free at Last, Free at Last, Thank God Almighty I'm Free at Last."

Recommended additional reading: Let the Trumpet Sound: The Life of Martin Luther King, Jr. *by Stephen B. Oates (Harper & Row, 1982), and* A Testament of Hope: The Essential Writings of Martin Luther King, Jr. *edited by James M. Washington (Harper & Row, 1986).*

Reagan's Rise

Gerard De Groot argues that exploitation of silent majority fears about 60s student protest is the key to understanding Ronald Reagan's rise to prominence in Californian politics.

Gerard J. De Groot

Gerard J. DeGroot is Lecturer in Modern History at the University of St. Andrews and author of Liberal Crusader: The Life of Sir Archibald Sinclair, *(Hurst and Co., 1993).*

The 1966 California gubernatorial race was supposed to be about big government, welfare and high taxation. But, after a few weeks of campaigning, the Republican candidate Ronald Reagan told his handlers:

> Look, I don't care if I'm in the mountains, the desert, the biggest cities of the state, the first question is: 'What are you going to do about Berkeley?'—and each time the question itself... get(s) applause.

By 'Berkeley' Reagan meant student unrest. The 'campus war' allowed Reagan to highlight the populist themes of his campaign: morality, law and order, strong leadership and traditional values. By skillfully manipulating this issue, Reagan won comfortably in 1966 and was re-elected in 1970. The campus confrontation brought enormous benefits: it embarrassed California liberals, it deflected attention from less successful areas of administration and it allowed the governor to gain nationwide recognition as the common man's hero.

As will be shown, other politicians (including S. I. Hayakawa and Spiro Agnew) benefited from tough stands on campus unrest. But no one benefited more than Reagan. His actions provide a blueprint for the perfect populist campaign. The supporters he attracted to his side as a result of this issue, namely working-class, high school educated Democrats, never deserted him.

Serious unrest first erupted at Berkeley with the Free Speech Movement demonstrations in late 1964. Images on the nightly news of unruly students holding police at bay angered and frightened ordinary California citizens. The instinctive liberalism of Governor Edmund G. Brown, a Democrat, prevented him from responding as aggressively as the outraged electorate demanded. This provided a golden opportunity for Reagan, the self-proclaimed 'citizen politician'. As he later related:

> I learned that the people of this state had a very, very deep and great pride in the university system. Because of that, they were emotionally involved and disturbed with what was happening to what they thought was the great pride of California.

Reagan's public expressions of disgust at the supposedly scandalous behaviour of students were cleverly calculated to keep public indignation on the boil. A notorious dance on the Berkeley campus in March 1966 conveniently occurred shortly after he declared his candidacy. Police reports of the dance somehow made it to Reagan's campaign headquarters, most likely via the Mameda County District Attorney, one Edwin Meese. Reagan claimed that the dance had turned into an orgy of sex and drugs and, as such, was evidence of the 'leadership gap' at Berkeley:

> The hall was entirely dark except for the light from the two movie screens. On these screens the nude torsos of men and women were portrayed, from time to time, in suggestive positions and movements. Three rock-and-roll bands played simultaneously. The smell of marijuana was thick throughout the hall. There were signs that some of those present had taken dope. There were indications of other happenings which cannot be mentioned.

Against this backdrop, Reagan seemed a stolid defender of civilised values. The difference between his campaign and Barry Goldwater's run for the presidency in 1964 could not have been more striking. Ideologically the two candidates were similar, yet in terms of style they were miles apart, as was revealed by a short film on the Berkeley problem which Goldwater aides offered to Reagan. 'I must tell you it was a hairy, hairy film', recalled Stuart Spencer, Reagan's public relations supremo. 'We killed it.... Reagan was on the right side of that issue. We didn't have to go out and do wild things about it'.

Reagan argued that a 'small minority of beatniks, radicals and filthy speech advocates have brought shame to... a great University. This has been allowed to go on in the name of academic freedom'. In fact, the Berkeley problem had little to do with academic freedom, which protected teachers, not students. But Reagan realised that there was little to gain from lambasting militant youngsters. If, however, those students could be shown to be supported (or, better, 'indoctrinated') by radical (or, better, 'Communist') professors, the problem would then be magnified and his call for tough action would seem more appropriate. And if the radical professors were defended—in the name of academic freedom—by liberal colleagues, then the list of enemies would grow conveniently longer. The UC administration could in

5. FROM THE COLD WAR TO THE 1990s

turn be blamed for failing to 'enforce a code based on decency, common sense and dedication to the high and noble purpose of the University' and Governor Brown for his 'policy of appeasement'. There was little the Brown camp could do to respond to this onslaught. Frederick Dutton, a Brown supporter, felt helpless:

> There was an especially hysterical element in the psychology of southern California in the fall of '66. If you look at Reagan's TV spots or a recording of 'the speech' he'd often give, it was his Berkeley reference which always got the explicit, noisy reaction. For Reagan to mention Berkeley was always a great crowd-gatherer. That was where the cutting edge of emotions were.

'The University thing drove us nuts', recalled Richard Kline, a Brown aide. 'It was a mystifying time and we were totally unprepared... I don't think we understood'.

Reagan promised to implement a 'code of conduct that would force (faculty) to serve as examples of good behaviour and decency'. Chancellors would be told to restore authority or face dismissal. Though a governor had no such power, these spurious threats served a dual purpose: they embarrassed Brown and enhanced Reagan's reputation as a man of action. The voters cared little about the nuances of higher education policy: what they wanted was a governor who would address their anxieties. They feared an ever more expensive education system and universities where children learned Marxism, revolution and sexual licentiousness. Yet these fears were in large part Reagan's creation.

At this stage activists constituted a miniscule proportion of students and faculty. In the midst of the unrest, Berkeley was judged the 'best balanced and distinguished university in the country' by the American Council of Education. But this news made less appealing copy than lurid tales of sex, drugs and Communism preferred by the predominantly pro-Reagan press.

Three weeks before the election, a Reagan aide admitted confidentially that 'If the disorders boil into public prominence again... on balance it would be good for our campaign'. Reagan responded by urging the Berkeley Student Non-Violent Coordinating Committee (SNCC), to cancel a meeting at which the black activist Stokely Carmichael was due to speak, arguing that Carmichael's appearance on the Berkeley campus so soon before the election will stir strong emotions'. The message to SNCC, released to all the major California papers, was a red rag waved intentionally at a hot-tempered bull. No self-respecting radical group would bow to this type of pressure, yet by going ahead with the rally SNCC cast a brighter light on Reagan's campaign.

Reagan won the election by over a million votes. As governor, he reacted to campus unrest exactly as he had during his campaign—in other words, with more bombast than understanding. Reagan, like his supporters, did not really understand student anger. But he did understand the gulf which had developed between the university community and ordinary citizens. The public found universities bewildering; the university treated the public with contempt. By his actions, Reagan widened this gulf, and the wider it became, the more he benefited. Supposedly 'off the cuff' remarks carefully echoed the people's chauvinism. On one occasion he told how a group of protesters:

> ...were carrying signs that said 'Make Love Not War'. The only trouble was they didn't look like they were capable of doing either. His hair was cut like Tarzan, and he acted like Jane, and he smelled like Cheetah.

Reagan's sensational statements fed public paranoia. He alleged, without foundation, that a group of demonstrators were all 'either on parole or have records of previous arrests'—thus suggesting that the predominantly middle-class student radicals were, in fact, hardened criminals. In February 1969, he claimed that thirty-five 'negroes' had attacked a university dean 'with switchblades at his throat' forcing him to admit them to classes. A subsequent investigation could not substantiate the story, yet Reagan's original yarn received considerably more coverage than did reports of its fabrication.

Perhaps the most outrageous misrepresentation came in June 1968 when, on a national television talk show, Reagan suggested that the Robert Kennedy assassination and the unrest on campuses were linked. 'A sick campus community in California in many ways is responsible for a sick community around those campuses', he argued. None of this should be surprising from a man who had a utilitarian attitude toward truth. As biographer Gary Wills has argued, the pretence was effective because most of the time Reagan did not realise he was pretending.

The governor often used military metaphors evocative to an older generation: campus radicals were compared to Hitler's Brownshirts with whom there was 'no longer any room for appeasement'. At other times, a more recent struggle was invoked: the campus became a battlefront in the Cold War; in Berkeley, as in South East Asia, the dominoes would not fall. According to Reagan, campus militants, like the Viet Cong, were highly organised, followed an alien ideology, employed guerrilla tactics, and were funded by Moscow and Peking. 'This is guerrilla warfare', Reagan maintained.

Even more striking was Reagan's actual use of military power. During the People's Park demonstrations of May 1969 massive force was mobilised. One demonstrator was killed, another blinded and on one occasion National Guard helicopters sprayed CS gas indiscriminately on the Berkeley campus. The outcry in some quarters was tremendous, and a subsequent inquiry judged the use of force excessive. But Reagan remained unrepentant, arguing that 'there was no alternative... once the dogs of war are unleashed, you must expect that things will happen and that people, being human, will make mistakes on both sides'.

Reagan's sometimes bizarre behaviour suggests a dangerous ignorance of higher education. He condemned universities for 'subsidizing intellectual curiosity' and was fond of pointing out that the University of Michigan awarded masters degrees in band instrument repair. This issue had nothing to do with the University of California, but frequent reference to it suggested that *all* universities were similarly absurd. When asked about providing ethnic history courses—a hot topic during a period of civil rights unrest—he surmised that the problem was one of bulk:

> History has grown, fifty more years history than fifty years ago. So the books either have to get thicker or they have to skim down some of the things that some of us learned earlier.

(He suggested that perhaps the problem could be solved by greater reliance upon film in teaching.)

Simplistic statements like these encouraged academics to underestimate Reagan, much to his advantage. But for the large number of Californians who found universities perplexing and esoteric, his anti-intellectualism was an attractive political creed The *San Diego Union,* a loud voice of low-brow conservatism, was reassured by the simple logic: 'his success has been due to his willingness to speak his mind, to speak common sense. Common sense may be 'simplistic', as the liberals like to call it. But the people understand it. And they can't act unless they understand the issues'.

'My idea of higher education', Reagan remarked, 'is four years on a campus with red brick walls and you leave with a tear in your eye'. His own experience as a student at Eureka College, a private religious college with just 187 students, was inadequate preparation for his stewardship over a massive, complex, sometimes impersonal institution devoted to excellence in research and graduate studies. Reagan expected University of California professors to be like those he remembered at Eureka: teachers concerned 'not only with the intellectual, but also the moral development of the students'. Those at Berkeley and other UC campuses were, he felt, failing as moral mentors because they neglected teaching in favour of research. In this moral vacuum, the universities had been turned into 'staging areas for insurrection', where left-wing professors peddled biased opinions.

Reagan repeatedly threatened to dismiss professors who participated in illegal demonstrations and toyed with the idea of introducing a political test. Yet he acted upon none of these threats. He was undoubtedly aware that he could not possibly win an academic freedom case in the courts and defeat would be too embarrassing. In any case, he needed the university to remain intact, if embattled. Despite all of his criticisms of esoteric research, he realised that the UC system was the foundation upon which California's high-tech industry was built. The state received 25 per cent of US defence department contracts. In any case, with Reagan, threats were more effective than action, because he usually achieved what he wanted with mere bluster.

Opinion polls revealed just how solidly the public backed Reagan on the campus unrest issue. In June 1969, a poll in the *Oakland Tribune* showed 84 per cent supported Reagan's desire to end the once sacred principle of free higher education. Respondents echoed the governor's simple logic that fees would 'weed out the non-serious student and promote respect for school property'. During his first term, Reagan's approval rating was always comfortably over 50 per cent, but his popularity was lowest in spring 1968, when the campuses were most quiet. It surged in 1969, after prolonged confrontations with militants at San Francisco State and Berkeley.

When the pollsters asked 'What things that the governor has done since he has been in office do you approve of?', his handling of student unrest was usually top of the achievements listed and always so during periods of crisis on campus. For instance, in February 1969, 50 per cent listed Reagan's handling of student unrest, followed by his budgetary measures at just 17 per cent and his taxation policy at 6 per cent. The People's Park crisis demonstrated that even the most aggressive action inspired enthusiastic public approval.

These polls reflected a nationwide tendency to support tough action against militancy. The escalation of violent protest at the end of the decade caused a distinct swing away from liberal values by the public. Support for the student's right to protest (even peacefully) steadily declined, to less than 40 per cent in 1969. A Gallup Poll in March 1969 found 82 per cent in favour of expelling militant students and 84 per cent in favour of withdrawing their federal student loans. What is ironic is that this trend occurred at the same time as a steady and rapid decline in public support for the Vietnam War. Sympathy for the students' main cause was not translated into sympathy for students.

The problem of campus unrest was a much-needed tonic for right-wing Republicans humiliated by the defeat of Goldwater in 1964. Reagan was Goldwater neatly re-packaged—a right-wing radical with a kind face. As one moderate Californian Republican complained:

> For the first time, the Republicans don't see the rainbow ending in the middle of the spectrum. In the past, Republican conservatives, to survive, had to move toward the middle. But the law and order issue and the Reagan phenomenon have created a view that it is dangerous to occupy the middle.

By defying campus dissidents with bravado and muscle, Reagan made himself into something akin to a war hero of the previous generation. He was ideally poised to exploit the voter's fondness for battling crusaders: as an actor he knew how to strike just the right authoritative pose and to deliver the appropriate stern warning. His voice and facial gestures suggested courage and determination. Those most impressed were blue-collar workers without a university education—by nature Democrats—who resented the shenanigans of privileged elites on campus. A poll taken in 1969 found that 'young people under thirty, people who have been to college and blacks tend to be much more sympathetic to student demonstrators than older, high school educated whites'. By assuming a firm line on student unrest, Reagan collected a windfall of support from 'Middle America'. Once he attracted this group to his side, they never left him.

Reagan was not the only one to benefit from this windfall. S. I. Hayakawa rocketed to prominence on the strength of one momentous act: in 1968 he pulled an electrical plug which deprived a rowdy group of demonstrators at San Francisco State College of their public address system. He shortly afterwards became president of the college, and later US Senator. Likewise, Spiro Agnew's brief popularity was due in large part to his ability to voice the common people's anger. Across the United States, conservative politicians (like Governor James Rhodes of Ohio) capitalised on this anger, especially in states or localities where student unrest was most pronounced. Nor is this attempt to create an internal enemy a phenomenon confined to the 1960s. The current Republican governor of California, Pete Wilson, a moderate compared to Reagan, launched a highly visible crusade against illegal Mexican immigrants when his popularity began to flag around 1992. Wilson's deployment of massive forces on the border echoed Reagan's mobilisation of National Guardsmen in Berkeley. The tactic appears to have paid off; in the November 1994 elections Wilson won what was

5. FROM THE COLD WAR TO THE 1990s

supposed to have been a close race against Kathleen Brown by over a million votes. At the same time, Californians passed Proposition 187, a bill denying state welfare benefits to illegal aliens. But one has to accept that Wilson benefited mostly from events beyond his control, namely the massive nationwide rejection of the Democrats.

But as George Bush's 'family values' crusade in 1992 demonstrates, an appeal to the electorate's base instincts does not always work. So why did it work for Reagan, arguably the most successful populist in American political history? His success arose from a number of factors, some his own creation, others fortuitous. It was, for instance, extraordinarily good fortune that student unrest was nowhere worse than in California. This brought Reagan an enormous amount of nationwide publicity; juxtaposed with long-haired, shabbily dressed, obscenity-shouting students, he could not help but shine. This publicity meant that California became an example to the rest of the nation both of the dangers of Brown-style permissive liberalism and the appropriateness of Reagan-style aggressiveness.

It was also fortunate that the student unrest issue grafted nicely onto Reagan's package of conservative policies. Brown's liberal regime of high spending, high taxation and ever expanding social welfare programmes had, according to Reagan, produced a state of social chaos in which campus unrest was only one of many crises. What, in other words, had liberalism wrought? Reagan's attack upon the political and social status quo in 1966 was successful precisely because he was an outsider, theoretically innocent of responsibility for the state of crisis. The great fallacy of Bush's family values campaign in 1992 was that he could not explain why a long period of Republican dominance had not arrested the moral decay which he promised to combat.

But beyond his good fortune, one must also credit Reagan's indubitable skill as a politician. Many commentators at the time, and historians since, have had difficulty giving Reagan credit where credit is due. He has been derided as a ventriloquist's dummy, expertly handled by public relations wizards. Yet in his early campaigns he was a skilled political professional who still had the vitality and innocence of an amateur. At weekly press conferences he took on hardened reporters, many of whom were openly hostile toward him. He invariably disarmed them through a perfect combination of facts, fables and anecdotes.

'He always kept his cool in all kinds of situations in which they tried to trap him', recalled Stanley Plog, Reagan's public relations guru during the 1966 campaign. 'The voting public began to say, "Hey, this guy's pretty cool, isn't he, man?"' His ability to digest data and recall it at will was prodigious—a perhaps ironic attribute given that during his presidency it was his lapses of memory which were most striking. But perhaps most important to his success was his personality: he appeared tough at the same time that he seemed warm, engaging, friendly and humorous. The great problem with populism is that it so often attracts boorish demagogues like Spiro Agnew or Joe McCarthy. Reagan displayed none of the repugnant characteristics which eventually ruined those men.

The great irony of Reagan's governorship was that the issue which brought him the most favourable publicity was also the area in which he was least successful. He never brought the campuses under control; militancy instead simply faded away with splits among activists and peace in Vietnam. Reagan did more to radicalise students than to tame them, and he also emasculated administrators who could have acted as a moderating influence in the crisis. But this failure did not matter, since he had found an acceptable substitute for success. Given the nature of public feeling, the student unrest issue was one on which he could not lose. If he won a skirmish with students, Californians cheered. But if he failed to control the unrest, his failure merely underscored how serious the threat of militancy was and how urgent the need for tough action.

A September 1969 poll found a majority of Californians agreeing that campus disorders were worse than when Reagan took office. But when asked about Reagan's approach, 32 per cent judged it about right, 39 per cent not tough enough, and only 18 per cent too tough. Even among Democrats, only one in four found Reagan too aggressive. His great skill was that he could sound ferocious without having to be ferocious. In April 1970, in response to trouble in Santa Barbara, he remarked: 'if it takes a bloodbath' to silence the demonstrators 'let's get it over with'. There was predictable outcry on the campuses and in liberal circles, but the remark delighted Reagan supporters. He claimed it was merely a slip of the tongue, but that seems improbable, given one so astute at telling the people what they wanted to hear.

In March 1969, Robert Newhall of the *San Francisco Chronicle* accused Reagan of creating the unrest 'in a very surgical way . . . There are people in this administration unscrupulous enough to wreck the University this way just to establish themselves better in power'. That criticism seems excessive. Reagan was no Machiavelli; he merely acted in the way he sincerely believed was right. As one of his aides remarked, his great success arose from the fact that he could satisfy the people's aspirations simply by being Ronald Reagan.

Like William Jennings Bryan, another great populist, Reagan could translate a complicated world which he barely comprehended into values he never questioned. He certainly remained convinced that his iron-handed response was singularly appropriate. 'We have proven and proven to the nation that this is the answer and this is the only way to handle it', he said. He perhaps did not realise how prophetic those words were. By turning a relatively small problem of campus unrest into a massive conspiracy to overthrow democratic society, and then by meeting that threat with maximum force, Reagan established himself as a leader worthy of national attention.

FOR FURTHER READING:

Bill Boyarsky, *The Rise of Ronald Reagan*, (Random House, 1968); Lou Cannon, *Reagan*, (G. R. Putnam & Sons, 1982) and *President Reagan: The Role of a Lifetime*, (Simon Schuster, 1991); Gary Wills, *Reagan's America: Innocence at Home*, (Doubleday, 1987); Kenneth J. Heineman, *Campus Wars*, (New York University Press, 1993); W. J. Rorabaugh, *Berkeley at War: The 1960s*, (Oxford University Press, 1989); Tom Wells, *The War Within: The Battle over Vietnam*, (University of California Press, 1994).

Looking Back at Watergate

The most harmful legacy was the erosion of Americans' faith in the rule of law.

Allen N. Sultan

Dr. Sultan is professor of law, University of Dayton (Ohio).

Two decades have passed since the resignation of Richard Nixon in the aftermath of the break-in at Democratic Party offices at the Watergate complex polarized the American people. Passions, however, usually are transient. The soothing effects of time offer inspection free of the divisive partisan politics that frequently accompany such precipitative events. Today, it is possible to reflect more coolly upon the trying months of Watergate, not as a political crisis, but, rather, as a most important event in the history and constitutional philosophy of the nation.

"I believe this [to be] the strongest government on earth....; the only one where every man... would fly to the standard of the law, and would meet invasions of the public order as his own personal concern," stated Thomas Jefferson in his Inaugural address, March 4, 1801.

On Oct. 18, 1973, the American people rose as one and "flew to the standard of the law" with an avalanche of telegrams to Washington, D.C., that would have made Jefferson and his colleagues swell with pride. Responding to what has become known as "The Saturday Night Massacre," they confirmed Jefferson's confidence and prediction that they "would meet an invasion of the public order as [their] own personal concern." They were, in effect, 20th-century minutemen (and women), armed with their freedoms of expression and petition, rather than a musket. On behalf of themselves and posterity, they kept faith with the heritage of liberty secured by the constitutional rule of law.

A second, fascinating parallel exists between pre-revolutionary colonial experience and the events leading up to that autumn evening 21 years ago. In the Declaration of Independence, Jefferson referred to the "history of repeated injuries and usurpations" by King George III. He also pointed out that human nature is more "disposed to suffer" endurable evils than to take politically precipitous action—until, in the words of Edmund Burke, "forbearance ceases to be a virtue."

Most are familiar with the injuries and usurpations of George III that are expressed so ably in the Declaration. Yet, how many, especially the voters of tomorrow, remember or have since learned about the transgressions of Richard Nixon and his immediate subordinates? Consider, as illustrations:

• An enemies list, declaring certain citizens to be "enemies" because they may not agree with some of the policies of their public servants.

• The political surveillance of citizens—the violation of their private lives and personal communications because they may hold independent views of public policy.

• Attempts at special tax audits to destroy various citizens whose only crime was to disagree with those who were temporarily in power.

• The stamp of national security and the claim of "implied powers" that were misused time and again for political gain.

• The sale of government favors—a premeditated campaign of Nixon officialdom furrowing out customers. Like so many magazine salesmen, they sought their patron in his nest with the message: Buy a piece of the people's government—or else! (Not surprisingly, the manager of that effort, former Secretary of Commerce Maurice Stans, proved to be the most successful money-raiser in the history of American politics.)

• A top government position being dangled before a Federal judge who was presiding over a major trial involving the reach or extent of the powers of the presidency.

• A secret, huge cache of funds to be used at the whim of those in power.

• Key documents involving possible criminal fraud that, for some strange reason, simply could not be found.

• An incredulous series of "flip-flops" by Nixon, one time claiming to have acted as president, another as an individual—whichever would have best served his particular dilemma at the time.

• Being told that seeking out the truth would permanently wound the office of the presidency, when, in fact, the President held the integrity of that office in his own hands. (All he had to do was speak the truth.)

• Being told about Nixon's two luxurious estates, of his half-million dollars in back taxes, of his White House guards ostentatiously dressed in the manner befitting the Austrian Hapsburgs, of blasting trumpets announcing his entrance at state dinners, and of the exorbitant refitting of Air Force One so his family would not have to pass through a public area on the plane.

• The deepest cut of all, the desecration of the vote—the refutation of democracy itself—by dirty tricks, burglary, and similar acts amounting to a vast conspiracy to destroy the fundamental constitutional right of all citizens to their free choice in an election.

STONEWALLING

After these many experiences, Americans still clung to their trust in the rule of law and the system it had created.

5. FROM THE COLD WAR TO THE 1990s

They patiently awaited action by the Special Prosecutor, Archibald Cox, an eminent constitutional authority at Harvard Law School. Upon taking office, Cox immediately sought out the evidence, no matter where it might lead.

The White House responded with unkept promises, delays, and general deception and evasion, building a stone wall between the White House and the people it served. On March 22, 1973, almost seven months before the Saturday Night Massacre, Nixon instructed Attorney General John Mitchell: "I want you to stonewall it, plead the Fifth Amendment, cover up or anything else."

Cox was fully aware of the compelling significance of his responsibilities to the future efficacy of the republic. He persisted, actively seeking out audio tapes of relevant White House conversations. Then, with the President and the Special Prosecutor eyeball to eyeball, Nixon stumbled, firing Cox. With him went Attorney General Elliot Richardson and his deputy, William Ruckelshouse, both resigning rather than carry the odious message.

With these dismissals on Oct. 18, 1973, Richard Nixon had crossed his Rubicon. By precipitating the Saturday Night Massacre, he had sealed his own fate. The voters were appalled. Political reality mandated that a new Special Prosecutor be appointed—and soon! The public outcry was uniform and vociferous.

The newly appointed Special Prosecutor, Leon Jaworski, a Texas attorney, continued the investigation in the manner and spirit of his predecessor. (In a report two years later, Jaworski referred to the dismissals triggering the avalanche of telegrams to Washington, near uniform condemnation by the media, and, in general, pervasive nationwide public reaction that buried the Nixon presidency. It was, the report said, no less than the American people rising up in anger, their sense of injustice painfully ignited.) Ever the political combatant, Nixon fought back:

• He offered a collection of transcripts of White House conversations concerning the break-in on national television and told the American people that they contained the complete facts. In truth, they were replete with distortions and omissions, as later proven by House of Representatives' transcripts of key, unedited tapes.

• The transcripts also evidenced no White House concern for the presidency, national security, or the operations of government—causing some historians later to characterize them as "the most self-incriminating document ever published by an American president."

• On a human level, the language of the President and his advisors astonished and outraged the American people. Most significantly, Nixon's words were "foul, vengeful and full of ethnic slurs . . . [reflecting both] fear and hate."

• When pressured to release the actual tapes, he responded with the claim that some were completely missing—in an administration where every moment was the subject of a memo and every presidential murmur an object for posterity.

• Nixon also wanted the public to accept unbelievable physical contortions by his personal secretary, followed by "a denial theory"—all in an attempt to explain erasures on other tapes that just happened to encompass extremely vital conversations.

• On July 24, 1974, a unanimous Supreme Court ruled that Nixon must release all of the actual audio tapes.

• Also on July 24, at 7:45 p.m., Rep. Peter Rodino (D.-N.J.), chairman of the House Judiciary Committee, rapped his gavel on nationwide television, opening the hearings that commenced the impeachment process. He said, "Make no mistake about it. This is a turning point—whatever we decide. . . . [O]ur judgment is not concerned with an individual but with a system of constitutional government. . . . We have been fair. Now the American people, the House of Representatives, and the whole history of our republic demand that we make up our minds."

Members of the committee then made their positions known. For instance, Rep. Barbara Jordan (D.-Tex.) declared, "My faith in the Constitution is whole, it is complete, it is total, and I am not going to sit here and be an idle spectator to the diminution, the subversion, the destruction of the Constitution." Rep. James Mann (D.-S.C.) stated, "If there be no accountability, another president will feel free to do as he chooses. The next time there may be no watchman in the night."

• Now completely in a corner, Nixon released more tapes on Aug. 5. They revealed that he was directly involved in the coverup—in the criminal obstruction of justice. One of them has come to be known as the "smoking gun" tape of a White House conversation of June 23, 1972. It contains Nixon's voice clearly directing his aide to demand that the CIA do whatever it can to restrain the FBI's investigation of Watergate. "Call the CIA people and tell them that further inquiry might lead to the whole Bay of Pigs thing." The CIA should call Acting FBI Director Patrick Grey and say, "Don't go further into this case. Period!"

Three days later, finding himself without any political support, Nixon resigned the presidency, effective the next day, Aug. 9, 1974. Thus ended the ominous ordeal known as Watergate. Although he had been respected for his political sagacity, Nixon's Saturday Night Massacre remains the most prominent example of the dangers of confusing knowledge with wisdom. His ill-fated decisions of that evening triggered a pervasive nationwide reaction that led to his inevitable fall from power. In the last analysis, Nixon lost his furious gamble because he did not understand the values of the nation and the attitudes of the people that he led, and because his acts were a dramatic insight into his true character.

To the amazement of much of the rest of the world, the most powerful office on Earth changed hands peaceably. True to the motto on the national seal—*Novus Ordo Seclorium* (a new cycle of the ages)—the U.S. still was teaching the rest of the world by example. The institutions of government remained firm; the soldiers remained in their barracks; the system based upon freedom of expression for both citizen and the press protected by an independent judiciary fully worked, as the Framers knew it would; and the constitutional rule of law prevailed.

The cashiering of a sitting president remains a momentous event. A sobering message can be inferred from the fact that no president ever had been forced out of office in almost 200 years until Nixon was. Jefferson expressed this imperative of political philosophy in the Declaration of Independence: "[A]ll experience hath shown, that mankind are more disposed to suffer, while evils are sufferable, than to right themselves by abolishing the forms to which they are accustomed."

Sound practical reasons also counsel against the removal of a sitting president. The Founding Fathers purposefully created a strong national executive, knowing that specific governmental objectives and unpredictable future challenges demanded that they do so. To compromise or erode this vital aspect of the national polity by Nixon's removal, therefore, created the real possibility of future weaknesses to the institution of the presidency.

WAS FORCING NIXON FROM OFFICE NECESSARY?

Thus, looking back, the ultimate constitutional question about the Watergate experience must be asked: Would it have been wiser for the American people to ride out the storm than to set such a potentially disabling precedent? Has subsequently available information indicated that forcing Nixon from office was really a *necessary* cleansing process of American democracy?

The record leaves little doubt that the correct choice was made. Post-Watergate revelations of the actions of Richard Nixon and the White House crew for which he set the tone fully support the need for political surgery. Indeed, given the following examples of those revelations, can any reasonable person doubt the wisdom of this conclusion?:

• In 1971, the following conversation took place between Nixon and his Chief of Staff, H.R. Haldeman. They were discussing the possibility of unleashing Teamster "thugs" against American citizens who were exercising their First Amendment rights of political expression, assembly, and petition in opposition to the Vietnam War:
Nixon: "They, they've got guys who'll go in and knock their heads off."
Haldeman: "Sure. Murderers. Guys that really, you know that's what they really do.... I mean go in ... and smash some noses."

• A second conversation took place a year later involving Nixon, Haldeman, and White House Counsel John Dean. The topic of the conversation was Nixon's suggestion that they steal files from the Internal Revenue Service. In their discussion, they appear to approve of the crime of burglary, the same felony that served as the fuse to Nixon's Watergate quagmire. The President asked Dean why they never had pulled the files of his Democratic opponent, George McGovern, in 1972.
Dean: "I had a tremendous time just trying to get [the file on Henry Kimmleman, one of McGovern's financial contributors].... The problem is this. There are so many damn Democrats [at the IRS].... It would have to have been an artful job to go down and get that file."
Nixon (later in the same conversation): "We have to do it artfully so that we don't create an issue by abusing the IRS politically ... and there are ways to do that. Goddamn it, sneak in in the middle of the night." This conversation took place *less than three months after* the arrest of the burglars following the Watergate break-in. Talk about the corruption of power!

• Pulitzer Prize-winning investigative reporter Seymour Hirsh unearthed Nixon's response to the attempted assassination of his Dixiecrat opponent, George Wallace. Nixon dispatched E. Howard Hunt to plant McGovern campaign material at the home of Arthur Bremer, the man who shot Wallace. The obvious objective was to tie the shooting to a McGovern supporter, leaving open the question, in the public mind, of his campaign participation.

• McGovern became Nixon's Democratic rival after Sen. Edmund Muskie (D.-Me.) dropped out of the 1972 primaries. Consider the following statement by Muskie's campaign manager, Berl Bernhard: "You go in expecting a campaign to be rough, even nasty.... You don't expect to be undercut every step of the way by criminal behavior. Phony memos misstating our positions. Scurrilous attacks on other candidates on our letterhead.... I'll never forget the day Muskie gave a major address on Israel at a Miami synagogue—he is, remember, Polish-Catholic—and he goes outside with all the cameras running, and a huge banner unfolds: 'Remember the Warsaw Ghetto.' It was filth—and it was everywhere.... They understood from the start that McGovern would be the weakest opponent, and they got him. All it took was undermining the democratic process."

• Finally, there are the musings of Nixon's White House men over whether—and how—to murder syndicated columnist Jack Anderson, a critic of the Administration long before Watergate. The mastermind of the Watergate burglary, G. Gordon Liddy, related the criminal conspiracy to Anderson on a television news show in June, 1991: "The rationale was to come up with a method of silencing you through killing you." After discussing the possibility of

32. Looking Back at Watergate

using the illegal drug LSD, "Finally they came up with striking your car on a turn and making it crash and burn.... It was written up in a memo and sent to the White House." This time, however, the Nixon White House said "No." According to Liddy, they felt that murder "was too severe a sanction."

Liddy's comments prompt reflection on what lesser sanction—if any—the men of the Nixon White House would approve. Anderson has indicated that he believes E. Howard Hunt carried the frustrating news to Liddy. At that time, Hunt worked for White House Special Counsel Chuck Colson.

These examples underscore why Americans, as a society, had to clean up the mess. They support the assertion that the nation responded correctly to Watergate. The book has not been closed on possible evidence of justification, however. With a large amount of the approximately 4,000 hours of Nixon White House tapes still not made public, there no doubt will be future tidings in the ongoing saga of Watergate. One can only speculate as to what juicy tidbits the future holds.

Retrospect raises additional questions containing important moral dimensions. Richard Nixon had, over the years, frequently served the nation well. His acumen and performance in foreign affairs was, and continued to be until his death in 1994, both valuable and obvious. In the domestic realm, his contributions as president included ending the draft, revaluation of the currency, proposing national health care reform two decades before it became a raging debate, and fostering the creation of the Environmental Protection Agency. As a result of his environmental leadership, Americans once again can swim and fish in the nation's waters and breathe virtually lead-free air. Indeed, at the time of Watergate, Nixon was recognized internationally as one of the most effective American leaders in the post-World War II era.

THE LESSONS OF WATERGATE

Why, after two decades, look back at Watergate? Since Nixon paid a significant price for his obviously improper behavior, why not simply focus upon the numerous contemporary challenges?

To respond properly requires asking a further question: What have been the

5. FROM THE COLD WAR TO THE 1990s

empirical effects of Watergate on U.S. society and on Americans' personal day-to-day interactions with each other and their government? If there have been no serious ongoing detriments from the national trauma, Watergate should be relegated to the history books. In that circumstance, there would be no need to (in Nixon's words) "wallow in Watergate."

However, if there has been and continues to be serious permanent damage to our society from Watergate, then we should (indeed, must) periodically review the very important lessons it teaches about the possible base abuse of political power so feared by the Founding Fathers. Like Holocaust history in Israel, compelling reasons would demand that it be taught anew to each generation; like Three Mile Island, next time we may not be so lucky!

Simple common sense suggests the greatest harmful legacy of Watergate—the possible erosion of faith in the rule of law. Probably the best articulation of the underlying relevant principle of political philosophy and its psychological ramifications on individual citizens came from the pen of Supreme Court Justice Louis Brandeis:

"Decency, security and liberty alike demand that government officials shall be subjected to the same rules of conduct that are commands to the citizen. In a government of laws, existence of the government will be imperiled if it fails to observe the law scrupulously. Our government is the potent, the omnipresent teacher. For good or for ill, it teaches the whole people by its example. Crime is contagious. If the government becomes a lawbreaker, it breeds contempt for law; it invites every man to become a law unto himself; it invites anarchy."

Admittedly, abuse of power, greed, and corruption are indigenous to human affairs, infesting leaders as well as many of those they, in theory, serve. Yet, Watergate remains in a class by itself. Its many characteristics cause it to be set apart from other political criminal enterprises. Its felons commanded the very apex of the political hierarchy; their crimes were so blatant; their ongoing conspiracies included so many culpable individuals; their arrogance towards their fellow citizens, including some of their own colleagues, at times challenged human imagination; their criminal activities continued for such a long time; and they executed so many crimes against social order.

These differences in degree have given Watergate its unique status, making it the pithy teacher of the present and future generations. It elucidates the necessity for diligence and demonstrates the dangers of indifference: That we all pay a steep price when we ignore Jefferson's call for "external vigilance" in the cause of freedom.

Take, for instance, the area of criminology and the administration of criminal justice. The penal law serves two functions: as a deterrent against criminal acts and as a hook to bring those who have not been deterred into the system of criminal justice. At the time Watergate shook the American public, the well-established purpose of prisons was the rehabilitation of the inmates. Choosing rehabilitation as *the* penal objective meant that practicality was wed with humanity to diminish both the more basic objective of incapacitation and the more primitive one of retribution. Rehabilitation also represented faith in the wisdom of juvenile courts, probation, parole, indeterminate (rather than mandated) sentences, and therapeutic assistance to inmates.

Watergate helped change all of these assumptions. To a considerable degree, the nation has turned away from these civilizing influences. Debating the validity of these changes takes one into such matters as the economic causes of crime and the changing rates of recidivism. Few, though, can doubt that these changes exist in the public attitude towards convicted criminals or that they are to some degree the logical consequence of the U.S. becoming a far more cynical society.

Like polluted soil and water, the national psyche eventually will be purified of the insidious defilement by the Watergate legacy. However, it undoubtedly will take a long, long time.

Final Days of South Vietnam

One of the last Americans out of Saigon looks back 20 years to the bitter aftermath of America's well-intended but fatally flawed war in southeast Asia.

Col. Harry G. Summers, Jr.

A combat veteran of both the Korean and Vietnam wars, Colonel Summers is the editor of Vietnam magazine. His books On Strategy: A Critical Analysis of the Vietnam War *(Presidio, 1982) and* Vietnam War Almanac *(Facts on File, 1985) are standard teaching and reference texts on the war. A third book,* Historical Atlas of the Vietnam War, *is published by Houghton Mifflin (1995).*

In an 1832 discussion of "centers of gravity" that he called the key to winning wars, the great Prussian strategist Carl von Clausewitz noted that "in small countries that rely on larger ones, the center of gravity is usually *the army of their protector.*"

Von Clausewitz's words were to prove sadly prophetic 143 years later, when, in April 1975, South Vietnam fell to a North Vietnamese Army (NVA) multidivision cross-border *blitzkrieg.* The key to the South Vietnamese defeat, to use the strategist's own words, was the absence of the "army of their protector." During the ten-year period leading up to that collapse, the role of the United States and the U.S. military in South Vietnam had completely reversed itself.

Two NVA campaigns in the Central Highlands define the changes that took place in America's commitment to South Vietnam during that decade. The first turning point came in the Ia Drang Valley in November 1965, when the U.S. 1st Cavalry Division (Airmobile) thwarted an attempt by NVA regulars to strike across the Central Highlands from their Cambodian sanctuaries and cut South Vietnam in two. At the time, *New York Times* war correspondent Neil Sheehan accurately noted that "this could be the most significant battle of the Vietnam War."

What had up to that point been a low-level guerrilla war became a major conflict involving the regular forces of both the United States and North Vietnam. It accelerated the U.S. military buildup from mostly an advisory effort to a half-million-man conventional fighting force, and to the U.S. takeover of the war. In December 1964, 23,300 Americans had been stationed in Vietnam; by December 1965 that figure grew to 184,300. At the peak of the buildup, in April 1969, the U.S. military commitment reached 543,400 men and women.

In March 1975 another watershed battle took place at Ban Me Thuot, just south of the Ia Drang. Where the Ia Drang had given proof that the United States intended to fight to prevent its South Vietnamese ally from being overrun by the North Vietnamese invaders, Ban Me Thout was final evidence that America no longer possessed the will to continue doing so. Ban Me Thuot conclusively reaffirmed what had been evidenced two months earlier at the battle for Phuoc Long province—that the U.S. had lost the determination to support South Vietnam militarily and was reneging on its January 1973 promises to reenter the war if the NVA violated the terms of the Paris Peace Accords.

Then national security advisor (and by 1975, Secretary of State) Henry Kissinger had personally assured South Vietnamese President Nguyen Van Thieu that the U.S. response to a major Communist violation of the accords would be "both swift and brutal," and President Richard Nixon had written him three letters confirming that very pledge. But it was obvious after Phuoc Long and Ban Me Thuot that those guarantees were now worthless.

The "conventional wisdom" about the fall of South Vietnam is that the United States had lost a guerrilla war in Asia. But such an assessment is wrong. For one thing, America was no longer there to lose, having withdrawn the last of its ground forces in August 1972, and the remainder of its armed forces in March 1973, in accordance with the Paris Peace Accords. Furthermore, the Viet Cong (VC) guerrillas had almost nothing to do with the final campaign, for they had been eliminated as a viable fighting force seven years earlier in the aftermath of the 1968 Tet Offensive. In his account of the war's final battles (including the battle for Saigon itself), General Van Tien Dung, the NVA commander barely mentions the Viet Cong.

"An NBC television crew caught one of the most significant pictures of the event," noted former CIA Director William Colby of the April 1975 fall of Saigon. "It filmed the huge North Vietnamese tank with its monstrous cannon as it broke open the main gate to the Presidential Palace. The people's war was over, not by the work of a barefoot guerrilla but by the most conventional of military forces.

"During the last days of the South Vietnamese collapse, as Colonel Harry G. Summers reports, one of the most trenchant comments was made by a naval fighter pilot flying cover for the helicopter evacuations. Returning to the USS *Coral Sea,* he said excitedly, 'They're fighting our war!'

"The ultimate irony was that the people's war launched in 1959 had been defeated," Colby concluded, "but the soldier's war, which the United States had insisted on fighting during the 1960s with massive military forces, was finally won by the enemy."

5. FROM THE COLD WAR TO THE 1990s

THREE WHO ESCAPED

For the Nguyen Family, the most unforgetable and uncertain hours of their lives began on the evening of April 29, 1975. Lu Nguyen, then a first lieutenant in the South Vietnamese Marines, was stationed at Vung Tau, a coastal city about three hours' travel east of Saigon.

Nguyen and his wife Tuoi need only two words to describe April 29—frantic fear. "People ran wildly around. Nobody knew where they were going," recalls Tuoi. "They knew that the line [between North and South Vietnam] had fallen, and they just wanted to get away. The sound of the exploding shells was so close that you thought your head would fly off."

Anticipating the worst, Lieutenant Nguyen sent two of his Marines to escort his wife and four-year-old daughter My Tuyet onto a small boat docked at the shore while he remained behind to fight. The boat, crammed full of people, soon got underway without a destination in mind, and after circling around endlessly, became lost. During the night it came upon an American ship, but that vessel was already so crowded with refugees that the crew fired shots to prevent the newcomers from boarding.

Not knowing what else to do, the boat's crew eventually anchored offshore. The situation grew uncomfortable, for in their rush to escape the refugees had brought little food or water. My Tuyet [who twenty years later conducted this interview with her parents] recalls being really hungry and having an aching back from having to sit up all night.

Finally, late on the afternoon of the 30th the little boat chanced upon a much larger Vietnamese civilian vessel, the *Tan Nam Viet,* and the refugees were allowed to board.

Lieutenant Nguyen, meanwhile, was taking part in the final defense of Vung Tau. At one point he told his radioman to remove his radio pack so that he could flee more quickly. But at that moment, while the soldier's hands were lifted, shrapnel flew by and sliced off his hand at the wrist.

Nguyen, who had known for some time that all was inevitably lost (because food and ammunition supplies were gone), radioed to the 150 men under his command to retreat to the shoreline. He then took the wounded man to headquarters for medical attention before heading for the shore himself. There he and many others swam about a mile out to sea, where Nguyen clung to an innertube while waiting for the shooting to subside and for a chance to escape.

After about three hours, a small Vietnamese naval vessel stopped nearby, and the hundreds of swimmers began to climb on board. Weighed down by so much humanity, the craft started to sink. Nguyen then swam over to a nearby oil barge and spent the night there.

On April 30, the barge's captain received word of South Vietnam's surrender. He decided to put to sea, and he radioed for help. As chance would have it, the ship that responded was the *Tan Nam Viet*—the same vessel that had picked up Nguyen's wife and daughter!

Reunited, the Nguyens were evacuated to a refugee camp in Guam for six weeks, then to another in Little Rock, Arkansas. A Lutheran Church in Pennsylvania offered to sponsor them, and the family moved to that state, where they continue to reside today.

Another lingering misperception about the Vietnam War is that the South Vietnamese military (officially the Republic of Vietnam Armed Forces, or RVNAF) played little part in the war—and that in any event its soldiers would rather run away than fight.

The truth is that South Vietnamese fighting men, far from being an army of cowards, took four times as many casualties as the U.S. military did every day of the war. As compared to the 47,244 Americans killed in action (and an additional 10,446 who died of other causes), South Vietnam suffered 233,748 service members killed in action—not including the uncounted numbers who perished in the final NVA offensive.

NVA commander General Van Tien Dung certainly did not regard the South Vietnamese as pushovers. He used three divisions in his assault on the RVNAF 53rd Regiment defending Ban Me Thuot. In his account of the battle, Dung declared that he won because he "achieved superiority over the enemy [i.e., the South Vietnamese].... As for infantry the ratio was 5.5 of our troops for each enemy soldier. As for tanks and armored vehicles, the ratio was 1.2 to 1. In heavy artillery the ratio was 2.1 to 1."

Two months earlier, Dung had used the same overwhelming force against South Vietnamese defenders in Phuoc Long province, pitting his two-division 301st Corps, supported by tanks and heavy artillery, against four RVNAF Regional Force battalions. After a three-week siege and under cover of a three-thousand-round artillery barrage, the NVA finally overwhelmed the defenders. Of 5,400 South Vietnamese committed to the battle, only 850 survived.

The NVA won more than a battle at Phuoc Long. It received the green light to begin its final campaign. In October 1974 the North Vietnamese Politburo had met to work out plans for the conquest of South Vietnam. The principal question, according to General Dung, was: "Would the United States be able to send its troops back to the South if we launched large-scale battles that would lead to the collapse of puppet troops?"

"The Watergate scandal had seriously affected the entire United States and precipitated the resignation of an extremely reactionary president—Nixon," the conference noted. "U.S. aid to the Saigon puppet regime was decreasing. Comrade Le Duan [Ho Chi Minh's successor] drew an important conclusion that became a resolution: 'Having already withdrawn from the South, the United States could hardly jump back in, and no matter how it might intervene, it would be unable to save the Saigon administration from collapse.'"

The battle of Phuoc Long confirmed Le Duan's assessment. "All the conferees analyzed the enemy's weakness which in itself heralded a new opportunity for us," said General Dung in his account of the Politburo meeting that followed the battle. "To fully exploit this great opportunity we had to conduct large-scale annihilating battles to destroy and disintegrate the enemy on a

33. Final Days of South Vietnam

ONE WHO WAS LEFT BEHIND

April 30, 1975 will live forever in the minds of millions of Vietnamese. It was a day filled with the spectrum of man's emotions: joy, sadness, anger, bitterness, and shame. For some, it was a great moment of liberation and triumph—but for many others it meant defeat and fathomless fear.

San Nguyen, a lieutenant colonel in the South Vietnamese Army, was one of the unfortunate ones. For Nguyen, April 30 marked the beginning of more than a decade of pain and suffering.

Nguyen and the soldiers under his command were fighting about twenty-five kilometers outside of Saigon, at Hoc Mon, when they heard that the Communists were triumphant and all was now lost. He and his men threw away their arms and uniforms and headed for home. Some escaped to freedom, but many others (including Nguyen) were captured and imprisoned, while some were shot on the spot.

Taken to Bach Dang, the North Vietnamese headquarters for interrogation in Saigon, Nguyen was held in solitary confinement and questioned about his and his family's involvement with the Americans, specifically the Central Intelligence Agency (CIA). "I told them I knew nothing, but the mere fact that I was born in South Vietnam made me guilty," says Nguyen.

After two weeks, Nguyen and others were released—only to be imprisoned again within days. Nguyen was confined at first in South Vietnam, but then moved every two or three months to another location farther north, until he finally reached Hanoi.

Each new prison camp was like the last. Nguyen's ordeal became a blur of endless days of solitary confinement in a dark, three-by-five-foot cell; deprivation of sleep, water, and food (turnips were the staple diet); and endless hours of hard manual labor. "Re-education" training began at 2:00 A.M. each morning, then the prisoners were awakened again at 4:00 A.M. for the two-hour walk to the worksite. "I went from 160 pounds to only 80 pounds within two months of entering the prison camps," Nguyen recalls. "My mother sent me a pair of jeans from the U.S. while I was in prison, and after only eight months they were totally shredded due to the amount of sweat that poured daily from my body."

The only relief during these horrific years was small care packages from family members and the annual fifteen-minute visits that he was allowed to have with his wife. Nghia Nguyen traveled for days from Ho Chi Minh City [formerly Saigon] to Hanoi for these precious minutes together.

After thirteen long years of "re-education," Nguyen finally was released in 1988. Then, in 1992 he was allowed to come to America as part of Vietnam's "Humanities Operations Program." "I never thought I would leave the prison camps," he says.

When asked if he wanted to come to the United States, Nguyen replies that "there's an old saying in Vietnam—even a lamppost would leave if it had feet."

Now, three years after his arrival in America, Nguyen lives in Pennsylvania with his wife and enjoys the freedom that he had so long dreamed of. "Of course there are also difficulties that I must endure in America, but compared to Vietnam this is like heaven," says Nguyen with a smile.

—Interview by My Tuyet Nguyen (no relation to San Nguyen).

---

large scale." Encouraged not only by the battle but by the U.S. reaction, the final NVA offensive was set in motion. Two months later three NVA divisions descended on Ban Me Thuot.

Casting aside security guarantees that it had made two years earlier, the United States limited its response to the NVAs blatant violation (and it was deliberately meant to be blatant in order to test the U.S. resolve) of the Paris Accords to an official diplomatic protest. And in a press conference on January 21, 1975, President Gerald Ford said he could foresee no circumstances in which the U.S. might actively reenter the Vietnam War.

It was now obvious to South Vietnam President Thieu that he was on his own. On March 14, 1975, as the battle for Ban Me Thuot drew to a close, he held a meeting at Cam Ranh Bay with Major General Pham Van Phu, the commander of Military Region II. Phu was ordered to withdraw his forces from Kontum and Pleiku in the Central Highlands to provide additional forces for the retaking of Ban Me Thout. The evacuation began on March 15, 1975—a day that marked the beginning of the end for South Vietnam.

Poorly planned and even more poorly executed, the withdrawal quickly disintegrated into chaos. "Not foreseeing the inevitable mass civilian exodus that would accompany the military column as soon as the population discovered what was going on," notes the official U.S. military history, "General Phu made no preparations to control the crowds which became entangled in combat formations, impeding their movement and ability to deploy and fight."

Disaster followed upon disaster. South Vietnam's defenses along the Demilitarized Zone (DMZ) between North and South Vietnam were manned by South Vietnamese Marines. When President Thieu ordered the Airborne Division, then in the line near Da Nang, to return to Saigon to provide a strategic reserve, the Military Region I commander, Lieutenant General Truong Ngo Quang, ordered one Marine brigade out of the line at Quang Tri along the DMZ and replaced it with Regional Force units.

This withdrawal, as earlier in the Central Highlands, sparked a mass exodus of civilians down QL 1, the main highway south. They were soon joined by civilians fleeing Hue city and as a result the highway from the Hai Van Pass north was blocked by refugees to the point where military movement was impossible.

The Hai Van Pass was a major topographical feature that separated the upper two provinces of South Vietnam from the rest of the country. North of the pass was the RVNAF's 1st Infantry Division. Like all RVNAF divisions (except the Airborne and Marine divisions) its soldiers were accompanied by their families. Then, what Major General Homer D. Smith—the senior U.S. military officer then in Vietnam—called the "family syndrome" began to manifest itself. This, not lack of a will to fight, would become the primary factor in the collapse of the South Vietnamese military.

"Men and officers set out to save their families," General Smith pointed

5. FROM THE COLD WAR TO THE 1990s

out. "It was that simple. Who else was going to do it? . . . It is difficult for the average American to conceive of a situation where a soldier's overwhelming desire to save his family—wife, children, mother, etc.—would cause him to leave his post. Not in this century at least, has a single American soldier been faced with the choice. We have always fought away from our own soil and our own families."

"We saw the family syndrome reassert itself time and again during the final days," Smith said. "Yet we never saw the lack of a will to fight. As the lines around Saigon tightened there was plenty of evidence of hard and skillful fighting . . . I know of no case where a member of a regular unit of the South failed to fight when his family was safe."

At Hue the RVNAF 1st Infantry Division fell prey to the family syndrome, then the 2nd Infantry Division at Da Nang, followed by the 3rd Infantry Division south and west of the city. Da Nang descended into anarchy as both civilians and armed mobs of South Vietnamese soldiers fought for space on evacuation boats and aircraft. As emotion overtook reason, pandemonium erupted. The mobs had literally wrested control of the city from all official authority. The last Americans out of Da Nang, along with the RVNAF military hierarchy escaped over the beach onto Vietnamese Navy craft. As General Smith noted, "the experience was shattering to all who participated." It was one that would haunt the subsequent evacuation of Saigon.

Meanwhile, what was left of the forces withdrawing from Pleiku and Kontum, still under attack by the pursuing 320th NVA Division, emerged at Tuy Hoa, south of Qui Nhon. The NVA had finally succeeded in doing what the Americans had prevented them from accomplishing ten years earlier. They had cut South Vietnam in half.

As the debacle continued to unfold, the MR II commander, Major General Phu (who would later commit suicide in disgrace), deserted his headquarters at Nha Trang and fled to Saigon. Nha Trang did not so much fall to the enemy as it was abandoned by its erstwhile defenders.

A counterpoint to Nha Trang, however, was the stand of the RVNAF 18th Infantry Division at Xuan Loc, the capital of Long Khanh province, forty miles northeast of Saigon. On March 17, Xuan Loc came under attack by the NVA 6th and 7th Divisions. These attacks were repulsed by the South Vietnamese 18th Infantry Division defenders, but on April 9, reinforced by the NVA 341st Division, the battle resumed. Even though the NVA was supported by a four-thousand-round artillery bombardment and T-54 medium tanks, the attack once again failed.

On April 15, the NVA reinforced yet again with their 325th Division and began bringing their 10th and 304th Divisions into position. Two days later, faced with overwhelming odds, the 18th Division was forced to give ground. But they had virtually destroyed three NVA divisions in the process.

"An uneasy quiet settled over the battlefield," notes the official history, "while the enemy made plans, conducted reconnaissance, and issued orders for the final drive. Sixteen NVA divisions were now in Military Region III and poised for a three-pronged attack on Saigon."

Meanwhile, those of us in the U.S. Mission in Saigon (i.e., the Embassy staff, the fifty military members of the Defense Attaché Office (DAO), and the six remaining members of the U.S. Delegation, Four Party Joint Military Team—Colonel John H. Madison, Jr., its chief; myself, the head of the Negotiations Division; my deputy Captain Stuart A. Herrington; Master Sergeant William Herron; Marine Sergeant Ernest Pace; and our interpreter, Specialist 7 Garrett "Bill" Bell) were busy with the fixed-wing evacuation of U.S. civilians and their families, as well as Vietnamese civilians whose past cooperation with the United States had put their lives in danger.*

The U.S. Ambassador to Vietnam, Graham Martin, had placed his defense attaché, General Smith, in charge of the evacuation. From his headquarters at the old MACV (Military Assistance Command Vietnam) compound at Tan Son Nhut airbase in the suburbs of Saigon, Smith organized the withdrawal.

One of the first evacuation flights was that of a U.S. Air Force (USAF) C-5A transport on April 4. Dubbed "Operation Baby Lift," it involved some 250 orphans, escorted by thirty-seven American women, mostly secretaries and staff personnel from the U.S. mission. Soon after departure, the transport suffered a massive structural failure and, while attempting to return to Tan Son Nhut, crashed short of the runway.

The many casualties in this tragedy included one of the plane's crew members, USAF aero-evacuation nurse Captain Mary Klinker, the last U.S. military officer to die in the war; my secretary Barbara Kavulia; and the wife and one child of Specialist Bell. Miraculously his other daughter survived the crash. But terrible as that incident was, the airlift continued apace. From April 6 to April 28 some 44,920 evacuees were processed through the DAO, primarily by USAF C-130 and C-141 cargo aircraft.

On April 29 the NVA began a rocket and artillery attack on Tan Son Nhut that brought the fixed-wing evacuation to a close. Killed in the attack were two U.S. Marine security guards, lance Corporal Darwin Judge and Corporal Charles McMahon, Jr.—the last American servicemen to die in action in the war.

Meanwhile, on April 25—accompanied by Specialist Bell, who had returned to Vietnam of his own volition after escorting his surviving daughter to his parent's home in the United States—I made a trip to Hanoi on a USAF C-130 to receive the North Vietnamese terms for the U.S. withdrawal. (The members of the U.S. Delegation, Four Party Joint Military Team were the only Americans to then have open diplomatic contact with the North Vietnamese. Regular FPJMT liaison flights to Hanoi had been conducted since 1973.)

It was a far cry from my first tour in Vietnam almost a decade earlier as operations officer of the 1st Battalion, 2nd Infantry Regiment in the U.S. 1st Infantry Division. For one thing, I now was on my own. "Damned if I know" was the answer I received when I asked the U.S. Embassy what I should do in Hanoi: "Do the best you can." For another, being in the enemies' capital on the eve of their victory was a surreal experience—made even more uncomfortable by their attempts to put me at ease.

"You have done more than enough . . . more than enough for the RVN [Republic of Vietnam]," said NVA Major Huyen, head of the official reception committee

---

*The Four Party Joint Military Team (FPJMT) had been set up by the Paris Accords to negotiate on the POW/MIA issue.

33. Final Days of South Vietnam

in Hanoi, "and you have no reason to feel badly." He then went on to give me the North Vietnamese terms for the U.S. withdrawal from Saigon.

"The U.S. Delegation, FPJMT *must* stay" he said, "to accomplish its humanitarian tasks." As usual he linked Article 8b of the Paris Accords relating to the MIA issue to Article 21 dealing with reparation aid. "The DAO *must* go," he said, "It is only the military advisors that must go."

"The Embassy must work out its own future," Major Huyen continued, going to great pains to make the point that there was no reason friendly relations could not be established between the U.S. and North Vietnam.

On the return flight to Saigon those terms were reiterated by Colonel Tu, head of the FPJMT's North Vietnamese Delegation. Earlier I had said to him, "You know you never beat us on the battlefield!" His reply was a short lesson in strategy. "That may be true," he said, "but it is also irrelevant."

On April 29—fully prepared to stay in-country after Saigon's fall—our six-man FPJMT contingent moved from our headquarters in the DAO compound to the U.S. Embassy downtown. We arrived just in time to find that Secretary Kissinger, reportedly in a pique over being "betrayed" by Le Duan, had ordered all U.S. personnel, including the FPJMT, out of Vietnam.

While the evacuation plan had called for an Air America helilift of some one hundred Embassy personnel from the roof to the main evacuation point at the DAO compound at Tan Son Nhut, we found some three thousand American, third-country and Vietnamese evacuees jammed within the Embassy walls. Near-chaos reigned, and Colonel Madison volunteered the services of his team to maintain order and organize the evacuation while the Marine guards manned the perimeter to keep out thousands of additional frantic Vietnamese.

The first order of business was to calm the evacuees, for the specter of the debacle at Da Nang where the mobs made evacuation impossible was ever-present. Thanks to Captain Herrington, Sergeants Herron and Pace, and Specialist Bell, all of whom spoke Vietnamese, the crowd was assured they would not be abandoned. With the help of Tom Stebbins, a missionary who spoke fluent Vietnamese, I too worked at calming the evacuees.

The main evacuation at the DAO compound began after initial delays at about 4:00 P.M. on April 29th as Marine CH-46 *Sea Knight* and CH-53 *Sea Stallion* helicopters started moving evacuees to ships of the U.S. fleet offshore. By 8:00 P.M. the DAO evacuation was complete, and at 12:12 A.M. on the 30th, the last of the Marine security force departed and the old MACV headquarters was destroyed by preset demolition charges.

Meanwhile the Embassy evacuation, although sporadic, continued apace. By 4:20 A.M. on April 30, only 460 evacuees remained within the Embassy walls. Six CH-53 helilifts would have completed the operation. But that was not to be. Because of a breakdown in communications, fleet commanders thought they were dealing with a bottomless pit and recommended that the evacuation be terminated. By order of President Ford, Ambassador Martin and his staff left at 4:45 A.M. and our FPJMT personnel at 5:30 A.M.

The 420 evacuees to whom we had given our solemn word, now realizing they had been abandoned, began pressing at the Marine guards as they withdrew into the Embassy. But it was all over.

The evacuation of the U.S. Embassy in Saigon had turned out to be the Vietnam War writ small. Our intentions were good, but the execution was fatally flawed. For those of us who were there, it was a shameful day to be an American.

Recommended additional reading: One of the best accounts of the Saigon evacuation is Stuart A. Herrington's Peace With Honor? (Presidio, 1983). For the final days, Arnold Isaac's Without Honor (Johns Hopkins University, 1983) is recommended, as is David Butler's The Fall of Saigon (Simon & Schuster, 1985).

How the Seventies Changed America

The "loser decade" that at first seemed nothing more than a breathing space between the high drama of the 1960s and whatever was coming next is beginning to reveal itself as a bigger time than we thought

Nicholas Lemann

Nicholas Lemann, a national correspondent for The Atlantic, *is the author of* The Promised Land: The Great Black Migration and How It Changed America, *published by Alfred A. Knopf [1991].*

"That's it," Daniel Patrick Moynihan, then U.S. ambassador to India, wrote to a colleague on the White House staff in 1973 on the subject of some issue of the moment. "Nothing will happen. But then nothing much is going to happen in the 1970s anyway."

Moynihan is a politician famous for his predictions, and this one seemed for a long time to be dead-on. The seventies, even while they were in progress, looked like an unimportant decade, a period of cooling down from the white-hot sixties. You had to go back to the teens to find another decade so lacking in crisp, epigrammatic definition. It only made matters worse for the seventies that the succeeding decade started with a bang. In 1980 the country elected the most conservative President in its history, and it was immediately clear that a new era had dawned. (In general the eighties, unlike the seventies, had a perfect dramatic arc. They peaked in the summer of 1984, with the Los Angeles Olympics and the Republican National Convention in Dallas, and began to peter out with the Iran-contra scandal in 1986 and the stock market crash in 1987.) It is nearly impossible to engage in magazine-writerly games like discovering "the day the seventies died" or "the spirit of the seventies"; and the style of the seventies—wide ties, sideburns, synthetic fabrics white shoes, disco—is so far interesting largely as something to make fun of.

But somehow the seventies seem to be creeping out of the loser-decade category. Their claim to importance is in the realm of sweeping historical trends, rather than memorable events, though there were some of those too. In the United States today a few basic propositions shape everything: The presidential electorate is conservative and Republican. Geopolitics revolves around a commodity (oil) and a religion (Islam) more than around an ideology (Marxism-Leninism). The national economy is no longer one in which practically every class, region, and industry is upwardly mobile. American culture is essentially individualistic, rather than communitarian, which means that notions like deferred gratification, sacrifice, and sustained national effort are a very tough sell. Anyone seeking to understand the roots of this situation has to go back to the seventies.

The underestimation of the seventies' importance, especially during the early years of the decade, is easy to forgive because the character of the seventies was substantially shaped at first by spillover from the sixties. Such sixties events as the killings of student protesters at Kent State and Orangeburg, the original Earth Day, the invasion of Cambodia, and a large portion of the war in Vietnam took place in the seventies. Although sixties radicals (cultural and political) spent the early seventies loudly bemoaning the end of the revolution, what was in fact going on was the working of the phenomena of the sixties into the mainstream of American life. Thus the first Nixon administration, which was decried by liberals at the time for being nightmarishly right-wing, was actually more liberal than the Johnson administration in many ways—less hawkish in Vietnam, more free-spending on social programs. The reason wasn't that Richard Nixon was a liberal but that the country as a whole had continued to move steadily to the left throughout the late sixties and early seventies; the political climate of institutions like the U.S. Congress and the boards of directors of big corporations was probably more liberal in 1972 than in any year before or since, and the Democratic party nominated its most liberal presidential candidate ever. Nixon had to go along with the tide.

In New Orleans, my hometown, the hippie movement peaked in 1972 or 1973. Long hair, crash pads, head shops, psychedelic posters, underground newspapers, and other Summer of Love-inspired institutions had been unknown there during the real Summer of Love, which was in 1967. It took even longer, until the middle or late seventies, for those aspects of hippie life that have endured to catch on with the general public. All over the country the likelihood that an average citizen would wear longish hair, smoke marijuana, and openly live with a lover before marriage was probably greater in 1980 than it was in 1970. The sixties' preoccupation with self-discovery became a mass phenomenon only in the seventies, through homebrew psychological therapies like est. In politics the impact of the black enfranchisement that took place in the 1960s barely began to be felt until the mid- to late 1970s. The tremendously influential feminist and gay-liberation movements were, at the dawn of the 1970s, barely under way in Manhattan, their headquarters, and certainly hadn't begun their

34. How the Seventies Changed America

spread across the whole country. The sixties took a long time for America to digest; the process went on throughout the seventies and even into the eighties.

The epochal event of the seventies as an era in its own right was the Organization of Petroleum Exporting Countries' oil embargo, which lasted for six months in the fall of 1973 and the spring of 1974. Everything that happened in the sixties was predicated on the assumption of economic prosperity and growth; concerns like personal fulfillment and social justice tend to emerge in the middle class only at times when people take it for granted that they'll be able to make a living. For thirty years—ever since the effects of World War II on the economy had begun to kick in—the average American's standard of living had been rising, to a remarkable extent. As the economy grew, indices like home ownership, automobile ownership, and access to higher education got up to levels unknown anywhere else in the world, and the United States could plausibly claim to have provided a better life materially for its working class than any society ever had. That ended with the OPEC embargo.

While it was going on, the embargo didn't fully register in the national consciousness. The country was absorbed by a different story, the Watergate scandal, which was really another sixties spillover, the final series of battles in the long war between the antiwar liberals and the rough-playing anti-Communists. Richard Nixon, having engaged in dirty tricks against leftish politicians for his whole career, didn't stop doing so as President; he only found new targets, like Daniel Ellsberg and Lawrence O'Brien. This time, however, he lost the Establishment, which was now far more kindly disposed to Nixon's enemies than it had been back in the 1950s. Therefore, the big-time press, the courts, and the Congress undertook the enthralling process of cranking up the deliberate, inexorable machinery of justice, and everybody was glued to the television for a year and a half. The embargo, on the other hand, was a nonvideo-friendly economic story and hence difficult to get hooked on. It pertained to two subcultures that were completely mysterious to most Americans—the oil industry and the Arab world—and it seemed at first to be merely an episode in the ongoing hostilities between Israel and its neighbors. But in retrospect it changed everything, much more than Watergate did.

By causing the price of oil to double, the embargo enriched—and therefore increased the wealth, power, and confidence of—oil-producing areas like Texas, while helping speed the decline of the automobile-producing upper Midwest; the rise of OPEC and the rise of the Sunbelt as a center of population and political influence went together. The embargo ushered in a long period of inflation, the reaction to which dominated the economics and politics of the rest of the decade. It demonstrated that America could now be "pushed around" by countries most us had thought of as minor powers.

MOST IMPORTANT OF ALL, THE EMBARGO now appears to have been the pivotal moment at which the mass upward economic mobility of American society ended, perhaps forever. Average weekly earnings, adjusted for inflation, peaked in 1973. Productivity—that is, economic output per man-hour—abruptly stopped growing. The nearly universal assumption in the post–World War II United States was that children would do better than their parents. Upward mobility wasn't just a characteristic of the national culture; it was the defining characteristic. As it slowly began to sink in that everybody wasn't going to be moving forward together anymore, the country became more fragmented, more internally rivalrous, and less sure of its mythology.

Richard Nixon resigned as President in August 1974, and the country settled into what appeared to be a quiet, folksy drama of national recuperation. In the White House good old Gerald Ford was succeeded by rural, sincere Jimmy Carter, who was the only President elevated to the office by the voters during the 1970s and so was the decade's emblematic political figure. In hindsight, though, it's impossible to miss a gathering conservative stridency in the politics of the late seventies. In 1976 Ronald Reagan, the retired governor of California, challenged Ford for the Republican presidential nomination. Reagan lost the opening primaries and seemed to be about to drop out of the race when, apparently to the surprise even of his own staff, he won the North Carolina primary in late March.

IT IS QUITE CLEAR WHAT CAUSED THE Reagan campaign to catch on: He had begun to attack Ford from the right on foreign policy matters. The night before the primary he bought a half-hour of statewide television time to press his case. Reagan's main substantive criticism was of the policy of détente with the Soviet Union, but his two most crowd-pleasing points were his promise, if elected, to fire Henry Kissinger as Secretary of State and his lusty denunciation of the elaborately negotiated treaty to turn nominal control of the Panama Canal over to the Panamanians. Less than a year earlier Communist forces had finally captured the South Vietnamese capital city of Saigon, as the staff of the American Embassy escaped in a wild scramble into helicopters. The oil embargo had ended, but the price of gasoline had not retreated. The United States appeared to have descended from the pinnacle of power and respect it had occupied at the close of World War II to a small, hounded position, and Reagan had hit on a symbolic way of expressing rage over that change. Most journalistic and academic opinion at the time was fairly cheerful about the course of American foreign policy—we were finally out of Vietnam, and we were getting over our silly Cold War phobia about dealing with China and the Soviet Union—but in the general public obviously the rage Reagan expressed was widely shared.

A couple of years later a conservative political cause even more out of the blue than opposition to the Panama Canal Treaty appeared: the tax revolt. Howard Jarvis, a seventy-five-year-old retired businessman who had been attacking taxation in California pretty much continuously since 1962, got onto the state ballot in 1978 an initiative, Proposition 13, that would substantially cut property taxes. Despite bad press and the strong opposition of most politicians, it passed by a two to one margin.

PROPOSITION 13 WAS TO SOME EXTENT another aftershock of the OPEC embargo. Inflation causes the value of hard assets to rise. The only substantial hard asset owned by most Americans is their home. As the prices of houses soared in the mid-seventies (causing people to dig deeper to buy housing, which sent the national savings rate plummeting and made real estate prices the great conversation starter in the social life of the middle class), so did property taxes, since they are based on the values of the houses. Hence, resentment over taxation became an issue in waiting.

The influence of Proposition 13 has been so great that it is now difficult to recall that taxes weren't a major concern

5. FROM THE COLD WAR TO THE 1990s

in national politics before it. Conservative opposition to government focused on its activities, not on its revenue base, and this put conservatism at a disadvantage, because most government programs are popular. Even before Proposition 13, conservative economic writers like Jude Wanniski and Arthur Laffer were inventing supply-side economics based on the idea that reducing taxes would bring prosperity. With Proposition 13 it was proved—as it has been proved over and over since—that tax cutting was one of the rare voguish policy ideas that turn out to be huge political winners. In switching from arguing against programs to arguing against taxes, conservatism had found another key element of its ascension to power

The tax revolt wouldn't have worked if the middle class hadn't been receptive to the notion that it was oppressed. This was remarkable in itself, since it had been assumed for decades that the American middle class was, in a world-historical sense, almost uniquely lucky. The emergence of a self-pitying strain in the middle class was in a sense yet another sixties spillover. At the dawn of the sixties, the idea that *anybody* in the United States was oppressed might have seemed absurd. Then blacks, who really were oppressed, were able to make the country see the truth about their situation. But that opened Pandora's box. The eloquent language of group rights that the civil rights movement had invented proved to be quite adaptable, and eventually it was used by college students, feminists, Native Americans, Chicanos, urban blue-collar "white ethnics," and, finally, suburban homeowners.

Meanwhile, the social programs started by Lyndon Johnson gave rise to another new, or long-quiescent, idea, which was that the government was wasting vast sums of money on harebrained schemes. In some ways the Great Society accomplished its goal of binding the country together, by making the federal government a nationwide provider of such favors as medical care and access to higher education; but in others it contributed to the seventies trend of each group's looking to government to provide it with benefits and being unconcerned with the general good. Especially after the economy turned sour, the middle class began to define its interests in terms of a rollback of government programs aimed at helping other groups.

As the country was becoming more fragmented, so was its essential social unit, the family. In 1965 only 14.9 percent of the population was single; by 1979 the figure had risen to 20 percent. The divorce rate went from 2.5 per thousand in 1965 to 5.3 per thousand in 1979. The percentage of births that were out of wedlock was 5.3 in 1960 and 16.3 in 1978. The likelihood that married women with young children would work doubled between the mid-sixties and the late seventies. These changes took place for a variety of reasons—feminism, improved birth control, the legalization of abortion, the spread across the country of the sixties youth culture's rejection of traditional mores—but what they added up to was that the nuclear family, consisting of a working husband and a nonworking wife, both in their first marriage, and their children, ceased to be so dominant a type of American household during the seventies. Also, people became more likely to organize themselves into communities based on their family status, so that the unmarried often lived in singles apartment complexes and retirees in senior citizens' developments. The overall effect was one of much greater personal freedom, which meant, as it always does, less social cohesion. Tom Wolfe's moniker for the seventies, the Me Decade, caught on because it was probably true that the country had placed relatively more emphasis on individual happiness and relatively less on loyalty to family and nation.

LIKE A SYMPHONY, THE SEVENTIES FINALLY built up in a crescendo that pulled together all its main themes. This occurred during the second half of 1979. First OPEC engineered the "second oil shock," in which, by holding down production, it got the price for its crude oil (and the price of gasoline at American service stations) to rise by more than 50 percent during the first six months of that year. With the onset of the summer vacation season, the automotive equivalent of the Depression's bank runs began. Everybody considered the possibility of not being able to get gas, panicked, and went off to fill the tank; the result was hours-long lines at gas stations all over the country.

It was a small inconvenience compared with what people in the Communist world and Latin America live through all the time, but the psychological effect was enormous. The summer of 1979 was the only time I can remember when, at the level of ordinary life as opposed to public affairs, things seemed to be out of control. Inflation was well above 10 percent and rising, and suddenly what seemed like a quarter of every day was spent on getting gasoline or thinking about getting gasoline—a task that previously had been completely routine, as it is again now. Black markets sprang up; rumors flew about well-connected people who had secret sources. One day that summer, after an hour's desperate and fruitless search, I ran out of gas on the Central Expressway in Dallas. I left my car sitting primly in the right lane and walked away in the hundred-degree heat; the people driving by looked at me without surprise, no doubt thinking, "Poor bastard, it could have happened to me just as easily."

In July President Carter scheduled a speech on the gas lines, then abruptly canceled it and repaired to Camp David to think deeply for ten days, which seemed like a pale substitute for somehow setting things aright. Aides, cabinet secretaries, intellectuals, religious leaders, tycoons, and other leading citizens were summoned to Carter's aerie to discuss with him what was wrong with the country's soul. On July 15 he made a television address to the nation, which has been enshrined in memory as the "malaise speech," although it didn't use that word. (Carter did, however, talk about "a crisis of confidence . . . that strikes at the very heart and soul and spirit of our national will.")

TO REREAD THE SPEECH TODAY IS TO BE struck by its spectacular political ineptitude. Didn't Carter realize that Presidents are not supposed to express doubts publicly or to lecture the American people about their shortcomings? Why couldn't he have just temporarily imposed gas rationing, which would have ended the lines overnight, instead of outlining a vague and immediately forgotten six-point program to promote energy conservation?

His describing the country's loss of confidence did not cause the country to gain confidence, needless to say. And it didn't help matters that upon his return to Washington he demanded letters of resignation from all members of his cabinet and accepted five of them. Carter seemed to be anything but an FDR-like reassuring, ebullient presence; he communicated a sense of wild flailing about as he tried (unsuccessfully) to get the situation under control.

34. How the Seventies Changed America

I REMEMBER BEING ENORMOUSLY IMpressed by Carter's speech at the time because it was a painfully honest and much thought-over attempt to grapple with the main problem of the decade. The American economy had ceased being an expanding pie, and by unfortunate coincidence this had happened just when an ethic of individual freedom as the highest good was spreading throughout the society, which meant people would respond to the changing economic conditions by looking out for themselves. Like most other members of the word-manipulating class whose leading figures had advised Carter at Camp David, I thought there *was* a malaise. What I didn't realize, and Carter obviously didn't either, was that there was a smarter way to play the situation politically. A President could maintain there was nothing wrong with America at all—that it hadn't become less powerful in the world, hadn't reached some kind of hard economic limit, and wasn't in crisis—and, instead of trying to reverse the powerful tide of individualism, ride along with it. At the same time, he could act more forcefully than Carter, especially against inflation, so that he didn't seem weak and ineffectual. All this is exactly what Carter's successor, Ronald Reagan, did.

Actually, Carter himself set in motion the process by which inflation was conquered a few months later, when he gave the chairmanship of the Federal Reserve Board to Paul Volcker, a man willing to put the economy into a severe recession to bring back price stability. But in November fate delivered the *coup de grâce* Carter in the form of the taking hostage of the staff of the American Embassy in Teheran, as a protest against the United States' harboring of Iran's former shah.

As with the malaise speech, what is most difficult to convey today about the hostage crisis is why Carter made what now looks like a huge, obvious error: playing up the crisis so much that it became a national obsession for more than a year. The fundamental problem with hostage taking is that the one sure remedy—refusing to negotiate and thus allowing the hostages to be killed—is politically unacceptable in the democratic media society we live in, at least when the hostages are middle-class sympathetic figures, as they were in Iran.

There isn't any good solution to this problem, but Carter's two successors in the White House demonstrated that it is possible at least to negotiate for the release of hostages in a low-profile way that will cause the press to lose interest and prevent the course of the hostage negotiations from completely defining the Presidency. During the last year of the Carter administration, by contrast, the hostage story absolutely dominated the television news (recall that the ABC show *Nightline* began as a half-hour five-times-a-week update on the hostage situation), and several of the hostages and their families became temporary celebrities. In Carter's defense, even among the many voices criticizing him for appearing weak and vacillating, there was none that I remember willing to say, "Just cut off negotiations and walk away." It was a situation that everyone regarded as terrible but in which there was a strong national consensus supporting the course Carter had chosen.

So ended the seventies. There was still enough of the sixties spillover phenomenon going on so that Carter, who is now regarded (with some affection) as having been too much the good-hearted liberal to maintain a hold on the presidential electorate, could be challenged for renomination by Ted Kennedy on the grounds that he was too conservative. Inflation was raging on; the consumer price index rose by 14.4 percent between May 1979 and May 1980. We were being humiliated by fanatically bitter, premodern Muslims whom we had expected to regard us with gratitude because we had helped ease out their dictator even though he was reliably pro-United States. The Soviet empire appeared (probably for the last time ever) to be on the march, having invaded Afghanistan to Carter's evident surprise and disillusionment. We had lost our most recent war. We couldn't pull together as a people. The puissant, unified, prospering America of the late 1940s seemed to be just a fading memory.

I WAS A REPORTER FOR THE *WASHINGTON Post* during the 1980 presidential campaign, and even on the *Post's* national desk, that legendary nerve center of politics, the idea that the campaign might end with Reagan's being elected President seemed fantastic, right up to the weekend before the election. At first Kennedy looked like a real threat to Carter; remember that up to that point no Kennedy had ever lost a campaign. While the Carter people were disposing of Kennedy, they were rooting for Reagan to win the Republican nomination because he would be such an easy mark.

He was too old, too unserious, and, most of all, too conservative. Look what had happened to Barry Goldwater (a sitting officeholder, at least) only sixteen years earlier, and Reagan was so divisive that a moderate from his own party, John Anderson, was running for President as a third-party candidate. It was not at all clear how much the related issues of inflation and national helplessness were dominating the public's mind. Kennedy, Carter, and Anderson were all, in their own way, selling national healing, that great postsixties obsession; Reagan, and only Reagan, was selling pure strength.

IN A SENSE REAGAN'S ELECTION REPResents the country's rejection of the idea of a sixties-style solution to the great problems of the seventies—economic stagnation, social fragmentation, and the need for a new world order revolving around relations between the oil-producing Arab world and the West. The idea of a scaled-back America—husbanding its resources, living more modestly, renouncing its restless mobility, withdrawing from full engagement with the politics of every spot on the globe, focusing on issues of internal comity—evidently didn't appeal. Reagan, and the country, had in effect found a satisfying pose to strike in response to the problems of the seventies, but that's different from finding a solution.

Today some of the issues that dominated the seventies have faded away. Reagan and Volcker did beat inflation. The "crisis of confidence" now seems a long-ago memory. But it is striking how early we still seem to be in the process of working out the implications of the oil embargo. We have just fought and won a war against the twin evils of Middle East despotism and interruptions in the oil supply, which began to trouble us in the seventies. We still have not really even begun to figure out how to deal with the cessation of across-the-board income gains, and as a result our domestic politics are still dominated by squabbling over the proper distribution of government's benefits and burdens. During the seventies themselves the new issues that were arising seemed nowhere near as important as those sixties legacies, minority rights and Vietnam and Watergate. But the runt of decades has wound up casting a much longer shadow than anyone imagined.

191

New Directions for American History

The cold war dominated American foreign policies for more than four decades. It spawned an arms race that threatened to destroy the planet and was the cause of numerous destructive wars. Despite disagreements over particular responses, it did provide a unifying theme for American diplomacy. That theme vanished along with the Soviet empire. What we have instead is a proliferation of conflicts around the globe, the relevance of which to American interests often is unclear. One merely has to look at the Balkans, at various nations in Africa, and at the Middle East to feel a sense of bewilderment over what, if anything, the United States should do. The last selection in this unit, "America after the Long War," predicts that the end of the cold war will have a profound effect on domestic affairs and "pose daunting new challenges for parties and presidents."

America is a mobile society. In "The Suburban Century Begins," William Schneider argues that the enormous growth of middle-class suburbia will exert an ever-greater impact on many aspects of American life. Suburbanites tend to vote differently than their urban counterparts, they shop in different environments, and they expect and demand participation in local government. Schneider evaluates the suburban phenomenon and its implications for the future of cities that are being abandoned by people.

The essays "The Disuniting of America" and "The Painful Demise of Eurocentrism" present opposing viewpoints on what has become known as "multiculturalism." Arthur Schlesinger, in the first essay, argues that although, of course, attention and respect should be accorded to all racial and ethnic groups, the new emphasis has been on those factors that divide Americans, not on what unites them. This emphasis, Schlesinger believes, can only result in the "Balkanization" of racial and ethnic communities. Then, Molefi Kete Asante, in "The Painful Demise of Eurocentrism," protests that what has passed as "unity" within the United States actually has been the domination of society by white males of European origins, who have structured the system to benefit themselves at the expense of others.

During the 1970s the American government abandoned the long-standing policy of trying to integrate Native Americans into the mainstream in favor of recognizing tribal sovereignty. The implications of this new approach are discussed in "Revolution in Indian Country." Fergus Bordewich contends that the process of taking control over their own destiny has obvious benefits for the various tribes, but at the same time it has caused generational friction among Native Americans and between them and whites living in tribal enclaves.

Many Americans have become concerned over the consequences of immigration from Asia, Latin America, and elsewhere. The complaints are many: that the newcomers take jobs away from American citizens, that they place a growing burden on already bloated welfare and health programs, and that their numbers and language problems threaten to swamp school systems. Earlier immigrants, it has been argued, had to pull themselves out of poverty by their own self-reliance without significant help from government at any level. Frederick Rose, in "Muddled Masses: The Growing Backlash against Immigration Includes Many Myths," takes a look at this proposition and declares that it is wrong.

When the first European settlers came to what is now the United States, they found vast lands of abundant resources peopled only lightly (in European terms) by those whom they chose to call "Indians." Over the course of centuries westward expansion and the subsequent growth of cities radically changed the environment. Forests were cut, land misused, rivers and the very air itself polluted. Some protested early on against this degradation, but only in recent years have major commitments been made to reverse the damages. The article "The American Environment: The Big Picture Is More Heartening than All the Little Ones" concludes that while there is a long way to go, a start has been made and the effort must be sustained.

Looking Ahead: Challenge Questions

Discuss the political, economic, and cultural implications of suburban development.

Few would argue against showing respect for all cultures. But will "multiculturalism" lead to disunity in the United States, or will it help liberate the society from what

UNIT 6

has been the dominant elite? Might it do both? What impact will continued immigration from various parts of the world have on the situation?

Americans traditionally have believed that they must be free to develop the resources they own without interference. Such an attitude has resulted in massive degradation of the environment. To what extent should society attempt to regulate enterprise for the benefit of the present and future generations?

Discuss the implications of the end of the cold war on American society. Why should the welcome demise of a costly and deadly rival cause social disarray?

The real meaning of the 1992 election*

The Suburban Century Begins

William Schneider

William Schneider is a contributing editor of The Atlantic Monthly *and a political analyst for Cable News Network. He is also a resident fellow at the American Enterprise Institute and is currently the Speaker Thomas P. O'Neill Jr. Visiting Professor of American Politics at Boston College.*

The United States is a nation of suburbs. The 1990 census makes it official. Nearly half the country's population now lives in suburbs, up from a quarter in 1950 and a third in 1960. This year will see the first presidential election in which a majority of the voters will in all likelihood be suburbanites—the first election of the suburban century.

That explains the obsessive focus on the middle class in the 1992 campaign. The middle class is who lives in the suburbs. The word that best describes the political identity of the middle class is "taxpayers." Democrats have been talking about "the forgotten middle class," and for good reason. For the past twenty-five years the Democrats have forgotten the middle class. And they have paid dearly.

---

*Editor's note: While many of the political references in this article refer to the elections of 1992, the data used to illustrate the population shift to the suburbs is from the 1990 Census—the most current available. The trends examined in this paper are ongoing, and they underscore the continuing urban problems regarding policies and politics incumbent in resident population losses.

They can't afford to do that anymore. The third century of American history is shaping up as the suburban century. Until 1920 most Americans lived in rural areas. By 1960 the country was a third urban, a third rural, and a third suburban. That balance didn't last long, however. By 1990 the urban population had slipped to 31 percent and the rural population was down to less than a quarter. We are now a suburban nation with an urban fringe and a rural fringe.

The first century of American life was dominated by the rural myth: the sturdy and self-reliant Jeffersonian farmer. By the end of the nineteenth century, however, Americans were getting off the farms as fast as they could, to escape the hardship and brutality of rural life. How could you keep them down on the farm after they'd seen Kansas City?

Most of the twentieth century has been dominated by the urban myth: the melting pot; New York, New York; the cities as the nation's great engines of prosperity and culture. All the while, however, Americans have been getting out of the cities as soon as they can afford to buy a house and a car. They want to escape the crowding and dangers of urban life. But there is more to it than escape. As Kenneth T. Jackson argues in *Crabgrass Frontier*, a history of suburbanization in the United States, the pull factors (cheap housing and the ideal of a suburban "dream house") have been as important as the push factors (population growth and racial prejudice).

The 1990 Census tells the story of the explosive growth of suburbs. That year fourteen states had a majority suburban population, including six of the ten most populous states (California, Pennsylvania, Ohio, Michigan, Florida, and New Jersey).

Five of the nation's ten fastest-growing counties were majority suburban; two others had considerable suburban development. Three were outside Atlanta. Nineteen of the nation's twenty-five fastest-growing "cities" were really suburbs. They included the Los Angeles-area suburbs of Moreno Valley, Rancho Cucamonga, and Irvine; the Phoenix suburbs of Mesa, Scottsdale, and Glendale; and the Dallas suburbs of Arlington, Mesquite, and Plano.

Suburban growth is not likely to end anytime soon. According to the polls, 43 percent of Boston residents, 48 percent of people who live in Los Angeles, and 60 percent of those who live in New York City say they would leave the city if they could. When the Gallup Poll asked Americans in 1989 what kind of place they would like to live in, only 19 percent said a city.

Is there a suburban myth? Sure there is. It has been a staple of American popular culture since the 1950s, from television shows like *The Adventures of Ozzie and Harriet* and *Leave It to Beaver* to movies like *E.T.* The suburban myth was challenged in highbrow culture as soon as it emerged, however, in books like David Riesman's *The Lonely Crowd* (which criticized suburbia's "other-directedness") and William H. Whyte Jr.'s *The Organization Man* (which called it "group-mindedness"). The debunking of the suburban myth has now reached American popular culture, where television comedies like *Roseanne* and *The Simpsons* portray the harsh realities of suburban life—unemployment, dysfunctional families, and, above all, stress.

In 1990 five of the nation's ten fastest-growing counties were majority suburban; two others had considerable suburban development. Nineteen of the twenty-five fastest-growing "cities" were really suburbs.

Suburban stress has not produced any large-scale countermovement back to the cities or out to the countryside, however. Instead, the larger suburbs have become what the author Joel Garreau calls "edge cities"—places where jobs have migrated to follow the population. These, in turn, have spawned more-distant suburbs of their own—"exurbs." The prevailing life-style in all these places remains distinctively suburban, meaning home-owning, homogeneous, and largely white.

The prevailing imperative of suburban life is security—both economic and physical. When I interviewed Dan Walters, a columnist for the *Sacramento Bee* and one of the keenest observers of California politics, he explained to me how the culture and life-style of the suburbs work to undermine political consensus.

"The theory of California," Walters explained, "is, 'I bought this house. It's mine. This is my little preserve.' The first thing the homeowner would do was put up a six-foot fence around his entire house. Then the developers started putting in the fences themselves.

"The next step after that was to put a fence around the entire development and put a guard at the gate. The development became a walled community. These walled communities created their own governmental structures. They might be private structures, like homeowners' associations, that exercised government-like powers. But in some cases they actually created public entities that served as private guardians."

Walters offered the following theory: "Personal security in a time of economic and social uncertainty is a very salable commodity. Developers are not selling security but a sense of security." The result, in his view, was "the loss of a sense of common purpose" in California. "We don't have a social consensus, he said, "so we cannot achieve a political consensus. All politics does is implement the social consensus."

THE DECLINING URBAN SECTOR

In the 1890s the social consensus broke down in this country when declining rural areas rose up in rebellion against urban America. The Populists spoke for the old rural America that was being displaced economically and culturally by immigration and the rise of great cities. The countryside was driven to radical extremes by economic pressure and the loss of political influence. In the election of 1896 the Democrats fused with the Populists and nominated William Jennings Bryan, shutting themselves out of presidential politics for most of the next thirty-six years.

The social consensus is breaking down again in the 1990s. Urban America is facing extreme economic pressure and the loss of political influence. The cities feel neglected, and with good reason: they are the declining sector of American life. Just as the Populists of the 1890s exalted the rural myth, urban leaders of the 1990s are trying to glorify the urban myth.

In 1990 the mayors of thirty-five of the nation's big cities held an "urban summit" in New York City. They published a position paper pleading the case that their urban agenda was, as the title suggested, "In the National Interest." "Urban centers are the focus of national vitality in trade, manufacturing, finance, law and communications," the mayors insisted. "American culture is profoundly affected by the artistic and intellectual communities that thrive in the compressed space of cities." Mayor Tom Bradley, of Los Angeles, warned, "If we do not save our cities, we shall not save this nation."

35. Suburban Century Begins

The mayors wanted to designate the 1990s "The Decade of the City." They called for "a public education campaign around the theme of why cities are essential." Finally, however, they gave in. They said "city" needs to be redefined "to include the entire urban region as a community." If you can't beat the suburbs, join them.

Like the Populists before them, today's urban activists react with rage and frustration to the neglect of their agenda. Jesse Jackson grumbles that the Democratic Party is turning away from its base. Last year he complained about "an unholy alliance between the two parties—leaving the electorate with two names but one party, one set of assumptions, and no options."

Jackson's mission in 1984 and 1988 was to rally the declining urban sector in a populist protest movement. But this year Jackson decided not to run—much to the relief of Democratic strategists, who dreaded the spectacle of Jackson's again extorting concessions from the party's nominee. They fear that Jackson is as out of step with suburban America today as Bryan was with urban America in the 1890s.

When the U.S. Conference of Mayors met in Washington, last January, the Democratic mayors decided not to rally around a presidential candidate. Mayor Raymond L. Flynn, of Boston, the conference president, complained that none of the major contenders performed strongly enough on the urban agenda. "I want a little fire in the belly here for America's cities," Flynn told *The New York Times*. "There's still this hesitancy among the candidates.... We want somebody who's really going to have a feeling of commitment to problems like homelessness and AIDS."

Actually, one Democratic candidate did draw a positive response from the mayors—Larry Agran, the former mayor of Irvine, California. Agran was regarded, of course, as a long shot for the nomination. The mayors' conference was one of the few candidate forums that included him. What he promised was $25 billion in direct, no-strings-attached aid to cities, paid for by a gigantic cut in military spending. Delighted, the mayors said he was the only candidate who understood the needs of urban America.

The mayors and other liberal activists worry that the Democrats are moving toward a suburban agenda. They are right.

6. NEW DIRECTIONS FOR AMERICAN HISTORY

The mayors know that problems like poverty, homelessness, and AIDS can't be solved with middle-class tax cuts and entitlement programs. Even robust economic growth doesn't do the cities much good, as the country discovered in the 1980s. What the cities need is targeted resources. But that's exactly what Democrats are afraid of—redistributive programs that take resources from the suburbs to pay for the problems of the cities. That sounds like the Great Society programs that got the Democrats in trouble with the suburban middle class in the 1960s. But isn't it "in the national interest" to bail out the cities? The suburbs have given their answer: walled communities.

Nowhere has the gap between city and suburb been more dramatically demonstrated than in the notorious not-guilty verdict in the trial of four Los Angeles police officers last April. The trial, which took place in Simi Valley, an overwhelmingly white suburb, produced an incomprehensible verdict. The reaction in the inner city of Los Angeles was one of incomprehensible violence.

THE REPUBLICANS' SUBURBAN EDGE

Presidential politics these days is a race between Democratic cities and Republican suburbs to see who can produce bigger margins. The suburbs are winning.

In 1960 urban areas cast 33 percent of the national vote, 20 percent Democratic and 13 percent Republican. So the Democrats came out of the cities with a seven-point lead. In 1988 the urban vote was down to 29 percent of the total. It split 18 percent for the Democrats and 11 percent for the Republicans. That's still a seven-point lead. Thus, from 1960 to 1988 two things happened to the urban vote: it became smaller, and it became more Democratic. As a result, the Democrats' lead coming out of the cities held constant.

Over the same period the rural vote became smaller and more Republican. So the Republican lead coming out of the countryside also stayed about the same (a two-point lead in 1960, a three-point lead in 1988).

What happened to the suburban vote from 1960 to 1988 was quite different. While the suburbs grew larger, they also became more Republican. In 1960 the suburbs generated a third of the national vote. The suburban third divided 18 percent for the Republicans and 15 percent for the Democrats. So the Republican Party came out of the suburbs that year with a three-point lead. In 1988 the suburbs accounted for 48 percent of the vote. And that vote split 28–20 for the Republicans. Thus they came out of the suburbs with an eight-point lead in 1988—enough to cancel out the Democrats' lead in the cities. The suburbs had arrived, politically.

Presidential politics these days is a race between Democratic cities and Republican suburbs. The suburbs are winning. They are growing larger faster than the cities are becoming Democratic.

The suburbs are growing larger faster than the cities are becoming more Democratic. That has tipped the balance to the Republicans in presidential elections in a number of key states.

Illinois is a case in point. In 1960 Chicago cast 35 percent of the Illinois presidential vote. With a little help from Richard J. Daley's machine, the city voted 63 percent Democratic that year. In 1988 Chicago's vote was down to 23 percent of the Illinois total. With no apparent help from the Daley machine, the city voted 69 percent Democratic.

At the same time, the suburban vote outside Chicago became slightly more Republican, moving from 60 percent for Nixon in 1960 to 62 percent for Bush in 1988. The number of voters in the suburbs grew enormously, however. The suburbs accounted for 26 percent of the Illinois vote in 1960—a quarter less than Chicago. They cast 38 percent of the Illinois vote in 1988—two thirds more than Chicago.

In 1960 the Democrats came out of Chicago with 456,000-vote lead for President. The Republicans came out of the suburbs 254,000 votes ahead. Illinois went Democratic. In 1988 the Democrats came out of a smaller but more Democratic Chicago with a 420,000-vote lead. But the Republican margin was 423,000 votes in the suburbs. Illinois went Republican.

In 1960 Detroit cast 22 percent of the Michigan vote. Seventy-one percent of those votes went Democratic. Kennedy got a 312,000-vote lead out of Detroit. The Detroit suburbs also went Democratic that year, by 84,000 votes. Michigan ended up in the Democratic column.

By 1988 Detroit voted a whopping 85 percent Democratic. But the city was down to eight percent of the Michigan vote. It gave Michael S. Dukakis a 217,000-vote lead. Detroit's suburbs were now voting 60 percent Republican. And they accounted for a third of the Michigan vote. The suburbs gave Bush a 230,000-vote lead. Michigan went Republican.

In 1960 Los Angeles County had two and a half times as many voters as the five suburban counties of southern California. But the Republican lead in the suburban counties (138,000 votes) was already large enough to offset the Democratic lead in Los Angeles County (21,000 votes). By 1988 L.A. County and the southern California suburbs were casting the same number of votes. The Democrats' lead of 133,000 votes in L.A. County was dwarfed by the Republicans' lead of 717,000 votes in the suburbs. A state that had gone Republican by 36,000 votes in 1960 went Republican by 353,000 votes in 1988.

How bad has it gotten for Democrats? Bush's margin in Ohio (477,000 votes) was far larger than his total vote in Cleveland (34,000 votes). His margin in Michigan (290,000) was greater than his total vote in Detroit (44,000). Ditto for Georgia and Atlanta. And for Louisiana and New Orleans. The same was very nearly true for Maryland and Baltimore and for California and Los Angeles. Bush's margin in Missouri (83,000 votes) was about the same as the total number of votes he got in St. Louis and Kansas City together (85,000).

In other words, Bush could have carried most of these states without getting a single vote in their largest cities. Republicans can afford to ignore the cities. But the Democrats, like many urban residents, have to worry about becoming trapped in them—exactly the way the Democrats got trapped in rural America in the 1890s.

THE SUBURBAN VIEW OF GOVERNMENT

Democrats have not done badly among suburban voters in elections below the presidential level. California, for instance, is a heavily suburban state that has voted for the Democratic ticket only once since Harry Truman (the 1964 LBJ landslide), but Democrats have won ten out of twenty-four elections for governor and senator since 1952, have held a majority of California's seats in the House of Representatives since 1958, and have controlled both houses of the state legislature since 1974.

Across the country suburban voters usually vote more Democratic in state elections than in presidential elections. The difference averages between five and eight points in nonsouthern states like California, Illinois, and Michigan. Among suburban voters in southern states like Texas and Florida, Democratic candidates for governor and senator typically do 15 to 25 points better than Democratic presidential candidates.

In 1990 a hundred and seventy congressional districts had majority suburban populations (according to data in the 1980 Census). That was substantially more than the number of majority urban (ninety-eight) or majority rural (eighty-eight) districts. (The remaining seventy-nine districts were "mixed.") Democrats represented more than 80 percent of the urban districts, almost 60 percent of the rural districts, and a bare 50 percent of the suburban districts. The Democrats' ability to sustain a majority in the House of Representatives depends on the party's continuing competitiveness in the suburbs.

And that, in turn, depends on the Democrats' ability to understand the suburban view of government. Suburbanization means the privatization of American life and culture. To move to the suburbs is to express a preference for the private over the public. The architects Andres Duany and Elizabeth Plater-Zyberk offer this disdainful characterization:

> The classic suburb is less a community than an agglomeration of houses, shops, and offices connected to one another by cars, not by the fabric of human life.... The structure of the suburb tends to confine people to their houses and cars; it discourages strolling, walking, mingling with neighbors. The suburb is the last word in privatization, perhaps even its lethal consummation, and it spells the end of authentic civic life.

There is a reason why people want to be confined to their houses and their cars. They want a secure and controlled environment. Suburban commuters show a determined preference for private over public transportation. Automobiles may not be efficient, but they give people a sense of security and control. With a car you can go anywhere you want, anytime you want, in the comfort of your own private space.

Entertainment has also been privatized. Suburbanites watch cable television and rent videos. They can watch anything they want, anytime they want, in the comfort of their own private space. People have control over what they see—remote control. And they don't have to put up with the insecurity and disorder of public spaces. Historically, enjoying public spaces was one of the reasons people lived in cities.

Even public activities like shopping have been privatized. The difference between a mall and a downtown is that a mall is a private space, a secure environment. Young people can hang out there. Old people can "mall walk" for exercise. Those are difficult and dangerous things to do in uncontrolled public spaces. Even the streets of a suburb are not really public areas. Suburban houses have decks, which protrude into private back yards. In the great American suburb there are no front porches.

A major reason people move out to the suburbs is simply to be able to buy their own government. These people resent it when politicians take their money and use it to solve other people's problems.

Suburbanites' preference for the private applies to government as well. Suburban voters buy "private" government—good schools and safe streets for the people who live there. They control their local government, including taxes, spending, schools, and police.

There are rich suburbs (Fairfax County, Virginia) and poor suburbs (Chelsea, Massachusetts); black suburbs (Prince Georges County, Maryland) and Hispanic suburbs (Hialeah, Florida); liberal suburbs (Marin County, California) and conservative suburbs (Orange County, California). Can suburban voters, then, be said to have a defining characteristic? Yes: suburban voters are predominantly property owners. And that makes them highly tax-sensitive.

A major reason people move out to the suburbs is simply to be able to buy their own government. These people resent it when politicians take their money and use it to solve other people's problems, especially when they don't believe that government can actually solve those problems. Two streams of opinion seem to be feeding the anti-government consensus as American politics enters the suburban era. One is resistance to taxes, which is strongest among middle-class suburban voters. The other is cynicism about government, which is strongest among the urban poor and the poorly educated.

Upscale voters are the most likely to say that government has too much power and influence, that taxes should be kept low, and that people should solve their problems for themselves. That's the "elitist" suburban view. Downscale voters express doubts about what government *can* do. They are the most likely to say that public officials don't know what they are doing, that most of them are crooks, that they don't pay attention to what people think, that government is run by a few big interests, and that you can't trust the government to do what is right. That's the cynical, "populist" view. Put the two together and you have a powerful, broad-based, anti-government, anti-tax coalition.

Polls show that people want government to do more about education, the environment, the infrastructure, and health care. But they trust it less than ever. The more expansive view of what government *should* do has been canceled out by the more constricted view of what government *can* do. No one wants to give politicians more money to spend, even if the nation's problems are becoming more serious.

6. NEW DIRECTIONS FOR AMERICAN HISTORY

The last time the nation was in this kind of anti-political frenzy was during the Progressive era, in the early decades of this century. Progressives, however, were anti-political but pro-government. The reforms of that era were aimed at curbing the power of political parties by expanding what Progressives saw as the rational, managerial authority of government (for example, having cities run by professional city managers instead of politicians). They used the attack on politics to justify an essentially liberal agenda: making government more professional.

Today the attack on politics serves an essentially conservative agenda: taking government out of the hands of a professional political elite and making it more responsive to the people. How? By limiting terms, limiting pay, limiting spending, and limiting taxes. In the suburban era, unlike the Progressive era, opposition to politics and opposition to government go hand in hand.

SPEND BROADLY, TAX NARROWLY

The suburbanization of the electorate raises a big problem for the Democrats: How can they sell activist government to a constituency that is hostile to government? The answer is, they have to learn how to talk about taxes and spending in ways palatable to the middle class. There are two lessons the Democrats should have learned by now.

One is that the only social programs that are politically secure are those that benefit everybody. Medicare, for example, is the principal enduring legacy of Lyndon Johnson's Great Society. Like Social Security, Medicare helps everybody, not just those in greatest financial need. The Democrats found it impossible to sustain support for LBJ's War on Poverty, however, precisely because it was not a universal entitlement. It was targeted at the poor.

Consider two kinds of government spending. Public-works spending is salable to middle-class voters. Social-welfare spending is not. Public-works spending involves benefits that are available to everyone and that people cannot provide for themselves—things like good schools, fast highways, safe streets, and a clean environment.

Social-welfare spending is targeted by need. It helps disadvantaged people get things that others are able to provide for themselves, like housing, food, and medical care. That is fine with middle-class voters, as long as they are persuaded that the benefits are going to the "truly needy" and that no one is taking advantage of the system. But middle-class voters tend to be suspicious of programs aimed at creating social change rather than providing public services.

Entitlement programs are like public works. By definition, entitlements are not based on need. People are entitled to a benefit because they belong to a certain category, and it is a category anyone can belong to—the elderly, children, veterans, disabled persons (everyone was once a child, everyone expects to get old, and everyone can join the service or become disabled). True, entitlement programs are wasteful, expensive, and inefficient ways to bring about social change. But that is not their purpose. Entitlement programs, like Social Security, are only incidentally redistributive. In effect, middle-class voters are bribed to support them because they get benefits too.

It is worth remembering that the New Deal was not a social-welfare program. The Great Depression was a natural disaster that affected everybody, the just and the unjust alike. When the Democrats took the White House in 1933, they did not attempt a tremendous program of social change. What they came up with was an ambitious program of public works.

The other lesson for Democrats comes from the Reagan era: Don't raise taxes that hurt everybody. Democrats saw what happened to Walter Mondale in 1984 when he proposed a general tax increase. Suburban middle-class voters, however, are willing to consider specifically targeted fees and taxes. That was the principle behind the highway bill passed in 1987 over President Reagan's veto. The bill designated revenues from the highway trust fund to pay for road and bridge construction. Congress proudly pointed to the fact that the bill did not do anything to increase the federal deficit. Of course, it did not do anything to reduce the deficit either.

An even more ingenious solution to the revenue problem is not to raise taxes or spend government money at all. Just mandate that employers pay more in benefits to their workers. Raise the minimum wage. Require employers to pay for health insurance and grant parental and medical leave. The idea is to expand "workers' rights" and "family rights"—that is, entitlements—by making business, not government, pay for them. These kinds of proposals elicit a great many complaints from business, particularly small business, which bears most of the burden. But they draw few complaints from taxpayers.

According to *The New York Times*, state and local governments have been relying increasingly on special-purpose taxes, revenues frequently raised from specific groups of taxpayers and used for specific purposes. Among the examples: a $10 increase in marriage-license fees in Colorado to pay for child-abuse prevention programs. Higher real-estate taxes for downtown property owners in an eighty-block area of Philadelphia to pay for enhanced security and special street-cleaning services. A dollar a year added to automobile insurance premiums in Michigan to pay for auto-theft prevention programs. Taxes on beer in several states to pay for anti-drunk-driving and alcohol rehabilitation programs.

"The logical place for this to wind up," the criminologist Lawrence W. Sherman told the *Times*, "is that every crime will have its own tax, except for the unpopular offenses that involve the poor or that are not important to middle-class voters." Precisely. Special-purpose taxes are the suburban ideal—not just private government but private taxes.

The message to Democrats is: In order to compete from a suburban electorate, keep spending as broad as possible and make taxes as specific as possible. That is the reverse of urban priorities.

The message to Democrats is: In order to compete for a suburban electorate, keep spending as broad as possible and make taxes as specific as possible.

That, of course, is the exact reverse of urban priorities. The urban agenda consists of broad-based taxes and targeted spending programs: tax as many people as possible in order to provide for the needs of specific disadvantaged groups. That requires means-testing. Probably the most difficult thing to do in politics these days is to sell means-tested programs to suburban voters. They know that they will end up paying for the programs and that the benefits will go to people of more modest means. To middle-class voters, a program that helps the few and taxes the many is an outrage. A program that helps the many and taxes the few seems eminently fair.

THE COLLAPSE OF "OPERATIONAL CONSERVATISM"?

Twenty-five years ago, in *The Political Beliefs of Americans*, Lloyd A. Free and Hadley Cantril described the American public as ideologically conservative and operationally liberal. Their polls showed that Americans professed a belief in small government but at the same time supported a wide range of government subsidies and spending programs. The Democrats ruled by appealing to those operational sentiments. "President Johnson was correct," Free and Cantril concluded, "when he indicated that the argument over the welfare state had been resolved in favor of federal action to achieve it."

The Reagan era appears to have reversed that formulation. During the 1980s public opinion grew more liberal on issues of government spending and intervention. Nevertheless, the anti-tax consensus has held fast. Today's "operational conservatism" is sustained by both continued public resistance to tax increases and widespread cynicism about what government can do. That operational conservatism has enabled Republicans to control the agenda since 1978.

The operational liberalism of the Johnson era was legitimized by the Democratic Party's ability to keep the country prosperous. The New Deal and the Second World War, with their unprecedented expansion of federal power, had saved the country from the Great Depression. Americans are pragmatists. They believe that if something works, it must be right. If liberalism meant prosperity, as it did from the 1930s through the 1960s, then it was all right with most Americans.

The operational conservatism of the Reagan era also had pragmatic roots. It was legitimized by the Republican Party's ability to keep the country prosperous. The Reagan Revolution, with its tax cuts and its unprecedented attack on federal power, saved the country from the Great Inflation. As long as low taxes and limited government worked, Americans had no quarrel with Reaganomics.

But Reaganomics isn't working anymore. *The Boston Globe* has reported that after four years in office, Bush is likely to end up with the poorest record of economic growth of any President since Harry Truman. Economists estimate that the country's average annual growth rate from 1989 through 1992 will be 1.6 percent—far lower than the yearly growth rate under Ronald Reagan (3.0 percent), Jimmy Carter (3.1 percent), Richard Nixon and Gerald Ford (2.2 percent), and Lyndon Johnson (4.6 percent). No President with that kind of record is supposed to be reelected. During his 1988 campaign Bush promised to create thirty million new jobs in eight years. At the rate he is going, fewer than five million will have been created by the end of 1996.

Bush's failure gives Democrats an opportunity to woo the middle-class vote on the economic issue—but only if they understand the middle-class view of government. In 1988 Michael Dukakis went after middle-class voters the same way Democrats have always gone after constituencies. His message was: You've got a problem; we've got a program.

Dukakis had a program to provide child care to families with working parents. He had a program to help young families afford home mortgages. He had a program to help students cope with college-tuition costs. He had a program to provide health insurance to all working Americans. His programs were, for the most part, ingeniously designed to be self-financing. The Democrats could do it all without a tax increase. How? All you had to do was read the position papers.

But middle-class voters were suspicious of government programs. They figured that they would end up paying for the programs while the benefits would go to someone else. George Bush's answer to "the middle-class squeeze" was far more persuasive. What he promised middle-class voters was prosperity. "I am optimistic and I believe we can keep this long expansion going," Bush said in the second campaign debate.

That's what the middle class wanted to hear. Their message to the candidates was: Just protect our jobs, keep the paychecks coming in, and hold taxes down. We'll solve our problems for ourselves. We'll send our kids to college. You just keep the recovery going.

But Bush didn't. And now he's in danger of losing the middle class. Some Republicans believe that if they lose middle-class votes on the economy, they can get them back with an appeal to values. A Republican strategist told *The New York Times* early this year, "If you look at the middle class as just this monolithic group driven by economic self-interest, I think that's wrong . . . that's what the Democrats are doing right now, and I think they'll get blindsided by a whole set of values and other issues that will appeal to these voters."

The problem with that argument is that middle-class voters are well educated and tend to be moderate on social issues. Democrats, too, can appeal to their values. If the Supreme Court votes to overturn *Roe* v. *Wade* this year, Republicans will find themselves on the defensive on values as well as economics.

On social issues, the suburban voters of the 1990s are quite different from the silent majority of the 1970s or the Reagan Democrats of the 1980s. They are not backlash voters. Look at California, the model for the new suburban electorate. Since the passage of Proposition 13, in 1978, California has tended to be tax-averse and stingy with public funds. But it is also one of the most environmentally conscious and pro-choice states in the country.

New Jersey Senator Bill Bradley knows these voters. He is one of them, and he almost got destroyed by their tax revolt in his own state. In a deeply felt and highly personal speech delivered in the Senate last July, Bradley accused President Bush of "inflaming racial tension to perpetuate power and then using that power to reward the rich and ignore the poor." Bradley said to Bush, "You have tried to turn the Willie Horton code of 1988 into the quotas code of 1992."

Bradley's message was a simple and powerful *"J'accuse."* He didn't accuse Bush of being a racist. He accused him of dividing the country and failing to provide moral leadership. And he came

6. NEW DIRECTIONS FOR AMERICAN HISTORY

THE SOUTHERN STRATEGY
Total electoral votes: 271

MAPS BY BETTE DUKE

close to accusing Bush of being a hypocrite. "We measure our leader by what he says and by what he does," Bradley said. "If both what he says and what he does are destructive of racial harmony, we must conclude that he wants to destroy racial harmony."

In an interview later in his office, Bradley told me that he believes there are a lot of voters out there who feel the way he does. He described them as "independent suburban voters who are under fifty and who care about civil rights, who care about America's role in the world, who are concerned about the budget deficit because they are starting to have kids."

He didn't think those voters could be reached by appealing to their racial or economic resentment. One had to appeal to their aspirations and ideals. "They define our national identity partly in terms of ethnic and racial harmony," Bradley explained. The Democrats can get them by exposing the Republicans as the party of divisiveness and intolerance. "They're going to turn off," Bradley said, once they know they're being asked to support "someone whose path to power has been to destroy that harmony, consciously, explicitly, and deliberately."

Bradley is on to something. The swing voters in the electorate today are young, well educated, moderate, and independent. They fill the suburbs of states like New Jersey and California. They have been voting Republican, not because of race but because they see the Democrats as either corrupt or fiscally incompetent. These voters are uncomfortable with the Republican positions on race and abortion; at least, they will be if the Republicans keep pursuing the "southern strategy"—that is, running on the same conservative social values they used in 1988 to portray Michael Dukakis as outside the national mainstream.

A SOUTHERN OR A SUBURBAN STRATEGY?

These days, democratic presidential candidates consistently do worse in the South than in any other part of the country. Even Carter could not hold the South against Reagan in 1980. Democrats can either try to win it back or pursue a suburban or "California" strategy—go for the industrial states of the West Coast, the Midwest, and the Northeast.

Which strategy seems more promising for 1992? If you rank the states by the average vote they gave Jimmy Carter in 1976 and 1980, you get the southern strategy. The two elections in which the Democrats did best in California, relative to the national average, were 1972 and 1988. Those were the years when the Democrats nominated New Politics liberals, George McGovern and Michael Dukakis. If you average the 1972 and 1988 Democratic votes and rank the states, you have the suburban strategy.

There are eleven states (plus the District of Columbia) that the Democrats would have to carry under either strategy to get an electoral-vote majority. The eleven states are West Virginia, Rhode Island, Minnesota, Maryland, Massachusetts, Delaware, New York, Hawaii, Missouri, Pennsylvania, and Wisconsin. These are the Democrats' base. Seven of them are in the North and East. The Democrats averaged 53.5 percent of the vote in these states and the District in 1988. Eight went for Dukakis, while the other four (Pennsylvania, Maryland, Missouri, and Delaware) voted for Bush.

Under the suburban strategy, the Democrats would need to carry eleven additional states, mostly on the West Coast and in the industrial Midwest. Only three of those states went Democratic in 1988. But the vote tended to be close. On average, the eleven states needed for the suburban strategy voted 48.4 percent Democratic In 1988.

The southern strategy also adds eleven new states to the Democratic base. All of them are southern. Not a single one voted for Dukakis in 1988.

200

35. Suburban Century Begins

THE SUBURBAN STRATEGY
Total electoral votes: 270

The Democrats averaged only 41.0 percent of the vote in these eleven states.

This means that it would take a much stronger swing to get the South to vote Democratic in 1992 than it would to build a winning coalition outside the South. Dukakis was supposed to be pursuing a suburban strategy in 1988. In fact, Dukakis did pretty well in the prototypical suburban state, California—47.6 percent, two points better than he did in the country as a whole. In both 1976 and 1980 Carter did worse in California than he did in the country as a whole. Nevertheless, Democrats know one thing about Dukakis: he was a disaster. He got wiped out in the South, despite the presence of Texas Senator Lloyd Bentsen on the ticket.

The southern strategy is the anti-Dukakis strategy. It targets Reagan Democrats, the white, blue-collar constituency that is Democratic by heritage but has abandoned the Democratic Party in presidential elections since the civil-rights movement of the 1960s. Reagan Democrats tend to be liberal on economic issues (pro-labor, pro-"fairness") and conservative on social issues (race, religion, and foreign policy). In other words, they are populists.

The southern strategy means going after the states where Dukakis was weakest in 1988—and where the Democrats have been weakest for twenty-five years.

The alternative is to build strength in the states where Dukakis did relatively well, like California. That requires a suburban strategy, which would target the so-called "new collar" Baby Boom voters. (Southern suburban voters, in contrast, are usually very conservative socially and economically, and therefore much harder for the Democrats to capture.) They are relatively affluent and well educated. They tend to be fiscally conservative and socially liberal, the antithesis of populism. They are independent by heritage and anti-establishment by inclination. They don't like racial politics. They are pro-choice on abortion. And they feel betrayed by George Bush on the economy.

Ross Perot's prospective candidacy as an independent helps make the case for the suburban strategy. The polls show Perot running strongest in the West. Perot could take enough votes from Bush to tilt this historically Republican region to the Democrats—but only if Clinton makes a credible showing in a region where he, too, is weak.

To win back the middle class, Democrats will have to regain credibility on the issue of economic growth. They will have to persuade the voters that Democrats can manage the economy better than Republicans. The recession gives the Democrats an opportunity—but only an opportunity—to do that.

Bill Clinton, the presumptive Democratic nominee, pitches his message directly at what he calls "the forgotten middle class." He calls on Democrats to abandon the "tax and spend" policies of the past. He criticizes congressional Democrats for contributing to the mismanagement of the economy during the 1980s. He talks about restoring a sense of personal responsibility. That's a subtle way of trying to change the Democratic Party's image. More personal responsibility means less government responsibility. It's a way of saying, "We're not going to have a program for every problem. People are basically responsible for themselves. That's the middle-class way."

If New York Governor Mario M. Cuomo had run for President, Bill Clinton would have been Gary Hart, the candidate of new ideas. Instead, after Paul Tsongas wan the New Hampshire primary, Clinton was thrust into the role of Walter Mondale, the fairness candidate.

Clinton is not an Old Politics Democrat, however. The candidate who came closest to that message in 1992 was Tom Harkin. Harkin's departure from the race in early March marked a turning point. He was the last New Dealer. None of the other Democrats defended the party's traditional message of taxing, spending, and big government, and its championing of big labor.

6. NEW DIRECTIONS FOR AMERICAN HISTORY

In fact, the three Democrats who have done best this year, Clinton, Tsongas, and Jerry Brown, share a skeptical, pragmatic view of government. Clinton, after all, chaired the Democratic Leadership Council, an organization whose objective has been to move the Democratic Party away from interest-group liberalism (and from Jesse Jackson, who has referred to the DLC as "Democrats for the Leisure Class"). Clinton's message, like that of Tsongas, is aimed squarely at the suburban middle class.

Clinton won the primaries by combining the South with the Democrats' shrinking urban base. That is not a formula for victory in November, however. The South is no longer solidly Democratic. And the urban base doesn't have enough votes anymore. The Democrats have to break into the suburbs by proving that they understand something they have never made an effort to understand in the past—namely, the values and priorities of suburban America.

Clinton may be able to do that. But he also has to do something else: overcome unusually strong personal negatives. In some ways Clinton is in the same situation that Ronald Reagan was in 1980. As unpopular as Carter was that year, the voters were afraid of Reagan. They saw him as a right-wing extremist who might start a war or throw old people out in the snow. The election remained a dead heat until the last few days of the campaign, when Reagan took advantage of the final debate to recast the election as a referendum on Carter's record ("Ask yourself, are you better off than you were four years ago?"). Reagan also reassured the voters that he was not a monster and would not do the foolish things he often said he wanted to do. Things were so bad under Carter that the voters finally decided they had to have change. The country couldn't keep going the way it was going. So they took a chance and elected Reagan.

Bill Clinton has a harder task. He must reassure voters of his basic integrity. He may be able to do it, because he is a skillful and accomplished politician. That is his strength. It is also his weakness, because 1992 is a year when the voters do not seem to be looking for a skillful and accomplished politician—as the rise of Perot, the populist billionaire anti-politician, indicates.

Clinton is a master at having everything both ways. As he tries to straddle the South and the suburbs, the shrinking Democratic base and the swing voters of the middle class, that quality of his political persona and his personal character will be put to the test. In fact, he will face two tests. One test is whether he can do it. The other is whether the voters want someone who can do it.

The Disuniting of America

Arthur M. Schlesinger, Jr.

The fading away of the cold war has brought an era of ideological conflict to an end. But it has not, as forecast, brought an end to history. One set of hatreds gives way to the next. Lifting the lid of ideological repression in eastern Europe releases ethnic antagonisms deeply rooted in experience and in memory. The disappearance of ideological competition in the third world removes superpower restraints on national and tribal confrontations. As the era of ideological conflict subsides, humanity enters—or, more precisely, re-enters—a possibly more dangerous era of ethnic and racial animosity.

For the mutual antipathy of tribes is one of the oldest things in the world. The history of our planet has been in great part the history of the mixing of peoples. Mass migrations produce mass antagonisms. The fear of the Other is among the most instinctive human reactions. Today, as the twentieth century draws to an end, a number of factors—not just the evaporation of the cold war but, more profoundly, the development of swifter modes of communication and transport, the acceleration of population growth, the breakdown of traditional social structures, the persistence of desperate poverty and want—converge to stimulate mass migrations across national frontiers and thereby to make the mixing of peoples a major problem for the century that lies darkly ahead.

What happens when people of different ethnic origins, speaking different languages and professing different religions, settle in the same geographical locality and live under the same political sovereignty? Unless a common purpose binds them together, tribal hostilities will drive them apart. Ethnic and racial conflict, it seems evident, will now replace the conflict of ideologies as the explosive issue of our times.

On every side today ethnicity is the cause of the breaking of nations. The Soviet Union, Yugoslavia, India, South Africa are all in crisis. Ethnic tensions disturb and divide Sri Lanka, Burma, Ethiopia, Indonesia, Iraq, Lebanon, Israel, Cyprus, Somalia, Nigeria, Liberia, Angola, Sudan, Zaire, Guyana, Trinidad—you name it. Even nations as stable and civilized as Britain and France, Belgium and Spain and Czechoslovakia, face growing ethnic and racial troubles. "The virus of tribalism," says the Economist, "risks becoming the AIDS of international politics—lying dormant for years, then flaring up to destroy countries."

Take the case of our neighbor to the north. Canada has long been considered the most sensible and placid of nations. "Rich, peaceful and, by the standards of almost anywhere else, enviably successful," the Economist observes: yet today "on the brink of bust-up." Michael Ignatieff (the English-resident son of a Russian-born Canadian diplomat and thus an example of the modern mixing of peoples) writes of Canada, "Here we have one of the five richest nations on earth, a country so uniquely blessed with space and opportunity that the world's poor are beating at the door to get in, and it is tearing itself apart. . . . If one of the top five developed nations on earth can't make a federal, multiethnic state work, who else can?"

The answer to that increasingly vital question has been, at least until recently, the United States.

Now how have Americans succeeded in pulling off this almost unprecedented trick? Other countries break up because they fail to give ethnically diverse peoples compelling reasons to see themselves as part of the same nation. The United States has worked, thus far, because it has offered such reasons. What is it then that, in the absence of a common ethnic origin, has held Americans together over two turbulent centuries? For America was a multiethnic country from the start. Hector St. John de Crèvecoeur emigrated from France to the American colonies in 1759, married an American

6. NEW DIRECTIONS FOR AMERICAN HISTORY

woman, settled on a farm in Orange County, New York, and published his *Letters from an American Farmer* during the American Revolution. This eighteenth-century French American marveled at the astonishing diversity of the other settlers—"a mixture of English, Scotch, Irish, French, Dutch, Germans, and Swedes," a "strange mixture of blood" that you could find in no other country.

Ethnic and racial conflict will now replace the conflict of ideologies as the explosive issue of our times.

He recalled one family whose grandfather was English, whose wife was Dutch, whose son married a Frenchwoman, and whose present four sons had married women of different nationalities. "From this promiscuous breed," he wrote, "that race now called Americans have arisen." (The word *race* as used in the eighteenth and nineteenth centuries meant what we mean by nationality today; thus people spoke of "the English race," "the German race," and so on.) What, Crèvecoeur mused, were the characteristics of this suddenly emergent American race? *Letters from an American Farmer* propounded a famous question: "What then is the American, this new man?" (Twentieth-century readers must overlook eighteenth-century male obliviousness to the existence of women.)

Crèvecoeur gave his own question its classic answer: *"He* is an American, who leaving behind him all his ancient prejudices and manners, receives new ones from the new mode of life he has embraced, the new government he obeys, and the new rank he holds. The American is a new man, who acts upon new principles. . . . *Here individuals of all nations are melted into a new race of men."*

E pluribus unum. The United States had a brilliant solution for the inherent divisibility of a multiethnic society: the creation of a brand-new national identity, carried forward by individuals who, in forsaking old loyalties and joining to make new lives, melted away ethnic differences. Those intrepid Europeans who had torn up their roots to brave the wild Atlantic *wanted* to forget a horrid past and to embrace a hopeful future. They *expected* to become Americans. Their goals were escape, deliverance, assimilation. They saw America as a transforming nation, banishing dismal yesterdays and developing a unique national character based on common political ideals and shared experiences. The point of America was not to preserve old cultures, but to forge a new *American* culture.

One reason why Canada, despite all its advantages, is so vulnerable to schism is that, as Canadians freely admit, their country lacks such a unique national identity. Attracted variously to Britain, France, and the United States, inclined for generous reasons to respect diverse ethnic inheritances, Canadians have never developed a strong sense of what it is to be a Canadian. As Sir John Macdonald, their first prime minister, put it, Canada has "too much geography and too little history."

The United States has had plenty of history. From the Revolution on, Americans have had a powerful national creed. The vigorous sense of national identity accounts for our relative success in converting Crèvecoeur's "promiscuous breed" into one people and thereby making a multiethnic society work.

This is not to say that the United States has ever fulfilled Crèvecoeur's ideal. New waves of immigration brought in people who fitted awkwardly into a society that was inescapably English in language, ideals, and institutions. For a long time the Anglo-Americans dominated American culture and politics. The pot did not melt everybody, not even all the white immigrants.

As for the nonwhite peoples—those long in America whom the European newcomers overran and massacred, or those others brought against their will from Africa and Asia—deeply bred racism put them all—red Americans, black Americans, yellow Americans, brown Americans—well outside the pale. The curse of racism was the great failure of the American experiment, the glaring contradiction of American ideals and the still crippling disease of American life.

Yet even nonwhite Americans, miserably treated as they were, contributed to the formation of the national identity. They became members, if third-class members, of American society and helped give the common culture new form and flavor. The infusion of non-Anglo stocks and the experience of the New World steadily reconfigured the British legacy and made the United States, as we all know, a very different country today from Britain.

Crèvecoeur's vision of America prevailed through most of the two centuries of the history of the United States. But the twentieth century has brought forth a new and opposing vision. One world war destroyed the old order of things and launched Woodrow Wilson's doctrine of the self-determination of peoples. Twenty years after, a second world war dissolved the western colonial empires and intensified ethnic and racial militancy around the planet. In the United States itself new laws eased entry for immigrants from South America, Asia, and Africa and altered the composition of the American people.

In a nation marked by an even stranger mixture of blood than Crèvecoeur had known, his celebrated question is asked once more, with a new passion—and a new answer. Today many Americans turn away from the historic goal of "a new race of man." The escape from origins has given way to the search for roots. The "ancient prejudices and manners" disowned by Crèvecoeur have made a surprising comeback. A cult of ethnicity has arisen both among non-Anglo whites and among nonwhite minorities.

The eruption of ethnicity had many good consequences. The American culture began at last to give shamefully overdue recognition to the achievements of minorities subordinated and spurned during the high noon of Anglo dominance. American education began at last to acknowledge the existence and significance of the great swirling world beyond Europe. All this was to the good. Of course history should be taught from a variety of perspectives. Let our children try to imagine the arrival of Columbus from the viewpoint of those who met him as well as from those who sent him. Living on a shrinking planet, aspiring to global leadership, Americans must learn much more about other races, other cultures, other continents. As they do, they acquire a more complex and invigorating sense of the world—and of themselves.

But, pressed too far, the cult of ethnicity has had bad consequences too. The new ethnic gospel rejects Crèvecoeur's vision of individuals from all nations melted into a new race. Its underlying philosophy is that America is not a nation of individuals at all but a nation of groups, that ethnicity is the defining experience for most Americans, that ethnic

The curse of racism was the great failure of the American experiment, the glaring contradiction of American ideals and the still crippling disease of American life.

ties are permanent and indelible, and that division into ethnic groups establishes the basic structure of American society and the basic meaning of American history.

Implicit in this philosophy is the classification of all Americans according to ethnic and racial criteria. But while the ethnic interpretation of American history like the economic interpretation, is valid and illuminating up to a point, it is fatally misleading and wrong when presented as the whole picture. The ethnic interpretation, moreover, reverses the historic theory of America—the theory that has thus far managed to keep American society whole.

Instead of a transformative nation with an identity all its own, America increasingly sees itself in this new light as preservative of diverse alien identities. Instead of a nation composed of individuals making their own unhampered choices, America increasingly sees itself as composed of groups more or less ineradicable in their ethnic character. The multiethnic dogma abandons historic purposes, replacing assimilation by fragmentation, integration by separatism. It belittles *unum* and glorifies *pluribus.*

The historic idea of a transcendent and unifying American identity is now in peril in many arenas—in our politics, our voluntary organizations, our churches, our language. And in no arena is the erosion of faith in an overriding national identity more crucial than in our system of education.

The schools and colleges of the republic train the citizens of the future. Our public schools in particular have been the historic mechanisms for the transmission of the ideal of "one people." What students are taught in schools affects the way they will thereafter see and treat other Americans, the way they will thereafter conceive the purposes of the republic. The debate about the curriculum is a debate about what it means to be an American.

The militants of ethnicity now contend that a main objective of public education should be the protection, strengthening, celebration, and perpetuation of ethnic origins and identities. Separatism, however, magnifies differences and stirs antagonisms. The consequent increase in ethnic and racial conflict lies behind the hullabaloo over "multiculturalism" and "political correctness," over the iniquities of the "Eurocentric" curriculum, and over the notion that history and literature should be taught not as intellectual disciplines but as therapies whose function is to raise minority self-esteem.

One wonders. Do not the ethnic militants see any dangers in a society divided into distinct and immutable ethnic and racial groups, each taught to cherish its own apartness from the rest? What is ultimately at stake is the shape of the American future. Will the center hold? or will the melting pot give way to the Tower of Babel?

I don't want to sound apocalyptic about these developments. Education is always in ferment, and a good thing too. Schools and colleges have always been battlegrounds for debates over beliefs, philosophies, values. The situation in our universities, I am confident, will soon right itself once the great silent majority of professors cry "enough" and challenge what they know to be voguish nonsense.

The impact of ethnic and racial pressures on our public schools is more troubling. The bonds of national cohesion are sufficiently fragile already. Public education should aim to strengthen those bonds, not to weaken them. If separatist tendencies go on unchecked, the result can only be the fragmentation, resegregation, and tribalization of American life.

I remain optimistic. My impression is that the historic forces driving toward "one people" have not lost their power. For most Americans this is still what the republic is all about. They resist extremes in the argument between "unity first" and "ethnicity first." "Most Americans," Governor Mario Cuomo has well said, "can understand both the need to recognize and encourage an enriched diversity as well as the need to ensure that such a broadened multicultural perspective leads to unity and an enriched sense of what being an American is, and not to a destructive factionalism that would tear us apart."

Whatever their self-appointed spokesmen may claim, most American-born members of minority groups, white or nonwhite, while they may cherish particular heritages, still see themselves primarily as Americans and not primarily as Irish or Hungarians or Jews or Africans or Asians. A telling indicator is the rising rate of intermarriage across ethnic, religious, even (increasingly) racial lines. The belief in a unique American identity is far from dead.

But the burden to unify the country does not fall exclusively on the minorities. Assimilation and integration constitute a two-way street. Those who want to join America must be received and welcomed by those who already think they own America. Racism, as I have noted, has been the great national tragedy. In recent times white America has at last begun to confront the racism so deeply and shamefully inbred in our history. But the triumph over racism is incomplete. When old-line Americans, for example, treat people of other nationalities and races as if they were indigestible elements to be shunned and barred, they must not be surprised if minorities gather bitterly unto themselves and damn everybody else. Not only must *they* want assimilation and integration; *we* must want assimilation and integration too. The burden to make this a unified country lies as much with the complacent majority as with the sullen and resentful minorities.

The American population has unquestionably grown more heterogeneous than ever in recent times. But this very heterogeneity makes the quest for unifying ideals and common culture all the more urgent. And in a world savagely rent by ethnic and racial antagonisms, it is all the more essential that the United States continue as an example of how a highly differentiated society holds itself together.

Low self-esteem is too deep a malady to be cured by hearing nice things about one's own ethnic past. Institutionalized separatism only crystallizes racial differences and magnifies racial tensions.

6. NEW DIRECTIONS FOR AMERICAN HISTORY

THE DECOMPOSITION OF AMERICA

Low self-esteem is too deep a malady to be cured by hearing nice things about one's own ethnic past. History is not likely to succeed where psychiatry fails. Afrocentrism in particular is an escape from the hard and expensive challenges of our society—the need for safer schools, better teachers, better teaching materials, greater investment in education; the need for stable families that can nourish self-discipline and aspiration; the need for jobs and income that can nourish stable families; the need to stop the ravages of drugs and crime; the need to overcome the racism still lurking in the interstices of American society. "The need," William Raspberry observes of his own people, "is not to reach back for some culture we never knew but to lay full claim to the culture in which we exist."

I

The ethnicity rage in general and Afrocentricity in particular not only divert attention from the real needs but exacerbate the problems. The recent apotheosis of ethnicity, black, brown, red, yellow, white, has revived the dismal prospect that in happy melting-pot days Americans thought the republic was moving safely beyond—that is, a society fragmented into ethnic groups. The cult of ethnicity exaggerates differences, intensifies resentments and antagonisms, drives ever deeper the awful wedges between races and nationalities. The end game is self-pity and self-ghettoization.

Now there is a reasonable argument in the black case for a measure of regrouping and self-reliance as part of the preparation for entry into an integrated society on an equal basis. Integration on any other basis, it is contended, would mean total capitulation to white standards. Affirmation of racial and cultural pride is thus essential to true integration. One can see this as a psychological point, but as a cultural point?

For generations blacks have grown up in an American culture, on which they have had significant influence and to which they have made significant contributions. Self-Africanization after 300 years in America is playacting. Afrocentricity as expounded by ethnic ideologues implies Europhobia, separatism, emotions of alienation, victimization, paranoia. Most curious and unexpected of all is a black demand for the return of black-white segregation.

"To separate [black children] from others of similar age and qualifications solely because of their race," Chief Justice Warren wrote in the school-integration case, "generates a feeling of inferiority as to their status in the community that may affect their hearts and minds in a way unlikely ever to be undone." In 40 years doctrine has come full circle. Now integration is held to bring feelings of inferiority, and segregation to bring the cure.

This revival of separatism will begin, if the black educator Felix Boateng has his way, in the earliest grades. "The use of standard English as the only language of instruction," Boateng argues, "aggravates the process of deculturalization." A "culturally relevant curriculum" for minority children would recognize "the home and community dialect they bring to school." (Not all black educators, it

---

The militants of ethnicity now contend that a main objective of public education should be the protection, strengthening, celebration, and perpetuation of ethnic origins and identities.

---

should be said, share this desire to handicap black children from infancy.) "One fact is clear," notes Janice Hale-Benson of Cleveland State University "Speaking standard English is a skill needed by Black children for upward mobility in American society and it should be taught in early childhood.")

If any educational institution should bring people together as individuals in friendly and civil association, it should be the university. But the fragmentation of campuses in recent years into a multitude of ethnic organizations is spectacular—and disconcerting.

One finds black dormitories, black student unions, black fraternities and sororities, black business and law societies, black homosexual and lesbian groups, black tables in dining halls. Stanford, Dinesh D'Souza reports, has "ethnic theme houses." The University of Pennsylvania gives blacks—6 percent of the enrollment—their own yearbook. Campuses today, according to one University of Pennsylvania professor, have "the cultural diversity of Beirut. There are separate armed camps. The black kids don't mix with the white kids. The Asians are off by themselves. Oppression is the great status symbol."

Oberlin was for a century and half the model of a racially integrated college. "Increasingly," Jacob Weisberg, an editor at *The New Republic,* reports, "Oberlin students think, act, study, and live apart." Asians live in Asia House, Jews in "J" House, Latinos in Spanish House, blacks in African-Heritage House, foreign students in Third World House. Even the Lesbian, Gay, and Bisexual Union has broken up into racial and gender factions. "The result is separate worlds."

Huddling is an understandable reaction for any minority group faced with new and scary challenges. But institutionalized separatism only crystallizes racial differences and magnifies racial tensions. "Certain activities are labeled white and black," says a black student at Central Michigan University. "If you don't just participate in black activities, you are shunned." A recent study by the black anthropologist Signithia Fordham of Rutgers concludes that a big reason for black underachievement is the fear that academic success will be taken as a sellout to the white world. "What appears to have emerged in some segments of the black community," Fordham says, "is a kind of cultural orientation which defines academic learning in school as 'acting white.' "

Militants further argue that because only blacks can comprehend the black experience, only blacks should teach black history and literature, as, in the view of some feminists, only women should teach women's history and literature. "True diversity," according to the faculty's Budget Committee at the University of California at Berkeley, requires that courses match the ethnic and gender identities of the professors.

The doctrine that *only* blacks can teach and write black history leads inexorably to the doctrine that blacks can teach and write *only* black history as well as to inescapable corollaries: Chinese must be restricted to Chinese history, women to women's history, and so on. Henry Louis Gates criticizes "ghettoized programs where students and members of the faculty sit around and argue about whether a white person can think a black

206

thought." As for the notion that there is a "mystique" about black studies that requires a person to have black skin in order to pursue them—that, John Hope Franklin observes succinctly, is "voodoo."

The voodoo principle is extended from scholarship to the arts. Thus the fine black playwright August Wilson insists on a black director for the film if his play *Fences*. "We have a different way of responding to the world," Wilson explains. "We have different ideas about religion, different manners of social intercourse. We have different ideas about style, about language. We have different esthetics [sic].... The job requires someone who shares the specifics of the culture of black Americans.... Let's make a rule. Blacks don't direct Italian films. Italians don't direct Jewish films. Jews don't direct black American films." What a terrible rule that would be!

In the same restrictive spirit, Actors' Equity tried to prevent the British actor Jonathan Pryce from playing in New York the role he created in London in *Miss Saigon,* announcing that it could not condone "the casting of a Caucasian actor in the role of a Eurasian." (Pryce responded that, if this doctrine prevails, "I'd be stuck playing Welshmen for the rest of my life.") Equity did not, however, apply the same principle to the black actors Morgan Freeman and Denzel Washington who were both acting in Shakespeare at that time in New York. *The Wall Street Journal* acidly suggested that, according to the principle invoked, not only whites but the disabled should protest the casting of Denzel Washington as Richard III because Washington lacked a hunchback.

The distinguished black social psychologist Kenneth B. Clark, whose findings influenced the Supreme Court's decision in the school-integration case, rejects the argument that blacks and whites must be separated "because they represent different cultures and that cultures, like oil and water, cannot mix." This, Clark says, is what white segregationists have argued for generations. He adds, "There is absolutely no evidence to support the contention that the inherent damage to human beings of primitive exclusion on the basis of race is any less damaging when demanded or enforced by the previous victims than when imposed by the dominant group."

II

The separatist impulse is by no means confined to the black community. Another salient expression is the bilingualism movement, ostensibly conducted in the interests of all non-English speakers but particularly a Hispanic-American project.

Bilingualism is hardly a new issue in American history. Seven years after the adoption of the Constitution, a proposal to print 3,000 sets of federal laws in German as well as English was narrowly defeated in the House of Representatives. (This incident gave rise to the myth, later cherished by Nazi propagandists like Colin Ross, that German had nearly displaced English as America's official language.) In the nineteenth century, newly arrived immigrants stayed for a season with their old language, used it in their homes, churches, newspapers, and not seldom in bilingual public schools, until acculturation reduced and the First World War discouraged the use of languages other than English.

The separatist impulse is by no means confined to the black community. Another salient expression is the bilingualism movement.

In recent years the combination of the ethnicity cult with a flood of immigration from Spanish-speaking countries has given bilingualism new impetus. The presumed purpose is transitional: to move non-English-speaking children as quickly as possible from bilingual into all-English classes. The Bilingual Education Act of 1968 supplies guidelines and funding; the 1974 Supreme Court decision in *Lau v. Nichols* (a Chinese-speaking case) requires school districts to provide special programs for children who do not know English.

Alas, bilingualism has not worked out as planned: rather the contrary. Testimony is mixed, but indications are that bilingual education retards rather than expedites the movement of Hispanic children into the English-speaking world and that it promotes segregation more than it does integration. Bilingualism shuts doors. It nourishes self-ghettoization, and ghettoization nourishes racial antagonism. Bilingualism "encourages concentrations of Hispanics to stay together and not be integrated," says Alfredo Mathew, Jr., a Hispanic civic leader, and it may well foster "a type of apartheid that will generate animosities with others, such as Blacks, in the competition for scarce resources, and further alienate the Hispanic from the larger society."

Using some language other than English dooms people to second-class citizenship in American society. "Those who have the most to lose in a bilingual America," says the Mexican-American writer Richard Rodriguez, "are the foreign-speaking poor." Rodriguez recalls his own boyhood: "It would have pleased me to hear my teachers address me in Spanish.... But I would have delayed ... having to learn the language of public society.... Only when I was able to think of myself as an American, no longer an alien in *gringo* society, could I seek the rights and opportunities necessary for full public individuality."

Monolingual education opens doors to the larger world. "I didn't speak English until I was about 8 years of age," Governor Mario Cuomo recently recalled, "and there was a kind of traumatic entry into public school. It made an immense impression on me." Traumatic or not, public school taught Cuomo the most effective English among politicos of his generation.

Yet a professor at the University of Massachusetts told Rosalie Pedalino Porter, whose long experience in bilingual education led to her excellent book *Forked Tongue,* that teaching English to children reared in another language is a form of political oppression. Her rejoinder seems admirable: "When we succeed in helping our students use the majority language fluently ... we are empowering our students rather than depriving them."

Panicky conservatives, fearful that the republic is over the hill, call for a constitutional amendment to make English the official language of the United States. Seventeen states already have such statutes. This is a poor idea. The English language does not need statutory reinforcement and the drive for an amendment will only increase racial discrimination and resentment.

Nonetheless, a common language is a necessary bond of national cohesion in so heterogeneous a nation as America. The bilingual campaign has created both an educational establishment with a vested interest in extending the bilingual empire and a political lobby with a vested interest in retaining a Hispanic constituency. Like Afrocentricity and the ethnicity cult, bilingualism is an elitist, not a popular, movement—"romantic ethnicity," as Myrdal called it; political ethnicity too. Still, institutionalized bilingualism remains another source of the fragmentation of America, another threat to the dream of "one people."

III

Most ominous about the separatist impulse is the meanness generated when one group is set against another. What Harold Isaacs, that acute student of racial sensitivities and resentments, called the "built-in we-they syndrome" has caused more dominating, fearing, hating, killing than any other single cause since time began.

Blacks, having suffered most grievously (at least in America) from persecution, have perhaps the greatest susceptibility to paranoia—remembering always that even paranoids may have real enemies. After all, considering what we now know about the plots against black Americans concocted by J. Edgar Hoover and executed by his FBI, who can blame blacks for being forever suspicious of white intentions?

Still, the *New York Times*—WCBS-TV poll of New Yorkers in 1990 is startling. Sixty percent of black respondents thought it true or possibly true that the government was making drugs available in black neighborhoods in order to harm black people. Twenty-nine percent thought it true or possibly true that the AIDS virus was invented by racist conspirators to kill blacks.

When Mayor Edward Koch invited the irrepressible Leonard Jeffries of CCNY to breakfast to discuss the "ice people-sun people" theory, Jeffries agreed to come "but said he would not eat because white people were trying to poison him. When he arrived," Koch reports, "I offered him coffee and danish, but he refused it. I then offered to be his food taster, but he still declined."

On another occasion, Jeffries observed that "AIDS coming out of a laboratory and finding itself localized in certain populations certainly has to be looked at as part of a conspiratorial process." After a Jeffries class, 10 black students told the *Times* reporter that AIDS and drugs were indeed part of a white conspiracy. "During the Carter administration," one said, "There was a document put out that said by the year 2000, one hundred million Africans had to be destroyed." "Because of who's being devastated the most, and growing up in the U.S. and knowing the history of slavery and racism in this country," an older black man said, "you can't be black and not feel that AIDS is some kind of experiment, some kind of plot to hit undesirable minority populations."

Nor is such speculation confined to the feverish sidewalks of New York. "Let me make a speech before a black audience," testifies William Raspberry, "and sometime during the Q & A someone is

---

A common language is a necessary bond of national cohesion in so heterogeneous a nation as America.

---

certain to ask if I believe there is a conspiracy against black Americans. It doesn't matter whether the subject is drugs or joblessness, school failure or teen pregnancy, politics or immigration. I can count on hearing some version of the conspiracy question."

The black case is only a more extreme version of the persecution complex—the feeling that someone is out to get them—to which nearly all minorities on occasion succumb. Mutual suspicion and hostility are bound to emerge in a society bent on defining itself in terms of jostling and competing groups.

IV

"The era that began with the dream of integration," Richard Rodriguez has observed, "ended up with scorn for assimilation." Instead of casting off the foreign skin, as John Quincy Adams had stipulated, never to resume it, the fashion is to resume the foreign skin as conspicuously as can be. The cult of ethnicity has reversed the movement of American history, producing a nation of minorities or at least of minority spokesmen—less interested in joining with the majority in common endeavor than in declaring their alienation from an oppressive, white, patriarchal, racist, sexist, classist society. The ethnic ideology inculcates the illusion that membership in one or another ethnic group is the basic American experience.

Most Americans, it is true, continue to see themselves primarily as individuals and only secondarily and trivially as adherents of a group. Nor is harm done when ethnic groups display pride in their historic past or in their contributions to the American present. But the division of society into fixed ethnicities nourishes a culture of victimization and a contagion of inflammable sensitivities. And when a vocal and visible minority pledges primary allegiance to their groups, whether ethnic, sexual, religious, or, in rare cases (communist, fascist), political, it presents a threat to the brittle bonds of national identity that hold this diverse and fractious society together.

A peculiarly ugly mood seems to have settled over the one arena where freedom of inquiry and expression should be most unconstrained and civility most respected—our colleges and universities. It is no fun running a university these days. Undergraduates can be wanton and cruel in their exclusion, their harassment, their heavy pranks, their wounding invective. Minority students, for the most understandable reasons, are often vulnerable and frightened. Racial cracks, slurs, insults, vilification pose difficult problems. Thus posters appear around the campus at the University of Michigan parodying the slogan of the United Negro College Fund: A MIND IS A TERRIBLE THING TO WASTE—ESPECIALLY ON A NIGGER. Decent white students join the protest against white bullies and thugs.

Presidents and deans begin to ask themselves, which is more important—protecting free speech or preventing racial persecution? The Constitution, Justice Holmes said, embodies "the principle of free thought—not free thought for those who agree with us but freedom for the thought that we hate." But suppose the thought we hate undercuts the Constitution's ideal of equal justice under law? Does not the First Amendment protect equality as well as liberty? How to draw a bright line between speech and behavior?

One has a certain sympathy for besieged administrators who, trying to do their best to help minority students, adopt regulations to restrict racist and sexist speech. More than a hundred institutions, according to the American Civil Liberties Union, had done so by February 1991. My own decided preference is to stand by the First Amendment and to fight speech by speech, not by censorship. But then, I am not there on the firing line.

The black case is only a more extreme version of the persecution complex to which nearly all minorities on occasion succumb.

One can even understand why administrators, not sure what best to do for minorities and eager to keep things quiet, accept—even subsidize—separatist remedies urged by student militants. They might, however, ponder Kenneth Clark's comment: "The white liberal . . . who concedes black separatism so hastily and benevolently must look to his own reasons, not the least of them perhaps an exquisite relief." And it is sad, though instructive, that the administrations especially disposed to encourage racial and ethnic enclaves—like Berkeley, Michigan, Oberlin, the University of Massachusetts at Amherst—are, Dinesh D'Souza (himself an Indian from India) points out, the ones experiencing the most racial tension. Troy Duster, a Berkeley sociologist, finds a correlation between group separatism and racial hostility among students.

Moderates who would prefer fending for themselves as individuals are bullied into going along with their group. Groups get committed to platforms and to we-they syndromes. Faculty members appease. A code of ideological orthodoxy emerges. The code's guiding principle is that nothing should be said that might give offense to members of minority groups (and, apparently, that anything can be said that gives offense to white males of European origin).

The Office of Student Affairs at Smith College has put out a bulletin listing types of oppression for people belatedly "realizing that they are oppressed." Some samples of the Smith litany of sins:

ABLEISM: Oppression of the differently abled by the temporarily able.

HETEROSEXISM: Oppression of those of sexual orientation other than heterosexual, such as gays, lesbians, and bisexuals; this can take place by not acknowledging their existence.

LOOKISM: The belief that appearance is an indicator of a person's value; the construction of a standard for beauty/attractiveness; and oppression through stereotypes and generalizations of both those who do not fit that standard and those who do.

Can they be kidding up there in Northampton? The code imposes standards of what is called, now rather derisively, "political correctness." What began as a means of controlling student incivility threatens to become, formally or informally, a means of controlling curricula and faculty too. Clark University asks professors proposing courses to explain how "pluralistic (minority, women, etc.) views and concerns are explored and integrated in this course." A philosopher declined to sign, doubting that the university would ask professors to explain how "patriotic and pro-family values are explored and integrated."

Two distinguished American historians at Harvard, Bernard Bailyn and Stephan Thernstrom, offered a course in population history called "The Peopling of America." Articles appeared in the *Harvard Crimson* criticizing the professors for "racial insensitivity," and black students eventually presented them with a bill of particulars. Thernstrom, an advocate of ethnic history, the editor of the *Harvard Encyclopedia* of *American Ethnic Groups,* was accused of racism. He had, it developed, used the term "Indians" instead of "Native Americans." He had also referred to "Oriental" religion—the adjective was deemed "colonial and imperialistic." Bailyn had recommended diaries of Southern planters without recommending slave narratives. And so on, for six single-spaced pages.

The episode reminds one of the right-wing students who in Joe McCarthy days used to haunt the classrooms of liberal Harvard professors (like me) hoping to catch whiffs of Marxism emanating from the podium. Thernstrom decided to hell with it and gave up the course. A signal triumph for political correctness.

Those who stand up for what they believe invite smear campaigns. A favorite target these days is Diane Ravitch of Columbia's Teachers College, a first-class historian of American education, an enlightened advocate of school reform, and a steadfast champion of cultural pluralism. She is dedicated to reasoned and temperate argument and is perseveringly conciliatory rather than polemical in her approach. Perhaps the fact that she is a woman persuades ethnic chauvinists that they can bully her. Despite nasty efforts at intimidation, she continues to expose the perils of ethnocentrism with calm lucidity.

Ravitch's unpardonable offense seems to be her concern about *unum* as well as about *pluribus*—her belief that history should help us understand how bonds of cohesion make us a nation rather than an irascible collection of unaffiliated groups. For in the end, the cult of ethnicity defines the republic not as a polity of individuals but as a congeries of distinct and inviolable cultures. When a student sent a memorandum to the "diversity education committee" at the University of Pennsylvania mentioning her "deep regard for the individual," a college administrator returned the paper with the word *individual* underlined: "This is a *red flag* phrase today, which is considered by many to be *racist*. Arguments that champion the individual over the group ultimately privileges [sic] the 'individuals' belonging to the largest or dominant group."

The contemporary sanctification of the group puts the old idea of a coherent society at stake. Multicultural zealots reject as hegemonic the notion of a shared commitment to common ideals. How far the discourse has come from Crèvecoeur's "new race" from Tocqueville's civic participation, from Emerson's "smelting pot," from Bryce's "amazing solvent," from Myrdal's "American Creed"!

Yet what has held the American people together in the absence of a common ethnic origin has been precisely a common adherence to ideals of democracy and human rights that, too often transgressed in practice, forever goad us to narrow the gap between practice and principle.

The American synthesis has an inevitable Anglo-Saxon coloration, but it is no longer an exercise in Anglo-Saxon domination. The republic embodies ideals that transcend ethnic, religious, and political lines. It is an experiment, reasonably successful for a while, in creating a common identity for people of diverse races, religions, languages, cultures. But

What has held the American people together has been precisely a common adherence to ideals of democracy and human rights that forever goad us to narrow the gap between practice and principle.

6. NEW DIRECTIONS FOR AMERICAN HISTORY

the experiment can continue to succeed only so long as Americans continue to believe in the goal. If the republic now turns away from Washington's old goal of "one people," what is its future?—disintegration of the national community, apartheid, Balkanization, tribalization?

"The one absolutely certain way of bringing this nation to ruin, of preventing all possibility of its continuing to be a nation at all," said Theodore Roosevelt, "would be to permit it to become a tangle of squabbling nationalities, an intricate knot of German-Americans, Irish-Americans, English-Americans, French-Americans, Scandinavian-Americans, or Italian-Americans, each preserving its separate nationality." Three-quarters of a century later we must add a few more nationalities to T.R.'s brew. This only strengthens his point.

The Painful Demise of Eurocentrism

Arthur Schlesinger cannot see his own Anglo-Saxon bias nor multiculturalism's nourishing contribution to America's core identity.

Molefi Kete Asante

Molefi Kete Asante is professor and chair of the Department of African American Studies at Temple University. He is the author of thirty-two books including three seminal works on the Afrocentric philosophy Afrocentricity, The Afrocentric Idea, *and* Kemet, Afrocentricity, and Knowledge.

Arthur Schlesinger, Jr., won Pulitzer prizes for his books *The Age of Jackson* (1945) and *A Thousand Days* (1965). These works and the *Age of Roosevelt, The Imperial Presidency,* and *Robert Kennedy and His Times* established him as a leading American historian. Yet Schlesinger's latest book, *The Disuniting of America,* serves to call into question his understanding of American history and his appreciation of diversity. As a designated great American historian, he is supposed to know something about what he writes. However, one of the most obvious manifestations of hegemonic thinking in cultural matters is pontification. Measuring the amount of pontification in *The Disuniting of America,* one comes away with a certain distrust of Schlesinger's writing as well as his perspective on American society. This is doubly so if one is an African American.

Schlesinger envisions an America rooted in the past, where whites, actually Anglo-Saxon whites, defined the protocols of American society, and white culture itself represented the example to which others were forced to aspire. He loves this vision because it provides a psychological justification for the dominance of European culture in America over others. In his vision, there is little history of enslavement, oppression, dispossession, racism, or exploitation. In effect, there is no disunion in the Union; adjustments need to be made, for sure, but they are minor ripples in the perfect society. Fortunately, many whites as well as African Americans see this vision as corrupted by the arrogance of political, academic, and cultural dominance. How, they ask, can one have such a vision of America with what we know of our history? Yet this is Schlesinger's perspective on American society.

Alas, the vision is clouded by Afrocentrists, the bad guys in Schlesinger's book, who bring disunity to this perfect world. Trapped in his own cultural prison, Schlesinger is unable to see the present American cultural reality, and I believe he has missed the point of the past as well. The evidence suggests that he holds a nearly static view of America. Perhaps the America of his youth—its academic life, social life, business environment, and political institutions—was framed for him in some version of the white American dream.

There is, of course, a nightmarish side to Schlesinger's vision or fantasy. He peoples his vision with negations, colored by axioms that support no truth but that are ultimately structured to uphold the status quo of white male privilege and domination. Had Schlesinger admitted this as a goal of his book, it would have allowed a more honest footing for discussion and debate. Nevertheless, this mixture of fact and fiction presents itself for analytical deinvention, not national disunity.

DISUNION AND DISBELIEF

Schlesinger might have cited any number of issues as disuniting America: unequal protection under the law, taxation without representation, gender strife, economic class antagonisms, corrupt politicians, rampant anti-Africanism, growing anti-Semitism, or pollution of the environment. Instead, he focuses on the African-American challenge to the educational system, calling it a disuniting element; indeed, he believes it is a frightening development. Why should an Afrocentric position—that is, a position where Africans describe themselves as subjects rather than objects—create such an uproar?[1]

Are we to conclude that Schlesinger does not see the hegemonic imposition of the Eurocentric idea? Or do we conclude that he sees it and understands it and supports it? If he does not see it, then he will not understand the substance of what I am saying in this essay. Hegemonic thinking is like a person standing on the lid of a manhole. The fact that another person will rise out of that manhole means that the person standing on the lid will have to change positions.

---

1. See Molefi Kete Assante, *The Afrocentric Idea* (Philadelphia: Temple University press, 1987).

36. Painful Demise of Eurocentrism

Will the Afrocentric perspective affect the Eurocentric hegemony on information and in education? Absolutely, because our perceptions are altered by new information whether we admit it or not. A lifetime of delusion that denies Africans and Africa a place in human history creates a basic disbelief in facts that are presented in an Afrocentric framework. Indeed, *The Age of Jackson* did not indicate any real appreciation of the nature of Jackson's racism and anti-Indian sentiments. Schlesinger's glorification of Andrew Jackson, whom even Davy Crockett considered a scoundrel, is demonstrative of Schlesinger's disregard for the multi-ethnic, multicultural, pluralistic reality of American society.

Schlesinger envisions an America rooted in the past, where whites, actually Anglo-Saxon whites, represented the example to which others were forced to aspire.

One must be factual, and in trying to be factual I have always believed primary description is better than secondary interpretation. Thus, when Afrocentrists say that George Washington and Thomas Jefferson were slaveowners, *inter alia,* who did not believe in the equality of Africans, that is a fact descriptive of those two individuals. One can excuse the fact on the grounds of interpretation, one can claim ignorance, one can argue that their good points outweighed their bad points, and so on; but the fact is that they believed in the inferiority of Africans. Students must be introduced to this factual information in order to make proper assessments and judgments. Schlesinger would insist that we not mention the racist heritage of the "founding fathers" because that would create disunity. If that be creating disunity, I am guilty, as he claims in his book, and I will create more disunity. Nothing is more valuable than the truth in bringing about national integration.

Eurocentric control of space and time in publishing and the media has meant that legitimate intellectual and scholarly voices of African Americans are seldom heard by whites who refuse to read African-American scholarly journals. The *Journal of Black Studies,* the *Journal of Negro Education,* the *Journal of African Civilizations, Western Journal of Black Studies,* and *Imhotep* are a few of the prominent journals that are accessible to scholars. They remain relatively unread by writers such as Schlesinger, who apparently believes that there is little outside of the "white" journals worth reading. That is a serious mistake in scholarship, because reading the African-American journals would greatly increase appreciation for new findings and new ideas.

Can Schlesinger really believe that only whites or blacks who believe they are white have reasonable ideas? Afrocentrists, who got their degrees from the same institutions as white scholars, tend to have a far broader reading program that allows for more critical leverage to analysis. The fact that cyclopean stone tombs dating from 5700 B.C., among the earliest in the world, have been found in the heart of the Central African Republic may not be a part of one's knowledge base, but if it were known, it would add to any discussion of historical time lines. Yet without reading any of my books or those of other Afrocentrists in depth, as far as I can discern, Schlesinger attempts to paint Afrocentrists as some kind of wild bunch out to create disunity in American society.

What this celebrated white American historian seeks is a dismissal of historical facts related to Africans as insignificant in the American nation. He seems to operate within a closed system of thought, and such systems are prodigious in producing closed minds. Education within such a system is found to produce those who speak a certain restrictive language, use a handed-down political vocabulary, and believe in elves.

The danger, quite frankly, is that Schlesinger's attitude toward difference creates insiders and outsiders, those who are free to define themselves and others and those who are the defined. There is no question in his mind about who will do the defining. Afrocentrists flatly reject this kind of thinking and insist on defining their own reality within the context of society.

To be Afrocentric is not to deny American citizenship. Just as to be a Chinese American, live in Chinatown, employ Chinese motifs in artistic expression, and worship Buddha is not anti-American, the person who believes that the African American must be recentered, relocated in terms of historical referent, is not anti-American. This is neither a destructive nor a disuniting behavior. It suggests the strengths of this country compared to other countries. The conviction that we will defend the rights of all cultural expressions, not just Greco-Roman-Hebraic-Germanic-Viking cultures, must be strongly embedded in our political psyches if the nation is to survive.

In this way we avoid what I call the Soviet problem, that is, the Russification of the empire. Respect for each other's culture must be the guiding principle for a truly remarkable society. Since the American idea is not a static but a dynamic one, we must constantly reinvent ourselves in the light of our diverse experiences. One reason this nation works the way it does is our diversity. Try to make Africans and Asians copies of Europeans and women copies of men and you will force the disunity Schlesinger fears. This does not mean, as some dishonest writers have said, that black children will be taught black information and white children will be taught white information and so forth. No Afrocentrist has articulated such a view, though it has been widely reported in the news.

UNITY IN AMERICA

The unity of America is based upon shared goals, a collective sense of mission, a common purpose, and mutual respect. It should be clear to the reader, upon reflection, that Schlesinger's view of America is too provincial; it is as if he has not outgrown the way of thinking he expressed in *The Age of Jackson.* I believe his view is planted in the narrow confines of a particular ethnic or racial identity. Thus, it cannot produce a harvest of unity. The unity of the American nation is not a unity of historical experiences or cultural backgrounds. Because each of us could give a different version of the same story, there must be an acceptance of pluralism without ethnic or cultural hegemony. Only in this manner can we build a common culture. For the present we have many cultures, occasionally interacting with each other, but we have only one society. This means that it is no longer viable for white cultures to parade as the only American culture.

I find it curious that Schlesinger, who has spent a lifetime championing an elit-

6. NEW DIRECTIONS FOR AMERICAN HISTORY

ist educational program, is now interested in a multicultural one. This may be a result of his professorship at City University of New York, or of the controversy surrounding a number of his colleagues at the City University. I should not be mistaken. I like the idea that Schlesinger sees multiculturalism as important; it is just that he would be the last person I would consider knowledgeable of this field.[2]

There is no particularist multiculturalism or pluralist multiculturalism; there is, quite simply, multiculturalism. I pointed out in response to Diane Ravitch (a deputy assistant secretary of education) who came up with the notions of particularist and pluralist multiculturalisms, that the first is an oxymoron and the second a redundancy. Multiculturalism is not a complicated proposition; it is clear and simple. In a multicultural society, there must be a multicultural curriculum, a multicultural approach to institution building, and so forth.

Afrocentrists say that one should not be able to declare competency in music in America without having been introduced to the spirituals, Duke Ellington, or the blues. Yet every year this happens in major American universities.

AN AFROCENTRIC ORIENTATION

What Schlesinger dislikes in the Afrocentric position is the emphasis on re-centering of African Americans in a subject position vis-à-vis history, culture, and science. However, 374 years of white domination have disoriented, dislocated, and displaced many African Americans. This is the legacy of stealing us from Africa, of dehumanizing and enslaving us. So fearful of Africans were the slave masters that they sought to rob us of our heritage, memory, languages, religion, customs, traditions, and history. In the end, it is true, some of us did lose our way and *our* minds, and decentered, disoriented, and often alienated—would claim that we came to America on the *Mayflower*.

Afrocentricity seeks to understand this phenomenon by beginning all analysis from the African person as human agent. In classes, it means that the African-American child must be connected, grounded to information presented in the same way that white children are grounded, when we discuss literature, history, mathematics, and science. Teachers who do not know this information when it comes to Africans must seek it out from those who do. Afrocentrists do not take anything away from white history except its aggressive urge to pose as universal.

The meaning of this school of thought is critical for all Americans. I make a claim that we must see ourselves within American society, with points of reference in our culture and history. Our children as well as other children must know about us in the context of our own history. The Afrocentric school of thought becomes useful for the expansion of dialogue and the widening of discourse—the proper function of education. The white self-esteem curriculum now present in most school systems is imposed as universal.

We know this curriculum is not universal, of course, but rather specific social studies and humanities information centered on a particular culture. There is nothing fundamentally wrong about a Eurocentric curriculum so long as other cultures are not denied. The real question is whether Eurocentrism can exist without denial of the Other. To speak arrogantly of this model as a conquest model is to assert a claim of right by force, not on the basis of facts nor on the ground of what is useful for this society. We ought to be able to develop a curriculum of instruction that affirms all people in their cultural heritages.

A FINISHED PARADIGM

It is bizarre to find that Schlesinger attacks my vision of a multicultural nation without having read any of my works. At the end of the twentieth century, the United States must be spared the intellectual intolerance, xenophobia, ethnic hatred, racist thinking, and hegemonic attitudes that now seem to be running rampant in Europe.

Schlesinger makes judicious use of the critical remarks of African-American scholars such as John Hope Franklin, Henry Louis Gates, and Frank Snow in order to divide African-American intellectuals into two camps. There are also women who accept the male view of history. There were Jews who accepted the German version of culture. There will always be members of the dominated group who will accept certain ideas from those dominating. We all experience our particular dislocations. But as for me, an American citizen of African descent, I shall never abandon my ancestors' history. Neither would I expect Schlesinger to abandon his, though that is his right. Whatever he does about it, I will not say he is sowing disunity.

Dividing African scholars in order to set off conflict is an old game, but it avoids raising the issue discussed by the Afrocentrists. Why should a monocultural experience and history dominate a multicultural and multiethnic nation? There is no good answer to this question, so Schlesinger believes in shoring up the old, "perfect" order as the best procedure. But it will not wash. His description is of a paradigm that is finished. It is not enough for Schlesinger to cite majority support, since popular belief and mass acceptance are not adequate for validating ideas. Description and demonstration are the principal calling cards of proof, not authoritative pronouncements, even if they come from a well-known historian. Neither hegemony nor power can determine truth.

NATIONALITY AND CULTURE

Schlesinger's book is unfortunate at this stage in national integration and development. He confuses American nationality with American culture. Whether by choice or circumstances, we are American in nationality. So one can say that my nationality and citizenship are American, but my historical and cultural origins are African. My ancestors did not arrive in this country from Europe. They did not see a mountain of possibility but a valley of despair.

It is this distinction, this historical cleavage, that cannot be resolved by some mythical idea that we all came here on the *Mayflower*. The preferred resolution of such dual experiences is a true multiculturalism, where Europeans are seen working for national purpose alongside other people, not in a hegemonic

---

2. There are a great number of intercultural communicationists who have written intelligently on this subject. Schlesinger might have looked at two of my works in this field, *Transracial Communication* and *Handbook of Intercultural Communication*. Others such as Andrea Rich, William Gudykunst, Erika Vora, Tulsi Saral, and Thomas Kochman, have written extensively on the question of culture and cultural interactions.

position. This takes a measure of humility that is not evident in Schlesinger's book. Without a reorientation from conquest, from dominance, from superiority, the whites in this country can never understand the discourse of unity expressed by Africans, Latinos, Asians, and Native Americans.

I agree with Franklin Roosevelt's observation that "Americanism is not a matter of race and ancestry but of adherence to the creed of liberty and democracy." This means that the litmus test for Americanism must not be how Eurocentric a person becomes but whether the person adheres to the idea of mutual individual and cultural respect. One cannot equate a Chinese American's love of Chinese motifs, food, decorations, and myths with a rejection of Americanism: It *is* Americanism. Of course, we all are free to reject our ethnic or cultural past, but that does not mean we do not possess culture.

Schlesinger writes in a very condescending manner: "Nor is there anything more natural than for generous-hearted people, black and white, to go along with Afrocentrism out of a decent sympathy for the insulted and injured of American society and of a decent concern to bind up the wounds." But Afrocentrism is not about sympathy or insult; it is about the proper presentation of factual information in a multicultural society. To frame an argument in the context of the generous hearted doing something for Africans is to miss the point. What we do by making America safe for diversity is to ensure the unity of the nation.

Schlesinger's continuation suggests that his condescension is unabated, "Still, doctrinaire ethnicity in general and the dogmatic black version in particular raise questions that deserve careful and dispassionate examination." This representation seeks to diminish the Afrocentric movement's rational arguments through hyperbole. Doctrinaire ethnicity, if it exists in America is not to be found in the African-American community. He is especially exercised by "the dogmatic black version," which he does not describe in any detail. Yet he says that the Afrocentric campaign most worries him. His problem with Afrocentric scholarship is that he cannot dismiss it. For example, he wants to question the African origin of civilization and counterposes Mesopotamia as the cradle of civilization. But this does not work, either in theory or reality.

THE AFRICAN ORIGIN OF CIVILIZATION

Cheikh Anta Diop wrote in *The African Origin of Civilization* that Africa is the cradle of human civilization. He expanded his argument in his massive work *Civilization and Barbarism,* assembling evidence from disparate sources such as linguistics, botany, osteology, history, and molecular biology. Numerous scholars have supported the arguments Diop made in those books. In fact, Theophile Obenga has shown the origin of medicine, theology, queenship, astronomy, mathematics, ethics, and philosophy in Africa. There is no comparable evidence of antiquity in any other continent.[3]

Mesopotamia does not figure in ancient civilization, either concretely *or* philosophically, at the same level as ancient Egypt. Even were one to take evidence from the ancient Egyptian, Hebrew, Greek, and Ethiopian peoples, one would find that the Nile Valley of Africa rather than the Tigris Euphrates Valley was considered the most ancient cradle of human civilization.

Plato's corpus includes twenty-eight extant dialogues; in twelve of those dialogues, he discusses Egypt, not Mesopotamia, Sumer, or Babylon. Of course, Plato himself was taught in Africa by Seknoufis and Kounoufis. He did not think of Mesopotamia as a high civilization on the level of Egypt. The Hebrew Bible mentions Egypt nearly one thousand times but refers to Mesopotamia no more than twenty times. The Ethiopians refer to Egypt, not to Mesopotamia, in their ancient sacred books, the *Kebra Nagast* and *The Book of Henok.* While I believe Mesopotamia is a significant civilization, I also believe that it is advanced as a sort of contemporary anti-African project, a kind of counterpoint to the African origin of civilization. This is why some writers claim that Mesopotamian civilization can be dated one hundred years prior to the First Egyptian Dynasty. However, dynastic Egypt was

---

3. Theophile Obenga, *African Philosophy in the Time of the Pharaohs* (Paris: Presence Africaine, 1991). Furthermore, the works of Maulana Karenga and Jacob Carruthers are useful documents. See *The Husia,* edited by Maulana Karenga (Los Angeles: University of San Kore Press) and Carruthers, *Essays in Ancient Kemetic Studies* (Los Angeles: University of San Kore Press, 1985).

36. Painful Demise of Eurocentrism

not the beginning of civilization in the Nile Valley. There had been at least sixteen kings of Upper (Southern) Egypt before Narmer (Menes), who is normally given as the first dynastic king. My point is that the ancients did not consider Mesopotamia more important than Egypt; this is preeminently a contemporary project.

Let us examine Schlesinger's assault on the Egyptian scholarship of African scholars. He admits that he is no expert on ancient Egypt and, in a broad stroke for justification, claims, "neither are the educators and psychologists who push Afrocentrism." I do not know what special criteria Schlesinger is using for expertise, but Cheikh Anta Diop, Theophile Obenga, Wade Nobles, Jacob Carruthers, Maulana Karenga, Asa Hilliard, and others have spent more than one hundred collective years in the study of ancient Africa. Their research and publications are accessible and well known to those of us who consider ourselves Afrocentrists. All of these scholars are students of ancient languages: Mdu Netr, the language of the ancient Egyptians, Ge'ez, Greek, and Latin. Although my knowledge of ancient languages is not nearly at the level of the scholars I have mentioned, my familiarity with the ancient literatures is indicated in many of the books that I have written. My book *Kemet, Afrocentricity and Knowledge* explores various aspects of the historiography of ancient Africa.

Schlesinger's attack seeks to undermine the Africanness of the ancient Egyptian. Indeed, he brings three witnesses to his case: Frank Snowden, Frank Yurco, and Miriam Lichtheim. All three of these people have deeply invested interests in the Eurocentric paradigm of history (that is, the projection of Eurocentric concepts in African people). Snowden, a retired Howard University professor, has written on the African image in Greece and Rome. He does not read Mdu Netr and certainly is no scholar of ancient Africa. Yurco, a librarian at the University of Chicago, has produced nothing of the caliber of any of the Afrocentrists. From his Regenstein Library desk at the University of Chicago, Yurco has made a career of responding to Diop, Carruthers, Bernl, Hilliard, and, lately, my book *Kemet, Afrocentricity, and Knowledge*. His ideological perspective appears to fog his analysis. His essay, cited by Schlesinger, in *Biblical Archaeology Review* is a nasty

213

6. NEW DIRECTIONS FOR AMERICAN HISTORY

little piece written against Martin Bernal.

Lichtheim is by far the best-known ancient Egyptian scholar, but the comment Schlesinger chooses to use from Lichtheim is rather strange.

I do not wish to waste any of my time refuting the errant nonsense which is being propagated in the American black community about the Egyptians being Nubians and the Nubians being black. The Egyptians were not Nubians, and the original Nubians were not black. Nubia gradually became black because black peoples migrated northward out of Central Africa. The "Nile Valley School" is obviously an attempt by American blacks to provide themselves with an ancient history linked to that of the high civilization of ancient Egypt.

Neither Schlesinger nor Lichtheim names or quotes any African or African-American scholar as saying anything "about the Egyptians being Nubians." However, it is possible to say that the difference between Nubians and Egyptians was much like that of Sicilians and Italians, Icelanders and Danes, or Germans and Austrians. Lichtheim's comment and Schlesinger's use of it is meant to suggest that the ancient Egyptians and ancient Nubians were of different races. Nubians and Egyptians looked alike and came from the same general culture. In addition, both were black-skinned peoples.

Lichtheim's denial of the blackness (that is, the black-skinnedness) of the ancient Nubians borders on intellectual incompetence because it disregards the available concrete evidence in texts, sculptures, paintings, and linguistics. Lichtheim's statement that the "Egyptians were not Nubians" is correct but misleading. One can say that the French are not Spanish or the Swedes are not Norwegians, but that is not a statement about the color of skin. I can say that the Yoruba are not Ibo, but that tells me something about ethnicity and perhaps national identity, not about their complexions. So to say that the Egyptians were not Nubians is to say no more than that the two people who lived along the Nile occupied different geographical areas.

The fact is that the Egyptians saw themselves and Nubians as looking exactly alike in physical appearance as well as dress. One only needs to know the first ethnology in the world, the Biban el-Moluk bas-relief from the tomb of Sesostris I, to see that Egyptians painted themselves and Nubians as coal black and whites and Asians as lighter in complexion. There are four people on the bas-relief, representing four different cultures: Egyptian, Nehasi (Nubian), Namou (Asian), and Tamhou (Aryan). The Egyptian and the Nehasi are exactly alike, even to their clothes. They are visibly different from the Namou and the Tamhou.

But the greater nonsense is Lichtheim's statement that the "original Nubians were not black." Does Lichtheim mean to imply that they were what we would call white today? Does she mean they were lighter complexioned blacks? Or does Lichtheim mean to suggest, as some white Egyptologists suggested in the past, that the people were black-skinned whites? The problem here is racialist thinking. Since the discourse under which white academics have often operated is Eurocentric, it is difficult for them to admit that civilization started in Africa and that it was black people who started it.

As far as we know, human beings originated on the African continent and migrated outward. No scientist suggests that the people who migrated outward and who peopled the continent of Africa were white.[4] Indeed, the monogenesis thesis argues that hominids, the Grimaldi, migrated to Europe and emerged after the Ice Age as white in complexion because of environmental and climatic factors.

The Nubians were not only black physically but shared with the Egyptians and others of the Nile Valley the same African cultural and philosophical modalities. Present-day Egypt, like present-day America, is not a reflection of its ancient past. Arabs came from Arabia with the jihads of the seventh century A.D. Therefore, Arabic is not indigenous to Africa, as English is not indigenous to the United States.

The aim of Schlesinger's remarks and Lichtheim's quote is not the Nubian issue but the question of the complexion of the ancient Egyptians. Afrocentrists claim that Eurocentric scholars have attempted to take Egypt out of Africa and to take Africans out of ancient Egypt in a whitening process of the earliest civilizations. Children's books still exist with Egyptians looking like Scandinavians.

The evidence of the blackness of the ancient Egyptians is overwhelming. The early Greeks said that the Egyptians were black. They never wrote that the Egyptians were white. In fact, Aristotle wrote in *Physiognomonica* that both the Egyptians and the Ethiopians (Nubians) were black. Herodotus writes in *Histories* that the people of Colchis must be Egyptians because "they are black-skinned and have woolly hair."[5] One could cite Sfrabo, Pindar, and Apollonius of Rhodes as making similar attestations about how the Egyptians looked.

Thus, Lichtheim's statement is not only errant but pure nonsense. It flies in the face of all available evidence and, beyond that, it defies logic. Perhaps this style of written pontification by white scholars is the source of confusion in the minds of the American public. Lichtheim proposes what Bernal has aptly called the Aryan Model of Ancient History, which suggests, among other things, that civilization could not have started in Africa, and, if civilization is found in Africa, it had to be the results of an external movement into Africa.

E PLURIBUS UNUM

Schlesinger likes to quote Diane Ravitch. But both Schlesinger and Ravitch are wrong when they suggest that *e pluribus unum* meant out of many cultures, one. Actually, this expression was initially applied to the fact that several colonies could produce one federal government. Thus, out of many colonies, one central government. To apply this term of political structure to the American cultural reality is to miss the point of both politics and culture. A nation of more than 130 cultural groups cannot hope to have all of them Anglo-Saxonized. Such a vision is disastrous and myopic. What we can wish for and realize is a society of mutual respect, dynamism, and decency. Rather than labeling or setting cultural groups against each other, we should empower a vision that sees the American kaleidoscope of cultures as uniquely fortunate. Schlesinger sees multiculturalism as a danger. I see it as a further indication that the shift to a new, more operable paradigm in this mighty nation is well on its way.

---

4. Martin Bernal, *Black Athena*, vols. 1 and 2 (New Brunswick: Rutgers University Press, 1987).

5. *The Works of Aristotle*, W. D. Ross, vol. VI, *Physiognomica* (Oxford: Clarendon Press, 1913), 812.

Revolution in Indian Country

After centuries of conflict over their rights and powers, Indian tribes now increasingly make and enforce their own laws, often answerable to no one in the United States government. Is this the rebirth of their ancient independence or a new kind of legalized segregation?

Fergus M. Bordewich

Fergus M. Bordewich's book Killing the White Man's Indian *was published in 1996 by Doubleday. He is also the author of* Cathay: A Journey in Search of Old China.

Micki's Cafe is, in its modest way, a bulwark against the encroachment of modern history and a symbol, amid the declining fortunes of prairie America, of the kind of gritty (and perhaps foolhardy) determination that in more self-confident times used to be called the frontier spirit. To Micki Hutchinson, the problem in the winter of 1991 seemed as plain as the grid of streets that white homesteaders had optimistically laid out in 1910, on the naked South Dakota prairie, to create the town of Isabel in the middle of what they were told was no longer the reservation of the Cheyenne River Sioux Tribe. It was not difficult for Hutchinson to decide what to do when the leaders of the tribal government ordered her to purchase a $250 tribal liquor license: She ignored them.

"They have no right to tell me what to do. I'm not Indian!" Hutchinson told me a year and a half later. She and other white business people had by then challenged the tribe's right to tax them in both tribal court and federal district court and had lost. The marks of prolonged tension showed on her tanned, angular, wary face. "If this were Indian land, it would make sense. But we're a non-Indian town. This is all homestead land, and the tribe was paid for it. I can't vote in tribal elections or on anything else that happens on the reservation. What they're talking about is taxation without representation."

When I visited, everyone in Isabel still remembered the screech of the warning siren that someone had set off on the morning of March 27, 1991, when the tribal police reached the edge of town, as if their arrival were some kind of natural disaster, like a tornado or fire. The convoy of gold-painted prowl cars rolled in from the prairie and then, when they came abreast of the café, swung sideways across the road. Thirty-eight tribal policemen surrounded the yellow brick building. The tribe's police chief, Marvin LeCompte, told Hutchinson that she was in contempt of tribal court. Officers ordered the morning breakfast crowd away from their fried eggs and coffee. Then they went back into the pine-paneled bar and confiscated Hutchinson's stock of beer and liquor—"contraband," as LeCompte described it—and drove off with it to the tribal government's offices at Eagle Butte.

A few days before I met Hutchinson, I had interviewed Gregg J. Bourland, the youthful chairman of the Cheyenne River Sioux Tribe. Bourland is widely reckoned to be one of the most effective tribal chairmen in the region and, with a degree in business from the state college in Spearfish, also one of the best educated. "Let them talk about taxation without representation," Bourland told me dismissively. "We're not a state. We're a separate nation, and the only way you can be represented in it is to be a member of the tribe. And they can't do that. They're not Indians. These folks are trespassers. They are within reservation boundaries, and they will follow reservation law. They've now had one hundred years with no tribal authority over them out here. Well, that's over."

More than Micki Hutchinson or than any of the other angry whites in their declining prairie hamlets, it was Bourland who understood that what was at stake was much more than small-town politics. The tax, the ostentatious convoy, and the lawsuit were part of a much larger political drama that was unfolding across the inland archipelago of reservations that make up modern Indian Country. They symbolized the reshaping of the American West, indeed of the United States itself. By the 1990s, almost unnoticed by the American public or media, a generation of legislation and court actions had profoundly remade Indian Country, canonizing ideas about tribal autonomy that would have shocked the lawmakers who a century before had seen the destruction of the reservations as the salvation of the American Indian. If Bourland was right, Micki Hutchinson and the white residents of Isabel were living in a sovereign tribal state. They were tolerated guests with an uncertain future.

Until the 1870s, reservations were established throughout the Dakota Territory and other parts of the West with the promise that they would be reserved in perpetuity for the Indians' exclusive use. Those promises were broken almost everywhere when reservations were opened to homesteading at the end of the century, usually with only perfunctory consultation with the tribes or none at all. As I listened to Gregg Bourland, it was easy to sympathize with the tribe's striving for some kind of control over forces that were felt to have in-

6. NEW DIRECTIONS FOR AMERICAN HISTORY

vaded their land and undermined their culture. Bourland justified the tax as a means both to raise revenue for the tribe and to control alcohol consumption on a reservation where more than 60 percent of the adults were unemployed and 53 percent were active alcoholics.

Micki Hutchinson and her white neighbors were told they were living in a tribal state, guests with an uncertain future.

But promises that had been made a century ago to the ancestors of settlers like Micki Hutchinson were now being broken too. From the 1880s until the 1930s, the cornerstone of federal Indian policy had been the popular program known as allotment, the systematic breaking up of most of the nation's reservations into private holdings. In its day allotment seemed the perfect panacea to resolve at a single stroke the perennial problems of white settlers' insatiable desire for new land and Indians' growing dependency on the federal government. Sen. Henry L. Dawes, the idealistic architect of the Allotment Act of 1881, which set the pattern for a generation of similar legislation, ringingly proclaimed that as a result of allotment, the Indian "shall be one of us, contributing his share to all that goes to make up the strength and glory of citizenship in the United States."

The means of the Indian's salvation was to be the family farm, which most people of the time had been taught to regard as the ultimate repository of American individualism and the democratic spirit. Each Indian allottee would receive 160 acres of land and eventual United States citizenship, along with money for seed, tools, and livestock. The "excess," or leftover, land would be offered for sale to white settlers, who would be free to form their own municipal governments. The promise of the allotment policy was twofold: that the nation would integrate Indians into white society and that non-Indian settlers would never be subject to tribal regimes.

At the time, the Commissioner of Indian Affairs dismissed notions of separate Indian nationality as mere sentimentality: "It is perfectly clear to my mind that the treaties never contemplated the un-American and absurd idea of a separate nationality in our midst, with power as they may choose to organize a government of their own." To maintain such a view, the commissioner added, was to acknowledge a foreign sovereignty upon American soil, "a theory utterly repugnant to the spirit and genius of our laws, and wholly unwarranted by the Constitution of the United States."

As I left Isabel, I wondered who really was the victim here and who the victimizer. Behind that nagging question lurked still more difficult ones that occupied me for many months, from one end of the United States to the other, in the course of researching what was to become *Killing the White Man's Indian,* an investigation into the political and cultural transformation of modern Indian Country. Are Native Americans so fundamentally different from other Americans that they occupy a special category to which conventional American values and laws should not apply? Or are they simply one more American group, whose special pleading is further evidence that the United States has become a balkanized tangle of ghettos and ethnic enclaves? Do we discriminate against Indians by failing to blend them more effectively into the national mainstream? Or is the very notion of "mainstreaming" Indians so inherently racist that it should not even be contemplated as a component of national policy? Are Indian reservations and the way of life they preserve a precious national resource that must be maintained without the taint of contact with white America? Or is tribal self-determination creating a new form of segregation that merely freezes decayed tribal cultures like ghettoized versions of Colonial Williamsburg? Who, ultimately, are Indians in the 1990s? What are they to other Americans, and the others to them?

Killing the White Man's Indian represented a return to familiar country. As a youth in the 1950s and early 1960s, I often accompanied my mother, who was the executive director of the Association on American Indian Affairs, in her travels around reservations, part of her tireless effort to prod the federal government into improving tribal economies, education, health care, and law and order. Vivid experiences were plentiful: participating in a nightlong peyote rite in a tepee on the Montana prairie; a journey by pirogue deep into the Louisiana bayous to meet with a forgotten band of Houmas who wanted Washington to take notice of their existence; walking the Little Bighorn Battlefield with an aged Cheyenne who, as a small boy, had witnessed the annihilation of Custer's command. Poverty shaded almost every experience. Staying with friends often meant wind fingering its way through gaps in the walls, a cheese and bologna sandwich for dinner, sleeping three or four in a bed with broken springs. It seemed there was always someone talking about an uncle who, drunk, had frozen to death on a lonely road or about a cousin already pregnant at sixteen. More generally those years left me with a sense of the tremendous diversity of the lives and communities that lay submerged within the catchall label of "Indians" and a recognition that Native Americans were not mere vestiges of a mythic past but modern men and women struggling to solve twentieth-century problems.

In the course of four years' research on my book, I visited reservations from upstate New York to southern California and from Mississippi to Washington State, meeting with tribal leaders, ranchers, farmers, educators, and hundreds of ordinary men and women, both Indian and white. In Michigan I sailed Lake Superior with waterborne Chippewa police, searching for poachers on tribal fisheries in the lake. In Oregon I hiked the Cascades with professional foresters from the Warm Springs Tribe, which with its several hydroelectric dams and thriving timber industry is one of Indian Country's great success stories. I sweated with a group of recovering Navajo alcoholics in a traditional sweat lodge in the New Mexico desert. I also spent many a night in dust-blown reservation towns where, as an old South Dakota song puts it, "There's nothing much to do except walk up and down." In a few places, as a result of childhood connections, I was welcomed as a friend. More frequently I met with suspicion rooted in the widespread belief that curiosity like mine

37. Revolution in Indian Country

Strangely enough, these conflicts—widespread, often bitter, and with profound ramifications for American institutions—seemed to be happening beyond the ken of most Americans, for whom Indians largely remain a people of myth and fantasy. Like no other inhabitants of the United States, Indians have nourished our imagination, weaving in us a complex skein of guilt, envy, and contempt; yet when we imagine we see "the Indian," we often see little more than the distorted reflection of our own fears, fancies, and unhappy longings. This was vividly brought home to me on a visit to the reservation of the two-hundred-member Campo Band of Mission Indians, in the arid hills an hour's drive east of San Diego. This reservation landscape is a profoundly discouraging one. It offers nothing to comfort the eye, produces nothing of value, and provides almost nothing to sustain life as it is enjoyed by most Americans today. The single resource that the Campos possess is wasteland. In 1987 the band learned that the city of San Diego had named the reservation as one of several potential dump sites for the city's refuse.

"We just need this one little thing to get us started," the band's chairman, Ralph Goff, told me as we walked through the redshank and yucca and ocher sand where the first trenches had been cut for the new landfill. "With it we can create our own destiny." Goff, a formidably built man with little formal education, grew up in the 1940s, when the only work available was as a cowhand or day laborer for whites. When there was no work, people went hungry. "You just had to wait until there was some more food." In the 1960s most of the unskilled jobs disappeared, and nearly every Campo family went on welfare. "We needed it, but it really wrecked us as people. It created idleness. People didn't have to do anything in order to get money."

If the Campos have their way, by the end of the decade daily freight trains will be carrying loads of municipal waste to a three-hundred-acre site on a hilltop at the southern end of the reservation. For the privilege of leasing the band's land, a waste-management firm will pay the Campos between two and five million dollars a year. Goff argued that the dump would put an end to the band's dependence on federal largess. It would create jobs for every adult Campo who is willing to work, provide long-

was just a form of exploitation and that whites are incapable of writing about Indians with objectivity and honesty.

My original intention had been to use the lives of several men and women whom I had known in the 1950s as a microcosm and through them to chart the changes that had been wrought in Indian Country during the intervening years. But I soon realized that such a focus would be far too narrow, for it had become clear to me that a virtual revolution was under way that was challenging the worn-out theology of Indians as losers and victims and was transforming tribes into powers to be reckoned with for years to come. It encompassed virtually every aspect of Indian life, from the revival of moribund tribal cultures and traditional religions to the development of aggressive tribal governments determined to remake the relationship between tribes and the United States. The ferment was not unalloyed, however. Alongside inspired idealism, I also found ethnic chauvinism, a crippling instinct to mistake isolation for independence, and a habit of interpreting present-day reality through the warping lens of the past.

In the 1970s, in a reversal of long-standing policies based on the conviction that Indians must be either persuaded or compelled to integrate themselves into mainstream America, the United States enshrined the concept of tribal sovereignty at the center of its policy toward the nation's more than three hundred tribes. In the watershed words of Richard Nixon, federal policy would henceforth be guided "by Indian acts and Indian decisions" and would be designed to "assure the Indian that he can assume control of his own life without being separated from the tribal group."

In 1975 the Indian Self-Determination and Education Assistance Act amplified this principle, calling for a "transition from Federal domination of programs for and services to Indians to effective and meaningful participation by the Indian people." This has been reflected in a national commitment to the strengthening of tribal governments and to more comprehensive tribal authority over reservation lands. More ambiguously, it has also led to the increasing development of a new sphere of political power that rivals, or at least claims to rival, that of the states and the national government and for which there is no foundation in the Constitution. In the mid-1990s I found tribal officials invoking "sovereign right" in debates over everything from highway maintenance and fishing quotas to law and order, toxic-waste disposal, and the transfer of federal services to tribal administrations, not to mention the rapid proliferation of tribally run gambling operations. Reflecting the sentiments of many tribal leaders, Tim Giago, the publisher of *Indian Country Today,* the most widely read Indian newspaper in the United States, likened state legislation that affects Indians to "letting France make laws that also become law in Italy."

To people like Micki Hutchinson, it often seemed that Indians were playing an entirely new game, and that no one but the Indians understood the rules. In Connecticut, and elsewhere, tribes were exploiting a principle of sovereignty unknown to the average American in order to build casinos that sucked colossal sums of money from neighboring regions. New Mexicans found that they were equally helpless in the face of the Mescalero Apaches' determination to establish a nuclear-waste facility on their reservation outside Alamogordo. In Wisconsin and in Washington State, recurrent violence had accompanied the judicially mandated enlargement of Indian fishing rights in accordance with nineteenth-century treaties. In Nevada farmers found themselves on the brink of failure as the Paiutes of Pyramid Lake gained political leverage over the watershed of the Truckee River.

Tribes were invoking a principle of sovereignty unknown to the average American in order to set up casino operations.

In some states Indian demands for the return of sacred lands posed significant threats to local economies, including, most prominently, the Black Hills region of South Dakota. Nor was science exempt. Tribal claims on ancestral bones and artifacts were depleting many of the most valuable anthropological collections in the country.

6. NEW DIRECTIONS FOR AMERICAN HISTORY

term investment capital for the band, supply money for full college scholarships for every school-age member of the band, and finance new homes for the families that now live in substandard housing. The dump would, in short, give the Campos financial independence for the first time in their modern history.

The landfill would be one of the most technically advanced in the United States; to regulate it, the Campos enacted an environmental code more stringent than the State of California's. Nevertheless, the dump generated fierce opposition in towns near the reservation, where thousands of non-Indians live. Geologists hired by the dump's opponents have suggested, but not proved, that seepage from the dump might contaminate the water supply of ranches beyond the reservation boundary. Environmentalists accused the band of irresponsibility toward the earth and charged that the Campos had been targeted in an "assault" on reservations by "renegade" waste-dumping companies. A bill was even introduced in the California legislature that would have made it a crime to deliver waste to the Campo landfill. Goff shrugged away the protests. "It's a sovereignty issue. It's our land, and we'll do what we want to with it."

"How can you say that the economic development of two hundred people is more important than the health and welfare of all the people in the surrounding area?" an angry and frustrated rancher, whose land lay just off the reservation, asked me. "It's hard making a living here. The fissures will carry that stuff right through here. We'll have all that stuff in our water and blowing down on us off the hills. If our water is spoiled, then everything's spoiled."

There were predictable elements to her rage: the instinctive resistance of most Americans to any kind of waste dump anywhere near their homes and the distress of many white Americans when they realize the implications of tribal sovereignty for the first time and find themselves subject to the will of a government in which they have no say. But there was something more, a sort of moral perplexity at Indians' having failed to behave according to expectation, an imputation that they were guilty of self-interest. Revealingly, I thought, on the wall of the rancher's trailer there was a poster decorated with Indian motifs. Entitled "Chief Seattle Speaks," it began, in words that are becoming as familiar to American schoolchildren as those of the Gettysburg Address once were: "How can you buy or sell the sky, the warmth of the land?" Here, in sight of the dump, the so-called testament of Chief Seattle was a reproach to the Campos, an argument rooted in what the rancher presumably believed to be Indians' profoundest values. "Before all this I had this ideal about Indian people and all they've been through," she told me. "I used to think they had this special feeling about the land."

More than any other single document, Seattle's twelve-hundred-word "testament" lends support to the increasingly common belief that to "real" Indians any disruption or commercialization of the earth's natural order is a kind of sacrilege and that the most moral, the most truly "Indian" relationship with the land is a kind of poetic passivity. Having been translated into dozens of languages and widely reproduced in school texts, the "testament" has attained a prophetic stature among environmentalists: In 1993 Greenpeace used it as the introduction to a scarifying report on toxic dumping, calling it "the most beautiful and profound statement on the environment ever made." Unfortunately, like much literature that purports to reveal the real nature of the Indians, the "testament" is basically a fiction. Seattle was indeed a historical figure, a slave-owning chief of the Duwamishes who sold land to the United States in the mid-1850s and welcomed the protection of the federal government against his local enemies. However, the "testament," as it is known to most Americans, was created from notes allegedly made thirty years after the fact by a white doctor who claimed to have been present when Seattle spoke, and which then were extravagantly embroidered by a well-meaning Texas scriptwriter by the name of Ted Perry as narration for a 1972 film on the environment, produced by the Southern Baptist Radio and Television Commission. How is it, I wondered, that Americans have so readily embraced such a spurious text, not only as a sacred screed of the ecology movement but also as a central document of "traditional" Native American culture?

Increasingly it became clear to me that to be able to describe the realities of modern Indian life and politics, I would have to strip away the myths that whites have spun around Native Americans ever since Columbus arbitrarily divided the peoples he encountered into noble Arawaks and savage Caribs, conflating European fantasies with presumed native reality and initiating a tradition that would eventually include Montesquieu, Locke, Hobbes, and Rousseau, as well as a vivid popular literature stretching from *The Last of the Mohicans* to *Dances With Wolves*. Untamable savage, child of nature, steward of the earth, the white man's ultimate victim: each age has imagined its own mythic version of what the historian Robert F. Berkhofer, Jr., termed the "white man's Indian."

The single resource that the Campo Indians possess is wasteland. The dump would give them financial independence for the first time.

Typically the Denver *Post* could declare, not long ago, in an editorial attacking the University of Arizona for a plan to build an observatory atop an allegedly sacred mountain: "At stake is the very survival of American Indian cultures. If these sacred places are destroyed, then the rituals unique to those places no longer will be performed and many tribes simply may cease to exist as distinct peoples." Such logic implies both that only Native Americans who profess to live like pre-Columbians are true Indians and that Indians are essentially hopeless and helpless and on the brink of extinction. Apparently it never occurred to the paper's editorialist that the religion of the great majority of Indians is not in fact some mystical form of traditionalism but a thriving Christianity.

In keeping with our essentially mythic approach to the history of Indians and whites, Americans were generally taught until a generation or so ago to view their national story as a soaring arc of unbroken successes, in which the defeat of the Indians reflected the inevitable and indeed spiritual triumph of civilization over barbarism. More recently, but not so differently, numerous revisionist works like Kirkpatrick Sale's *The Conquest of Paradise: Christopher Columbus and the Columbian Legacy* and Richard Drinnon's *Facing West: The Metaphysics of Indian-Hating and Empire Building* have tended to portray the settlement of North America as a prolonged story of unredeemed tragedy and failure, in which the destruction of the Indians stands as proof of a fundamental ruthlessness at the heart of American civilization. Such beliefs have steadily percolated into the wider culture—to be embodied in New Age Westerns like *Dances With Wolves* and popular books like the best-selling *Indian Givers: How the Indians of the Americas Transformed the World*, which purports to show how practically every aspect of modern life from potatoes to democracy derives from the generosity of American Indians—and into the consciences of journalists, clergy, and others who shape public opinion.

On the whole the complex and intricate relationship between whites and Indians has been presented as one of irreconcilable conflict between conqueror and victim, corruption and innocence, Euro-American "materialism" and native "spirituality." The real story, of course, is an often contradictory one, disfigured by periods of harsh discrimination and occasional acts of genocide but also marked by considerable Indian pragmatism and adaptability as well as by the persistent, if sometimes shortsighted, idealism of whites determined to protect Indians from annihilation and find some place for them in mainstream America.

For instance, in contradiction of the notion that Indians were innocent of even the most elementary business sense, it was clear during negotiations over the Black Hills in the 1870s that Sioux leaders had a perfectly good grasp of finance and that indeed they were determined to drive the best bargain they could. "The Black Hills are the house of Gold for our Indians," Chief Little Bear said at the time. "If a man owns anything, of course he wants to make something out of it to get rich on." Another chief, Spotted Tail, added: "I want to live on the interest of my money. The amount must be so large as to support us." Similarly, in contrast with the popular belief that the United States government was committed to a policy of exterminating the Indian (no such policy ever existed, in fact), Senator Dawes publicly described the history of Indians in the United States as one "of spoliation, of wars, and of humiliation," and he firmly stated that the Indian should be treated "as an individual, and not as an insoluble substance that the civilization of this country has been unable, hitherto, to digest."

Indeed, the impulse behind the allotment of tribal lands and the national commitment to Indians was dramatically (and, with the benefit of hindsight, poignantly) acted out in a rite of citizenship that after 1887 was staged at Timber Lake, in the heart of the Cheyenne River Sioux country, and at many other places in the freshly allotted lands of other tribes. In the presence of representatives of the federal government, new allottees stood resplendent in the feathers and buckskins of a bygone age. One by one, each man stepped out of a tepee and shot an arrow to symbolize the life he was leaving behind. He then put his hands on a plow and accepted a purse that indicated that he was to save what he earned. Finally, holding the American flag, the Indian repeated these words: "Forasmuch as the President has said that I am worthy to be a citizen of the United States, I now promise this flag that I will give my hands, my head, and my heart to the doing of all that will make me a true American citizen." It was the culminating, transformative moment of which Senator Dawes had dreamed.

It is true enough, however, that, as so often in Indian history, reality failed to live up to good intentions. Unscrupulous speculators soon infested the allotted reservations, offering worthless securities and credit in return for land. Within a few years it was found that of those who had received patents to their land at Cheyenne River, 95 percent had sold or mortgaged their properties. When the Allotment Act was passed in 1881, there were 155 million acres of Indian land in the United States. By the time allotment was finally brought to a halt in 1934, Indian Country had shrunk by nearly 70 percent to 48 million acres, and two-thirds of Indians either were completely landless or did not have enough land left to make a living from it. In the mid-1990s Indian Country as a whole is still a daunting and impoverished landscape whose inhabitants are twice as likely as other Americans to be murdered or commit suicide, three times as likely to die in an automobile accident, and five times as likely to die from cirrhosis of the liver. On some reservations unemployment surpasses 80 percent, and 50 percent of young Indians drop out of high school, despite progressively increased access to education.

Our people live in a limbo culture that is not quite Indian and not quite white either. . . . a house without a foundation.

Is the tribal-sovereignty movement a panacea for otherwise intractable social problems? In the cultural sphere, at least, its importance cannot be underestimated. "Our people live in a limbo culture that is not quite Indian and not quite white either," said Dennis Hastings, surrounded by books, gazing out toward the Iowa plains through the window of the sky blue trailer where he lives in a cow pasture. Hastings, a burly former Marine and the tribal historian of the Omaha Nation, which is in northeastern Nebraska, has almost singlehandedly led an effort to recover tribal history as a foundation for community renewal that is probably unmatched by any other small tribe in the United States. "It's like living in a house without a foundation. You can't go back to the old buffalo days, stop speaking English and just use our own language, and ignore whites and everything in white culture. If we did that, we'd become stuck in history, become dinosaurs."

Teasing small grants and the help of volunteer scholars from institutions around the country, Hastings has initiated an oral-history project to collect memories of fading tribal traditions. "We go into each family, get an anthropologist to record everything right from how you wake up in the morning," he said. Hundreds of historic photographs of early reservation life have been collected and deposited with the State Historical Society, in Lincoln. A friendly

6. NEW DIRECTIONS FOR AMERICAN HISTORY

scholar from the University of Indiana recovered a trove of forgotten Omaha songs recorded in the 1920s on wax cylinders. Another at the University of New Mexico undertook a collective genealogy that would trace the lineage of more than five thousand Omahas back to the eighteenth century. Hastings explained, "Until now everything was oral. Some people knew the names of their ancestors, and some knew nothing at all. There was a loss of connection with the past. Now people can come back and find out who their ancestors were." In sharp contrast with the combative chauvinism of some tribes, the Omahas invited scientists from the University of Nebraska and the Smithsonian Institution to examine repatriated skeletons to see what they could discover about the lives of their ancestors. In 1989, astonishing perhaps even themselves, tribal leaders brought home Waxthe'xe, the True Omaha, the sacred cottonwood pole that is the living embodiment of the Omaha people, which had lain for a hundred years in Harvard's Peabody Museum; at the July powwow that year, weeping hundreds bent to touch it as if it were the true cross or the ark of the covenant.

"We want the benefits of modern society," Hastings told me in his nasal Midwestern drawl. "But America is still dangerous for us. The question is then, How do we take the science that America used against us and make it work for us? The answer is, we try to build on the past. It's like a puzzle. First you see where the culture broke and fragmented. Then you try to build on it where people have been practicing it all along. Then people start to think in a healthy way about what they were in the past. If you can get each person to be proud of himself, little by little, you can get the whole tribe to become proud. We're going to dream big and be consistent with that dream."

In its broadest sense the tribal sovereignty movement is demonstrating that the more than three hundred Indian tribes in the lower forty-eight states (more than five hundred if you count Alaskan native groups) are distinct communities, each with its unique history, traditions, and political environment, for whom a single one-size-fits-all federal policy will no longer suffice. Greater autonomy will surely enable well-governed and economically self-sufficient tribes—mostly those located near big cities and those with valuable natural resources—to manage their own development in imaginative ways. For many others, however, far from airports and interstate highways, populated by ill-trained workers and governed, in some cases, by politicians who do not abide by the most basic democratic rules, the future is much less assured.

There is nothing abstract about such concerns in Timber Lake, South Dakota, which lies a short drive east from Isabel across the rolling plains of the Cheyenne River Sioux Reservation. Like Isabel, Timber Lake has been battered by the general decline of a region that is hemorrhaging jobs and people. Timber Lake is one of the relatively lucky places, kept alive by the presence of the Dewey County offices, the rural electric co-op, the central school, and a cheese factory. Even so, one hundred of the six hundred people who lived there a decade ago have moved away to places with better prospects and more hope. Isabel's population has dropped by half, to three hundred. Trail City has shrunk from three hundred and fifty to thirty, Firesteel to a single general store, and Landeau has disappeared completely. Entire towns have lost their doctors, banks, and schools. From a certain angle of vision, Sioux demands for the restoration of the reservation to its original nineteenth-century limits are simply an anticlimax.

The people of Timber Lake—the mechanics, the teachers, the co-op clerks, the men who work at the grain elevator, the retired farmers—are the human fruit of allotment, the flesh-and-blood culmination of the cultural blending that Senator Dawes envisioned. "Everyone here has relatives who are Indian," said Steve Aberle, a local attorney whose Russian-German father married into the Ducheneaux, a prominent clan of Cheyenne River Sioux. Aberle, who is thirty-five, is one-eighth Sioux; he is a voting member of the tribe and served for two and a half years as chairman of the tribal police commission. Nevertheless he shares the uneasiness of non-Indians who feel themselves slipping toward a kind of second-class citizenship within the reservation's boundaries. "It would be better to be in a situation where everybody works together and deals with people as people, but it's hard to do that when people know they pay taxes but are excluded from benefits and services," Aberle told me. "When my grandparents came from Russia, the United States government told them that they would be full citizens if they moved out here. Now I see people being told that they can't even take part in a government that wants to regulate them. Something is inherently wrong when you can't be a citizen where you live because of your race. It just doesn't fit with the traditional notion of being a U.S. citizen. At some point there has to be a collision between the notion of tribal sovereignty and the notion of being United States citizens. Anytime you have a group not represented in the political process they will be discriminated against. There's going to be more and more friction. It's going to hurt these communities. People start looking for jobs elsewhere."

The Sioux were the victims of nineteenth-century social engineering that decimated their reservation. But the descendants of the adventurous emigrants who settled the land are also the victims of an unexpected historical prank, the trick of the disappearing and now magically reappearing reservation. Reasonably enough, the rhetoric of tribal sovereignty asks for tribes a degree of self-government that is taken for granted by other Americans. However, the achievement of a sovereignty that drives away taxpayers, consumers, and enterprise may be at best but a Pyrrhic victory over withered communities that beg for cooperation and innovation to survive at all.

With little debate outside the parochial circles of Indian affairs, a generation of policymaking has jettisoned the long-standing American ideal of racial unity as a positive good and replaced it with a doctrine that, seen from a more critical angle, seems disturbingly like an idealized form of segregation, a fact apparently invisible to a nation that has become accustomed to looking at Indians only through the twin lenses of romance and guilt and in an era that has made a secular religion of passionate ethnicity. Much of the thinking that underlies tribal sovereignty seems to presuppose that cultural purity can and ought to be preserved, as if Indian bloodlines, economies, and histories were not already inextricably enmeshed with those of white, Hispanic, and black Americans.

Such concerns will be further exacerbated in the years to come as Indian identity grows increasingly ambiguous. Virtually all Indians are moving along a continuum of biological fusion with other American populations. "A point will be reached... when it will no longer make sense to define American Indians in generic terms [but] only as tribal members or as people of Indian ancestry or ethnicity," writes Russell Thornton, a Cherokee anthropologist and demographer at the University of Southern California, in *American Indian Holocaust and Survival,* a study of fluctuations in native populations. Statistically, according to Thornton, Indians are marrying outside their ethnic group at a faster rate than any other Americans. More than 50 percent of Indians are already married to non-Indians, and Congress has estimated that by the year 2080 less than 8 percent of Native Americans will have one-half or more Indian blood.

How much ethnic blending can occur before Indians finally cease to be Indians? The question is sure to loom ever larger for coming generations, as the United States increasingly finds itself in "government-to-government" relationships with tribes that are becoming less "Indian" by the decade. Within two or three generations the nation will possess hundreds of "tribes" that may consist of the great-great-grandchildren of Indians but whose native heritage consists mainly of autonomous governments and special privileges that are denied to other Americans.

Much thinking that underlies tribal sovereignty seems to presuppose that cultural purity can and should be preserved.

Insofar as there is a political solution to the Indian future, I have come to believe that it lies in the rejection of policies that lead to segregation and in acknowledgment of the fact that the racially and ethnically variegated peoples whom we call "Indian" share not only common blood but also a common history and a common future with other Americans. The past generation has seen the development of a national consensus on a number of aspects of the nation's history that were long obscured by racism or shame; there is, for instance, little dispute today among Americans of any ethnic background over the meaning of slavery or of the internment of Japanese-Americans during the Second World War. There is as yet no such consensus, however, with respect to the shared history of Indians and whites, who both still tend to see the past as a collision of irreconcilable opposites and competing martyrdoms.

That history was not only one of wars, removals, and death but also one of calculated compromises, mutual accommodation, and deliberately chosen risks, a story of Indian communities and individuals continually remaking themselves in order to survive. To see change as failure, as some kind of cultural corruption, is to condemn Indians to solitary confinement in a prison of myth that whites invented for them in the first place. Self-determination gives Indian tribes the ability to manage the speed and style of integration but not the power to stop it, at least for long. Integration may well mean the eventual diminishing of conventional notions of "tribal identity," but it must also bring many new individual opportunities, along with membership in the larger human community. "People and their cultures perish in isolation, but they are born or reborn in contact with other men and women, with man and woman of another culture, another creed, another race," the Mexican novelist Carlos Fuentes has written. Tribes will survive, if anything, as stronger entities than they have been for many generations. The question is whether they will attempt to survive as isolated islands or as vital communities that recognize a commonality of interest and destiny with other Americans.

Muddled Masses: The Growing Backlash against Immigration Includes Many Myths

Folklore Says Great-Grandpa Didn't Take Handouts; Actually, He Took Plenty

Newcomers Today Cost Less

Frederick Rose

Staff Reporter of The Wall Street Journal

Some images seem etched forever in the national memory: stark photos of Ellis Island's weary arrivals, turn-of-the-century tenements, grim-faced children in sweatshops across industrial America—and millions of newcomers pulling themselves up solely by dint of their own Herculean efforts.

Some quite different views seem widely accepted about today's immigrants: Many are on welfare, make excessive demands on the health-care system, are overrunning schools—and are costing Americans billions of tax dollars.

Call it the Immigration Gap, a profound divide between perspectives of past and present. "My ancestors, and most of our ancestors, came to this country not with their hands out for welfare checks," Texas Rep. Bill Archer, chairman of the Ways and Means Committee, told the House of Representatives as it passed a bill last month denying welfare to most legal immigrants. "They came here for the opportunity for freedom and the opportunity to work." His views are backed up by opinion polls and by voters such as those in California who supported Proposition 187, the controversial measure that cuts off services to illegal immigrants.

But there is a problem with the conventional wisdom about yesterday's self-reliant immigrants. It's wrong.

THE HAZE OF HISTORY

Forgotten in a haze of history and family lore are the nation's struggles near the turn of the century to accommodate the tidal wave of new arrivals from which so many of today's Americans are descended. There is no denying that today's costs are high, but in many cases those of a century ago were, proportionally, even higher, as a review of census documents, government investigations and yellowing academic tomes shows.

Contrary to popular myth, for example, more than half of public welfare recipients nationwide in 1909 were immigrant families, making new arrivals three times more likely than natives to be on the public dole, according to research accumulated by a 1911 commission on immigration. In Chicago, two-thirds of those receiving public assistance were foreign born. And, with their native-born children, these immigrants made up four out of five of the city's welfare recipients.

Today, the weight of newcomers is proportionately far smaller. According to calculations from the 1990 census, 9% of immigrant households received welfare payments, compared with 7.4% of households headed by natives, although today's more elaborate welfare system is costly. Including noncash programs such as food stamps, the federal government alone spends more than $5 billion annually on welfare for immigrants.

Moreover, at the turn of the century, a third of those in public hospitals and insane asylums were foreign-born, more than twice the proportion of foreign-born in the general population. In 1906, Thomas Darlington, president of the

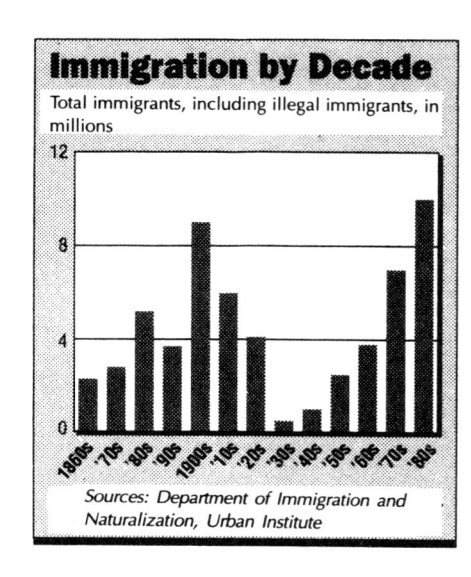

Immigration by Decade
Total immigrants, including illegal immigrants, in millions

Sources: Department of Immigration and Naturalization, Urban Institute

New York Board of Health, complained that nearly half the spending at city hospitals went to treat the immigrant poor. Such proportions are a far cry from today, when only about 6.5% of all Medicaid recipients (a figure including hospital as well as office patients) are immigrants.

A TEMPORARY DESTINATION

Schooling that lifted succeeding generations of new Americans to better economic circumstances drained budgets everywhere. In the nation's 30 biggest cities, more than half the students in public schools were from immigrant families during the early years of this century. In New York alone, nearly three quarters were the children of new arrivals. In Chicago, it was more than two thirds. The national burden today, estimated at a bit over 5%, is comparatively light.

The conventional wisdom that yesterday's immigrants came seeking a permanent new home with freedom and opportunity also doesn't always meet the test of historical accuracy. In reality, America for many wasn't a final destination at all, but instead was a temporary escape from a jobless and famine-ridden Europe.

Historians estimate that as many as a third of the nearly 30 million foreigners who arrived between the Civil War and World War I moved back to their native countries. At times, the homeward flow of these "birds of passage," as the itinerants were known, was huge. In 1908, for example, a time of world-wide economic depression, a quarter more Italians went home than arrived in the U.S. Those who did stay sent home four out of every five dollars they earned, according to Italian estimates—attracting the wrath of Americans who accused them of draining the U.S. economy.

All of this clashes with the current romanticized picture of immigration, of Mayflower-like pilgrim arrivals and of "huddled masses yearning to breathe free," in the poet Emma Lazarus's words.

"Emma Lazarus's image, which has endured for generations, needs serious revision," suggests Caroline Golub, a historian and author of "Immigrant Destinations," a study of turn-of-the-century arrivals. Many American families today, for instance, are accidents of history. "A lot of people were planning to go back when World War I broke out," Ms. Golub says. "That was a great Americanizer."

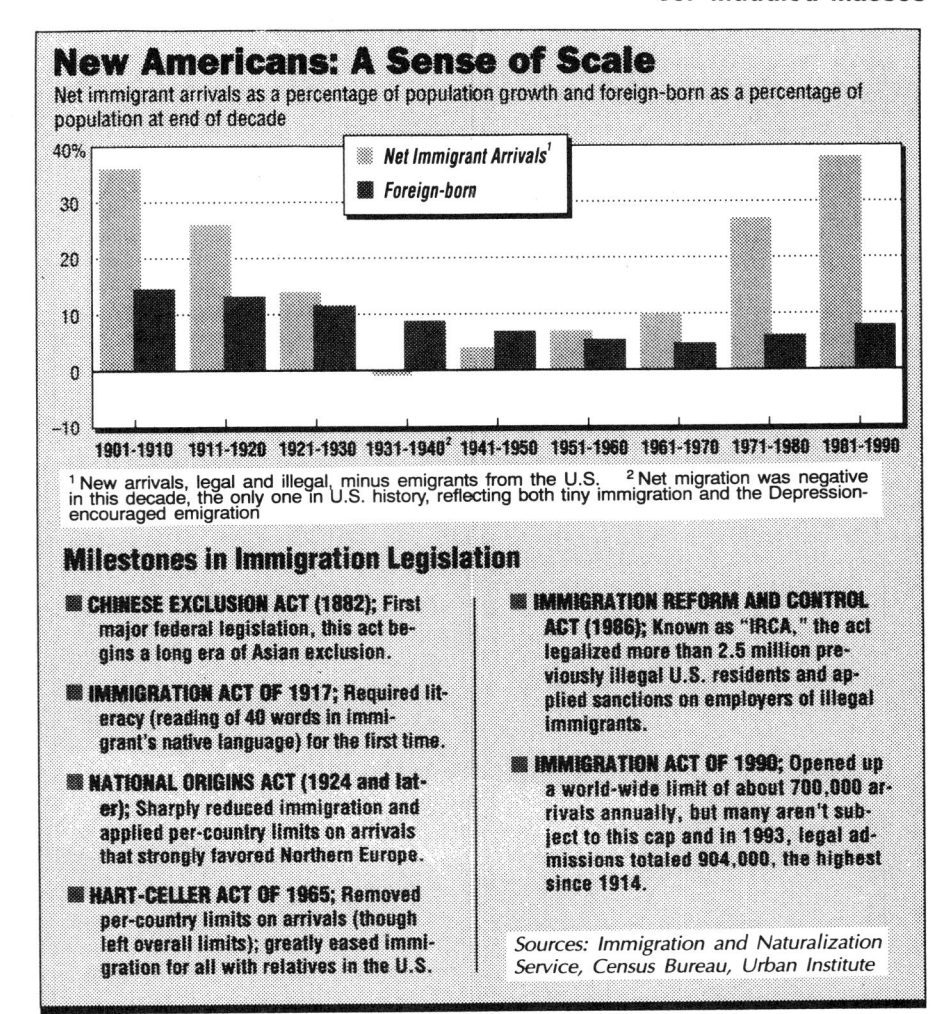

Life a century ago was hard for all working people, whether immigrant or native, adds Lawrence H. Fuchs, immigration historian at Brandeis University and a vice chairman of the U.S. Commission on Immigration Reform. "But the idea that immigrants had no charity available, no welfare, is crazy," he says.

DUELING COST ESTIMATES

Total welfare and other costs for immigrants weren't compiled at the turn of the century. But two respected analysts have tried to estimate public costs of today's immigration—with vastly different conclusions.

Jeffrey Passel and other analysts at the Urban Institute, a Washington-based think tank, found that immigrants are responsible for an economic net gain of $27 billion. But Donald Huddle, an economist at Rice University, found immigrants impose on taxpayers a yearly net burden of $43 billion in expenditures. The latter figure has been seized on by increasingly vocal critics who advocate more limits on immigration.

The two studies differ by about $10 billion in the estimated costs immigrants impose on government programs. A much wider gap, more than $50 billion, results from different estimates of how much immigrants pay in taxes. Neither calculation charges to immigrants a portion of the costs of law enforcement, roads, defense or any other public services used by newcomers and natives alike.

'BLIND, IDIOTIC, CRIPPLED'

Whatever the cost—or burden—of immigrants, they were as much a lightning rod for criticism a century ago as they are today. In 1880, in a charge that would echo exactly 100 years later in

---

New Americans: A Sense of Scale
Net immigrant arrivals as a percentage of population growth and foreign-born as a percentage of population at end of decade

[Bar chart showing Net Immigrant Arrivals¹ and Foreign-born percentages for decades 1901-1910 through 1981-1990]

¹ New arrivals, legal and illegal, minus emigrants from the U.S.   ² Net migration was negative in this decade, the only one in U.S. history, reflecting both tiny immigration and the Depression-encouraged emigration

Milestones in Immigration Legislation

- **CHINESE EXCLUSION ACT (1882):** First major federal legislation, this act begins a long era of Asian exclusion.
- **IMMIGRATION ACT OF 1917:** Required literacy (reading of 40 words in immigrant's native language) for the first time.
- **NATIONAL ORIGINS ACT (1924 and later):** Sharply reduced immigration and applied per-country limits on arrivals that strongly favored Northern Europe.
- **HART-CELLER ACT OF 1965:** Removed per-country limits on arrivals (though left overall limits); greatly eased immigration for all with relatives in the U.S.
- **IMMIGRATION REFORM AND CONTROL ACT (1986):** Known as "IRCA," the act legalized more than 2.5 million previously illegal U.S. residents and applied sanctions on employers of illegal immigrants.
- **IMMIGRATION ACT OF 1990:** Opened up a world-wide limit of about 700,000 arrivals annually, but many aren't subject to this cap and in 1993, legal admissions totaled 904,000, the highest since 1914.

Sources: Immigration and Naturalization Service, Census Bureau, Urban Institute

6. NEW DIRECTIONS FOR AMERICAN HISTORY

the Mariel boatlift when occupants of Cuba's prisons and mental hospitals were cast adrift to the U.S., the New York State Board of Charities complained that Europe was sending its "blind, idiotic, crippled, epileptic, lunatic, and other infirm paupers, incapable of supporting themselves, in order thereby to avoid the burden of their support." A steerage ticket to America, the board noted, was a lot cheaper than caring for such dependents in their home country.

In 1888, a Congressional committee complained of immigrant paupers showing up in New York City poorhouses a mere two days after entering the U.S. through the backdoor of Canadian ports. It was hardly the last of such criticism.

"Nativist" groups have argued since colonial times that American culture and principles were being diluted by the influx of foreigners. Benjamin Franklin griped in the 18th century that Pennsylvania's German arrivals would never fit in.

But, as the immigrant influx soared in the 19th century, arguments focused on economic as well as cultural reasons to close the door. Bit by bit, through the late 19th and early 20th centuries, rules emerged requiring that new arrivals possess a modicum of money, good health and, eventually, literacy.

SLAMMING THE DOOR

Finally the door slammed nearly shut. The 1924 National Origins Act and amendments soon after put a ceiling of about 150,000 annually on European immigration (or barely 10% of the peak inflow), barred most Asians and limited the entrance of all national groups to their 1890 proportion of the population, effectively cutting off the flow from Eastern and Southern Europe.

The nature of immigration changed dramatically and, with the intervening years, so did the collective memory of its origins. Among other things, the changes imbued the immigration tale with an extraordinary and sweeping sense of success.

With legal changes in the 1920s, a huge flow of mostly unskilled immigrants came to a halt. Among the trickle that still could get in, education and skill levels soared, climbing from well below American averages to well above, beginning in the late 1920s. Flight from Nazism, Communism and war brought a sizable chunk of Europe's intellectual elite to America. Immediately after the war, entrants from Western Europe and Canada dominated, and they were quick to assimilate. Some countries, notably Britain and Canada, worried openly about a "brain drain" as some of their best-educated citizens emigrated to the U.S.

"It was an anomaly, a time when some immigrants literally were rocket scientists," notes Lawrence Katz, a Harvard University economist. "The halls of academe today are still filled with people who came in this period."

In an era when the immigrant down the street was as likely to be a chemist as an unskilled laborer, perceptions of immigration changed. World War II and military service were a common cause in which Americans, native stock and newly arrived alike, had a part. Antagonisms that had crested in the 1920s seemed to fade, although the 1950s also saw the Immigration and Naturalization Service launch now-infamous sweeps against Mexican agricultural workers in the Southwest.

John F. Kennedy's 1958 book, "A Nation of Immigrants," reflected the reverent tone toward newcomers. "There is no part of our nation that has not been touched by our immigrant background; everywhere immigrants have enriched and strengthened the fabric of American life," the great-grandson of an Irish immigrant wrote. He went on to praise not just the laborers, but immigrant scientists, inventors and industrialists.

Even today, recollections of an immigrant elite dominate discussions. "We've been led down the golden path by that period," says Claudia Goldin, an economic historian at Harvard. But a recent analysis indicates that past immigrants' progress may have been overstated.

As better-educated immigrants arrived in midcentury, relatively unskilled immigrants from decades earlier and their descendants still were climbing far lower rungs on the educational and economic ladder. On the whole, census data showed rising levels of immigrant education and income. But in the mid-1980s, economist George Borjas, now at the University of California at San Diego, noted a statistical conundrum: The accomplishments of midcentury immigrants seemed to have masked a slower-than-expected rise by turn-of-the-century immigrants and their descendants. Mr. Borjas combined statistical analysis with 1980 census material to reach his conclusions.

Analysts have long believed that it takes three generations on average for immigrant families to reach educational and economic parity with natives. But according to Mr. Borjas's calculations, it takes four generations, or 100 years. "In the great scheme of things, that's not a very long time," he says. "But for Americans, it's half of this country's history."

According to Mr. Borjas's research, differences in education and skill levels among different national groups arriving near the turn of the century still are visible in their grandchildren today. For instance, the 1910 census reported that literacy rates of Danish-born men were more than double those of Mexican-born men—and the 1980 census found Danish descendants averaged three more years of education than their Mexican counterparts. "The melting pot is working, but clearly it has been simmering, not boiling," he says.

Though still hotly contested in some quarters, the thrust of Mr. Borjas's interpretations is increasingly accepted in academic circles. "The progress of immigrant families now seems to be slower than earlier research suggested," says Mr. Katz, the Harvard economist, who until recently was chief economist at the U.S. Labor Department.

QUESTIONS FOR THE FUTURE

That's both troubling and meaningful for future immigration because today, as nearly a century ago, the nation's immigrant flow includes millions of low-skilled workers. This time, economists and historians worry, these newcomers are colliding with an economy that increasingly requires highly skilled workers.

At the same time, the current backlash against these newcomers—and the legislative assault that those attitudes are spawning—may mean today's immigrants will receive even less help than their predecessors. If immigrants, even with extensive government and private aid, take 100 years to reach the skill levels of natives, what will happen if that aid is scaled back? The growing divide between the ever-more-technological economy and the stream of often unskilled workers compounds the problem. Says Ms. Goldin, the economic historian, "It's the country that's different—not, perhaps, the immigrants."

The American Environment

The Big Picture Is More Heartening than All the Little Ones

John Steele Gordon

John Steele Gordon writes the "Business of America" column for American Heritage.

The Cuyahoga River died for our sins. In 1796 The Cuyahoga, which promised easy transportation into the wilderness of the Ohio country from Lake Erie, prompted the city of Cleveland into existence. Over the next 170 years a primitive frontier town grew into a mighty industrial city, one that stretched for miles along the banks of its seminal river.

By the mid-twentieth century, however, the river no longer served as a major artery of transportation, having been superseded by railroads and highways. Now, instead of carrying the products of civilization into the vast interior, it carried the effluent of a far more technically advanced civilization out into the lake. The once crystalline waters of the river had become turbid and rank with its new cargo of chemicals and sewage. Its once abundant wildlife had long since fled, leaving only a few carps and suckers to eke out a living in the foul sullage on its bottom, testifying thereby to the very tenacity of life itself.

Finally, late in the morning of June 22, 1969, the Cuyahoga could no longer bear the burden humankind had placed upon it. In a sort of fluvial *cri de coeur,* the river burst into flames.

The fire was no will-o'-the-wisp flickering over a transient oil slick. Rather, it roared five stories into the sky, reduced wooden railroad trestles to ruins, and demonstrated to the people of Cleveland and the nation as no scientific study or news report ever could that the burden being placed on the environment was reaching limits that could be crossed only at the peril of the future.

Less than a year later, on April 22, 1970, Earth Day was held, one of the most remarkable happenings in the history of democracy. Fully 10 percent of the population of the country, twenty million people, demonstrated their support for redeeming the American environment. They attended events in every state and nearly every city and county. American politics and public policy would never be the same again.

Today, nearly a quarter-century after the fire, sunlight once more sparkles off the surface of the Cuyahoga. Boaters cruise its waters for pleasure, and diners eat at riverside restaurants. Mayflies—so characteristic of a Great Lakes spring—once more dance in the air above it in their millions while their larvae provide food for at least twenty-seven species of fish that have returned to its waters.

The Cuyahoga is not pristine, and barring an alteration in human priorities and circumstances beyond anything now imagined, it will not become so. But it has changed greatly for the better and continues to improve. It is once more a living river.

The Cuyahoga and its history is a microcosm of the American environment. For the history of that environment is the story of the interaction between a constantly changing, ever-more-powerful technology and an only slowly shifting paradigm of humankind's proper relationship with the natural world.

"DOMINION . . . OVER EVERY LIVING THING"

Human beings evolved in the Old World, a fact that more than once would have sudden and drastic consequences for the New.

The beginning of the Upper Paleolithic period was marked by a dramatic technological development as humans acquired tools and weapons that were far more sophisticated than any known before and became the most formidable hunters the world has ever known. In the Old World both our prey and our competitors, evolving alongside, quickly learned to treat the emerging biological superpower with the greatest respect, and most were able to adapt successfully. But the New World lay in innocence while human hunters perfected their newfound skills in the Old.

The first settlers saw the wilderness not as beautiful but as barren and threatening.

When the land bridge that was a temporary consequence of the last ice age allowed humans to migrate into it, the results were swift and devastating: much of the North American Pleistocene fauna went extinct. Horses, camels, mastodons, mammoths, true elephants, several species of deer, bison, and antelope, ground sloths, glyptodonts, and giant beavers vanished, as did their associated predators, such as saber-toothed cats, giant lions, and cheetahs.

It cannot be known for sure to what extent the arrival of human hunters affected this great extinction, but there is little doubt that it was an important, perhaps fundamental, factor. But the evolutionary equilibrium that had been shattered by the arrival of the super-hunters eventually returned, for the human population of the New World, limited by numerous other factors besides food supply, remained low. And the surviving among the species they had encountered quickly adapted to the new conditions.

Thus the next human culture that appeared in the New World, the Euro-

6. NEW DIRECTIONS FOR AMERICAN HISTORY

The Kansas-Pacific Railway touts its bison-hunting parties with a show of the animals' heads, 1870.

peans, found it to possess a biological abundance and diversity of, to them, astounding proportions. But these newcomers failed almost entirely to appreciate this aspect of the New World, for hunting in their culture had been reduced to, at most, a secondary source of food.

They were heirs to the agricultural revolution that began in the Old World at the end of the last ice age. It, too, was marked by a profound leap in technology. In turn the more settled conditions of agricultural communities allowed the development of still more elaborate technologies as well as social and political organizations of unprecedented complexity. The result was what we call civilization.

But the early civilizations were acutely aware that they were small islands surrounded by vast seas of wilderness from which savage beasts, and savage men, might come at any time and wipe them out. Thus their inhabitants came to look on the wilderness as an alien place, separate and apart. Not surprisingly under these circumstances, the religions that developed in the Near East in the wake of the agricultural revolution reflected this worldview, sanctioned it, and codified it. Because it became, quite literally, Holy Writ, it persisted unquestioned for centuries.

The Book of Genesis, in fact, could hardly be more direct on the subject. "God said unto [man], Be fruitful, and multiply, and replenish [i.e., fill up] the earth, and subdue it: and have dominion over the fish of the sea, and over the fowl of the air, and over every living thing that moveth upon the earth."

Over the next more than two thousand years, humans operating with this worldview in mind transformed the continent of Europe, and by the time they began to expand overseas, wilderness had disappeared from all but the margins of that continent.

Thus the world they encountered in North America was unlike anything they had ever seen. The greatest temperate forest in the world, teeming with life, stretched almost unbroken from the Atlantic seaboard to well west of the Mississippi. The grasslands that filled the Great Plains in the rain shadow of the Rocky Mountains also abounded with animal life as millions of bison, pronghorn antelope, elk, white-tailed and mule deer roamed it, as did their associated predators, the wolf, the mountain lion, the bear, and the jaguar.

Farther west still, the forests of the Northwest and the deserts of the Southwest reached to the Pacific.

A "HOWLING DESART"

When the new settlers arrived, they did not see the beauty or abundance of the wilderness that greeted them. Far from it; they regarded it as barren and threatening because the ancient paradigm that dated to the dawn of civilization still molded their thinking. Thus they regarded their first task in the New World to be a re-creation of what they had known in the Old, an environment shaped by the hand of man, for man's benefit.

But while they sought, as nearly as possible, to re-create the Europe they had left behind, converting the "remote, rocky, barren, bushy, wild-woody wilderness" into a "second England for fertility," there was one way in which the New World was utterly unlike the Old: it possessed an abundance of land so great that it seemed to the early settlers, and to their descendants for many generations, to verge upon the infinite. "The great happiness of my country," wrote the Swiss-born Albert Gallatin, Jefferson's Secretary of the Treasury, "arises from the great plenty of land."

Because the supply seemed without end, the value placed on each unit was small. It is only common sense to husband the scarce and let the plentiful take care of itself. Caring for the land, an inescapable necessity in Europe, was simply not cost-effective here. After all, the settlers could always move on to new, rich land farther west. For three hundred years they did exactly that, with ever-increasing speed.

Americans also developed other habits in the early days that stemmed directly from the wealth of land and scarcity of the population. Today, when American archaeologists investigate a site, they know that the place to look for the garbage dump is on the far side of the fence or stone wall that was nearest to the dwelling. In Europe that was likely to belong to a neighbor; in America it was often wilderness and thus beyond the human universe. This out-of-sight-out-of-mind attitude would have no small consequences when technology increased the waste stream by orders of magnitude.

The early settlers, while they greatly altered the landscape of the Eastern seaboard, clearing whole stretches of the primeval forest and converting the land to fields, pastures, and meadows, did not greatly diminish the biological diversity. They opened up the best land for farming but left untouched the steep or rocky areas as well as, to a great extent, the wetlands and mountains. Indeed in some ways the early settlers increased the diversity by expanding habitat for such grassland species as bluebirds, ground hogs, and meadowlarks. The ecosystem as a whole remained intact.

North America was transformed within a century. There was a vast price to pay.

Only in the South, where plantation agriculture became the rule in areas to which it was suited, did monocultural husbandry greatly diminish the fertility and texture of the soil. Virginia, the largest and, thanks to its tobacco exports, most powerful of the colonies, found its yields declining sharply toward the end of the eighteenth century as the best land was exploited and exhausted. Erosion became an increasing problem. As early as the 1780s Patrick Henry thought that "the greatest patriot is he who fills the most gullies."

"A THOUSAND YEARS"

Meanwhile, as a new civilization was being built out of the wilderness of North America, new attitudes toward wilderness itself were emerging in Europe. The ancient paradigm that had gripped Western thinking since Genesis was beginning, partially, to shift at last.

In the seventeenth century, wilderness had been universally regarded as at best a waste, if not an evil. In the eighteenth, however, it began to be seen for the first time as a thing of beauty. Mountains came to be viewed as majestic, not just as an impediment to travel or a barrier against invasion.

In Britain the aristocracy began to lay out gardens, such as those by Capability Brown, that were highly stylized versions of nature itself, rather than the direct refutation of it that seventeenth-century gardens, like those at Versailles, had been.

Biology became a systematic science (although the word itself would enter the language only in the early nineteenth century). Linnaeus studied the relationships of plants and animals. Georges Cuvier, William Smith, and others began to examine fossils and to sense, for the first time, a history of the earth that was at variance with the account given in Genesis.

The new attitude toward wilderness soon came to this country and contributed to the growing American sense of uniqueness. James Fenimore Cooper's novels and Thoreau's essays displayed a love of wilderness that would have been inconceivable a century earlier.

Of course, in Europe wilderness was largely an abstraction. In America it was just down the road. At the end of the Revolution, it nowhere lay more than a few days on horseback from the Atlantic shore, and Thomas Jefferson, no mean observer, thought it would be "a thousand years" before settlement reached the Pacific.

Jefferson was wrong. He did not realize—no one could have—that a third technological revolution was just getting under way, one that would give humankind the power to transform the world far beyond anything provided by the first two. It had taken millennia to reshape the face of Europe to human ends. North America would be transformed in less than a century. But there would be a vast price to pay for this miracle.

The steam engine and its technological successors allowed energy in almost unlimited quantity to be brought to bear on any task. So forests could be cut, fields cleared, dams built, mines worked with unprecedented speed. As a result, in less than a single human lifetime an area of eastern North America larger than all Europe was deforested. Virtually uninhabited by Europeans as late as 1820, the state of Michigan by 1897 had shipped 160 billion board feet of white pine lumber, leaving less than 6 billion still standing.

As early as the 1850s it was clear that something irreplaceable was disappearing.

But the new engines needed fuel. At first waste wood supplied much of it, and later coal and then oil. The byproducts of this combustion were dumped into the atmosphere as they had always been, but now their quantity was increasing geometrically. In 1850 Americans were utilizing more than eight million horsepower, animal and mechanical. By 1900 nearly sixty-four million, almost all mechanical, was being used by what economists call prime movers.

The factory system and mechanization brought many commodities within the financial reach of millions, while new transportation systems created national markets and made economies of scale both possible and necessary. This, in turn, caused the demand for raw materials to soar. The great mineral wealth that was being discovered under the American landscape was exploited with ever-increasing speed. Again the waste products were dumped at the lowest possible cost, which meant, in effect, on the far side of the nearest stone wall.

6. NEW DIRECTIONS FOR AMERICAN HISTORY

Increasing wealth and the new technologies allowed cities to bring in fresh, clean water for their rapidly increasing populations. This water was used to flush away the dirt and sewage of human existence, but only into the nearest body of water. The quality of life in the human environment was immeasurably improved by this, as the squalor that had characterized the urban landscape since Roman times disappeared. But the quality of the nation's waterways sharply deteriorated.

The new technology allowed us to turn more and more of the landscape to human use. The old-fashioned moldboard plow, in use since medieval times, could not deal easily with the rich, heavy soils and deep sod of the American Midwest. The steel plow invented by John Deere in 1837 quickly opened up what would become the breadbasket of the world. Wetlands could now be drained economically and made productive. Millions of acres vanished, and their vast and wholly unappreciated biological productivity vanished too.

So rapid an alteration of the landscape could only have a severe impact on the ecosystem as a whole. The loss of so much forest caused runoff to increase sharply, eroding the land and burdening the waters with silt, destroying more wetlands. Many animals' habitats disappeared. And because the ancient biblical notion that humans had dominion over the earth still held, others vanished entirely.

The beautiful Carolina parakeet, North America's only native parrot, proved a major agricultural pest. Because it lived in large, cohesive flocks, it made an easy target for farmers with the shotguns that the Industrial Revolution made cheap. It was extinct in the wild by the turn of the century; the last known specimen died in the Cincinnati Zoo in 1914.

Another avian casualty was the passenger pigeon, one of the great natural wonders of America, as amazing as Niagara Falls or the Grand Canyon. The passenger pigeon almost certainly existed in larger numbers than any other bird in the world. Moreover, it was concentrated in flocks of unbelievable immensity. Audubon reported one flock that took a total of three days to pass overhead and estimated that, at times, the birds flew by at the rate of three hundred million an hour.

The passenger pigeon nested in heavily forested areas in colonies that were often several miles wide and up to forty miles long, containing billions of birds. Trees within the colony each had hundreds of nests, and limbs often broke under the weight. The squabs, too heavy to fly when abandoned by their parents at the end of the nesting season, were easy prey. With railroads able to ship the fresh-killed birds to the great Eastern cities quickly, hunters slaughtered them in the millions to meet the demand.

Unfortunately it turned out that passenger pigeons needed the company of huge numbers of their fellows to stimulate breeding behavior. Once the size of the flocks fell below a certain very large minimum, the birds stopped reproducing, and the population crashed. Just as with the Carolina parakeet, the last passenger pigeon died in the Cincinnati Zoo in 1914.

The herds of the Great Plains also fell to hunters. It is estimated that upward of thirty million bison roamed the grasslands of North America in the middle of the nineteenth century. By the dawn of the twentieth, less than a thousand remained alive.

"FOREVER WILD"

As early as the 1850s it was clear to the more thoughtful that something precious and irreplaceable was rapidly disappearing. The wilderness that had helped define the country seemed ever more remote. It was now recognized the natural world could provide refreshment whose need was becoming more and more keenly felt.

Urban parks, such as New York City's incomparable Central and Prospect parks, were intended to provide the population with a taste of nature that many could now obtain no other way. But these parks were, like the aristocratic gardens created in eighteenth-century Britain, wholly manmade and no more truly natural than a sculpture is a rock outcropping.

Movements began to take hold to preserve portions of the fast-vanishing wilderness itself. As early as the 1830s the painter George Catlin put forward the idea of a wild prairie reservation, a suggestion that, alas, was not implemented before nearly all of the country's prairie ecosystem was destroyed. But the movement took root, and in 1864 the first act of preservation was undertaken when ownership of the Yosemite Valley and a stand of sequoias was transferred from the public lands of the United States to the state of California.

In 1872 the first national park in the world was created when reports of the splendors of Yellowstone were delivered to Congress. James Bryce, British ambassador to the United States, called the national parks the best idea America ever had. Certainly they have been widely copied around the world. Today American national parks protect 47,783,680 acres, an area considerably larger than the state of Missouri.

States, too, began to set aside land to protect what was left of the wilderness. New York turned five million acres—15 percent of the state's land area—into the Adirondack Park and Forest Preserve, to remain "forever wild."

In the 1870s Carl Schurz, Secretary of the Interior, began moving for the preservation of federally owned forests. Born in Europe, where forests had long since become scarce and thus precious, and where forest-management techniques were far more advanced than those in this country, Schurz and many others helped create a new concern for America's fast-dwindling woodlands. By the end of Theodore Roosevelt's Presidency, almost sixty million acres were in the forest reserve system.

Today hundreds of millions of acres in this country enjoy various levels of protection from development, and more are added every year. But while the parks and reserves created by this movement are national treasures that have greatly enriched the quality of life, their creation was predicated on the part of the ancient paradigm that still survived. That part held that the natural world and the human one were two separate and distinct places. And it was still thought that each had little effect on the other.

"THE HARMONIES OF NATURE"

It was George Perkins Marsh, lawyer, businessman, newspaper editor, member of Congress, diplomat, Vermont fish commissioner, and lover and keen observer of nature, who first recognized the folly of this unexamined assumption. Growing up in Vermont, he had seen how the clear-cutting of the forests and poor farming practices had degraded the state's environment.

In 1864 he published *Man and Nature*, which he expanded ten years later and published as *The Earth as Modified by Human Action*. Individual instances of human effect on the natural world had been noted earlier, but Marsh, like Darwin with evolution, gathered innumerable examples together and argued the general case. He decisively demonstrated that the impress of humankind on the whole world was deep, abiding, and because it was largely unnoticed, overwhelmingly adverse. "Man is everywhere a disturbing agent," he wrote. "Wherever he plants his foot, the harmonies of nature are turned to discords."

Recognizing that technology, energy use, population, food production, resource exploitation, and human waste all were increasing on curves that were hyperbolic when plotted against time, he feared for the future. "It is certain," he wrote, "that a desolation, like that which overwhelmed many once beautiful and fertile regions of Europe, awaits an important part of the territory of the United States . . . unless prompt measures are taken."

Marsh observed in 1864, "Man is everywhere a disturbing agent." Nobody listened.

Darwin's book *On the Origin of Species* provoked a fire storm of controversy in the intellectual world of his time when it was published in 1859. It changed humankind's perception of the world profoundly and immediately. But *Man and Nature* changed nothing. Published only five years later, it met with profound indifference, and its author sank into the undeserved oblivion of those who are out of sync with their times. As late as 1966, when the science of ecology he was instrumental in founding was already well developed, so commodious a reference work as the *Encyclopaedia Britannica* made no mention of him whatever.

Perhaps the difference was that Darwin's ideas had only philosophical, religious, and scientific implication. Marsh's ideas, on the other hand, had profound economic consequences. An America rapidly becoming the world's foremost industrial power did not want to hear them, even though as early as 1881 the mayor of Cleveland could describe the Cuyahoga River as "an open sewer through the center of the city."

"A DIFFERENT WORLD"

In fact, the seeds of the country's first great man-made ecological disaster were being planted even as Marsh wrote.

In the 1860s railroads pushed across the Great Plains and opened them up to settlement by connecting them to Eastern markets. On the high plains toward the Rockies, as hunters slaughtered bison and pronghorns by the millions, ranchers replaced them with cattle, which overgrazed the land. Then farmers began moving in.

World War I greatly increased the demand for wheat, while the tractor made plowing the tough, deep sod of the high plains a more practical proposition. The number of farms in the area east of the Rocky Mountains burgeoned in the 1920s, taking over more and more of the ranchland.

The mean annual rainfall in this area varied between ten and twenty inches, not enough for crop farming except in the best of years. But the early decades of the century happened to see many such years. Then, in the late twenties, the rains slacked off, and drought swept the plains.

This had happened hundreds of times in the past, and the plants and animals that had evolved there were adapted to it. Wheat and cattle were not. Worse, over the last few years, the sod, the deep net of grass roots that had bound the soil together, had been broken over millions of acres by the farmers with their plows. The topsoil, without which no plant can grow nor animal live, now lay exposed to the ceaseless, drying winds.

In 1933 no rain fell for months in western Kansas, and little elsewhere. The crops withered, the livestock died of thirst or starvation, and the dust, bound by neither sod nor moisture, began to blow. On November 11 a howling, rainless storm sprang up. "By midmorning," a reporter wrote of a farm in South Dakota, "a gale was blowing cold and black. By noon it was blacker than night, because one can see through the night and this was an opaque black. It was a wall of dirt one's eyes could not penetrate, but it could penetrate the eyes and ears and nose. It could penetrate to the lungs until one coughed up black. . . .

"When the wind died and the sun shone forth again, it was on a different world. There were no fields, only sand drifting into mounds and eddies that

George Perkins Marsh around 1880, two decades after his *Man and Nature* showed how humans unbalance nature.

6. NEW DIRECTIONS FOR AMERICAN HISTORY

swirled in what was now but an autumn breeze. There was no longer a section-line road fifty feet from the front door. It was obliterated. In the farmyard, fences, machinery, and trees were gone, buried. The roofs of sheds stuck out through drifts deeper than a man is tall."

The dust of this storm, uncountable millions of tons of topsoil, darkened the skies of Chicago the following day and those of Albany, New York, the day after that. Terrible as it was, the storm proved but the first of many that ravaged the high plains in the next several years, as the drought tightened its grip and the unforgiving winds blew and blew. In the middle years of the 1930s, they laid waste thousands of square miles of what had been, just a few years earlier, a vibrant ecosystem. It was now the Dust Bowl. Upward of two hundred thousand people were forced to abandon their farms and trek westward in desperate search of the necessities of life itself.

The rains finally came again, and in the 1940s the discovery of the Oglala aquifer, a vast reservoir of water that underlies much of the Midwest, rescued the farmers who remained. Tapped by ever-deeper wells, the aquifer is now seriously depleted. And economics is slowly rescuing the land as the price of water increases every year.

It was always marginal for farming, and so it remains. Even with many, though mostly ill-conceived, federal programs, the farmers on the high plains are finding it ever harder to compete in world markets. Every year more and more farms are abandoned, and the land reverts to what in a perfect world it would never have ceased to be—short-grass prairie.

"A PHRASE CONCEIVED IN ARROGANCE"

The technological leap that had begun in Jefferson's day only accelerated in the twentieth century. The burdens that had been placed on the environment in the nineteenth century by such things as fuel use and sewage disposal increased sharply as the population expanded and new technologies spread across the land.

The limits of the ability of the environment to cope with the load were being reached more and more often. In October 1947 a thermal inversion settled over Donora, Pennsylvania. The town is set in a natural basin and was home to much heavy industry. The layer of cold air trapped the effluent of that industry and of the cars and furnaces of the population. By the time the inversion ended, four days later, twenty people were dead and six thousand ill enough to require treatment.

To an astonishing extent—at least as viewed from today's perspective—the people of the time accepted such happenings as the price of the Industrial Revolution that had brought them so much wealth and material comfort. A *New Yorker* cartoon of the day showed a woman sitting at a table set for lunch in the garden of a New York brownstone. "Hurry, darling," she calls to her unseen husband, "your soup is getting dirty."

New burdens were also added. The chemical industry grew quickly in this century, fueled by an explosion in knowledge. The disposition of chemicals was, as always, over the nearest stone wall: into a landfill or convenient body of water.

Agriculture became more businesslike as farms grew in size, became much more mechanized, and increasingly specialized in one or two crops. Of course, even Patrick Henry had known, two centuries earlier, that monocultural farming depletes the soil and is vulnerable to insects and other pests. But now the chemical industry could overcome this, thanks to synthetic fertilizers and pesticides.

Such chemicals as DDT were greeted as miracles of modern science when they first became available, and their use spread rapidly. In 1947 the United States produced 124,259,000 pounds of chemical pesticides. Only thirteen years later, in 1960, production was up to 637,666,000 pounds of often far more potent pesticides.

Diseases such as malaria and agricultural pests such as the boll weevil were declared on the verge of eradication. And the "control of nature," the final realization of the dominion enjoined by Genesis, was said to be at hand. DDT and other pesticides sprayed from airplanes blanketed vast areas, to kill gypsy moths, budworms, and mosquitoes.

But there were troubling signs for the few who looked. The pesticides were nondiscriminatory; they killed all the insects they touched. Honeybees, essential for the pollination of many crops and innumerable natural plants, were often wiped out by spraying programs aimed at other insects. Beekeepers began to fight back with lawsuits. "It is a very distressful thing," one beekeeper wrote, "to walk into a yard in May and not hear a bee buzz."

More than two hundred new pesticides were introduced in the years following World War II. The reason was that the older ones became increasingly ineffective. Many species of insects go through numerous generations a year and can evolve very rapidly, especially when a severe pressure such as a new pesticide is applied. In a monument to the vigor with which life clings to existence, they did exactly that.

And birdwatchers noticed a troubling decline in the numbers of some species, especially the large raptors that lived at the top of the food chains. Charles Broley, a retired banker, banded bald eagles in Florida beginning in 1939 as a hobby. He usually banded about a hundred and fifty young birds a year on the stretch of coast he patrolled. Beginning in 1947, more and more nests were empty or held eggs that had failed to hatch. In 1957 he found only eight eaglets, the following year only one.

But these troubling events were scattered, knowledge of them dispersed over a huge country and many scientific disciplines. They were no match for the chemical companies. But these, it turned out, were no match for a frail middle-aged woman named Rachel Carson.

Within a few years of Silent Spring, *the demand for action became irresistible.*

Rachel Carson was trained as a marine biologist, but she was a born writer. In 1952 her book *The Sea Around Us* was published with a very modest first printing. To everyone's astonishment—most of all hers—it became a titanic bestseller that made its author famous across America. Ten years later she published *Silent Spring*. It changed the world.

Again a huge bestseller, *Silent Spring* detailed in lucid, often poetic, and always accessible prose how pesticides were playing havoc with the air, land, and water of the country and how their uncontrolled use was doing far more harm than good. Further, it introduced millions of Americans to the concept that the natural world was an intimately interconnected web. This web, Carson made clear, included humans quite as much as every other living thing that shared planet Earth. What killed insects would, if not handled carefully, one day kill us too. George Perkins Marsh had said much the same thing a hundred years earlier. This time the people read and believed.

The ancient paradigm from the dawn of civilization, when man was frail and nature omnipotent, was dead at last. Dead with it was what had been in theory a dream and in fact a nightmare—the control of nature. It had been, Rachel Carson wrote on the last page of *Silent Spring,* "a phrase conceived in arrogance."

"THE SKY IS FALLING"

Within a few years the public demand for action in behalf of the environment became irresistible, and it caught a complacent government by surprise. John C. Whitaker, Nixon's cabinet secretary, later recalled that "we were totally unprepared for the tidal wave of public opinion in favor of cleaning up the environment."

Earth Day cleared up any lingering doubts about the public's opinion on the matter. Federal government agencies such as the Environmental Protection Agency were created, and goals and timetables for air and water quality were established. We Americans set out on a crusade to rescue the land from ourselves. In many ways we shared the fervor with which the medieval world had set out to rescue the holy Land from the infidel.

Today, nearly a quarter-century after the crusade to the new Jerusalem of a clean environment began, there is vast progress to report. In 1959, 24.9 million tons of particulate matter—soot—were emitted into the air in the United States. By 1985, 7.2 million were, and less every year. In 1970, 28.4 million tons of sulfur oxides, a prime contributor to smog, were released by power plants and automobiles. In 1990, 21.2 million tons were, a drop of nearly 25 percent. Carbon monoxide emission has fallen by 40 percent since 1970, and lead has been eliminated as an additive to gasoline.

Cars being manufactured in the 1990s emit only a fifth as much pollution as those made before 1975. Thus 80 percent of all automobile pollution today is generated by just 10 percent of the cars on the road. In the next few years, as these clunkers end up on the scrap heap, automobile pollution will decrease sharply.

Already the number of days per year when the air quality is below standards in most of the country's cities has fallen significantly, by 38 percent in the 1980s alone. Even Los Angeles, the smog capital of the country thanks to its geography and automobile-oriented infrastructure, has enjoyed a 25 percent decline in smog-alert days.

In 1960 only about 50 million Americans were served by municipal sewage plants that provided secondary or tertiary treatment. Today more than half the population is. As a result, many urban waterways are now cleaner than they have been since the early 1800s. New York used to dump the sewage of eight million people into the Hudson, Harlem, and East rivers. Today, in a development that would have stunned turn-of-the-century New Yorkers, there is an annual swimming race around Manhattan Island.

Rural rivers too have greatly benefited. Most of the Connecticut River's four-hundred-mile length was declared "suitable only for transportation of sewage and industrial wastes" in the 1960s. Today 125 new or upgraded water treatment plants, costing $900 million, have transformed it. Fishing and swimming are now allowed almost everywhere, and wildlife such as ospreys, bald eagles, blue crabs, and salmon has returned in numbers.

The sludge that is the end product of sewage treatment was until very recently dumped in the ocean or into landfills. Now it is increasingly being sought by farmers as cheap fertilizer and soil conditioner. New York City produces 385 tons a day, all of it once dumped beyond the continental shelf. One hundred tons of that is being used by farmers in Colorado and Arizona. Initially skeptical, fifty of those farmers recently sent New York's mayor a letter asking for more. He's likely to oblige. Boston sludge now fertilizes Florida citrus groves. And because sewage sludge not only fertilizes but improves soil quality, it is displacing chemical fertilizers.

As old factories reach the end of their productive lives and are replaced by new ones built under stringent controls, the non-sewage pollution of the waterways is also steadily declining. The violation rate (the percentage of tests where the amount of pollutants was found to be above standards) for lead and cadmium fell to less than one percent. Dissolved oxygen is an important measure of a water body's biological viability. The percentage of times it was found to be below standard fell 60 percent in the 1980s.

Many bodies of water, such as Lake Erie, declared dead in the 1970s, have bounded back with the improved situation and with the help of life's ferocious determination to go on living. The amounts of pesticides being used every year fell by more than a quarter in the 1980s, and those in use today are far less persistent and far less toxic than most of those in widespread use in the 1960s. The level of DDT present in human fatty tissue, a fair measure of its presence in the environment, was 7.95 parts per million in 1970. By 1983 it had fallen to 1.67 parts per million. Today, ten years latter, no one even bothers to gather the statistic.

The land, too, has improved. In the eastern part of the United States, the area of forest land has been increasing for more than a century, as clear-cut areas have been allowed to regenerate. It will be another hundred years, at least, before they reach the climax stage, but they are on their way. And today 28 percent of all farmland is no longer plowed at all, and the percentage is growing quickly. Conservation tillage is used instead; the method sharply reduces erosion and improves soil quality while slashing costs, producing crops for as much as 30 percent less.

Programs to reduce the use of chemical fertilizers are being tried in more and more areas as farmers learn new techniques. In Iowa in 1989 and 1990 a joint EPA-state program helped farmers cut their use of nitrogen fertilizer by four hundred million pounds without sacrificing crop yields. Because agricultural fertilizers and pesticides now account for more than 65 percent of all water pollution (factories account for only 7 percent), this trend has no small implication for the future.

Wildlife is on the mend in many ways. To be sure, the number of species on the endangered list has grown sharply in the last two decades, but that is much more an artifact of increased knowledge than of a still-deteriorating situation.

Many species have rebounded sharply, thanks in some cases to protection and in others to the explosion of biological and ecological knowledge that has so marked the last twenty-five years. To give just two examples, alligators, once hunted mercilessly for their skins, are no longer on the list at all. And peregrine falcons, almost extirpated in the Eastern United

One Town's Environment
The ebb and flow of tooth and claw, fifty miles from Times Square

One winter Sunday morning a few years ago, I happened to look out my bedroom window as I was getting dressed. There on the lawn below was the carcass of a deer, its hindquarters half-eaten by whatever had brought it down. Tufts of its fur were scattered across the grass. Its eyes, glassy in death, stared back at me sightless. A coyote, slat-thin and mangy, was taking furtive bites, looking up every few seconds as if expecting to be attacked. A few feet away three turkey vultures were walking about in that peculiar loping gait unique to vultures, waiting their turn at the carcass.

This nature-red-in-tooth-and-claw scene was so reminiscent of the "Nature" series on PBS that I half-expected George Page to come around the corner at any moment, camera crew in tow. But what is most astonishing of all, perhaps, is that I do not live in some remote part of the country. Far from it. I live in North Salem, New York, less than fifty miles from Times Square. That so vibrant a habitat could exist so close to the center of the nation's largest city is powerful evidence that life is far more resourceful and tenacious than many environmental activists would like to admit.

North Salem is a small place. The town occupies twenty-two square miles (about the size of Manhattan Island), but only forty-eight hundred people call it home. Economically they range from getting by to *Forbes*-four-hundred rich. There is only one traffic light, a recent and much-resented addition. The hamlet of Purdys has a First Street but no longer has a Second Street. In the hamlet of Croton Falls, a local bank occupies a corner of the fishing-supplies store.

Although there is a town historian and an active historical society, precious little history beyond the purely local has ever taken place here. Ogden Mills, a major figure in California history, was born in North Salem, and his house still stands, now a small herb farm. General Rochambeau and his troops marched through in 1781 on the way to the siege of Yorktown. The expedition that resulted in the capture of the British spy Major André was supposedly planned at the Yerkes Tavern, whose foundation—all that remains of it—is on my property, and whose front door is now the front door of my house. But that's about it, and even the Yerkes Tavern plot, alas, is almost certainly a myth.

Altogether it's the sort of place where most people feel no need to lock their doors, where neighbors leave excess zucchini on your front porch unasked, knowing you don't have a garden, where everyone calls the town officials by their first names, even when bawling the hell out of them at town board meetings. I suspect Thornton Wilder would have liked North Salem.

The crest of Keeler Hill includes the highest point in Westchester County, and from it one can see, across rolling hills and fields, clear to the Hudson River, twenty miles away, and even Bear Mountain on the far side. The landscape is peaceful, gentle, and apparently timeless.

It is not. The beautiful lake that you can see from Keeler Hill dates only to 1893, when New York City dammed the town's major waterway, the Titicus River, and created a new reservoir for its ever-growing thirst. Even the spruce forest that runs up one side of Turkey Hill, a mile or so away, is only about sixty years old, planted by Tom Purdy when he wanted to cut down on the number of fields that had to be mowed during the Great Depression.

In the last hundred years wave after wave of ecological change has swept over North Salem. Even in the not quite half a century of my existence, the changes have been many, and I have marked them. For it has been my pleasant fate to spend much of my life here, first as a constant visitor to the farm my grandparents used as a summer place and for the last thirteen years as a resident on a piece of that farm, living in a small eighteenth-century house that my grandmother lovingly restored sixty years ago, her own mini-Williamsburg project.

Like most of the rest of the northeast part of the country, North Salem before the arrival of Europeans was heavily forested with deciduous trees, oaks and hickories predominating on the higher, drier slopes, maples, sycamores, and tulip trees marking the wetter areas. The local Indians practiced agriculture using slash-and-burn techniques that created open areas and a good deal of edge, the part of woodlands most attractive to game such as deer and wild turkeys.

North Salem was first established by Europeans in 1731, but the effect of Europeans on its environment began a century earlier.

The Dutch came to this area to trade for furs. By the time farming began in North Salem, beavers, martens, minks, and many other fur-bearing animals had long since been extirpated or greatly reduced. The major carnivores too, such as bears, mountain lions, wolves, and coyotes, soon vanished.

The farmers moving in girdled the trees to kill them and created pastures for their livestock and fields for their crops. By 1800 much of the original forest had vanished, replaced by open fields, meadows, and pastures. Only the wetlands and steeper slopes remained covered by trees. With the loss of most of the edge, game declined in numbers, and human hunters added to the pressure. Wild turkeys were gone by the middle of the nineteenth century, and deer became vanishingly rare.

But North Salem was never rich farming country. Its soil is thin in most parts of the town, for there is little bottomland and much hillside. The glacier that retreated about ten thousand years ago scoured the bedrock clean and left an infinity of stones behind as it melted. One boulder left by the glacier and weighing about sixty tons rests on five smaller stones. The Balanced Rock, as it is called, is the town's distinctly modest—but only—tourist attraction.

While the glacier provided North Salem with what one local calls "our answer to the Grand Canyon," it also gave the early farmers a big problem. Before fields could be plowed, they had to be cleared of the stones the glacier had left. At a cost in human and animal labor that staggers the imagination, the early farmers built hundreds of miles of stone walls on the edges of their fields, walls made so well that most remain to this day and provide the modern landscape with its most abiding characteristic.

Because the land was relatively poor, dairy farming and orchards were always the dominant forms of agriculture, and most field crops that were grown—principally hay—were for local consumption.

Like all towns before the Industrial Revolution, North Salem had to provide for virtually all its own needs. Individual households made most items. But blacksmith shops, slaughterhouses, flour mills, nail factories, and others supplied the rest. This local industry was powered mostly by the

States by DDT, have been with infinite care and effort put on the road to recovery. Today there is a pair nesting on the Verrazano Bridge at the entrance to New York's Upper Bay, and there is even a pair nesting on the top of the Met Life (formerly Pan Am) building in midtown, exploiting the distinctly unendangered local pigeon population.

Nor has public interest in rescuing the environment slackened. *The New York Times Index* for 1960 needed less than 19

Titicus River, which runs east to west through the center of the town, and the Croton River, which forms the town's western border. Both those waterways also, of course, served as giant disposal systems and were foul and smelly for most of the nineteenth century. The part of town where many of these small factories were concentrated, along what is now called Titicus Road, was known then as Bedbug Hollow. Today it is the center of the town's most affluent area.

In the 1840s the railroad reached North Salem. New York City had been, at best, a long day's journey away; it was now a two-hour ride. The railroads also soon connected the Middle Western grainlands and upstate dairy areas to the Eastern seaboard. Marginal agricultural areas close to the city, which had prospered by their proximity, prospered no more. North Salem's population, which had doubled since the Revolution, peaked in the 1840s and then began a long, slow decline that lasted until 1950, when the town's population was back to what it had been when Rochambeau marched through.

The railroads also spelled the slow death of the local industries. As manufacturing enterprises of national scope evolved in the late nineteenth century, the local factories shut down one by one. The Titicus and Croton rivers soon cleansed themselves and sparkled once more in the sunlight.

By 1900, 90 percent of the land was still open fields, but around that time agriculture began, slowly, field by field, to disappear from the town. The poorest pastures were let go and were soon tangles of brush, briars, and saplings, difficult to walk through but a paradise for many birds, such as song and field sparrows, whose numbers increased.

Soon the abandoned fields were second-growth forests, on their way back to the climax deciduous forest that had once covered the town. As this process, called succession, began, the habitat diversified, and more and more species of birds returned or increased their numbers. Just in the last ten years, as second-growth forests grew old enough to produce a substantial number of dead trees, the magnificent pileated woodpecker reappeared. Its strident cry and air-hammer-like drilling now resound through North Salem's woods.

Today perhaps 70 percent of the town is forest, nearly a reversal of the situation at the beginning of the century, and agriculture is nearly gone. There is a vineyard, producing a variety of wines (memo to Mouton Rothschild: Don't worry), and Outhouse Orchards, which produces vegetables as well as fruits and cider.But the last dairy farm closed down ten years ago, and today the farms are only horse farms, really boarding stables.

Still the horse farms and the open fields maintained by wealthy, mostly horse-loving landowners preserve much open space. This open land allows the continuation of a major fox hunt in North Salem, adding vast color and cheerful noise to the landscape and, because years go by between kills, doing little harm.

The patchwork of open fields and small woods that now characterizes the town provides much edge, and with the decline of hunting (only bow and arrow can be used), it has sparked a major revival of game species. Wild turkey are once again present (just the other day a hen strolled across my back lawn as though she owned the place, as, in a sense, I suppose she does).

Deer, seldom seen when I was a child in North Salem, are now a thoroughgoing pest to gardeners and a serious threat to the habitat as a whole. For while North Salem's ecosystem is a vibrant one, it is not a complete one. Coyotes have returned in numbers, and bobcats are to be found, but they are merely hunters of opportunity when it comes to deer. The major carnivores are gone forever. With human hunting light, nothing checks the population of deer, and they tend to breed up to the limit of the food supply, doing much damage to diversity as they extirpate favored species of plants and destroy the forest understory. It is not at all uncommon to see herds of twenty or more browsing in open fields.

Control of the deer population is largely a political problem. Hunters' license fees fund the state's Department of Environmental Conservation, and hunters' interests—because there's a rich supply of animals to shoot at—get first attention as a result. Many animal lovers, who apparently studied ecology only at Walt Disney University, fiercely resist any control measures at all. As a result, Westchester County has one of the densest deer populations in the country.

But except for the deer, North Salem's environment is in better shape and more diversified and richly populated than it has been since before the coming of the Europeans. In my lifetime the improvement has been noticeable. Although I've been walking the town's fields and woods with binoculars since I was old enough to focus them, I was thirty-four before I ever saw a bluebird. Today the bird that wears the sky on its back (as Thoreau described it) is once again common, thanks to hundreds, perhaps thousands, of birdhouses that dot the town. Last year even a bald eagle was spotted.

Has anything gotten worse? Yes, two things. One, the night sky has seriously deteriorated. The glow of lights to the south, where the population has increased much more rapidly than it has in North Salem, blots out most stars in that direction. And today the Danbury Mall, although more than ten miles away, gives the northeast sky a pink glow as unnecessary as it is obnoxious. Towns with major astronomical observatories, such as Flagstaff, Arizona, have developed ordinances to protect the observatories while maintaining safety and convenience. The adoption of these ordinances nationwide would give us back the night sky and save very significant amounts of energy as well, a win-win situation if ever there was one.

The other deterioration is the noise. When I was a child, I loved to wander off into the fields of my grandparents' farm. There, sitting on a stone wall or lying in the grass, I would listen, just listen. All I would hear were the sounds of the earth that Oscar Hammerstein II thought were music itself: the lowing of cattle, a distant dog, the rustle of the wind through the hay, the song of meadowlarks, the caw of crows.

Today human-generated noise always intrudes, like someone jingling coins at a concert. There is always the hum of traffic from the interstate, although it is three and a half miles from my house. Small planes buzz around the sky in astonishing numbers. Somewhere there is always a chain saw working, or a weed whacker running, or a police siren racing to the scene of an accident.

If there is a solution to this problem (beyond my increasing deafness), I do not know it. I do know I miss the silence that was so full of music.

—J.S.G.

---

inches to list all the references to air pollution that year, and only 15 for water pollution. In 1991 the two subjects required 87 and 107 inches respectively.

Local organizations monitoring local situations have multiplied across the country. Many hire professionals, such as the Hudson River Fisherman's Association, whose "river-keeper" patrols the Eastern seaboard's most beautiful waterway.

And public opinion has become a powerful force. In the fall of 1992 the

6. NEW DIRECTIONS FOR AMERICAN HISTORY

governor of Alaska proposed culling the number of wolves in the state in order to increase the number of moose and caribou for human hunters. It was not long before he wished he hadn't. The state, heavily dependent on tourist dollars, was soon backpedaling furiously before the onslaught of intensely negative public reaction.

So is the American environment once more pristine? Of course not. Many pollutants have proved unexpectedly stubborn and persistent. Many businesses have resisted changing their ways. In most cities the storm and waste sewers are still one and the same, and sewage overflows in bad weather. It will take many years and billions of dollars to correct that. An unknowable number of species are still threatened by human activity.

But the nation's water, air, land, and wildlife are all better, in many respects, than they have been in a century, and they continue to improve. To put it another way, if the task of cleaning up the American environment were a journey from Boston to Los Angles, we would be well past the Appalachians and might even have the Mississippi in sight.

Then why is the impression so widespread that we are, at best, entering Worcester, if not actually marching backward somewhere in Maine? There are many reasons, and as so often happens, human nature lies at the root of all of them.

A first reason is that environmental bureaucrats, like all bureaucrats, want to maximize the personnel and budgets of their departments. So from their point of view, it simply makes good sense to highlight new problems and to minimize news about the old ones that have been successfully addressed. Similarly, environmental organizations live and die by fundraising. The-sky-is-falling stories are simply more effective in getting someone to reach for a checkbook than are things-are-looking-up stories. And environmental bureaucrats and lobbyists alike know that they must struggle hard to maintain their constituencies and budgets to fight the serious problems that do persist. They fear, not without reason, that if they don't play up the troubles that endure, they may lose the ability to address them at all—and we might lose much of what we've won.

A second reason is that the media have often failed to evaluate environmental stories with scientific competence and sometimes even honesty. As fundraising, bad news sells better than good news.

As a result, tentative data have often been presented as irrefutable fact, and short-term or local trends have been extrapolated into global catastrophes. In the 1970s there were many stories about the coming ice age. Ten years later global warming was destined to extinguish civilization.

A third reason that things often seem to be getting worse here at home is extremists. Extremists are always present in great reform movements, and the goal of environmental extremists is not a clean environment but a perfect one. They are few in number, compared with the legions now dedicated to cleaning the American environment, but like many extremists, they are often gifted propagandists and they are willing to use ignoble means to further noble ends.

Consider the support given by some environmental organizations to the Delaney Clause. This law, passed in 1958, requires that even the slightest residue of pesticides that have been shown to cause cancer in laboratory animals may not be present in processed foods. The Delaney Clause made some sense in the 1950s, when our ability to detect chemicals was limited to about one part in a million and our knowledge of carcinogenesis rudimentary at best. Today it is nothing short of ludicrous, for we can now detect chemicals in amounts of one part in a quintillion. To get some idea of what that means, here is the recipe for making a martini in the ratio of 1:1,000,000,000,000,000,000: Fill up the Great lakes—all five of them—with gin. Add one tablespoon of vermouth, stir will, and serve.

As a result, to give just one example, propargite, a nonpersistent pesticide that controls mites on raisins, can't be used because it has been shown to cause cancer when fed to rats in massive doses. But a human being would have to eat eleven tons of raisins a day to ingest the amount of propargite needed to induce cancer in laboratory rats. Had it been available in the 1950s, propargite's use would have been perfectly legal because the infinitesimal residue would have been completely undetectable.

Every first-year medical student knows it is the dosage that makes the poison. Yet many environmental organizations are adamantly against any revision of the Delaney Clause for reasons that amount to nothing less than scientific know-nothingism. They are wasting time, money, and, most important, credibility on the chimera of perfection.

But time, money, and most of all credibility are precious commodities. For even if we are at the Mississippi on the journey to clean up the American environment, we still have two-thirds of the journey to go. And it will be the most difficult part.

For as we proceed, the problems will become more and more intractable, and thus more and more expensive to deal with. For instance, it was easy to get a lot of lead out of the atmosphere. We simply stopped adding it to gasoline as an antiknock agent, virtually the sole source of atmospheric lead. But getting the fertilizers and pesticides out of agricultural runoff—now far and away the greatest source of water pollution in the country—will be another matter altogether, especially if we are to keep the price of food from rising sharply.

Part of the problem is the iron law of diminishing returns. Getting, say, 90 percent of a pollutant out of the environment may be easy and relatively cheap. But the next 9 percent might cost as much as the first 90, and so might the next .9 percent, and so on. At some point we have to say, "That's clean enough." Where that point will be, in case after case, is going to have to be decided politically, and democratic politics requires give and take on all sides to work.

Another part of the problem is that, increasingly, environmental regulations have been impinging on private-property rights. In the early days, the environmental movement was largely about cleaning up the commons—the air and water that belong to us all. The rule of thumb was easy: He who pollutes—whether the factory owner or the commuter in his automobile—should bear the cost of cleaning up now and of preventing that pollution in the future. Today, however, new regulations are more likely to affect the ways in which someone can use his or her own property and thus gravely affect its economic value.

There is a genuine clash of basic rights here. One is the individual right to hold, enjoy, and profit from private property. The other is the general right to pass on to our children a healthy and self-sustaining environment.

To give just one specific example of how these rights can clash, a man in South Carolina bought beachfront property in the 1980s for $600,000. The property was worth that much because it

234

consisted of two buildable lots. He intended to build two houses, one for himself and one to sell. But the state then changed the regulations, to protect the delicate shoreline ecosystem, and his property became unbuildable. Its value plummeted from $600,000 to perhaps $30,000.

Not surprisingly, the owner sued for the economic loss he had suffered. But the state ruled that it was merely regulating in the public interest and that no compensation was due as it was not a "taking": the property still belonged to the owner. The property owner argued that the regulations, however valuable a public purpose they served, had indeed effected a taking, because the state had sucked the economic value out of his property, leaving him the dried husk of legal title.

This case is still in the courts, and cases like it are multiplying. A general acknowledgment of the validity of both sides' rights and motives is necessary if difficult matters such as these are to be resolved successfully.

Still a third problem is that, increasingly, environmental issues are global issues, beyond the reach of individual sovereign states. Worse, scientists have been studying the earth as a single, interlocking ecosystem for only the last few decades. Global weather and ocean temperature data nowhere stretch back more than a hundred and fifty years and usually much less. The amount of data we possess, therefore, is often insufficient to allow for the drawing of significant conclusions. Has the recent increase in atmospheric carbon dioxide caused an increase in average temperatures, or has a normal cyclical increase in temperature caused an increase in carbon dioxide? We just don't know the answer to that question. But billions, perhaps trillions of dollars in spending may depend on the answer.

Another issue is growth versus the environment. Many feel that economic growth and increased pollution are two sides of the same coin, that it is impossible to have the one without the other. Others feel that economic growth is the very key to cleaning up the environment because it alone can provide the wealth to do so.

Obviously, in some absolute sense, the more production of goods and services, the more waste products that must be dealt with. But if the wealth produced greatly exceeds the pollution produced, the pollution can be dealt with while standards of living continue to rise. Certainly among the world's densely populated countries, the correlation between wealth and environmental quality is striking. People cannot worry about the problem of tomorrow's environment if the problem of tonight's supper looms large. It is landless peasants, more than timber barons, who are cutting down the Amazon rain forest.

So far there has been no flagging of the pace or weakening of the spirit on the crusade to a clean American environment. The commitment of the American people is firm. Doubtless it will remain firm, too, if, in the midst of the ferocious political debates sure to come, we all keep in mind the fact that honorable people can disagree about means without disagreeing about ends; that there is more than one road to the New Jerusalem; and, especially, that cleaning up the American environment is far too important to be left to bureaucrats, activists, journalists, and fanatics. This is our crusade.

America After the Long War

"Nothing is inevitable in politics, but there is evidence that the domestic order forged by the cold war is coming apart, ushering in a period of political disarray and posing daunting new challenges for parties and presidents. This decay and the tasks it implies will increasingly define the fault lines in American politics."

Daniel Deudney and G. John Ikenberry

Daniel Deudney is an assistant professor of social sciences at the University of Pennsylvania and author of the forthcoming book, Pax Atomica: Planetary Geopolitics and Republicanism.

G. John Ikenberry is an associate professor of political science at the University of Pennsylvania and author of After Victory: Power, Social Purpose, and the Recreation of Order After Major War.

There is universal recognition that the end of the cold war marks the close of one era and the beginning of another. The collapse of the Soviet threat promises both improved global security and a hefty worldwide peace dividend. American politics without the cold war, however, may not be so benign—the end of the East-West conflict holds deeper implications for the American polity than has been recognized.

Despite the widespread expectation that relations between the Western democracies would be disrupted with the end of the cold war, it is the case that relations within those democracies have been more profoundly disturbed. At the moment of victory of Western institutions over their rivals, Western polities are disioriented and dispirited, and Western leaders have unprecedentedly low approval ratings. While the domestic disarray in the West does not begin to approach that in the former Yugoslavia and Soviet Union, it is surprising and reveals a darker legacy of the cold war era.

The aftershocks of the cold war's end have been slower to register in the United States than in front-line countries, but the effects are already visible and growing. The war's end weighed heavily in the reelection bid of George Bush, the quintessential cold war president whose foreign policy accomplishments could not prevent a precipitous drop in popularity from an unprecedented high to electoral defeat in less than a year. Domestic political coalitions have begun to unravel, seen most dramatically in the strongest third party presidential showing since 1912 in the 1992 presidential election. The dramatic Republican capture of both houses of Congress in the 1994 midterm elections underscores the volatility of post–cold war American politics. Public support for American involvement in the world is waning—particularly in areas of foreign aid, military involvement, and United Nations support. Unlike the Soviet threat, which stimulated national unity, the emerging politics of global trade and finance pit region against region, and class against class.

The diplomatic historian John Lewis Gaddis has dubbed the cold war era "the long peace": the lengthiest period of general peace in Europe in modern times. But from the American public's standpoint, it has been "the long war." Since the late 1930s, the United States has sustained a nearly continuous military mobilization for global war, an effort that has profoundly shaped and changed the country. In the flush of triumph and optimism, it is easy to overlook the key historical fact that the great half-century struggle with fascism and communism made it easier—perhaps even possible—to cope with a wide array of domestic problems. Mobilization during the long war set a new mold for relations between the state and society, between the institutions of government, and between the parties, and it reshaped the national identity.

Foreign struggle had great domestic benefits for the United States. Mobilization for global conflict required a "social bargain" that effectively modernized and democratized American institutions. It is easy to forget that before World War II, the American political system had reached an impasse in responding to the demands of industrialization and state building. The permanency and pervasiveness of international conflict, beginning in the 1940s, required and enabled the United States to build a strong modern state, manage an industrial economy, reduce social inequalities, and foster national cohesion. It was the fascist and communist challenges from abroad that stimulated the progressive development of American capitalism.

The end of the cold war threatens to unravel these accomplishments and return the United States to the impasses of the 1920s and 1930s. If modernization and democratization were accidental side effects of this struggle, then it may be beyond the capacity of the American polity to sustain this institutional legacy. As the social bargain unravels, it will have to be rewoven. The tasks ahead are not simply manipulation of the budget, but reconstitution of the underlying domestic consensus on an activist state, social welfare provisions, and the political bases of national identity. This reweaving will be inextricably connected to the redefinition and reordering of the parties and the presidency. The future holds not a return to mythical or halcyon normalcy, but rather a potentially divisive struggle over the basic principles of the American political and economic order.

PREWAR DOMESTIC DILEMMAS

To understand the domestic impact of the cold war, it is necessary to recall the underlying trajectories and dilemmas of American political development before permanent global engagement. Since the middle of the nineteenth century, American institutions, like those in other major countries such as Germany, Japan, and Russia, have had to cope with and adapt to the manifold imperatives of spreading industrialization. Industrialization brought with it capitalist cycles of boom and bust, which generated demands for elaborate and powerful mechanisms for state intervention and management of the economy. In addition, the emergence of a mass urban working class produced the "social problem" and the attendant need for a social "safety net" of labor laws, unemployment insurance, retirement income, and welfare provisions. Finally industrial societies tended to become much more occupationally and socially stratified while at the same time more densely linked and integrated, thus generating the need for new forms of national identity and cohesion.

In the United States, efforts to cope with these dilemmas ran against the grain of the American system. America was better equipped to deal with these problems than countries with feudal social and autocratic political systems—such as Germany, Russia, and Japan, where violent revolution ensued. But the twin pillars of the American political system—individualism and limited government—imposed formidable political constraints. In the late nineteenth and early twentieth centuries, the populist and progressive reform movements met with only modest success in mobilizing sufficient political power to restructure American institutions.

In the decade immediately before World War II, however, the United States was mired in economic collapse and political impasse. Although the populist-progressive coalition had a working majority entrenched opposition to modern state building had blocked important institutional change. By the mid-1930s, when the first New Deal programs had lost momentum, America suffered from chronic economic stagnation, class warfare, and political disarray. Despite the magnitude of the problems and the breadth of the awareness that change was necessary the decentralized American political system hindered the mobilization of necessary political power to restructure core American social, political, and economic institutions. Without external pressures, these features of the American regime impeded the emergence of a modern state and the realization of progressive social goals set in the industrial era.

THE COLD WAR ORDER

The domestic political order of the United States has been profoundly altered by a half century of global engagement. Beginning with rearmament in anticipation of World War II, intensifying during the struggle with the Axis powers, and routinized with the four decades of cold war, American political development took a new direction. America's rise to global engagement required major institutional innovation that broke through the impasse of political development and accomplished much of the progressive agenda. Fifty years of global engagement produced changes in four domestic areas: the strength of the state, economic management, social equity and welfare, and national identity. The United States, in effect, reaped the benefits of such change without mobilizing a national political consensus for domestic modernization. The long war forged a social bargain, but it was an accidental one.

War and state building have been intimately connected throughout history, and the United States is no exception. From the Declaration of Independence to the beginning of World War II, war played a crucial role in the expansion of central state power. The need for a sufficiently strong central government to fend off European economic and military predations was a decisive factor in the ratification of the Constitution. During the Civil War the strength of the central government grew with the establishment of the federal banking system, conscription, direct taxation of individuals, the transcontinental railroad, and the Homestead Act; the war also saw the strengthening of the presidency within the national government. The demands of War World I led to further expansion of the powers and resources of the central government. In each case, the return to prewar normalcy was marked by the partial dismantlement of war-born institutions and powers—but much remained.

In the twentieth century America's struggle to maintain a global balance of power greatly altered the domestic balance of power. The demands of war enhanced the power and prestige of the central government at the expense of the states. Within the federal government, the power of the executive grew at the expense of the judicial and legislative branches. As leader of the free world and sole commander-in-chief of nuclear forces with global reach, the American presidency gained an almost monarchical aura.

Permanent global engagement also generated requirements for centralized economic management. In the conditions of total war, it was politically possible for the federal government to effectively manage labor and capital in pursuit of maximum economic output. As war raged abroad, the fear of class struggles at home gave way to an administered peace. After World War II, the actual system of wage and price controls was ended, but the techniques of Keynesian macroeconomic management and a commitment to federal responsibility for full employment were maintained. During the postwar struggle, direct federal involvement tended to concentrate in key technological sectors. In the cases of atomic energy, aeronautics, and space, the federal government called whole industries into existence and dramatically quickened the pace of innovation. During the 1950s, measures such as the expansion of the federal highway system and the science and education system were justified as national defense measures.

The cold war's impact on equity, class, and social welfare was equally significant, if less direct. The expansion of the defense budget and related manpower requirements led to programs and

6. NEW DIRECTIONS FOR AMERICAN HISTORY

institutions that advanced social equity and mobility. Veterans' benefits, especially the G.I. Bill, opened the door to the middle class for millions of Americans. The post-Sputnik commitment to improve education further broadened social opportunity. Moreover, the initial success of radical integration in the armed services gave impetus to racial integration in American society.

American sensitivity to social and class issues was heightened by the distinctive nature of the Soviet Union and communism. Unlike the Japanese and German threats, the communist challenge contained an ideological commitment to build a "workers' paradise" as well as a great power military threat. In this context, especially in the 1950s and 1960s, the performance of American capitalism in meeting social goals such as full employment, health care, and adequate housing had international ideological importance. At the same time, the communist threat delegitimized radical programs and comprehensive agendas for change. Ironically, the struggle with Soviet communism aided American capitalism in overcoming many of the flaws and instabilities present in the 1930s.

The cold war's end forces us to ask a fundamental question about the future of American politics: can the accidental social bargain be sustained in the absence of a global external challenge?

Finally, the mobilization of the American polity to a semipermanent war footing strengthened American national identity. This unifying threat helped overcome the extreme centrifugal tendencies of American society rooted in ethnic and sectional differences and the ideological heritage of individualism. The long war was especially important in integrating the South and the West into the national economy and society. Moreover, the fact that the United States was the leader of the "free world" and advancing itself as a model for people elsewhere infused American citizens and leaders with a sense of high purpose and responsibility with domestic as well as international consequences.

The net result of this half century of global struggle was the forging of a social bargain that met many progressive goals but did not depend on the establishment of a domestic progressive consensus. The cold war was neither always necessary nor always strongly felt. The effect of this competition was greatest between the late-1930s and the mid-1960s, and had already begun to wane in subsequent decades. Domestic constituencies for progressive change existed, but the cold war gave them a decisive boost. Because of this conflict, American institutions are more modern—more centralized, more democratic, and more cohesive.

THE DEMISE OF ORDER?

The cold war's end forces us to ask a fundamental question about the future of American politics: can the accidental social bargain be sustained in the absence of a global external challenge? Nothing is inevitable in politics, but there is evidence that the domestic order forged by the cold war is coming apart, ushering in a period of political disarray and posing daunting new challenges for parties and presidents. This decay and the tasks it implies will increasingly define the fault lines in American politics. Trouble ahead is visible in four areas.

First, power at the center of the political system is weakening. At the federal level the power of the presidency is eroding. Presidential authority is greatest in foreign and military policy. Without foreign threats, the salience of the presidency wanes. Outside foreign and military policy, the presumption of presidential preeminence is lacking, and many strong domestic groups and interests impede action. Similarly the overall importance of the federal government is in decline. Even if the size of the federal government remains large because of spending on domestic social programs, its political complexion will change.

Second, the ability to justify federal support for technological innovation and industrial development will decline, and state capacities for economic management could weaken. Without the cold war threat it will be necessary to justify industrial policies supporting promising future technologies on their own merits. National security agencies such as the Defense Advanced Research Projects Agency have played a comparable role to Japan's Ministry for International Trade and Investment in stimulating high-tech development, but they lack an explicit mandate to help the civilian sector despite their long record of technological stimulus. American industrial policy debate must move into the open political arena where the cacophony of competing corporate, sectional, and ideological divisions weakens the chances for their survival. Without the cloak of national security secrecy, decisions on technology funding become more contentious and difficult to resolve.

Third, the cold war's end will make the achievement of domestic social equity and welfare more difficult, and will thereby reinvigorate class division and conflict. In the absence of a major foreign military threat, the size of the military will continue to decline, thus shrinking this vehicle for social mobility. Moreover, no longer faced with an ideological challenge to capitalism, the political costs of severe social inequity decline. Domestic concern for social equity will be further eroded as the relevant standard of comparison shifts to third world countries teeming with cheap labor, blighted by severe class inequity and bereft of rudimentary social programs. The American welfare state, already under fiscal pressure and lacking a strong constituency, is further weakened by the changing international environment.

Finally, the end of the long war will tend to erode national political cohesion, thus allowing ethnic and sectional differences to dominate politics. With the triumph of capitalism and the spread of liberal democracy, the distinctiveness of the United States as a "free" people will be diminished. If, as many argue, we are shifting from an age of geopolitics to geoeconomics, then national unity and cohesiveness are likely to weaken as deep sectional economic differences rooted in geography assert themselves. Also, the centrifugal tendencies in American culture will increasingly lack a national counterbalance, thereby eroding a common collective identity.

Is this bleak picture the entire story? Skeptics might raise several doubts. The social bargain, though accidental in origin, may have achieved sufficient momentum and constituency to endure absent the conditions that generated it. Institutions tend to persist and create their own constituencies. Whatever the ultimate merits of this view, it is probably true that institutional inertia will slow the decay. But it is unlikely to prevent it, especially in an era of extreme fiscal limits.

Another possibility is that a new foreign threat will arise to reinvigorate the institutions of the long war. The most likely candidates are China, Japan, Germany or a united Europe. All are capitalist states and potential economic rivals, but aside from China they are also strong security allies of the United States. Although conflict among capitalist states may increase, the lines of conflict are not as clear-cut and alliances across national lines are as likely as those between them. Barring the unlikely degeneration of intracapitalist conflict into military confrontation, these conflicts are not likely to evoke measures of the sort needed to underpin the unraveling social bargain.

PRESIDENTS AND PARTIES

The end of the long war is also likely to significantly alter the balance of power between the parties and their ability to capture the White House. Since the 1940s, the Republican Party has dominated presidential politics, in large measure because of its stance toward the communist threat. When faced with an ominous foreign threat, the president's job description asked him to be "tough but responsible," something at which the Republicans excel. To be president during the cold war was to be the leader of the Western alliance—the man with the finger on the button—and candidates were judged accordingly. The first post–cold war presidential election in 1992 provides evidence of a new political pattern.

Republicans must find new ways to unify themselves. Political commentator George Will has tellingly observed that the Democrats are the party of government, but it is equally true that the Republicans—at least when in comes to foreign policy—are the party of the state. Although opposed to a strong state in domestic affairs, the Republicans have been the most vigorous advocates of the national security establishment. With a consistently smaller bloc of registered voters, the Republicans captured the White House in seven of eleven races. In all seven victories (Eisenhower twice, Nixon twice, Reagan twice, and Bush once) the Republicans were clearly positioned to the right on issues of anticommunism. The Republican presidential candidates lost in 1948, 1960, and 1976 when Democrats appeared to be at least, if not more, anticommunist than the Republican candidates. (The anomaly of 1964 resulted from the fact that Johnson, a hawkish Texas Democrat, was strongly anticommunist, while Goldwater seemed threateningly irresponsible.) For the Republican Party, anticommunism in the postwar era served to rally supporters in much the same way that the ghost of Herbert Hoover and the Great Depression worked for the Democrats and "waving the bloody shirt" worked for the Republicans after the Civil War.

The 1992 presidential election marked the first defeat of an incumbent elected Republican president since Hoover, and it revealed the contours of a fundamentally new post–cold war political landscape. Like previous Republican presidents, Bush's strong suit was foreign and military affairs. He believed that victory in the Persian Gulf War would sustain his electoral support, but found that the popular impact of this episode quickly faded. Saddam Hussein may have looked like Hitler, but the American people were able to see that he represented an altogether different caliber of threat. Without a strong foreign threat, the presidential election turned on domestic issues that had long been overshadowed.

Taking the traditional Republican line, Bush hammered away on the issue of seasoned judgment and foreign policy experience, but with little consequence. The plausibility of Ross Perot as a presidential candidate was made possible by the fact that the public did not assess him with the old cold war standard—as a man who could calmly lead through crises in the shadow of nuclear war. That Perot's legendary volatility and his long record of gun-slinging hypernationalism were hardly mentioned, let alone disqualifying, revealed just how little the American public remembered the standards by which it had so carefully judged previous candidates.

Republican liabilities were Democratic opportunities. Questions about Bill Clinton's character and military service record were much debated, but they did not have the impact they might have had in previous elections. Furthermore, Clinton was able to largely ignore foreign and military policy during the campaign without political cost.

The long war's end has opened a fissure in the Republican Party on foreign affairs that has yet to be fully explored. With the end of the cold war, the Republicans have lost an electoral trump card. More important, the party contains radically opposing impulses on foreign policy. One powerful impulse is inward looking and suspicious of the federal government. The new era has released a torrent of latent Republican isolationism and antistatism. During the cold war, even the most ardent antigovernment conservatives saw a strong central government as a crucial counterbalance to the menace of international communism. With the demise of the Soviet Union, conservatives increasingly see Washington as the "Evil Empire." The Oklahoma City bombing this April brought to public prominence a current in far-right thinking that is far more paranoid of federal power and foreign entanglement than perhaps at any time in American history. The intense fear of totalitarianism that was cultivated on the right during the cold war seems not to have ended, but to have been displaced toward the institutions of government and anything seen as foreign. This impulse is a more strident echo of the pre-cold war isolationism of the Republican Midwest and West that was exemplified by Senator Robert Taft of Ohio.

At the same time, a strong opposing impulse in Republican foreign policy thought is also evident. Over the last 50 years there has been a decisive shift in the American business community away from the inward-looking, Midwestern-centered capitalism of "Main Street" toward globally oriented, multinational, and outward-looking free traders. It is revealing that the most active support for NAFTA and the most recent GATT trade round came from the mainstream business community. It is difficult, therefore, to see how the free trade global village of business elites can be squared with nationalist, nativist, and protectionist factions.

THE BEGINNING OF THE NEW POLITICS

Many of these dynamics are already evident in the Clinton era. In the aftermath

6. NEW DIRECTIONS FOR AMERICAN HISTORY

of the long war, the powers of the presidency, public expectations about the post, and the tasks commanding attention are being transformed.

The office of the presidency is ill-designed for achieving a domestic agenda. The powers of the office are not interchangeable: institutions created to do one thing cannot easily do another. The instruments assembled to wage global war against the Soviet Union do not readily lend themselves to cleaning up the environment, providing health care, or controlling street crime. There will be a strong temptation to view domestic problems through lenses left over from the cold war—declaring a "war on drugs" or proclaiming environmental degradation a national security threat. Doing so reflects the greater ease with which resources can be mobilized, consensus achieved, and powers deployed when national security is at stake. Unfortunately the national security rationale does not travel well. As the gridlock over energy policy in the 1970s demonstrated, it is difficult to resolve complex domestic problems even when they can be credibly linked with traditional national security concerns.

These constraints were vividly revealed during the first two years of the Clinton administration. Clinton came to office believing that he had a strong mandate to address the country's health care crisis. Following the long war pattern, Clinton cast the problem as one of "health care security" and sought a major expansion of the federal role in this area. Despite the high priority he attached to this issue and the control of both houses of Congress by the Democratic Party, Clinton's health care reform program was completely stymied.

The long war has also left expectations about the president and standards for measuring his performance in office; these will weigh heavily on future presidencies, with important ramifications for the legitimacy of the political system. During the cold war the president was first and foremost expected to be a successful leader of the anticommunist alliance. A central ingredient in a successful presidency during that era was the ability to display the toughness, resolve, and judgment on the grave issues at play on the world stage. If the public continues to judge presidencies by these wartime standards, presidents will appear chronically deficient. The combination of presidential incapacity and public expectation is likely to fuel the growing sense that political institutions are unresponsive to public demands.

Future presidents will also find themselves at an impasse in conducting foreign affairs. Given the way the office is structured and the difficulty in making major headway in dealing with domestic problems, it will be natural for post–cold war presidents to turn to foreign affairs—however strong their desire to focus on domestic policy. It is here that a president can operate as the spokesman for the nation, thus setting himself above the partisan struggles of mere politicians. But in this area presidents will also face frustration. The American public is now less concerned about foreign events and much less willing to pay the costs for international leadership. Fearful of diminishing its standing, the military has grown increasingly unwilling to see force used and suffer casualties, unless backed by overwhelming public support and core national security interests. With these constraints, the lofty trappings of presidential leadership are increasingly meaningless.

This pattern is present in the Clinton administration. Despite having been elected to refocus the power of the presidency on domestic problems, Clinton has been drawn into the foreign arena. In part this was inevitable, given the expectations and commitments the United States has around the world. The continuing crisis in Bosnia and Herzegovina clearly reveals the new political terrain. As leader of NATO and advocate of an expanded UN role in peacekeeping, the United States was looked on to orchestrate a solution to the problem, thus prompting Clinton to focus extensively on it. But the antipathy of the American public to seeing its soldiers killed in battle meant that the threats and promises of the United States were empty. As a result, not only the credibility of the United States but the prestige and authority of the Clinton administration were badly tarnished. The post–cold war environment appears to offer few opportunities to act boldly and effectively, especially with military force. Indeed, many of the trouble spots beckoning American military intervention look like quagmires and promise to frustrate presidential initiative and divide public sentiment.

ERASING THE POLITICAL DEFICIT

Without the overriding mission of the long war, American politics is undergoing fundamental change. Even if the contours of this new era are undefined, the American political system is losing important and underappreciated sources of progressive modernization. The cold war forged and nurtured many central American institutions. As this period fades into history, there is reason to worry about the ability of America's parties and presidents to build coalitions and form a consensus around the management of a modern society and economy.

The current debate about the prospects for domestic renewal overlooks this deep-seated problem that strikes at the heart of the American polity. In effect, what the United States faces is yet another deficit—this one political. The American political system has enjoyed the benefits of public institutions whose formation did not require an explicit consensus on their behalf. Now American politics must confront the gap between the institutions it has come to depend on and the political support that undergirds them. The challenge for presidents and other would-be political leaders in the years ahead is to find ways to legitimate and build support for an activist state and a progressive political agenda without the easy rationale of an external threat. A new social bargain must be found. Only then will the long war really give way to a long peace.

Index

abstention, from alcohol, 79–80
abuse, child, 12–16
Adee, Alvee, 37, 40
Afrocentrism, 206, 210–214
Agnew, Spiro, 175, 177, 178
Aguinaldo y Famy, Emilio, 30, 32, 33, 35, 36
AIDS, 195, 196, 208
airplanes, and the Wright brothers, 49–55
air-raid drills, during World War II, 118–119, 124
alcohol, in American history, 77–82
Allotment Act of 1881, 216, 219
Ambrose, Stephen, 130–131, 162
ambushes, and Philippine-American War, 30–36
American Temperance Society, 78, 79
Anderson, Thomas, 32–33
Anti-Saloon League, 78, 80, 81
archaeology, historic, Custer's Last Stand and, 17–23
Armat, Thomas, 56, 61
Arthur, Chester A., 24, 161
Atlantic Charter, 136, 138
automobile industry, Henry Ford and, 87, 101

Banana Wars, and U.S. intervention in the Caribbean, 37–43
battle archaeology, Custer's Last Stand and, 17–23
Bell, Alexander Graham, 45, 51
benevolent pacification, and Philippine-American War, 30–36
Bennett, Harry, 99, 100
Benteen, Frederick W., 18, 19, 22, 23
Bergh, Henry, 13–16
Beveridge, Albert, 32, 65
bilingualism, 207–208
Birth of a Nation, 6, 61, 102
black market, during World War II, 126
blackouts, during World War II, 118, 119
blacks, 122; Ku Klux Klan and, 102–103; Madam C. J. Walker and, 72–76; and *Plessy v. Ferguson*, 28–29; Reconstruction and, 6–11. *See also* civil rights; racial issues
Bolo War. *See* Philippine-American War of 1898–1902
booby traps, and Philippine-American War, 30–36
boycott, Montgomery bus, civil rights movement and, 166–168, 170–171
Bradley, Bill, 199–200
Brandeis, Louis D., 69, 70, 182
Britain, 66, 70, 81, 107, 109, 117, 135, 136, 146, 147, 148, 149, 170, 203, 204, 224, 227
Brown, Edmund G., 175, 176
Brown, Henry, 28–29
Brown v. Board of Education of Topeka, Kansas, 29
Bryan, William Jennings, 32, 178, 195
Bulgaria, 147, 149
bureaucracy, civil service and, 24–25
Bush, George, 43, 66, 149, 161, 178, 196, 199–200, 201, 236, 239

Canada, 203, 224
CAP (Civil Air Patrol), 119–120
capitalism, 106, 146

Caribbean, U.S. intervention in, 37–43
carpetbaggers, Reconstruction and, 6–11
Carson, Rachel, 230–231
Carter, Jimmy, 162, 189, 190–191, 200, 202, 208
centenarians, recollections of, 44–48
Chanute, Octave, 51, 53–54
Cheyenne people, Custer's Last Stand and, 17–23
Chiang Kai-shek, 154, 155
children: and 1950s television, 160; rights for, 12–16; during World War II, 122–123, 124
China, 107, 137, 138, 143, 189, 239; Korean conflict and, 154–155
Churchill, Winston, 109, 117, 132, 133, 137, 138, 142–143, 147
civil rights, 7, 48, 190, 200; and *Plessy v. Ferguson*, 28–29; Martin Luther King Jr. and, 165–168, 169–174
civil service, bureaucracy and, 24–25
Civil War, 37, 61, 75, 112, 123; Reconstruction and, 6–11
Clark, Kenneth B. 207, 209
Cleveland, Grover, 32, 39
Clifford-Elsey memo, 147–148
Clinton, Bill, 24, 43, 86, 201, 202, 239, 240
clothing, at the turn of the century, 47
CO (Conscientious Objector), 115
Cold War, 37, 66, 102, 137, 138, 149, 154, 176, 189, 203; end of, 236–240
Columbia, 37, 38, 40
common man, FDR and, 106–108
communism, 43, 106, 110, 146, 148, 149, 163, 173, 175, 224, 238; Korean conflict and, 154–155
conservatism, collapse of operational, 199–200
Constitution, U.S. *See* individual amendments
containment, of Soviet expansionism, 148–149, 163
conveniences, at the turn of the century, 44–45
Coolidge, Calvin, 42–64
corruption: civil service and, 24; Reconstruction and, 6–11
Couzens, James, 90, 95
Crazy Horse, 21, 23
Crèvecoeur, Hector St. John de, 203, 209
crime shows, on 1950s television, 159
Cuba, U.S. intervention in, 37–43
Cuomo, Mario, 201, 205, 207
Custer's Last Stand, 216, 219; historic archaeology and, 17–23
Czechoslovakia, 107, 149, 203

daily life, at the turn of the century, 44–48
Daley, Richard, 173, 196
Darlington, Thomas, 222, 223
Dawes, Henry L., 216, 219, 220
D-Day, 130–131
DDT, 230, 231, 232
DeShaney v. Winnebago County, 12
defense industry, during World War II, 121–123
Dewey, George, 30, 32, 39
Dewey, Thomas, 162–163
Dewson, Molly, 85–86

Dinnerstein, Harvey, illustrations of, 167
disuniting, of America, 203–210; reaction to, 210–214
Dominican Republic, U.S. intervention in, 37–43
Douglas, William O., 146, 152
draft, military, during World War II, 109–115, 116–117
drama, live television, in the 1950s 158
drunk driving, 77–78
D'Souza, Dinesh, 206, 209
Du Bois, W. E. B., 7, 11, 72
Dukakis, Michael, 196, 199, 200, 201
dust bowl, 108, 230

Earth Day, 225, 231
Edison, Thomas, 55, 56
education, G.I. Bill and, 150–153, 165; and student protests in the 1960s, 175–178
Eighteenth Amendment, to the U.S. Constitution, 107
Eisenhower, Dwight D., 130, 141, 154, 159; presidential leadership of, 161–165
elections, 1992, suburban century and, 194–202
entrepreneur, Madam C. J. Walker as, 72–76
environmental issues, 226–235; Native Americans and, 217–218
Ethiopia, 154, 203, 213, 214
ethnic issues, and disuniting of America, 203–210
Eurocentrism, 205; demise of, 210–214
examinations, civil service, 24–25
expansionsim, Soviet, U.S. isolationism and, 146–149
extinction, species, 226, 228

fascism, 135, 136, 154
FBI (Federal Bureau of Investigation), 173, 174, 180, 208
Federal Reserve Act, 69–70, 191
feminism, 86, 88, 190
fetal alcohol syndrome, 78–79
Fifteenth Amendment, to the U.S. Constitution, 7
Fifth Amendment, to the U.S. Constitution, 180
films, early, 56–61
First Amendment, to the U.S. Constitution, 208
flight, and the Wright brothers, 49–55
Flying Hawk, 21, 22
Ford, Edsel, 97–100
Ford, Gerald, 162, 185, 187, 189, 199
Ford, Henry, II, 87–101, 103, 121
Ford, Henry (II), 100–101
Forrestal, James, 140–146
Four Freedoms, 136, 138
Fourteenth Amendment, to the U.S. Constitution, 7, 12; *Plessy v. Ferguson* and, 28–29
France, 70, 136, 148, 149, 203, 204
Franklin, John Hope, 207, 212
freedmen, Reconstruction and, 6–11
free-fire zones, and Philippine-American War, 30–36

Gall, 20, 21, 22, 23

game shows, on 1950s television, 159-160
Ghandi, Mohandas, 161, 166, 170, 171, 174
Gates, Henry Louis, 206, 212
Germany, 70, 106, 107, 146, 148, 237, 239. *See also* World War I; World War II
Gerry, Elbridge T., 13-16
G.I. Bill, 150-153, 165, 238
Goldwater, Barry, 165, 175, 177, 191, 239
Gore, Al, 24, 86
Grant, Ulysses S., 23, 163
Great Depression, 41, 81, 85, 100, 106-108, 129, 136, 150, 151, 165, 190, 198, 199, 239
Great Society, 190, 196, 198
Greece, 147, 148, 149
Greenstein, Fred, 162, 164
Grenada, U.S. intervention in, 37-43
guerrilla warfare, and Philippine-American War, 30-36

Haiti, U.S. intervention in, 37-43
Harriman, Averell, 135, 136
Hastings, Dennis, 219-220
Hayakawa, S. I., 175, 177
Hayes, Rutherford B., 25, 32
health issues: early movie theaters and, 59-60; at the turn of the century, 45-46
Herrington, Stuart A., 186, 187
Herron, William, 186, 187
Hirohito, Emperor, 110, 143
historic archaeology, Custer's Last Stand and, 17-23
Hitler, Adolf, 106, 107, 109, 110, 114, 130-131, 135, 136, 138, 142, 176
Ho Chi Minh, 43, 154, 184
Hollow Horn Bear, 20, 22
home front, during World War II, 116-129
homelessness, 195, 196
Hoover, Herbert, 43, 84, 106, 134, 162, 239
Hoover, J. Edgar, 173, 208
housing, during World War II, 123-124
Hull, Cordell, 134, 137

immigration, myths of, 222-224
imperialism: Banana Wars and, 37-43; and Philippine-American War, 30-36
India, 170, 171, 188, 203
intervention, U.S., in the Caribbean, 37-43
Iran, 147, 191
Iraq, 66, 203
Iron Curtain, 147, 148
isolationism, 66, 110, 132, 134, 138, 163; end of U.S., 146-149
Italy, 70, 148, 149

Jackson, Andrew, 24, 211
Jackson, Jesse, 195, 202
Japan, 155, 237, 238, 239; U.S. atomic bombing of, 139-143. *See also* World War II
Jefferson, Thomas, 179, 180, 182, 211, 227, 230
Jenckes, Thomas A., 24-25
Jenkins, C. Francis, 56, 61
Jim Crow laws, and *Plessy v. Ferguson*, 28-29
Johnson, Andrew, 25; Reconstruction and, 6-11
Johnson, Lyndon B., 43, 66, 69, 133, 161, 162, 163, 174, 188, 190, 197, 198, 199, 239
jungle warfare, and Philippine-American War, 30-36

Kennan, George, 146, 148-149
Kennedy, John F., 161, 162, 164, 171, 191, 196, 224
Kennedy, Robert, 171, 173, 176, 210

Keogh, Myles, 20, 21
Keynes, John Maynard, 134, 237
Kim Il Sung, 154, 155
King, Martin Luther, Jr., civil rights movement and, 166-168, 169-174
Kissinger, Henry, 183, 187, 189
Knox, George, 72, 73
Knudsen, Bill, 96-97, 99
Korean conflict, 154-155, 164
Ku Klux Klan, 8, 11, 102-103, 169, 170-171

Laemmle, Carl, 60-61
Landon, Alf, 106, 107
Langley, Samuel, 50, 51, 53
Lau v. Nichols, 207
Lawrence, Florence, 60-61
League of Nations, 66, 70, 134, 135
Leahy, William D., 139, 140, 147
Leninism, 136, 188
Lichtheim, Miriam, 213-214
Lights, 21, 22
Lilienthal, Otto, 50, 51
Lincoln, Abraham, 6, 24
Lippmann, Walter, 133, 136-137, 148
Little Big Horn, Battle of, 17-23, 216
loser decade, 1970s as, 188-191
lynching, 75-76, 102, 169

Macabebes, 35, 36
MacArthur, Arthur, 35-36
MacArthur, Douglas, 140, 142, 146, 162; Korean conflict and, 154-155
MADD (Mothers Against Drunk Driving), 78, 82
Madison, John H., 186, 187
Mahan, Alfred Thayer, 32, 134
Manchuria, 154, 155
Manifest Destiny, 37
manners, at the turn of the century, 47
manufacturing, defense, during World War II, 121-123
Marsh, George Perkins, 228-229; 231
Marshall, George, 109, 140, 142, 162
Marshall Plan, 147, 148, 149
Marxism, 136, 146, 173, 176, 188, 209
McCarthy, Joseph R., 159, 164, 165, 178, 209
McCormack, Mary Ellen, 12-16
McGovern, George, 181, 200
McKinley, William, 39, 134; and Philippine-American War, 30-37
Me Decade, 1970s as, 190
media, 6, 107; and 1950s television, 156-160; during World War II, 127. *See also* movies
Merritt, Wesley, 30, 32, 33
military draft, during World War II, 109-115, 116-117
Miller, Arjay, 100-101
Moley, Raymond, 106-107, 134
Mondale, Walter, 198, 201
Montgomery bus boycott, civil rights movement and, 166-168, 170-171
Montgomery, John, 51, 54
Moskowitz, Belle Lindner, 84, 85, 86
movies, early, 56-61, 107, 109
multicultural issues, 203-209, 210-214
Murrow, Edward R., 156, 159, 160
music, during World War II, 128
Mussolini, Benito, 110, 142, 154

NAACP (National Association for the Advancement of Colored People), 72, 75, 171, 173, 174
National Origins Act, 223, 224

national parks, 228
nationality, culture and, 212-213
Native Americans, 35, 44; Custer's Last Stand and, 17-23; tribal sovereignty and, 215-221
NATO (North Atlantic Treaty Organization), 147, 149, 240
Nevins, Allan, 10, 96
"new collar" workers, 201
New Deal, 64-65, 106, 108, 134, 135, 136, 163, 165, 198, 199, 237
New Freedom, 69, 70
New Nationalism, 69
news programs, on 1950s television, 159
Nicaragua, U.S. intervention in, 37-43
nickelodeon, 58-60
Nimitz, Chester W., 140-141
1950s, television in, 156-160, 194-195
1970s, as loser decade, 188-191
1992 elections, suburban century and, 194-202
Nixon, Richard, 159, 161-162, 163, 183, 188, 189, 196, 199, 217, 231; Watergate scandal and, 179-182
nuclear weapons, 154, 164, 237; use of, during World War II, 139-143

OCD (Office of Civilian Defense), 118-120
oil industry, 93, 189
operational conservatism, collapse of, 199-200
OSAP (Office of Substance Abuse Prevention), 78, 81
OSS (Office of Strategic Services), 141, 142

Panama, 189; U.S. intervention in, 37-43
patronage, civil service and, 24-25
Pearl Harbor, Japanese attack on, 112, 113, 114, 128, 131, 136, 138
Pendleton Act, 24-25
Pendleton, Joseph, 41, 42
Perkins, Frances, 85, 86
Perot, Ross, 201, 202, 239
pesticides, 230, 231
Philippines, 39, 143, 162; and Philippine-American War of 1898-1902, 30-36
plantations, Southern, Reconstruction and, 6-11
Plessy v. Ferguson, 28-29
Poland, 137, 147, 149
politician, Woodrow Wilson as, 66-71
politics, women in American, 83-86
populism, 195, 197, 201, 202
progressivism, 70, 103, 198
Prohibition, 47, 60, 77, 80, 81-82, 107
Proposition 13, 189-190, 199
Proposition 187, 178, 222
Public Law 346, 150-153
Pure Food and Drug Act, 64-65

racial issues, 48, 122; and disuniting of America, 203-214; Ku Klux Klan and, 102-103; and Philippine-American War, 30-32. *See also* blacks; civil rights
Radical Reconstruction, 7-11
Raspberry, William, 206, 208
rationing, during World War II, 124-125
Ravitch, Diane, 209, 212, 214
Reagan, Ronald, 147, 149, 161, 162, 165, 189, 191, 198, 199, 200, 201, 202; student protest and, 175-178
Reconstruction, 25, 28, 102; new view of, 6-11

Reno, Marcus, 19, 20, 23
revisionist history, of Reconstruction, 6–11
Rhee, Syngman, 154, 155
RID (Remove Intoxicated Drivers), 77–78, 82
Roe v. Wade, 199
Rommel, Erwin, 130, 131
Roosevelt, Eleanor, 80, 84–85, 86
Roosevelt, Franklin D., 66, 69, 71, 84, 100, 110, 111, 113, 114, 116, 120, 122, 128, 140, 142, 147, 150, 151, 153, 157, 162, 163, 190, 213; and common man, 106–108; as man of the century, 132–138
Roosevelt, Theodore, 32, 39, 40, 42, 65, 66, 69, 134, 210, 228
Runsted, Gerd von, 130, 131
Rush, Benjamin, 79, 80
Russia, 70, 106, 132, 133, 136, 141, 142. *See also* Soviet Union

saboteurs, World War II, 120
Santos-Dumont, Albert, 51, 54
Sato, Nastaki, 141–142
scalawags, Reconstruction and, 6–11
Schlesinger, Arthur, 161, 163
SCLC (Southern Christian Leadership Conference), 171, 172, 173, 174
scrap drives, during World War II, 125–126
search-and-destroy missions, and Philippine-American War, 30–36
Selective Training and Service Act, 110–111, 116–117
Servicemen's Readjustment Act of 1944, 150–153
Sherwood, Robert, 109, 132
Silverman, Burt, illustrations of, 168
Sioux people, 36, 215, 219, 220; Custer's Last Stand and, 17–23
situation comedies, on 1950s television, 159
slavery, Reconstruction and, 6–11
Smith, Alfred E., 84, 85
Smith, Homer D., 185–186
SNCC (Student Nonviolent Coordinating Committee), 169, 171, 176
Sorenson, Charles, 91, 94, 96, 99, 100
sovereignty, tribal, Native Americans and, 215–221
Soviet Union, 66, 189, 191, 203; and end of cold war, 236–240; and end of U.S. isolationism, 146–149; Korean conflict and, 154–155. *See also* Russia
Spain, 39, 203
Spalding, Elizabeth, 146, 149
Spanish-American War, 30–31, 37, 39
SPCC (Society for the Prevention of Cruelty to Children), 15–16
Spindletop oil field, 93
sports, during World War II, 109, 128
Stalin, Joseph, 136, 137, 141, 146, 154, 155
Standing Bear, 21, 22
Stephenson, David C., 102–103
Stevens, Thaddeus, 7, 9
Stimson, Henry, 42, 43, 114, 136, 140, 141
stonewalling, Watergate scandal and, 179–180
strategic hamlets, and Philippine-American War, 30–36
student protest, Ronald Reagan and, 175–178
suburban century, 194–202
suffrage, women's 83–86
Supreme Court, 12, 107, 166, 171, 182, 199, 207; and *Plessy v. Ferguson*, 28–29

Taft, Robert, 163, 239
Taft, William H., 36, 41, 65, 69
taxes, during World War II, 126–127
telephone, invention of, 45
television, in the 1950s, 156–160, 194–195
temperance movement, 78, 79, 80–81
terrorism, and Philippine-American War, 30–36
Terry, Alfred, 17, 18, 19, 20, 23
Thomas, Norman, 109–110
Thoreau, Henry David, 170, 227
Tocqueville, Alexis de, 11, 209
totalitarianism, 109, 136
tribal sovereignty, Native Americans and, 215–221
tribalism, and disuniting of America, 203–210
Truman, Harry S., 66, 127, 147, 154, 161, 163, 164, 197, 199; use of nuclear weapons during World War II and, 139–143
Tsongas, Paul, 201, 202
Turkey, 147, 148, 149
Two Moons, 22, 23

UN (United Nations), 66, 85, 138, 141, 146, 240; Korean conflict and, 154–155
Urban League, 173, 174
USO (United Service Organization), 127–128

Vandenberg, Arthur, 146–147
variety shows, on 1950s television, 158–159
victory gardens, 120, 126, 128
Vietnam War, 42, 133, 154, 161, 162, 165, 173–174, 176, 178, 188, 191; comparison of, to Philippine-American War, 30–36; fall of, 183–187
vitascope, 56–57

Walker, Madam C. J., 72–76
Wallace, George, 20, 181
War on Poverty, 161, 198
Washington, Booker T., 72, 73, 74
Washington, George, 24, 80, 133, 211
Watergate scandal, 161–162, 179, 182, 189, 191
Welles, Sumner, 134, 135, 137
westerns, on 1950s television, 159
Wheeler, Etta, 12–16
White Bull, 20, 21, 23
Whitney, William C., 38–39
Wiener, Jonathan, 8–9
Wiley, Harvey, 64–65
Wills, Gary, 176, 162
Wilson, Pete, 177–178
Wilson, Woodrow, 41, 42, 61, 75, 134, 136, 138, 162; as politician, 66–71
women: in American politics, 83–86; and Madam C. J. Walker as black entrepreneur, 72–76; and temperance movement, 80–81; working, 46, 121–122, 128
World War I, 40, 41, 61, 66, 88, 94, 96, 103, 112, 113, 134, 136, 146, 153, 223, 229
World War II, 48, 66, 81, 85, 146, 157, 163, 165, 189, 199, 230, 237; D-Day and, 130–131; G.I. Bill and, 150–153; home front during, 116–129; military draft and, 109–115; nuclear weapons and, 139–143; Franklin Roosevelt and, 132–138
Wright, Wilbur and Orville, 49–55

YMCA (Young Men's Christian Association), 72, 73, 74
Yugoslavia, 147, 203

Credits/Acknowledgments

Cover design by Charles Vitelli

1. Reconstruction and the Gilded Age
Facing overview—Photo from the National Archives.

2. The Emergence of Modern America
Facing overview—Photo from the Library of Congress.

3. From Progressivism to the 1920s
Facing overview—Photo from the Library of Congress.

4. From the Great Depression to World War II
Facing overview—Photo from the National Archives.

5. From the Cold War to the 1990s
Facing overview—AP/Wide World photo.

6. New Directions for American History
Facing overview—New York Stock Exchange photo.

PHOTOCOPY THIS PAGE!!!

ANNUAL EDITIONS ARTICLE REVIEW FORM

■ NAME: _____ DATE: _____

■ TITLE AND NUMBER OF ARTICLE: _____

■ BRIEFLY STATE THE MAIN IDEA OF THIS ARTICLE: _____
_____

■ LIST THREE IMPORTANT FACTS THAT THE AUTHOR USES TO SUPPORT THE MAIN IDEA:
_____
_____
_____
_____

■ WHAT INFORMATION OR IDEAS DISCUSSED IN THIS ARTICLE ARE ALSO DISCUSSED IN YOUR TEXTBOOK OR OTHER READINGS THAT YOU HAVE DONE? LIST THE TEXTBOOK CHAPTERS AND PAGE NUMBERS:
_____
_____
_____
_____

■ LIST ANY EXAMPLES OF BIAS OR FAULTY REASONING THAT YOU FOUND IN THE ARTICLE:
_____
_____
_____
_____

■ LIST ANY NEW TERMS/CONCEPTS THAT WERE DISCUSSED IN THE ARTICLE, AND WRITE A SHORT DEFINITION:
_____
_____
_____
_____

*Your instructor may require you to use this ANNUAL EDITIONS Article Review Form in any number of ways: for articles that are assigned, for extra credit, as a tool to assist in developing assigned papers, or simply for your own reference. Even if it is not required, we encourage you to photocopy and use this page; you will find that reflecting on the articles will greatly enhance the information from your text.

We Want Your Advice

ANNUAL EDITIONS revisions depend on two major opinion sources: one is our Advisory Board, listed in the front of this volume, which works with us in scanning the thousands of articles published in the public press each year; the other is you—the person actually using the book. Please help us and the users of the next edition by completing the prepaid article rating form on this page and returning it to us. Thank you for your help!

ANNUAL EDITIONS: AMERICAN HISTORY, VOLUME II, 14/E
Article Rating Form

Here is an opportunity for you to have direct input into the next revision of this volume. We would like you to rate each of the 40 articles listed below, using the following scale:

1. **Excellent: should definitely be retained**
2. **Above average: should probably be retained**
3. **Below average: should probably be deleted**
4. **Poor: should definitely be deleted**

Rating	Article	Rating	Article
	1. The New View of Reconstruction		23. The Biggest Decision: Why We Had to Drop the Atomic Bomb
	2. The First Chapter of Children's Rights		24. Good-Bye to Isolationism
	3. A New View of Custer's Last Battle		25. The G.I. Bill May Be the Best Deal Ever Made by Uncle Sam
	4. Reinventing Government, 1882		26. Echoes of a Distant War
	5. *Plessy v. Ferguson* Mandate		27. TV's Wonder Years
	6. Our First Southeast Asian War		28. Looking Back on Ike
	7. Intervention		29. The Boycott That Changed Dr. King's Life
	8. How We Lived		30. Trumpet of Conscience: A Portrait of Martin Luther King Jr
	9. Wings for Man		31. Reagan's Rise
	10. Learning to Go to the Movies		32. Looking Back at Watergate
	11. Doctor Wiley and His Poison Squad		33. Final Days of South Vietnam
	12. Woodrow Wilson, Politician		34. How the Seventies Changed America
	13. Madam C. J. Walker		35. The Suburban Century Begins
	14. Alcohol in American History		36. The Disuniting of America and The Painful Demise of Eurocentrism
	15. Why Suffrage for American Women Was Not Enough		37. Revolution in Indian Country
	16. Citizen Ford		38. Muddled Masses: The Growing Backlash against Immigration Includes Many Myths
	17. When White Hoods Were in Flower		39. The American Environment: The Big Picture Is More Heartening than All the Little Ones
	18. 1933: The Rise of the Common Man		40. America after the Long War
	19. The Draft		
	20. Home Front		
	21. Operation Overlord from the Inside		
	22. The Man of the Century		

(Continued on next page)

ABOUT YOU

Name _____ Date _____

Are you a teacher? ❑ Or a student? ❑
Your school name _____
Department _____
Address _____
City _____ State _____ Zip _____
School telephone # _____

YOUR COMMENTS ARE IMPORTANT TO US!

Please fill in the following information:
For which course did you use this book? _____
Did you use a text with this ANNUAL EDITION? ❑ yes ❑ no
What was the title of the text? _____
What are your general reactions to the Annual Editions concept?

Have you read any particular articles recently that you think should be included in the next edition?

Are there any articles you feel should be replaced in the next edition? Why?

Are there other areas that you feel would utilize an ANNUAL EDITION?

May we contact you for editorial input?

May we quote you from above?

ANNUAL EDITIONS: AMERICAN HISTORY, Volume II, 14/E

BUSINESS REPLY MAIL		
First Class	Permit No. 84	Guilford, CT

Postage will be paid by addressee

**Dushkin Publishing Group/
Brown & Benchmark Publishers**
Sluice Dock
Guilford, Connecticut 06437

No Postage
Necessary
if Mailed
in the
United States